Concert
of
Voices

Second Edition

"To redeem the word from the superstition of the word is to humanize it, to make it participate once more in a living concert of voices…"
— Geoffrey Hartman, *Beyond Formalism*

Concert
of
Voices

An Anthology of
World Writing
in English

SECOND

EDITION

Edited by

Victor J. Ramraj

broadview press

Library and Archives Canada Cataloguing in Publication

Concert of voices : an anthology of world writing in English / edited by Victor J. Ramraj. — 2nd ed.

Includes indexes.
ISBN 978-1-55111-977-9

1. English literature — 20th century. I. Ramraj, Victor Jammona, 1941-

PN6014.C625 2009   820.8'0091   C2009-903455-7

Broadview Press is an independent, international publishing house, incorporated in 1985. Broadview believes in shared ownership, both with its employees and with the general public; since the year 2000 Broadview shares have traded publicly on the Toronto Venture Exchange under the symbol BDP.

We welcome comments and suggestions regarding any aspect of our publications — please feel free to contact us at the addresses below or at broadview@broadviewpress.com.

North America
PO Box 1243, Peterborough, Ontario, Canada K9J 7H5
2215 Kenmore Ave., Buffalo, New York, USA 14207
Tel: (705) 743-8990; Fax: (705) 743-8353
email: customerservice@broadviewpress.com

UK, Ireland, and continental Europe
NBN International, Estover Road, Plymouth, UK PL6 7PY
Tel: 44 (0) 1752 202300; Fax: 44 (0) 1752 202330
email: enquiries@nbninternational.com

Australia and New Zealand
NewSouth Books
c/o TL Distribution
15-23 Helles Ave., Moorebank, NSW, 2170
Tel: (02) 8778 9999; Fax: (02) 8778 9944
email: orders@tldistribution.com.au

www.broadviewpress.com

Broadview Press acknowledges the financial support of the Government of Canada through the Book Publishing Industry Development Program (BPIDP) for our publishing activities.

Edited by Martin Boyne.
Cover design by Lisa Brawn Text designed by Chris Rowat Design, Daiva Villa

This book is printed on paper containing 100% post-consumer fibre.

PRINTED IN CANADA

Contents

Editor's Note to the Second Edition

The informing tenet of the first edition — that postcolonial literature, despite its preoccupation with historical and cultural specificities, is as much concerned with human commonalities — is what guided me again in preparing this new edition. For various reasons, but primarily to include recent writers, I have replaced more than one-third of the original items and added as many more. The additions include a few nineteenth-century pieces that exhibit the imperial attitude toward the colonies (such as Willie Collins's "A Sermon for Sepoys" [1858]) and others that overtly demonstrate the "writing-back" or corrective characteristic of postcolonial litera- tures (Rudyard Kipling's "The White Man's Burden" and Ernest Crosby's "The Real 'White Man's Burden'" [1899]). I have doubled the number of essays/memoirs; they now cover a wider range of issues, including Salman Rushdie's corrective on depic- tions of India in print and on screen ("Outside the Whale"), the contentious read- ings of Joseph Conrad's *Heart of Darkness* (Caryl Phillip's "Out of Africa: The Case Against Conrad"), Henry Louis Gates, Jr.'s interview with Wole Soyinka on Africa's relationship with Europe, and the diaspora longing for food of the homeland (Janice Shinebourne's "Red Bean Cake: London and New York"). I have extended the biographical notes and supplemented them with extensive critical and back- ground notes and a fair number of explanatory footnotes. Several readers asked for these supplementary materials.

I have retained and added pieces that range over the various issues particular to postcolonial writings related to in-betweenness, ambivalence, camouflage mimicry, English language as political and artistic tool, writing back, exile, immigration, and diaspora. But there are also pieces — such as Wong May's "The Shroud" and Mervyn Morris's "Little Boy Crying" — that tellingly are bereft of cultural markers and tran- scend specifics of time and place. And we now have three indexes — by title, genre, and region — having eliminated the cumbersome listing by genre and region in the Table of Contents of the first edition.

I cannot thank enough the many individuals who helped me in bringing this anthology out: Piper-Lee Blackey, Tony Boxill, Martin Boyne, Brigitte Clarke, Julia Gaunce, Chris Griffin, Clara Joseph, Marjorie Mather, Rod McGillis, Ken McGoogan, Sharon Ramraj-Thompson, Victor V. Ramraj, Myrna Sentes, Rowland Smith, Saroj Tiwari, Tara Trueman, Camille van der Meer, Shaobo Xie, Don LePan (on whose initiative this anthology came about), and Ruby Ramraj, who keeps me on even keel. I want to express my gratitude also to the students in my International English classes over the years, to those writers, both prominent and up-and-com- ing, who generously allowed me to use their work in this anthology, and to the many readers and instructors around the world who provided me with feedback. Please continue to do so.

Introduction to the First Edition

The literary community from which *Concert of Voices: An Anthology of World Writing in English* draws its material is one linked by a common language imposed by centuries of British imperial expansion. In many instances, the language has acquired local linguistic features but the various versions retain strong affinities with each other and with British English. This vast literary community extends into every continent and encompasses many different cultures and traditions and hundreds of poets, essayists, novelists, and dramatists, whose works have appeared in a range of local and international publications. To select for this anthology a representative set of short essays, fiction, plays, and poems from the multifarious literary community was a formidable task, one that eventually required reining in ambitiousness with practicality and tempering selectivity with arbitrariness. Although a number of anthologies of national or regional writings are readily available, it is difficult to find one that spans these contiguous literatures and addresses the requirements of survey courses or the needs of readers who want an introductory overview. *Concert of Voices* is an attempt to provide such a text.

The parameter this collection adopts to cope with the formidable quantity of material is to regard itself as an anthology of work by writers who have had to define themselves in relation to current or residual imperial presences, or to dominant cultures within their societies (whether it is the Japanese-Canadian Joy Kogawa in Canada, the Aboriginal Jack Davis in Australia, or the Welsh-Dominican Jean Rhys in the Caribbean), or to both. As such, the anthology is both cross-cultural and multicultural in scope. The intention in the first instance is to provide an *alternative* text to anthologies of traditional and established writings (in which the new writings in English invariably are displaced and marginalized) and at the same time to *complement* these anthologies. In this regard, the word "other" — which points up apartness and division — was found wanting and dropped from the main title. Its omission draws attention to a concept (and conviction) operative in the construction of the anthology: despite historical and cultural specificities (the focus of cross-cultural and multicultural studies), commonalities and affinities exist among these writings and between writings on both sides of the hegemonic divide. The anthology, then, is not intended simply as an offering of sociological or anthropological insights into these "different" peoples. The selections can be used to show that literature alerts us to the common and shared in human experience, whatever our own particular cultural, ethnic, historical, national, or political attachments. As Timothy Mo's protagonist puts it in *An Insular Possession*, under "the different veneers of varying laws, institutions, and civilizations ... the Old Adam is the same. His nature contains the same admixture of bad and good ... whether ... subsumed under an integument which is yellow, black, red, white, coffee, or any combination of fleshly tints" (257). The pieces in *Concert of Voices* demonstrate that imaginative writings can evolve from the cocoon of particularities into what can be called — modifying a catch-phrase of certain other disciplines — Literature Without Borders. To put it another way, they illustrate what Northrop Frye identified as *primary* and *secondary* concerns in literature: *primary* concerns, according to Frye, are akin to Wordsworth's notion of the "primary laws of our nature," which are shared by all peoples of all times and include the "essential passions of the heart" and the desire to live comfortably with food, shelter, and companionship. *Secondary* concerns include "loyalty to one's place in the class structure, and in short to everything that comes under the heading of ideology" (21).

These *secondary* concerns are much in evidence in many of the selections in this text, particularly in the writers' responses to centuries of domination by imperial cultures. Many of these writers whose languages and cultures were (and are) relegated to the margins in their own communities and dismissed as inferior by the imperial centre or the dominant culture now reclaim and celebrate their distinct identities and traditions. Others, possessed of a bicultural or multicultural imagination that encompasses both the local and the metropolitan, the marginal and the dominant, exhibit ambivalences and divided psyches, which — if and when they are resolved — may result in denial of one side of their bipolarity or in a philosophical recognition of the complementarity of their binary opposites.

Similar responses are to be seen in the writers' relationship with the English language. Those who perceive language to be inseparable from cultural identity and interpret continued use of imposed imperial languages as a prolonging of colonialism reject English in favour of indigenous languages. (They are likely to contend that an anthology of this kind, which takes its selection from former English-speaking colonies, is complicitly engaged in perpetuating colonialism.) Others who have lost touch with the languages of their ancestors and for whom English is their first and often only language continue to use it self-consciously, and are aware of the irony of their situation, particularly when they employ it to write back to the centre. For others yet English is a lingua franca — in which as much as three-quarters of its words are foreign-born; it belongs to them; it is theirs to master and, if they so wish, to modify and transform into nation languages to serve local needs.

The colonial-imperial, marginal-central binary informs much of the writings of this linguistic community but it is not the exclusive or overriding preoccupation of the writers. They do not confine themselves to political and ideological issues or subsume beneath them other geneses and dimensions of experiences of love, ambition, resentment, envy, generosity, anger, and the range of responses that make humans human. To do so would be to simplify and falsify their complex lives. Moreover, to trace all experiences to hegemonic politics is to deny individuals and communities agency and responsibility for their own fates, and to ignore that in some locations home-grown tyrants have supplanted foreign imperialists, and that individuals can have feelings and thoughts only tangentially related to the political and ideological, if at all.

The subtitle claims that this is an anthology of "World Writing in English." What might this mean? A decade or two ago, perhaps the term "Commonwealth Literature" would have been used to cover a great deal of this material, but that would have meant dispensing with such writings in English as those by Natives in the USA and by South Africans. Moreover, nowadays for many this is an outmoded term for works forged in and by an age of decolonization and dissolution of imperial ties. The currently fashionable term "Postcolonial Literature," on the other hand, is not confined to writings in English; and it is considered by some as yet another political concept that now imposes coloniality on all current issues, forces homogeneity on countries and regions with different histories of colonization, and ignores that colonialism in various guises is still around. "New Literatures in English" may appear to be politically neutral, but for some it relegates to a junior status literatures some of which have been around for more than two centuries. This anthology therefore settled on "World Writing in English" as the most convenient term, even though it excludes — like its affiliates "World Literature Written in English" or "International English Literature" — traditional and established texts from the USA and the UK. (Once again, the book is quite consciously an *alternative* to traditional mainstream anthologies.)

Concert of Voices attempts to include many of the established writers with solid reputations at home and abroad and to balance these with new and not-so-well-known voices, yet — as is to be expected of a short anthology — a number of significant writers and writings had to be omitted even within the set parameters. To do justice to this body of writing and to do anything more than provide a limited sampling of the writings and the ideological, artistic, and cultural underpinnings of these literatures would require a multi-volume anthology. Perhaps survey courses of these literatures could compensate for these omissions by supplementing the works included here with a selection of novels and extended plays from the different regions and communities.

The selections are organized alphabetically under the authors' names, and to serve the needs of those who would like regional or genre access to the authors and works, two additional indexes are provided. The regional index groups the selections under Africa, Canada, the Caribbean, the Indian Subcontinent, South-East Asia, the South Pacific, and the UK and USA. Authors with dual national or regional affiliations are listed in both regions. In the genre index, selections are grouped under fiction, poetry, drama, and essays. An index of titles and brief biographical notes on each author are included. I would like to thank my colleagues and friends in the field of International English Literature (or whatever term they deem appropriate) for their very helpful comments on my selections: Karin Beeler, Frank Birbalsingh, Anthony Boxill, Cherry Clayton, Saros Cowasjee, Kwame Dawes, Susan Gingell, Robert Hamner, Kelly Hewson, Shamsul Islam, Chelva Kanaganayakam, Carol Morrell, Kenneth Ramchand, Sumana Sen-Bagchee, Pat Srebrnik, John Thieme, George Fitzpatrick, Jennifer Kelly, Don LePan, and Guangtian Li all had a hand in the production of this anthology, and I acknowledge with thanks their assistance. I am indebted to Myrna Sentes and Saroj Tiwari, who generously let me avail myself of their faxing and word-processing skills. And I am particularly grateful to Ruby Ramraj, without whose support and assistance this anthology would not have seen publication.

Works Cited

Frye, Northrop. "Literary and Linguistic Scholarship in a Postliterate World." *Myth and Metaphor: Collected Essays 1974-1988*. Ed. Robert Denham. Charlotteville: U of Virginia P, 1990.

Mo, Timothy. *An Insular Possession*. London: Chatto & Windus, 1986.

Chinua Achebe

Chinua Achebe (b. 1930) was born in Ogidi, Nigeria. He studied in Ibadan and London. His novels include *Things Fall Apart* (1958), *A Man of the People* (1966), and *Anthills of the Savannah* (1986). He has published stories, poetry, and essays—including *Home and Exile* (essays, 2000) and *Collected Poems* (2004)—and has held teaching positions in Nigeria and the United States. He has been awarded honorary degrees from such universities as Harvard, Ife (Nigeria), and Toronto.

Achebe's "Girls at War" is set in the Biafran War (Nigeria's Civil War, 1967-70). The story invites reading—on one level—as a feminist text. With whom are the girls at war? Is Nwankwo's assessment of Gladys accurate? Is it invalidated by Gladys's heroic act at the end of the story? It is also a postcolonial text, addressing the imperial-colonial divide, complicated by racial issues. The story can be compared with Ama Ata Aidoo's "No Sweetness Here" as a feminist and postcolonial text. Achebe spurns the European conception of universalism but not the idea of human commonality: "I should like to see the word 'universal' banned altogether from discussions of African literature *until* such a time as people cease to use it as a synonym for the narrow, self-serving parochialism of Europe" (emphasis added).[1] He advises the postcolonial writer not "to run after universality," noting that if writers are faithful to their particular experiences and perspectives, "there is enough that is in common between peoples, between one people and another, for what [they say] to be appreciated."[2] Does "Girls at War" support Achebe's contention? Is it more than just a postcolonial, feminist text but rather a broader indictment of the physical and emotional devastation of wars? Is the echo at the end of the story of the last line of T.S. Eliot's "The Love Song of J. Alfred Prufrock"— waking up to "human voices"—of any significance?

Girls at War

The first time their paths crossed nothing happened. That was in the first heady days of warlike preparation when thousands of young men (and sometimes women too) were daily turned away from enlistment centres because far too many of them were coming forward burning with readiness to bear arms in defence of the exciting new nation.

The second time they met was at a check-point at Awka. Then the war had started and was slowly moving southwards from the distant northern sector. He was driving from Onitsha to Enugu and was in a hurry.[3] Although intellectually he approved

---

[1] Chinua Achebe, "Colonialist Criticism," *The Post-Colonial Studies Reader*, ed. Bill Ashcroft, Gareth Griffiths, and Helen Tiffin (London: Routledge, 1995) 57–61.

[2] Quoted in Kate Turkington, *Chinua Achebe: "Things Fall Apart"* (London: Edward Arnold, 1977) 10.

[3] *Awka ... Enugu* Awka is the capital of Anambra State; Onitsha is a commercial centre and river port on the Niger River; Enugu is the capital city of Enugu State. All three are in Nigeria.

of thorough searches at road-blocks, emotionally he was always offended whenever he had to submit to them. He would probably not admit it but the feeling people got was that if you were put through a search then you could not really be one of the big people. Generally he got away without a search by pronouncing in his deep, authoritative voice: "Reginald Nwankwo, Ministry of Justice." That almost always did it. But sometimes either through ignorance or sheer cussedness the crowd at the odd check-point would refuse to be impressed. As happened now at Awka. Two constables carrying heavy Mark 4 rifles were watching distantly from the roadside leaving the actual searching to local vigilantes.

"I am in a hurry," he said to the girl who now came up to his car. "My name is Reginald Nwankwo, Ministry of Justice."

"Good afternoon, sir. I want to see your boot."

"Oh Christ! What do you think is in the boot?"

"I don't know, sir."

He got out of the car in suppressed rage, stalked to the back, opened the boot and holding the lid up with his left hand he motioned with the right as if to say: After you!

"Are you satisfied?" he demanded.

"Yes, sir. Can I see your pigeon-hole?"

"Christ Almighty!"

"Sorry to delay you, sir. But you people gave us this job to do."

"Never mind. You are damn right. It's just that I happen to be in a hurry. But never mind. That's the glove-box. Nothing there as you can see."

"All right sir, close it." Then she opened the rear door and bent down to inspect under the seats. It was then he took the first real look at her, starting from behind. She was a beautiful girl in a breasty blue jersey, khaki jeans and canvas shoes with the new-style hair-plait which gave a girl a defiant look and which they called — for reasons of their own — "air force base"; and she looked vaguely familiar.

"I am all right, sir," she said at last meaning she was through with her task. "You don't recognize me?"

"No. Should I?"

"You gave me a lift to Enugu that time I left my school to go and join the militia."

"Ah, yes, you were the girl. I told you, didn't I, to go back to school because girls were not required in the militia. What happened?"

"They told me to go back to my school or join the Red Cross."

"You see I was right. So, what are you doing now?"

"Just patching up with Civil Defence."

"Well, good luck to you. Believe me you are a great girl."

That was the day he finally believed there might be something in this talk about revolution. He had seen plenty of girls and women marching and demonstrating before now. But somehow he had never been able to give it much thought. He didn't doubt that the girls and the women took themselves seriously, they obviously did. But so did the little kids who marched up and down the streets at the time drilling

2

with sticks and wearing their mothers' soup bowls for steel helmets. The prime joke of the time among his friends was the contingent of girls from a local secondary school marching behind a banner: WE ARE IMPREGNABLE!

But after that encounter at the Awka check-point he simply could not sneer at the girls again, nor at the talk of revolution, for he had seen it in action in that young woman whose devotion had simply and without self-righteousness convicted him of gross levity. What were her words? We are doing the work you asked us to do. She wasn't going to make an exception even for one who once did her a favour. He was sure she would have searched her own father just as rigorously.

When their paths crossed a third time, at least eighteen months later, things had got very bad. Death and starvation having long chased out the headiness of the early days, now left in some places blank resignation, in others a rock-like, even suicidal, defiance. But surprisingly enough there were many at this time who had no other desire than to corner whatever good things were still going and to enjoy themselves to the limit. For such people a strange normalcy had returned to the world. All those nervous check-points disappeared. Girls became girls once more and boys boys. It was a tight, blockaded and desperate world but none the less a world—with some goodness and some badness and plenty of heroism which, however, happened most times far, far below the eye-level of the people in this story—in out-of-the-way refugee camps, in the damp tatters, in the hungry and bare-handed courage of the first line of fire.

Reginald Nwankwo lived in Owerri[1] then. But that day he had gone to Nkwerri in search of relief. He had got from Caritas in Owerri a few heads of stock-fish, some tinned meat, and the dreadful American stuff called Formula Two which he felt certain was some kind of animal feed. But he always had a vague suspicion that not being a Catholic put one at a disadvantage with Caritas. So he went now to see an old friend who ran the WCC depot at Nkwerri to get other items like rice, beans and that excellent cereal commonly called Gabon gari.[2]

He left Owerri at six in the morning so as to catch his friend at the depot where he was known never to linger beyond 8.30 for fear of air-raids. Nwankwo was very fortunate that day. The depot had received on the previous day large supplies of new stock as a result of an unusual number of plane landings a few nights earlier. As his driver loaded tins and bags and cartons into his car the starved crowds that perpetually hung around relief centres made crude, ungracious remarks like "War Can Continue!" meaning the WCC! Somebody else shouted "Irevolu!" and his friends replied "shum!" "Irevolu!" "shum!" "Isofeli?" "shum!" "Isofeli?" "Mba!"

Nwankwo was deeply embarrassed not by the jeers of this scarecrow crowd of rags and floating ribs but by the independent accusation of their wasted bodies and sunken eyes. Indeed he would probably have felt much worse had they said nothing,

---

[1] *Owerri* The capital of Imo State, southeastern Nigeria. Nkwerri (Nkwerre) is about 30 kilometres from Owerri.

[2] *gari* A dough made of manioc (also known as cassava and tapioca).

simply looked on in silence, as his boot was loaded with milk, and powdered egg and oats and tinned meat and stock-fish. By nature such singular good fortune in the midst of a general desolation was certain to embarrass him. But what could a man do? He had a wife and four children living in the remote village of Ogbu and completely dependent on what relief he could find and send them. He couldn't abandon them to kwashiokor. The best he could do—and did do as a matter of fact—was to make sure that whenever he got sizeable supplies like now he made over some of it to his driver, Johnson, with a wife and six, or was it seven?, children and a salary of ten pounds a month when gari in the market was climbing to one pound per cigarette cup. In such a situation one could do nothing at all for crowds; at best one could try to be of some use to one's immediate neighbours. That was all.

On his way back to Owerri a very attractive girl by the roadside waved for a lift. He ordered the driver to stop. Scores of pedestrians, dusty and exhausted, some military, some civil, swooped down on the car from all directions.

"No, no, no," said Nwankwo firmly. "It's the young woman I stopped for. I have a bad tyre and can only take one person. Sorry."

"My son, please," cried one old woman in despair, gripping the door-handle.

"Old woman, you want to be killed?" shouted the driver as he pulled away, shaking her off. Nwankwo had already opened a book and sunk his eyes there. For at least a mile after that he did not even look at the girl until she finding, perhaps, the silence too heavy said:

"You've saved me today. Thank you."

"Not at all. Where are you going?"

"To Owerri. You don't recognize me?"

"Oh yes, of course. What a fool I am . . . You are . . . "

"Gladys."

"That's right, the militia girl. You've changed, Gladys. You were always beautiful of course, but now you are a beauty queen. What do you do these days?"

"I am in the Fuel Directorate."

"That's wonderful."

It was wonderful, he thought, but even more it was tragic. She wore a high-tinted wig and a very expensive skirt and low-cut blouse. Her shoes, obviously from Gabon, must have cost a fortune. In short, thought Nwankwo, she had to be in the keep of some well-placed gentleman, one of those piling up money out of the war.

"I broke my rule today to give you a lift. I never give lifts these days."

"Why?"

"How many people can you carry? It is better not to try at all. Look at that old woman."

"I thought you would carry her."

He said nothing to that and after another spell of silence Gladys thought maybe he was offended and so added: "Thank you for breaking your rule for me." She was scanning his face, turned slightly away. He smiled, turned, and tapped her on the lap.

"What are you going to Owerri to do?"

"I am going to visit my girl friend."

"Girl friend? You sure?"

"Why not?...If you drop me at her house you can see her. Only I pray God she hasn't gone on weekend today; it will be serious."

"Why?"

"Because if she is not at home I will sleep on the road today."

"I pray to God that she is not at home."

"Why?"

"Because if she is not at home I will offer you bed and breakfast...What is that?" he asked the driver who had brought the car to an abrupt stop. There was no need for an answer. The small crowd ahead was looking upwards. The three scrambled out of the car and stumbled for the bush, necks twisted in a backward search of the sky. But the alarm was false. The sky was silent and clear except for two high-flying vultures. A humorist in the crowd called them Fighter and Bomber and everyone laughed in relief. The three climbed into their car again and continued their journey.

"It is much too early for raids," he said to Gladys, who had both her palms on her breast as though to still a thumping heart. "They rarely come before ten o'clock."

But she remained tongue-tied from her recent fright. Nwankwo saw an opportunity there and took it at once.

"Where does your friend live?"

"250 Douglas Road."

"Ah! that's the very centre of town — a terrible place. No bunkers, nothing. I won't advise you to go there before 6 p.m.; it's not safe. If you don't mind I will take you to my place where there is a good bunker and then as soon as it is safe, around six, I shall drive you to your friend. How's that?"

"It's all right," she said lifelessly. "I am so frightened of this thing. That's why I refused to work in Owerri. I don't even know who asked me to come out today."

"You'll be all right. We are used to it."

"But your family is not there with you?"

"No," he said. "Nobody has his family there. We like to say it is because of air-raids but I can assure you there is more to it. Owerri is a real swinging town and we live the life of gay bachelors."

"That is what I have heard."

"You will not just hear it; you will see it today. I shall take you to a real swinging party. A friend of mine, a Lieutenant-Colonel, is having a birthday party. He's hired the Sound Smashers to play. I'm sure you'll enjoy it."

He was immediately and thoroughly ashamed of himself. He hated the parties and frivolities to which his friends clung like drowning men. And to talk so approvingly of them because he wanted to take a girl home! And this particular girl too, who had once had such beautiful faith in the struggle and was betrayed (no doubt about it) by some man like him out for a good time. He shook his head sadly.

"What is it?" asked Gladys.

"Nothing. Just my thoughts."

They made the rest of the journey to Owerri practically in silence.

She made herself at home very quickly as if she was a regular girl friend of his. She changed into a house dress and put away her auburn wig.

"That is a lovely hair-do. Why do you hide it with a wig?"

"Thank you," she said leaving his question unanswered for a while. Then she said: "Men are funny."

"Why do you say that?"

"You are now a beauty queen," she mimicked.

"Oh, that! I mean every word of it." He pulled her to him and kissed her. She neither refused nor yielded fully, which he liked for a start. Too many girls were simply too easy those days. War sickness, some called it.

He drove off a little later to look in at the office and she busied herself in the kitchen helping his boy with lunch. It must have been literally a look-in, for he was back within half an hour, rubbing his hands and saying he could not stay away too long from his beauty queen.

As they sat down to lunch she said: "You have nothing in your fridge."

"Like what?" he asked, half-offended.

"Like meat," she replied undaunted.

"Do you still eat meat?" he challenged.

"Who am I? But other big men like you eat."

"I don't know which big men you have in mind. But they are not like me. I don't make money trading with the enemy or selling relief or ..."

"Augusta's boy friend doesn't do that. He just gets foreign exchange."

"How does he get it? He swindles the government—that's how he gets foreign exchange, whoever he is. Who is Augusta, by the way?"

"My girl friend."

"I see."

"She gave me three dollars last time which I changed to forty-five pounds. The man gave her fifty dollars."

"Well, my dear girl, I don't traffic in foreign exchange and I don't have meat in my fridge. We are fighting a war and I happen to know that some young boys at the front drink gari and water once in three days."

"It is true," she said simply. "Monkey de work, baboon de chop."

"It is not even that; it is worse," he said, his voice beginning to shake. "People are dying every day. As we talk now somebody is dying."

"It is true," she said again.

"Plane!" screamed his boy from the kitchen.

"My mother!" screamed Gladys. As they scuttled towards the bunker of palm stems and red earth, covering their heads with their hands and stooping slightly in their flight, the entire sky was exploding with the clamour of jets and the huge noise of home-made anti-aircraft rockets.

Inside the bunker she clung to him even after the plane had gone and the guns, late to start and also to end, had all died down again.

"It was only passing," he told her, his voice a little shaky. "It didn't drop anything. From its direction I should say it was going to the war front. Perhaps our people are pressing them. That's what they always do. Whenever our boys press them, they send an SOS to the Russians and Egyptians to bring the planes." He drew a long breath.

She said nothing, just clung to him. They could hear his boy telling the servant from the next house that there were two of them and one dived like this and the other dived like that.

"I see dem well well," said the other with equal excitement. "If no to say de ting de kill porson e for sweet for eye. To God."

"Imagine!" said Gladys, finding her voice at last. She had a way, he thought, of conveying with a few words or even a single word whole layers of meaning. Now it was at once her astonishment as well as reproof, tinged perhaps with grudging admiration for people who could be so light-hearted about these bringers of death.

"Don't be so scared," he said. She moved closer and he began to kiss her and squeeze her breasts. She yielded more and more and then fully. The bunker was dark and unswept and might harbour crawling things. He thought of bringing a mat from the main house but reluctantly decided against it. Another plane might pass and send a neighbour or simply a chance passer-by crashing into them. That would be only slightly better than a certain gentleman in another air-raid who was seen in broad daylight fleeing his bedroom for his bunker stark-naked pursued by a woman in a similar state!

Just as Gladys had feared, her friend was not in town. It would seem her power-ful boy friend had wangled for her a flight to Libreville to shop. So her neighbours thought anyway.

"Great!" said Nwankwo as they drove away. "She will come back on an arms plane loaded with shoes, wigs, pants, bras, cosmetics and what have you, which she will then sell and make thousands of pounds. You girls are really at war, aren't you?"

She said nothing and he thought he had got through at last to her. Then sud-denly she said, "That is what you men want us to do."

"Well," he said, "here is one man who doesn't want you to do that. Do you remember that girl in khaki jeans who searched me without mercy at the check-point?"

She began to laugh.

"That is the girl I want you to become again. Do you remember her? No wig. I don't even think she had any earrings ..."

"Ah, na lie-o. I had earrings."

"All right. But you know what I mean."

"That time done pass. Now everybody want survival. They call it number six. You put your number six; I put my number six. Everything all right."

The Lieutenant-Colonel's party turned into something quite unexpected. But before it did things had been going well enough. There was goat-meat, some chicken and rice and plenty of home-made spirits. There was one fiery brand nicknamed "tracer" which indeed sent a flame down your gullet. The funny thing was looking at it in the bottle it had the innocent appearance of an orange drink. But the thing that caused the greatest stir was the bread—one little roll for each person! It was the size of a golf-ball and about the same consistency too! But it was real bread. The band was good too and there were many girls. And to improve matters even further two white Red Cross people soon arrived with a bottle of Courvoisier and a bottle of Scotch! The party gave them a standing ovation and then scrambled to get a drop. It soon turned out from his general behaviour, however, that one of the white men had probably drunk too much already. And the reason it would seem was that a pilot he knew well had been killed in a crash at the airport last night, flying in relief in awful weather.

Few people at the party had heard of the crash by then. So there was an immediate damping of the air. Some dancing couples went back to their seats and the band stopped. Then for some strange reason the drunken Red Cross man just exploded.

"Why should a man, a decent man, throw away his life. For nothing! Charley didn't need to die. Not for this stinking place. Yes, everything stinks here. Even these girls who come here all dolled up and smiling, what are they worth? Don't I know? A head of stock-fish, that's all, or one American dollar and they are ready to tumble into bed."

In the threatening silence following the explosion one of the young officers walked up to him and gave him three thundering slaps—right! left! right!—pulled him up from his seat and (there were things like tears in his eyes) shoved him outside. His friend, who had tried in vain to shut him up, followed him out and the silenced party heard them drive off. The officer who did the job returned dusting his palms.

"Fucking beast!" said he with an impressive coolness. And all the girls showed with their eyes that they rated him a man and a hero.

"Do you know him?" Gladys asked Nwankwo.

He didn't answer her. Instead he spoke generally to the party:

"The fellow was clearly drunk," he said.

"I don't care," said the officer. "It is when a man is drunk that he speaks what is on his mind."

"So you beat him for what was on his mind," said the host, "that is the spirit, Joe."

"Thank you, sir," said Joe, saluting.

"His name is Joe," Gladys and the girl on her left said in unison, turning to each other.

At the same time Nwankwo and a friend on the other side of him were saying quietly, very quietly, that although the man had been rude and offensive what he had said about the girls was unfortunately the bitter truth, only he was the wrong man to say it.

When the dancing resumed Captain Joe came to Gladys for a dance. She sprang to her feet even before the word was out of his mouth. Then she remembered immediately and turned round to take permission from Nwankwo. At the same time the Captain also turned to him and said, "Excuse me."

"Go ahead," said Nwankwo, looking somewhere between the two.

It was a long dance and he followed them with his eyes without appearing to do so. Occasionally a relief plane passed overhead and somebody immediately switched off the lights saying it might be the Intruder. But it was only an excuse to dance in the dark and make the girls giggle, for the sound of the Intruder was well known.

Gladys came back feeling very self-conscious and asked Nwankwo to dance with her. But he wouldn't. "Don't bother about me," he said, "I am enjoying myself perfectly sitting here and watching those of you who dance."

"Then let's go," she said, "if you won't dance."

"But I never dance, believe me. So please enjoy yourself."

She danced next with the Lieutenant-Colonel and again with Captain Joe, and then Nwankwo agreed to take her home.

"I am sorry I didn't dance," he said as they drove away. "But I swore never to dance as long as this war lasts."

She said nothing.

"When I think of somebody like that pilot who got killed last night. And he had no hand whatever in the quarrel. All his concern was to bring us food ..."

"I hope that his friend is not like him," said Gladys.

"The man was just upset by his friend's death. But what I am saying is that with people like that getting killed and our own boys suffering and dying at the war fronts I don't see why we should sit around throwing parties and dancing."

"You took me there," said she in final revolt. "They are your friends. I don't know them before."

"Look, my dear, I am not blaming you. I am merely telling you why I personally refuse to dance. Anyway, let's change the subject ... Do you still say you want to go back tomorrow? My driver can take you early enough on Monday morning for you to go to work. No? All right, just as you wish. You are the boss."

She gave him a shock by the readiness with which she followed him to bed and by her language.

"You want to shell?" she asked. And without waiting for an answer said, "Go ahead but don't pour in troops!"

He didn't want to pour in troops either and so it was all right. But she wanted visual assurance and so he showed her.

One of the ingenious economics taught by the war was that a rubber condom could be used over and over again. All you had to do was wash it out, dry it and shake a lot of talcum powder over it to prevent its sticking; and it was as good as new. It had to be the real British thing, though, not some of the cheap stuff they brought in from Lisbon which was about as strong as a dry cocoyam leaf in the harmattan.

He had his pleasure but wrote the girl off. He might just as well have slept with a prostitute, he thought. It was clear as daylight to him now that she was kept by some army officer. What a terrible transformation in the short period of less than two years! Wasn't it a miracle that she still had memories of the other life, that she even remembered her name? If the affair of the drunken Red Cross man should happen again now, he said to himself, he would stand up beside the fellow and tell the party that here was a man of truth. What a terrible fate to befall a whole generation! The mothers of tomorrow!

By morning he was feeling a little better and more generous in his judgements. Gladys, he thought, was just a mirror reflecting a society that had gone completely rotten and maggotty at the centre. The mirror itself was intact; a lot of smudge but no more. All that was needed was a clean duster. "I have a duty to her," he told himself, "the little girl that once revealed to me our situation. Now she is in danger, under some terrible influence."

He wanted to get to the bottom of this deadly influence. It was clearly not just her good-time girl friend, Augusta, or whatever her name was. There must be some man at the centre of it, perhaps one of these heartless attack-traders who traffic in foreign currencies and make their hundreds of thousands by sending young men to hazard their lives bartering looted goods for cigarettes behind enemy lines, or one of those contractors who receive piles of money daily for food they never deliver to the army. Or perhaps some vulgar and cowardly army officer full of filthy barrack talk and fictitious stories of heroism. He decided he had to find out. Last night he had thought of sending his driver alone to take her home. But no, he must go and see for himself where she lived. Something was bound to reveal itself there. Something on which he could anchor his saving operation. As he prepared for the trip his feeling towards her softened with every passing minute. He assembled for her half of the food he had received at the relief centre the day before. Difficult as things were, he thought, a girl who had something to eat would be spared, not all, but some of the temptation. He would arrange with his friend at the WCC to deliver something to her every fortnight.

Tears came to Gladys's eyes when she saw the gifts. Nwankwo didn't have too much cash on him but he got together twenty pounds and handed it over to her.

"I don't have foreign exchange, and I know this won't go far at all, but ..."

She just came and threw herself at him, sobbing. He kissed her lips and eyes and mumbled something about victims of circumstance, which went over her head. In deference to him, he thought with exultation, she had put away her high-tinted wig in her bag.

"I want you to promise me something," he said.

"What?"

"Never use that expression about shelling again."

She smiled with tears in her eyes. "You don't like it? That's what all the girls call it."

"Well, you are different from all the girls. Will you promise?"

"OK."

Naturally their departure had become a little delayed. And when they got into the car it refused to start. After poking around the engine the driver decided that the battery was flat. Nwankwo was aghast. He had that very week paid thirty-four pounds to change two of the cells and the mechanic who performed it had promised him six months' service. A new battery, which was then running at two hundred and fifty pounds was simply out of the question. The driver must have been careless with something, he thought.

"It must be because of last night," said the driver.

"What happened last night?" asked Nwankwo sharply, wondering what insolence was on the way. But none was intended.

"Because we use the head light."

"Am I supposed not to use my light then? Go and get some people and try pushing it." He got out again with Gladys and returned to the house while the driver went over to neighbouring houses to seek the help of other servants.

After at least half an hour of pushing it up and down the street, and a lot of noisy advice from the pushers, the car finally spluttered to life shooting out enormous clouds of black smoke from the exhaust.

It was eight-thirty by his watch when they set out. A few miles away a disabled soldier waved for a lift.

"Stop!" screamed Nwankwo. The driver jammed his foot on the brakes and then turned his head towards his master in bewilderment.

"Don't you see the soldier waving? Reverse and pick him up!"

"Sorry, sir," said the driver. "I don't know Master wan to pick him."

"If you don't know you should ask. Reverse back."

The soldier, a mere boy, in filthy khaki drenched in sweat lacked his right leg from the knee down. He seemed not only grateful that a car should stop for him but greatly surprised. He first handed in his crude wooden crutches which the driver arranged between the two front seats, then painfully he levered himself in.

"Thank sir," he said turning his neck to look at the back and completely out of breath.

"I am very grateful. Madame, thank you."

"The pleasure is ours," said Nwankwo. "Where did you get your wound?"

"At Azumini, sir. On tenth of January."

"Never mind. Everything will be all right. We are proud of you boys and will make sure you receive your due reward when it is all over."

"I pray God, sir."

They drove on in silence for the next half-hour or so. Then as the car sped down a slope towards a bridge somebody screamed—perhaps the driver, perhaps the soldier—"They have come!" The screech of the brakes merged into the scream and the shattering of the sky overhead. The doors flew open even before the car had come to a stop and they were fleeing blindly to the bush. Gladys was a little ahead of Nwankwo when they heard through the drowning tumult the soldier's voice crying: "Please come and open for me!" Vaguely he saw Gladys stop; he pushed past her shouting to her at the same time to come on. Then a high whistle descended like a spear through the chaos and exploded in a vast noise and motion that smashed up everything. A tree he had embraced flung him away through the bush. Then another terrible whistle starting high up and ending again in a monumental crash of the world; and then another, and Nwankwo heard no more.

He woke up to human voices and weeping and the smell and smoke of a charred world. He dragged himself up and staggered towards the source of the sounds.

From afar he saw his driver running towards him in tears and blood. He saw the remains of his car smoking and the entangled remains of the girl and the soldier. And he let out a piercing cry and fell down again.

1972

Ama Ata Aidoo

Ama Ata (Christina) Aidoo (b. 1942) was born in Gold Coast, now Ghana, was educated there and at Stanford University, and now lives in the United States. A poet, playwright, and novelist, she has written the novels *Our Sister Killjoy, or Reflections from a Black-Eyed Squint* (1977) and *Changes* (1991), the plays *The Dilemma of a Ghost* (1965) and *Anowa* (1970), and several short stories, some of which are included in *No Sweetness Here and other Stories* (1970) and *The Girl Who Can and Other Stories* (1999). Aidoo has taught for many years in Kenya and the United States.

Aidoo's "No Sweetness Here" provides a graphic portrayal of the life of women (and children) in a small village in rural Ghana in the latter half of the twentieth century. The story juxtaposes and compares two women, one a housewife who has never left her village and the other a Westernized teacher. What do they learn from each other? Is the teacher caught between her traditional and her Westernized values? Are the two ways of telling time (the sinking sun and the watch) at the end of the story significant? Do they reflect the teacher's dual heritages? Compare Aidoo's portrayal of women with Bessie Head's in "The Collector of Treasures" and Chinua Achebe's in "Girls at War." Do they all portray strong female protagonists who prevail in adverse situations?

No Sweetness Here

He was beautiful, but that was not important. Beauty does not play such a vital role in a man's life as it does in a woman's, or so people think. If a man's beauty is so ill-mannered as to be noticeable, people discreetly ignore its existence. Only an immodest girl like me would dare comment on a boy's beauty. "Kwesi is so handsome," I was always telling his mother. "If ever I am transferred from this place, I will kidnap him." I enjoyed teasing the dear woman and she enjoyed being teased about him. She would look scandalised, pleased and alarmed all in one fleeting moment.

"Ei, Chicha.[1] You should not say such things. The boy is not very handsome really." But she knew she was lying. "Besides, Chicha, who cares whether a boy is handsome or not?" Again she knew that at least she cared, for, after all, didn't the boy's wonderful personality throw a warm light on the mother's lively though already waning beauty? Then gingerly, but in a remarkably matter-of-fact tone, she would voice out her gnawing fear. "Please Chicha, I always know you are just making fun of me, but please, promise me you won't take Kwesi away with you." Almost at once her tiny mouth would quiver and she would hide her eyes in her cloth as if ashamed of her great love and her fears. But I understood. "O, Maami, don't cry, you know I don't mean it."

"Chicha I am sorry, and I trust you. Only I can't help fearing, can I? What will I do, Chicha, what would I do, should something happen to my child?" She would raise her pretty eyes, glistening with unshed tears.

---

[1] *Chicha* Demotic English for "teacher."

"Nothing will happen to him," I would assure her. "He is a good boy. He does not fight and therefore there is no chance of anyone beating him. He is not dull, at least not too dull, which means he does not get more cane-lashes than the rest of his mates...."

"Chicha, I shall willingly submit to your canes if he gets his sums wrong," she would hastily intervene.

"Don't be funny. A little warming-up on a cold morning wouldn't do him any harm. But if you say so, I won't object to hitting that soft flesh of yours." At this, the tension would break and both of us begin laughing. Yet I always went away with the image of her quivering mouth and unshed tears in my mind.

Maami Ama loved her son; and this is a silly statement, as silly as saying Maami Ama is a woman. Which mother would not? At the time of this story, he had just turned ten years old. He was in Primary Class Four and quite tall for his age. His skin was as smooth as shea-butter and as dark as charcoal. His black hair was as soft as his mother's. His eyes were of the kind that always remind one of a long dream on a hot afternoon. It is indecent to dwell on a boy's physical appearance, but then Kwesi's beauty was indecent.

The evening was not yet come. My watch read 4.15 p.m., that ambiguous time of the day which these people, despite their great ancient astronomic knowledge, have always failed to identify. For the very young and very old, it is certainly evening, for they've stayed at home all day and they begin to persuade themselves that the day is ending. Bored with their own company, they sprawl in the market-place or by their own walls. The children begin to whimper for their mothers, for they are tired with playing "house." Fancying themselves starving, they go back to what was left of their lunch, but really they only pray that mother will come home from the farm soon. The very old certainly do not go back on lunch remains but they do bite back at old conversational topics which were fresh at ten o'clock.

"I say, Kwame, as I was saying this morning, my first wife was a most beautiful woman," old Kofi would say.

"Oh! Yes, yes, she was an unusually beautiful girl. I remember her." Old Kwame would nod his head but the truth was he was tired of the story and he was sleepy. "It's high time the young people came back from the farm."

But I was a teacher, and I went the white man's way. School was over. Maami Ama's hut was at one end of the village and the school was at the other. Nevertheless it was not a long walk from the school to her place because Bamso is not really a big village. I had left my books to little Grace Ason to take home for me; so I had only my little clock in my hand and I was walking in a leisurely way. As I passed the old people, they shouted their greetings. It was always the fantasised form of English.

"Kudiimin-o,[1] Chicha." Then I would answer, "Kudiimin, Nana." When I greeted first, the response was "Tanchiw."[2]

"Chicha, how are you?"

---

[1] *Kudiimin-o* Demotic English for "good morning."

[2] *Tanchiw* Demotic English for "thank you."

"Nana, I am well."

"And how are the children?"

"Nana, they are well."

"*Yoo*, that is good." When an old man felt inclined to be talkative, especially if he had more than me for audience, he would compliment me on the work I was doing. Then he would go on to the assets of education, especially female education, ending up with quoting Dr. Aggrey.

So this evening too, I was delayed: but it was as well, for when I arrived at the hut, Maami Ama had just arrived from the farm. The door opened, facing the village, and so I could see her. Oh, that picture is still vivid in my mind. She was sitting on a low stool with her load before her. Like all the loads the other women would bring from the farms into their homes, it was colourful with miscellaneous articles. At the very bottom of the wide wooden tray were the cassava and yam tubers, rich muddy brown, the colour of the earth. Next were the plantain, of the green colour of the woods from which they came. Then there were the gay vegetables, the scarlet pepper, garden eggs, golden pawpaw and crimson tomatoes. Over this riot of colours the little woman's eyes were fixed, absorbed, while the tiny hands delicately picked the pepper. I made a scratchy noise at the door. She looked up and smiled. Her smile was a wonderful flashing whiteness.

"Oh Chicha, I have just arrived."

"So I see. *Ayekoo.*"

"*Yaa*, my own. And how are you, my child?"

"Very well, Mother. And you?"

"Tanchiw. Do sit down, there's a stool in that corner. Sit down. Mmmm.... Life is a battle. What can we do? We are just trying, my daughter."

"Why were you longer at the farm today?"

"After weeding that plot I told you about last week, I thought I would go for one or two yams."

"Ah!" I cried.

"You know tomorrow is Ahobaa. Even if one does not feel happy, one must have some yam for old Ahor."[1]

"Yes. So I understand. The old saviour deserves it. After all it is not often that a man offers himself as a sacrifice to the gods to save his people from a pestilence."

"No, Chicha, we were so lucky."

"But Maami Ama, why do you look so sad? After all, the yams are quite big." She gave me a small grin, looking at the yams she had now packed at the corner.

"Do you think so? Well, they are the best of the lot. My daughter, when life fails you, it fails you totally. One's yams reflect the total sum of one's life. And mine look wretched enough."

---

[1] *Ahobaa... Ahor* Ahobaa is a festival in Ghana that commemorates the sacrifice of Egya Ahor, a member of royalty, during a devastating epidemic that killed numerous people; his sacrifice (of his life) stopped the deadly epidemic.

"O, Maami, why are you always speaking in this way? Look at Kwesi, how many mothers can boast of such a son? Even though he is only one, consider those who have none at all. Perhaps some woman is sitting at some corner envying you."

She chuckled. "What an unhappy woman she must be who would envy Ama! But thank you, I should be grateful for Kwesi."

After that we were quiet for a while. I always loved to see her moving quietly about her work. Having finished unpacking, she knocked the dirt out of the tray and started making fire to prepare the evening meal. She started humming a religious lyric. She was a Methodist.

We are fighting
We are fighting
We are fighting for Canaan, the Heavenly Kingdom above.

I watched her and my eyes became misty, she looked so much like my own mother. Presently, the fire began to smoke. She turned round. "Chicha."

"Maami Ama."

"Do you know that tomorrow I am going to have a formal divorce?"

"Oh!" And I could not help the dismay in my voice.

I had heard, soon after my arrival in the village, that the parents of that most beautiful boy were as good as divorced. I had hoped they would come to a respectful understanding for the boy's sake. Later on when I got to know his mother, I had wished for this, for her own sweet self's sake too. But as time went on I had realised this could not be or was not even desirable. Kodjo Fi was a selfish and bullying man, whom no decent woman ought to have married. He got on marvellously with his two other wives but they were three of a feather. Yet I was sorry to hear Maami was going to have a final breach with him.

"Yes, I am," she went on. "I should. What am I going on like this for? What is man struggling after? Seven years is a long time to bear ill-usage from a man coupled with contempt and insults from his wives. What have I done to deserve the abuse of his sisters? And his mother!"

"Does she insult you too?" I exclaimed.

"Why not? Don't you think she would? Considering that I don't buy her the most expensive cloths on the market and I don't give her the best fish from my soup, like her daughters-in-law do."

I laughed. "The mean old witch!"

"Chicha, don't laugh. I am quite sure she wanted to eat Kwesi but I baptised him and she couldn't."

"Oh, don't say that, Maami. I am quite sure they all like you, only you don't know."

"My child, they don't. They hate me."

"But what happened?" I asked the question I had wanted to ask for so long.

"You would ask, Chicha! I don't know. They suddenly began hating me when Kwesi was barely two. Kodjo Fi reduced my housekeeping money and sometimes he refused to give me anything at all. He wouldn't eat my food. At first, I used to ask him why. He always replied, 'It is nothing.' If I had not been such an unlucky woman, his mother and sisters might have taken my side, but for me there was no one. That planting time, although I was his first wife, he allotted to me the smallest, thorniest plot."

"Ei, what did you say about it?"

"What could I say? At that time my mother was alive, though my father was already dead. When I complained to her about the treatment I was getting from my husband, she told me that in marriage, a woman must sometimes be a fool. But I have been a fool for far too long a time."

"Oh!" I frowned.

"Mother has died and left me and I was an only child too. My aunts are very busy looking after the affairs of their own daughters. I've told my uncles several times but they never take me seriously. They feel I am only a discontented woman."

"You?" I asked in surprise.

"Perhaps you would not think so. But there are several who do feel like that in this village."

She paused for a while, while she stared at the floor.

"You don't know, but I've been the topic of gossip for many years. Now, I only want to live on my own looking after my child. I don't think I will ever get any more children. Chicha, our people say a bad marriage kills the soul. Mine is fit for burial."

"Maami, don't grieve."

"My daughter, my mother and father who brought me to this world have left me alone and I've stopped grieving for them. When death summoned them, they were glad to lay down their tools and go to their parents. Yes, they loved me all right but even they had to leave me. Why should I make myself unhappy about a man for whom I ceased to exist a long time ago?"

She went to the big basket, took out some cassava and plantain, and sitting down began peeling them. Remembering she had forgotten the wooden bowl into which she would put the food, she got up to go for it.

"In this case," I continued the conversation, "what will happen to Kwesi?"

"What will happen to him?" she asked in surprise. "This is no problem. They may tell me to give him to his father."

"And would you?"

"No, I wouldn't."

"And would you succeed in keeping him if his father insisted?"

"Well, I would struggle, for my son is his father's child but he belongs to my family."

I sat there listening to these references to the age-old customs of which I had been ignorant. I was surprised. She washed the food, now cut into lumps, and arranged it in the cooking-pot. She added water and put it on the fire. She blew at it and it burst into flames.

"Maami Ama, has not your husband got a right to take Kwesi from you?" I asked her.

"He has, I suppose, but not entirely. Anyway, if the elders who would make the divorce settlement ask me to let him go and stay with his father, I wouldn't refuse."

"You are a brave woman."

"Life has taught me to be brave," she said, looking at me and smiling, "By the way, what is the time?"

I told her, "It is six minutes to six o'clock."

"And Kwesi has not yet come home?" she exclaimed.

"Mama, here I am," a piping voice announced.

"My husband, my brother, my father, my all-in-all, where are you?" And there he was. All at once, for the care-worn village woman, the sun might well have been rising from the east instead of setting behind the coconut palms. Her eyes shone. Kwesi saluted me and then his mother. He was a little shy of me and he ran away to the inner chamber. There was a thud which meant he had thrown his books down.

"Kwesi," his mother called out to him. "I have always told you to put your books down gently. I did not buy them with sand, and you ought to be careful with them."

He returned to where we were. I looked at him. He was very dirty. There was sand in his hair, ears and eyes. His uniform was smeared with mud, crayon and berry-juice. His braces were hanging down on one side. His mother gave an affectionate frown. "Kwesi, you are very dirty, just look at yourself. You are a disgrace to me. Anyone would think your mother does not look after you well." I was very much amused, for I knew she meant this for my ears. Kwesi just stood there, without a care in the world.

"Can't you play without putting sand in your hair?" his mother persisted.

"I am hungry," he announced. I laughed.

"Shame, shame, and your chicha is here. Chicha, you see? He does not fetch me water. He does not fetch me firewood. He does not weed my farm on Saturdays as other schoolboys do for their mothers. He only eats and eats." I looked at him; he fled again into the inner chamber for shame. We both started laughing at him. After a time I got up to go.

"Chicha, I would have liked you to eat before you went away; that's why I am hurrying up with the food." Maami tried to detain me.

"Oh, it does not matter. You know I eat here when I come, but today I must go away. I have the children's books to mark."

"Then I must not keep you away from your work."

"Tomorrow I will come to see you," I promised.

"*Yoo*, thank you."

"Sleep well, Maami."

"Sleep well, my daughter." I stepped into the open air. The sun was far receding. I walked slowly away. Just before I was out of earshot, Maami shouted after me, "And remember, if Kwesi gets his sums wrong, I will come to school to receive his lashes, if only you would tell me."

"*Yoo*," I shouted back. Then I went away.

The next day was Ahobaada. It was a day of rejoicing for everyone. In the morning, old family quarrels were being patched up. In Maami Ama's family all became peaceful. Her aunts had — or thought they had — reconciled themselves to the fact that, when Maami Ama's mother was dying, she had instructed her sisters, much to their chagrin, to give all her jewels to her only child. This had been one of the reasons why the aunts and cousins had left Ama so much to her own devices. "After all, she has her mother's goods, what else does she need?" they were often saying. However, today, aunts, cousins and nieces have come to a better understanding. Ahobaa is a season of goodwill! Nevertheless, Ama is going to have a formal divorce today....

It had not been laid down anywhere in the Education Ordinance that school-children were to be given holidays during local festivals. And so no matter how much I sympathised with the kids, I could not give them a holiday, although Ahobaa was such an important occasion for them; they naturally felt it a grievance to be forced to go to school while their friends at home were eating so much yam and meat. But they had their revenge on me. They fidgeted the whole day. What was worse, the schoolroom was actually just one big shed. When I left the Class One chicks to look at the older ones, they chattered; when I turned to them, Class Two and Class Three began shouting. Oh, it was a fine situation. In the afternoon, after having gone home to taste some of the festival dishes, they nearly drove me mad. So I was relieved when it was three o'clock. Feeling no sense of guilt, I turned them all out to play. They rushed out to the field. I packed my books on the table for little Grace to take home. My intention was to go and see the divorce proceedings which had begun at one o'clock and then come back at four to dismiss them. These divorce cases took hours to settle, and I hoped I would hear some of it.

As I walked down between the rows of desks, I hit my leg against one. The books on it tumbled down. As I picked them up I saw they belonged to Kwesi. It was the desk he shared with a little girl. I began thinking about him and the unhappy con-nection he had with what was going on at that moment down in the village. I remembered every word of the conversation I had had with his mother the previous evening. I became sad at the prospect of a possible separation from the mother who loved him so much and whom he loved. From his infancy they had known only each other, a lonely mother and a lonely son. Through the hot sun, she had carried him on her back as she weeded her cornfield. How could she dare to put him down under a tree in the shade when there was no one to look after him? Other women had their own younger sisters or those of their husbands to help with the baby; but she had had no one. The only face the little one had known was his mother's. And now ...

"But," I told myself, "I am sure it will be all right with him."

"Will it?" I asked myself.

"Why not? He is a happy child."

"Does that solve the problem?"

"Not altogether, but ... "

"No buts; one should think of the house into which he would be taken now. He may not be a favourite there."

But my other voice told me that a child need not be a favourite to be happy.

I had to bring the one-man argument to an end. I had to hurry. Passing by the field, I saw some of the boys playing football. At the goal at the further end was a headful of hair shining in the afternoon sun. I knew the body to which it belonged. A goalkeeper is a dubious character in infant soccer. He is either a good goalkeeper and that is why he is at the goal, which is usually difficult to know in a child, or he is a bad player. If he is a bad player, he might as well be in the goal as anywhere else. Kwesi loved football, that was certain, and he was always the goalkeeper. Whether he was good or not I had never been able to see. Just as I passed, he caught a ball and his team clapped. I heard him give the little squeaky noise that passed for his laugh. No doubt he was a happy child.

Now I really ran into the village. I immediately made my way to Nana Kum's house, for the case was going on there. There was a great crowd in front of the house. Why were there so many people about? Then I remembered that it being a holiday, everyone was at home. And of course, after the eating and the drinking of palm-wine in the morning and midday, divorce proceedings certainly provide an agreeable diversion, especially when other people are involved and not ourselves.

The courtyard was a long one and as I jostled to where Maami Ama was sitting, pieces of comments floated into my ears. "The elders certainly have settled the case fairly," someone was saying. "But it seemed as if Kodjo Fi had no strong proofs for his arguments," another was saying. "Well, they both have been sensible. If one feels one can't live with a woman, one might as well divorce her. And I hate a woman who cringes to a man," a third said. Finally I reached her side. Around her were her family, her two aunts, Esi and Ama, her two cousins and the two uncles. To the right were the elders who were judging the case; opposite were Kodjo Fi and his family.

"I have come, Maami Ama," I announced myself.

She looked at me. "You ought to have been here earlier, the case has been settled already."

"And how are things?" I inquired.

"I am a divorced woman."

"What were his grounds for wanting to divorce you?"

"He said I had done nothing, he only wanted to ... "

"Eh! Only the two of you know what went wrong," the younger aunt cried out, reproachfully. "If after his saying that, you had refused to be divorced, he would have had to pay the Ejecting Fee, but now he has got the better of you."

"But aunt," Maami protested, "how could I refuse to be divorced?"

"It's up to you. I know it's your own affair, only I wouldn't like your mother's ghost to think that we haven't looked after you well."

"I agree with you," the elder aunt said.

"Maami Ama, what was your debt?" I asked her.

"It is quite a big sum."

"I hope you too had something to reckon against him?"

"I did. He reckoned the dowry, the ten cloths he gave me, the Knocking Fee...."

All this had been heard by Kodjo Fi and his family and soon they made us aware of it.

"Kodjo," his youngest sister burst out, "you forgot to reckon the Knife Fee."

"No. *Yaa*, I did not forget," Kodjo Fi told her. "She had no brothers to whom I would give the fee."

"It's all right then," his second sister added.

But the rest of his womenfolk took this to be a signal for more free comments.

"She is a bad woman and I think you are well rid of her," one aunt screamed.

"I think she is a witch," the youngest sister said.

"Oh, that she is. Anyway, only witches have no brothers or sisters. They eat them in the mother's womb long before they are born."

Ama's aunts and cousins had said nothing so far. They were inclined to believe Ama was a witch too. But Maami sat still. When the comments had gone down a bit, she resumed the conversation with me.

"As I was saying, Chicha, he also reckoned the price of the trunk he had given me and all the cost of the medicine he gave me to make me have more children. There was only the Cooking Cost for me to reckon against his."

"Have you got money to pay the debt?" I asked her.

"No, but I am not going to pay it. My uncles will pay it out of the family fund and put the debt down against my name."

"Oh!"

"But you are a fool," Maami Ama's eldest aunt shouted at her.

"I say you are a fool," she insisted.

"But aunt ..." Maami Ama began to protest.

"Yes! And I hope you are not going to answer back. I was born before your mother and now that she is dead, I'm your mother! Besides, when she was alive I could scold her when she went wrong, and now I say you are a fool. For seven years you have struggled to look after a child. Whether he ate or not was your affair alone. Whether he had any cloth or not did not concern any other person. When Kwesi was a child he had no father. When he nearly died of measles, no grandmother looked in. As for aunts, he began getting them when he started going to school. And now you are allowing them to take him away from you. Now that he is grown enough to be counted among the living, a father knows he has got a son."

"So, so!" Kodjo Fi's mother sneered at her. "What did you think? That Kodjo would give his son as a present to you, eh? The boy belongs to his family, but he must be of some service to his father too."

"Have I called your name?" Ama's aunt asked the old woman.

"You have not called her name but you were speaking against her son." This again was from Kodjo Fi's youngest sister.

"And who are you to answer my mother back?" Ama's two cousins demanded of her.

"Go away. But who are you people?"

"Go away, too, you greedy lot."

"It is you who are greedy, witches."

"You are always calling other people witches. Only a witch can know a witch."

Soon everyone was shouting at everyone else. The people who had come started going home, and only the most curious ones stood by to listen. Maami Ama was murmuring something under her breath which I could not hear. I persuaded her to come with me. All that time no word had passed between her and her ex-husband. As we turned to go, Kodjo Fi's mother shouted at her, "You are hurt. But that is what you deserve. We will get the child. We will! What did you want to do with him?"

Maami Ama turned round to look at her. "What are you putting yourself to so much trouble for? When Nana Kum said the boy ought to go and stay with his father, did I make any objection? He is at the school. Go and fetch him. Tomorrow, you can send your carriers to come and fetch his belongings from my hut." These words were said quietly.

Then I remembered suddenly that I had to hurry to school to dismiss the children. I told Maami Ama to go home but that I would try to see her before night.

This time I did not go by the main street. I took the back door through back streets and lanes. It was past four already. As I hurried along, I heard a loud roaring sound which I took to be echoes of the quarrel, so I went my way. When I reached the school, I did not like what I saw. There was not a single childish soul anywhere. But everyone's books were there. The shed was as untidy as ever. Little Grace had left my books too.

Of course I was more than puzzled. "How naughty these children are. How did they dare to disobey me when I had told them to wait here until I came to dismiss them?" It was no use looking around the place. They were not there. "They need discipline," I threatened to the empty shed. I picked up my books and clock. Then I noticed that Kwesi's desk was clean of all his books. Nothing need be queer about this; he had probably taken his home. As I was descending the hill the second time that afternoon, I saw that the whole school was at the other end of the main street. What were the children doing so near Maami Ama's place? I ran towards them.

I was not prepared for what I saw. As if intentionally, the children had formed a circle. When some of them saw me, they all began to tell me what had happened. But I did not hear a word. In the middle of the circle, Kwesi was lying flat on his back. His shirt was off. His right arm was swollen to the size of his head. I simply stood there with my mouth open. From the back yard, Maami Ama screamed, "I am drowning people of Bamso, come and save me!" Soon the whole village was there.

What is the matter? What has happened? Kwesi has been bitten by a snake. Where? Where? At school. He was playing football. Where? What has happened? Bitten by a snake, a snake, a snake.

Questions and answers were tossed from mouth to mouth in the shocked evening air. Meanwhile, those who knew about snake-bites were giving the names of different cures. Kwesi's father was looking anxiously at his son. That strong powerful man was almost stupid with shock and alarm. Dose upon dose was forced down the reluctant throat but nothing seemed to have any effect. Women paced up and down around the hut, totally oblivious of the fact that they had left their festival meals half prepared. Each one was trying to imagine how she would have felt if

Kwesi had been her child, and in imagination they suffered more than the suffering mother. "The gods and spirits of our fathers protect us from calamity!"

After what seemed an unbearably long time, the messenger who had been earlier sent to Surdo, the village next to Bamso, to summon the chief medicine man arrived, followed by the eminent doctor himself. He was renowned for his cure of snake-bites. When he appeared, everyone gave a sigh of relief. They all remembered someone, perhaps a father, brother or husband, he had snatched from the jaws of death. When he gave his potion to the boy, he would be violently sick, and then of course, he would be out of danger. The potion was given. Thirty minutes; an hour; two hours; three, four hours. He had not retched. Before midnight, he was dead. No grown-up in Bamso village slept that night. Kwesi was the first boy to have died since the school was inaugurated some six years previously. "And he was his mother's only child. She has no one now. We do not understand it. Life is not sweet!" Thus ran the verdict.

The morning was very beautiful. It seemed as if every natural object in and around the village had kept vigil too. So they too were tired. I was tired too. I had gone to bed at about five o'clock in the morning and since it was a Saturday I could have a long sleep. At ten o'clock, I was suddenly roused from sleep by shouting. I opened my window but I could not see the speakers. Presently Kweku Sam, one of the young men in the village, came past my window. "Good morning, Chicha." He shouted his greeting to me.

"Good morning, Kweku," I responded. "What is the shouting about?"

"They are quarrelling."

"And what are they quarrelling about now?"

"Each is accusing the other of having been responsible for the boy's death."

"How?"

"Chicha, I don't know. Only women make too much trouble for themselves. It seems as if they are never content to sit quiet but they must always hurl abuse at each other. What has happened is too serious to be a subject for quarrels. Perhaps the village has displeased the gods in some unknown way and that is why they have taken away this boy." He sighed. I could not say anything to that. I could not explain it myself, and if the villagers believed there was something more in Kwesi's death than the ordinary human mind could explain, who was I to argue?

"Is Maami Ama herself there?"

"No, I have not seen her there."

He was quiet and I was quiet.

"Chicha, I think I should go away now. I have just heard that my sister has given birth to a girl."

"So," I smiled to myself. "Give her my congratulations and tell her I will come to see her tomorrow."

"*Yoo.*"

He walked away to greet his new niece. I stood for a long time at the window staring at nothing, while I heard snatches of words and phrases from the quarrel. And these were mingled with weeping. Then I turned from the window. Looking into the little mirror on the wall, I was not surprised to see my whole face bathed in unconscious tears. I did not feel like going to bed. I did not feel like doing anything at all. I toyed with the idea of going to see Maami Ama and then finally decided against it. I could not bear to face her; at least, not yet. So I sat down thinking about him. I went over the most presumptuous daydreams I had indulged in on his account. "I would have taken him away with me in spite of his mother's protests." She was just being absurd. "The child is a boy, and sooner or later, she must learn to live without him. The highest class here is Primary Six and when I am going away, I will take him. I will give him a grammar education. Perhaps, who knows, one day he may win a scholarship to the university." In my daydreams, I had never determined what career he would have followed, but he would be famous, that was certain. Devastatingly handsome, he would be the idol of women and the envy of every man. He would visit Britain, America and all those countries we have heard so much about. He would see all the seven wonders of the world. "Maami shall be happy in the end," I had told myself. "People will flock to see the mother of such an illustrious man. Although she has not had many children, she will be surrounded by her grandchildren. Of course, away from the village." In all these reveries his father never had a place, but there was I, and there was Maami Ama, and there was his father, and he, that bone of contention, was lost to all three. I saw the highest castles I had built for him come tumbling down, noiselessly and swiftly.

He was buried at four o'clock. I had taken the schoolchildren to where he lay in state. When his different relatives saw the little uniformed figure they all forgot their differences and burst into loud lamentations. "Chicha, O Chicha, what shall I do now that Kwesi is dead?" His grandmother addressed me. "Kwesi, my Beauty, Kwesi my Master, Kwesi-my-own-Kwesi," one aunt was chanting, "Father Death has done me an ill turn."

"Chicha," the grandmother continued, "my washing days are over, for who will give me water? My eating days are over, for who will give me food?" I stood there, saying nothing. I had let the children sing "Saviour Blessed Saviour." And we had gone to the cemetery with him.

After the funeral, I went to the House of Mourning as one should do after a burial. No one was supposed to weep again for the rest of the day. I sat there listening to visitors who had come from the neighbouring villages.

"This is certainly sad, and it is most strange. School has become like business; those who found it earlier for their children are eating more than the children themselves. To have a schoolboy snatched away like this is unbearable indeed," one woman said.

"Ah, do not speak," his father's youngest sister broke in. "We have lost a treasure."

"My daughter," said the grandmother again, "Kwesi is gone, gone for ever to our forefathers. And what can we do?"

"What can we do indeed? When flour is scattered in the sand, who can sift it? But this is the saddest I've heard, that he was his mother's only one."

"Is that so?" another visitor cried. "I always thought she had other children. What does one do, when one's only water-pot breaks?" she whispered. The question was left hanging in the air. No one dared say anything more.

I went out. I never knew how I got there, but I saw myself approaching Maami Ama's hut. As usual, the door was open. I entered the outer room. She was not there. Only sheep and goats from the village were busy munching at the cassava and the yams. I looked into the inner chamber. She was there. Still clad in the cloth she had worn to the divorce proceedings, she was not sitting, standing or lying down. She was kneeling, and like one drowning who catches at a straw, she was clutching Kwesi's books and school uniform to her breast. "Maami Ama, Maami Ama," I called out to her. She did not move. I left her alone. Having driven the sheep and goats away, I went out, shutting the door behind me. "I must go home now," I spoke to myself once more. The sun was sinking behind the coconut palm. I looked at my watch. It was six o'clock; but this time, I did not run.

1970

Meena Alexander

Meena Alexander (b. 1951) was born in Allahabad, India, to a family of Syrian Christians. Christened Mary Elizabeth, she changed her name to Meena on her fifteenth birthday—a name that she says in her autobiography *Fault Lines* (1993) reflects her "truer self, stripped free of the colonial burden." She lives in the United States, where she teaches at the City University of New York. Essayist, poet, and novelist, among her publications are *Nampally Road* (novel, 1991), *The Shock of Arrival: Reflections on Postcolonial Experience* (poems and essays, 1996), *River and Bridge* (poems, 1996), and *Manhattan Music* (novel, 1997).

Alexander's "Port Sudan" is a poem that records the speaker's return to what was once her home. Port Sudan is the Republic of Sudan's most important port city. Alexander lived from age 5 to 18 in this city, where her father worked with the Sudanese government soon after Sudan gained independence in 1956. Compare the poem with Dionne Brand's "Return I" and Eunice de Souza's "Return." The poem also links language with identity. The poet has said in her autobiography, "Colonialism seems intrinsic to the burden of English in India, and I felt robbed of literacy in my own mother tongue." In this regard, compare this poem with Derek Walcott's "Midsummer: LII."

Port Sudan

I listen to my father's voice on the phone.
He wants me to come from America to see him.
He does not want to die and be put in the earth,
my sweet father who held me so high
above the waters of the Red Sea, when I was five.
Who saw the white ship, the *S.S. Jehangir* docking
at Port Sudan and came sprinting for me,
through a crowd of labourers forced
to raise bales of cotton to their heads.

Someone cried: "KefHalek!"[1]
My skirt spun in the wind
and Arabic came into my mouth
and rested alongside all my other languages.
Now I know the truth of my tongue
starts where translations perish.
Where voices cease
and I face the image of the Pharaoh

---

[1] *KefHalek* "Kefhalek" is a greeting used among people who know each other well, a more intimate form of "Salaam Aliekum."

The one who murmured at the hour of his death
throat turned towards the restless waters:
"If I forget Upper Egypt, cut off my right hand.
Here lies memory."[1]
The same man loved his daughter so
he knew she needed knowledge of the imprints of earth,
glyphs cut in granite
inscriptions on rough cloth
underwater moorings and the black sun of death.

2002

---

[1] *If I… memory* The poet made up this comment by the Pharaoh.

Agha Shahid Ali

Agha Shahid Ali (1949-2001) was born in New Delhi; his ancestry and upbringing are Kashmiri. He was educated in Kashmir, New Delhi, and the United States. At the time of his death he was living in the United States, where he had taught at several universities and colleges, particularly Princeton and Penn State. His publications include *The Half-Inch Himalayas* (1987) and *A Nostalgist's Map of America* (1990).

In "Snowmen," Ali proclaims his ancestry and identity as South Asian ("Himalayan snow") but he always thought of his work as being unquestionably within a modern Western tradition. This in-betweenness is a hallmark of postcolonialism. Is there any evidence of this duality in "Snowmen"? Is there tension between form and content, East and West, or has the poet successfully integrated the antithetical elements? Compare Ali's treatment of ancestry and origins with Jean Arasanayagam's "I Have No Country," Edward Kamau Brathwaite's "Red Rising," and Shirley Lim's "Passports."

Snowmen

My ancestor, a man
of Himalayan snow,
came to Kashmir[1] from Samarkand,
carrying a bag
of whale bones:
heirlooms from sea funerals.
His skeleton
carved from glaciers, his breath
arctic,
he froze women in his embrace.
His wife thawed into stony water,
her old age a clear
evaporation.

This heirloom,
his skeleton under my skin, passed
from son to grandson,
generations of snowmen on my back.
They tap every year on my window,
their voices hushed to ice.

---

[1] *Kashmir* The northwestern region of the Indian subcontinent, at the foothills of the Himalayas.

No, they won't let me out of winter,
and I've promised myself,
even if I'm the last snowman,
that I'll ride into spring
on their melting shoulders.

1987

Lillian Allen

Lillian Allen (b. 1951) moved to Toronto from Jamaica in 1969. She is acclaimed as the originator in Canada of the genre of dub poetry, a form of oral poetry set to music and characterized
by strong political sentiments. She has published *Women Do This Every Day: Selected Poems*
(1993). She also writes plays and short fiction, produces films, and has made award-winning
recordings. She has one album for children and four for adults, including *Nothing But a Hero*
(1992).

"Rub A Dub Style Inna Regent Park" tries to capture as much as it can on the printed page the
oral and strongly musical element of dub poetry. It has to be heard, of course, to be appreciated fully. It pleads the case of the impoverished immigrant worker who is portrayed as
today's slave. The form of English used here could be compared with Louise Bennett's in
"Anancy an Ticks" and Arthur Yap's "2 Mothers in a HDB Playground."

Rub A Dub Style Inna[1] Regent Park[2]

Monday morning broke
News of a robbery
Pam mind went
couldn't hold the load
dem took her to the station
a paddy wagon
screaming...
her Johnny got a gun from an ex-policeman
Oh Lawd Oh Lawd Oh Lawd eh ya
a wey dis ya society a do
to wi sons[3]
Rub a dub style
inna Regent Park
mon a dub it inna dance
inna Regent Park
Oh Lawd Oh Lawd

"forget yu troubles and dance"[4]
forget yu bills dem

---

[1] *Inna* In a.

[2] Regent Park is a culturally diverse neighbourhood in Toronto.

[3] *a wey dis...sons* What is this society doing to our sons.

[4] Bob Marley's lyrics from "Them Belly Full (But We Hungry)," in the album *Natty Dread* (1975).

an irie up yuself[1]
forget yu dreams gathering dusts
on the shelves
dj rapper hear im[2] chant
pumps a musical track
for im platform
cut it wild
say de system vile
dubbing it inna dance
frustration pile
a different style
inna Regent Park

could have been a gun
but's a mike in his hand
could've been a gun spilling out the lines
    but is a mike
      is a mike
is a mike
Oh Lawd Oh Lawd Oh Lawd

riddim line vessel im ache
from im heart outside
culture carry im past
an steady im mind
man tek[3] a draw an feeling time
words cut harsh I   try to find
explanations
de sufferings of de times

"forget yu troubles and dance"
forget yu bills dem
an irie up yuself
forget yu dreams gatherin
dust dust dust

is a long time wi sweating here
is a long time wi waiting here

---

[1] *an irie up yuself* And cheer yourself up.

[2] *im* Him.

[3] *tek* Take.

to join society's rites
is a long time wi beating down yu door

is a long time since we mek[1] the trip
cross the Atlantic
on the slave shipppppppp
is a long time wi knocking
an every time yu slam the door
sey: no job
discrimination — injustice
a feel the whip lick
an is the same boat
   the same boat
      the same boat
Oh Lawd Oh Lawd Oh Lawd eh ya

dj chant out cutting it wild
sey one hay fi dub it inna different style
when doors close down on society's rites
windows will pry open
in the middle of the night
dashed hopes run wild
in the middle of the night
Oh Lawd Oh Lawd Oh Lawd eh

1993 (Recorded 1986)

---

[1] *mek* Make.

32

Mulk Raj Anand

Mulk Raj Anand (1905-2004) was born in Peshawar, India (now in Pakistan). He was educated in Punjab and London and earned his PhD in Philosophy in 1929. Actively involved in India's struggle for independence, he served later as cultural advisor to the government. *Untouchable* (1935) was the first of his many novels, which include also *The Village* (1939), *Across the Black Waters* (1940), *The Sword and the Sickle* (1942), and *The Private Life of an Indian Prince* (1953). He has written on such diverse topics as *The Indian Theatre* (1950), *Is There a Contemporary Indian Civilization?* (1963), and *Indian Ivories* (1970).

Anand's "Duty" was written during the colonial period in India, but colonial and postcolonial issues are subsumed beneath a portrayal of a slice of Indian society that is conscious of class (and caste) hierarchy. It can be compared in this regard with such stories as Saros Cowasjee's "His Father's Medals" and Anita Desai's "Surface Textures." Is the title significant? The opening paragraph provides an extended introduction to the midday sun of Indian summers. How important is the natural setting? Is there an element of social Darwinism here?

Duty

The midday sun blasts everything in the Indian summer: it scorches the earth till its upper layers crack into a million fissures; it sets fire to the water till the lakes and pools and swamps bubble, evaporate and dry up; it shrivels up the lives of birds, beasts and flowers; it burns into one like red pepper and leaves one gasping for breath with a bulging tongue till one spends one's time looking for some shady spot for even the most precarious shelter.

Mangal Singh, the policeman who had been posted on duty at the point where the branch road from the village of Vadala enters the Mall Road of Chetpur, had taken shelter under the sparse foliage of a kikar tree[1] beyond the layers of white dust, after having stood in the sun for five and a half hours since dawn. In a little while sepoy[2] Rahmat-Ullah would come and relieve him, and he felt that he could cool down a little and prepare to go to the barracks.

The sun was penetrating even the leaves of the wayside trees, and there was not much comfort in the humid airless atmosphere, but after the cracking heat of the open, Mangal felt that this comparative shade was a blessing.

He was not, of course, like the delicate Lallas, rich Hindu merchants, who rode out into the gardens early in the morning and withdrew after "eating" the fresh air at sunrise and never appeared till sunset, sitting in the laps of their wives drinking

---

[1] *kikar tree* A small thorny tree used primarily for timber and fuel.

[2] *sepoy* The term used in the British Indian Army (and still used in the modern Indian Army) for an infantry private.

milk-water or lying sprawled about on the front boards of their shops under the cool air of electric fans.... No, he didn't say as they would: "I go for a pice[1] worth of salt, bring me a palanquin."[2] Nor could he "quench his thirst by drinking dew." No, he was proud that he came from strong peasant stock and was a hardy policeman who could rough it: indeed, this police service was not active enough for him and he felt it a pity that he had not become a real sepoy; for there was more pay in the paltans[3] and there were better uniforms, also free mufti and free rations. So he had heard after he had put the mark of his thumb down and joined the police force — but once done cannot be undone. And it was the blessing of the Gurus, as there was little chance of earning any extra money in the military; while, apart from the fifteen rupees' pay, there were other small sums so long as confectioners continued to mix milk with water and so long as there was a murder or two in the prostitutes' bazaar, and so long as there were respectable Lallas who would pay rather than have their names mentioned.... Why, even here on point-duty in the waste land — "your own is your own and another's is also yours." For if the peasants offered tokens of grain and butter and sugar to the Munshi at the customs house, then why not to the police? That skinny little Babu at the octroi[4] post had not the strong arm of the sepoy to protect them when they were being looted by the thugs in the market.... He knew. After wisdom the club. If only he had been able to pay a nazar to the Tehsildar he would never have lost his land to Seth Jhinda Ram.... But God's work was well done, man's badly. And, truly, if he had not pressed the limbs of the landlord he would never have got the recommendation to join the police. And you learnt a great deal in the service of the Sarkar.[5] And there was nothing better than service: no worry, and there was so much izzat[6] in it that these very cowardly city folk who laughed at you if you were a peasant joined their hands in obeisance to you if you wielded a truncheon. And the rustics who had no notion of discipline or duty could be made to obey authority with the might of the stave, and if they didn't obey that, the fear of the handcuff — even a daring robber like Barkat Ali could not escape because one could blow the whistle and call the entire police force out. And the Sarkar is truly powerful. Like Alamgir,[7] it leaves no fire in the hearth, nor water in the jar, to bring a man to justice....

He glanced at his dust-covered feet in the regulation shoes of rough cow-hide, even as he congratulated himself on his lucky position as a member of the much-feared police service and wished he had really been in the army, for there the sepoys had boots given them. His puttees too were old and faded and there was something

---

[1] *pice* Paise, an Indian coin.

[2] *palanquin* A covered sedan or chair.

[3] *paltans* British Bengali colonial regiment (probably derived from "platoon").

[4] *octroi* Local tax-collector.

[5] *Sarkar* The government or the powers-that-be.

[6] *izzat* The honour or reputation of a person, organization or institution.

[7] *Alamgir* Rulers of the Mogul Empire (in India): Alamgir I (1658–1707); Alamgir II (1754–59).

loose about the khaki uniform with the black belt. The uniform of the army was so tight-fitting. Perhaps the whistle-chain and the truncheon improved this and the red-and-blue turban was nice, but—he lifted his hand to caress the folds of his headdress and to adjust it, as it was heavy and got soaked with the sweat that flowed from his fuming scalp burdened by long hair on the lower edges....

The sun poured down a flood of fire on the earth, and it seemed as if the desolate fields covered with dense brown thickets and stalks of grass and cacti were crackling like cinders and would soon be reduced to ashes. A partridge hummed in its nest somewhere and a dove cooed from the tree overhead, giving that depth to the shade which fills the air with long, endless silences and with the desolate peace of loneliness.

Mangal Singh drifted a few steps from where he was standing and halted on a spot where the shade was thicker than it was anywhere else under the kikar trees. And, blowing a hot breath, he cupped his palms over the knob of his stave and leaned his chin on the knuckles of his joined hands and stood contemplating the scene with half-closed eyes like a dog who rests his muzzle on his front paws and lies in wait for his prey.

Layers of white-sheeted mist floated past his eyes in the sun-soaked fields, the anguish of a thousand heat-singed bushes, while the parched leaves of the hanging boughs of the wayside trees rustled at the touch of a scorching breeze.

One breath, a thousand hopes, they say, and there never comes a day without evening—but it would be very difficult to walk down to the barracks through this terrible heat. And he wished his duty was not up, that someone could fetch his food for him and that he could borrow a charpai[1] from the octroi and go to sleep in the grove of neem trees by the garden of Rais Jagjiwan Das, or sit and talk to the grass-cutter's wife who had breasts like turnips. Only Rahmat-Ullah had an eye on her too, and he was sure to be here, as he preferred the desolate afternoon, thinking that he might get a chance when no one was about.

"I will have to walk back to the lines," he muttered to himself and yawned. He felt heavy and tired at the prospect and his legs seemed to weaken from the knowledge of the unending trudge of three miles. He shook his head and tried to be alert, but the invisible presence of some overwhelming force seemed to be descending on him and his heavy-lidded eyes were closing against his will. He took a deep breath and made another effort to open his eyes wide through the drowsy stupor of the shade that weighed down from the trees. For a moment his body steadied and his eyes half opened. But how hateful was the glare, and how cruel, how meaningless, was life outside.... And what peace, what quiet below the trees, beneath the eyes....

If a God should be standing here he could not help closing his eyes for a minute, he felt; and sleep came creeping into his bones with a whiff of breeze that was like a soft beauty retreating coyly before the thousand glares of the torrid sun which burnt so passionately above the silent fields.... The heat seemed to be melting the

---

[1] *charpai* A portable string cot.

fat in his head and to be blinding his eyes, and he let himself be seduced by the placid stillness into a trance of half-sleep....

Through sleepy eyes he was conscious of the whispering elements as he dozed, and his body still stood more or less erect, though his head was bent on the knuckles of his hand above the stave, and the corners of his mouth dribbled slightly....

"Shoop ... shoop ... shoop ..." a snake seemed to lash his face at the same time as he saw the soothing vision of a dim city through the stealthy corners of whose lanes he was passing suavely into a house was effaced....

"Shoop ... shoop...."

He came to suddenly and saw Thanedar Abdul Kerim standing before him, his young face red with anger under the affected Afghan turban, his tall lanky form tight — stretched, a cane in his hand, and his bicycle leaning against his legs....

"Wake up! Wake up, you ox of a Sikh! Is it because it is past twelve that your senses have left you?"

Mangal reeled, then steadied himself, his hands climbing automatically to his turban which had been shaken by the Inspector's onslaught.

"Shoop ... shoop," the cane struck his side again and stung his skin like a hundred scorpions. And a welter of abuse fell upon his ears: "Bahin chod, the D.S.P. might have passed, and you are supposed to be on *duty*. Wake up and come to your senses, Madar chod!"[1]

Quite involuntarily Mangal's right hand left the turban and shot up to his forehead in a salute, and his thick, trembling lips phewed some hot stale breath: "Huzoor Mai-bap."[2]

"You eat the bread of illegality," the Thanedar shouted. "I will be reprimanded and my promotion stopped, you swine!"

And he lifted his cane to strike Mangal again, but the sepoy was shaking with fright so that his stave dropped from his hand.

Mangal bent and picked up his lathi.[3]

"Go and be on your point-duty!" ordered the Thanedar sternly and, putting his foot on the pedal, rode shakily away on his bicycle.

Mangal walked out of the shade, his shins and thighs still trembling and his heart thumping in spite of himself, though he was less afraid than conscience-stricken for neglecting his duty.

The heat of the sun made the skin of his face smart with a sharp pain where the perspiration flowed profusely down his neck. He rubbed his hand across it and felt the sweat tingle like a raw wound.

He shook himself and his head twitched, and he looked about in order to see if anyone had seen him being beaten. He wanted to bear the pain like a man. But his

---

[1] *Bahin chod* Sister-fucker; *Madar chod* Mother-fucker.

[2] *Huzoor Mai-bap* O lord, mother-father.

[3] *lathi* A stick or baton, used by Indian policemen.

eyes, startled by the suddenness with which they had opened, were full of a boiling liquid that melted into fumes as he raised his head.

His throat was parched dry and he coughed with an effort so that his big brown face above the shaggy beard reddened. Then he paused to spit on the road and felt his legs trembling and shaking more than ever. He twisted his face in the endeavour to control his limbs and lunged forward....

"Ohe, may you die, ohe asses, ohe, may you die," came a voice from behind him.

As he turned round he saw a herd of donkeys come stampeding up the road in a wild rush, which became wilder as their driver trotted fast behind them in an attempt to keep them from entering the Mall Road at that pace.

For a moment the cloud of dust the herd had raised on the sides of the deeply rutted Vadala Road obscured Mangal's view of the man, but then suddenly he could hear him shouting: "Ohe, may you die, asses!"

Mangal ran with his stave upraised in a wild scurry towards the driver of the stampeding donkeys, scattering them helter-skelter till some of them cantered the more quickly into the Mall and the others turned back and came to a standstill. He caught the driver up before the man had escaped into a ditch by the banana field. And, grinding a half-expressed curse between his teeth, he struck him with his stave hard, hard, harder, so that the blows fell edgewise on a donkey's neck, on the driver's arms, on a donkey's back, on a donkey's head, on the man's legs....

"Oh, forgive, Sarkar, it is not my fault," the man shouted in an angry, indignant voice while he rubbed his limbs and spread his hands to ward off more blows.

"You, son of a dog," hissed Mangal as he struck again and again, harder and harder as if he had gone mad, till his stave seemed to ring as a bamboo stick does when it is splitting into shreds.

1938

Jean Arasanayagam

Jean Arasanayagam (b. 1940) was born in Kandy, Sri Lanka (Ceylon), into a Dutch Burgher family (that is, of mixed Dutch and local ancestry; her birth-name was Jean Solomons). She was educated there and in Scotland. She has published several volumes of poetry and fiction, including *A Colonial Inheritance and Other Poems* (1985), *Out of our Prisons We Emerge* (poems, 1987), *Red Water Flows Clear* (poems, 1991), *The Cry of the Kite* (stories, 1984), *The Outsider* (novel, 1989), and *The Famished Waterfall* (novel, 2004).

In "I Have No Country" Arasanayagam examines the plight of a postcolonial individual (most likely living in Sri Lanka) who feels there is no hope for a better world for her, in her homeland or elsewhere. The poet deliberately echoes Tennyson's high-spirited speaker in "Ulysses" to underline contrastingly her speaker's dismay. Compare this poem with Edwin Thumboo's "Ulysses by the Merlion" and Agha Shahid Ali's "Snowmen."

I Have No Country

I have no country now but self
I mark my boundaries extend demesnes
Even beyond the darkness of those regions
Still to be explored, chart my ocean voyages
In blood or stay becalmed watching a gull
Impale its shadow on a thorn of wave.
Waiting for the winds to blow to set once more
In motion the pattern of the sea, a ripple stir
Into a wave that sweeps, tidal, wide horizons,
Rises above a cloud to drench the sky
And pours its deluge on the stars to drown
All lights and in that darkness find again
New brightness from a self created firmament
The cosmic mind imagines, to choose one star
Out of a galaxy or constellation, constant as
The Pole's unmoving light[1] whose spokes glittered
On the waves to guide through an unknown and
Blinding dark, the voyages of ancient mariners
Through oceans to reach those lands as yet unmapped
And undiscovered.

---

[1] *Pole's unmoving light* The Pole star is Polaris (the "north star"). Other stars' positions change throughout the night in the sky, but not the Pole star's. It is depended on to indicate the direction north.

Once more to journey on a chartered course
To reach which country? One that I must know
Before this birth or one that others more intrepid
Had discovered so that for me there's no new
Adventure left and nothing new for exploration
Except the landmarks racing through my blood
Or found in ruined fortresses and artefacts
In archives and in museums.

What subterfuge of islands draw me near
Destruction, here, snares already set, the pit is staked
With poisoned thorns and ragged branches,
My footsteps trapped with guile, I fell headlong
Through the camouflage, the hunt made easy
For both hunter and for poacher. And remain
My gait now fractured, couched on a bed of thorns
Wait for what death will come, through knife or bullet.
This was perhaps my choice. So I stay here
Iconoclastic of all statues, images
Covering the walls of sacred places,
The saints too good, too pure and too unreal
To be my guides although they too follow paths
That can only spell new dangers.
Heretical my thought and that of all unbelievers
Yet out of a loss of faith
For our salvation, we seek once more
A stronger faith; my fear is that escape
From martyrdom makes our complexion and
Our stature, coward. Cowering for safety
In the camps to which we flee for refuge
And remain with other fugitives who have escaped
From fire and slaughter for all time disinherited.

1991

Louise Bennett

Louise Bennett (-Coverley; 1919-2006) was born in Jamaica. A folklorist, writer, and performing artiste, she originally wrote poems in Standard English but abandoned that for Jamaican creole or "nation language." She went to England on a drama scholarship and had a regular program on the BBC. She spent the last years of her life based in Toronto after years of residing in Jamaica. Her publications include *Jamaica Labrish* (1966), *Aunty Roachy Seh* (1993), and retold Jamaican folk tales in such published collections as *Anancy and Miss Lou* (1979).

Bennett's "Anancy an Ticks" is a well-known Caribbean comic folktale about the trickster spider Anancy (first told by Philip Sherlock in *Anansi the Spider Man*, 1954; see his "The Warau People Discover the Earth"), whose cunning allows him to exist in a world of hardship primarily by taking advantage of those not as smart as he. In this story, Anancy outwits Ticks into feeling guilty about the loss of a goat. This etiological tale accounts for why ticks infest the hides of cows. Note that the language used here is considered a demotic version of English. Throughout the former British Empire, English evolved into various local versions (just as Latin had evolved into such Romance languages as French, Italian, and Spanish). Compare Bennett's English with Arthur Yap's "Singlish" (Singaporean English) in his poem "2 Mothers in a HDB Playground."

Anancy an Ticks

Once upon a time Anancy an Ticks use to live nex door to one anada. Anancy had a goat an Ticks had a cow, but Anancy coulda read an Ticks couldn't read. An eena dem days dem nevah got no Literacy Campaign.

Well, one day Anancy read eena newspaper seh dat a gentleman want a cow an a man fi hire, an de man haffi ride de cow fi do certain kine a job wat de gentleman had. Anancy memba Bredda Ticks cow an him study a brain fi work pon Ticks.

One evenin wen Ticks was a put up him cow fi de night, Anancy chop off him goat head an push it eena de tick bush between him an Ticks yard. Him hole awn pon de head an gwan like him a try fi pulli out.

Hear him: "Mmmmmi woan come out, mmmmi fasten."

Bredda Ticks seh: "Wat happen, Anancy?"

Hear Anancy: "Me goat, Bredda Ticks—him fasten ina de bush yah, an all de draw me dah draw me cyan get him out. Come help me, Bredda Ticks."

Ticks like a big fool go ovah Anancy yard, hole awn pon de goat head an meck one pull wid all him strengt. Plaps! De goat head come out ina him han.

Anancy jump up ina tempa an seh: "Eehi now, Bredda Ticks, yuh see weh yuh do? De one deggeh goat me got yuh teck grudgeful kill him! Bredda Ticks, i naw go soh! Bad tings a goh happen between me an yuh!"

Po Ticks so frighten, hear him: "Cho, Anancy—noh gwan so. Is accident."

Hear Anancy: "Me goat jine tird party insurance an is bans a truvel fi yuh, Bredda Ticks. Me an yuh dah go a law, an yuh wi haffi pay fi me goat weh yuh kill!"

Po Ticks start cry an seh: "Bredda Anancy, me noh got noh money, as yuh know— all me got is a cow!"

Anancy seh: "Well yuh wi haffi gi me de cow."

Ticks seh: "Ef me gi yuh di cow is wat me gwine teck meck me livin?"

Hear Anancy: "Bredda Ticks, ah sorry fi yuh, so ah gwine ease yuh up. Ef yuh willin fi work yuh cow an pay me back fi me goat, me know a way how yuh can do it."

Ticks seh: "Yes, Bredda Nancy, me wi tenkful."

Anancy seh: "Me know a gentleman wat want smaddy fi ride a cow an do some work fi him. Meck we go to him now, an yuh work an pay me, back."

So Anancy teck Ticks to de man an hire him out wid de cow, an Anancy collec de pay. An up to now Ticks no done pay Anancy yet. Das why till teday Ticks still live in a cow back. Is Anancy meck it.

Jack Mandora, me noh choose none.[1]

HERE IS A LITERAL RENDITION OF THE STORY IN MORE OR LESS STANDARD ENGLISH:

Once upon a time, Anancy and Ticks used to live next door to each other. Anancy had a goat and Ticks had a cow, but Anancy could read and Ticks couldn't read. And in those days they never had any Literacy Campaign.

Well, one day Anancy reads in the newspaper that a gentleman wants a cow and a man for hire, and the man has to ride the cow to do certain kinds of job that the gentleman has. Anancy remembers Brother Ticks's cow and he studies [racks his brain to come up with] a plan to work on Ticks.

One evening when Ticks is putting his cow up for the night, Anancy chops off his [own] goat's head and pushes it in the thick bush between his and Ticks's yards. He holds on to the head and goes on [pretends] like he is trying to pull it out.

Hear him: "Mmmmm, it won't come out; mmmm, it fasten."

Brother Ticks says: "What happen, Anancy?"

Hear Anancy: "My goat, Brother Ticks — he's fastened in the bush here and all the draw [pull] I draw I can't get him out. Come help me, Brother Ticks."

Ticks, like a big fool, goes over to Anancy's yard; he holds on to the goat's head and makes one pull with all his strength. Plaps! The goat's head comes out in his hand.

Anancy jumps up in a temper and says: "Eh-eh, now, Brother Ticks, you see what you do? The one and only goat I got you take [and] grudgefully kill him! Brother Ticks, I'm not going [to behave] so! Bad things are going to happen between me and you!"

---

[1] *me noh choose none* Many Anancy stories end with this declaration. Jack Mandora is "keeper of heaven's door." "Me no choose none" is a disclaimer by the storyteller; it means literally "It is not of my choosing" or "Don't blame me; I'm not responsible for the action/morals of the story."

Poor Ticks is so frightened, hear him: "Cho, Anancy— don't go on so. Is [an] accident."

Hear Anancy: "My goat join third party insurance and is lots a trouble for you, Brother Ticks. Me and you will go to law [court], and you'll have to pay for my goat that you killed!"

Poor Ticks starts to cry and says: "Brother Anancy, I've no money, as you know—all I got is a cow!"

Anancy says: "Well, you will have to give me the cow."

Ticks says: "If I give you the cow, how am I going to make my living?"

Hear Anancy: "Brother Ticks, I'm sorry for you so I'm going to ease up on you. If you're willing to work your cow and pay me back for my goat, I know a way how you can do it."

Ticks says: "Yes, Brother 'Nancy; I'll be thankful."

Anancy says: "I know a gentleman who wants somebody to ride a cow and do some work for him. Let us go to him now, and you work and pay me back."

So Anancy takes Ticks to the man and hires him out with the cow, and Anancy collects the pay. And up to now Ticks hasn't done paying Anancy yet.

That's why until today ticks still live in cows' back. It is Anancy who is responsible for this.

Jack Mandora, it is not of my choosing.

1975 [1957]

Neil Bissoondath

Neil Bissoondath (b. 1955) was born and educated in Arima, Trinidad; he immigrated to Canada in 1973 to attend York University. He currently lives in Quebec City, Canada. His publications include *Digging Up the Mountains* (stories, 1986), *A Casual Brutality* (novel, 1988), *Doing the Heart Good* (novel, 2002), and *The Unyielding Clamour of the Night* (novel, 2005). An outspoken critic of Canada's multiculturalism policy, he has published *Selling Illusions: The Cult of Multiculturalism in Canada* (1994).

Bissoondath's "Man as Plaything, Life as Mockery" illustrates the author's belief in the commonality of human experience. He contends (like such writers as Timothy Mo and Rohinton Mistry) that he writes about human rather than specifically ethnic experiences. Is this why in his story the protagonist-refugee to Canada remains unnamed and his country of origin unidentified? Does this technique help to point up the universality of the refugee experience? Would the story be more realistic/authentic if his country of origin and the particular sociopolitical context were revealed? Compare this story with Austin Clarke's "The Man," which depicts the life of an immigrant in Toronto whose ethnic and cultural particulars are most evident.

Man as Plaything, Life as Mockery

It had rained earlier that morning. Then a wind had arisen and driven away the clouds that had made a rumpled grey sweater of the morning sky. Aspect changed dramatically: the wind, cold and with a bite, brought in its own cloud, low, white, rapid with the urgency of a miracle sky. There was a play of light and shadow that altered the view more rapidly than the eye could seize it. It was like viewing, in rapid succession, the positive and negative of the same photograph: the vision was tricked, the substantial lost, so that even the angular concrete of the airport carpark across the way was emptied, became unreal.

His stance, feet apart, hands clasped behind his back, was casual. It was an attitude struck, a pose. Only the fingers could give him away: even intertwined, they were in motion, playing with one another, rubbing at one another, dissipating energy in small spurts, like dust. They held a scrap of paper that might have been a large theatre ticket, or a grocery list. But a closer glance revealed more history, its creases and lines filled in with the luminous brown that comes not from dirt but from years of handling.

He unclasped his hands, taking the paper in his right palm. He raised it but didn't look at it immediately. A lengthy darkening of the outside view caused his reflection to be etched in the glass wall in front of him and for a moment he studied his face: square, pudgy, with inexpressive eyes caught in the middle of thick, circular spectacle frames, hair so thinned that in the muted light he looked bald. Then his body: a raincoat of unarresting cut, an impression of bulk compressed onto a small frame, a sturdiness that surprised him.

The sun flashed suddenly and his image was effaced. Outside, a man in white coveralls, carrying a broom and a garbage bag, shuffled by chasing a wayward paper cup. The absurd figure, a tragi-comedy on legs, irritated him. He turned his lips down, deepening the hollows that defined his cheeks, and finally, as if in anger, looked at the paper in his hand.

It was a photograph, the outlines of black, white, and grey blurring through time into a desperate fuzziness, so that there was no distinction, no sharpness to the image, like an ink drawing on cheap paper. But his memory sharpened the lines, defined the contours, and to his practised eye a youthful female face came clear. Her smile was thin, not hesitant but threadbare, a gesture, he could tell, summoned for the camera from a carefully rationed reserve.

The photograph produced no effect in him. It had become too familiar over the years and he searched it now only for the way things might have gone: how the cheeks might have sagged, the eyes bagged, the forehead crinkled. But the effort was beyond him. The image was too static, had replaced the vivid elasticity of memory so that the face was no longer a face but a frozen combination of features.

The woman, his wife, had almost ceased to be real.

He slipped the photograph into his coat pocket, half-turning to glance at the arrival monitor that hung from the far wall behind him. There had been a change: the letters ARR now commented on her flight number.

Something within him jumped.

It was not that he had hoped to avoid memory. That would have required an effort beyond his resources.

And he had recognized that, for him, it could never be myth. The transformation would have depleted him, would have used him up; and that depletion, that sense of a life gone by, would have been bequeathed to their daughter, an unfair inheritance. So that what for him could never be myth had, for their daughter, quickly taken on atmosphere. She was denied perspective, save for that of the novel. He saw this as strength: it was a way of moving forward.

She was now twenty-seven. Then she had been five.

He was now fifty-four. Then he had been thirty-two.

Twenty-two years: it was a lifetime.

Still, he remembered. The rain, the mud turning the night into a glutinous surge: the thunder of heavy guns, seeming always close, gouging then dulling the senses; the banks of black smoke for days on end defining the sun into a circle of red-hot metal; the corpses and pieces of corpses backing up in the ditches by night, rotting in the ditches by day; and the flow of people—in front, beside, behind— men, women, children, faces blank with misery, possessions abandoned, moving without urgency, like people stripped of all but the automatic, offered nothing now but a knowledge of loss and a numbing sense of violation, victims of a mass rape. Even terror, then, had been beyond them.

And yet no memory was as vivid as the warmth that had filled his hand, that had pressed limply against his chest, exuding exhaustion.

He had shielded his daughter from nothing. She saw, as he did, the severed head of a neighbour lying beside the road; had helped him fight off the dogs driven crazy by hunger; had foraged for roots in soil long dredged; had watched, with him in a torpor, as a mother prepared to carve her husband's body so her children, hollow-eyed approximations of themselves, could eat.

He was grateful that none of this had remained with her. She recalled only playing with sand, playing with dogs, faces and movement; memories edited of carnage.

He himself had lost none of it. But he had retained too the memory of her warmth, a warmth that held its own terror, of night, of contemplated infanticide, of horror of his own hands, of utter senselessness. And yet, in an unfathomable way, it was a positive memory.

It had been a grey violent time, a time in which the rules of human life had been usurped by human madness, an experience of images that formed no whole, that took no shape, an experience without parentheses. It was history in the making, episodic, he and his daughter particles insignificant in the upheaval of event. None of the usual prejudices applied. It was an extraordinary time, requiring extraordinary responses, eliciting extraordinary ends. The centre had been lost, all had become unpredictable.

So they had trudged, father and daughter, across the bridge of black iron that offered an unrelieving safety, separated from the wife, the mother, by hundreds, by thousands of miles of chaos, just another attenuated refugee family among countless other attenuated refugee families, misery blending them into a whole for the news photographers who scurried around, absorbed, flashbulbs popping.

Attenuated: by profession, by civil war. The wounded needed a doctor; his right hand was bulbous with pus from a wound by an infected scalpel. His wife, a surgeon more skilful than he, went off into the night with her bundle of instruments. He knew the horrors that awaited her: amputations without anaesthetic, stomachs that spilled their contents, bodies with more rips than pores, blood less precious than water. The images, red, gleaming, startling in their intensity, had come to him through a feverish haze as he watched her retreating back, her bundle. He knew he had felt pain; he had retained the knowledge of it. Pain, he had learnt, could not be a memory; the mind resisted, and only the absence of well-being could be submitted to review, in a withdrawn, intellectual way.

Hours, days, weeks: he didn't know how much time passed. Night and day switched places, and back again. His wife didn't return. He didn't know where she had gone, which of the many groups she had left with. Heavy artillery blended dusk with dawn as the fight closed in. Still she didn't return. And when the guns caused their town to split in two, spilling its guts like an overripe corpse, he fled with his daughter, following the ride.

No one talked of safety. No one talked of direction. No one talked. They trudged, through a landscape overturned.

He remembered the first evening of safety, a night spent in a churchyard, in a rain that couldn't cleanse. The church had been crowded, the pews, the altar, the corners disappearing under black, heaving bundles of sighs. He had found a spot against an outside wall, had sat, his back to the wall, his raised knees covered by a piece of cardboard, his daughter asleep on the ground under the cardboard.

Sleep had eluded him on that night: around him thin chests collapsing in an oblique light, apparitions of limp bodies, arms, legs dangling, being carted away by shadowed figures. A night of death in mime.

Just before dawn, the man lying next to him—a stranger of familiar clothes and unfamiliar dialect—very quietly pressed a six-inch knife into his own side, up to the wooden hilt and then beyond. He made no sound; there was little blood. He sighed as if in satisfaction and a thin trickle of red crept from the left corner of his mouth, slashed rapidly down across his cheek, like a wound opening itself.

He had watched, had made no attempt to interfere, had offered a mute compassion which, he knew, denied his profession. It had been a private act, silent, relieving, like the swallowing of a pill.

He had watched as the rain eased, then stopped, and the sun, creating steam, sliced more deeply into the churchyard, the ground black with people stirring tentatively, in disbelief of life.

His neighbour drained, already shrunken, one hand still clutching what was left of the knife hilt, attracted no attention.

Safety. It provided no answers. They had to be made.

He remembered, but no longer really cared to, the trek through the city solidified with refugees in search of further flight. Papers, stamps, signatures; documents newly printed, crackling with the fresh and the official he could have believed no longer existed; tiny pleasures that surprised him, like being asked to sign his name and discovering that once more, in some miraculous way, it counted for something beyond the simplest of identification. He was asked for his medical papers. He didn't have them. But he was a doctor, he had a profession. It struck him as extraordinary, and he wondered, but only for a moment, that he could have watched with equanimity the suicide of his churchyard neighbor. That this could be construed as a denial of his profession seemed to him now only a passing fancy.

He managed, through contacts, to get the necessary papers. Everything could be managed somehow, even from a country still convulsed against itself—everything but his wife. Paper, if not destroyed, stayed put, could be traced, retrieved; but a person moved, was driven by spasm beyond human control like a piece of meat moving through intestine. Her rescue was the one thing he couldn't manage. She was too distant, out of his reach.

Wait, they said, wait for the war to end.

Wait for things to settle down. Settle yourself first.

Here's your visa. Take your daughter. Go. Wait.

One man, an official in white shirt with sleeves rolled stylishly, incongruously, to his elbow, meaning to be kind but in the hurried way survival demanded, said,

"You've lost everything. You've lost your wife. Count her for dead. Take your daughter and go."

And he had thought: Yes.

So he had emigrated, got himself accredited, begun to build a base in a land alien to him. Here, the war was remote, a small item on the world-news page of the local newspaper. Then the war ended and the land he had left, quickly grown alien, withdrew into itself, became hermetic. It sealed his wife in.

He noted the withdrawal with calm. He was building his base. Much of the period he recalled only through a haze, as of fatigue, and it was his eviscerating effort that now offered itself as myth to him. His wife, the memory of her, began to evade him and after a while — he didn't know how long; time revealed its man-made fragility, divested itself of context — he stopped the unconscious calculation of time's breach. It had become pointless in every way.

His daughter grew quickly and, in a way that he found inexplicable, began to slip from his grasp. She was, he realized one evening, no longer an asexual being. She was becoming aware of differences, and his clumsiness only increased her apprehension. He was a doctor, he knew the technical details. But how to explain them to his daughter? For a time, he thought of his wife, as of a stranger, with blame. And then he thought of her no more.

Back then, the city which had become his had been grey and stolid. Nothing sparkled. The foreign was distrusted. People kept to themselves. They worked and, afterwards, retreated to family, to a privacy that was itself hermetic.

So it surprised him when, at the hospital, Marya began seeking him out to talk: about her flight from Soviet armies at the end of the war, about the family she had had to abandon, about the man who had brought her then discarded her for a middle-aged artist who promised mothering and an Oedipal sexuality. She went, from the first, to the heart of the personal.

No reply came to him; he felt a sense of caution, a wariness. He asked, with unmerited rudeness, why she had singled him out.

It was, she said, because she recognized in him someone who might understand: they shared a quality, a quality of absorption. In the grey city, it marked him.

He remained guarded.

She talked, and as she talked, weaving images, conjuring horror, his reserve broke.

He told her about his flight, his daughter, his problems, his wife, too, but almost incidentally: she was just another element.

Marya offered to help with his daughter.

He hesitated; he was a doctor, she a floor-cleaner. He often passed her in the corridor, he clasping a chart, she a mop, each acknowledging the other only by the merest of pauses, the way a bee might react before an artificial flower, with surprise and a mild confusion. Then, after a night of thought, he accepted her offer.

At first, his daughter resisted, but Marya was persistent. Over time they grew close, Marya, his daughter, and him. And the first time he slept with Marya he was surprised at the warmth and pliability of her flesh. Every day at the hospital he touched patients, but with her his fingers trembled, lost their professional edge, offered a thrill without memory, and culminated in an act that was, to him, startling in its exclusiveness. He discovered in his hands a set of abilities he thought he had lost. It was like a gift.

When, eventually, Marya moved in—she had only two suitcases and a box of assorted papers, pictures, mementoes, knick-knacks that assumed value only to an attenuated life—it seemed the natural thing to do, even, yet especially, in the grey city.

One evening he took a mental step outside his life and gazed back at it with what he thought was objectivity, and he was struck by what a perfect family they made. He thought with a gentle awe: I am happy.

I am happy. Yet, with lucidity, he refused to indulge the thought. It was an attitude not only of the present but also of the future; it reached beyond the graspable to the uncertainties of hope, dream, and expectation. He had seen too much, been through too much, been too much the pawn of the unpredictable. He would deal with what he could see, feel, smell, touch, hear, understand. He rejected the nebulous; he would not speculate.

His life then, to his relief, became uneventful. He worked. He bought a house. Marya became a housewife. His daughter grew. Years passed in unthinking contentment. His base expanded. His hair thinned, he took on a squat appearance.

When the letter arrived bearing stamps of a familiar style, yet less lyrical than those he'd known, extolling now the virtues of trains and pick-axes, it was as if some unexplored part of his mind had always known it would. He was not surprised. He was angered. Not at his wife: that she was alive after so many years was just a fact. His anger was, rather, at the unpredictable, at those elements that fitted no pattern, that came at random to disrupt. For his wife he felt no sorrow, no pity, a little relief. It had been too long.

Her letter told of hardship and distress, of years of physical labor on the farm to which she had been banished. Her words, unadorned, shorn of stylistic flourish, impressed him as would a relic. The country in which she was caught remained so remote; the letter was like a communication from the distantly dead.

His reply was passionless. He could not pretend. He gave her, briefly, the details of autobiography. He sent her some money, as he would continue to do every month for years even as the country, sealed, convulsed once more unto itself. He didn't mention Marya; there was no point. The two would never meet, they could never affect one another. To mention her might simply have caused an unnecessary distress.

The letters—fragments of self, in the style of the memo—continued to come, if infrequently. He replied, also in the style of the memo, communication of the flimsiest kind, reminders of existence rather than exchanges of thought.

His daughter grew. Marya continued to live as his wife. The letters, with their intricate, colourful stamps, continued to come. He sent her money, automatically, as if paying the telephone bill; it was no hardship, he saw it not as duty but simply as something that had to be done, like a household chore.

Sometimes he would read the letters to his daughter, translating from the language of which she had, over the years, retained only a few words. The daughter never made a comment, just asked at the end for the stamp. Once she said, "I wish she'd use different stamps, I have lots of these red ones already." He felt her attitude was correct.

After his daughter had moved into her own apartment, he continued ripping out the stamps for her. She never asked to hear the letters. After a while she stopped collecting stamps.

Marya took over the collection.

Of course, in the end, it had all been a matter of choice. "You had no choice": the words formed of themselves in his mind.

But he'd wanted to avoid such preparation. It hinted at self-defence, at justification of action in a time that had made thought, will, decision absurd.

He sought distraction. A crowd had gathered at the exit of the Customs Hall. In front of the doors — of an opaque glass that revealed the movements of shadowed ghosts — was a small old man in a casual blue and white uniform that lent him little air of authority. He faced the crowd, his blue peaked cap pushed to the back of his head. What was he? A guard? A guide? A porter? He joked with people in the crowd, he looked stern, he stood at attention, he leaned loosely on the wrought-iron rail that marked off the path from the doors; he was like a man who couldn't decide on a function, on an appropriate image, as if, despite himself, he was infected by those around him.

He felt sorry for the little old man in his anonymous uniform: he looked lost.

"You had no choice." The words formed once again, like a chant of response in the church he had attended for a time every Sunday morning twenty-two years before in order to improve his comprehension of English. And the thought pursued itself: "You had no choice. I did. For myself. For our daughter. Should I have refused? What is this loyalty that would deny life? To what does it aspire?" Words. Forming in his mind, they thickened the saliva in his mouth: he wanted to spit. Words now could only confuse.

He had long accepted that he would never again see his wife, and that she was here now affected him only in that it revealed his essential insignificance: man as plaything, life as mockery.

He had had no hesitation in bringing her out, not, he knew, from love but from duty, unquestioned, unquestioning, the way one lays flowers on the grave of a relative dead twenty years. His action carried no moral weight; the automatic never could. It had just been, just was.

He slipped his hands, suddenly cold, into his coat pockets. Nervousness: he caught it, slipped momentarily into confusion. In that eternity of seconds he lost his name, his memory, his place in the world; his very existence seemed to slip from him. His fingers, grasping at the rough cloth of the coat pocket, seeking stability, brushed the picture. He took hold of it between two fingers, withdrew it.

But then a face that had changed little in its essence, much in its detail, slid past the little old man. His mind took a step backwards so that, observing her advance towards him, he observed himself and, on yet another level—not that of the observer of self but of another, less photographic, more judgmental—he remarked on his composure. She was here, he was greeting her, like an appointed official fulfilling duty.

The second level of his mind persisted, observing her with what the third level thought an interesting dispassion. She wore a plain coat, light grey, with no pretension to style. She was smaller now than before but less soft, with a rigidity in her forehead, her eyes, her mouth. Her skin was bronzed and a single thought—the picture, the past, the present—fused the levels of his mind: she used to be proud of her pure, unblemished skin, her only vanity.

In her left hand, the arm crooked at the elbow to accommodate a cheap plastic handbag, she held, like an amulet, a blue air-letter, his own, he guessed, probably the last he had sent, the one in which he had told her what to do, what to expect, on arrival at the airport. He supposed she made a touching sight.

With a tremor of panic, he clutched the photograph into his left fist, now gone moist.

Then she was before him, looking somehow tragically short.

They shook hands.

Hers was small, dry, rough, with a strong grip, a hand that no longer knew the syringe, that had been transformed by plough and hoe and shovel. He held it for a few unthinking seconds while her eyes—revealing a reserve, a puzzle, blank yet questioning, signalling a sense of betrayal yet a compassion he couldn't grasp—looked frankly into his own.

He knew, then, that she knew about Marya. And he knew, too, that he felt no guilt, no shame: relief, rather, and an enigmatic gratitude.

She took her hand away with a masculine briskness.

He said, "How are you?" After twenty-two years, in a language so long unused, the words, simplistic, meaningless, without weight, offered a measure of himself: he couldn't pretend.

"I am well, thank you, and how are you?"

"I am well."

"And how is our daughter?"

"She is well." Then: "She is longing to see you."

He sensed her unasked question and was grateful for her tact. Or was it fear? No, he decided, she was not a weak woman, she was a survivor in a way that he had never been. Could he, a doctor, who took a pure pride in the intellect, have survived those years in the fields as she had? Millions had died; starvation and execution had raked the ranks of their generation. Survival demanded a skill that was not his. He needed to see a future. He could build, but merely to survive: for this, strength evaded him.

"She had to work. She couldn't come with me." Transparent, he knew: this too revealed his weakness. But she said nothing, in no way acknowledged his lies, and once more he was grateful. He said, too hurriedly, "We have a lot to talk about."

"There is nothing to talk about."

"I have rented an apartment for you. I will take care of all your needs." Like an invalid, he thought, regretting his words.

"You owe me nothing."

He took her suitcase — of cheap plastic, like her handbag — tipped the porter, led her in silence to the exit. The doors slipped open. Outside, the air was cool, given bite by the wind. The sky was once more grey. There was no sun: the carpark across the way took on the aspect of monolith.

"Is she beautiful?"

His calm pleased him, but he couldn't look at her: "No, but she is a good woman. She has been a good mother to our daughter."

"I meant our daughter." Her voice did not change, was neutral.

Stupid, he thought. He had answered the two unstated questions, had revealed all in a manner more abrupt, more crushing, than he'd intended.

But she was a survivor.

"Yes," he said, "our daughter is beautiful."

The wind fingered down his neck, struck his chest. He shivered. The suitcase in his hand was light, the photograph in his left a more onerous weight. With an effort of will, he opened his palm. The photograph fluttered out. The wind picked it up, flung it into a gutter. He picked up his pace: there were things to do.

Presently not long after they had driven off, the old man in white coveralls, carrying a broom and a garbage bag, came along on yet another turn past the carpark. He saw the photograph, the outlines of black, white, and grey blurred into a desperate fuzziness, so that there was no distinction, no sharpness to the image, like an ink drawing on cheap paper. His mind couldn't sharpen the lines, couldn't define the contours.

He swept it into the garbage bag and went off in his unsteady shuffle after a fluttering candy-wrapper.

1985

Dionne Brand

Dionne Brand (b. 1953) was born in Guayaguayare, Trinidad. She immigrated to Canada in 1970 and is involved in the black community and in the educational system in Toronto. She has published several volumes of poetry, including *Chronicles of the Hostile Sun* (1984), *No Language is Neutral* (1990), and *Inventory* (2006). Her fiction publications include *Sans Souci and Other Stories* (1988), *In Another Place, Not Here* (novel, 1996), and *At the Full & Change of the Moon* (novel, 2004). In addition to her poetry and fiction, Brand has published essays on race, gender, and politics in contemporary Canadian culture. Some are collected in *Bread Out of Stone* (1994).

Dionne Brand's "Return I" is — until the last line — a nostalgic piece by someone returning to her home (here most likely a West Indian island). It portrays vividly various aspects of the land. The final line adds a political perspective that suppresses and replaces the nostalgia. (See the effect of the last line of Marilyn Chin's "Elegy for Chloe Nguyen [1955-1988].") Compare this poem with David Dabydeen's "Catching Crabs" and Derek Walcott's "Ruins of a Great House." "Amelia" is an elegy that evokes the immediate circumambient setting of the death of Amelia. How functional is the change of pronouns (from first person to third, back to first)? Would you agree that without the place name "guayguayare" (the place of birth of the poet, in Trinidad), it would have been impossible reading just the poem to contextualize the experience regionally, specifically as a West Indian poem? Compare the poem in this regard with Wong May's "The Shroud," Claire Harris's "Death in Summer," and Mervyn Morris's "Little Boy Crying."

Return I

So the street is still there, still melting with sun
still the shining waves of heat at one o'clock
the eyelashes scorched, staring the distance of the
park to the parade stand, still razor grass burnt and
cropped, everything made indistinguishable from dirt
by age and custom, white washed, and the people ...
still I suppose the scorpion orchid by the road, that
fine red tongue of flamboyant and orange lips
muzzling the air, that green plum turning fat and
crimson, still the crazy bougainvillea fancying and
nettling itself purple, pink, red, white, still the trickle of
sweat and cold flush of heat raising the smell of
cotton and skin ... still the dank rank of breadfruit milk,
their bash and rain on steps, still the bridge this side
the sea that side, the rotting ship barnacle eaten still
the butcher's blood staining the walls of the market,

the ascent of hills, stony and breathless, the dry
yellow patches of earth still threaten to swamp at the
next deluge ... so the road, that stretch of sand and
pitch struggling up, glimpses sea, village, earth
bare-footed hot, women worried, still the faces,
masked in sweat and sweetness, still the eyes
watery, ancient, still the hard, distinct, brittle smell of
slavery.

1990

Amelia[1]

I know that lying there in that bed
in that room
smelling of wet coconut fibres
and children's urine
bundled up in a mound
under the pink chenille and cold
sweating sheets
you wanted to escape,
run from that room
and children huddling against you
with the rain falling outside
and flies and mud
and a criminal for a son
and the scent of the sewer heightened
by the rain falling.
On those days
she tried to roll herself
into the tiniest of balls on the bed
on those days she did not succeed
except in turning the bed into a ship
and she, the stranded one
in that sea of a room
floating and dipping
into the waves, the swell
of a life anchored.

---

[1] Brand's grandmother (who parented her) was named Amelia Virginia Brand (née Noray).

I think that she would have been better
by the sea
in guayguayare,[1]
but in the town
hot with neighbours and want
she withered and swelled
and died and left me
after years of hiding
and finally her feet fearful and nervous
could not step on asphalt
or find a pair of shoes.
Swimming in the brutish rain
at once she lost her voice
since all of its words contained her downfall.
She gargled instead the coarse water from her eyes
the incessant nights
the crickets call
and the drooping tree,
breathed, in gasps
what was left in the air
after husband and two generations of children.
Lying in a hospital bed
you could not live by then
without the contradictions
of your own aggrieved room
with only me to describe the parking lot outside
and your promise, impossible,
to buy me a bicycle,
when they brought your body home
I smiled a child's smile of conspiracy
and kissed your face.

1984

---

[1] *guayguayare* A fishing village (now a petroleum centre also) in southeast Trinidad, the place of birth of
    the poet. (Spelled also *Guayaguayare*; pronounced "gwuy-a-gwuy-a-ree.")

Edward Kamau Brathwaite

Edward Kamau Brathwaite (b. 1930) was born in Barbados, West Indies. He was educated at Harrison College, Barbados, and Cambridge University. His many volumes of poems include *The Arrivants: A New World Trilogy* (1973), *Mask* (1968), *Sun Poems* (1982), *X/self* (1987), and *Roots* (1993). He has lectured in history at the Mona Campus of the University of the West Indies in Jamaica and has written several studies of Caribbean social and cultural history, including "History of the Voice: The Development of Nation Language in Anglophone Caribbean Poetry" (1986). His *Born to Slow Horses* (2005) was winner of the 2006 International Griffin Poetry Prize.

Braithwaite's "Red Rising" (a phrase originally used in Longfellow's "Keats") combines Western and African images and myths, a hallmark of Brathwaite's style. Brathwaite makes a conscious effort to acknowledge and celebrate his African heritage in his writings. Compare his response to his African ancestry with Claire Harris's in "Backstage at the Glenbow Museum, Calgary." Note Brathwaite's helpful annotation to the poem (found at the end of the poem), which is similar to T.S. Eliot's in "The Waste Land," a seminal early-twentieth-century poem that is one of Brathwaite's influences.

Red Rising

1

When the earth was made
when the wheels of the sky were being fashioned
when my songs were first heard in the voice of the coot of the owl
hillaby soufriere and kilimanjaro were standing towards me with water with fire

at the centre of the air

there
in the keel of the blue
the son of my song, father-giver, the sun/sum
walks the four corners of the magnet, caught in the wind, blind

in the eye of ihs own hurricane

and the trees on the mountain become mine: living eye of my branches
of bone; flute
where is my hope hope where is my psalter

my children wear masks dancing towards me the mews of their origen earth

so that this place which is called mine
which will never know that cold scalpel of skull, hill of dearth

brain corals ignite and ignore it

and that this place which is called now
which will never again glow: coal balloon anthracite: into cross-

roads of hollows

black spot of my life: *jah*
blue spot of my life: *love*
yellow spot of my life: *iises*
red spot of my dream that still flowers flowers flowers

let us give thanks

when the earth was made
when the sky first spoke with the voice of the rain/bow
when the wind gave milk to its music
when the suns of my morning walked out of their shallow thrill/dren

2

So that for centuries now have i fought against these opposites
how i am sucked from water into air
how the air surrounds me blue all the way

from ocean to the other shore
from halleluja to the black hole of hell

from this white furnace where i burn
to those green sandy ant-hills where you grow your yam

you would think that i would hate eclipses
my power powdered over as it were

but it's hallucination my fine friend
a fan a feather; some

one else's breath of shadow
the moon's cool or some plan/et's
but can you ever guess how i
who have wracked

you wrong
long too to be black

be
come part of that hool that shrinks us all to stars

how i
with all these loco

motives in me
would like to straighten

strangle eye/self out

grow a beard wear dark glasses
driving the pack straight far

ward into indigo and vi
olet and on into ice like a miss

ile

rather than this surrendered curve
this habit forming bicycle of rains and seasons
weathers when i tear my hair

i will never i now know make it over the atlantic of that nebula

but that you may live my fond retreating future
i will accept i will accept the bonds that blind me
turning my face down/wards to my approaching past these morning chill/dren

Poet's Notes

Red Rising: dawn, the first voice of the rainbow.

Stanza I

l.4. *hillaby soufriere and kilimanjaro*: mountain landmarks of the Third World: Hillaby, Barbados (though less than 1,000 ft!); Soufriere, St. Vincent, active volcano; Kilimanjaro, Tanzania.

l.8. *sun/sum: sunsum*: Akan word for soul, origin of spiritual life.

l.10. *ihs*: natural/divine version of its/his

l.15. *mews*: sound-word (news/mews)

l.15. *origen*: origin, *originem*, and the Early Christian (Neo-platonist) theologian of Alexandria (c. 155-253). The "rainbow" sense (literal, moral, mystical) of "origin."

l.24. *iises*: Rastafarian version of "praises." *Jah, love* and *thanks* are also Rasta ritual words, juxtaposed here with N. American Indian sacred colours: black, blue, yellow, red.

Stanza 2

l.19. *hool*: hole, whirlpool, galactic black hole.

1982

Dennis Brutus

Dennis Brutus (b. 1924) was born in Zimbabwe (formerly Rhodesia). He was educated in South Africa, where he studied English and law. Because of his opposition to apartheid, he was banned from South Africa and made his home in the United States. He was on the faculty at the University of Pittsburgh and Northwestern University. His poetry collection, *Letters to Martha and Other Poems from a South African Prison* (1968), tells of his experiences of violence and degradation in prison; he was jailed for 18 months in South Africa's infamous Robben Island. Other volumes include *Still the Sirens* (1993) and *Poetry and Protest: A Dennis Brutus Reader* (2006).

Brutus's "By the Waters of Babylon" is, as its biblical title (taken from Psalm 137) indicates, a lament of the exiled. (The King James translation is "by the rivers of Babylon.") Like the Israelites in exile in Babylon, the speaker (who, if linked with the poet, is South African) is a refugee in Bamako, the capital of Mali (an African country just south of Algeria, north of Ghana). Though it is a beautiful place — and is on his home continent of Africa — it is nevertheless a place of exile for this South African. Compare the poem with NourbeSe Philip's "Sprung Rhythm" and Sasenarine Persaud's "Gifting the Light of the Soul."

By the Waters of Babylon

By the waters of Babylon[1]
   the brackish wastes of alienness
   lie like dust on heart and throat,
   contour and curve of hill and field
   unspeaking and meaningless
   as a barbarous foreign tongue

by the waters of Babylon
we sat down and wept
   the mind yearns over the low horizon
   to other familiar friendly haunts
   not unlike these gracious scenes

when we remembered thee
O Zion
   these trees; these hills; this sky, this sun
   evoke a dearness that lacerates;
   the heart heels from this wounding loveliness

---

[1] *the waters of Babylon* A quotation from the Bible, Psalm 137; the Israelites are lamenting their exile in Babylon.

How can we sing our songs
in a strange land?
    Wordlessly
    one turns from such beauty and such pain:
    weeps.

In strange land.
By the waters of Babylon
we sat down
and wept

Bamako,[1] *Mali*

1970

---

[1] *Bamako* The capital of Mali.

Buhkwujjenene

Buhkwujjenene (c.1815-1900) was the Ojibway chief who, in 1878, told a group of Englishmen the story of Nanaboozhoo creating the world.

Buhkwujjenene's "Nanaboozhoo Creates the World" noticeably echoes Noah's flood and the re-creation of the world. Compare this Canadian tale with Philip Sherlock's "The Warau People Discover the Earth," derived from West Indian Amerindians, and Ngitji Ngitji's Australian legend "The Possum Woman." Consider these stories in the light of James Fraser's belief in common, universal myths in his study *The Golden Bough* (1890). Wilson Harris has a similar credo — look at his Amerindian story set in Guyana, "Kanaima."

Nanaboozhoo Creates the World

Nanaboozhoo[1] ... had a son. He loved his son. He told his son never to go near the water lest evil should come to him. The son disobeyed his father, he went out in a canoe and was never seen or heard of more. Nanaboozhoo then vowed vengeance against the gods of the water who had destroyed his son. There were two of these gods and one day they lay sleeping on the shore. Nanaboozhoo was looking everywhere for them, determined to kill them. A loon offered to show him where they were sleeping. He followed the loon till he found them, and then he made short work of them with his tomahawk and his war-club. But lo and behold no sooner were the gods dead than the waters of the great lake rose up in vengeance; they pursued Nanaboozhoo up on to the dry land, and he had to run for his life. He sought the highest mountain and climbed to the top of the highest pine tree. Still the waters pursued him. They rose higher and higher. What could he do! He broke off a few of the topmost branches and made a raft upon which he got and saved himself. He saved also a number of the animals that were kicking and struggling in the water all around him. At length he bethought himself of making a new world. How should he do it? Could he but procure a little of the old world he might manage it. He selected the beaver from among the animals, and sent it to dive after some earth. When it came up it was dead. He sent the otter, but it died also. At length he tried the muskrat. The muskrat dived. When it came up it was dead. But in its claws was clenched a little earth. Nanaboozhoo carefully took this earth, rubbed it in his fingers till it was dry, then placed it in the palm of his hand, and blew it gently over the surface of the water. A new world was thus formed, and Nanaboozhoo and all the

---

[1] *Nanaboozhoo* In Ojibway mythology, Nanaboozhoo (or *Nanabozho* or *Manabozho*) is a prominent spirit who plays a significant role in stories of the creation of the world.

animals landed. Nanaboozhoo sent out a wolf to see how big the world was. He was gone a month. Again he sent him out and he was gone a year. Then he sent out a very young wolf. This young wolf died of old age before it could get back. So Nanaboozhoo said the world was big enough, and might stop growing.

1879

Willi Chen

Willi Chen (b. 1934) was born in Trinidad, where he currently resides. He is a short-story writer, poet, dramatist, painter, and sculptor. Some of his stories are collected in *King of the Carnival and Other Stories* (1988) and *Chutney Power and Other Stories* (2006).

Chen is one of the first writers of Chinese extraction in West Indian literature. "Assam's Iron Chest," set in rural Trinidad, is a classic story of villains outsmarting each other. If we accept that satire uses laughter mockingly, comedy sympathetically, and farce purposelessly (that is, just to amuse), is this story satire, comedy, or farce? How does it compare with the tone in V.S. Naipaul's "B. Wordsworth" and Thomas King's "A Coyote Columbus Story"? In many of his other stories, Chen shows an awareness of the sad undercurrents (and violence) in the lives of his characters. Is any of this evident in this story? Is this story in the tradition of the trickster figure in Louise Bennett's "Anancy an Ticks"?

Assam's Iron Chest

A dull moon glowed in the country-night darkness. They came out of hiding from behind the caimette tree, avoiding the crackle of dead leaves underfoot. Into the pale light stepped big, loudmouthed Mathias, Boyo, with his matted dreadlocks wrapped up in a "Marvingay" hat, and laglee-chewing[1] Sagamouth, so nicknamed because of his grotesque lips and the smattering noises they made.

In the little clearing overlooking Assam's shopyard, they waited patiently behind large tannia leaves that shielded them from the light of passing motorists. They waited for the last bus to rattle by on its return journey to town and for the soft glow of Assam's Coleman lamp, whirring moths and beetles striking against the lampshade, to go out.

Boyo puffed at the carmine-tipped stick of ganja that brightened his face as he slapped at mosquitoes. Sagamouth's lips continued slurping noisily.

"Keep quiet, man. Christ! You goh wake up the whole damn village," Mathias hissed between clenched teeth.

"Look, the light out," Sagamouth whispered excitedly.

"Yea, but keep your flapping mouth shut. I could see. Who in charge here?"

"Boyo, put out that weed. Whole place stink ah grass," Mathias warned.

At the galvanised paling surrounding the shop-yard, a flimsy steel sheet suddenly loosened in the moonlight and fell aside, allowing three figures to squeeze through the narrow space into the shop-yard. They were confronted by stacks of empty soft

---

[1] *Laglee (Lagli)* A gum made from the sap of certain trees (balata, breadfruit, etc.), used to trap birds.

drink crates, discarded cartons, pitch oil tins and, against the shed, bundles of stacked crocus bags.

Remembering the action in the motion picture *Bataan*, and with the dramatic invasion in *Desert Fox* still fresh in his mind, Mathias crouched on all fours, leading his platoon across the yard.

"Sssh," he cautioned them as he sat on his buttocks before the big door. They paused in the darkness. Mathias' hands felt for the door frame. He inserted a pig foot into the crevice. With both feet against the wall he pried the door, throwing his whole weight on it. A slow cracking noise erupted as the nails lifted off the hinges and the door came up. A dank odour of wet oilmeal, soap and stale mackerel greeted them. They crawled in, feeling their way between the stacks of packaged goods. Further inside, they saw a table with a lighted lamp and a red spot of mosquito coil under it. A big square mosquito net hung over a four-poster bed out of which floated Assam's snores in grating spasms.

Convinced that Assam was sound asleep, Mathias struck a match and immediately shadows jumped across the walls, on the shelves of bottles and over tinned stuffs. On the floor, crowding the aisles, was the paraphernalia of jumbled haberdashery, pots and pans, and bags of peas and beans. Moving in the crowded interior, Mathias came to the room where, over a small table, bills hung pinned to the wall, next to a Chinese calendar. Cupping the lighted match in his hand, Mathias tiptoed further inside. More bags, packed in rows, and bales of macaroni and cornmeal. Flagons of cider and an old rum cask stood on the floor. In the corner, the square block of metal stood on a rough framework of local timber; a squat, dull hunk of iron with a circular dial of brass. It was the iron chest. Mathias came up to it and tested its weight. Boyo braced himself in readiness.

With Sagamouth holding the light, Mathias and Boyo heaved at the heavy hulk of iron. They pushed until the wooden stand inched along the floor.

"Damn thing must be full," Boyo said.

"Canefarmer pay, choopid," Sagamouth replied, spraying them with his spittle.

"All you keep quiet," Mathias entreated.

Pitting themselves against the heavy load, they worked with caution. Twice they heard Assam cough. Their hands glided, slipped over the smooth surface of the chest. After some strenuous efforts, they managed to push the chest to the doorway. Finally the whole bulk of metal was heaved outside, catapulting, digging into the yard with a dull thud.

The cool night breeze invigorated their bodies. The sight of the chest inspired their minds with the promise of new things in life. Sagamouth disappeared into the bushes and returned with a crocus bag containing a crowbar, a sledge hammer and a flambeau. Behind him he dragged a large piece of board, the underside of which was lined with plain galvanised sheeting. At one end was tied a long piece of rope. They eased their cargo on to the wooden contraption. Mathias again directed the operations. Standing before the metal chest, he tied the end of the rope around his waist and leant forward. Boyo and Sagamouth were pushing at the rear.

They hauled the makeshift sledge along the grassy side tracks. With the heavy iron chest strapped to it, it skidded and scuttled across the bare ground. Their backs shone like their faces, which streamed with perspiration. Boyo puffed like a trace mule. Sagamouth's mouth continued its feeble movements. They halted behind a silk cotton tree. Mathias swung the axe in long, measured strokes against the chest. The sounds echoed deep into the woods. The heavy blows ricocheted over the door. Now and then he stopped to inspect the shallow indentations. The brass handle had fallen off, the dial long warped under the punishing blows. Yet the door remained sealed. They persevered, taking turns with the sledge hammer and the crowbar, until Mathias, bringing the heavy hammer from high overhead, struck the chest with such force that they heard a loud cracking noise.

Instantly they sprang forward, their eager hands reached out for the door. Three pairs of hands churned inside the chest, as their eyes opened in anticipation. Then Sagamouth withdrew exclaiming, "Empty."

"Christ, you mean the damn thing en't have a cent, boy."

"All dis damn trouble," Boyo said.

Mathias stood up wearily and looked at the others, his arms sore and wet, as he whispered, "Dat damn Chinese smart like hell! Ah never cud believe it. You mean he move out all de damn money, boy?"

Sagamouth's dribbling stopped. Boyo looked up at the sky.

One day, some three months afterwards, when the notorious episode was almost forgotten in the little village and the blue police van had long completed its trips to Assam's on investigation, Sagamouth came into Assam's shop. He stood at the counter and called for a pound of saltbeef. There was no one in the shop except for a well-dressed man. A briefcase was on the counter and he was busily scribbling on a pad.

"Yes, please sign on this, Mr. Assam," the man said in his mellow voice. Assam, spectacles tied to his ear with a piece of flour-bag string, leant over the counter and scrawled on the pad.

"Have everything dong, Mister Blong?"

"Yes, all that you have told me," Mr. Brown replied. "$1,000 in US, $15,000 in Canadian and $2,100 in TT[1] cash. $89 in silver and that solid gold chain from China. But as I said, I'm not sure that the company will pay the foreign money."

Assam placed a large brown paper bag containing two bottles of rum on the counter before Mr. Brown.

"Well, check all in TT dollars then," Assam said, taking out another brown bag from below the counter.

Mr. Brown smiled and pointed to the last item on the list. "Ah—that is the iron chest, Mr. Assam. The company will pay you the $8,000 you have claimed."

"Yes, sah," Assam said smiling, "velly goot," his eyes two narrow slits behind thick lenses.

Sagamouth stood dumb, rooted in front of the counter, unmoving, as he listened

---

[1] *TT* Trinidad and Tobago (twin-island West Indian nation).

to the conversation. His lips had suddenly lost all sense of movement. They hung droopily over the counter, nearly falling into the shop-scale pan.

1988

Marilyn Chin

Marilyn (Mei Ling) Chin (b. 1955) was born in Hong Kong; she now lives in San Francisco and San Diego, where she is on the faculty of the MFA Program at San Diego State University. She is a graduate of the Iowa Writers' Workshop. Her poetry publications include *The Dwarf Bamboo* (1987), *The Phoenix Gone, The Terrace Empty* (1994), and *Rhapsody in Plain Yellow* (2002).

Chin's "Elegy for Chloe Nguyen (1955-1988)" has a surprising matter-of-fact tone for an elegy. Perhaps this has to do with the fact that the speaker has suffered the deaths of many family members. Does she see death as the equalizer? With all her learning and fortune, her friend could not escape death. What does the last line do to the tone and meaning of the poem? Does it add another dimension to this elegy? (See the effect of the last line of Dionne Brand's "Return I.") Compare this poem with Sally Ito's "Of the Wave."

Elegy For Chloe Nguyen (1955-1988)

Chloe's father is a professor of linguistics.
Mine runs a quick-you-do-it Laundromat in Chinatown.
If not pretty at least I'm clean.

Bipedal in five months, trilingual in a year;
at eleven she had her first lover.

Here's a photo of Chloe's mother in the kitchen
making petit fours, petit fours that are very pretty.
Here's my mother picking pears, picking pears
for a self-made millionaire grower.

The night when Chloe died, her father sighed,
"Chloe was my heart; Chloe was my life!"

One day under an earthen-black sky
and the breeze brushing our adolescent pinafores,
a star fell — or was it a satellite
exploding into a bonfire at the horizon?
Chloe said, "This is how I want to die,
with a bang and not with a flicker."

Oh, Chloe, eternally sophomore and soporific!
Friend of remote moribund languages!
Chloe read Serbo-Croatian, the Latin of Horace.

She understood Egyptian hieroglyphics, the writing of the tombs.
The tongues of the living, the slangs of the dead —
in learning she had no rival.

Then came the lovers of many languages
to quell her hunger, her despair.
Each night they whispered, "Chloe, you are beautiful."
Then, left her with an empty sky in the morning.
Chloe, can you hear me? Is it better in heaven?

Are you happier in hell? This week I don't understand the lesson
being a slow learner — except for the one about survival.
And Death I know him well …

He followed my grandfather as a puff of opium,
my father as a brand new car.
Rowed the boat with my grandmother,
blowing gales into my mother's ear.
Wrapped his arms around my asthmatic sister,
but his comforting never won us over.

Yes, Death is a beautiful man,
and the poor don't need dowries to court him.
His grassy hand, his caliph — you thought you could master.

Chloe, we are finally Americans now. Chloe, we are here!

1994

Austin Clarke

Austin Clarke (b. 1934) was born and educated in Barbados. He came to Canada in 1955 to study economics but decided on a writing career. He has published several novels — including *Survivors of the Crossing* (1964), *The Meeting Point* (1967), *The Polished Hoe* (2002), and *More* (2008) — and several collections of short stories, including *Nine Men Who Laughed* (1986), *In This City* (1992), and *There Are No Elders* (1993). *Growing Up Stupid Under the Union Jack* (1980) and *Pigtails 'n' Breadfruit: The Rituals of Slave Food, A Barbadian Memoir* (1999) are two of his memoirs.

Austin Clarke's "The Man," a portrait of an immigrant from Barbados living in Toronto, can be compared with Neil Bissoondath's immigrant story "Man as Plaything, Life as Mockery." Clarke gives cultural and historical particulars, and he identifies the original home of the protagonist. Bissoondath subsumes particulars in his effort to point up the commonality of immigrant human experiences. Clarke appears to be doing so as well in his generic title and at the beginning of the story, but then he begins to particularize the world of the protagonist. Is one form of narration more effective than the other?

The Man

The man passes the five open doors on two floors that shut as he passes, moving slowly in the dark, humid rooming house. Slowly, pausing every few feet, almost on every other step, he climbs like a man at the end of a double shift in a noisy factory, burdened down also by the weight of time spent on his feet, and by the more obvious weight of his clothes on his fat body, clothes that were seldom cleaned and changed. Heavy with the smell of his body and the weight of paper which he carries with him, in all nine pockets of trousers and jacket and one in his shirt, he climbs, leaving behind an acrid smell of his presence in the already odorous house.

When he first moved into this house, to live in the third-floor room, the landlady was a young wife. She is widowed now, and past sixty. The man smells like the oldness of the house. It is a smell like that which comes off fishermen when they come home from the rum shop after returning from the deep sea. And sometimes, especially in the evening, when the man comes home, the smell stings you and makes you turn your head, as your nostril receives a tingling sensation.

The man ascends the stairs. Old cooking rises and you think you can touch it on walls that have four coats of paint on them, put there by four different previous owners of the house. Or in four moods of decoration. The man pauses again. He inhales. He puts his hands on his hips. Makes a noise of regained strength and determination. And climbs again.

The man is dressed in a suit. The jacket is from a time when shoulders were worn wide and tailored broad. His shoulders are padded high, as his pockets are padded wide by the letters and the pieces of paper with notes on them, and clippings from the *Globe and Mail*, and envelopes with scribbling on them: addresses and telephone numbers. And the printed words he carries in his ten pockets make him look stuffed and overweight and important, and also like a man older than he really is. His hips are like those of a woman who has not always followed her diet to reduce. He meticulously puts on the same suit every day, as he has done for years. He is a man of some order and orderliness. His shirt was once white. He wears only shirts that were white when they were bought. He buys them second-hand from the bins of the Goodwill store on Jarvis Street and wears them until they turn grey. He changes them only when they are too soiled to be worn another day; and then he buys another one from the same large picked-over bins of the Goodwill store.

He washes his trousers in a yellow plastic pail only if a stain is too conspicuous, and presses them under his mattress; and he puts them on before they are completely dry. He walks most of the day, and at eight each night he sits at his stiff, wooden, sturdy-legged table writing letters to men and women all over the world who have distinguished themselves in politics, in government and in universities.

He lives as a bat. Secret and self-assured and self-contained as an island, high above the others in the rooming house; cut off from people, sitting and writing his important personal letters, or reading, or listening to classical music on the radio and the news on shortwave until three or four in the morning. And when morning comes, at eight o'clock he hits the streets, walking in the same two square miles from his home, rummaging through libraries for British and American newspapers, for new words and ideas for letters; then along Bloor Street, Jarvis Street, College Street, and he completes the perimeter at Bathurst Street. His room is the centre of gravity from which he is spilled out at eight each morning in all temperatures and weather, and from which he wanders no farther than these two square miles.

The man used to work as a mover with Maislin Transport in Montreal. Most of the workers came from Quebec and spoke French better than they spoke English. And one day he and a young man dressed in jeans and a red-and-black checkered shirt, resembling a man ready for the woods of lumberjacks and tall trees, were lifting a refrigerator that had two doors; and the man said "Left." He misunderstood the man's English and began to turn left through the small apartment door. He turned old suddenly. His back went out, as the saying goes. And he developed "goadies," a swelling of the testicles so large that they can never be hidden beneath the most restraining jockstrap. That was the end of his moving career.

This former animal of a man, who could lift the heaviest stove if only he was given the correct word, was now a shadow of his former muscle and sinews, with sore back and callused hands, moving slowly through a literary life, with the assistance of a private pension from Maislin Transport. He has become a different kind of animal now, prowling during the daytime through shelves of books in stores and in libraries, and visiting slight acquaintances as if they were friends whenever he smelled a drink or a meal; and attending public functions.

His pension cheque came every month at the same time, written in too much

French for the rude bank teller, who said each time he presented it, even after two years, "Do you have some *identification?*"

He used to be sociable. He would nod his head to strangers, flick his eyes on the legs of women and at the faces of foreign-language men on College Street, all the way west of Spadina Avenue. He would even stop to ask for a light, and once or twice for a cigarette, and become confused in phrase-book phrases of easy, conversational Greek, Portuguese and Italian.

Until one evening. He was walking on a shaded street in Forest Hill Village when a policeman looked through the window of his yellow cruiser, stopped him in his wandering tracks and said, "What the hell're you doing up here, *boy?*" He had been walking and stopping, unsure along this street, looking at every mansion which seemed larger than the one before, when he heard the brutal voice. "Git in! Git your black ass in here!"

The policeman threw open the rear door of the cruiser. The man looked behind him, expecting to see a delinquent teenager who had earned the policeman's raw hostility. The man was stunned. There was no other person on the street. But somehow he made the effort to walk to the cruiser. The door was slammed behind him. The policeman talked on a stuttering radio and used figures and numbers instead of words, and the man became alarmed at the policeman's mathematical illiteracy. And then the cruiser sped off, scorching the peace of Forest Hill, burning rubber on its shaded quiet streets.

The cruiser stopped somewhere in the suburbs. He thought he saw Don Mills on a sign post. It stopped here, with the same temperamental disposition as it had stopped the first time in Forest Hill Village. The policeman made no further conversation of numerals and figures with the radio. He merely said, "*Git!*" The man was put out three miles from any street or intersection that he knew.

It was soon after this that he became violent. He made three pillows into the form of a man. He found a second-hand tunic and a pair of trousers that had a red stripe in them, and a hat that had a yellow band instead of a red one, and he dressed up the pillows and transformed them into a dummy of a policeman. And each morning at seven when he woke up, and late at night before he went to bed, after he washed out his mouth with salt water, he kicked the "policeman" twice — once in the flat feathery section where a man's testicles would be, and again at the back of the pillow in the dummy's ass. His hatred did not disappear with the blows. But soon he forgot about the effigy and the policeman.

Today he had been roaming the streets, like every day, tearing pieces of information from the *Globe and Mail* he took from a secretary's basket at the CBC, from *Saturday Night* and *Canadian Forum* magazines. And the moment he reached his attic room, he would begin to compose letters to great men and women around the world, inspired by the bits of information he had gathered.

And now, as he climbs, the doors of the roomers on each floor close as he passes, like an evil wind. But they close too late, for his scent and the wind of his presence have already touched them.

With each separation and denial, he is left alone in the dim light to which he is accustomed, and in the dust on the stairs; and he guides his hand along the shining banister, the same sheen as the wallpaper, stained with the smells and specks of cooking. He walks slowly because the linoleum on the stairs is shiny too, and dangerous and tricky under the feet.

Now, on his last flight to his room for the night, his strength seems to leave his body, and he pauses and rests his hands, one on the banister and the other on his right hip.

The cheque from Montreal will arrive tomorrow.

He feels the bulkiness of the paper in his pockets, and the weight of his poverty in this country he never grew to love. There was more love in Barbados. On many a hot afternoon, he used to watch his grandfather rest his callused hand on his hip as he stood in a field of endless potatoes, a field so large and quiet and cruel that he thought he was alone in the measureless sea of green waves, and not on a plantation. Alone perhaps now too, in the village, in the country, because of his unending work of bending his back to pull up the roots, and returning home when everyone else is long in bed.

And now he, the grandson, not really concerned with that stained ancestry, not really comparing himself with his grandfather, stands for a breath-catching moment on this landing in this house in which he is a stranger. He regards his room as the country. It is strange and familiar. It is foreign, yet it is home. It is dirty. And at the first signs of summer and warmth, he would go down on his hands and knees in what would have been an unmanly act and scrub the small space outside his door, and the four or five steps he had to climb to reach it. He would drop soap into the water, and still the space around the door remained dirty. The house had passed that stage when it could be cleaned. It had grown old like a human body. And not even ambition and cleanliness could purify it of this scent. It could be cleaned only by burning. But he had become accustomed to the dirt, as he was accustomed to the thought of burning. In the same way, he had become accustomed to the small room which bulged, like his ten pockets, with the possessions of his strange literary life.

He is strong again. Enough to climb the last three or four steps and take out his keys on the shining ring of silver, after putting down the plastic bag of four items he had bought through the express check-out of Dominion around the corner, and then the collection of newspapers — two morning and two afternoon and two evening editions. He flips each key over, and it makes a dim somersault, until he reaches the last key on the ring which he knows has to be the key he's looking for.

Under the naked light bulb he had opened and shut, locked and unlocked this same blue-painted door when it was painted green and red and black, so many times that he thought he was becoming colour-blind. But he could have picked out the key even if he was blind; for it was the only key in the bunch which had the shape of the fleur de lys at its head. He went through all the keys on the ring in a kind of elimination process. It was his own private joke. A ritual for taking up time.

He spent time as if he thought it would not end: walking along College Street and Spadina Avenue when he was not thinking of letters to be written; looking at the clusters of men and women from different countries at the corner of Bathurst and Bloor; at the men passing their eyes slowly over the breasts and backsides of the women; at the women shopping at Dominion and the open-air stalls, or amongst the fibres of cheap materials and dresses, not quite pure silk, not one hundred percent cotton, which they tore as they searched for and tore from each other's hands to get at cheaper prices than those advertised at Honest Ed's bargain store. And he would watch how these women expressed satisfaction with their purchases in their halting new English.

And now in the last few months, along those streets he had walked and known, all of a sudden the names on stores and the signs on posts appeared in the hieroglyphics of Chinese. Or Japanese? He no longer felt safe, tumbling in the warmth and shouts of a washing machine in a public laundromat in this technicoloured new world of strangers.

He had loved those warm months and those warm people before their names and homes were written in signs. They were real until someone turned them into Chinese characters which he could not read. And he spent the warm months of summer writing letters to the leaders of the world, in the hope of getting back a reply, no matter how short or impersonal, with their signatures, which he intended to sell to the highest bidder.

He came from a colony, a country and a culture where the written word spelled freedom. An island where the firm touch of the pen on paper meant freedom. Where the pen gripped firmly in the hand was sturdier than a soldier holding a gun, and which meant liberation. And the appearance of words on paper, the meaning and transformation they gave to the paper, and the way they rendered the paper priceless, meant that he could now escape permanently from the profuse sweat and the sharp smell of perspiration on the old khaki trousers and the thick-smelling flannel worn next to the skin. This sweat was the uniform, and had been the profession of poor black grandfathers. Now pen and paper mean the sudden and unaccountable and miraculous disappearance from a colonial tradition where young bodies graduated from the play and games and beaches of children into the dark, steamy and bee-droning caverns and caves of warehouses in which sat white men in white drill suits and white cork hats, their white skin turning red from too much rum and too much sun, and from their too-deep appetites for food and local women. For years before this graduation, he could find himself placed like a lamp post, permanent and blissful in one job, in one spot, in one position, until perhaps a storm came, or a fierce hurricane, and felled him like the chattels of houses and spewed him into the gutter.

So he learned the power of the *word*. And kept close to it. When others filled the streets and danced in a Caribana festival and wore colours hot as summer in a new spring of life, this man remained in his isolation; and he cut himself off from those frivolous, ordinary pleasures of life that had surrounded his streets for years, just as the immigrants surrounded the open-air Kensington Market. He thought and lived and expressed himself in this hermitage of solitary joy, writing letters to President de Gaulle, President Carter, Willy Brandt (whose name he never learned to spell), to Mao Tse Tung, Dr. Martin Luther King and Prime Minister Indira Gandhi.

The few acquaintances he called friends and met for drinks on the eighteenth-floor bar of the Park Plaza Hotel, and those he visited and talked with and drank with in their homes, all thought he was mad. And perhaps he was mad. Perhaps his obsession with the word had sent him off.

The persons to whom he wrote were all unknown to him. He did not care for their politics or their talent. But he made a fortune out of time spent in addressing them. It was an international intrusion on their serious lives: *Dear Prime Minister, I saw your name and picture in the Toronto Globe and Mail this morning. I must say I was most impressed by some of the things you have said. You are one of the most indispensable personages in this western world. This western world would come to its end of influence were it not for you. You and you alone can save it and save us. Long may you have this power. Yours very sincerely, William Jefferson.*

"Look what I pulled off!" he told Alonzo. He held the glass of cold beer bought for him on the account of friendship, and a smile came to his face. The smile was the smile of literary success. He had just promised Alonzo that he would defray all his loans with the sale of his private correspondence. A smile came to Alonzo's face. It was the smile of accepted social indebtedness. "The university would just *love* to get its hands on this!" *This* was the reply from the Prime Minister: a plain white post card on which was written, *Thank you very much, Mr. Jefferson, for your thoughtfulness.*

He would charge the university one hundred dollars for the reply from Prime Minister Gandhi. Perhaps he could sell them his entire correspondence! Why not? Even publish them in *The Private Correspondence of William Jefferson with the Great Men and Great Women of the Twentieth Century.*

Alonzo did not know whether to continue smiling or laugh right out. He could not decide if his friend was slightly off the head. He needed more proof. The letter from Mrs. Gandhi, which he did not show, could supply the proof. But it was a man's private business, a man's private correspondence; and not even the postman who delivered it had the right to see it. If this correspondence went on, Alonzo thought, who knows, perhaps one day he may be drinking beer and associating with a man of great fame, a famous man of letters, hounded by universities to get a glimpse of this correspondence....

While the man is trying to unlock his door, the urge overtakes him. The keyhole had not answered the key. And the urge to pee swells over his body like a high wave. This urge would overcome him almost always when a porcelain oval hole was not immediately available. It would take him into its grip and turn his entire body into a cramping, stuttering muscle-bound fist. Always on the wrong side of the street, too.

He was on Bloor Street once, in that stretch of shops and stores and restaurants where women wear furs and carry merchandise in shopping bags with Creeds and Holt Renfrew and Birks proclaimed on them, where the restaurants look like country clubs and the shops like chapels and banks, where he could not get the nerve to enter the stained-glass door with heraldry on it, jerk a tense glance in *that* direction and receive the direction to *there* or get a sign to show him the complicated carpeted route to *washrooms* printed on a brass plate. Not dressed the way he was. Not without giving some explanation. Not without alarming the waitresses dressed more like nurses and the waiters who looked like fashion models.

Once he dashed into Holt Renfrew. It was the last desperate haven. The water was heavy on his nerves, on his bladder. His eyes were red and watery. He barely had strength to speak his wish. Experience with this urge had cautioned him, as he stood before the glass case of ladies' silk underwear, that to open his mouth at that moment, when the association of this urge with ladies' panties was in full view, meant a relaxation of his grip on the water inside him. Then it would pour out onto the carpeted floor of Persian silence, perhaps even dribble onto the feet of the young clerk whose legs he could see beneath the thinness of her almost transparent dress.

The young woman saw his stiffness and posture, and with a smile and a wave, showed him the nearest haven. It had *Employees Only* inscribed on the shining brass. When he was finished, he could not move immediately. The loss of weight and water was like the loss of energy. "Have a good day, sir!" Her smile was brighter then.

He was still outside his room. The key was still in the hole. He did not have the strength to go down two flights of stairs to the second-floor bathroom beside the room of the woman who lived on welfare.

To have to go down now, with this weight making his head heavier, did something with his hand and the key turned.

He was safe inside his room. Relieved and safe. He did it in the pail. He keeps this pail in a corner, under the table, on which is a two-ringed hot plate. In times of urgency, he uses it, and in times of laziness and late at night. He adds soap flakes to the steaming liquid to hide its smell and composition, and when he carries the plastic pail down, the woman on welfare cannot smell or detect his business. He relishes his privacy.

Sometimes he has no flakes of soap, so he drops a pair of soiled underwear into the urine and walks with it, pretending there is no smell; and if the coast is clear, he bolts the lock on the bathroom door and does his business and laundry like a man hiding from his superstition.

He had heard that a famous Indian politician used to drink his own pee. And it overcame him.

He is safe inside his room. He breathes more easily now. He is home. His room relaxes him. It is like a library of a man obsessed with books and eccentric about the majesty of books.

Red building blocks which he stole two at a time are placed in fours at each end of the white-painted three-ply shelves. And the shelves end, as a scaffold should, at the end of available space, the ceiling. The same construction occupies all four walls. There are books of all sizes, all topics, all tastes.

The space between the bottom shelf and the floor is crammed with newspapers which are now yellow. There are magazines with their backs missing through frequent use. Each new magazine goes into the space which can get no larger. Statements of great political and international significance, the photograph of a man or a woman to be written to, are torn out from their sources and pinned to the three-ply shelves with common pins; and there are framed photographs of writers whom this man regards as the great writers of the world. No one else has heard of them.

He has collected relics of his daily passage throughout the city, in the same two square miles, not going beyond this perimeter. He has never again ventured into that part of the suburbs where the policeman had picked him up. Among his relics are jars and bottles, and one beautiful piece of pottery that looks as if it had been unearthed in an archaeological digging somewhere in the distant world. It is brown and has a mark like antiquity around its swelling girth; and where it stands on an old trunk that could have belonged to a sea captain, or to an immigrant from Europe or the West Indies, large enough to transport memories and possessions from a poorer life to this new country, this little brown jug gives age and seriousness to the other useless but priceless pieces in his room.

In all the jars and bottles, and in this brown "antique" jug, are dried branches of trees, flowers, sprigs and brambles. Dead beyond recognition.

The man collects dead things. Leaves and brambles and flowers and twigs. And he must like this death in things because there is nothing that lives in his room. Nothing but the man himself. He does not see them as dead things, or as meaning death.

He has five clocks. They are all miraculously set at the same, precise time, with not a second's difference. Every morning, using the time on the CBC radio as his standard and barometer, he checks and re-checks each of his five clocks; and when this is done, he sits on his old-fashioned, large and comfortable couch, upholstered in green velvet that now has patches like sores in the coat of a dog, with knobs of dull mahogany at the ends where the fingers touch, or rest, or agitate (if he is writing or thinking about a letter to an important personage in the world). He would sit here, now that he has set his time, and listen to the ticking, secure ordering of the meaning of time; pretending he is back home in the island that consumes time, where all the clocks ticked at various dispositions and carried different times. Canada has taught him important discipline. And he has learned about time. He has learned always to be *in* time.

Paper bags are stuffed between books, folded in their original creases and placed there, anxious for when they can be used a second time. A cupboard in the room is used as a clothes closet, a pantry and a storeroom. It contains more paper bags of all sizes, of all origins, from all supermarkets; but most are from Dominion. They are tied and made snug and tidy by elastic bands whose first use he has obviously forgotten. On the bottom shelf of the cupboard are plastic bags imprinted with barely visible names of stores and shops, folded in a new improvised crease and placed into a large brown paper bag.

All this time, he is walking the four short lengths of floor bordered by his books, stopping in front of one shelf, running his fingers absentmindedly over the titles of books. The linoleum floor is punctuated by the nails in his shoes that walk up and down, late into the night of thoughtfulness, of worrying about a correct address or a correct salutation. Now he stands beside a large wooden table made by immigrants or early settlers on farms, in the style of large sturdy legs the size and shape of their own husky peasant form. This table does not move. It cannot move. On it he has storeroomed his food and his drinks, his "eatables and drinkables," and it functions as his pantry of dishes and pots and pans. At one end of the table is the gas hot plate, the only implement for cooking that is allowed in this illegally-small living space.

On the hot plate is a shining aluminium saucepan battered around its girth by temper, hunger and burned rice.

He uncovers the saucepan. The food is old. Its age, two or three days, has thickened its smell, and makes it look like wet cement. The swollen black-eyed peas sit permanently among hunks of pig tails. He is hungry all of a sudden. These two urges, peeing and eating, come upon him without notice and with no regard to the last time he has eaten or peed. So he digs a "pot spoon" into the heart of the thick drying cement of food and uproots the swollen hunks of pig tails whose oily taste brings water and nostalgia to his eyes, and he half shuts his eyes to eat the first mouthful.

He replaces the lid. He puts the "pot spoon" between the saucepan rim and the lid, and pats the battered side of the saucepan the way a trainer would pat a horse that has just won on a long-shot bet.

He takes off his jacket. It is two sizes too large. Then he takes off his red woollen sweater, and another one of cotton, and long-sleeved; and then a third, grey, long-sleeved, round-necked and marked *Property of the Athletic Department, University of Toronto.*

He is a man of words, and the printed claim of ownership on his third pullover never ceases to amaze and impress him.

Stripped now of his clothes, he is left in a pair of grey long johns. And it is in these that he walks about the wordy room, ruminating as he struggles late into the night to compose the correct arrangement of words that would bring him replies from the pens of the great. Sometimes his own words do not flow as easily as he would wish. And this literary constipation aborts the urge to pee. At such times he runs to his Javex box, where he keeps all the replies he has ever received. He reads them now, praying for an easier movement of words from the bowels of his brain.

Dear Mr. Jefferson, Thank you for your letter.

That was all from one great personage, But it was good enough. It was a reply. And an official one at that. A rubber stamp of the signature tells you of the disinterest or the thick appointment book of the sender, that perhaps the sender does not understand the archival significance of the letter he has received from Mr. William Jefferson.

This is to acknowledge receipt of your letter.

Another reply from a great personage. Even the stamp, print and address are reproductions of the original. But the man believes that some value lies even in this impersonal reply.

Dear Mr. Jefferson, We are very glad to know that, as a Barbadian, you have intro-duced us to the archives of the University of Toronto, which is considering maintaining a Barbados collection. We wish you every success in your significant venture.

This is his most valuable letter. It is signed by someone who lives! A human hand has signed it. But he cannot untangle the name from its spidery script. He does not know who has replied to him. For typed beneath the script is only the person's offi-cial position: *Secretary.*

He understands more than any other living person the archival importance of these letters. And he treasures them within a vast imagination of large expectations, in this large brown box which contained Javex for bleaching clothes before it fell into his possession.

He has been nervous all week. And this nervousness erupted in strong urges to pee, strong and strange even for his weak bladder. The nervousness was linked to the price of his collection. This afternoon he had spoken to someone at the univer-sity. Over the telephone the voice told him, "Of course! Of course, Mr. Jefferson. We'll be interested in seeing your collection." It was a polite reply, like the written ones in his Javex box. But as a man obsessed by his relics, who attaches great signifi-cance to their esoteric value, he inflates that significance. He is also a man who would read an offer to purchase in a polite reply from the university. He is a man who hears more words than those that are spoken.

He starts to count his fortune. This letter to him from a living Prime Minister would be the basis of his fortune. His friend Alonzo would get a free round of beer at the Park Plaza roof bar. He would pay his rent six months in advance. He would have more time to spend on his private correspondence with the great men and women of the world.

He holds the Prime Minister's letter in his hand and examines the almost invisi-ble water marks on which it is typed. He studies the quality of the official stationery made in Britain and used by the West Indies, and compares it to that of Canada and the United States. He decides that the British and West Indies knew more about prestigious stationery. He continues to feel the paper between big thumb and two adjoining fingers, rubbing and rubbing and feeling a kind of orgasm coming on; and in this trance, he reads another letter.

Dear Mr. Jefferson, Thank you for your kind and thoughtful letter. Yours, Prime Minister's Office.

Above this line, "Margaret Thatcher" is stamped in fading ink. Still, it is a mark on history; "a first" from a poor woman whom history had singled out to be great.

When he is in his creative mood, he moves like a man afraid to cause commo-tion in a room in which he is a guest, like a man moving amongst bric-a-brac, price-less mementos of glass and china and silver locked in a glass cabinet. He moves about his room soundlessly, preparing his writing materials and deepening his mood for writing.

His stationery is personalized. *William Jefferson, Esquire* is printed in bold letters at the top of the blue page. And below that, his address. He writes with a fountain pen. And when he fills it from the bottle of black ink, he always smiles when the pen makes its sucking noise. This sucking noise takes him back years to another room in another country when he formed his first letters. And he likes the bottle that contains the ink. It has a white label, with a squeezed circle like an alert eye; and through this eye, through the middle of this eye, is an arrow which pierces it. *Parker super quick ink. Permanent black.* It suggests strength and longevity. It is like his life: determined and traditional, poised outside the mainstream but fixed in habit and custom. Whenever he uses this fountain pen, his index finger and the finger next to that, and his thumb, bear the verdict and the evidence of this permanent blackness. This *noire*. He sometimes wishes that he could use the language of Frenchmen who slip words and the sounds of those words over their tongues like raw oysters going down the throat!

"What a remarkable use of the tongue the French have! That back of the throat sensation!" he told Alonzo one afternoon, but in such a way as if he were speaking to the entire room in the Park Plaza Hotel bar.

Noire.

Many years ago, in 1955, the minute his feet touched French soil at Dorval in Quebec, the first greeting he heard was "*Noire!*" The sound held him in its grip, and changed his view of ordinary things, and made him fastidious and proper and suspicious. The only word he retained was *noire*. It was not a new word to him. For years even before that greeting, and in Barbados on a Sunday afternoon after the heavy midday meal, he used to sit at the back door looking out onto the cackling of hens, one of which he had eaten earlier, inhaling with the freshness of stomach and glorious weather the strong smell of Nugget shoe polish as he lathered it on his shoes and on his father's shoes and his mother's shoes and his grandfather's shoes. So he had already dipped his hands into *noire* long before Canada.

He had known *noire* for years. But no one had addressed him as *noire*.

He likes the *noire* of the ink he uses, as he liked the *noire* in the Nugget which gave his shoes longer life and made them immortal and left its proud, industrious and indelible stain on his fingers.

Tomorrow the University of Toronto is coming to buy his papers. He runs his hands over his letters in the Javex box, hundreds of them, and thinks of money and certified cheques. He empties all his pockets and puts the papers on the table. He picks up each piece like a man picking flesh from a carcass of bones. Who should he write to tonight?

The silent books around him, their words encased in covers, do not offer advice. But he knows what they would answer. He finds it difficult to concentrate. Tomorrow is too near. The money from his papers, cash or certified cheque, is too close at hand. He spends time spending it in his mind. And the things contained in tomorrow, like the things contained in his Javex box, have at last delivered him, just as his articulate use of the pen confirmed the value of the word and delivered him from the raving crowds of new immigrants. He has gained peace and a respectable distance from those aggressive men and women because of his use of the word.

"Should I write to the President of Yale University?"

The books, thick in their shelves around him, and few of which he has read from cover to cover, all these books remain uncommunicative and have no words of advice.

"Should I write to President Reagan?"

His five electric clocks continue to keep constant time, and in their regulated determination, refuse to disclose a tick of assistance.

"The Prime Minister of Barbados?"

Barbados is no longer home. Home, he had told Alonzo ten years ago, "is where I pee and eat and write."

He gets up and turns on the flame of the hot plate under the saucepan. "While the grass is growing, the horse is starving," he tells the saucepan. He smiles at his own wisdom. The heat makes the saucepan crackle. "While the grass is growing ..." The thin saucepan makes a smothered crackling sound. The hot plate seems to be melting the coagulated black-eyed peas and rice and pig tails. The hot plate is crackling as if it is intent upon melting the cheap alloy of the saucepan and turning the meal into soft hot lead, and then spreading its flame over the letters on the table, and then the table itself, and then the room. He lowers the flame.

"Fire cleans everything," he tells the hot plate. The saucepan stops laughing with the heat. His meal has settled down to being re-cooked.

But he is soon smelling things. The nostalgia of food and the perspiration from his mother's forehead as she cooked the food, and the strong, rich smell of pork. He smells also the lasting wetness of flannel shirts worn in the fields back on the small island.

He gets accustomed to these smells. And he thinks again of new correspondence since all these on the table before him would be gone by tomorrow, sold, archived among other literary riches. A hand-rubbing enthusiasm and contentment brings a smile to his face.

"I'll write the Prime Minister of Barbados!"

The smell comes up again. With the help of the smell, he is back on the small island, witnessing spires of blue smoke pouring out from each small castle of patched tin and rotting wood where his village stood. He can hear the waves and the turbulent sea, so much like the turbulence of water he boiled in the same thin-skin saucepan to make tea. As he thinks back, his eyes pass over used tea bags spread in disarray, an action caught in the midst of an important letter when he would sometimes drop a used tea bag into the yellow plastic pail.

Dear Prime Minister ...

He reaches over to the hot plate and raises the flame. He sees it change from yellow to blue, and smiles. "The horse is starving ..."

Certain important universities have asked me to act as a liaison to encourage you to submit your ...

The fragile aluminium saucepan is losing its battle in the heat of warming the food. But it is the smell. The smell takes his mind off the letter, and off the great sums of money, cash and certified cheques. He is a boy again, running home from school, colliding with palings and dogs and the rising smells of boiled pork reddened in tomatoes and bubbling over rice like the thick tar which the road workers poured over a raw road under construction.

He can taste his country now. Clearly. And see the face of the Prime Minister, greedy to make a name for himself in a foreign institution of higher learning, and obtain foreign currency for his foreign account.

... I have lived a solitary life, apart from the demonstrations and protests of the mainstream of immigrants. I have become a different man. A man of letters. I am more concerned with cultural things, radio, books and libraries, than with reports ...

Something is wrong with his pen. The flow is clogged and constricted, just like when he's caught with his pants up in a sudden urge to pee, and having forced it inwards, cannot get it outwards. And he gets up and heads downstairs. Just as he's moving away from his door, still on the first three or four steps going down, he turns back. "My pen is my penis," he tells the door.

He picks up the yellow plastic pail. He throws a shirt and underwear into the brown stagnant water. It looks like stale beer. Before he goes through the door again, he picks up the unfinished letter to the Prime Minister of Barbados, and in his long johns, armed with pail and paper, he creeps out.

The stairs are still dim. And he smiles. He moves down slowly, hoping that when he reaches the second floor the woman on welfare who occupies the toilet longer than any other tenant would not be there.

The saucepan has now begun to boil, although there are more solids than liquids within its thin frame. Popcorn comes into his mind. He doesn't even eat popcorn! He doesn't even go to the movies! The saucepan is turning red at the bottom. If he was in his room, he could not tell where the saucepan's bottom began and where the ring of the hot plate ended.

He thinks of roast corn as he reaches the closed door of the only bathroom in the house. He stands. He listens. He smells. He inhales. And he exhales. He puts his hand on the door and pushes gently, and the door opens with a small creak. He stands motionless, alarmed to see that the bathroom is indeed empty. Where is the woman on welfare?

... at night, back home, in the crop season when the sugar canes are cut and harvested, they burn the corn over coals....

Right then, above his head, the saucepan explodes. He doesn't hear it. The blackeyed peas and rice burst out, pelting the cover before it, and the table top is splattered like careless punctuation marks. It falls on his fine blue stationery.

The explosion comes just as he holds the yellow pail at a tilt, over the growling toilet bowl. In the same hand as the pail is the unfinished letter. The urine is flowing into the bowl and he stands thinking, when he sees the first clouds of smoke crawling down the stairs, past the open bathroom door.

The smoke becomes heavier and makes tears come into his eyes. He is crying and passing his hands in front of his face, trying to clear a passage from the second floor, through the thickening smoke rising like high waves. Up and up he goes, no faster than when he entered the house that afternoon, struggling through the smoke until he reaches the steps in front of his door. And as he gets there, it seems as if all the books, all the letters, all the bags of plastic and paper shout at once in an even greater explosion.

Before he can get downstairs to call for help from the woman on welfare, he thinks he hears all five of his clocks alarming. And then, in the way a man who has been struck by a deadening blow waits for the second one to land, he stands, expecting the five clocks to do something else. It is then that he hears one clock striking the hour. He counts aloud until he reaches eight, and then he refuses to count any longer.

1985

Wilkie Collins

Wilkie Collins (1824-89), born in London, was called to the bar in 1851. He never practiced law, choosing instead to be a writer. He was a close friend of Charles Dickens. Well liked by Victorian readers, he wrote at least 50 short stories, 15 plays, and 100 non-fiction pieces. He published 25 novels, including *The Woman in White* (1860) and *The Moonstone* (1868).

Collins's "A Sermon for Sepoys" originally appeared in *Household Words: A Weekly Journal* 414 (27 Feb. 1858): 244-47. I have included it here to give readers an idea of some Victorian writers' perception of Britain's relationship with its colonial possessions. Less than a year after what Britain called "The Indian Mutiny" (now viewed by Indians as the first Indian war for independence against British rule), Collins wrote this piece, which complements his single chapter in a story loosely based on the mutiny that he co-authored with Charles Dickens to celebrate British "heroics" in India: "The Perils of Certain English Prisoners." While Dickens exhibits—surprisingly for one who sided with the "subaltern" in his novels—undisguised racism in his two chapters, Collins is much more sensitive toward matters of ethnicity in his chapter. In "A Sermon for Sepoys," rather than demonize the Indians as Dickens had done, or imply that they are uncivilized, Collins reminds us of the benevolent Shah Jehan or Jahan (1592-1666), during whose reign the Taj Mahal was built. Collins's Indians are not barbaric, but thoughtful and philosophical. At the end of this piece, however, we wonder about Collins's perception of the rebellious Indians as "Betrayers" and "Assassins."

A Sermon for Sepoys[1]

While we are still fighting for the possession of India, benevolent men of various religious denominations are making their arrangements for taming the human tigers in that country by Christian means. Assuming that this well-meant scheme is not an entirely hopeless one, it might, perhaps, not be amiss to preach to the people of India, in the first instance, out of some of their own books—or, in other words,

---

[1] *Sepoy* The term used in the British Indian Army (and still used in the modern Indian Army) for an infantry private. Wilkie Collins wrote this essay less than a year after what is termed "The Sepoy Rebellion" or the "Indian Mutiny" of 1857 (but seen by Indian scholars as The Indian War of Independence of 1857). Muddled, exaggerated, and sensationalized reporting in the British press of atrocities of Indians against English men, women, and children during this Indian uprising had served to incense the British against Indians. Collins wrote this piece to provide a more balanced view of the "mutiny." Even his friend Charles Dickens, whose novels are sympathetic to the downtrodden, said vengefully in "The Perils of Certain English Prisoners," in the Christmas 1857 issue of *Household Words*: "I wish I were a commander in chief in India. The first thing I would do [is] to strike that Oriental Race with amazement [and] I should do my utmost to exterminate the race upon whom the stain of the late cruelties rested." Such sentiments led to bloody reprisals on the part of the British— and eventually to the handing over of the control of India by the East India Company to the crown.

to begin the attempt to purify their minds by referring them to excellent moral lessons which they may learn from their own Oriental literature. Such lessons exist in the shape of ancient parables, once addressed to the ancestors of the sepoys, and still quite sufficient for the purpose of teaching each man among them his duty towards his neighbour, before he gets on to higher things. Here is a specimen of one of these Oriental apologues. Is there reason why it should not be turned to account, as a familiar introduction to the Christian sermon addressed to pacified native congregation in the city of Delhi?

In the seventeenth century of the Christian era, the Emperor Shah Jehan — the wise, the bountiful, the builder of the new city of Delhi — saw fit to appoint the pious Vizir,[1] Gazee Ed Din, to the government of all districts of Morodabad.

The period of the Vizir's administration was gratefully acknowledged by the people whom he governed as the period of the most-precious blessings they had ever enjoyed. He protected innocence, he honoured learning, he rewarded industry. He was an object for the admiration of all eyes — a subject for the praise of all tongues. But the grateful people observed, with grief, that the merciful ruler who made them all happy, was himself never seen to smile. His time in the palace passed in mournful solitude. On the few occasions when he appeared in the public walks, his face was gloomy, his gait was slow, his eyes were fixed on the ground. Time passed, and there was no change in him for the better. One morning the whole population was astonished and afflicted by the news that he had resigned the reins of government and had gone to justify himself before the emperor at Delhi.

Admitted to the presence of Shah Jehan, the Vizir made his obeisance, and spoke these words: "Wise and mighty Ruler, condescend to pardon the humblest of your servants if he presumes to lay at your feet the honours which you have deigned to confer on him in the loveliest country on the earth. The longest life, oh bountiful Master, hardly grants time enough to man to prepare himself for death. Compared with the performance of that first of duties, all other human employments are vain as the feeble toil of an ant on the highway, which the foot of the first traveller crushes to nothing! Permit me, then, to prepare myself for the approach of eternity. Permit me, by the aid of solitude and silence, to familiarize my mind with the sublime mysteries of religion; and to wait reverently for the moment when eternity unveils itself to my eyes, and the last summons calls me my account before the Judgment Seat."

The Vizir said these words, knelt down, laid his forehead on the earth, and was silent. After a minute of reflection, the emperor answered him in these terms: "Faithful servant! Your discourse has filled my mind with perplexity and fear. The apprehensions which you have caused me are like those felt by a man who finds himself standing, unawares, on the edge of a precipice. Nevertheless, I cannot decide whether the sense of trouble that you have awakened within me is justified by sound reason or not. My days, like yours, however long they may be, are but an

---

[1] *Vizir* A high-ranking political or religious adviser or minister to a Muslim emperor.

instant compared with eternity. But, if I thought as you do, if all men capable of doing good followed your example, who would remain to guide the faithful? Surely the duties of government would then fall to the share of those men only who are brutally careless of the future that awaits them beyond the grave—who are insensible to all feelings which are not connected with their earthly passions and their earthly interests? In that case, should I not be—should you not be—responsible before the Supreme Being for the miseries, without number, which would then be let loose on the world. Ponder that well, Vizir! And while I, on my side, consider the same subject attentively, depart in peace to the abode which I have prepared to receive you, since your arrival in this city. May Heaven direct us both into the way which it is safest best to take!"

The Vizir withdrew. For three days he remained in his retirement, and received no message from the emperor. At the end of the third day, he sent to the palace to beg for a second audience. The request was immediately granted.

When he again appeared in the presence of his sovereign, his countenance expressed the tranquility of his mind. He drew a letter from his bosom, kissed it, and presented it to the emperor on his knees. Shah Jehan having given him permission to speak, he expressed himself, thereupon, in these words:

"Sovereign Lord and master! The letter which you have deigned to take from my hands has been addressed to me by the sage, Abbas, who now stands with me in the light of your presence, and who has lent me the assistance of his wisdom to unravel the scruples and perplexities which have beset my mind. Thanks to the lesson I have learned from him, I can now look back on my past life with pleasure, and contemplate the future with hope. Thanks to the wisdom which I have imbibed from his teaching, I can now conscientiously bow my head before the honours which your bounty showers on me, and can gladly offer myself again to be the shadow of your power in the province of Morodabad."

Shah Jehan, who had listened to the Vizir with amazement and curiosity, directed that the letter should be given to the sage, Abbas, and ordered him to read aloud the words of wisdom that he had written to Gazee Ed Din. The venerable man stood forth in the midst of the Court, and, obeying the Emperor, read these lines: "May the pious and merciful Vizir, to whom the wise generosity of our sovereign lord and master has entrusted the government of a province, enjoy to the end of his days the blessing of perfect health!

"I was grieved in my inmost heart when I heard that you had deprived the millions of souls who inhabit Morodabad of the advantages which they enjoyed under your authority. Modesty and respect prevent me from combating your scruples of conscience while you were describing them in the presence of the Emperor. I hasten, therefore, to write the words which I could not venture to speak. My purpose is to clear your mind of the doubts which now darken it, by relating to you the history of my own youth. The anxious thoughts which trouble you, were once the thoughts which troubled me also. May your soul be relieved of the burden that oppresses it, as mine was relieved in the bygone time!

"My early manhood was passed in studying the science of medicine. I learnt all the secrets of my art, and practised it for the benefit of my species. In time, however, the fearful scenes of suffering and death which perpetually offered themselves to my eyes, so far affected my mind as to make me tremble for my own life. Wherever I went, my grave seemed to be yawning at my feet. The awful necessity of preparing myself for eternity impressed itself upon my soul, and withdrew my thoughts from every earthly consideration. I resolved to retire from the world, to despise the acquisition of all mortal knowledge, and to devote my remaining days to the severest practices of a purely religious life. In accordance with this idea, I resolved to humble myself by suffering the hardship of voluntary poverty. After much consideration, I came to the conclusion that those who stood in need of my money were the persons who were least worthy of being benefited by it; and that those who really deserved the exercise of my charity were too modest, or too high-minded, to accept my help. Under the influence of this delusion, I buried in earth all the treasure that I possessed, and took refuge from human society in the wildest and most inaccessible mountains of my native country. My abode was in the darkest corner of a huge cavern; my drink was the running water; my food consisted of the herbs and fruits that I could gather in the woods. To add to the severe self-restraint which had now become the guiding principle of my life, I frequently passed whole nights in watching—on such occasions, keeping my face turned towards the East, and waiting till the mercy of the Prophet should find me out, and unveil the mysteries of Heaven to my mortal view.

"One morning, after my customary night of watching, exhaustion overpowered me, at the hour of sunrise; and I sank prostrate in spite of myself, on the ground at the entrance of my cave.

"I slept, and a vision appeared to me.

"I was still at the mouth of the cave, and still looking at the rays of the rising sun. Suddenly a dark object passed between me and the morning light. I looked at it attentively, and saw that it was an eagle, descending slowly to the earth. As the bird floated nearer and nearer to the ground, a fox dragged himself painfully out of a thicket near at hand. Observing the animal, as he sank exhausted close by me, I discovered that both his fore legs were broken. While I was looking at him, the eagle touched the earth, laid before the crippled fox a morsel of goat's flesh that he carried in his talons, flapped his huge wings, and, rising again into the air, slowly disappeared from sight.

"On coming to my senses again, I bowed my forehead to the earth, and addressed my thanksgivings to the Prophet for the vision which be had revealed to me. I interpreted it in this manner. 'The divine Power,' I said to myself, 'accepts the sacrifice that I have made in withdrawing myself from contaminations of the world; but reveals to me, at the same time, that there is still some taint of mortal doubt clinging to my mind, and rendering the trust which it is my duty to place in the mercy of Heaven less absolute and unconditional than it ought to be, so long as I waste even the smallest portion of my time in the base employment of providing for my own daily wants, so long my confidence in Providence be imperfect, and my mind be incapable of wholly abstracting itself from earthly cares. This is what the vision is designed to teach me. If the bounty of Heaven condescends to employ an eagle to provide for the wants of a crippled fox, how sure may I feel that the same mercy will extend the same benefits to me! Let me wholly devote myself, then, to the service of my Creator, and commit the preservation of my life to the means which His wisdom is sure to supply.'

"Strong in this conviction, I searched the woods no more for the herbs and fruits which had hitherto served me for food. I sat at the mouth of my cavern, and waited through the day, and no heavenly messenger appeared to provide for my wants. The night passed; and I was still alone. The new morning came; and my languid eyes could hardly lift themselves to the light, my trembling limbs failed to sustain me when I strove to rise. I lay back against the wall of my cavern, and resigned myself to die.

"The consciousness of my own existence seemed to be just passing from me, when the voice of an invisible being sounded close at my ear. I listened, and heard myself addressed in these words: 'Abbas,' said the supernatural voice, 'I am the Angel whose charge it is to search out and register your inmost thoughts. I am sent to you on a mission of reproof. Vain man! do you pretend to be wiser than the wisdom which is revealed to you? The blindness of your vision and the vainglory of your heart have together perverted a lesson which was mercifully intended to teach you the duties that your Creator expects you to perform. Are you crippled like the fox? Has not nature, on the contrary, endowed you with the strength of the eagle? Rise and bestir yourself! Rise, and let the example of the eagle guide you, henceforth, in the right direction. Go back to the city from which you have fled. Be, for the future, the messenger of health and life to those who groan on the hard bed of sickness. Ill-judging mortal! the virtue that dies in solitude, lives in the world from which you have withdrawn. Prove your gratitude to your Creator by the good that you do among his helpless and afflicted creatures. There is the way that leads you from earth to Heaven. Rise, Abbas, rise humbly, and take it!'

"An unseen hand lifted me from ground, an unseen hand guided me back to the city. Humbled, repentant, enlightened at last, I drew my treasure from its hiding place, and employed it in helping the poor. Again I devoted all my energies to the blessed work of healing the sick. Years passed and found me contented and industrious in my vocation. As the infirmities of age approached, I assumed the sacred robe, comforted the souls of my fellow-creatures, as I had formerly comforted their bodies. Never have I forgotten the lesson that I learnt in my hermitage on the mountain. You see me now, high in the favour of my Sovereign—Know that I have deserved my honours, because I have done good in my generation, among the people over whom he rules.

"Such, oh, pious Vizir, is the story of my youth. May the lesson which enlightened me do the same good office for you. I make no pretensions to wisdom: I speak only of such things as I know. Believe me, all wisdom which extends no farther than yourself is unworthy of you. A life sacrificed to subtle speculations is a life wasted.

Let the eagle be the object of your emulation as he was of mine. The more gifts you have received, the better use it is expected you will make of them. Although the All-Powerful alone can implant virtue in the human heart, it is still possible for you, as the dreaded representative of authority, to excite to deeds of benevolence, even those who have no better motive for doing good, than the motive of serving their own interests. With time, you may teach them the knowledge of higher things. Meanwhile, it will matter little to the poor who are succoured whether it is mere ostentation or genuine charity that relieves them. Spread the example, therefore, of your own benevolence, beyond the circle of those only who are wise and good. Widen the sphere of your usefulness among your fellow-creatures, with every day; and fortify your mind with the blessed conviction that the life you will then lead, will be of all lives the most acceptable in the eyes of the Supreme Being.

"Farewell. May the blessings of a happy people follow you wherever you go. May your name, when you are gathered to your fathers, be found written in the imperishable page — in the Volume of the Book of Life!"

Abbas ceased. As he bowed his head, and folded up the scroll, the emperor beckoned him to the foot of the throne, and thanked the sage for the lesson that he had read to his Sovereign and to all the Court. The next day, the Vizir was sent back to his government at Morodabad. Shah Jehan also caused copies of the letter to be taken, and ordered them to be read to the people in the high places of the city. When that had been done, he further commanded that this inscription should be engraved on the palace gates, in letters of gold, which men could read easily, even from afar off:

THE LIFE THAT IS MOST ACCEPTABLE TO THE SUPREME BEING, IS THE LIFE THAT IS MOST USEFUL TO THE HUMAN RACE.

Surely not a bad Indian lesson, to begin with, when Betrayers and Assassins are the pupils to be taught?

1858

Saros Cowasjee

Saros Cowasjee (b. 1931) was born in India. He studied at Agra University and the University of Leeds. Later he taught at the University of Regina, and he is now Professor Emeritus there. His novels include *Goodbye to Elsa* (1974) and *My Dear Maura* (2005). He has published several collections of stories, as well as essays and commentaries, and has edited such volumes of Indian stories as *A Raj Collection* (2005).

Cowasjee's "His Father's Medals," like Mulk Raj Anand's "Duty" or R.K. Narayan's "Mother and Son," is virtually free of issues related overtly to the postcolonial imperial-colonial divide. All three stories could be compared on this level—and on others. Cowasjee focuses on family attachments and caste (class) conflicts in an Indian community. Is there an irony of life here that lifts this story beyond being just a cultural documentary of an individual's day-to-day life in an Indian village?

His Father's Medals

Ramu sat on the doorstep of his hut in a far corner of Thakur Madan Singh's compound, a good distance away from the quarters of the other servants better placed in life than himself. He spat on the silver medal and with the bottom edge of his shirt rubbed it hard till it shone with a dull lustre. "That's better," he said, dropping it gently into his shirt pocket and pulling out the other two—these of bronze. He again spat and polished them—in the same manner. If I had only dug my little finger in the polish on the lavatory shelf, he thought, these would have glittered like gold. And nobody would have suspected, for what has a sweeper boy to do with polish?

Three medals were all that his father, Ramji Lal, had left him. Dying, the medals still on his famished chest, he fought to keep back his last breath—not that life had much to give, but that death would take even the little he had. Ramji Lal died and the prized proof of a lifetime's devotion to duty passed on to Ramu, his only child. Ramu looked fondly at the medals. They were no mere tokens of affection—a link between a dead father and a living son—but a flaming ideal towards which he must strive. He pressed them to his heart and tears welled up in his eyes; his dear, dear father had left them in his care.

Three medals! The two large ones of bronze from the British Government for cleaning the officers' latrines through the Burma Campaign, and the little silver one from the Colonel himself as a mark of appreciation that they were well cleaned. He looked at the medals intently. Who was this bald, point-bearded man with the face of a butcher, waging wars and distributing medals? His father had often talked of him —a great king who ruled the world and did justice to all. Justice to all? What justice was done to his father? Two ribbons to decorate his breast while the heart beneath was starved of blood. Ah, but that was being too hard on the king. What could a king do but sit on a golden seat and empty his bowels in a silver pot? A silver pot—glistening like his little medal. How he would love to be a king's sweeper and handle silver pots!

Ramu shook himself. He was demanding too much from life. What God had given was good enough: it was not everybody who became a sweeper in the household of Thakur Madan Singh, BA. There were Goodan, Murari, Sona and Ravi and a horde of others sweeping the public streets from morning to night and envying him his honoured position.

The back door of the palatial house facing Ramu's quarters was flung open and Sultan Singh, the cook, clad in his yellow turban, called out: "Ramu! O Ramu! Come here and clean this."

Ramu dropped the medals in his pocket, jumped down the single step that led to his hut, and hurried towards the latrines. He lifted the lids off the commodes and expertly pulled out the pots. It was for the eleventh time this morning that he was cleaning them; yesterday he had had to attend to them some sixteen times, though only five people lived in this capacious house. God! What do they eat that they must go some twenty times a day? But it was good that they frequented the latrines, for were they habituated like the poor how could he have found full-time employment in a respectable home? As he gracefully carried the pots, his head thrown back to avoid the stink, he could not help musing that at least in this there was no difference between rich and poor except in its frequency; that whatever delicacies the rich might relish, it must come down to this, this that he carried at arm's length, and that kept him at arm's length from his fellow men.

Having done a good job, he sat down again on the doorstep. Once a sweeper, always a sweeper. He had given up all attempts to break through the social barrier. His life and his future must be decided by his own class, the Untouchable.[1] Nothing could ever break through the rigid class system, no, not even love. There stood Kamala, now engaged to a lorry driver's son. He had loved her passionately, would have done anything to win her, but she had asked of him the impossible—to forget her. As children they had played together, planned together. He was not then a sweeper's son nor she a Rajput's daughter. But as Kamala grew to maidenhood, under the vigilance of her father Sultan Singh, and the providential care of Thakur Madan Singh, dignity and distance silenced her feeble pulse of love.

He remembered how he had once playfully caught her hand and the fear that had come into her eyes. "Leave me," she had begged. "Oh, let me go!" He had pulled back his hand, to see her rush back to her quarters. Through the half-open door he had seen her washing herself clean. He had turned his face aside, the humiliation sticking in his throat: he was an Untouchable. A sweeper holding the hand of a Rajput's daughter! Did you ever hear of that?

No, he had never heard. He had given up all thought of possessing her, all thought and those rash promises of boyhood without a struggle. Love could live on,

---

[1] *Untouchable* In the Indian caste system, a Dalit, often called an Untouchable or Outcaste.

just as hope lives on, deep in the core of the poor man's heart. He would keep her memory alive, would keep the twisted hairpin and the broken bangles she had dropped into the litter bin close to his heart. And he would give her something: a little token that would remind her of Ramu and tell her that even a sweeper boy has a heart. A sweeper boy has a heart! Did you hear that?

A pathetic smile dissolved into anguish on his lips as he stood up and put his hands into the loose, patched trousers, which had once belonged to Thakur Madan Singh. He pulled out all the bits of copper and added them up. They made a little over two rupees. Enough to buy a handsome present, he said. If I run short I can sell off one of my father's medals. No, he would never sell his dear father's medals: not for love, not for this world — for what are love and a world to a sweeper boy?

He sauntered till he came to the market. He walked on, unable to decide where he should take his first peep. On the pavement Shivaji, notorious for his prices, had spread his fancy goods. He thought he could take a look; it would give him some idea of the things he could buy for Kamala. He came to the shop and stood in the midst of the little group that was examining the goods. His eager, boyish face beamed with excitement as he viewed the glittering array of bangles, hairpins, rings, bead necklaces, mirrors, till it came to rest on a pair of brilliant anklets. Shining silver anklets! He would put them round Kamala's ankles with his own hands, would give just a little press to her delicate feet; she would not object to that, no, not as long as he kept to her feet. But, ah, they must be expensive. Silver anklets cost a lot of money. Yet sometimes they are sold cheap, sometimes when they are false, sometimes when they are stolen....

"How much do you want for these?" he asked hesitantly, pointing to the anklets.

"Fifteen rupees and nothing less," replied Shivaji.

Ramu stepped back. He felt as if somebody had given him a punch in the face. He turned to go.

"Wait," said Shivaji. "How much can you give?"

"I can't afford them. I don't want them," said Ramu.

"You do, you do. Give anything and take them."

Ramu blushed. "No, no."

"Can you give four rupees?" asked Shivaji, holding an anklet high to display it.

Ramu felt the weight of the copper in his pocket and taking courage said, "Two rupees."

Shivaji burst into a loud, coarse laugh. "Ha, ha, ha, ha. Silver anklets for two rupees!" And turning to the group of buyers he remarked, "Wants anklets for two rupees to put round the feet of some hussy!" Then with a malicious grin he swore at Ramu: "By God, how much do you pay her for a ride?"

The little crowd seemed to enjoy Shivaji's remarks and pressed closer to get a better view of Ramu. One from the crowd mockingly reprimanded Shivaji: "You mustn't be so hard on the poor fellow, Master. It may be for his mother!"

Burning rage gave him courage; the low jibe of Shivaji made him dare. He would teach him a lesson — and now. He looked to the left and then to the right. The street was surging with people. With one rush he snatched the anklet from Shivaji's hand and darted off to mingle in the crowd.

A hand lay on his shoulder. Two policemen tightly gripped him by the arms and stood on either side of him, while a jeering mob pressed around him.

"Move out of the way," yelled one of the policemen. "Let us take this son of a pig to the police station."

"The pimp," swore the other. "Thinks we police and justice are dead."

"That he will find out when the strap licks his bloody arse and leaves it as red as a monkey's bum," rejoined the first.

"As a monkey's bum," echoed one from the crowd. "Give him a monkey's bum. The fool is stealing in broad daylight, when nowadays it is not advisable even at night, because of our vigilant police."

The two policemen, sensing the irony in the remark, cut through the crowd and triumphantly marched away with their prey. Having got clear off the busy street, they began searching Ramu's pockets.

"Just two rupees! That's not much," said the first policeman. "What's in your shirt pocket?"

"Nothing, nothing," implored Ramu.

The second policeman dug his hand into Ramu's pocket and pulled out the medals. "Eh, where did you get these from?"

"I did not steal them, I did not steal them. They are my father's medals. Please give them back to me."

"Give them back to you, eh! Your father's medals! Where did he steal them from? Out with it, or my boot will be at your bottom. Quick."

"My father was not a thief. They were given to him for his services," wept Ramu, tears running down his cheeks.

"Services? What services? You and your father are not good enough to clean our latrines. Now march on fast," said the first policeman, hitting Ramu across the calves with his cane, "or you will find this creeping up your arse."

1986

Rienzi Crusz

Rienzi Crusz (b. 1925) was born in Sri Lanka (Ceylon) of Portuguese and Sinhalese ancestry. He was educated at St. Joseph's College in Colombo and later taught there. In 1951, he studied library science in London, England. He immigrated to Canada in 1965 and worked as a librarian. His volumes of poetry include *Flesh and Thorn* (1974), *A Time for Loving* (1986), *Lord of the Mountain: the Sardiel Poems* (1999), and *Gambolling with the Devine* (2003).

Crusz's "Roots" traces the lineage of the Sri Lankan speaker, who is a burgher (that is, an individual of mixed Portuguese—or Dutch—and Sri Lankan ancestry). Here is the common postcolonial experience of being caught between two worlds. Compare this poem with Agha Shahid Ali's "Snowmen," Jean Arasanayagam's "I Have No Country," and Kamala Das's "An Introduction." In "In the Idiom of the Sun," the immigrant-speaker (to whom the sun is a metaphor for his original tropical home) sees himself as a subaltern in his adopted country and feels he must temporize and hold his tongue when insulted.

Roots

For Cleta Marcellina Nora Serpanchy

What the end usually demands
is something of the beginning,
and so
I conjure history from a cup
of warm Portuguese blood
from my forefathers,
black diamond eyes, charcoal hair
from my Sinhalese mothers;
the beached catamaran,
gravel voices of the fishermen,
the catch still beating like a heart
under the pelting sun;
how the pariah dogs looked urgent
with fish meal in their brains,
the children romped, sagged,
then melted into the sand.

A Portuguese captain holds
the soft brown hand of my Sinhala mother.

It's the year 1515 A.D.,[1]
when two civilizations kissed and merged,
and I, burgher[2] of that hot embrace,
write a poem of history
as if it were only the romance
of a lonely soldier on a crowded beach
in Southern Ceylon.

1986

In the Idiom of the Sun

It would have been somewhat different
in green Sri Lanka, where I touched
the sun's fire daily
with my warm finger tips.

I wouldn't have hesitated
to call you a bastard
and for emphasis, might have even
thrown in the four-letter word.
The blood would have shuddered a little
under your Aryan skull,
but you would have held my honesty
like a Temple flower in full bloom,
forgiven my unholy idiom.

Here in this white land,
the senses forged to iron silence,
the mind trapped in a snow-boot,
I must hold my black tongue.

The blood has wintered,
and icicles hang like cobwebs

---

[1] *1515 A.D.* Early in the sixteenth century, the Portuguese Captain Odoardo Barbosa made contact with
the island now known as Sri Lanka (Ceylon).

[2] *burgher* In Sri Lanka burghers constitute a Eurasian ethnic group mostly of Portuguese or Dutch and
local Sinhalese ancestry.

from the roof of my cold mouth.
I can now only spit frozen-eyed,
and gently demur.

2005

Cyril Dabydeen

Cyril Dabydeen (b. 1945) was born in Guyana. He came to Canada in 1970 and attended Queen's University. A poet and fiction writer, he has published several volumes of poetry, including *Distances* (1977) and *Coastland* (1989); two volumes of short stories, *Black Jesus and Other Stories* (1996) and *My Brahmin Days and Other Stories* (2000); and a handful of novellas, including *The Wizard Swami* (1985) and *Drums of My Flesh* (2007).

Dabydeen's poem "My Mother" explores an issue faced by many immigrants — to what extent must they try to assimilate; to what extent must they accommodate the mutual give-and-take between the minority and the majority in the formation of the nation? How conscious is the speaker of the complexity of his assimilationist approach? Is there a difference in tone between the two parts of the poem? Compare Dabydeen's perspective here with Marilyn Chin's in "Elegy for Chloe Nguyen (1955-1988)" and Dennis Brutus's in "By the Waters of Babylon."

My Mother

I

I am doing it again:
I've fallen into the old trap,
telling my mother
she must forsake the old ways,
she must go out in the snow
day or night and start jogging.

She who has lived most of her life in the tropics,[1]
raising her children, us,
having toiled all the years long;
suddenly I want her to be in the fashion magazines,
to live her life with panache, be confident,
or overbearing in her dealings with other people;

Never to be a quiet woman any more,
as I tell her to change her diet in Canada
so as to overcome stress —
to exercise regularly. She must!
She balks, though never protesting loudly,

---

[1] *the tropics* It is very likely the speaker is referring to Guyana, the original home of the poet.

and she yearns to do as I tell her—
I, her eldest, who has attended university,
who figures he knows it all—
what's best for her because I have been here longest;

Telling her again and again, as brothers and sisters
listen, and say I'm too demanding—
yet I continue to berate her each time I visit,
imagining a life of newness, her changed behaviour.
See, we're in Canada, the Great White North!
This is the land of people taking control,
land of people living with determined zest,
people always in command, controlling destiny—
… but she quickly laughs
and tells me to mind my manners, finally.

II

That night I imagine my mother skiing,
coming down a mountain with breakneck speed
as she loudly calls out to me,
then telling the others what she's achieved;
but I see her tumble and fall,
but she is miraculously up again—

Making her mark on the prismatic Canadian
landscape or soil, where else?
Who can doubt her zest?
Who can blame her for not trying hard?

A gin and tonic next.
I mull over my words, feeling guilty
thinking I must leave her alone
in her silence, her memory intact,
despite her daily watching soap opera,
and all other acts on the TV—
still in deepest silence
in the regular living room.

My siblings, they mutter softly,
sometimes alone with her when I'm not there
as she yet ponders going out when the wind whistles—
the cold and the snow piling up—

imagining the outside with closed eyes,
her brows furrowed,
eyes dilating next, blinking,
as in the everlasting tropical sun.

1996

David Dabydeen

David Dabydeen (b. 1955) was born in Berbice, Guyana. He immigrated to England when he was thirteen years old. He attended the universities of Cambridge and London. His publications include such scholarly works as *Hogarth's Blacks* (1987), several volumes of poetry, including *Slave Song* (1984), and several novels, including *The Intended* (1991), *Our Lady of Demerara* (2004), and *Molly and the Muslim Stick* (2008).

Dabydeen's "Catching Crabs" portrays a speaker caught up in nostalgia, recalling his youthful days in his original homeland—very likely Guyana, if the poem is derived from the poet's experience. Even though the poem itself is not sentimental, the speaker is nostalgic; it portrays unflinchingly the pain of separation. Has the speaker actually returned to his mother's home or is he imagining this in his Cambridge flat? Compare this poem with Dionne Brand's "Return I" and Sasenarine Persaud's "Gifting the Light of the Soul." The speaker of Dabydeen's "The New Poetry" is annoyed with a woman he knows who, absorbed with her own Arcadian world, feigns indifference to his recitation of colonial exploitation. The setting appears to be somewhere in the United Kingdom. Is the woman necessarily white? Is this relevant?

Catching Crabs

Ruby and me stalking savannah[1]
Crab season with cutlass and sack like big folk.
Hiding behind stones or clumps of bush
Crabs locked knee-deep in mud mating
And Ruby seven years old feeling strange at the sex
And me horrified to pick them up
Plunge them into the darkness of bag,
So all day we scout to catch the lonesome ones
Who don't mind cooking because they got no prospect
Of family, and squelching through the mud,
Cutlass clearing bush at our feet,
We come home tired slow, weighed down with plenty
Which Ma throw live into boiling pot piece-piece.
Tonight we'll have one big happy curry feed,
We'll test out who teeth and jaw strongest
Who will grow up to be the biggest
Or who will make most terrible cannibal.

---

[1] *savannah* The savannahs of the coastlands of Guyana become muddy wetlands during the rainy season.

We leave behind a mess of bones and shell
And come to England and America
Where Ruby hustles in a New York tenement
And me writing poetry at Cambridge,
Death long catch Ma, the house boarded up
Breeding wasps, woodlice in its dark-sack belly:
I am afraid to walk through weed yard,
Reach the door, prise open, look,
In case the pot still bubbles magical
On the fireside, and I see Ma
Working a ladle, slow —
Limbed, crustacean-old, alone,
In case the woodsmoke and curry steam
Burn my child-eye and make it cry.

1988

The New Poetry

She wanted to be alone with her world, vexed
Always by his prehistoric eye,
The strange usurping tales of anthropophagi
And recitation of colonial texts.

Britannia is serviced by new machines
Humming and twinkling as they work,
The creak of mule-drawn punt or old slave feet,
The exhalation of the aborigines

Are esoteric notes in a scholar's curious book:
The new poetry quietly observes
The ways a leaf spirals neutrally to earth,
The shades of moon, the tides, the shepherd's timeless crook.

She forsook as tedious his confession,
His alien unbridgeable babble of words,
Settling comfortably on the sofa
She would turn the television on

And see confirmed the greetings beamed through space
Of natives singing by some runway,
The bone-shaped plane of fat white men and foreign aid
Met by loud spears and women jigging waist.

1988

Fred D'Aguiar

Fred D'Aguiar (b. 1960) was born in London to Guyanese parents. He spent his early years in Guyana, returning to England in 1972, where he currently resides (with extended stays in the United States). Recently he was professor of Creative Writing at the University of Miami and at Virginia Tech University. A poet, novelist, and dramatist, his volumes of poems include *Mama Dot* (1985), *Airy Hall* (1989), and *Continental Shelf* (2009). His fourth novel *Bethany/Bettany* won the Guyana Prize for Fiction, 2004.

D'Aguiar's "Home" is a fine example of the ambivalence to the imperial centre of postcolonial individuals, whether they reside there (as does the speaker of this poem, who, if we identify him with the poet, is a London-born Guyanese resident of the United Kingdom) or in the former colonies. This poem can be compared with Janice Shinebourne's "Red Bean Cakes: London and New York" and Jamaica Kincaid's "On Seeing England for the First Time." D'Aguiar's memoir piece "A Son in Shadow" (which was published in *Harper's* and won the Best American Essay 2002 award) is a poetic evocation of a father he never knew and of the estrangement of his parents.

Home

These days when I'm away too long,
anything I happen to clap eyes on,
that red phone box, somehow makes me
miss here like nothing I can name.

My heart performs its jazz drum solo
when the bared crow's feet on the 747
scrape down at Heathrow. H.M. Customs ...
I'm resigned to the usual inquisition,

telling me with Surrey loam caked
on the tongue, home is always elsewhere.
I take it like an English middleweight
with a questionable chin, knowing

my passport photo's too open-faced,
haircut wrong (an afro) for the decade;
the stamp, British Citizen not bold enough
for my liking and too much for theirs.

The cockney cab driver begins chirpily
but can't or won't steer clear of race,

so rounds on Asians. I lock eyes with him
in the rearview when I say I'm one.

He settles to his task, grudgingly,
in a huffed silence. Cha![1] Drive man!
I have legal tender burning in my pocket
to move on, like a cross in Transylvania.

At my front door, why doesn't the lock
recognize me and budge? As I fight it,
I think intruder then see with the clarity
of a torture victim the exact detail:

in my case that extra twist necessary,
falling forward over the threshold
then mail or junk felicitations,
into a cool reception in the hall.

Grey light and close skies I love you.
Choky streets, roundabouts and streetlamps
with tires round them, I love you.
Police Officer, your boots need re-heeling.

Robin Redbreast; special request: burst
with calypso, bring the Michelin-rung[2] worm
winding, carnival-style to the surface.
We must all sing for our suppers or else.

1993

A Son in Shadow: Remembering, in Fragments, a Lost Parent

I know nothing about how they meet. She is a schoolgirl. He is at work, probably a government clerk in a building near her school. At the hour when school and office are out for lunch their lives intersect at sandwich counters, soft-drink stands, traffic

---

[1] *Cha* A West Indian (mainly Jamaican) expression of annoyance.

[2] *Michelin-rung* Most likely a reference to the cartoon-like figure of the Michelin Man.

lights, market squares. Their eyes meet or their bodies collide at one of these food queues. He says something suggestive, complimentary. She suppresses a smile or traps one beneath her hands. He takes this as encouragement (as if any reaction of hers would have been read as anything else) and keeps on talking and following her and probably misses lunch that day. All the while she walks and eats and drinks and soaks up his praise, his sweet body-talk, his erotic chatter and sexy pitter-patter, his idle boast and ample toasts to his life, his dreams about their future, the world their oyster together.

Am I going too fast on my father's behalf? Should there have been an immediate and cutting rebuttal from her and several days before another meeting? Does he leave work early to catch her at the end of the school day and follow her home just to see where she lives and to extend the boundaries of their courtship? Throwing it from day to night, from school to home, from childhood play to serious adult intent? Georgetown's two-lane streets with trenches on either side mean a mostly single-file walk, she in front probably looking over her shoulder when he says something worthy of a glance, or a cut-eye look if his suggestions about her body or what he will do with it if given half a chance exceed the decorum of the day—which is what, in mid-fifties Guyana? From my grandmother it's, "Don't talk to a man unless you think you're a big woman. Man will bring you trouble. Man want just one thing from you. Don't listen to he. Don't get ruined for he. A young lady must cork her ears and keep her eye straight in front of she when these men start to flock around. The gentleman among them will find his way to her front door. The gentleman will make contact with the parents first. Woo them first before muttering one thing to the young lady. Man who go directly to young ladies only want to ruin them. Don't want to make them into respectable young women—just whores. Mark my words." My grandfather simply thinks that his little girl is not ready for the attentions of any man, that none of them is good enough for his little girl, and so the man who comes to his front door had better have a good pretext for disturbing his reverie. He had better know something about merchant seamen and the character of the sea, and about silence—how to keep it so that it signifies authority and dignity, so when you speak you are heard and your words, every one of them, are rivets. That man would have to be a genius to get past my grandfather, a genius or a gentleman. And since my father is neither, it's out of the question that he'll even use the front door of worship. His route will have to be the yard and the street of ruination.

So he stands in full view of her house at dusk. It takes a few nights before her parents realize he is there for their daughter. Then one day her father comes out and tells him to take his dog behavior to someone else's front door, and the young man quickly turns on his heel and walks away. Another time her mother opens the upstairs window and curses him, and he laughs and saunters off as if her words were a broom gently ushering him out of her yard. But he returns the next night and the next, and the daughter can't believe his determination. She is embarrassed that her body has been a magnet for trouble, that she is the cause of the uproar, then angry with him for his keen regard of her at the expense of her dignity, not to mention his. Neighbors tease her about him. They take pity on the boy, offer him drinks, some ice-cold mauby,[1] a bite to eat, a dhal-pouri,[2] all of which he declines at first, then dutifully accepts. One neighbor even offers him a chair, and on one night of pestilential showers an umbrella, since he does not budge from his spot while all around him people dash for shelter, abandoning a night of liming (loitering) and gaffing (talking) to the persistence and chatter of the rain. Not my father. He stands his ground with only the back of his tight hand up to his brow to shelter his eyes zeroed in on her house. She steals a glance at him after days of seeming to ignore the idea of him, though his presence burns brightly inside her heart. She can't believe his vigilance is for her. She stops to stare in the mirror and for the first time sees her full lips, long straight nose, shoulder-length brunette hair, and dark green eyes with their slight oval shape. Her high cheek-bones. Her ears close to her skull. She runs her fingers lightly over these places as if to touch is to believe. Her lips tingle. Her hair shines. Her eyes smile. And she knows from this young man's perseverance that she is beautiful, desirable. She abandons herself to chores, and suppresses a smile and a song. She walks past windows as much as possible to feed the young man's hungry eyes with a morsel of that which he has venerated to the point of indignity. She rewards his eyes by doing unnecessary half-turns at the upstairs window. A flash of clavicle, a hand slowly putting her hair off her face and setting it down behind her ears, and then a smile, a demure glance, her head inclined a little, her eyes raised, her eyelids batted a few times — she performs for him though she feels silly and self-conscious. What else is there for a girl to do? Things befitting a lady that she picked up from the cinema. Not the sauciness of a tramp.

Her mother pulls her by one of those beautiful close-skulled ears from the window and curses her as if she were a ten-cent whore, then throws open the window and hurtles a long list of insults at this tall, silent, rude, good-for-nothing streak of impertinence darkening her street. The father folds his paper and gets up, but by the time he gets to the window the young man is gone.

My mother cries into the basin of dishes. She rubs a saucer so hard that it comes apart in her hands. She is lucky not to cut herself. She will have to answer to her mother for that breakage. In the past it meant at least a few slaps and many minutes of curses for bringing only trouble into her mother's house. Tonight her mother is even angrier. Her father has turned his fury against her for rearing a daughter who is a fool for men. Her mother finds her in the kitchen holding the two pieces of the saucer together and then apart — as if her dread and sheer desire for reparation would magically weld them whole. Her tears fall like drops of solder on that divided saucer. Her mother grabs her hands and strikes her and curses her into her face so that my mother may as well have been standing over a steaming, spluttering pot on

---

[1] *mauby* A drink made from the mauby bark.

[2] *dhal-pouri* A type of Indian flat, unleavened bread, stuffed with ground peas.

the stove. She drops the two pieces of saucer and they become six pieces. Her mother looks down and strides over the mess with threats about what will happen if her feet find a splinter. She cries but finds every piece, and to be sure to get the splinters too she runs her palms along the floor, this way and that, and with her nails she prizes out whatever her hand picks up. She cries herself to sleep.

The next night he is back at his station, and her mother and father, their voices, their words, their blows sound a little farther off, fall a little lighter. His presence, the bare-faced courage of it, becomes a suit of armor for her to don against her mother's and father's attacks. She flies through her chores. She manages under her mother's watchful eye to show both sides of her clavicle, even a little of the definition down the middle of her chest — that small trench her inflated chest digs which catches the light and takes the breath away, that line drawn from the throat to the uppermost rib exuding warmth and tension, drawing the eye twenty-five yards away with its radiance in the half-light of dusk, promising more than it can possibly contain, than the eye can hold, and triggering a normal heart into palpitations, a normal breath into shallowness and rapidity.

"Miss Isiah, howdy! How come you house so clean on the west side and not so clean on the east? It lopsided. Dirt have a preference in your house. Or is that saga boy hanging around the west side of your house a dirt repellent?" The gossip must have been rampant in the surrounding yards, yards seemingly designed deliberately so people could see into one another's homes and catch anything spilling out of them — quarrels, courtships, cooking pots, music — and sometimes a clash of houses, a reaction against the claustrophobia of the yard, but enough yards, not enough room to procure a necessary privacy in order to maintain a badly sought-after dignity — clean, well dressed, head high in the air on Sundays — impossible if the night before there is a fight and everyone hears you beg not to be hit any more, or else such a stream of obscenities gushes from your mouth that the sealed red lips of Sunday morning just don't cut it.

My father maintains his vigil. Granny threatens to save the contents of her chamber pot from the night before and empty it on his head. Could she have thrown it from her living room window to his shaded spot by the street? Luckily she never tries. She may well be telling him that he doesn't deserve even that amount of attention. If there is any creature lower than a gutter rat — one too low to merit even her worst display of disdain — then he is it. How does my father take that? As a qualification he can do without? How much of that kind of water is he able to let run off his back? Poor man. He has to be in love. He has to be wearing his own suit of armor. Lashed to his mast like Odysseus, he hears the most taunting, terrible things, but what saves him, restores him, are the ropes, the armor of his love for my mother. Others without this charm would have withered away, but my father smiles and shrugs at the barrage of looks, insults, gestures, silence, loneliness.

Watch his body there under that breadfruit or sapodilla tree; the shine of his status as sentry and his conviction are twin headlights that blind her parents. They redouble their efforts to get rid of his particular glare, then are divided by the sense of his inevitability in their daughter's life. My grandmother stops shouting at him while my grandfather still raises his cane and causes the young man to walk away briskly. My grandmother then opens the windows on the west side, ostensibly to let in the sea breeze but really to exhibit in all those window frames a new and friendly demeanor. My grandfather shouts at her that he can smell the rank intent of that black boy, rotten as a fish market, blowing into his living room and spoiling his thoughts. But the windows stay open. And my mother at them. With the love Morse of her clavicles and her cleavage as she grows bolder. Smiling, then waving. And no hand in sight to box her or grip her by the ear and draw her away from there. Until one night she boldly leaves the house and goes to him and they talk for five minutes rapidly as if words are about to run out in the Southern Hemisphere.

My father's parents wonder what has become of their Gordon.
"The boy only intend to visit town."
"Town swallow him up."
"No, one woman turn he head, stick it in a butter churn and swill it."
"He lost to us now."
"True."
They say this to each other but hardly speak to him except to make pronouncements on the size of foreign lands.
"Guyana small."
"What's the boy talking about?"
"Why, England and Scotland combined are the size of Guyana."
"How much room does a man need?"
"That woman take he common sense in a mortar and pound it with a pestle."
The two voices are one voice.
Opportunity is here now. The English are letting go of the reins, a whole new land is about to be fashioned. And he is planning to leave! What kind of woman has done this to our boy? The boy is lost. Talking to him is like harnessing a stubborn donkey. This isn't love but voodoo, obeah, juju, some concoction in a drink, some spell thrown in his locus. A little salt over the shoulder, an iodine shower, a rabbit foot on a string, a duck's bill or snake head dried and deposited into the left trouser pocket, a precious stone, lapis lazuli, amethyst, or anything on the middle finger, a good old reliable crucifix around the neck, made of silver, not gold, and at least one ounce in weight and two inches in diameter. A psalm in papyrus folded in a shirt pocket next to the heart. A blessing from a priest, a breathing of nothing but incense with a towel over the head. A bout of fasting, one night without sleep, a dreamless night, and a dreamless, sleepless, youngest son restored to them. He wants to stay around the house, he shows them why he loves his mummy and poppy and the bounteous land. There is no plan to flee. There is no city woman with his heart in her hand. And his brain is not ablaze in his pants. His head is not an empty, airless room.

They have one cardboard suitcase each, apart from her purse and his envelope tied with a string that contain their passports and tickets, birth certificate and, for him, a document that he is indeed a clerk with X amount of experience at such-and-such a government office, signed "supervisor" — a worthless piece of shit, of course, in the eyes of any British employer. But for the time being, these little things are emblematic of the towering, staggering optimism that propels them out of Georgetown, Guyana, over the sea to London, England.

So what do they do? My mother is a shy woman. My father, in the two photos I've seen of him, is equally reserved. Not liable to experimentation. The big risk has been taken — that of leaving everything they know for all that is alien to them. My mother knows next to nothing about sex, except perhaps a bit about kissing. My father may have experimented a little, as boys tend to do, but he, too, when faced with the female body, confronts unfamiliar territory. Each burns for the other, enough to pull up roots and take off into the unknown. Yet I want to believe that they improvise around the idea of her purity and respect it until their marriage night. That they keep intact some of the moral system they come from even as they dismantle and ignore every other stricture placed on them by Guyanese society: honor your father and mother; fear a just and loving God; pledge allegiance to the flag; lust is the devil's oxygen. All that circles in their veins.

Over the twelve days at sea they examine what they have left and what they are heading toward. At sea they are in between lives: one life is over but the other has not yet begun. The talking they do on that ship without any duties to perform at all! My mother tells how her father, despite his routine as a merchant seaman, finds time to memorize whole poems by the Victorians: Tennyson, Longfellow, Browning, Jean Ingelow, Arnold, and Hopkins. The sea is his workplace, yet he makes time to do this marvellous thing. She tells how when he comes back to land he gathers them all in the living room and performs "The Charge of the Light Brigade" or "Maud" or "My Last Duchess" or "Fra Lippo Lippi" or "The High Tide on the Coast of Lincolnshire" or "Dover Beach" or "The Kingfisher" or "The Wreck of the Deutschland."[1] He recites these poems to his creole-thinking children, who sit there and marvel at the English they are hearing, not that of the policeman or the teacher or the priest, but even more difficult to decipher, full of twists and impossible turns that throw you off the bicycle of your creole reasoning into the sand. If any of them interrupts my grandfather he stops in mid-flow, tells them off in creole, and resumes his poem where he left off. When particularly miffed by the disturbance he starts the poem from the beginning again. Does my grandfather recite these verses before or after he gets drunk, swears at the top of his voice, and chases my grandmother around the house with his broad leather belt?

---

[1] *The Charge … Deutschland* These are all poems by British poets: Tennyson's "The Charge of the Light Brigade" and "Maud," Robert Browning's "My Last Duchess" and "Fra Lippo Lippi," Jean Ingelow's "The High Tide on the Coast of Lincolnshire," Matthew Arnold's "Dover Beach," and Gerard Manley Hopkins's "The Kingfisher" (or "As Kingfishers Catch Fire") and "The Wreck of the Deutschland."

But when my parents are out at sea, they have only the King James Bible in their possession. What they plan and rehearse is every aspect of their new life.

"Children. I want children."

"Me too. Plenty of them."

"I can work between births."

"Yes, both of us. Until we have enough money for a house. Then you can stay home with the kids."

"A nanny. Someone to watch the kids while we work. What kind of house?"

"Three bedrooms. A garden at the front, small, and back, large. A car — a Morris Minor. With all that room in the back for the children and real indicators and a wood finish." Neither has a notebook or dreamed of keeping one. They do not write their thoughts, they utter them. If something is committed to memory, there has to be a quotidian reason for it, apart from bits of the Bible and a few calypsos. My grandfather's labor of love, his settling down with a copy of Palgrave's *Golden Treasury* and memorizing lines that bear no practical relationship to his life, must seem bizarre to his children. Yet by doing so he demonstrates his love of words, their music, the sense of their sound, their approximation to the heartbeat and breath, their holding out of an alternative world to the one surrounding him, their confirmation of a past and another's life and thoughts, their luxury of composition, deliberation, their balancing and rebalancing of a skewered life. I imagine my mother benefits from this exposure in some oblique way — that the Victorians stick to her mental makeup whether she cares for them or not, that a little of them comes off on me in the wash of my gestation in her.

There is an old black-and-white photo (isn't there always?) and fragments of stories about his comings and goings, his carryings-on, as the West Indian speak goes, his mischief. "Look pan that smooth face, them two big, dark eye them, don't they win trust quick-time? Is hard to tie the man with them eye in him head to any woman and she pickney[1] them. He face clean-shaven like he never shave. He curly black hair, dougla-look, but trim neat-neat. The man got topside." His hair, thick and wavy because of the "dougla" mix of East Indian and black, exaggerates an already high forehead. Automatically we credit such an appearance, in the Caribbean and elsewhere, with intelligence — "topside." And European nose, not broad, with high bridge (good breeding, though the nostrils flare a bit — sign of a quick temper!). And lips that invite kisses. "They full-full and pout like a kiss" with the sound of a kiss way behind, long after that kiss come and gone. He is six feet tall and thin but not skinny, that brand of thin that women refer to as elegant, since the result is long fingers and economic gestures. Notice I say economic and not cheap. A man of few words. A watcher. "But when he relax in company he know and trust, then he the centre of wit and idle philosophizing. He shoot back a few rums, neat no chaser, with anyone, and hold his own with men more inclined to gin and tonic. He know when to mind he Ps

---

[1] *pickney* A young child usually of black parentage.

and Qs and when to gaff in the most lewd Georgetown, rumshop[1] talk with the boys
What chance a sixteen-year-old closeted lady got against such a man, I ask you?"

But most of the puzzle is missing. So I start to draw links from one fragment to
the next. He begins to belong — fleetingly, at first — in my life. As a man in poor light
seen crossing a road mercifully free of traffic, its tar-macadam steamy with a recent
down-pour. As a tall, lank body glimpsed ducking under the awning of a shop front
and disappearing inside and never emerging no matter how long I wait across the
street, watching the door with its reflecting plate glass and listening for the little jin-
gle of the bell that announces the arrival and departure of customers.

Or I cross Blackheath Hill entranced by the urgent belief that my father is in one
of the cars speeding up and down it. Blackheath Hill curves a little with a steep gra-
dient — less than one in six in places. It's more of a ski slope than a hill. Cars and
trucks, motorbikes and cyclists all come down the road as if in a race for a finish
line. Going up it is no different. Vehicles race to the top as if with the fear that their
engines might cut off and they will slide back down. I want to be seen by my father.
I have to be close to his car so that he does not miss me. I measure the traffic and
watch myself get halfway, then, after a pause to allow a couple of cars to pass on
their way up, a brisk walk, if I time it right to allow the rest of the traffic to catch up
to me, to see the kid who seems to be in no particular hurry to get out of their way
looking at them. I step onto the sidewalk and cherish the breeze of the nearest vehicle at my back — Father, this is your son you have just missed. Isn't he big? Pull over
and call his name. Take him in your arms. Admonish him. Remind him that cars
can kill and his little body would not survive a hit at these high speeds. Tell him to
look for his father under less dangerous circumstances.

I am searching the only way I know how, by rumination, contemplation, conjecture, supposition. I try to fill the gaps, try to piece together the father I never knew. I
imagine everything where there is little or nothing to go on. And yet, in going back,
in raking up bits and pieces of a shattered and erased existence, I know that I am
courting rejection from a source hitherto silent and beyond me. I am conjuring up
a father safely out of reach and taking the risk that the lips I help to move, the lung I
force to breathe will simply say "No." No to everything I ask of them, even the merest crumb of recognition.

"Father." The noun rings hollowly when I say it, my head is empty of any meaning the word might have. I shout it in a dark cave but none of the expected bats
come flapping out. Just weaker and weaker divisions of my call. "Father." It is my
incantation to bring him back from the grave to the responsibility of his name. But
how, when I only know his wife, my mother, and her sudden, moody silence whenever he crops up in conversation?

You ever have anyone sweet-talk you? Fill your ears with their kind of wax, rub that
wax with their tongue all over your body with more promises than the promised

---

[1] *rumshop* A bar or liquor lounge.

land itself contains, fill your head with their sweet drone, their buzz that shuts out your parents, friends, your own mind from its own house? That's your father, the bumblebee, paying attention to me.

My sixteenth birthday was a month behind. He was nearly twenty. A big man in my eyes. What did he want with me? A smooth tongue in my ears. Mostly, though, he watched me, my house, my backside when he followed me home from school. His eyes gleamed in the early evening, the whites of his eyes. He stood so still by the side of the road outside my house that he might have been a lamppost, planted there, shining just for me.

My father cursed him, my mother joined in, my sisters laughed at his silence, his stillness. They all said he had to be the most stupid man in Georgetown, a dunce, a bat in need of a perch, out in the sun too long, sun fry his brain, cat take his tongue, his head empty like a calabash, his tongue cut out, he look like a beggar. They felt sorry for him standing there like a paling, his face a yard long, his tongue a slab of useless plywood in his mouth. "Look what Ingrid gone and bring to the house, shame, dumbness, blackness follow she here to we house to paint shame all over it and us. Go away, black boy, take your dumb misery somewhere else, crawl back to your pen in the country, leave we sister alone, she got more beauty than sense to listen to a fool like you, to let you follow her, to encourage you by not cursing the day you was born and the two people who got together to born you and your people and the whole sorry village you crawl out of to come and plant yourself here in front of we house on William Street, a decent street, in Kitty, in we capital."

I should have thanked my sisters; instead I begged them to leave him alone. Ignore him and he'll go away. My father left the house to get hold of the boy by the scruff of his neck and boot his backside out of Kitty, but he ran off when my father appeared in the door frame. With the light of the house behind him and casting a long, dark shadow, he must have looked twice his size and in no mood to bargain. Your father sprinted away, melting into the darkness. I watched for his return by checking that the windows I'd bolted earlier really were bolted, convincing myself that I had overlooked one of them, using my hands to feel the latch as I searched the street for him. But he was gone for the night. My knight. Shining eyes for armor.

My mother cursed him from the living room window, flung it open and pointed at him and with her tongue reduced him to a pile of rubble and scattered that rubble over a wide area then picked her way through the strewn wreckage to make sure her destruction was complete: "Country boy, what you want with my daughter? What make you think you man enough for her? What you got between your legs that give you the right to plant yourself in front of my house? What kind of blight you is? You fungus!"

As she cursed him and he retreated from the house sheepishly, she watched her husband for approval. These were mild curses for her, dutiful curses, a warm-up. When she really got going her face reddened and her left arm carved up the air in front of her as if it were the meat of her opponent being dissected into bite-size bits. That's how I knew she was searching for a way to help me but hadn't yet found it.

Not as long as my father was at home. Soon he would be at sea, away for weeks, and things would be different.

That is, if my onlooker, my remote watcher, my far-off admirer wasn't scared off forever. And what if he was? Then he didn't deserve me in the first place. If he couldn't take a few curses he wasn't good for anything. If I wasn't worth taking a few curses for … well, I didn't want a man who didn't think I was worth taking a few curses for! I loved him for coming back night after night when all he got from me was a glance at the window. Sometimes less than a glance. Just me passing across the window frame as I dashed from chore to chore under four baleful eyes.

It seemed like he was saving all his breath and words for when he could be alone with me. Then he turned on the bumblebee of himself and I was the hapless flower of his attentions. He told me about my skin that it was silk, that all the colours of the rainbow put together still didn't come close to my beautiful skin. That my face, my eyes, my mouth, my nose, the tip of my nose, my ears, my fingertips, each was a precious jewel, precious stone. He likened the rest of me to things I had read about but had never seen, had dreamed about but had never dreamed I would see: dandelions, apples, snow, spring in England's shires, the white cliffs of Dover. In his eyes my body, me, was everything I dreamed of becoming.

That was your father before any of you were a twinkle in his eye. More accurately, that was my lover and then my husband. Your father was a different man altogether. Suddenly a stranger occupied my bed. His tongue now turned to wood. All the laughter of my sisters, the half-hearted curses of my mother, my father's promise of blue misery, all came true in this strange man, this father, this latter-day husband and lover.

I saw the change in him. My hands were full with you children. He went out of reach. He cradled you as if he didn't know which side was up, which down. He held you at arm's length to avoid the tar and feathers of you babies. Soon I earned the same treatment, but if you children were tar and feathers I was refuse. His face creased when he came near me. What had become of my silk skin? My precious features disappeared into my face, earning neither praise nor blame — just his silence, his wooden tongue, and that bad-smell look of his. I kept quiet for as long as I could. I watched him retreat from all of us, hoping he'd reel himself back in since the line between us was strong and I thought unbreakable; but no. I had to shout to get him to hear me. I shouted like my mother standing at the upstairs window to some rude stranger in the street twenty-five yards away. I sounded like my father filling the door frame. My jeering sisters insinuated their way into my voice. And your father simply kept walking away.

Believe me, I pulled my hair and beat the ground with my hands and feet to get at him in my head and in the ground he walked on that I worshipped. Hadn't he delivered England to me and all the seasons of England, all England's shires and the fog he'd left out of his serenades, no doubt just to keep some surprise in store for me? The first morning I opened the door that autumn and shouted, "Fire" when I saw all that smoke, thinking the whole street on fire, all the streets, London burning, and slammed the door and ran into his arms and his laughter, and he took me out into it in my nightdress, he in his pajamas, and all the time I followed him, not ashamed to be seen outside in my thin, flimsy nylon (if anyone could see through that blanket) because he was in his pajamas, the blue, striped ones, and his voice, his sweet drone, told me it was fine, this smoke without fire was fine, "This is fog."

He walked away and everything started to be erased by that fog. That smoke without fire crossed the ocean into my past and obliterated Kitty, Georgetown, the house on William Street, everything he had touched, every place I had known him in. I swallowed that fog. It poured into my ears, nose, eyes, mouth. He was gone. I got a chest pain and breathlessness that made me panic. There wasn't just me. There were you children. I had to breathe for you children. The pain in my chest that was your father had to be plucked out, otherwise I too would be lost to you all, and to myself.

The first time I see him is the last time I see him. I can't wait to get to the front of the queue to have him all to myself. When I get there my eyes travel up and down his body. From those few gray hairs that decorate his temples and his forehead and his nose to the cuffs at his ankles and sparkling black shoes. He wears a black suit, a double-breasted number with three brass buttons on the cuff of each sleeve. He lies on his back with his hands clasped over his flat stomach. There is too much powder on his face. Let's get out of this mournful place, Dad. We have a lot of catching up to do. He has the rare look — of holding his breath, of not breathing, in between inhaling and exhaling — that exquisitely beautiful corpses capture. For a moment after I invite him to leave with me, I expect his chest to inflate, his lids to open, and those clasped hands to unfold and pull him upright into a sitting position as if he really were just napping because he has dressed way too early for the ball.

There are myths about this sort of thing. Father enslaves son. Son hates father, bides his time, waits for the strong father to weaken. Son pounces one day, pounces hard and definite, and the father is overwhelmed, broken, destroyed with hardly any resistance, except that of surprise and then resignation. Son washes his hands but finds he is washing hands that are not bloodstained, not marked or blemished in any way. He is simply scrubbing hands that no longer belong to him — they are his father's hands, attached to his arms, his shoulders, his body. He has removed a shadow all the more to see unencumbered the father in himself. There is the widow he has made of his mother. He cannot love her as his father might. While his father lived he thought he could. The moment his father expired he knew his mother would remain unloved.

I alight too soon from a number 53 bus on Blackheath Hill, disembark while the bus is moving, and stumble, trip from two legs onto all fours, hands like feet, transforming, sprouting more limbs, becoming a spider and breaking my fall. That same fall is now a tumble, a dozen somersaults that end with me standing upright and quite still on two legs with the other limbs dangling. Onlookers, who fully expected disaster, applaud. I walk back up the hill to the block of council flats as a man might, upright, on two legs. My other limbs dangle, swing as if they are two hands. Some days I will be out of breath, I will gasp and exhale, and the cloud before me will not be my winter's breath but the silken strands of a web, or worse, fire. Other days I might look at a bed of geraniums planted on the council estate and turn all their numberless petals into stone. A diamond held between my thumb and index finger crumbles in this mood, in this light, like the powdery wings of a butterfly.

I stare out of an apartment on the twenty-fourth floor of a tower block overlooking the nut-brown Thames. That wasp on the windowpane nibbling up and down the glass for a pore to exit through, back into the air and heat, tries to sting what it can feel but cannot see. My father is the window. I am the wasp. Sometimes a helping hand comes along and lifts the window, and the wasp slides out. Other times a shadow descends, there is a displacement of air, and it is the last thing the wasp knows. Which of those times is this? I want to know. I don't want to know. I am not nibbling nor trying to sting. I am kissing, repeatedly, rapidly, the featureless face of my father. It feels like summer light. It reflects a garden. Whose is that interfering hand? Why that interrupting shadow? My child's hand. My child's shadow. My son or my father? My son and my father. Two sons, two fathers. Yet three people. We walk behind a father's name, shoulder a father's memory. Wear another's walk, another's gait. Wait for what has happened to their bodies, the same scars, maladies, aches, to surface in ours.

I want to shed my skin. Walk away from my shadow. Leave my name in a place I cannot return to. To be nameless, bodiless. To swim to Wallace Stevens's Key West,[1] which is shoreless, horizonless. Blackheath Hill becomes Auden's Bristol Street,[2] an occasion for wonder and lament. Blackheath at 5:45 A.M. on a foggy winter morning becomes Peckham Rye. There are no trees on Blackheath, but angels hang in the air if only Blake were there to see them. On the twenty-fourth floor towering above the Thames, water, not land, surrounds me. Everything seems to rise out of that water. Look up at ambling clouds and the tower betrays its drift out to sea.

1999

---

[1] *Wallace Stevens's Key West* Stevens wrote a poem, "The Idea of Order at Key West"; the title indicates the theme.

[2] *Auden's Bristol Street* An image from W.H. Auden's poem "As I Walked Out One Evening" (1940), which opens with the lines "As I walked out one evening, / Walking down Bristol Street" and goes on to say that "Love has no ending."

Kamala Das

Kamala Das (1934-2009) was born and educated in Kerala, India. She wrote several volumes of poetry, including *The Descendants* (1967), *The Anamalai Poems* (1985), *Only the Soul Knows How to Sing* (1996), and *Yaa Allah* (2001). Her publications include *My Story* (autobiography, 1975), *Alphabet of Lust* (novel, 1977), and *Padmavati the Harlot and Other Stories* (stories, 1992). She wrote in Malayalam as well as English; it should be noted that her preferred genre in Malayalam was fiction, which she wrote under the pen-name of Madhavikutty.

Das's "An Introduction" has a speaker who is affronted by people simplifying and falsifying her psyche culturally and politically. She asserts that she is a complex human being with independent views of womanhood, feminism, and eroticism. Her poem can be compared with several pieces in this anthology, including Agha Shahid Ali's "Snowmen," Jean Arasanayagam's "I Have No Country," and Sally Ito's "Of the Wave." The speaker of Das's "The Looking Glass" employs an equally personal but less argumentative, more poignant voice in declaring her love for her husband.

An Introduction

I don't know politics but I know the names
Of those in power, and can repeat them like
Days of week, or names of months, beginning with
Nehru.[1] I am Indian, very brown, born in
Malabar, I speak three languages, write in
Two, dream in one. Don't write in English, they said,
English is not your mother-tongue. Why not leave
Me alone, critics, friends, visiting cousins,
Every one of you? Why not let me speak in
Any language I like? The language I speak
Becomes mine, its distortions, its queernesses
All mine, mine alone. It is half English, half
Indian, funny perhaps, but it is honest,
It is as human as I am human, don't
You see? It voices my joys, my longings, my
Hopes, and it is useful to me as cawing
Is to crows or roaring to the lions, it
Is human speech, the speech of the mind that is

---

[1] *Nehru* Jawaharlal Nehru was the first Prime Minister of India after its independence from Britain in 1947.

Here and not there, a mind that sees and hears and
Is aware. Not the deaf, blind speech
Of trees in storm or of monsoon clouds or of rain or the
Incoherent mutterings of the blazing
Funeral pyre. I was child, and later they
Told me I grew, for I became tall, my limbs
Swelled and one or two places sprouted hair. When
I asked for love, not knowing what else to ask
For, he drew a youth of sixteen into the
Bedroom and closed the door. He did not beat me
But my sad woman-body felt so beaten.

The weight of my breasts and womb crushed me. I shrank
Pitifully. Then ... I wore a shirt and my
Brother's trousers, cut my hair short and ignored
My womanliness. Dress in sarees, be girl
Be wife, they said. Be embroiderer, be cook,
Be a quarreller with servants. Fit in. Oh,
Belong, cried the categorizers. Don't sit
On walls or peep in through our lace-draped windows.
Be Amy, or be Kamala. Or, better
Still, be Madhavikutty.[1] It is time to
Choose a name, a role. Don't play pretending games.
Don't play at schizophrenia or be a
Nympho. Don't cry embarrassingly loud when
Jilted in love ... I met a man, loved him. Call
Him not by any name, he is every man
Who wants a woman, just as I am every
Woman who seeks love. In him ... the hungry haste
Of rivers, in me ... the oceans' tireless
Waiting. Who are you, I ask each and everyone,
The answer is, it is I. Anywhere and,
Everywhere, I see the one who calls himself
If in this world, he is tightly packed like the
Sword in its sheath. It is I who drink lonely
Drinks at twelve, midnight, in hotels of strange towns,
It is I who laugh, it is I who make love
And then, feel shame, it is I who lie dying
With a rattle in my throat. I am sinner,
I am saint. I am the beloved and the

---

[1] *Madhavikutty* Das's pen-name as a short-story writer in Malayalam, her native language.

Betrayed. I have no joys which are not yours, no
Aches which are not yours. I too call myself I.

1965

The Looking Glass

Getting a man to love you is easy
Only be honest about your wants as
Woman. Stand nude before the glass with him
So that he sees himself the stronger one
And believes it so, and you so much more
Softer, younger, lovelier.... Admit your
Admiration. Notice the perfection
Of his limbs, his eyes reddening under
Shower, the shy walk across the bathroom floor,
Dropping towels, and the jerky way he
Urinates. All the fond details that make
Him male and your only man. Gift him all,
Gift him what makes you woman, the scent of
Long hair, the musk of sweat between the breasts,
The warm shock of menstrual blood, and all your
Endless female hungers. Oh yes, getting
A man to love is easy, but living
Without him afterward may have to be
Faced. A living without life when you move
Around, meeting strangers, with your eyes that
Gave up their search, with ears that hear only
His last voice calling out your name and your
Body which once under his touch had gleamed
Like burnished brass, now drab and destitute.

1967

Jack Davis

Jack Davis (1917-2000), a Noongar Aboriginal, was born in Western Australia. He was active as a poet, dramatist, and critic (beginning in the 1960s) and was the editor of the Aboriginal magazine *Identity*. His poetry collections include *The First-Born and Other Poems* (1970), *John Pat and Other Poems* (1988), and *Black Life* (1992). Known more as a playwright than as a poet, he wrote several plays, including *Kullark* (1978) and *In Our Town* (1990). A handful of his stories appear in *Paperbark: A Collection of Black Australian Writings* (1992).

Davis's "Pay Back" and "White Fantasy — Black Fact" are both set in the Aboriginal community of Australia. They address the questions raised in postcolonial discourse regarding the effect of British imperialism and white racism on Aboriginal peoples. Both sides engage in stereotyping, racism, and cultural insensitivities. Does "Pay Back" have a more pessimistic tone than "White Fantasy — Black Fact"? Note the dehumanization of both groups of people in "Pay Back," and compare their anger with the sound of laughter from the two groups in "White Fantasy — Black Fact." Note the importance of the titles of both stories. Compare these stories with Archie Weller's "Pension Day" and Eva Johnson's "Murras."

White Fantasy — Black Fact

The bus driver was tired. He had been awakened several times during last night's hot summer hours, by the crying of the baby. His wife Anne had walked around with the child seemingly for hours. He hoped she had taken the child around to the Clinic today. After all it was the first summer of the child's existence, and it was really hot. Really hot.

The bus churned along the narrow bitumen road. He heard the slap, slap of the overhanging branches of roadside gums on the rooftop of the bus. His gaze flitted automatically to the approaching bus stop. He slowed the bus, but seeing nobody on the seat, he pushed the gear lever in a quick interchange of movement between foot on clutch pedal and hand on gear lever. The bus growled and surged ahead, sweeping back onto the centre of its laneway.

His mind slid back to the baby. They had called it Peggy Sue after Anne's mother. Anne had been so grateful when he had agreed with the name of their first child, Peggy Sue. He wondered what she would be like when she grew up. He knew she would be pretty. Blonde haired, blue eyed, and with a nice figure. Both him and Anne were well-built. He wondered what she would be character-wise. Anne was a calm practical even-tempered person. While he was almost the complete opposite. He hated untidiness, people with loud voices. He disliked violence, cruelty to animals. Both he and his wife sent money to overseas missions. He thought of the starving millions in Asia, and the resultant death and disease. Cholera, hook worm, sleeping sickness. His mind flitted through the explanatory brochures that he recalled to his mind, which were sent to him and his wife by the overseas mission people. He was glad that he lived in a country that was white, where there was plenty for all, where nobody starved, and everyone was equal. He saw the next bus stop ahead of him and he imperceptibly guided the bus off the bitumen. As he drew almost level with the stop he saw the small group of people. There were eight of them.

One man of indeterminate age, but old, was drunk and coughing, softly but violently. The paroxysms of his coughing shook his bony frame. He was accompanied by a man and woman and five children. The man was also affected by liquor. They were all scruffily dressed and untidy, and a faint whiff of body odour wafted into the interior of the empty bus. The bus driver stared blankly as the small group began gathering their belongings. The old man, his coughing subsiding into sporadic bursts, staggered forward and placed one hand on the bus door. The bus driver looked at the gnarled brown dirty broken finger-nailed hand. He had a mad kaleidoscopic vision of unparalleled sickness right there within the bus.

He thought of little Peggy Sue, her fair skin scabrous with sores. He thought of Anne, her body broken, lying in the back-yard. He thought this must not happen, this cannot be. The old man began to heave himself onto the bus, the others ready to climb aboard behind him. The bus driver bent forward and spoke hoarsely, "You are not allowed on this bus, let go the door." The old man glowered at him, replying, "Why aren't I?" The woman lifted her head and stared at the bus driver, she spoke loudly, shrilly. "Why ain't we allowed, we're people ain't we?" The other man evidently her husband chipped in, saying: "Driver you can't stop us from gettin on that bus. We got money don't worry about us," he opened his hand to show a crumpled two dollar note.

The bus driver rose from his seat and pushed the old man's hand quickly, but firmly, from the frame of the door and then grasping the lever he closed the door. He wrenched the gear stick downwards, and the engine snarled as if in protest against the unexpected call for power. The bus lurched back onto the bitumen sending a cloud of dust and leaves over the little Aboriginal group left standing at the side of the road.

Molly looked at the rapidly receding bus, tears of angry frustration in her eyes. She had to get the baby to the children's hospital that afternoon. She glanced at Peter, her husband, and the old man, her grandfather. She harangued them angrily, her voice rising high above their denunciation of the bus driver. "I told you to stop drinking," she said. "Now if the baby misses her appointment you'll be the one to blame, not the bus driver."

She looked at the long stretch of bitumen, it would be hours before another one traversed the road. The baby began to cry. Molly looked at the four other children. Three were her own. The eldest, Katey, a child of eight, was a parentless stray belonging to some distant relation who through circumstances had become part of her and Peter's brood. She had not wanted to bring them on the long journey from

Geraldton[1] to Perth. But as she had no one to leave them with she had been forced to bring them. They also had to bring the old man, grandfather Joshua. It had been his pension day when they had left Geraldton, and his money was needed to assist the group on the long journey. The old HR Holden had travelled well. But near Caversham in attempting a short cut to Guildford it had given up the mechanical ghost.

Peter and Joshua had pushed the car on to the side of the road. After gathering their essential belongings (Joshua carefully retrieved his remaining flagon) and locking the rickety doors, the small group had made their way to the Guildford road and the nearest bus stop. Two-years-old Tandy began whimpering for water. Molly surmised there would be water in the small creek some 159 metres down the road. The old man and Peter lay in the shade. She looked at them in disgust, disregarding her husband's half-hearted offer to obtain water. She emptied the collection of half-eaten food from a can and with the baby on her hip, and the children following, she made her way down the road where a small trickle of weed-covered water meandered slowly under a culvert then through the paddock bordering the road.

Molly and the children stood at the edge of the culvert. She looked dubiously down the sloping reed-covered bank. She spoke softly to Katey, "Looks like you'll have to get the water Katey Doll." The eight-year-old stepped forward eager to help. With the can in her hand she slithered agilely down the bank, her mother and the other children calling directions and encouragement. Katey stepped into the mud, her feet making delicious squelching sounds as she wriggled her toes in its coolness. She looked up at the small group above her, white teeth flashing, brown eyes full of merriment, enjoying her endeavours. She stepped toward the roof of the culvert where the water underneath was cleaner, deeper. She placed one slim hand on the woodwork to steady herself, and glanced to find a place to grasp the culvert ledge.

Then for one terror filled second her fingers were a fraction of an inch away from the snake. Her reflexes were instant, but even as she snatched her hand away, it struck, and with such blinding speed and force that its fangs became embedded in the back of her tiny hand, and swinging off balance, Katey Doll screamed and flung the snake in an arc, where it landed some two metres away. Then slithering in the water it vanished among the reeds. Molly saw it all as if in slow motion. She tried to call out but her voice choked off. With the baby in her arms she leapt down the bank. She grabbed the trembling Katey who stood frozen clutching her hand to her crotch. Her eyes were enormous, dilated with fear. "Mummy," she cried, "it bit me, it bit me. Will I die? Oh, Mummy will I die?" And realising the horror and the enormity of it all, the woman and the child screamed together.

Peter heard the screaming. With one leap he was standing on the road. He saw the way the children were running towards him, something was amiss. "Gawd," he muttered. "What's happened?" he ran. Upon reaching the culvert he sprang down the bank grabbing Katey. He saw the two long tips in the skin of her hand. He did not hesitate. He pulled the now mute child to a sitting position, and knelt beside her

---

[1] *Geraldton* Geraldton is 424 kilometres (254 miles) north of Perth, on Australia's west coast.

and gripping her wrist tightly, he began sucking hard and deep over the ragged perforations.

Joshua stood on the road, looking at them aghast. Molly handed the baby up to him. She struggled up the bank, calling to the old man. "If a car comes flag it down." Even as she spoke they heard the hum of an approaching vehicle. Molly standing on the road stood waving her hands frantically. The car came fast. Behind it another. Molly screamed her plea. "Stop! Please! Help! Help!" Both cars roared past, the drivers looking at them with the curious detached look of the unconcerned.

Molly sank on her knees and cried, "O God, please help us." The children were all crying. Peter began pulling the trembling Katey up the bank, still endeavouring to suck the poison from the small frail body. They all knelt at the side of the road. They heard the purr of an engine. Joshua thrust the baby into Molly's arms. He stood almost in the centre of the road, his arms waving wildly. Molly breathed a gasping sigh of relief as she saw the car slow to a crawl. It came opposite the old man, who stepped forward to speak to the driver. Then with a screech of tortured tyres it leaped forward, and an epithet, mingling with the sound of laughter, sprang at them like barbed wire from the interior of the speeding car. The old man stood crouched at the side of the road crying hoarsely, "Aw, you bastards, you bloody, rotten mongrel bastards!" Tears of anger flowed down his thin cheeks.

It was obvious now that the poison and shock were having an effect on Katey Doll, her eyes were closed, her breathing shallow, and a small trace of vomit lingered at the corner of her mouth. Peter knew he had to keep her awake. He shook the child hard, her head, arms and legs were marionette like, limp and flaccid. The old man crouched on the road verge, his voice keeping low, in the beginning of a death chant. Molly turned to him and said fiercely, "Stop that! Do you hear me? She can hear you and that'll make her worse." Suddenly, the little group became aware of a sound, a strange almost frightening sound. Now the noise was around them. The motor bikes were black and gleaming and the riders helmeted, goggled and dressed in black leather. The whole thirty of them had the skull and crossbones emblem stencilled on their jackets. The roar of the bikes began to lessen, becoming staccato as if wolf-like they had to snap and snarl at one another. A thin blonde-haired youth was the first to dismount from his machine and he spoke to the frightened Molly. "What's wrong lady? Are you havin' trouble?" Pointing to the tableau of Peter and Katey Doll, Molly replied "My, my little girl, snake bite!" The youth swore softly and yelled: "Christ, where's the Doc? Get him someone, this kid's been bitten by a bloody snake."

A towering red-headed, red-bearded giant of two metres or more threaded his way swiftly through the mass of machines, he knelt beside the exhausted Peter sucking the back of the girl's hand. He clasped one huge paw on Katey Doll's wrist and spoke softly to Peter, "Come on let's have a look, mate." There were calls from the riders now watching intently. "How she doin' Red Doc?" The man called "Red Doc" (two years at medical school had given him that unofficial title) gently picked up the child. He spoke quickly, quietly. "We have to move fast. Go Bo, Slit Eyes, get going to the nearest phone box, and ring for an ambulance. Tell them to bring anti-venom and to meet us on the northern highway to Perth Hospital."

Three bikes leapt to life and with a full-throated roar, they swept down the road in a blinding acceleration of rising speed. Big Red Doc climbed onto his enormous Harley with Katey Doll cradled in his arms, her hand with a tourniquet applied, suspended by a belt tied around his neck. He looked at Peter, grinned and said, "Right mate, on the back." Red Doc spoke to the others. "OK you guys, you organise getting a car and get the rest of these people into town, better bring them to the hospital."

A half dozen of the bikies with Joshua and the children sat in the waiting room. Everybody was tense not knowing how Katey Doll was faring. The doctors had guessed correctly that the snake was a death adder, usually fatal. They saw the doctor with Peter and Molly walking toward them, and they knew suddenly, everything was alright. Peter spoke first, his hand groping for the massive paw of Big Red. "She gonna be OK. Thanks fellas, thanks a million." Molly began to cry quietly as reaction set in. The doctor smiling, spoke: "She's going to be alright. She is a lucky little girl, the only reason she is alive is because she had prompt attention."

Molly looked at the group of leather-jacketed men and smiling, spoke softly. "You know when you all came down the road this afternoon, I thought you were a pack of devils, but instead you were all angels on chariots, surely sent by God." Old Joshua looked up and cackled, "And it's the first time I reckon, they rode motor bikes."

Slit Eye spoke cheerfully, "Now that's why we got kicked out of Northam. It was all that 'upstairs guy's' fault." And in the late hour of the evening, the hospital waiting room echoed their laughter.

1992

Pay Back

Munda had been trailing the party of three whites since early morning. He hated them. Yet within this hate was a mixture of fear. There were reasons. At the last moon, a party of white men had poisoned one of their centuries old water holes and several members of his group had died in agony. But these were not the men actually responsible. He had photographed the heavy foot marks of the men in his mind of those who had killed, and those imprints would remain in his mind forever. But he knew they were the same type of man. He also knew the party was heading into waterless country.

The searing summer heat burnt into the very minds of the white men. Liles' party headed in the direction they were travelling four weeks before them. Although they had zig-zagged across the desert for nearly two weeks they had been unsuccessful in cutting across the other exploring party's tracks. Wargoton, the leader of the group, knew that to survive they would have to find water within the next twenty hours. He was a tall man, bearded, lean and sunburnt to a deep brown. The same description applied to his two companions, Lorrest and Wicknell.

One of their three camels had died a week ago. All their possessions, cut down to bare needs, were now being carried by their two remaining beasts. They made camp in the middle of the day's heat. They were wise in the ways of the desert, and knew it was better to conserve their energy, by travelling in the early morning and late afternoon.

Wargoton shook the canteen containing the last of their precious water. He looked at his two companions crouched together with him, in the six feet of shade thrown by the ledge of rock under which they crouched. He spoke hoarsely.

"Well we're down to about four mouthfuls of water each."

Wicknell replied, "I've had a feeling all morning that the blacks are trailing us, why the hell don't they show themselves."

"Why should they?" said Wargoton. "They'll trail and watch us keep watching until we perish then they'll spear the camels for food then share what we leave."

They lapsed into a moody silence. The sun began to move on its downward path, but the day was still viciously hot. The small patch of shade began to diminish.

Wargoton groaned between seared lips in his attempt to speak. "If we're going to sit in the sun, we might as well move." They struggled to their feet. Wargoton poured out three measures of water and said grimly. "Last drink until sundown and God help us tomorrow."

Even as he spoke, the three men saw the black, standing no more than twenty yards from them. At the sight of him they knew their immediate need was solved. He was of average height, thin build and stark naked. In one hand he held a hunting spear pointing carefully downwards. In the other he held a nulla nulla.[1] In a hair belt around his left arm was a blade of quartz and around his forehead was a belt of hair tied low. He stood looking at the three whites with an almost bovine expression on his bearded face.

It was Wicknell who broke the long sounds of silence. He raised one hand and pointed to the canteens strapped to one of their camels. "Water, where is water?" he said. Munda pointed to the sun then swept his arm half way down from its destination. "Good," said Lorrest. "The bastard understands us. That looks to be about two hours from here." "What if he's lying?" replied Wicknell. "No," said Wargoton. "He's telling the truth, but I think we should take care of ourselves, by the simple method of making him need water as much as we do."

Wargoton offered Munda the compass. His curiosity overcame his caution; he stepped forward, eager to take the offered object. They grabbed him. He offered little resistance, but moaned and jabbered in his own tongue as they bore him to his knees in the red desert sand.

Wicknell finding untapped energy ran to one of the camels. Rummaging quickly in the pack saddle he returned with a double cupped handful of salt.

---

[1] *nulla nulla* A hardwood club.

Wargoton and Lorrest held the pitiful figure firmly, while Wicknell rammed the salt into the bearded mouth.

It was as if he realised their intentions, because he did not struggle. They let him go. He lay on his side in protest as the salt bit into his throat. He began retching, the spasms doubling him up in their intensity. Lorrest stepped forward, kicked him and pointing at the sun, said hoarsely, "Water, and bloody quick." Wicknell aimed his rifle in the black's direction. Munda climbed painfully to his feet clutching his throat, and the strange procession began.

The three whites finished the last of their water. They knew now that the black was their only chance of survival. Their victim was now nearly two hundred feet in advance of them. They let him lead. Once when he widened the distance, Wicknell slowed him with a rifle shot fired skyward.

They came to a claypan[1] some quarter of a mile across. The black stumbling, headed across it with the men still trailing him. At the claypan's outer edge the black suddenly veered sideways. He stopped, then pointed left to a spot where long low sandhills ringed the claypan.

Wargoton spoke hoarsely jubilant. "We've won, we've won. I can see the ground damp from here." They ran forward eagerly. They saw the black running for the safety of the sandhill. Wicknell stopped and raised his rifle. Wargoton still running forward, called out, "Let him go, we've got what we want."

The three men flung themselves down at the soak's edge gulping the tepid water greedily, and splashing it over their faces. They lay on their sides allowing the two camels to quench their thirst.

It was Wargoton who felt the first swordlike thrust of pain. Then agony struck Lorrest then Wicknell. Wargoton looked at his companions' eyes bulging. He gasped, "Liles, that bloody Liles has been here before us. He's always trying to wipe out the blacks, the soak has been poisoned."

Munda looked dispassionately at the scene below him. His woman came walking along the ridge of the sandhill, a kullamun[2] of water balanced on her head. Munda drank and together, turning their backs on the scene of death below them, they walked down the sandhill and into the distance of their land.

1992

---

[1] *claypan* A relatively compact and impervious sub-layer of clay.

[2] *kullamun* A kullamun (also "coolamon") is an Australian Aboriginal term for a wooden dish made of light wood for carrying such things as water (and even young babies).

Anita Desai

Anita Desai (b. 1937) was born in Mussoorie, a hill station north of Delhi, India, to a German mother and Bengali father. She has written several novels — including *Cry, The Peacock* (1963), *Fire on the Mountain* (1977), *Clear Light of Day* (1980), *Baumgartner's Bombay* (1988), *Fasting, Feasting* (1999), and *The Zigzag Way* (2004) — children's books, and two volumes of short stories, *Games at Twilight* (1978) and *Diamond Dust and Other Stories* (2000). She has taught in universities in the United States and India.

Desai's "Surface Textures" is a many-layered story. It is, on the most obvious level, a narrative of the widening emotional distance between an Indian couple, but it is also about the art of interpretation (which is what I am doing right now). Are we satisfied with the "surface" of the text? Is there a deeper level? Is the text making fun of exegesis and "deeper" analysis? Is there a biblical interpretation hinted at in such phrases as "apple of knowledge" and "bite into it"? Is this a study of how humans create their gods? In its apparent lack of overt political, postcolonial sentiments, the story can be compared with Saros Cowasjee's "His Father's Medals" and Mulk Raj Anand's "Duty."

Surface Textures

It was all her own fault, she later knew — but how could she have helped it? When she stood, puckering her lips, before the fruit barrow in the market and, after sullen consideration, at last plucked a rather small but nicely ripened melon out of a heap on display, her only thought had been Is it worth a *rupee* and fifty *paise*?[1] The lichees looked more poetic, in large clusters like some prickly grapes of a charming rose colour, their long stalks and stiff grey leaves tied in a bunch above them — but were expensive. Mangoes were what the children were eagerly waiting for — the boys, she knew, were raiding the mango trees in the school compound daily and their stomachaches were a result, she told them, of the unripe mangoes they ate and for which they carried paper packets of salt to school in their pockets instead of handkerchiefs — but, leave alone the expense, the ones the fruiterer held up to her enticingly were bound to be sharp and sour for all their parakeet shades of rose and saffron; it was still too early for mangoes. So she put the melon in her string bag, rather angrily — paid the man his one *rupee* and fifty *paise* which altered his expression from one of promise and enticement to that of disappointment and contempt, and trailed off towards the vegetable barrow.

That, she later saw, was the beginning of it all, for if the melon seemed puny to her and boring to the children, from the start her husband regarded it with eyes that

---

[1] *rupee and paise (pice)* Currency used in India.

seemed newly opened. One would have thought he had never seen a melon before. All through the meal his eyes remained fixed on the plate in the centre of the table with its big button of a yellow melon. He left most of his rice and pulses on his plate, to her indignation. While she scolded, he reached out to touch the melon that so captivated him. With one finger he stroked the coarse grain of its rind, rough with the upraised criss-cross of pale veins. Then he ran his fingers up and down the green streaks that divided it into even quarters as by green silk threads, so tenderly. She was clearing away the plates and did not notice till she came back from the kitchen.

"Aren't you going to cut it for us?" she asked, pushing the knife across to him.

He gave her a reproachful look as he picked up the knife and went about dividing the melon into quarter-moon portions with sighs that showed how it pained him.

"Come on, come on," she said, roughly, "the boys have to get back to school."

He handed them their portions and watched them scoop out the icy orange flesh with a fearful expression on his face — as though he were observing cannibals at a feast. She had not the time to pay any attention to it then but later described it as horror. And he did not eat his own slice. When the boys rushed away, he bowed his head over his plate and regarded it.

"Are you going to fall asleep?" she cried, a little frightened.

"Oh no," he said, in that low mumble that always exasperated her — it seemed a sign to her of evasiveness and pusillanimity, this mumble — "Oh no, no." Yet he did not object when she seized the plate and carried it off to the kitchen, merely picked up the knife that was left behind and, picking a flat melon seed off its edge where it had remained stuck, he held it between two fingers, fondling it delicately. Continuing to do this, he left the house.

The melon might have been the apple of knowledge for Harish — so deadly its poison that he did not even need to bite into it to imbibe it: that long, devoted look had been enough. As he walked back to his office which issued ration cards to the population of their town, he looked about him vaguely but with hunger, his eyes resting not on the things on which people's eyes normally rest — signboards, the traffic, the number of an approaching bus — but on such things, normally considered nondescript and unimportant, as the paving stones on which their feet momentarily pressed, the length of wire in a railing at the side of the road, a pattern of grime on the windowpane of a disused printing press.... Amongst such things his eyes roved and hunted and, when he was seated at his desk in the office, his eyes continued to slide about — that was Sheila's phrase later: "slide about" — in a musing, calculating way, over the surface of the crowded desk, about the corners of the room, even across the ceiling. He seemed unable to focus them on a file or a card long enough to put to them his signature — they lay unsigned and the people in the queue outside went for another day without rice and sugar and kerosene for their lamps and Janta cookers. Harish searched — slid about, hunted, gazed — and at last found sufficiently interesting a thick book of rules that lay beneath a stack of files. Then his hand reached out — not to pull the book to him or open it, but to run the ball of his thumb across the edge of the pages. In their large number and irregular cut, so closely laid out like some crisp palimpsest, his eyes seemed to find something of riveting interest and his thumb of tactile wonder. All afternoon he massaged the cut edges of the book's seven hundred odd pages — tenderly, wonderingly. All afternoon his eyes gazed upon them with strange devotion. At five o'clock, punctually, the office shut and the queue disintegrated into vociferous grumbles and threats as people went home instead of to the ration shops, empty-handed instead of loaded with those necessary but, to Harish, so dull comestibles.

Although Government service is as hard to depart from as to enter — so many letters to be written, forms to be filled, files to be circulated, petitions to be made that it hardly seems worthwhile — Harish was, after some time, dismissed — time he happily spent judging the difference between white blotting paper and pink (pink is flatter, denser, white spongier) and the texture of blotting paper stained with ink and that which is fresh, that which has been put to melt in a saucer of cold tea and that which has been doused in a pot of ink. Harish was dismissed.

The first few days Sheila stormed and screamed like some shrill, wet hurricane about the house. "How am I to go to market and buy vegetables for dinner? I don't even have enough for that. What am I to feed the boys tonight? No more milk for them. The washerwoman is asking for her bill to be paid. Do you hear? Do you *hear*? And we shall have to leave this flat. Where shall we go?" He listened — or didn't — sitting on a cushion before her mirror, fingering the small silver box in which she kept the red *kum-kum*[1] that daily cut a gash from one end of her scalp to the other after her toilet. It was of dark, almost blackened silver, with a whole forest embossed on it — banana groves, elephants, peacocks and jackals. He rubbed his thumb over its cold, raised surface.

After that, she wept. She lay on her bed in a bath of tears and perspiration, and it was only because of the kindness of their neighbours that they did not starve to death the very first week, for even those who most disliked and distrusted Harish — "Always said he looks like a hungry hyena," said Mr. Bhatia who lived below their flat, "not human at all, but like a hungry, hunchbacked hyena hunting along the road" — felt for the distraught wife and the hungry children (who did not really mind as long as there were sour green mangoes to steal and devour) and looked to them. Such delicacies as Harish's family had never known before arrived in stainless steel and brass dishes, with delicate unobtrusiveness. For a while wife and children gorged on sweetmeats made with fresh buffalo milk, on pulses cooked according to grandmother's recipes, on stuffed bread and the first pomegranates of the season. But, although delicious, these offerings came in small quantities and irregularly and soon they were really starving.

"I suppose you want me to take the boys home to my parents," said Sheila bitterly, getting up from the bed. "Any other man would regard that as the worst disgrace of all — but not you. What is my shame to you? I will have to hang my head and crawl

---

[1] *kum-kum* Festival powders.

home and beg my father to look after us since you won't," and that was what she did. He was sorry, very sorry to see her pack the little silver *kum-kum* box in her black trunk and carry it away.

Soon after, officials of the Ministry of Works, Housing and Land Development came and turned Harish out, cleaned and painted the flat and let in the new tenants who could hardly believe their luck—they had been told so often they couldn't expect a flat in that locality for at least another two years.

The neighbours lost sight of Harish. Once some children reported they had seen him lying under the *pipal* tree at the corner of their school compound, staring fixedly at the red gashes cut into the papery bark and, later, a boy who commuted to school on a suburban train claimed to have seen him on the railway platform, sitting against a railing like some tattered beggar, staring across the criss-cross of shining rails. But next day, when the boy got off the train, he did not see Harish again.

Harish had gone hunting. His slow, silent walk gave him the appearance of sliding rather than walking over the surface of the roads and fields, rather like a snail except that his movement was not as smooth as a snail's but stumbling as if he had only recently become one and was still unused to the pace. Not only his eyes and his hands but even his bare feet seemed to be feeling the earth carefully, in search of an interesting surface. Once he found it, he would pause, his whole body would gently collapse across it and hours—perhaps days—would be devoted to its investigation and worship. Outside the town the land was rocky and bare and this was Harish's especial paradise, each rock having a surface of such exquisite roughness, of such perfection in shape and design, as to keep him occupied and ecstatic for weeks together. Then the river beyond the rock quarries drew him away and there he discovered the joy of fingering silk-smooth stalks and reeds, stems and leaves.

Shepherd children, seeing him stumble about the reeds, plunging thigh-deep into the water in order to pull out a water lily with its cool, sinuous stem, fled screaming, not certain whether this was a man or a hairy water snake. Their mothers came, some with stones and some with canes at the ready, but when they saw Harish, his skin parched to a violet shade, sitting on the bank and gazing at the transparent stem of the lotus, they fell back, crying, "Wah!" gathered closer together, advanced, dropped their canes and stones, held their children still by their hair and shoulders, and came to bow to him. Then they hurried back to the village, chattering. They had never had a Swami[1] to themselves, in these arid parts. Nor had they seen a Swami who looked holier, more inhuman than Harish with his matted hair, his blue, starved skin and single-focused eyes. So, in the evening, one brought him a brass vessel of milk, another a little rice. They pushed their children before them and made them drop flowers at his feet. When Harish stooped and felt among the offerings for something his fingers could respond to, they were pleased, they felt accepted. "Swamiji," they whispered, "speak."

---

[1] *Swami* Title given to a Hindu religious teacher.

Harish did not speak and his silence made him still holier, safer. So they worshipped him, fed and watched over him, interpreting his moves in their own fashion, and Harish, in turn, watched over their offerings and worshipped.

1978

Eunice de Souza

Eunice de Souza (b. 1940) was born in Poona (Pune), India. She was educated in the United States and in Bombay, where she was head of the English Literature Department at St. Xavier's before her retirement. She has written three volumes of poetry, including *Ways of Belonging* (1990) and *Selected and New Poems* (1994), and two novels: *Dangerlok* (2001) and *Dev & Simran: A Novel* (2003).

De Souza's "Catholic Mother" makes a strong, ironical statement about the role of the woman in an Indian Catholic family. In "Return," the speaker is happy to return from London to familiar Indian places and people, despite the sad changes wrought by time. The poem can be compared with Dionne Brand's "Return I" and David Dabydeen's "Catching Crabs."

Catholic Mother

Francis X. D'Souza
father of the year.
Here he is top left
the one smiling.
By the Grace of God he says
we've had seven children
(in seven years)
We're One Big Happy Family
God Always Provides
India will Suffer for
her Wicked Ways
(these Hindu buggers got no ethics)

Pillar of the Church
says the parish priest
Lovely Catholic Family
says Mother Superior

the pillar's wife
says nothing.

1990

Return

I

The old wrought iron gate has gone
with the tall, tangled grass
and the mosquitoes.
The priest is chanting his blessings
on the stone of the new building.
Squirrels chase each other up and down
the two mango trees left standing.

My neighbours want to know,
did I enjoy?
Thinking of the old wrought iron gate
and the cotton flower tree
that managed only one flower every summer
I agree, perhaps enjoyment
should have no object.

II

It was the sound of the shenai[1]
in a London flat
that brought me scurrying back
to catch this train
to be again among
these old hills
stray bougainvillea
and the peasant women
with only a handful of berries to sell.
I want to touch this earth
and let its fierce sadness
blossom in my song.

III

Tuka,[2] forgive my familiarity.
I have loved your pithy verses
ever since that French priest
everyone thought mad

---

[1] *shenai* The shenai (or shehnai) is a north Indian oboe.

[2] *Tuka* The Marathi poet "Tuka" or Tukaram (1608–49) was a wandering monk who fled society when
famine killed his family and destroyed his grain business. He is one of India's best known and loved poets.

recited them, and told us
of his journey with your people.
They have broken down whole streets
of houses in Pandarpur,[1] to widen
the road to the shrine.
The priests do not sound like you
but I'll offer a coconut anyway
for someone I love.
You made life hard for your wife
and I'm not sure I approve of that.
Nor did you heed her last request:
Come back soon.

1990

---

[1] *Pandarpur* One of the most frequented pilgrimage sites in Maharashtra state, western India. Tukaram
is associated with this site.

Nissim Ezekiel

Nissim Ezekiel (1924-2004) was born in Bombay, India, of Jewish parents in Mumbai's tiny, Marathi-speaking, Bene Israel Jewish community. He was educated in Bombay and London and worked as a journalist, broadcaster, and teacher. He was professor of English and reader in American literature at the University of Mumbai in the 1990s. He wrote several volumes of poetry — including *Time To Change* (1952), *The Unfinished Man* (1960), and *Hymns in Darkness* (1976) — plays, reviews, and art criticism.

Ezekiel's "In India" is a perfect example of the wry humour that is the hallmark of his poetic commentaries on modern India. To what extent is the speaker mocking the individuals and groups he portrays? Is his tone comic (kind humour), satiric (mocking humour), or farcical (purposeless humour)? Does the speaker make fun of himself as well? Compare his tone with that of Jayanta Mahapatra in "Freedom" and "The Portrait," that of Eunice de Souza in "Return," and that of Dionne Brand in "Return I."

In India

1

Always, in the sun's eye,
Here among the beggars,
Hawkers, pavement sleepers,
Hutment[1] dwellers, slums,
Dead souls of men and gods,
Burnt-out mothers, frightened
Virgins, wasted child
And tortured animal,
All in noisy silence
Suffering the place and time,
I ride my elephant of thought,
A Cézanne[2] slung around my neck.

2

The Roman Catholic Goan boys[3]
The whitewashed Anglo-Indian[4] boys
The musclebound Islamic boys

---

[1] *Hutment* An encampment of huts (usually military).

[2] *Cézanne* A miniature of a Paul Cézanne painting (French Impressionist).

[3] *Goan boys* Goa, a Portuguese colony (for 450 years) on the west coast of India, was ceded to India in 1961.

[4] *Anglo-Indian* Someone of English and Indian descent.

Were earnest in their prayers.
They copied, bullied, stole in pairs
They bragged about their love affairs
They carved the tables, broke the chairs
But never missed their prayers.
The Roman Catholic Goan boys
Confessed their solitary joys
Confessed their games with high-heeled toys
And hastened to the prayers.
The Anglo-Indian gentlemen
Drank whisky in some Jewish den
With Muslims slowly creeping in
Before or after prayers.

3

To celebrate the year's end:
men in grey or black, so
women, bosom semi-bare,
twenty-three of us in all,
six nations represented.
The wives of India sit apart.
They do not drink,
they do not talk,
of course, they do not kiss.
The men are quite at home
among the foreign styles
(What fun the flirting is!),
I myself, decorously,
press a thigh or two in sly innocence.
The party is a great success.
Then someone says: we can't
enjoy it, somehow, don't you think?
The atmosphere corrupt,
and look at our wooden wives...
I take him out to get some air.

4

This, she said to herself,
As she sat at table
With the English boss,
Is IT. This is the promise:
The long evenings
In the large apartment

With cold beer and Western music,
Lucid talk of art and literature,
And of all "the changes India needs."
At the second meeting
In the large apartment
After cold beer and the music on,
She sat in disarray.
The struggle had been hard
And not altogether successful.
Certainly the blouse
Would not be used again.
But with true British courtesy
He lent her a safety pin
Before she took the elevator down.

1953

Lorna Goodison

Lorna Goodison (b. 1947) was born in Jamaica. She attended the University of Iowa and Radcliffe College. She has been a visiting fellow at the University of Michigan, Radcliffe College, and University of Toronto. She divides her time among Toronto, Michigan (where she teaches creative writing), and Jamaica. An artist and poet, she has written several volumes of poetry, including *I Am Becoming My Mother* (1986), *Heartease* (1988), *Travelling Mercies* (2001), and *Controlling the Silver* (2005), and two collections of short stories: *Baby Mother and the King of Swords* (1990) and *Fool-fool Rose is Leaving Labour-in-Vain Savannah* (2005). Her non-fiction includes *From Harvey River: A Memoir of My Mother and Her People* (2008).

Goodison's "Survivor" could be read allegorically as a poem celebrating the rekindled postcolonial spirit that survives imperial plundering. The poem has no identifiable setting other than an exploited environment. The extinct bird with half-extended wings could perhaps be the dodo, but the poem is not restricted to Mauritius, the home of that unfortunate bird. Note the poet's clever use of Adam's ribs for birth and rebirth. Is there a contrast set up between the bone flute music and the ankle bells song? "Lessons Learned from the Royal Primer" refers to the elementary school series that was used throughout the British Empire and to the merciless King Léopold of Belgium, whose cruel deeds are ignored in the Royal Reader. Goodison mentions ironically the possibility that a vulgar Jamaican term (associated with sanitary napkins) may have originated from this school text (see footnotes to the poem).

Survivor

The strangers passed through here
for years
laying waste the countryside.
They took most living things
even some rare species
with half extended wings.
They took them all.
Now that genus is extinct
Lord, they were thorough
in their plunderings.
So, here the wind plays
mourning notes
on bones that once were ribs
(savages) they broke them
when they'd finished eating
and you know how creative
God is with ribs.
That survivor over there

with bare feet and bound hair
has some seeds stored
under her tongue
and one remaining barrel
of rain
She will go indoors
when her planting is done
loosen her hair
and tend to her son
and over the bone flute music
and the dead story it tells,
listen for grace songs
from her ankle bells.

1988

Lessons Learned from the Royal Primer[1]

For Velma Pollard

Taught us how Bombo lived in the Congo
in a round grass hut. Bombo was the boy
who sported a white cloth about his loins,
causing one of our linguists to conjecture
that perhaps Bombo's rough garment gave
the name to one of Jamaica's curse-cloths.[2]

Now we were never told exactly what
that little boy Bombo was doing, except
just dwelling as a dark Congolese native
in his round-domed grass ancestral hut,
supported by a thorny center pole. But
what the Royal Primer forgot to tell us

was this, It seemed that it was the king
of Belgium who gave strict instructions

---

[1] *Royal Primer* An elementary or primary school text used in most schools throughout the British Empire.

[2] *Bomboclot(h)* An obscene term for sanitary cloth napkins and female genitals. Richard Allsopp (in *Dictionary of Caribbean Usage*, Oxford UP, 1996) traces its origins to the African word "mbumbu."

to his soldiers to cleanly chop off both
the little boy Bombo's hands, on account
of the fact that balls of rubber cultivated
by Bombo were deemed too lightweight
and not enough for the needs of Leopold.[1]

2005

---

[1] *Leopold* King Léopold II of Belgium (1835–1909) virtually owned the Congo Free State (later Belgian
Congo and Zaire, and now the Democratic Republic of the Congo) as his personal property; he later
transferred most of it to the Belgian nation. He turned the country into a vast labour camp for harvest-
ing rubber and ivory. His rule was brutal. Not only did his agents chop off hands as punishment, but
also, according to Adam Hochchild in *King Leopold's Ghost* (1998), he is responsible for the death of
perhaps 10 million Congolese. Mark Twain called Léopold the slayer of 15 million Congolese and a
"greedy, grasping, avaricious, cynical, bloodthirsty old goat" ("King Léopold's Soliloquy: A Defence of
His Congo Rule").

Nadine Gordimer

Nadine Gordimer (b. 1923) was born in Springs, near Johannesburg, South Africa. She attended the University of Witwatersrand, and she became increasingly active in the anti-apartheid movement after the South African Sharpeville massacre in 1960. She published her first collection of stories, *Face to Face*, in 1949. Since then she has published many other volumes of stories, including *Loot: And Other Stories* (2003), and such novels as *The Conservationist* (1974), *My Son's Story* (1990), and *Beethoven Was One-Sixteenth Black* (2007). She was awarded the Nobel Prize for Literature in 1991.

Gordimer's "Is There Nowhere Else Where We Can Meet?," set in South Africa of the apartheid period, examines what keeps peoples apart and what are the possibilities of reconciliation between them. Note the dominance in the opening paragraphs of symbolic (allegorical?) images that link or intertwine opposites, such as the inversion of sky and earth and greyness (mixture of white and black). Is there an antithesis set up between the inhabited and the uninhabited environment? Does the protagonist choose to seek refuge in the gated house or to continue her journey — of reconciliation — even though she is limping? Are the "black-jacks" she pulls off her stockings significant? Do they represent her fear of and bias toward the black stranger? A crucial aspect of the narrative is the woman's paralyzing anxiety that the man will rob or hurt her. Is he actually robbing her or possibly helping her by picking up the fallen parcel? (Keep in mind that we are getting her terrified perception of what is happening.) Is this ambiguous? If it is, why does Gordimer employ ambiguity here? Compare this story with Njabulo Ndebele's observations on racial relationships in "Guilt and Atonement."

Is There Nowhere Else Where We Can Meet?

It was a cool grey morning and the air was like smoke. In that reversal of the elements that sometimes takes place, the grey, soft, muffled sky moved like the sea on a silent day.

The coat collar pressed rough against her neck and her cheeks were softly cold as if they had been washed in ice water. She breathed gently with the air; on the left a strip of veld fire curled silently, flameless. Overhead a dove purred. She went on over the flat straw grass, following the trees, now on, now off the path. Away ahead, over the scribble of twigs, the sloping lines of black and platinum grass — all merging, tones but no colour, like an etching — was the horizon, the shore at which cloud lapped.

Damp burnt grass puffed black, faint dust from beneath her feet. She could hear herself swallow.

A long way off she saw a figure with something red on its head, and she drew from it the sense of balance she had felt at the particular placing of the dot of a figure in a picture. She was here: someone was over there.... Then the red dot was gone, lost in the curve of the trees. She changed her bag and parcel from one arm to the other and felt the morning, palpable, deeply cold and clinging against her eyes.

She came to the end of a direct stretch of path and turned with it round a dark-fringed pine and a shrub, now delicately boned, that she remembered hung with bunches of white flowers like crystals in the summer. There was a native in a red woollen cap standing at the next clump of trees, where the path crossed a ditch and was bordered by white-splashed stones. She had pulled a little sheath of pine needles, three in a twist of thin brown tissue, and as she walked she ran them against her thumb. Down; smooth and stiff. Up; catching in gentle resistance as the minute serrations snagged at the skin. He was standing with his back towards her, looking along the way he had come; she pricked the ball of her thumb with the needle-ends. His one trouser leg was torn off above the knee, and the back of the naked leg and half-turned heel showed the peculiarly dead, powdery black of cold. She was nearer to him now, but she knew he did not hear her coming over the damp dust of the path. She was level with him, passing him; and he turned slowly and looked beyond her, without a flicker of interest, as a cow sees you go.

The eyes were red, as if he had not slept for a long time, and the strong smell of old sweat burned at her nostrils. Once past, she wanted to cough, but a pang of guilt at the red-weary eyes stopped her. And he had only a filthy rag—part of an old shirt? —without sleeves and frayed away into a great gap from underarm to waist. It lifted in the currents of cold as she passed. She had dropped the neat trio of pine needles somewhere, she did not know at what moment, so now, remembering something from childhood, she lifted her hand to her face and sniffed: yes, it was as she remembered, not as chemists pretend it in the bath salts, but a dusty green scent, vegetable rather than flower. It was clean, unhuman. Slightly sticky too; tacky on her fingers. She must wash them as soon as she got there. Unless her hands were quite clean, she could not lose consciousness of them, they obtruded upon her.

She felt a thudding through the ground like the sound of a hare running in fear and she was going to turn around and then he was there in front of her, so startling, so utterly unexpected, panting right into her face. He stood dead still and she stood dead still. Every vestige of control, of sense, of thought, went out of her as a room plunges into dark at the failure of power and she found herself whimpering like an idiot or a child. Animal sounds came out of her throat. She gibbered. For a moment it was Fear itself that had her by the arms, the legs, the throat; not fear of the man, of any single menace he might present, but Fear, absolute, abstract. If the earth had opened up in fire at her feet, if a wild beast had opened its terrible mouth to receive her, she could not have been reduced to less than she was now.

There was a chest heaving through the tear in front of her; a face panting; beneath the red hairy woollen cap the yellowish-red eyes holding her in distrust. One foot, cracked from exposure until it looked like broken wood, moved, only to restore balance in the dizziness that follows running, but any move seemed towards her and she tried to scream and the awfulness of dreams came true and nothing would come out. She wanted to throw the handbag and the parcel at him, and as she fumbled crazily for them she heard him draw a deep, hoarse breath and he grabbed out at her and — ah! It came. His hand clutched her shoulder.

Now she fought with him and she trembled with strength as they struggled. The dust puffed round her shoes and his scuffling toes. The smell of him choked her. — It was an old pyjama jacket, not a shirt — His face was sullen and there was a pink place where the skin had been grazed off. He sniffed desperately, out of breath. Her teeth chattered, wildly she battered him with her head, broke away, but he snatched at the skirt of her coat and jerked her back. Her face swung up and she saw the waves of a grey sky and a crane breasting them, beautiful as the figurehead of a ship. She staggered for balance and the handbag and parcel fell. At once he was upon them, and she wheeled about; but as she was about to fall on her knees to get there first, a sudden relief, like a rush of tears, came to her and instead, she ran. She ran and ran, stumbling wildly off through the stalks of dead grass, turning over her heels against hard winter tussocks, blundering through trees and bushes. The young mimosas closed in, lowering a thicket of twigs right to the ground, but she tore herself through, feeling the dust in her eyes and the scaly twigs hooking at her hair. There was a ditch, knee-high in blackjacks;[1] like pins responding to a magnet they fastened along her legs, but on the other side there was a fence and then the road . . . She clawed at the fence — her hands were capable of nothing — and tried to drag herself between the wires, but her coat got caught on a barb, and she was imprisoned there, bent in half, whilst waves of terror swept over her in heat and trembling. At last the wire tore through its hold on the cloth; wobbling, frantic, she climbed over the fence.

And she was out. She was out on the road. A little way on there were houses, with gardens, postboxes, a child's swing. A small dog sat at a gate. She could hear a faint hum, as of life, of talk somewhere, or perhaps telephone wires.

She was trembling so that she could not stand. She had to keep on walking, quickly, down the road. It was quiet and grey, like the morning. And cool. Now she could feel the cold air round her mouth and between her brows, where the skin stood out in sweat. And in the cold wetness that soaked down beneath her armpits and between her buttocks. Her heart thumped slowly and stiffly. Yes, the wind was cold; she was suddenly cold, damp-cold, all through. She raised her hand, still fluttering uncontrollably, and smoothed her hair; it was wet at the hairline. She guided her hand into her pocket and found a handkerchief to blow her nose.

There was the gate of the first house, before her.

She thought of the woman coming to the door, of the explanations, of the woman's face, and the police. Why did I fight, she thought suddenly. What did I fight for? Why didn't I give him the money and let him go? His red eyes, and the

---

[1] *blackjacks* Flowering plants that are widespread as a weed on cultivated lands and along roadsides in South Africa.

smell and those cracks in his feet, fissures, erosion. She shuddered. The cold of the morning flowed into her.

She turned away from the gate and went down the road slowly, like an invalid, beginning to pick the blackjacks from her stockings.

1949

Jessica Hagedorn

Jessica Hagedorn (b. 1949) was born and raised in the Philippines; she now lives in the United States. She has performed in the theatre and has published numerous poems, reviews, essays, and fiction—including the collection of poems *Danger and Beauty* (1993) and such novels as *Dogeaters* (1990) and *Dream Jungle* (2003).

Hagedorn's "The Song of Bullets" has an ironic title. She portrays well the helplessness of those living in a society riddled by war and the uncertainty of everyday life—friends missing, people committing suicide. Comment on the effect of juxtaposing the image of "Assassins cruising the streets" and "sunbathers idle on the beach," or of "snipers and poets" cast in the same light. Is the tone one of pessimism, acceptance, or revulsion? Compare the tone of this poem with that of Achebe's story "Girls at War."

The Song of Bullets

Formalized
by middle age
we avoid crowds
but still
love music.

Day after day
with less surprise
we sit
in apartments
and count
the dead.

Awake,
my daughter croons
her sudden cries
and growls
my new language.
While she sleeps
we memorize
a list of casualties:

The photographer's brother
the doctor is missing.
Or I could say:

"Victor's brother Oscar
has been gone for two years ...
It's easier for the family
to think of him dead."

Victor sends
a Christmas card
from El Salvador:
"Things still the same."

And there are others
who don't play
by the rules —
someone else's brother
perhaps mine
languishes in a hospital;
everyone's grown tired
of his nightmares
and pretends
he's not there.

Someone else's father
perhaps mine
will be executed
when the time comes.
Someone else's mother
perhaps mine
telephones incessantly
her husband is absent
her son has gone mad
her lover has committed suicide
she's a survivor
who can't appreciate
herself.

The sight
of my daughter's
pink and luscious flesh
undoes me.
I fight
my weakening rage
I must remember
to commit

those names to memory
and stay angry.

Friends send postcards:
"Alternating between hectic
social Manila life & rural wonders
of Sagata[1] ... on to Hongkong and Bangkok —
Love ..."

Assassins cruise the streets
in obtrusive limousines
sunbathers idle
on the beach

War is predicted
in five years
ten years
any day now
I always thought
it was already happening

snipers and poets locked
in a secret embrace
the country
my child may never see

a heritage
of women in heat
and men
skilled at betrayal

dancing
to the song
of bullets.

1988

---

[1] *Sagata* Sagata, known for its caves and mountain scenery, is a ten-hour drive from Manila, Philippines.

Kaiser Haq

Kaiser Haq (b. 1950) was born in Bangladesh (or East Pakistan, as it was known then). He is a professor of English at Dhaka University, Bangladesh, where he has taught since 1975. He was a Senior Fulbright Scholar at the University of Wisconsin. His volumes of poems include *A Happy Farewell* (1994), *Black Orchid* (1996), *The Wonders of Vilayet* (1998), and *Published in the Streets of Dhaka, Collected Poems 1966-2006* (2007).

In Haq's poem "Strange Pleasures," the speaker and his friend employ black humour (that is, the use of humour in a situation that requires serious or sympathetic treatment) to cope with recurring political violence in their homeland. The speaker warns at the end of the poem that poets "are not to be entirely trusted." Does he really mean this or is he suggesting that his friend may have exaggerated the incident of the accidental shooting of the ear-cleaner and his customer to make a point?

Strange Pleasures

The last time we had prolonged
    political disturbances (which
are regular as cyclones or,
    in happier lands, carnivals)
nobody knew anything
    beyond their own anger
or despair, shops were half-
    shuttered, buses ran half-way,
a half-hearted coup aborted,
    the isle of tranquilizers
went up, foreign exchange reserves
    went down, and nobody bothered
to keep count of bodies sent to morgues.

Mercifully, phones still worked,
    were kept busy with chat.
A friend rang to tell me
    how people still tried
to get on with life, indoors
    and out: one man wished
to have his ear cleaned, another
    who made a living by satisfying

such wishes[1] got down to work.
    The client sat on a stool
beside a pavement[2] near a crossroads,
    eyes meditatively half-shut;
the other sighted like a marksman
    along a thin steel rod —
on his concentration depended
    pleasure and hygiene or pain and infection.
Not far away a few random shots were fired:
    one entered the sitting man's ear,
came out his other ear, entered
    the ear-cleaner's eye, ruining
for good his delicate concentration.

How the phones rang with our laughter:
    politics affords strange pleasures.
But I ought to add
    my informant was a poet
and poets, as everybody knows,
    are not to be entirely trusted.

1998

---

[1] *made a living… such wishes* Ear-cleaners are common in Asian cities; the art or trade can be traced
back to the medieval period.
[2] *pavement* Sidewalk.

Claire Harris

Claire Harris (b. 1937) was born in Trinidad and educated there and in Ireland, Jamaica, and Lagos, Nigeria. She now lives in Calgary but travels widely. A poet, short-story writer, and essayist, she has written many volumes of poetry, including *Fables from the Women's Quarters* (1984), *The Conception of Winter* (1988), *Dipped in Shadow* (1996), and *She* (2000).

Harris's poems "Death in Summer" and "Backstage at the Glenbow Museum, Calgary" both deal with her sense of place, placelessness, and ancestral longing as an Afro-Trinidadian living in Canada. Does the poetic form of "Backstage at the Glenbow Museum, Calgary" appropriately convey the persona's response to Africa? The poet was asked to advise the Glenbow Museum (in Alberta, Canada) on displaying an African exhibition. Though black but not in fact an African, the poet says that she has "a kind of duty" to do so. How effective is the repetition of this phrase? Is the form of the poem (particularly the untraditional lineation) effective? Have you noticed that this is a concrete (or shape) poem? There are outlines of animals in the typographical arrangement of the stanzas. "Death in Summer" depicts a speaker learning of the death of a loved one in her original homeland thousands of miles from her immigrant home. This poem could be compared with Derek Walcott's "A Letter from Brooklyn" and Dionne Brand's "Amelia."

Backstage at the Glenbow Museum, Calgary

out of the pale life of northern streets into the hushed dim
of mausoleums   no need to rush   ideas suspended in silence
dead   and i can't quite believe i've come here knowing this
though i have a kind of duty i suppose   even to these shells

"Do come down ... we have some wonderful things in the archives"
"I don't write on demand ..."
"You can come down early ... any day ... I'll show you
around ... these things should be seen ..."

i have a kind of duty i suppose

        drop by drop i dive in
      where tall cupboards
        hold ancient
           other   music frozen
                       masks/gourds/stools

other worlds into
feathered brilliances
boats/mats/statues
i float down aisles thru preserving light   temperature   humidity
ignoring ghostly canoes launched silent into corners the parrots'
muffled squawk and sigh   fat brown giggles clustering on window
sills fingers like roots weaving hailing   exotic   not mine not
mine   smoke   pots of red ochre   cedar leans cooking fires playing
ceilings   hooked on needs i bleed on must
a kind of duty i suppose
so   break water into
musty silence   a dun beach behind
which other silences should roll and tower
should roll & tower in the usual endless peaks
but don't

nothing
nothing here
nothing luminous
here

perhaps behind the doors
perhaps a cry racing entirely backwards
a space i can enter
to find what?
through murk and formless
i
wanting
come to the third cupboard on the third reef
doors open silence of sharks
or books
i need
a waterfall
africaafricaafricaafrica
AFRIC
africaAFRICAafrica
af   af   af   afr
ric   ric ric rica
A F R I C
Aaaaaa
brown rivers/plains/mountains/red earth/deserts/thorn
grass/forests/great herds/beasts/red/white/black/brown

in flight and swarm/market places/drums/stamping feet
pestles/baskets/flutes/songs/peoples   staring through
it all   as through cloud drifts
         orisas[1]
     challenge their fate
             Oluwa wa Olu wa wa O lu
                    wa wa
nothing

      shards   the past
    broken bits ab/truth
a row of faces on a dusty shelf lean drunkenly cheek
    to cheek
      hanging with them that smell   bargaining

i have a kind of duty i suppose

     nothing but art
                         it is May 1994 Calgary
cold and sunny in the afternoon clouds rain High 13 Low 3
       how Africa eludes my every effort
     wraps itself in abysses
       in drums
         in the terrible distances
       of pop images
              Serengetti
                            Mandela
                Buthelezi
       Kenya
                  Timbuktu

R(u)wanda[2]   and i am here in this clear blue city   beached on
heads hacked off   Africa dripping from the mouths of dogs
                       the hands of men

i have a kind of duty i suppose

1994

---

[1] *orisas* Orisas (also Orishas) are spirits that reflect one of the manifestations of *Olodumare* (God) in the Yoruba religious beliefs. They are similar in attributes to Hindu and ancient Greek/Roman gods and goddesses.

[2] *Serengetti... R(u)wanda* Serengetti, Kenya, Timbuktu, and Rwanda are all places in Africa; Nelson Mandela and Zulu Chief Buthelezi are major figures in the struggle to rid South Africa of apartheid.

Death in Summer

One known at home[1] our mail relays something of her
early summons awash in the proverbial bed

its final currents strip her of luggage she
nevertheless clings I watch from this shore

four thousand miles away her desperate drowning motions
I try to decipher what works what doesn't

how to save ourselves who no longer believe
in winged souls caged in flesh nor yet

believe in shared rounds in organic growth
and becoming I shall drift through this city

alive to the possibility of this edge if one
so vigorous … nothing between me and the grave

I shall laugh shall leave my stain here and there
dark energy of flawed creatures confused and clinging

to the bars They say her face transparent under
the shock of black hair lifts with each morning's light

which she watches intently as if to be sure
she has seen

I know fading angels move through her as eagles
through the upper air

1995

---

[1] *home* If the speaker's experience is based on the poet's, home is Trinidad, West Indies.

Wilson Harris

Wilson Harris (b. 1921) was born and educated in Guyana, and immigrated in 1959 to England. Among his novels are *Palace of the Peacock* (1960), *The Secret Ladder* (1963), *Ascent to Omai* (1970), *Carnival* (1985), *Resurrection at Sorrow Hill* (1993), *The Mask of the Beggar* (2003), and *The Ghost of Memory* (2006). He has written poetry and essays, including *History, Fable and Myth in the Caribbean and Guianas* (1970), *The Womb of Space: The Cross-Cultural Imagination* (1983), and *The Radical Imagination* (1992). A strong advocate of common ancestral memory and human commonality, he has lectured widely at universities around the world.

Harris's "Kanaima" is set in the Guyanese hinterland, a recurring setting of his fiction, including his classic first novel *Palace of the Peacock* (1960). For the Amerindians of Guyana, Kanaima is an avenging, evil spirit, perceived by some tribes as the hereditary enemy of humans. This story captures well the feel of the Guyanese interior and introduces us to the myth of Kanaima. Is it also an allegory (like Nadine Gordimer's and Ngugi wa Thiong'o's stories in this text)? Harris believes in common, universal myths. Are there Kanaima-figures in other cultures? Compare this story with Ngitji Ngitji's "The Possum Woman" and Philip Sherlock's "The Warau People Discover the Earth."

Kanaima

Tumatumari is a tiny dying village on the bank of the Potaro River,[1] overlooking roaring rapids. The bursting stream foams and bunches itself into a series of smooth cascading shells enveloping backs of stone. Standing on the top of the hill one feels the gulley and river sliding treacherously and beautifully as though everything was slipping into its own curious violent inner concentration and energy, and one turns away and faces the tiny encampment and village with a sensation of loss — as of something alive and vibrant and wholehearted whose swift lure and summons one evades once again to return to the shell of this standing death.

A beaten trail that keeps its distance from the dangerous brink of the gorge winds its spirit over the hill, through the village, like the patient skin of a snake, lying on the ground with entrails hanging high as husks of vine, dangling and rotting in the ancient forest.

The village seems to hold its own against the proliferation of the jungle with great difficulty, dying slowly in a valiant effort to live, eternally addressed by the deep voice of the falls, conscious too of a high far witness across the slanting sky — a blue line of mountains upholding a fiction of cloud....

A tiny procession — about a dozen persons in all, mostly women and children — was making its way across the trail. The man who led them, a rather stocky Indian, had stopped. His face bore the mooning fateful look of the Macusi Indians, travel-

---

[1] *Tumatumari...Potaro River* Tumatumari and the Potaro River are actual places in the Guyana hinterland.

ling far from home. They lived mostly in the high Rupununi savannahs stretching to Brazil, a long way off, and the village encampment at Tumatumari was composed of African and negro pork-knockers,[1] most of whom were absent at this time, digging the interior creeks for diamonds. They had left a couple of old watchmen behind them at Tumatumari but otherwise the village (which they used as a base camp) was empty. The leader of the newcomers reconnoitred the situation, looking around him with brooding eyes, rolling a black globule and charm on his tongue and exhibiting this every now and then against his teeth — under his curling lips — with the inward defiance of an experienced hunter who watched always for the curse of men and animals.

The six o'clock parrots flew screeching overhead. The Indians looked at the sun and corrected their mental time-piece. It could not have been later than four. The sky was still glowing bright on the mountain's shoulder. In the bush the hour was growing dark, but here on the snake's trail — which coiled around the huts and the shattered houses — the air still swam with the yellow butter of the sun.

One of the old decrepit watchmen — left by the negro pork-knockers — was approaching the Macusis. He shambled along, eyeing the strangers in an inhospitable, barren way. "Is no use," he said, when he reached them, shaking his head at them with an ominous spirit, "Kanaima been here already." The Indians remained silent and sullen, but in reality they were deeply shaken by the news. They started chattering all of a sudden like the discordant premature parrots that had passed a few moments ago overhead. The sound of their matching voices rose and died as swiftly as it had begun. Their stocky leader — with the black fluid beetle on his tongue — addressed the old watchman, summoning all the resources of the pork-knocker's language he was learning to use. "When Kanaima," he spoke the dreadful name softly, hoping that its conversion into broken English utterance deprived it of calling all harm, and looking around as if the ground and the trees had black ears — "when Kanaima come here?" he asked. "And which way he pass and gone?" His eyes, like charms betokening all guarded fear, watched the watchman before him. They glanced at the sky as if to eclipse the sentence of time and looked to the rim of the conjuring mountains where the approach of sunset burned indifferently, as though it stood on the after-threshold of dawn, rather than against the closing window of night.

"He gone so — that way." The old negro pointed to the golden mountains of heaven. "He say to tell you ..." his voice croaked a little ... "he expect you here today and he coming tonight to get you. He know every step of the way you come since you run away from home and is no use you hiding any more now. I believe ..." he dropped his voice almost to a whisper ... "I believe if you can pass him and shake him off your trail in the forest tonight — you got your only chance."

The Indians had listened attentively and their chattering rose again, full of staccato, wounded cries above the muffled voice of the waterfall, dying into helpless

---

[1] *pork-knockers* A Guyanese demotic term for independent prospectors for gold and diamonds along the rivers of Guyana's hinterland.

silence and submersion at last. "We got take rest," the leader of the party declared heavily and slowly, pronouncing each word with difficulty. He pointed to everyone's condition, indicating that they stood on the very edge of collapse. They had come a long way—days and weeks—across steep ridges and through treacherous valleys. They must stop now—even if it was only for four or five hours of recuperative sleep. The burden of flight would be too great if they left immediately and entered the trail in the night.

"Is no use," the old man said. Nevertheless he turned and shambled towards a shattered hut which stood against the wall of the jungle. It was all he was prepared to offer them. The truth was he wanted them to go away from his village. His name was Jordan. Twenty years of pork-knocking—living on next to nothing—expending nearly every drop of heart's blood in the fever and lust of the diamond bush—had reduced him to a scarecrow of ill-omen always seeing doom, and Kanaima—the avenging Amerindian god, who could wear any shape he wished, man or bird or beast—had come to signify— almost without Jordan being aware of it—the speculative fantasy of his own life; the sight of strange Indians invariably disturbed him and reminded him of the uselessness of time like a photograph of ghosts animated to stir memories of injustice and misfortune. He always pictured them as bringing trouble or flying from trouble. They were a conquered race, were they not? Everybody knew that. It was best to hold them at arm's length though it seemed nothing could prevent their scattered fictions from trespassing on ground where he alone wanted to be.

The light of afternoon began to lose its last vivid shooting colour, the blazing gold became silver, and the resplendent silver was painted over by the haze of dusk. In the east the sky had turned to a deep purple shell, while an intensity of steel appeared in the west, against which—on the topmost ridge of the ghostly mountains—the trees were black smudges of valiant charcoal emphasising the spectral earth and the reflection of fury. A few unwinking stars stood at almost vanishing point in the changing spirit of heaven.

The Indians witnessed the drama of sunset, as if it were the last they would see, through the long rifts in the roof of the house, and out beyond the open places in the desolate walls. The stupor of their long day enveloped them, the ancient worship of the sun, the mirage of space and the curse of the generations.

Kanaima had been on their heels now for weeks and months. Their home and village—comprising about sixty persons—had been stricken. First, there had been an unexpected drought. Then the game had run away in the forest and across the savannahs. After that, people had started dropping down dead. Kanaima planted his signature clear at last in the fire he lit no one knew when and where; it came suddenly running along the already withered spaces of the savannahs, leaving great black charred circles upon the bitten grass everywhere, and snaking into the village-compound where it lifted its writhing self like a spiritual warning in the headman's presence before climbing up the air into space.

They knew then it was no use quarrelling with fate. Day after day they had travelled, looking for somewhere to set up a new encampment, their numbers dwindling all the time, and every situation they came to, it was always to find that Kanaima had passed through before them. If it was not nature's indifference — lack of water or poor soil — they stumbled upon barren human looks and evil counsel, the huts they saw were always tumbling down, and the signs upon the walls they visited were as arid and terrible as flame, as their own home had looked when they had left to search for a new place. It was as if the world they saw and knew was dying everywhere, and no one could dream what would take its place. The time had surely come to stop wherever they were and let whatever had to happen, happen.

It was a hot, stifling night that fell pitch-black upon them. Jordan and the other aged watchman the pork-knockers had left at Tumatumari had nevertheless lit a fire in the village, over which they roasted a bush cow they had shot that morning. It was rare good fortune at a time when the country was yielding little game. The flame blazed steadily, painting a screen on the trees and the shadows of the two men seemed to race hither and thither out of a crowded darkness and back into multitudes still standing on the edge of the forested night. It seemed all of a sudden that another man was there in the open, a sombre reticent spectator. His shadow might have been an illusion of a glaring moment on the earth, or a curious blending of two living shapes into the settlement of a third moving presence.

He was taller than the two blind watchmen over whom he stood. He studied them from behind a fence of flaming stakes, a volcanic hallucinated gateway that might have belonged to some ancient overshadowed primeval garden. It was as if— though he stood near — he was always too far for anyone to see his flowing garb. It appeared as if his feet were buried in a voluminous cloak whose material swept into a black hole in the ground, yet when he moved it was with perfect freedom and without a sign of stumbling entanglement. He occasionally glided over the enfolding majestic snake of his garment that obeyed his footsteps.

All at once the sparks flew and his shadow seemed to part the two men in a rain of comets, dispatching one with a great leg of beef to the hut where the Indians were, while with another imperious gesture his muffled hand turned the roasting cow into a comfortable position for the one who remained by the fire to slice a share of the breast for dinner. It was the tenderest part of the meat and the stranger devoured a ghostly portion. A distant breeze stirred the whole forest and the fire lifted a tongue up to heaven as though a nest of crucial stars remaining just above a mass of dark trees had finally blown down on earth's leaves.

All around the fire and under the stars the night had grown blacker than ever. The crowding phantoms of the bush had vanished turning faceless and impotent and one with Kanaima's cloak of trailing darkness: the strong meat of life over which the lord of death stood had satisfied them and driven them down into the blackest hole at his feet. The aged watchmen too had their fill and seemed unable to rise from their squatting heels, dreaming of a pile of diamonds under the waterfall. The Macusi headman came to the door of the hut and stood looking towards every hidden snake and trail in the jungle. His companions were sound asleep after their unexpected meal. They had picked the bone clean and then tossed it into the uncanny depths of the lost pit outside their window. Even if they had wanted to resume their journey, the headman felt, it was impossible to do so now. The sound of the Tumatumari Falls rose into the air like sympathetic magic and universal pouring rain. But not a drop descended anywhere out of a sky which was on fire, burning with powder and dust and choked with silver and gold, a great pork-knocker's blackboard and riddle, infinitely rich with the diamonds of space and infinitely poor with the wandering skeletons of eternity.

The headman let his chin drop slowly upon his breast, half-asleep in awe and with nameless fatigue and misery. It was no use complaining he said to himself. Tumatumari was the same as every other village through which they had come, uniform as the river's fall and the drought standing all over the forgotten land from which they had fled, insignificant as every buried grave over which they had crossed. All the trails were vanishing into a running hole in the ground and there was nothing more to do than wait for another joint of roasting meat to fall upon them from the stars that smoked over their head.

There was a movement in the hut behind him, the shaking of a hammock, and a woman appeared in the door beside him. He recognised her in the dim light. She was his wife. She said something to him and began descending the steps, rolling a little like a balloon and half-crouching like an animal feeling for sand before it defecates.

The headman suddenly raised an alarm. He realised she had taken the wrong direction, her eyes half-bandaged by sleep. She had misjudged the trail and had blundered towards the waterfall. His voice was hardly out of his throat when her answering shriek pierced him. She had come to the yawning blind gulley, had tried to scramble for the foothold she was losing, and had only succeeded in slipping deeper and deeper. The headman continued to shout, running forward at the same time. He perceived the cloud of unknowing darkness where the chasm commenced and far below he felt he saw the white spit of foam illumined by starshine, blue and treacherous as a devil. The voices of his companions had followed him and were flying around him like a chorus of shrieks, and it seemed their cry also came from below. The two village-watchmen had also been aroused and they were heaving at the low fire, squandering a host of sparks, until they had acquired flaming branches in their hands. They began to approach the gulley. The flaring billowing light forked into the momentous presence of their infused companion, the shadow of the god who had attended the feast. He had been crouching at the fire beside them as though he presided over each jealous spark, his being shaped by the curious flux of their own bodies which wove his shape on the ground. Now his waving cloak swirled towards the great pit and it seemed that no one realised he was there until the headman of the Macusis saw him coming at last, a vast figure and extension of the dense frightful trees shaking everywhere and shepherding the watchmen along.

"Kanaima," he screamed. The whole company was startled almost out of their wits, and Jordan—who had met the Indians that afternoon when they arrived in the village—"I tell you so." He repeated like a rigmarole—"I tell you so."

Then indeed—as if they were proving what they had known all along—they perceived him, his head raised far in the burning sky and his swirling trunk and body sliding over the illuminated cloud above the waterfall. Yet—in spite of themselves—they were all drawn towards the precipice and the roaring invisible rainfall in the night. The flaring torches in their hands picked out the snaking garment which streamed upon the hideous glitter of the angry river, whose jaws gaped with an evil intent. They were lost in wonder at what they saw. The woman who had fallen hung against the side of the cliff, half-sitting upon a jutting nose of rock, her hands clasping a dark trailing vine that wreathed itself upwards along a ragged descending face in the wall. The torches lit up her blind countenance and her pin-point terrified eyes were enabled to see grinning massive teeth in the face on the wall. Tremblingly holding the vine—as if it were a lock of beloved hair—she began to climb upon the staircased-teeth, brushing lips of stone that seemed to support her, and yet not knowing whether at any moment she would be devoured by falling into the roaring jaws of death.

The watchers waited and beheld the groping muse of all their humanity: Kanaima alone knew whether she would reach the cliff top.

1964

Bessie Head

Bessie Head (1937-86) was born in South Africa of a Scottish mother and a black father. A teacher and journalist, she left South Africa in 1964 and spent the rest of her life in Botswana. She wrote four novels, including *Maru* (1971) and *A Question of Power* (1974), and two short-story collections: *The Collector of Treasures and Other Botswana Village Tales* (1977) and *Tales of Tenderness and Power* (published posthumously in 1989).

Head's "The Collector of Treasures," like her other stories, is primarily about the fate of women in African society from a postcolonial and feminist perspective. This story sets up a contrast between two husbands, one considerate and caring, the other selfish and lustful. The text shows how inappropriate it is to make sweeping sociological observations about the African male since the two in this story bring different values to bear on their marriages. The title is ironic; what the protagonist collects are hurts, not treasures. Compare this story's treatment of women with Ama Ata Aidoo's "No Sweetness Here" and Chinua Achebe's "Girls at War."

The Collector of Treasures

The long-term central state prison in the south was a whole day's journey away from the villages of the northern part of the country. They had left the village of Puleng at about nine that morning and all day long the police truck droned as it sped southwards on the wide, dusty cross-country track-road. The everyday world of ploughed fields, grazing cattle, and vast expanses of bush and forest seemed indifferent to the hungry eyes of the prisoner who gazed out at them through the wire mesh grating at the back of the police truck. At some point during the journey, the prisoner seemed to strike at some ultimate source of pain and loneliness within her being and, overcome by it, she slowly crumpled forward in a wasted heap, oblivious to everything but her pain. Sunset swept by, then dusk, then dark and still the truck droned on, impersonally, uncaring.

At first, faintly on the horizon, the orange glow of the city lights of the new independence town of Gaborone,[1] appeared like an astonishing phantom in the overwhelming darkness of the bush, until the truck struck tarred roads, neon lights, shops and cinemas, and made the bush a phantom amidst a blaze of light. All this passed untimed, unwatched by the crumpled prisoner; she did not stir as the truck finally droned to a halt outside the prison gates. The torchlight struck the side of her face like an agonising blow. Thinking she was asleep, the policeman called out briskly:

"You must awaken now. We have arrived."

He struggled with the lock in the dark and pulled open the grating. She crawled painfully forward, in silence.

---

[1] *Gaborone* The capital of Botswana; it is 15 kilometres (9 miles) from the South African border.

Together, they walked up a short flight of stairs and waited awhile as the man tapped lightly, several times, on the heavy iron prison door. The night-duty attendant opened the door a crack, peered out and then opened the door a little wider for them to enter. He quietly and casually led the way to a small office, looked at his colleague and asked: "What do we have here?"

"It's the husband murder case from Puleng village," the other replied, handing over a file.

The attendant took the file and sat down at a table on which lay open a large record book. In a big, bold scrawl he recorded the details: Dikeledi Mokopi. Charge: Man-slaughter. Sentence: Life. A night-duty wardress appeared and led the prisoner away to a side cubicle, where she was asked to undress.

"Have you any money on you?" the wardress queried, handing her a plain, green cotton dress which was the prison uniform. The prisoner silently shook her head.

"So, you have killed your husband, have you?" the wardress remarked, with a flicker of humour. "You'll be in good company. We have four other women here for the same crime. It's becoming the fashion these days. Come with me," and she led the way along a corridor, turned left and stopped at an iron gate which she opened with a key, waited for the prisoner to walk in ahead of her and then locked it with the key again. They entered a small, immensely high-walled courtyard. On one side were toilets, showers, and a cupboard. On the other, an empty concrete quadrangle. The wardress walked to the cupboard, unlocked it and took out a thick roll of clean-smelling blankets which she handed to the prisoner. At the lower end of the walled courtyard was a heavy iron door which led to the cell. The wardress walked up to this door, banged on it loudly and called out: "I say, will you women in there light your candle?"

A voice within called out: "All right," and they could hear the scratch-scratch of a match. The wardress again inserted a key, opened the door and watched for a while as the prisoner spread out her blankets on the floor. The four women prisoners already confined in the cell sat up briefly, and stared silently at their new companion. As the door was locked, they all greeted her quietly and one of the women asked: "Where do you come from?"

"Puleng," the newcomer replied, and seemingly satisfied with that, the light was blown out and the women lay down to continue their interrupted sleep. And as though she had reached the end of her destination, the new prisoner too fell into a deep sleep as soon as she had pulled her blankets about her.

The breakfast gong sounded at six the next morning. The women stirred themselves for their daily routine. They stood up, shook out their blankets and rolled them up into neat bundles. The day-duty wardress rattled the key in the lock and let them out into the small concrete courtyard so that they could perform their morning toilet. Then, with a loud clatter of pails and plates, two male prisoners appeared at the gate with breakfast. The men handed each woman a plate of porridge and a mug of black tea and they settled themselves on the concrete floor to eat. They turned and looked at their new companion and one of the women, a spokesman for the group said kindly:

"You should take care. The tea has no sugar in it. What we usually do is scoop the sugar off the porridge and put it into the tea."

The woman, Dikeledi, looked up and smiled. She had experienced such terror during the awaiting-trial period that she looked more like a skeleton than a human being. The skin creaked tautly over her cheeks. The other woman smiled, but after her own fashion. Her face permanently wore a look of cynical, whimsical humour. She had a full, plump figure. She introduced herself and her companions: "My name is Kebonye. Then that's Otsetswe, Galeboe, and Monwana. What may your name be?"

"Dikeledi Mokopi."

"How is it that you have such a tragic name," Kebonye observed. "Why did your parents have to name you *tears*?"

"My father passed away at that time and it is my mother's tears that I am named after," Dikeledi said, then added: "She herself passed away six years later and I was brought up by my uncle."

Kebonye shook her head sympathetically, slowly raising a spoonful of porridge to her mouth. That swallowed, she asked next:

"And what may your crime be?"

"I have killed my husband."

"We are all here for the same crime," Kebonye said, then with her cynical smile asked: "Do you feel any sorrow about the crime?"

"Not really," the other woman replied.

"How did you kill him?"

"I cut off all his special parts with a knife," Dikeledi said.

"I did it with a razor," Kebonye said. She sighed and added: "I have had a troubled life."

A little silence followed while they all busied themselves with their food, then Kebonye continued musingly:

"Our men do not think that we need tenderness and care. You know, my husband used to kick me between the legs when he wanted that. I once aborted with a child, due to this treatment. I could see that there was no way to appeal to him if I felt ill, so I once said to him that if he liked he could keep some other woman as well because I couldn't manage to satisfy all his needs. Well, he was an education-officer and each year he used to suspend about seventeen male teachers for making school girls pregnant, but he used to do the same. The last time it happened the parents of the girl were very angry and came to report the matter to me. I told them: 'You leave it to me. I have seen enough.' And so I killed him."

They sat in silence and completed their meal, then they took their plates and cups to rinse them in the wash-room. The wardress produced some pails and a broom. The sleeping quarters had to be flushed out with water; there was not a speck of dirt anywhere, but that was prison routine. All that was left was an inspection by the director of the prison. Here again Kebonye turned to the newcomer and warned:

"You must be careful when the chief comes to inspect. He is mad about one thing—attention! Stand up straight! Hands at your sides! If this is not done you should see how he stands here and curses. He does not mind anything but that. He is mad about that."

Inspection over, the women were taken through a number of gates to an open, sunny yard, fenced in by high, barbed-wire where they did their daily work. The prison was a rehabilitation centre where the prisoners produced goods which were sold in the prison store; the women produced garments of cloth and wool; the men did carpentry, shoe-making, brick-making, and vegetable production.

Dikeledi had a number of skills — she could knit, sew, and weave baskets. All the women at present were busy knitting woollen garments; some were learners and did their work slowly and painstakingly. They looked at Dikeledi with interest as she took a ball of wool and a pair of knitting needles and rapidly cast on stitches. She had soft, caressing, almost boneless, hands of strange power — work of a beautiful design grew from those hands. By mid-morning she had completed the front part of a jersey and they all stopped to admire the pattern she had invented in her own head.

"You are a gifted person," Kebonye remarked, admiringly.

"All my friends say so," Dikeledi replied smiling. "You know, I am the woman whose thatch does not leak. Whenever my friends wanted to thatch their huts, I was there. They would never do it without me. I was always busy and employed because it was with these hands that I fed and reared my children. My husband left me after four years of marriage but I managed well enough to feed those mouths. If people did not pay me in money for my work, they paid me with gifts of food."

"It's not so bad here," Kebonye said. "We get a little money saved for us out of the sale of our work, and if you work like that you can still produce money for your children. How many children do you have?"

"I have three sons."

"Are they in good care?"

"Yes."

"I like lunch," Kebonye said, oddly turning the conversation. "It is the best meal of the day. We get samp and meat and vegetables."

So the day passed pleasantly enough with chatter and work and at sunset the women were once more taken back to the cell for lock-up time. They unrolled their blankets and prepared their beds, and with the candle lit continued to talk a while longer. Just as they were about to retire for the night, Dikeledi nodded to her new-found friend, Kebonye:

"Thank you for all your kindness to me," she said, softly.

"We must help each other," Kebonye replied, with her amused, cynical smile. "This is a terrible world. There is only misery here."

And so the woman Dikeledi began phase three of a life that had been ashen in its loneliness and unhappiness. And yet she had always found gold amidst the ash, deep loves that had joined her heart to the hearts of others. She smiled tenderly at Kebonye because she knew already that she had found another such love. She was the collector of such treasures.

* * *

There were really only two kinds of men in the society. The one kind created such misery and chaos that he could be broadly damned as evil. If one watched the village dogs chasing a bitch on heat, they usually moved around in packs of four or five. As the mating progressed one dog would attempt to gain dominance over the festivities and oust all the others from the bitch's vulva. The rest of the hapless dogs would stand around yapping and snapping in its face while the top dog indulged in a continuous spurt of orgasms, day and night until he was exhausted. No doubt, during that Herculean feat, the dog imagined he was the only penis in the world and that there had to be a scramble for it. That kind of man lived near the animal level and behaved just the same. Like the dogs and bulls and donkeys, he also accepted no responsibility for the young he procreated and like the dogs and bulls and donkeys, he also made females abort. Since that kind of man was in the majority in the society, he needed a little analysing as he was responsible for the complete breakdown of family life. He could be analysed over three time-spans. In the old days, before the colonial invasion of Africa, he was a man who lived by the traditions and taboos outlined for all the people by the forefathers of the tribe. He had little individual freedom to assess whether these traditions were compassionate or not — they demanded that he comply and obey the rules, without thought. But when the laws of the ancestors are examined, they appear on the whole to have been vast, external disciplines for the good of the society as a whole, with little attention given to individual preferences and needs. The ancestors made so many errors and one of the most bitter-making things was that they relegated to men a superior position in the tribe, while women were regarded, in a congenital sense, as being an inferior form of human life. To this day, women still suffered from all the calamities that befall an inferior form of human life. The colonial era and the period of migratory mining labour to South Africa was a further affliction visited on this man. It broke the hold of the ancestors. It broke the old, traditional form of family life and for long periods a man was separated from his wife and children while he worked for a pittance in another land in order to raise the money to pay his British Colonial poll-tax. British Colonialism scarcely enriched his life. He then became "the boy" of the white man and a machine-tool of the South African mines. African independence seemed merely one more affliction on top of the afflictions that had visited this man's life. Independence suddenly and dramatically changed the pattern of colonial subservience. More jobs became available under the new government's localization programme and salaries sky-rocketed at the same time. It provided the first occasion for family life of a new order, above the childlike discipline of custom, the degradation of colonialism. Men and women, in order to survive, had to turn inwards to their own resources. It was the man who arrived at this turning point, a broken wreck with no inner resources at all. It was as though he was hideous to himself and in an effort to flee his own inner emptiness, he spun away from himself in a dizzy kind of death dance of wild destruction and dissipation.

One such man was Garesego Mokopi, the husband of Dikeledi. For four years prior to independence, he had worked as a clerk in the district administration service, at a steady salary of R50.00[1] a month. Soon after independence his salary shot up to R200.00 per month. Even during his lean days he had had a taste for womanising and drink; now he had the resources for a real spree. He was not seen at home again and lived and slept around the village, from woman to woman. He left his wife and three sons—Banabothe, the eldest, aged four; Inalame, aged three; and the youngest, Motsomi, aged one—to their own resources. Perhaps he did so because she was the boring, semi-literate traditional sort, and there were a lot of exciting new women around. Independence produced marvels indeed.

There was another kind of man in the society with the power to create himself anew. He turned all his resources, both emotional and material, towards his family life and he went on and on with his own quiet rhythm: like a river. He was a poem of tenderness.

One such man was Paul Thebolo and he and his wife, Kenalepe, and their three children, came to live in the village of Puleng in 1966, the year of independence. Paul Thebolo had been offered the principalship of a primary school in the village. They were allocated an empty field beside the yard of Dikeledi Mokopi, for their new home.

Neighbours are the centre of the universe to each other. They help each other at all times and mutually loan each other's goods. Dikeledi Mokopi kept an interested eye on the yard of her new neighbours. At first, only the man appeared with some workmen to erect the fence, which was set up with incredible speed and efficiency. The man impressed her immediately when she went around to introduce herself and find out a little about the newcomers. He was tall, large-boned, slow-moving. He was so peaceful as a person that the sunlight and shadow played all kinds of tricks with his eyes, making it difficult to determine their exact colour. When he stood still and looked reflective, the sunlight liked to creep into his eyes and nestle there; so sometimes his eyes were the colour of shade, and sometimes light brown.

He turned and smiled at her in a friendly way when she introduced herself and explained that he and his wife were on transfer from the village of Bobonong. His wife and children were living with relatives in the village until the yard was prepared. He was in a hurry to settle down as the school term would start in a month's time. They were, he said, going to erect two mud huts first and later he intended setting up a small house of bricks. His wife would be coming around in a few days with some women to erect the mud walls of the huts.

"I would like to offer my help too," Dikeledi said. "If work always starts early in the morning and there are about six of us, we can get both walls erected in a week. If you want one of the huts done in woman's thatch, all my friends know that I am the woman whose thatch does not leak."

The man smilingly replied that he would impart all this information to his wife, then he added charmingly that he thought she would like his wife when they met. His wife was a very friendly person; everyone liked her.

---

[1] *R50.00* The currency in Botswana was (at the time of the setting of this narrative) the South African rand; since 1976 it has been the Botswana pula.

Dikeledi walked back to her own yard with a high heart. She had few callers. None of her relatives called for fear that since her husband had left her she would become dependent on them for many things. The people who called did business with her; they wanted her to make dresses for their children or knit jerseys for the winter time and at times when she had no orders at all, she made baskets which she sold. In these ways she supported herself and the three children but she was lonely for true friends.

All turned out as the husband had said—he had a lovely wife. She was fairly tall and thin with a bright, vivacious manner. She made no effort to conceal that normally, and every day, she was a very happy person. And all turned out as Dikeledi had said. The work-party of six women erected the mud walls of the huts in one week; two weeks later, the thatch was complete. The Thebolo family moved into their new abode and Dikeledi Mokopi moved into one of the most prosperous and happy periods of her life. Her life took a big, wide upward curve. Her relationship with the Thebolo family was more than the usual friendly exchange of neighbours. It was rich and creative.

It was not long before the two women had going one of those deep, affectionate, sharing-everything kind of friendships that only women know how to have. It seemed that Kenalepe wanted endless amounts of dresses made for herself and her three little girls. Since Dikeledi would not accept cash for these services—she protested about the many benefits she received from her good neighbours—Paul Thebolo arranged that she be paid in household goods for these services so that for some years Dikeledi was always assured of her basic household needs—the full bag of corn, sugar, tea, powdered milk, and cooking oil. Kenalepe was also the kind of woman who made the whole world spin around her; her attractive personality attracted a whole range of women to her yard and also a whole range of customers for her dressmaking friend, Dikeledi. Eventually, Dikeledi became swamped with work, was forced to buy a second sewing-machine and employ a helper. The two women did everything together—they were forever together at weddings, funerals, and parties in the village. In their leisure hours they freely discussed all their intimate affairs with each other, so that each knew thoroughly the details of the other's life.

"You are a lucky someone," Dikeledi remarked one day, wistfully. "Not everyone has the gift of a husband like Paul."

"Oh yes," Kenalepe said happily. "He is an honest somebody." She knew a little of Dikeledi's list of woes and queried: "But why did you marry a man like Garesego? I looked carefully at him when you pointed him out to me near the shops the other day and I could see at one glance that he is a butterfly."

"I think I mostly wanted to get out of my uncle's yard," Dikeledi replied. "I never liked my uncle. Rich as he was, he was a hard man and very selfish. I was only a servant there and pushed about. I went there when I was six years old when my mother died, and it was not a happy life. All his children despised me because I was their servant. Uncle paid for my education for six years, then he said I must leave school. I longed for more because as you know, education opens up the world for one.

Garesego was a friend of my uncle and he was the only man who proposed for me. They discussed it between themselves and then my uncle said: "You'd better marry Garesego because you're just hanging around here like a chain on my neck." I agreed, just to get away from that terrible man. Garesego said at that time that he'd rather be married to my sort than the educated kind because those women were stubborn and wanted to lay down the rules for men. Really, I did not ever protest when he started running about. You know what the other women do. They chase after the man from one hut to another and beat up the girlfriends. The man just runs into another hut, that's all. So you don't really win. I wasn't going to do anything like that. I am satisfied I have children. They are a blessing to me."

"Oh, it isn't enough," her friend said, shaking her head in deep sympathy. "I am amazed at how life imparts its gifts. Some people get too much. Others get nothing at all. I have always been lucky in life. One day my parents will visit—they live in the south—and you'll see the fuss they make over me. Paul is just the same. He takes care of everything so that I never have a day of worry...."

The man Paul attracted as wide a range of male friends as his wife. They had guests every evening: illiterate men who wanted him to fill in tax forms or write letters for them, or his own colleagues who wanted to debate the political issues of the day—there was always something new happening every day now that the country had independence. The two women sat on the edge of these debates and listened with fascinated ears, but they never participated. The following day they would chew over the debates with wise, earnest expressions.

"Men's minds travel widely and boldly," Kenalepe would comment. "It makes me shiver the way they freely criticise our new government. Did you hear what Petros said last night? He said he knew all those bastards and they were just a lot of crooks who would pull a lot of dirty tricks. Oh dear! I shivered so much when he said that. The way they talk about the government makes you feel in your bones that this is not a safe world to be in, not like the old days when we didn't have governments. And Lentswe said that ten per cent of the population in England really control all the wealth of the country, while the rest live at starvation level. And he said communism would sort all this out. I gathered from the way they discussed this matter that our government is not in favour of communism. I trembled so much when this became clear to me ..." She paused and laughed proudly. "I've heard Paul say this several times: 'The British only ruled us for eighty years.' I wonder why Paul is so fond of saying that?"

And so a completely new world opened up for Dikeledi. It was so impossibly rich and happy that, as the days went by, she immersed herself more deeply in it and quite overlooked the barrenness of her own life. But it hung there like a nagging ache in the mind of her friend, Kenalepe.

"You ought to find another man," she urged one day, when they had one of their personal discussions. "It's not good for a woman to live alone."

"And who would that be?" Dikeledi asked, disillusioned. "I'd only be bringing trouble into my life whereas now it is all in order. I have my eldest son at school and I can manage to pay the school fees. That's all I really care about."

I mean," said Kenalepe, "we are also here to make love and enjoy it."

"Oh I never really cared for it," the other replied. "When you experience the worst of it, it just puts you off altogether."

"What do you mean by that?" Kenalepe asked, wide-eyed.

"I mean it was just jump on and jump off and I used to wonder what it was all about. I developed a dislike for it."

"You mean Garesego was like that!" Kenalepe said, flabbergasted. "Why, that's just like a cock hopping from hen to hen. I wonder what he is doing with all those women. I'm sure they are just after his money and so they flatter him ..." She paused and then added earnestly: "That's really all the more reason you should find another man. Oh, if you knew what it was really like, you would long for it, I can tell you! I sometimes think I enjoy that side of life far too much. Paul knows a lot about all that. And he always has some new trick with which to surprise me. He has a certain way of smiling when he has thought up something new and I shiver a little and say to myself: 'Ha, what is Paul going to do tonight!'"

Kenalepe paused and smiled at her friend, slyly.

"I can loan Paul to you if you like," she said, then raised one hand to block the protest on her friend's face. "I would do it because I have never had a friend like you in my life before whom I trust so much. Paul had other girls you know, before he married me, so it's not such an uncommon thing to him. Besides, we used to make love long before we got married and I never got pregnant. He takes care of that side too. I wouldn't mind loaning him because I am expecting another child and I don't feel so well these days ..."

Dikeledi stared at the ground for a long moment, then she looked up at her friend with tears in her eyes.

"I cannot accept such a gift from you," she said, deeply moved. "But if you are ill I will wash for you and cook for you."

Not put off by her friend's refusal of her generous offer, Kenalepe mentioned the discussion to her husband that very night. He was so taken off-guard by the unexpectedness of the subject that at first he looked slightly astonished, and burst out into loud laughter and for such a lengthy time that he seemed unable to stop.

"Why are you laughing like that?" Kenalepe asked, surprised.

He laughed a bit more, then suddenly turned very serious and thoughtful and was lost in his own thoughts for some time. When she asked him what he was thinking he merely replied: "I don't want to tell you everything. I want to keep some of my secrets to myself."

The next day Kenalepe reported this to her friend.

"Now whatever does he mean by that? I want to keep some of my secrets to myself?"

"I think," Dikeledi said smiling, "I think he has a conceit about being a good man. Also, when someone loves someone too much, it hurts them to say so. They'd rather keep silent."

Shortly after this Kenalepe had a miscarriage and had to be admitted to hospital for a minor operation. Dikeledi kept her promise "to wash and cook" for her friend. She ran both their homes, fed the children and kept everything in order. Also, people complained about the poorness of the hospital diet and each day she scoured the village for eggs and chicken, cooked them, and took them to Kenalepe every day at the lunch-hour.

One evening Dikeledi ran into a snag with her routine. She had just dished up supper for the Thebolo children when a customer came around with an urgent request for an alteration on a wedding dress. The wedding was to take place the next day. She left the children seated around the fire eating and returned to her own home. An hour later, her own children asleep and settled, she thought she would check the Thebolo yard to see if all was well there. She entered the children's hut and noted that they had put themselves to bed and were fast asleep. Their supper plates lay scattered and unwashed around the fire. The hut which Paul and Kenalepe shared was in darkness. It meant that Paul had not yet returned from his usual evening visit to his wife. Dikeledi collected the plates and washed them, then poured the dirty dishwater on the still-glowing embers of the outdoor fire. She piled the plates one on top of the other and carried them to the third additional hut which was used as a kitchen. Just then Paul Thebolo entered the yard, noted the lamp and movement in the kitchen hut and walked over to it. He paused at the open door.

"What are you doing now, Mma-Banabothe?" he asked, addressing her affectionately in the customary way by the name of her eldest son, Banabothe.

"I know quite well what I am doing," Dikeledi replied happily. She turned around to say that it was not a good thing to leave dirty dishes standing overnight but her mouth flew open with surprise. Two soft pools of cool liquid light were in his eyes and something infinitely sweet passed between them; it was too beautiful to be love.

"You are a very good woman, Mma-Banabothe," he said softly.

It was the truth and the gift was offered like a nugget of gold. Only men like Paul Thebolo could offer such gifts. She took it and stored another treasure in her heart. She bowed her knee in the traditional curtsey and walked quietly away to her own home.

* * *

Eight years passed for Dikeledi in a quiet rhythm of work and friendship with the Thebolos. The crisis came with the eldest son, Banabothe. He had to take his primary school leaving examination at the end of the year. This serious event sobered him up considerably as like all boys he was very fond of playtime. He brought his books home and told his mother that he would like to study in the evenings. He would like to pass with a "Grade A" to please her. With a flushed and proud face Dikeledi mentioned this to her friend, Kenalepe.

"Banabothe is studying every night now," she said. "He never really cared for studies. I am so pleased about this that I bought him a spare lamp and removed him from the children's hut to my own hut where things will be peaceful for him. We both sit up late at night now. I sew on buttons and fix hems and he does his studies ..."

She also opened a savings account at the post office in order to have some standby money to pay the fees for his secondary education. They were rather high—R85.00. But in spite of all her hoarding of odd cents, towards the end of the year, she was short on R20.00 to cover the fees. Midway during the Christmas school holidays the results were announced. Banabothe passed with a "Grade A." His mother was almost hysterical in her joy at his achievement. But what to do? The two youngest sons had already started primary school and she would never manage to cover all their fees from her resources. She decided to remind Garesego Mokopi that he was the father of the children. She had not seen him in eight years except as a passer-by in the village. Sometimes he waved but he had never talked to her or enquired about her life or that of the children. It did not matter. She was a lower form of human life. Then this unpleasant something turned up at his office one day, just as he was about to leave for lunch. She had heard from village gossip, that he had eventually settled down with a married woman who had a brood of children of her own. He had ousted her husband, in a typical village sensation of brawls, curses, and abuse. Most probably the husband did not care because there were always arms outstretched towards a man, as long as he looked like a man. The attraction of this particular woman for Garesego Mokopi, so her former lovers said with a snicker, was that she went in for heady forms of love-making like biting and scratching.

Garesego Mokopi walked out of his office and looked irritably at the ghost from his past, his wife. She obviously wanted to talk to him and he walked towards her, looking at his watch all the while. Like all the new "success men," he had developed a paunch, his eyes were blood-shot, his face was bloated, and the odour of the beer and sex from the previous night clung faintly around him. He indicated with his eyes that they should move around to the back of the office block where they could talk in privacy.

"You must hurry with whatever you want to say," he said impatiently. "The lunch-hour is very short and I have to be back at the office by two."

Not to him could she talk of the pride she felt in Banabothe's achievement, so she said simply and quietly: "Garesego, I beg you to help me pay Banabothe's fees for secondary school. He has passed with a "Grade A" and as you know, the school fees must be produced on the first day of school or else he will be turned away. I have struggled to save money the whole year but I am short by R20.00."

She handed him her post office savings book, which he took, glanced at and handed back to her. Then he smiled, a smirky know-all smile, and thought he was delivering her a blow in the face.

"Why don't you ask Paul Thebolo for the money?" he said. "Everyone knows he's keeping two homes and that you are his spare. Everyone knows about that full bag of corn he delivers to your home every six months so why can't he pay the school fees as well?"

She neither denied this, nor confirmed it. The blow glanced off her face which she raised slightly, in pride. Then she walked away.

As was their habit, the two women got together that afternoon and Dikeledi reported this conversation with her husband to Kenalepe who tossed back her head in anger and said fiercely: "The filthy pig himself! He thinks every man is like him, does he? I shall report this matter to Paul, then he'll see something."

And indeed Garesego did see something but it was just up his alley. He was a female prostitute in his innermost being and like all professional prostitutes, he enjoyed publicity and sensation—it promoted his cause. He smiled genially and expansively when a madly angry Paul Thebolo came up to the door of his house where he lived with *his* concubine. Garesego had been through a lot of these dramas over those eight years and he almost knew by rote the dialogue that would follow.

"You bastard!" Paul Thebolo spat out. "Your wife isn't my concubine, do you hear?"

"Then why are you keeping her in food?" Garesego drawled. "Men only do that for women they fuck! They never do it for nothing."

Paul Thebolo rested one hand against the wall, half dizzy with anger, and he said tensely: "You defile life, Garesego Mokopi. There's nothing else in your world but defilement. Mma-Banabothe makes clothes for my wife and children and she will never accept money from me so how else must I pay her?"

"It only proves the story both ways," the other replied, vilely. "Women do that for men who fuck them."

Paul Thebolo shot out the other hand, punched him soundly in one grinning eye and walked away. Who could hide a livid, swollen eye? To every surprised enquiry, he replied with an injured air:

"It was done by my wife's lover, Paul Thebolo."

It certainly brought the attention of the whole village upon him, which was all he really wanted. Those kinds of men were the bottom rung of government. They secretly hungered to be the President with all eyes on them. He worked up the sensation a little further. He announced that he would pay the school fees of the child of his concubine, who was also to enter secondary school, but not the school fees of his own child, Banabothe. People half liked the smear on Paul Thebolo; he was too good to be true. They delighted in making him a part of the general dirt of the village, so they turned on Garesego and scolded: "Your wife might be getting things from Paul Thebolo but it's beyond the purse of any man to pay the school fees of his own children as well as the school fees of another man's children. Banabothe wouldn't be there had you not procreated him, Garesego, so it is your duty to care for him. Besides, it's your fault if your wife takes another man. You left her alone all these years."

So that story was lived with for two weeks, mostly because people wanted to say that Paul Thebolo was a part of life too and as uncertain of his morals as they were. But the story took such a dramatic turn that it made all the men shudder with horror. It was some weeks before they could find the courage to go to bed with women; they preferred to do something else.

Garesego's obscene thought processes were his own undoing. He really believed that another man had a stake in his hen-pen and like any cock, his hair was up about it. He thought he'd walk in and re-establish his own claim to it and so, after two weeks, once the swelling in his eye had died down, he espied Banabothe in the village and asked him to take a note to his mother. He said the child should bring a reply. The note read: "Dear Mother, I am coming home again so that we may settle our differences. Will you prepare a meal for me and some hot water that I might take a bath? Gare."

Dikeledi took the note, read it and shook with rage. All its overtones were clear to her. He was coming home for some sex. They had had no differences. They had not even talked to each other.

"Banabothe," she said. "Will you play nearby? I want to think a bit then I will send you to your father with the reply."

Her thought processes were not very clear to her. There was something she could not immediately touch upon. Her life had become holy to her during all those years she had struggled to maintain herself and the children. She had filled her life with treasures of kindness and love she had gathered from others and it was all this that she wanted to protect from defilement by an evil man. Her first panic-stricken thought was to gather up the children and flee the village. But where to go? Garesego did not want a divorce, she had left him to approach her about the matter, she had desisted from taking any other man. She turned her thoughts this way and that and could find no way out except to face him. If she wrote back, don't you dare put foot in the yard I don't want to see you, he would ignore it. Black women didn't have that kind of power. A thoughtful, brooding look came over her face. At last, at peace with herself, she went into her hut and wrote a reply: "Sir, I shall prepare everything as you have said. Dikeledi."

It was about midday when Banabothe sped back with the reply to his father. All afternoon Dikeledi busied herself making preparations for the appearance of her husband at sunset. At one point Kenalepe approached the yard and looked around in amazement at the massive preparations, the large iron water pot full of water with a fire burning under it, the extra cooking pots on the fire. Only later Kenalepe brought the knife into focus. But it was only a vague blur, a large kitchen knife used to cut meat and Dikeledi knelt at a grinding-stone and sharpened it slowly and methodically. What was in focus then was the final and tragic expression on the upturned face of her friend. It threw her into confusion and blocked their usual free and easy feminine chatter. When Dikeledi said: "I am making some preparations for Garesego. He is coming home tonight," Kenalepe beat a hasty retreat to her own home terrified. They knew they were involved because when she mentioned this to Paul he was distracted and uneasy for the rest of the day. He kept on doing upside-down sorts of things, not replying to questions, absent-mindedly leaving a cup of tea until it got quite cold, and every now and again he stood up and paced about, lost in his own thoughts. So deep was their sense of disturbance that towards evening they no longer made a pretence of talking. They just sat in silence in their hut. Then, at about nine o'clock, they heard those wild and agonized bellows. They both rushed out together to the yard of Dikeledi Mokopi.

* * *

He came home at sunset and found everything ready for him as he had requested, and he settled himself down to enjoy a man's life. He had brought a pack of beer along and sat outdoors slowly savouring it while every now and then his eye swept over the Thebolo yard. Only the woman and children moved about the yard. The man was out of sight. Garesego smiled to himself, pleased that he could crow as loud as he liked with no answering challenge.

A basin of warm water was placed before him to wash his hands and then Dikeledi served him his meal. At a separate distance she also served the children and then instructed them to wash and prepare for bed. She noted that Garesego displayed no interest in the children whatsoever. He was entirely wrapped up in himself and thought only of himself and his own comfort. Any tenderness he offered the children might have broken her and swerved her mind away from the deed she had carefully planned all that afternoon. She was beneath his regard and notice too for when she eventually brought her own plate of food and sat near him, he never once glanced at her face. He drank his beer and cast his glance every now and again at the Thebolo yard. Not once did the man of the yard appear until it became too dark to distinguish anything any more. He was completely satisfied with that. He could repeat the performance every day until he broke the mettle of the other cock again and forced him into angry abuse. He liked that sort of thing.

"Garesego, do you think you could help me with Banabothe's school fees?" Dikeledi asked at one point.

"Oh, I'll think about it," he replied casually.

She stood up and carried buckets of water into the hut, which she poured into a large tin bath that he might bathe himself, then while he took his bath she busied herself tidying up and completing the last of the household chores. Those done, she entered the children's hut. They played hard during the day and they had already fallen asleep with exhaustion. She knelt down near their sleeping mats and stared at them for a long while, with an extremely tender expression. Then she blew out their lamp and walked to her own hut. Garesego lay sprawled across the bed in such a manner that indicated he only thought of himself and did not intend sharing the bed with anyone else. Satiated with food and drink, he had fallen into a deep, heavy sleep the moment his head touched the pillow. His concubine had no doubt taught him that the correct way for a man to go to bed, was naked.

So he lay, unguarded and defenceless, sprawled across the bed on his back.

The bath made a loud clatter as Dikeledi removed it from the room, but still he slept on, lost to the world. She re-entered the hut and closed the door. Then she bent down and reached for the knife under the bed which she had merely concealed with a cloth. With the precision and skill of her hardworking hands, she grasped hold of his genitals and cut them off with one stroke. In doing so, she slit the main artery which ran on the inside of the groin. A massive spurt of blood arched its way across the bed. And Garesego bellowed. He bellowed his anguish. Then all was silent. She stood and watched his death anguish with an intent and brooding look, missing not one detail of it. A knock on the door stirred her out of her reverie. It was the boy, Banabothe. She opened the door and stared at him, speechless. He was trembling violently.

"Mother," he said, in a terrified whisper. "Didn't I hear father cry?"

"I have killed him," she said, waving her hand in the air with a gesture that said — well, that's that. Then she added sharply: "Banabothe, go and call the police."

He turned and fled into the night. A second pair of footsteps followed hard on his heels. It was Kenalepe running back to her own yard, half out of her mind with fear. Out of the dark Paul Thebolo stepped towards the hut and entered it. He took in every detail and then he turned and looked at Dikeledi with such a tortured expression that for a time words failed him. At last he said: "You don't have to worry about the children, Mma-Banabothe. I'll take them as my own and give them all a secondary school education."

1977

A.D. Hope

Alec D. Hope (1907-2000) was born in Cooma, New South Wales, Australia. Educated at Oxford and Sydney, he was a vocational psychologist and later became Professor of English at Australian National University. A literary critic and poet, he published *The Wandering Island* (poems, 1955), *The Pack of Autolycus* (essays, 1978), *Ladies from the Sea* (drama, 1987), and *Orpheus* (poems, 1991).

Hope's "Man Friday" is yet another reassessment of Friday's relationship with Robinson Crusoe. See, for instance, J.M. Coetzee's *Foe* (1986), Charles Martin's *Passages from Friday* (1983), Derek Walcott's play *Pantomime* (1978), and Sam Selvon's *Moses Ascending* (1975). See also the opening of Selvon's story in this anthology, "Brackley and the Bed." In "Man Friday," Hope sets up a contrast between Crusoe and Friday: Friday lacks Crusoe's material resources and has to depend on his inner strength to cope with his lot. Is Friday portrayed here simply as a noble savage? (See notes to the poem.) Hope has a pervasive ironical, witty tone in most of his poems. Against whom is his satire directed when he says that Friday's stay in England transformed him into "an Englishman. / Brushed, barbered, hatted, trousered and baptized"?

Man Friday

For John Pringle

Saved at long last through Him whose power to save
Kept from the walking, as the watery grave,
Crusoe[1] returned to England and his kind,
Proof that an unimaginative mind
And sober industry and commonsense
May supplement the work of Providence.
He, no less providential, and no less
Inscrutably resolved to save and bless,
Eager to share his fortune with the weak
And faithful servants whom he taught to speak,
By all his years of exile undeterred,
Took into exile Friday and the bird.

The bird no doubt was well enough content.
She had her corn—what matter where she went?
Except when once a week he walked to church,
She had her master's shoulder as a perch,

---

[1] *Crusoe* Hope is rewriting the resolution of the Robinson Crusoe-Friday narrative in Daniel Defoe's *Robinson Crusoe* (1719) and *The Further Adventures of Robinson Crusoe* (1719).

She shared the notice of the crowds he drew
Who praised her language and her plumage too,
And like a rational female could be gay
On admiration and three meals a day.

But Friday, the dark Caribbean man,[1]
Picture his situation if you can:
The gentle savage, taught to speak and pray,
On England's Desert Island cast away,
No godlike Crusoe issuing from his cave
Comes with his thunderstick to slay and save;
Instead from caves of stone, as thick as trees,
More dreadful than ten thousand savages,
In their strange clothes and monstrous mats of hair,
The pale-eyed English swarm to joke and stare,
With endless questions round him crowd and press
Curious to see and touch his loneliness.

Unlike his master Crusoe long before
Crawling half-drowned upon the desolate shore,
Mere ingenuity useless in his need,
No wreck supplies him biscuit, nails and seed,
No fort to build, no call to bake, to brew,
Make pots and pipkins,[2] cobble coat and shoe,
Gather his rice and milk his goats, and rise
Daily to some absorbing enterprise.

And yet no less than Crusoe he must find
Some shelter for the solitary mind;
Some daily occupation to contrive
To warm his wits and keep the heart alive;
Protect among the cultured, if he can,
The "noble savage" and the "natural man."[3]
As Crusoe made his clothes, so he no less
Must labour to invent his nakedness

---

[1] *Caribbean man* The island of Tobago in the Caribbean was thought to be the real-life counterpart of Defoe's fictional island.

[2] *pipkins* Small earthenware pots or pans.

[3] *noble savage ... natural man* Jean-Jacques Rousseau, Swiss-French eighteenth-century writer-philosopher contended that "Natural Man" living enviably away from the corrupting influence of "civilization" was a "noble savage."

And, lest their alien customs without trace
Absorb him, tell the legends of his race
Each night aloud in the soft native tongue,
That filled his world when, bare and brown and young thusly,
His brown, bare mother held him at her breast,
Then say his English prayers and sink to rest.
And each day waking in his English sheets,
Hearing the waggons in the cobbled streets,
The morning bells, the clatter and cries of trade,
He must recall, within their palisade,
The sleeping cabins in the tropic dawn,
The rapt, leaf-breathing silence, and the yawn
Of naked children as they wake and drowse,
The women chattering round their fires, the prows
Of wet canoes nosing the still lagoon;
At each meal, handling alien fork or spoon,
Remember the spiced mess of yam and fish
And the brown fingers meeting in the dish;
Remember too those island feasts, the sweet
Blood frenzy and the taste of human meat.
Thus he piled memories against his need:
In vain! For still he found the past recede.
Try as he would, recall, relive, rehearse,
The cloudy images would still disperse,
Till, as in dreams, the island world he knew
Confounded the fantastic with the true,
While England, less unreal day by day,
The Cannibal Island, ate his past away.
But for the brooding eye, the swarthy skin,
That witnessed to the Natural Man within,
Year following year, by inches, as they ran,
Transformed the savage to an Englishman.
Brushed, barbered, hatted, trousered and baptized,
He looked, if not completely civilized,
What came increasingly to be the case:
An upper servant, conscious of his place,
Friendly but not familiar in address
And prompt to please, without obsequiousness,
Adept to dress, to shave, to carve, to pour
And skilled to open or refuse the door,
To keep on terms with housekeeper and cook,
But quell the maids and footmen with a look.

And now his master, thoughtful for his need,
Bought him a wife and gave him leave to breed.
A fine mulatto,[1] once a lady's maid,
She thought herself superior to Trade
And, reared on a Plantation, much too good
For a low native Indian from the wood;
Yet they contrived at last to rub along
For he was strong and kind, and she was young,
And soon a father, then a family man,
Friday took root in England and began
To be well thought of in the little town,
And quoted in discussions at "The Crown,"
Whether the Funds would fall, the French would treat
Or the new ministry could hold its seat.
For though he seldom spoke, the rumour ran
The master had no secrets from his man,
And Crusoe's ventures prospered so, in short,
It was concluded he had friends at Court.

Yet as the years of exile came and went,
Though first he grew resigned and then content,
Had you observed him close, you might surprise
A stranger looking through the servant's eyes.
Some colouring of speech, some glint of pride,
Not born of hope, for hope long since had died,
Not even desire, scarce memory at last,
Preserved that stubborn vestige of the past.

It happened once that man and master made
A trip together on affairs of trade;
A ship reported foundered in the Downs
Brought them to visit several seaport towns.
At one of these, Great Yarmouth or King's Lynn,[2]
Their business done, they baited at an inn,
And in the night were haunted by the roar
Of a wild wind and tide against the shore.
Crusoe soon slept again, but Friday lay
Awake and listening till the dawn of day.
For the first time in all his exiled years
The thunder of the ocean filled his ears;

---

[1] *Mulatto* A person of black and white parentage.

[2] *Great Yarmouth or King's Lynn* Seaports in Norfolk, England.

And that tremendous voice so long unheard
Released and filled and drew him, till he stirred
And left the house and passed the town, to reach
At last the dunes and rocks and open beach:
Pale, bare and gleaming in the break of day
A sweep of new-washed sand around the bay,
And spindrift driving up the bluffs like smoke,
As the long combers reared their crests and broke.
There in the sand beside him Friday saw
A single naked footprint on the shore.
His heart stood still, for as he stared, he knew
The foot that made it never had worn shoe
And, at a glance, that no such walker could
Have been a man of European blood.
From such a footprint once he could describe
If not the owner's name, at least his tribe,
And tell his purpose as men read a face
And still his skill sufficed to know the race;
For this was such a print as long ago
He too had made and taught his eyes to know.
There could be no mistake. Awhile he stood
Staring at that grey German Ocean's[1] flood;
And suddenly he saw those shores again
Where Orinoco[2] pours into the main,
And, stunned with an incredible surmise,
Heard in his native tongue once more the cries
Of spirits silent now for many a day;
And all his years of exile fell away.

The sun was nearly to the height before
Crusoe arrived hallooing at the shore,
Followed the footprints to the beach and found
The clothes and shoes and thought his servant drowned.
Much grieved he sought him up and down the bay
But never guessed, when later in the day
They found the body drifting in the foam,
That Friday had been rescued and gone home.

1959

---

[1] *German Ocean* An old name for the North Sea.

[2] *Orinoco* A river in South America that flows into the Atlantic Ocean, north of the Amazon River.

Nalo Hopkinson

Nalo Hopkinson (b. 1960) was born in Jamaica; her father was Slade Hopkinson, a Guyanese poet, playwright, and actor. She has lived in Toronto since 1977 and is one of a handful of postcolonial writers in the science fiction/fantasy genre. Her publications include *Brown Girl in the Ring* (1998), *Midnight Robber* (2000)—which was nominated for both the Hugo and Nebula awards—*Skin Folk* (2001), *The Salt Roads* (2003), and *The New Moon's Arms* (2007). She has edited *Whispers from the Cotton Tree Root: Caribbean Fabulist Fiction* (2000) and *So Long Been Dreaming* (2004).

Hopkinson's "A Habit of Waste," from *Skin Folk*, combines elements of science fiction and postcolonialism to produce a story that raises some important social and ethical issues about racial relationship. If it is possible to change one's body from black to white or white to black, should this be done? The black protagonist undergoes such a change and creates problems for her family and herself. Is her decision right, given that black people in futuristic Toronto have to struggle still with poverty, racism, and neglect? Hopkinson uses demotic Caribbean English to authenticate the lives of the immigrant residents in Toronto. Compare her use of such language with Louise Bennett's in "Anancy an Ticks" and Arthur Yap's in "2 Mothers in a HDB Playground."

A Habit of Waste

These are the latitudes of ex-colonised,
of degradation still unmollified,
imported managers, styles in art,
second-hand subsistence of the spirit,
the habit of waste,
mayhem committed on the personality,
and everywhere the wrecked or scuttled mind.
Scholars, more brilliant than I could hope to be,
advised that if I valued poetry,
I should eschew all sociology.
    Slade Hopkinson,
    "The Madwoman of Papine: Two Cartoons with Captions"

I was nodding off on the streetcar home from work when I saw the woman getting on. She was wearing the body I used to have! The shock woke me right up: It was my original, the body I had replaced two years before, same full, tarty-looking lips; same fat thighs, rubbing together with every step; same outsize ass; same narrow torso that seemed grafted onto a lower body a good three sizes bigger, as though God had glued left over parts together.

On my pay, I'd had to save for five years before I could afford the switch. When I ordered the catalogue from MediPerfiction, I pored over it for a month, drooling at the different options: Arrow-slim "Cindies" had long, long legs ("*supermodel qual-ity*"). "Indiras" came with creamy brown skin, falls of straight, dark hair, and curvaceous bodies ("exotic grace"). I finally chose one of the "Dianas," with their lithe muscles and small, firm breasts ("*boyish beauty*"). They downloaded me into her as soon as I could get the time off work. I was back on the job in four days, although my fine muscle control was still a little shaky.

And now, here was someone wearing my old castoff. She must have been in a bad accident: too bad for the body to be salvaged. If she couldn't afford cloning, the doctors would have just downloaded her brain into any donated discard. Mine, for instance. Poor thing, I thought. I wonder how she's handling that chafing problem. It used to drive me mad in the summer.

I watched her put her ticket in the box. The driver gave her a melting smile. What did he see to grin at?

I studied my former body carefully as it made its way down the centre of the streetcar. I hated what she'd done to the hair—let it go natural, for Christ's sake—sectioned it off, and coiled black thread tightly around each section, with a puff of hair on the end of every stalk. Man, I hated that back-to-Africa nostalgia shit. She looked like a Doctor Seuss character. There's no excuse for that nappy-headed nonsense. She had a lot of nerve, too, wrapping that behind in a flower-print sarong miniskirt. Sort of like making your ass into a billboard. When it was my body, I always covered its butt in long skirts or loose pants. Her skirt was so short that I could see the edges of the bike shorts peeking out below it. Well, it's one way to deal with the chafing.

Strange, though; on her, the little peek of black shorts looked stylish and sexy all at once. Far from looking graceless, her high, round bottom twitched confidently with each step, giving her a proud sexiness that I had never had. Her upper body was sheathed in a white sleeveless T-shirt. White! Such a plain colour. To tell the truth, though, the clingy material emphasized her tiny waist, and the white looked really good against her dark skin. Had my old skin always had that glow to it? Such firm, strong arms...

All the seats on the streetcar were taken. Good. Let the bitch stand. I hoped my fallen arches were giving her hell.

Home at last, I stripped off and headed straight for the mirror. The boyish body was still slim, thighs still thin, tiny-perfect apple breasts still perky. I presented my behind to the mirror. A little flabby, perhaps? I wasn't sure. I turned around again, got up close to the mirror so that I could inspect my face. Did my skin have that glow that my old body's had? And weren't those the beginning of crow's-feet around my eyes? Shit. White people aged so quickly. I spent the evening sprawled on the sofa, watching reruns and eating pork and beans straight from the can.

That Friday afternoon at work, Old Man Morris came in for the usual. I stacked his order on the counter between us and keyed the contents into the computer. It bleeped at me: "This selection does not meet the customer's dietary requirements."

As if I didn't know that, I tried to talk him into beefing up the carbs and beta-carotene. "All right, then," I said heartily, "what else will you have today? Some of that creamed corn? We just got a big batch of tins in. I bet you'd like some of that, eh?" I always sounded so artificial, but I couldn't help it. The food bank customers made me uncomfortable. Eleanor didn't react that way, though. She was so at ease in the job, cheerful, dispensing cans of tuna with an easy goodwill. She always chattered away to the clients, knew them all by name.

"No thanks, dear," Mr. Morris replied with his polite smile. "I never could stomach the tinned vegetables. When I can, I eat them fresh, you know?"

"Yeah, Cynthia," Eleanor teased, "you know that Mr. Morris hates canned veggies. Too much like baby food, eh, Mr. Morris?"

Always the same cute banter between those two. He'd flattened out his Caribbean accent for the benefit of us two white girls. I couldn't place which island he was from. I sighed and overrode the computer's objections. Eleanor and Old Man Morris grinned at each other while I packed up his weekend ration. Fresh, right. When could a poor old man ever afford the fresh stuff? I couldn't imagine what his diet was like. He always asked us for the same things: soup mix, powdered milk, and cans of beans. We tried to give him his nutritional quota, but he politely refused offers of creamed corn or canned tuna. I was sure he was always constipated. His problem, though.

I bet my parents could tell me where in the Caribbean he was from. Give them any inkling that someone's from "back home," and they'd be on him like a dirty shirt, badgering him with questions: *Which island you from? How long you been here in Canada? You have family here? When last you go back home?*

Old Man Morris signed for his order and left. One of the volunteers would deliver it later that evening. I watched him walk away. He looked to be in his sixties, but he was probably younger; hard life wears a person down. Tallish, with a brown, wrinkled face and tightly curled salt-and-pepper hair, he had a strong, upright walk for someone in his circumstances. Even in summer, I had never seen him without that old tweed jacket, its pockets stuffed to bursting with God knew what type of scavenge; half-smoked cigarette butts that people had dropped on the street, I supposed, and pop cans he would return for the deposit money. At least he seemed clean.

I went down to shipping to check on a big donation of food we'd received from a nearby supermarket. Someone was sure to have made a mistake sorting the cans. Someone always did.

My parents had been beside themselves when they found out I'd switched bodies. I guess it wasn't very diplomatic of me, showing up without warning on their suburban doorstep, this white woman with her flippy blond hair, claiming to be their daughter. I'd made sure my new body would have the same vocal range as the old one, so when Mom and Dad heard my voice coming out of a stranger's body, they flipped. Didn't even want to let me in the door, at first. Made me pass my new i.d. and the doctor's certificate through the letter slot.

"Mom, give me a break," I yelled. "I told you last year that I was thinking about doing this!"

"But Cyn-Cyn, that ain't even look like you!" My mother's voice was close to a shriek. Her next words were for my dad:

"What the child want to go and do this kind of stupidness for? Nothing ain't wrong with the way she look!"

A giggled response from my father, "True, she behind had a way to remain in a room long after she leave, but she get that from you, sweetheart, and you know how much I love that behind!"

He'd aimed that dig for my ears, I just knew it. I'd had enough. "So, are the two of you going to let me in, or what?" I hated it when they carried on the way they were doing. All that drama. And I really wished they'd drop the Banana Boat accents. They'd come to Canada five years before I was even born, for Christ's sake, and I was now twenty-eight.

They did finally open the door, and after that they just had to get used to the new me.

I wondered if I should start saving for another switch. It's really a rich people's thing. I couldn't afford to keep doing it every few years, like some kind of vid queen. Shit.

"What's griping you?" Eleanor asked after I'd chewed out one of the volunteers for some little mistake. "You've been cranky for days now."

Damn. "Sorry. I know I've been bitchy. I've been really down, you know? No real reason. I just don't feel like myself."

"Yeah. Well." Eleanor was used to my moodiness. "I guess it *is* Thanksgiving weekend. People always get a little edgy around the holidays. Maybe you need a change. Tell you what; why don't you deliver Old Man Morris's ration, make sure he's okay for the weekend?"

"Morris? You want me to go to where he lives?" I couldn't imagine anything less appealing. "Where is that, anyway? In a park or something?"

Eleanor frowned at that. "So, even if he does, so what? You need to get over yourself, girl."

I didn't say anything, just thought my peevishness at her. She strode over to the terminal at her desk, punched in Mr. Morris's name, handed me the printout. "Just go over to this address, and take him his ration. Chat with him a little bit. This might be a lonely weekend for him. And keep the car till Tuesday. We won't be needing it."

Mr. Morris lived on the creepy side of Sherbourne. I had to slow the car down to dodge the first wave of drunken suits lurching out of the strip club, on their boozy way home after the usual Friday afternoon three-hour liquid lunch. I stared at the storey-high poster that covered one outside wall of the strip club. I hoped to God they'd used a fisheye lens to make that babe's boobs look like that. Those couldn't be natural.

Shit. Shouldn't have slowed down. One of the prostitutes on the corner began to twitch her way over to the car, bending low so she could see inside, giving me a flash of her tits into the bargain: "Hey, darlin', you wanna go out? I can swing lezzie." I floored it out of there.

Searching for the street helped to keep my mind off some of the more theatrical sights of Cabbagetown West[1] on a Friday evening. I didn't know that the police could conduct a full strip search over the hood of a car, right out in the open.

The next street was Old Man Morris's. Tenement row houses slumped along one side of the short street, marked by sagging roofs and knocked-out steps. There were rotting piles of garbage in front of many of the houses. I thought I could hear the flies buzzing from where I was. The smell was like clotted carrion. A few people hung out on dilapidated porches, just staring. Two guys hunched into denim jackets stopped talking as I drove by. A dirty, greasy-haired kid was riding a bicycle up and down the sidewalk, dodging the garbage. The bike was too small for him and it had no seat. He stood on the pedals and pumped them furiously.

Mr. Morris lived in an ancient apartment building on the other side of the street. I had to double-park in front. I hauled the dolly out of the trunk and loaded Mr. Morris's boxes onto it. I activated the car's screamer alarm and headed into the building, praying that no weirdness would go down on the street before I could make it inside.

Thank God, he answered the buzzer right away. "Mr. Morris? It's Cynthia; from the food bank?"

The party going on in the lobby was only a few gropes away from becoming an orgy. The threesome writhing and sighing on the couch ignored me. Two men, one woman. I stepped over a pungent yellow liquid that was beetling its way down one leg of the bench, creeping through the cracks in the tile floor. I hoped it was just booze. I took the elevator up to the sixth floor.

The dingy, musty corridor walls were dark grey, peeling in places to reveal a bilious pink underneath. It was probably a blessing that there was so much dirt ground into the balding carpet. What I could glimpse of the original design made me queasy. Someone was frying Spam for dinner ("canned horse's cock," my dad called it). I found Mr. Morris's door and knocked. Inside, I could hear the sound of locks turning, and the curt "quack" of an alarm being deactivated. Mr. Morris opened the door to let me in.

"Come in quick, child," he said, wiping his hands on a kitchen towel. "I can't let the pot boil over. Don't Jake does deliver my goods?" He bustled back into a room I guessed was the kitchen. I wheeled the dolly inside. "Eleanor sent Jake home early today, Mr. Morris. Holiday treat."

He chuckled. "That young lady is so thoughtful, oui? It ain't have plenty people like she anymore."

I took a quick glance around the little apartment. It was dark in there. The only light was from the kitchen, and from four candles stuck in pop bottles on the living room windowsill. The living room held one small, rump-sprung couch, two aluminum chairs, and a tiny card table. The gaudy flower-print cloth that barely covered the table was faded from years of being ironed. I was surprised; the place was spotless, if a little shabby. I perched on the edge of the love seat.

---

[1] *Cabbagetown* A district in downtown Toronto (*Cabbagetown West* is fictional).

His head poked round the corner. "Yes," he said, "that's right. Siddown on the settee and rest yourself."

Settee. Oui. In his own home, he spoke in a more natural accent. "You from Trinidad, Mr. Morris?"

His face crinkled into an astonished grin. "Yes, doux-doux. How you know that?"

"That's where my parents are from. They talk just like you."

"You is from Trinidad?" he asked delightedly. "Is true Trini people come in all colours, but with that accent, I really take you for a Canadian, born and bred."

I hated explaining this, but I guess I'd asked for it, letting him know something about my life. "I was born here, but my parents are black. And so was I, but I've had a body switch."

A bemused expression came over his face. He stepped into the living room to take a closer look at me. "For true? I hear about people doin' this thing, but I don't think I ever meet anybody who make the switch. You mean to tell me, you change from a black woman body into this one? Lord, the things you young people does do for fashion, eh?"

I stood up and plastered a smile on my face. "Well, you've got your weekend ration, Mr. Morris; just wanted to be sure you wouldn't go hungry on Thanksgiving, okay?"

He looked pensively at the freeze-dried turkey dinner and the cans of creamed corn (I'd made sure to put them in his ration this time). "Thanks, doux-doux. True I ain't go be hungry, but…"

"But what, Mr. Morris?"

"Well, I don't like to eat alone. My wife pass away ten years now, but you know, I does still miss she some times. You goin' by you mummy and daddy for Thanksgiving?"

The question caught me off guard. "Yes, I'm going to see them on Sunday."

"But you not doing anything tonight?"

"Uh, well, a movie, maybe, something like that."

He gave me a sweet, wheedling smile. "You want to have a early Thanksgiving with a ol' man from back home?"

"*I'm not from 'back home*,'" I almost said. The hope on his face was more than I could stand. "Well, I …"

"I making a nice, nice dinner," he pleaded.

Eleanor would stay and keep the old man company for a few minutes, if it were her. I sat back down.

Mr. Morris's grin was incandescent. "You going to stay? All right, doux-doux. Dinner almost finish, you hear? Just pile up the ration out of the way for me." He bustled back into the kitchen. I could hear humming, pots and pans clattering, water running.

I packed the food up against one wall, a running argument playing in my head the whole time. Why was I doing this? I'd driven our pathetic excuse for a company car through the most dangerous part of town, just begging for a baseball bat through the window, and all to have dinner with an old bum. What would he serve anyway? Peanut butter and crackers? I knew the shit that man ate—I'd given it to him myself, every Friday at the food bank! And what if he pulled some kind of sleazy, toothless come-on? The police would say I asked for it!

A wonderful smell began to waft from the kitchen. Some kind of roasting meat, with spices. Whatever Mr. Morris was cooking, he couldn't have done it on food bank rations.

"You need a hand, Mr. Morris?"

"Not in here, darling. I nearly ready. Just sit yourself down at the table, and I go bring dinner out. I was going to freeze all the extra, but now I have a guest to share it with."

When he brought out the main course, arms straining under the weight of the platter, my mouth fell open. And it was just the beginning. He loaded the table with plate after plate of food: roasted chicken with a giblet stuffing, rich, creamy gravy, tossed salad with exotic greens; huge mounds of mashed potatoes, some kind of fruit preserve. He refused to answer my questions. "I go tell you all about it after, doux-doux. Now is time to eat."

It certainly was. I was so busy trying to figure out if he could have turned food bank rations into this feast, that I forgot all about calories and daily allowable grams of fat; I just ate. After the meal, though, my curiosity kicked in again.

"So, Mr. Morris, tell me the truth; you snowing the food bank? Making some money on the side?" I grinned at him. He wouldn't be the first one to run a scam like that, working for cash so that he could still claim welfare.

"No, doux-doux." He gave me a mischievous smile. "I see how it look that way to you, but this meal cost me next to nothing. You just have to know where to, um, *procure* your food, that is all. You see this fancy salad?" He pointed to a few frilly purple leaves that were all that remained of the salad. "You know what that is?"

"Yeah. Flowering kale. Rich people's cabbage."

Mr. Morris laughed. "Yes, but I bet you see it some where else, besides the grocery store."

I frowned, trying to think what he meant. He went on: "You know the Dominion Bank? The big one at Bathurst and Queen?" I nodded, still mystified. His smile got even broader. "You ever look at the plants they use to decorate the front?"

I almost spat the salad out. "Ornamental cabbage? We're eating ornamental cabbage that you stole from the front of a building?"

His rich laugh filled the tiny room. "Not 'ornamental cabbage,' darlin': 'flowering kale.' And I figure, I ain't really stealin' it; I recyclin' it! They does pull it all up and throw it away when the weather turn cold. All that food. It does taste nice on a Sunday morning, fry-up with a piece of saltfish and some small-leaf thyme. I does grow the herbs-them on the windowsill, in the sun."

Salted cod and cabbage. Flavoured with French thyme and hot pepper. My mother made that on Sunday mornings too, with big fried flour dumplings on the side and huge mugs of cocoa. Not the cocoa powder from the tin, either; she bought the raw chocolate in chestnut-sized lumps from the Jamaican store, and grated it into boiling water, with vanilla, cinnamon, and condensed milk. Sitting in Mr. Morris's living room, even with the remains of dinner on the table, I could almost smell that pure chocolate aroma. Full of fat, too. I didn't let my mom serve it to me anymore when I visited. I'd spent too much money on my tight little butt.

Still, I didn't believe what Old Man Morris was telling me. "So, you mean to say that you just…take stuff? From off the street?"

"Yes."

"What about the chicken?"

He laughed. "Chicken? Doux-doux, you ever see chicken with four drumstick? That is a wild rabbit I catch meself and bring home."

"Are you *crazy*? Do you know what's in wild food? What kind of diseases it might carry? Why didn't you tell me what we were eating?" But he was so pleased with himself, he didn't seem to notice how upset I was.

"Nah, nah, don't worry 'bout diseases, darlin'! I been eatin' like this for five-six years now, and I healthy like hog. De doctor say he never see a seventy-four-year-old man in such good shape."

He's seventy-four! He does look pretty damned good for such an old man. I'm still not convinced, though: "Mr. Morris, this is nuts; you can't just go around helping yourself to leaves off the trees, and people's ornamental plants, and killing things and eating them! Besides, um, how do you catch a wild rabbit, anyway?"

"Well, that is the sweet part." He jumped up from his chair, started rummaging around in the pockets of his old tweed jacket that was hanging in the hallway. He came back to the table, clutching a fistful of small rocks and brandishing a thick, Y-shaped twig with a loose rubber strap attached. So that's what he kept in those pockets — whatever it was.

"This is a slingshot. When I was a small boy back home, I was aces with one of these!" He stretched the rubber strap tight with one hand, aimed the slingshot at one of his potted plants, and pretended to let off a shot. "*Plai*! Like so. Me and the boys-them used to practice shooting at all kind of ol' tin can and thing, but I was the best. One time, I catch a coral snake in me mother kitchen, and I send one boulderstone straight through it eye with me first shot!" He chuckled. "The stone break the window, too, but me mother was only too glad that I kill the poison snake. Well, doux-doux, I does take me slingshot down into the ravine, and sometimes I get lucky and catch something."

I was horrified. "You mean, you used that thing to kill a rabbit? And we just ate it?"

Mr. Morris's face finally got serious. He sat back down at the table. "You mus' understan', Cynthia; I is a poor man. Me and my Rita, we work hard when we come to this country, and we manage to buy this little apartment, but when the last depression hit we, I get lay off at the car plant. After that, I couldn't find no work again; I was already past fifty years old, nobody would hire me. We get by on Rita nurse work until she retire and then hard times catch we ass. My Rita was a wonderful woman, girl; she could take a half pound of mince beef and two potatoes and make a meal that have you feelin' like you never taste food before. She used to tell me, 'Never mind, Johnny; so long as I have a little meat to put in this cook pot, we not goin' to starve.'

"Then them find out that Rita have cancer. She only live a few months after that, getting weaker till she waste away and gone. Lord, child, I thought my heart woulda break. I did wish to dead too. That first year after Rita pass away, I couldn't tell you how I get by; I don't even remember all of it. I let the place get dirty, dirty, and I was eatin' any ol' kaka from the corner store, not even self goin' to the grocery. When I get the letter from the government, telling me that them cuttin' off Rita pension, I didn't know what to do. My one little pension wasn't goin' to support me. I put on me coat, and went outside, headin' for the train tracks to throw myself down, oui? Is must be God did make me walk through the park."

"What happened?"

"I see a ol' woman sittin' on a bench, wearing a tear up coat and two different one-side boots. She was feedin' stale bread to the pigeons, and smiling at them. That ol' lady with she rip-up clothes could still find something to make she happy.

"I went back home, and things start to look up a little bit from then. But pride nearly make me starve before I find meself inside the food bank to beg some bread."

"It's not begging, Mr. Morris," I interrupted.

"I know, doux-doux, but in my place, I sure you woulda feel the same way. And too besides, even though I was eatin' steady from the food bank, I wasn't eatin' good, you know? You can't live all you days on tuna fish and tin peas!"

I thought of all the tins of tuna I'd just brought him. I felt myself blushing. Two years in this body, and I still wasn't used to how easily blushes showed on its pale cheeks. "So, what gave you the idea to start foraging like this?"

"I was eatin' lunch one day, cheese spread and crackers and pop. One paipsy,[1] tasteless lunch, you see? And I start thinkin' about how I never woulda go hungry back home as a small boy, how even if I wasn't home to eat me mother food, it always had some kinda fruit tree or something round the place. I start to remember Julie mango, how it sweet, and chataigne and peewah[2] that me mother would boil up in a big pot a' salt water, and how my father always had he little kitchen garden, growin' dasheen leaf and pigeon peas and yam and thing. And I say to meself, 'But eh-eh, Johnny, ain't this country have plants and trees and fruit and thing too? The squirrels-them always looking fat and happy; they mus' be eatin' something. And the Indian people-them-self too; they must be did eat something else besides corn before the white people come and take over the place!'

"That same day, I find my ass in the library, and I tell them I want to find out about plants that you could eat. Them sit me down with all kinda book and computer, and I come to find out it have plenty to eat, right here in this city, growing

---

[1] *paipsy* Insipid, pale, or weak (Caribbean).

[2] *chataigne* The seed of the breadnut fruit, closely resembling a chestnut in appearance and taste; *peewah* A small round fruit roasted or boiled for eating.

wild by the roadside. Some of these books even had recipes in them, doux-doux!

"So I drag out all of Rita frying pan and cook spoon from the kitchen cupboard, and I teach meself to feed meself, yes!" He chuckled again. "Now I does eat fresh mulberries in the summer. I does dig up chicory root to take the bitterness from my coffee, I even make rowan berry jam. All these things all around we for free, and people still starving, oui? You have to learn to make use of what you have.

"But I still think the slingshot was a master stroke, though. Nobody ain't expect a ol' black man to be hunting with a slingshot down in the ravine!"

I was still chuckling as I left Mr. Morris's building later that evening. He'd loaded me down with a container full of stuffed rabbit and a bottle of crabapple preserves. I deactivated the screamer alarm on the car, and I was just about to open the door when I felt a hand sliding down the back of my thigh.

"Yesss, stay just like that, Ain't that pretty? We'll get to that later. Where's your money, sweetheart? In this purse here?" The press of a smelly body pinned me over the hood. I tried to turn my head, to scream, but he clamped a filthy hand across my face. I couldn't breathe. The bottle of preserves crashed to the ground. Broken glass sprayed my calf.

"Shit! What'd you do that for? Stupid bitch!"

His hand tightened over my face. I couldn't *breathe*! In fury and terror, I bit down hard, felt my teeth meet in the flesh of his palm. He swore, yanked his hand away, slammed a hard fist against my ear. Things started to go black, and I almost fell. I hung on to the car door, dragged myself to my feet, scrambled out of his reach. I didn't dare turn away to run. I backed away, screaming, "Get away from me! Get away!" He kept coming, and he was big and muscular, and angry. Suddenly, he jerked, yelled, slapped one hand to his shoulder. "What the fuck...?" I could see wetness seeping through the shoulder of his grimy sweatshirt. Blood? He yelled again, clapped a hand to his knee. This time, I had seen the missile whiz through the air to strike him. Yes! I crouched down to give Mr. Morris a clear shot. My teeth were bared in a fighter's grin. The mugger was still limping towards me, howling with rage. The next stone glanced by his head, leaving a deep gash on his temple. Behind him, I heard the sound of breaking glass as the stone crashed through the car window. He'd had enough. He ran, holding his injured leg.

Standing in the middle of the street, I looked up to Mr. Morris's sixth-floor window. He was on the balcony, waving frantically at me. In the dark, I could just see the Y of the slingshot in his hand. He shouted, "Go and stand in the entranceway, girl! I comin' down!" He disappeared inside, and I headed back towards the building. By the time I got there, I was weak-kneed and shaky; reaction was setting in, and my head was spinning from the blow I'd taken. I didn't think I'd ever get the taste of that man's flesh out of my mouth. I leaned against the inside door, waiting for Mr. Morris. It wasn't long before he came bustling out of the elevator, let me inside, and sat me down on the couch in the lobby, fussing the whole time.

"Jesus Christ, child! Is a good thing I decide to watch from the balcony to make sure you reach the car safe! Lawd, look at what happen to you, eh? Just because you had the kindness to spen' a little time with a ol' man like me! I sorry, girl; I sorry can't done!"

"It's okay, Mr. Morris; it's not your fault. I'm all right. I'm just glad that you were watching." I was getting a little hysterical. "I come to rescue you with my food bank freeze-dried turkey dinner, and you end up rescuing me instead! I have to ask you, though, Mr. Morris; how come every time you rescue a lady, you end up breaking her windows?"

That Sunday, I drove over to my parents' place for Thanksgiving dinner. I was wearing a beret, cocked at a chic angle over the cauliflower ear that the mugger had given me. No sense panicking my mom and dad. I had gone to the emergency hospital on Friday night, and they'd disinfected and bandaged me. I was all right; in fact, I was so happy that two days later, I still felt giddy. So nice to know that there wouldn't be photos of my dead body on the covers of the tabloids that week.

As I pulled up in the car, I could see my parents through the living room window, sitting and watching television. I went inside.

"Mom! Dad! Happy Thanksgiving!" I gave my mother a kiss, smiled at my dad.

"Cynthia, child," he said, "I glad you reach; I could start making the gravy now."

"Marvin, don't be so stupidee," my mother scolded. "You know she won't eat no gravy; she mindin' she figure!"

"It's okay, Mom; it's Thanksgiving, and I'm going to eat everything you put on my plate. If I get too fat, I'm just going to have to start walking to work. You've got to work with what you've got, after all." She looked surprised, but didn't say anything.

I poked around in the kitchen, like I always did. Dad stood at the stove, stirring the gravy. There was another saucepan on the stove, with the remains of that morning's cocoa in it. It smelt wonderful. I reached around my father to turn on the burner under the cocoa. He frowned at me.

"Is cocoa-tea, Cyn-Cyn. You don't drink that no more."

"I just want to finish what's left in the pot, Dad. I mean, you don't want it to go to waste, do you?"

2001

Keri Hulme

Keri Hulme (b. 1947) was born in New Zealand and lives in Okarito on the west coast. She is of Maori (Kai Tahu) and Pakeha (European) ancestry. She has written poetry and fiction. Her publications include a novella, *Lost Possessions* (1985), two short-story collections, *The Windeater/ Te Kaihau* (1982) and *Stonefish* (2004), and a poetry volume, *Strands* (1991). Her novel *The Bone People* (1984) won the Pegasus Prize for Maori literature and the 1985 Booker Prize.

Hulme's "Hooks and Feelers," which won the 1975 Katherine Mansfield Memorial Award, has been criticized along with her other pieces of fiction for not privileging the Maori language, and this is because Hulme provided glossaries for Maori words in her texts, which was seen as relegating the language to a second-class status. Her critics argue that New Zealand made Maori an official language in 1987 (Maori Language Act). She has responded that the Act does not remove its second-class status in practice and that non-Maori readers require glossaries. Critics also accuse her of having an ambivalent attitude toward violence. Do you think this criticism is valid? Dialogue and dramatic scenes generally convey external conflicts effectively but they can also evoke inner complexity. Do you think that Hulme's narrative form conveys the psychological complexity of her Maori characters?

Hooks and Feelers

On the morning before it happened, her fingers were covered with grey, soft clay.

"Charleston,"[1] she says. "It comes from Charleston. It's really a modeller's clay, but it'll make nice cups. I envisage," gesturing in the air, "tall fluted goblets. I'll glaze them sea blue and we'll drink wine together, all of us."

I went out to the shed and knocked on the door. There's no word of welcome, but the kerosene lamp is burning brightly, so I push on in.

She's pumping the treadle potter's wheel with a terrible urgency, but she's not making pots. Just tall, wavery cones. I don't know what they are. I've never seen her make them before. The floor, the shelves, the bench — the place is spikey with them.

"They've rung," I say.

She doesn't look up.

"They said he'll be home tomorrow."

The wheel slowed, stopped.

"So?"

"Well, will you get him?"

"No."

---

[1] *Charleston* Charleston (South Island, New Zealand) is renowned for its deposits of clay and coal; the clay is superb for ceramics and pottery.

The wheel starts purring. Another cone begins to grow under her fingers.

"What are you making those for?"

She still won't look at me.

"You go," she says, and the wheel begins to hum.

Well, you can't win.

I go and get him and come home, chattering brightly all the way.

He is silent.

I carry him inside, pointing out that I've repainted everywhere, that we've got a new stove and did you like your present? And he ignores it all.

But he says, very quietly, to his ma, "Hello." Very cool.

She looks at him, over him, round him, eyes going up and down but always avoiding the one place where she should be looking. She says "Hello," back.

"Put me down please," he says to me then.

No "Thanks for getting me." Not a word of appreciation for the new clothes. Just that polite, expressionless, "Put me down please."

Not another word.

He went into his bedroom and shut the door.

"Well, it's just the shock of being back home, eh?"

I look at her, and she looks at me. I go across and slide my hands around her shoulders, draw her close to me, nuzzle her ear, and for a moment it's peace.

Then she draws away.

"Make a coffee," she says brusquely. "I'm tired."

I don't take offence. After grinding the beans, I ask, "What are you making the cones for?"

She shrugs.

"It's just an idea."

The smell from the crushed coffee beans is rich and heavy, almost sickening.

His door opens.

He has his doll in his hand. Or rather, parts of his doll. He's torn the head off, the arms and legs apart.

"I don't want this anymore," he says into the silence.

He goes to the fire, and flings the parts in. And then he reaches in among the burning coals and plucks out the head, which is melted and smoking. He says, "On second thoughts, I'll keep this."

The smoke curls round the steel and lingers, acridly.

Soon after, she went back to the shed.

I went down to the pub.

"Hey!" yells Mata, "c'mon over here!"

"Look at that," he says, grinning hugely, waving a crumpled bit of paper. It's a Golden Kiwi ticket. "Bugger's won me four hundred dollars." He sways. "Whatta yer drinking?"

I never have won anything. I reach across, grab his hand, shake it. It's warm and calloused, hard and real.

"Bloody oath, Mat, what good luck!"

He smiles more widely still, his eyes crinkling almost shut. "Shout you eh?"

"Too right you can. Double whisky."

And I get that from him and a jug and another couple of doubles and another jug. I am warm and happy until someone turns the radio up.

"Hands across the water, hands across the sea …" the voices thunder and beat by my ears, and pianos and violins wail and wind round the words.

The shed's in darkness.

I push the door open, gingerly.

"Are you there?"

I hear her move.

"Yes."

"How about a little light on the subject?" I'm trying to sound happily drunk, but the words have a nasty callous ring to them.

"The lamp is on the bench beside you."

I reach for it and encounter a soft, still wet, cone of clay. I snatch my fingers away hurriedly.

"Are you revealing to the world what the cones are for yet?"

I've found the lamp, fumble for my matches. My fingers are clumsy, but at last the wick catches a light, glows and grows.

She sniffs.

"Give me the matches please."

I throw the box across and she snatches them from the air.

She touches a match to a cigarette; the match shows blue and then flares bright, steady, gold. The cigarette pulses redly. The lamp isn't trimmed very well.

She sighs and the smoke flows thickly out of her month and nose.

"I put nearly all of them back in the stodge-box today."

What? Oh yes, the cones. The stodge-box is her special term for the pile of clay that gets reworked.

"Oh." I add after a moment, apologetically, "I sort of squashed one reaching for the lamp."

"It doesn't matter," she says, blowing out another stream of smoke.

"I was going to kill that one too."

I take my battered, old, guitar and begin to play. I play badly. I've never learned to play properly.

He says, out of the dark, "Why are you sad?"

"What makes you think I am?"

"Because you're playing without the lights on."

I sigh. "A man can play in the dark if he wants."

"Besides I heard you crying."

My dear cool son.

"... so I cry sometimes ..."

"Why are you sad?" he asks again.

Everlasting questions ever since he began to talk.

"Shut up."

"Because of me?" he persists. He pauses, long enough to check whether I'm going to move.

"Or because of her?"

"Because of me, now get out of here," I answer roughly, and bang the guitar down. It groans. The strings shiver.

He doesn't move.

"You've been to the pub?"

I prop the guitar against the wall and get up.

"You've been to the pub," he states, and drifts back into his room.

My mother came to visit the next day, all agog to see the wreckage. She has a nice instinct for disasters. She used to be a strong little woman but she's run to frailty and brittle bones now. Alas; all small and powdery, with a thick fine down over her face that manages, somehow, to protrude through her make-up. It'd look so much better if she didn't pile powder and stuff on, but I can't imagine her face without pink gunk clogging the pores. That much has never changed.

She brought a bag of blackballs for him. When he accepts them, reluctantly, she coos and pats him and strokes his hair. He has always hated that.

"Oh dear," she says, "your poor careless mother," and "You poor little man" and (aside to me) "It's just as well you didn't have a daughter, it'd be so much worse for a girl." (He heard that, and smiled blandly.)

She asks him, "However are you going to manage now? Your guitar and football and all? Hmmm?"

He says, steadily, "It's very awkward to wipe my arse now. That's all."

For a moment I like him very much.

My mother flutters and tchs, "Oh, goodness me, dear, you mustn't say ..."

He's already turned away.

As soon as my mother left, I went out to the shed.

"You could have come in and said hello," I say reproachfully.

"It would have only led to a fight." She sits hunched up on the floor. Her face is in shadow.

I look round. The shed's been tidied up. All the stray bits and pieces are hidden away. There's an innovation, however, an ominous one. The crucifix she keeps on the wall opposite her wheel has been covered with black cloth. The only part that shows is a hand, nailed to the wooden cross.

"Is that a reminder for penitence? Or are you mourning?"
She doesn't reply.

Early in the morning, while it's still quite dark, I awake to hear him sobbing. I lift the bedclothes gently—she didn't stir, drowned in sleep, her black hair wreathed about her body like seaweed—and creep away to his room.

The sobbing is part stifled, a rhythmic choking and gasping, rough with misery.
"Hello?"
"E pa ..." he turns over and round from his pillow and reaches out his arms. He doesn't do that. He hasn't done that since he was a baby.
I pick him up, cradling him, cuddling him.
"I can still feel it pa. I can feel it still." He is desperate in his insistence and wild with crying. But he is also coldly angry at himself.
"I know it's not there anymore," he struck himself a blow, "but I can *feel* it still...."
I kiss and soothe and bring a tranquilliser that the people at the hospital gave me. He sobs himself back to sleep, leaning, in the end, away from me. And I go back to bed.

Her ocean, her ocean, te moananui a Kiwa,[1] drowns me. Far away on the beach I can hear him calling, but I must keep on going down into the greeny deeps, down to where her face is, to where the soft anemone tentacles of her fingers beckon and sway and sweep me onward to the weeping heart of the world.

He stays home from school for another week. It's probably just as well, for once, the first time he ventured outside the house, the next door neighbour's kids shouted crudities at him.

I watched him walk over to them, talk, and gesture, the hook flashing bravely in the sun. The next door neighbour's kids fell silent, drew together in a scared huddled group.
"What did you do to stop that?" I ask, after he has stalked proudly back inside.
He shook his head.
"Tell me."
"I didn't have to do anything." He smiles.
"Oh?"
"I don't imagine," he says it so coolly, "that anyone wants this in their eyes."
The hair on the back of my neck bristles with shock.
"Don't you dare threaten anybody like that! No matter what they say!" I shout at him in rage, in horror. "I'll beat you silly if you do that again."
He shrugs. "Okay, if you say so pa."
(Imagine that cruel, steel curve reaching for your eyes. That pincer of unfeeling metal gouging in.) The steel hook glints as he moves away.

---

[1] *te moananui a Kiwa* The Great Ocean of Kiwa or, as the Portuguese explorer Ferdinand Magellan named it in 1520, the Pacific Ocean.

How can he be my son and have so little of me in him? Oh, he has my colouring, fair hair and steel-grey eyes, just as he has her colour and bone structure; a brown thick-set chunk of a boy.

But his strange cold nature comes from neither of us. Well, it certainly doesn't come from me.

Later on that day—we are reading in front of the fire—a coal falls out. He reaches for it.

"Careful, it's hot," I warn.

"I don't care how hot it is," he says, grinning.

The two steel fingers pick up the piece of coal and slowly crush the fire out of it.

It hasn't taken long for him to get very deft with those pincers. He can pluck up minute things, like pins, or the smallest of buttons. I suspect he practises doing so, in the secrecy of his bedroom. He can handle almost anything as skilfully as he could before.

At night, after he's had a shower, I ask, "Let me look?"

"No."

"Ahh, come on."

He holds it out, silently.

All his wrist bones are gone. There remains a scarred purplish area with two smooth, rounded knobs on either side. In the centre is a small socket. The hook, which is mounted on a kind of swivel, slots into there. I don't understand how it works, but it looks like a nice practical piece of machinery.

He is looking away.

"You don't like it?"

"It's all right... will you string my guitar backwards? I tried, and I can't do it."

"Of course."

I fetch his guitar and begin immediately.

"There is something quite new we can do, you know." The specialist draws a deep breath of smoke and doesn't exhale any of it.

The smell of antiseptic is making me feel sick. This room is painted a dull grey. There are flyspots on the light. I bring my eyes down to him and smile, rigidly.

"Ahh, yes?"

"Immediately after amputation, we can attach an undamaged portion of sinew and nerve to this nyloprene socket."

He holds out a gadget, spins it round between his lean fingers, and snatches it away again, out of sight.

"It is a permanent implant, with a special prosthesis that fits into it, but the child will retain a good deal of control over his, umm, hand movements."

He sucks in more smoke and eyes me beadily, eagerly. Then he suddenly lets the whole, stale lungful go, right in my face.

"So you agree to that then?"

"Ahh, yes."

Later, at night, she says, "Are you still awake too?"

"Yes."

"What are you thinking of?"

"Nothing really. I was just listening to you breathe." Her hand creeps to my side, feeling along until it finds a warm handful.

"I am thinking of the door," she says thoughtfully.

You know the way a car door crunches shut, with a sort of definite, echoing thunk?

Well, there was that. Her hurried footsteps. A split second of complete silence. And then the screaming started, piercing, agonized, desperate. We spun round. He was nailed, pinioned against the side of the car by his trapped hand.

She stood, going, "O my god! O my god!" and biting down on her hand. She didn't make another move, frozen where she stood, getting whiter and whiter and whiter.

I had to open the door.

"I know it's silly," she continues, still holding me warmly, "but if we hadn't bought that packet of peanuts, we wouldn't have spilled them. I wouldn't have got angry. I wouldn't have stormed out of the car. I wouldn't have slammed the door without looking. Without looking."

"You bought the nuts, remember?" she adds irrelevantly.

I don't answer.

There are other things in her ocean now. Massive black shadows that loom up near me without revealing what they are. Something glints. The shadows waver and retreat.

They stuck a needle attached to a clear, plastic tube into his arm. The tube filled with blood. Then, the blood cleared away and the dope ran into his vein. His eyelids dragged down. He slept, unwillingly, the tears of horror and anguish still wet on his face.

The ruined hand lay on a white, shiny bench, already apart from him. It was like a lump of raw, swollen meat with small, shattered, bluish bones through it.

"We'll have to amputate that, I'm afraid. It's absolutely unsalvageable."

"Okay," I say. "Whatever you think best."

They say that hearing is the last of the senses to die, when you are unconscious. They are wrong, at least for me. Images, or what is worse, not-quite images, flare and burst and fade before I sink into the dreamless sea of sleep.

I went out to the shed.

"Tea is nearly ready," I call through the open door.

"Good," she replies. "Come in and look."

She has made a hundred, more than a hundred, large shallow wine cups. "Kraters," she says, smiling to me briefly.

I grin back, delighted.

"Well, they should sell well."

She bends her head, scraping at a patch of dried clay on the bench.

"What were the cones?"

She looks up at me, the smile gone entirely. "Nothing important," she says. "Nothing important."

When she's washing the dishes, however, the magic happens again. For the first time since the door slammed shut, I look at her, and she looks willingly back and her eyes become deep and endless dark waters, beckoning to my soul. Drown in me...find yourself. I reach out flailing, groping for her hard, real body. Ahh, my hands encounter tense muscles, fasten on to them. I stroke and knead, rousing the long-dormant woman in her. Feel in the taut, secret places, rub the tender moist groove, caress her all over with sweet, probing fingers.

"Bait," says a cold, sneering voice.

She gasps and goes rigid again.

"Get away to bed with you," she says without turning round.

"I'm going to watch."

An overwhelming anger floods through me. I whip around and my erstwhile gentle hands harden and clench.

"No," she says, "no," touching me, warning me.

She goes across and kneels before him.

(I see he's trembling.)

She kisses his face.

She kisses his hand.

She kisses the hook.

"Now go to bed e tama."[1]

He stands, undecided, swaying in the doorway.

Then, too quickly for it to be stopped, he lashes out with the hook. It strikes her on her left breast.

I storm forward, full of rage, and reach for him.

"No," she says again, kneeling there, motionless. "No," yet again.

"Go to bed, tama," she says to him.

Her voice is warm and friendly. Her face is serene.

He turns obediently, and walks away into the dark.

At the weekend, I suggested we go for a picnic.

"Another one?" she asks, her black eyebrows raised.

"Well, we could gather pauas,[2] maybe some cress, have a meal on the beach. It'd be good to get out of the house for a while. This hasn't been too good a week for me, you know."

---

[1] *e tama* Son (*e* functions as a particle).

[2] *pauas* Abalones.

They both shrugged.

"Okay," he says.

"I will get the paua," she says, and begins stripping off her jeans.

"You get the cress," she says to him.

"I'll go with you and help," I add.

He just looks at me. Those steely eyes in that brown face. Then he pouted, picked up the kete,[1] and headed for the stream.

He selects a stalk and pinches it suddenly. The plant tissue thins to nothing. It's like he's executing the cress. He adds it to the pile in the kete. He doesn't look at me, or talk. He is absorbed in killing cress.

There's not much I can do.

So I put on my mask and flippers and wade into the water, slide down under the sea. I spend a long peaceful time there, detaching whelks and watching them wobble down to the bottom. I cruise along the undersea rock shelf, plucking bits of weed and letting them drift away. Eventually, I reach the end of the reef, and I can hear the boom and mutter of the real ocean. It's getting too close; I surface.

One hundred yards away, fighting a current that is moving him remorselessly out, is my son.

When I gained the beach, I was exhausted.

I stand, panting, him in my arms.

His face is grey and waxy and the water runs off us both, dropping constantly on the sand.

"You were too far out...."

He cries.

"Where is she?"

Where is she? Gathering paua somewhere ... but suddenly I don't know if that is so. I put my mask back on, leave him on the beach, and dive back under the waves, looking.

When I find her, as I find her, she is floating on her back amidst bullkelp. The brown weed curves sinuously over her body, like dark limp hands.

I splash and slobber over, sobbing to her. "God, your son nearly died trying to find you. Why didn't you tell us?"

She opens her brown eyes lazily.

No, not lazily: with defeat, with weariness.

"What on earth gave you the idea I was going to drown?" She rubs the towel roughly over her skin.

---

[1] *kete* Basket.

I say, haltingly, "Uh well, he was sure that …"

(He is curled up near the fire I've lit, peacefully asleep.)

"Sure of what?"

"I don't know. He went looking for you, got scared. We couldn't see you anywhere."

A sort of shudder, a ripple runs through her.

"The idea was right," she says, very quietly. She lets the towel fall. She cups her hand under her left breast and points.

"Feel there."

There is a hard, oval, clump amidst the soft tissue.

"God, did he do …"

"No. It's been growing there for the past month. Probably for longer than that, but I have only felt it recently." She rubs her armpit, thoughtfully. "It's there too and under here," gesturing to her jaw. "It'll have to come out." I can't stop it. I groan.

Do you understand that if I hadn't been there, both of them would have drowned?

There was one last thing.

We were all together in the living room.

I am in the lefthand chair, she is opposite me.

He is crooning to himself, sprawled in front of the fire.

"Loo-lie, loo-lay, loo-lie, loo-lay, the falcon hath borne my make away," he sings. He pronounces it, "the fawcon have borne my make away."

"What is that?" I ask.

"A song."

He looks across to his ma and they smile slyly, at one another, smiles like invisible hands reaching out, caressing secretly, weaving and touching.

I washed my hands.

I wept.

I went out to the shed and banged the door finally shut.

I wept a little longer.

And then, because there was nothing else to do, I went down to the pub.

I had been drinking double whiskies for more than an hour when Mata came across and laid his arm over my shoulder.

He is shaking.

"E man," he whispers. His voice grows a little stronger. "E man, don't drink by yourself. That's no good eh?" His arm presses down. "Come across to us?"

The hubbub of voices hushes.

I snivel.

"Mat, when I first knew, her fingers were covered in clay, soft grey clay. And she smiled and said it's Charleston, we'll call him Charleston. It's too soft really, but I'll make a nice cup from it. Cups. Tall fluted goblets she said."

His hand pats my shoulder with commiseration, with solicitude.
His eyes are dark with horror.
"I'll glaze them sea blue and we'll drink red wine together, all three of us."
We never did.

1975

Witi Ihimaera

Witi Ihimaera (-Smiler, b. 1944) was born in New Zealand of Maori and Scottish ancestry. He has published several novels and stories, including *Pounamu, Pounamu* (stories, 1970), *Tangi* (1973), *The Whale Rider* (1987), *Dear Miss Mansfield* (stories, 1989), *The Uncle's Story* (2000), *Woman Far Walking* (2000), *Sky Dancer* (2004), and *Band of Angels* (2005). He has also written an opera, *Waituhi: The Life of the Village* (1985) and a cultural history, *Maori* (1975). He is currently a professor in the Department of English, University of Auckland, New Zealand.

Ihimaera's "This Life Is Weary" is a rewriting of Katherine Mansfield's "The Garden Party" from the point of view of a working-class protagonist, which Ihimaera intends as a deliberate contrast to that of the upper-class Laura of Mansfield's story. "Writing back" is a characteristic of postcolonial literature; a postcolonial writer rewrites a pre-text to correct its ideological or cultural assumptions, to mock or ridicule it, to show high regard for it, or to mimic it blindly. What do you think the text reveals of Ihimaera's intention? It is significant that "This Life Is Weary," unlike Ihimaera's other stories, uses few if any Maori words (and has a Maori character with only a walk-on role).

This Life Is Weary

1.

The little cottages were in a lane to themselves at the very bottom of a steep rise. At the top was the house that the children called *The Big House*—everybody called it that because it was oh so lovely with its lovely house and gardens lived in by its lovely owners—like another world really, one much nicer than down here below the broad road which ran between. But Dadda would always laugh whenever the children were too filled to the brim about the goings on up there, and he would remind them that "We are all equal in the sight of God" or "Remember—the lilies of the field—" This was Dadda's way of saying that no envy should be attached to *The Big House*, nor malice against its gilded inhabitants.

The children loved their Dadda so much, especially Celia the eldest, who thought he was the most wonderful, most handsome, most perfect man in the whole world. Truth to tell, Celia was not far wrong about him—Jack Scott was a fine man. His face was strong and open and was topped with blond curly hair. His shoulders were broad and, altogether, he was a fine figure of a man. But Dadda was more than physically attractive—he possessed a sense of goodness and wholeness, as if his physical beauty merely reflected an inner purity untouched by coarseness. "When I grow up, Dadda," Celia would say, "I shall marry someone just like you." To this Jack Scott would laugh again—her dear, laughing Dadda—and caution Celia that beauty or handsomeness faded with years and, "Oh, my sweet Celia, follow your heart and, wherever it leads, to ugly plump thin or brown, there lie you down."

This kind of simple honesty was what made Dadda so greatly loved in this land of chocolate-brown houses. Although the very smoke coming out of the chimneys might be poverty-stricken — not at all like the great silvery plumes that uncurled from *The Big House* — one could hear the larks sing whenever the carter, Jack Scott, was around. "'ere you, Old Faithful," the washerwomen would call as Dadda whistled past. "'ow come you're always so 'appy of a mornin'?" Dadda would answer, "God has given us another beautiful day, ladies, and there are so many beautiful things in it." And the washerwomen would blush, for they took his remarks as declarations of romance and they loved him all the more — not lasciviously, mind, because they were decent women and beyond the age of temptation. "Oh my, Jack Scott," they would call, "you 'ave a way with the words, but be off with you!" Ah yes, and the men loved Dadda too because of his uprightness and fairness. "You're a good lad, Jack," the old pensioners would tell him when ever he was able to spare them some victuals. "Yes, you're a good mate," the young men agreed. There was not a finer friend to the young men than Dadda.

He was not old, was Dadda, being only twenty-nine, and his responsibilities as a good husband and father had not brought weariness to him. In the case of Mam, though, Celia could see that life's travails had changed her greatly from the little slip of a thing whom Dadda had met on the ship bringing settlers from England. Romance had blossomed below decks between Jack and Em — and Em's parents had not put a stop to it, for they could tell that Jack would make honest passage through the world and, given his good head for business, a profitable one. Nobody could want better for a daughter of fifteen years. So, on arrival in Wellington, Jack and Em had become man and wife, and they had fulfilled God's commandment to be fruitful by producing Celia, Margaret and Thomas within the first three years of marriage. The doctor had cautioned Jack, saying, "Give Em some peace now, lad, and let her body recover from the childbearing." Dadda had laughed and said, "It's not for my want of trying, Doctor, but the babies just seem to come and, if it is God's will" — And God willed that there should be two more, the babes Matthew and Mark.

The Big House was regarded with simple awe by many who lived in the little cottages below. Others were not so awestruck, looking upon *The Big House* with a sense of grievance, for it represented everything that they had hoped to escape from when they had left England. Even Dadda was not untouched by the angry murmurs of the working men at meetings of an evening. But above all else, he truly believed that Work and Self-improvement would win the changes that all strived for.

Dadda went to work every morning before dawn. He would slip out of bed and creep with candle up into the loft to see his little ones. "Blessed be the new day," he would whisper, "and God keep you all safe and well." Then he would be gone, often not returning until long after dark. Mam had the babes to tend to and, whenever she could, she took small mending work from *The Big House* — she had artistic fingers for embroidery. As for the children, they went off to school during the week. Mam was very firm about this and did not want them swarming in the little crowded lanes like many of the other children who were kept at home.

However, Saturday afternoons were free for the children to do as they pleased and, without fail, this meant going up to *The Big House*, crossing quickly over the broad road between, to watch the house and the comings and goings of the lovely people who lived or visited there. Celia had found a special place — you had to slip between the rose bushes and under the karaka trees to get to it — right by the tennis court. Under the trees was an old wrought-iron loveseat, just ideal for the children. The seat had obviously been thrown out many years ago but it was comfortable enough — once you wiped away the birds' droppings — and perfect to observe from. There was the house, side on to the sun, gleaming like a two-storeyed dolls' house. The driveway was at the front with a circle of green in the middle. Oh, what excitement was occasioned whenever the front gateway opened and a carriage came in! There was a back gateway also and, there, the delivery vans and storemen would enter, bringing the groceries, meat and other supplies to Cook. Once, the children had seen the familiar figure of Dadda himself and that night they couldn't wait to tell him, "Dadda, oh Dadda! We saw you at *The Big House* today" — as if grace and divinity had been suddenly bestowed on him. The house was surrounded with broad swathes of bright green lawn bordered by daisy plants. Just beyond the borders were the roses — hundreds and hundreds of glorious dark red roses of the kind that the children had seen on chocolate boxes.

It was Celia, of course, who thought of keeping notebooks on *The Big House*. Celia had always been an imaginative child and it only seemed natural that simple observation should lead to something more formal — like setting it all down in writing. Dadda and Mam were amused at first but grew to be thoroughly approving. "Better that the children should be constructive," Mam would say, "than down here wasting their lives away." And Dadda had said, "Who knows? Some of what they see might rub off on them!" So it soon became part of the Saturday routine for Mam to sharpen pencils and, when the children became more serious about keeping notebooks, to let them take a simple lunch — a crust of bread each and a bottle with water in it — with them. "Be back before dark!" Mam would cry as the children scampered off. "We will, Mam, we will!" Celia would reply — because telling Mam and Dadda, right after supper, about what they had seen at *The Big House* became part of the Saturday excursions also. And the children knew that Mam and Dadda welcomed their reports, taking them as signs that their children would do better than they had to make good lives for themselves.

Although Celia had never been to any theatre, watching *The Big House* was just as she imagined a play would be. Like all theatrical settings, the weather was always ideal up there and the days perfect and made to order. The backdrop was windless and warm, with a light blue sky flecked with gold. It was all so unlike the dark and dirty eyesore which cluttered the area the children came from. Indeed, sometimes it was difficult for the children to accept that this world was as real as their own — it really was as if they had paid a penny to go to His Majesty's Royal Theatre for a few hours of a drab Saturday afternoon. But what fun! Naturally, the house itself was the main stage prop, particularly the verandahs, top and bottom, and the french doors on to the verandahs. From out of these doors would come the lovely people of *The Big House*, the main actors of every Saturday afternoon performance. Head of the Household was Mr. Sheridan, who worked in the city and never seemed to be around very much. He generally slept late on Saturdays, sometimes not appearing until 2 p.m., all hairy and drumming his chest after a wash. Mistress of the House was Mrs. Sheridan, prone to sitting on a chair off the main bedroom and fanning herself like a lady in a magazine. Once, so Margaret swore, Mrs. Sheridan actually waved to the children where they sat. "Impossible," Celia replied. Her version appeared that night, after supper, when she produced a sketch of Mrs. Sheridan trying to swat at something going bbbzzzz—Mam and Dadda thought that was very funny, but Margaret was cross.

Mr. and Mrs. Sheridan had three daughters, Meg, Jose and Laura, and a son, Laurie—and it was on these four fascinating golden creatures that the children focused all their attention. Celia would scribble like mad in her notebook as Margaret and Thomas described every appearance: "Meg has just washed her hair," Margaret would say, in awe, because washing one's hair in the afternoon was the prerogative of the wealthy. "Oh, look, there's Jose! She has put on her lovely silk petticoat and the kimono jacket." And Thomas would reflect, "Do you think she got the jacket from the Chinamen who play pakapoo?" To which Celia, the expert on fashion, would say, "Kimonos come from Japan, Thomas, not China." But Margaret might interrupt, "Oh, quick, here comes Meg again! Doesn't she look pretty? I'll bet a beau is coming to call." And sure enough, half an hour later, the gateway would open and a fine hansom would deposit a grave but hopeful young man. "Oh, he's not right for Meg," Celia would say. "Pooh, no!" Thomas and Margaret would agree, for they knew that without doubt Meg was going to be a famous pianist. Her life was not to be squandered away on silly young men! Wasn't it true that every afternoon Meg practised the piano and showed signs of improving?—why, only four mistakes in the "Für Elise" last Saturday! As for Jose, oh dear, she would just have to give up any thought of an operatic career. While her voice was strong enough, alas, her sense of timing was woeful. Worse still, she could never hold the tune. Apart from which, nobody could sing "This Life is Weary" better than Dadda—

This Life is *Wee*-ary,
A Tear—a Sigh.
A Love that *Chan-ges*,
This Life is *Wee*-ary,
A Tear—a Sigh.
A Love that *Chan*-ges.
And then ... Good-bye!

No, Jose would be better off receiving silly young men herself. In this manner, the children would observe, ponder, dream and hope that the characters whom they had come to love would grow, prosper and make the right decisions.

The children's main interest was in the heroine of the Sheridan family, the one whom they thought was most like themselves—Laura. Her every entrance was greeted in the same way as a diva by a star-struck audience—with a hushed indrawn breath, moment of recognition, long sigh of release and joyous acclamation. Laura was Celia's age—at least, that's what Celia insisted—and could do no wrong. She was the one whom the children most wanted to have as a friend, if class would ever allow it. Their notebooks were filled, positively to the very margins, with anecdotes, drawings and notes about Laura in all her moods. To even get a good likeness was difficult enough, for Laura was always flying in and out, here and there, to and fro. Often the children would have to compare their drawings for accuracy and, "No, she didn't look like that," Celia would say, "she looked like this." Then Margaret would interject, "But she wasn't wearing the blue pinafore, she was wearing the yellow one with the tiny wee apron." To which Thomas would respond, "Well, she was just perfect as she was, a perfect little princess." This was, in fact, patently inaccurate, because perfect little princesses were not tomboys—and there was a streak of this in Laura. Perfect little princesses did not do cartwheels on the front lawn or thumb their noses at beaux they didn't like. Oh, she was such a character sometimes! "I wonder what her bedroom is like?" Margaret would wonder. "Does it have a huge bed and are all her dolls propped up on the pillows?" Interrupting, Thomas would venture, "And would there be a rockinghorse?" To which Celia would purse her lips and say, "Perhaps. Rockinghorses are really for boys but—yes, Laura is bound to have one."

On most occasions, the appearances by the Sheridans were seen from afar. There was one magical moment, however—the children had to pinch themselves to make sure they weren't dreaming—when Hans, one of the servants, brought a small table and four chairs on to the tennis court right in front of the children. Laura appeared with three of her dolls, placed them on chairs and proceeded to have afternoon tea with cakes and biscuits. "Lady Elizabeth," Laura said, "would you care for some milk? Sugar? One lump or two?" Then, with a laugh, "Oh, quite, Countess Mitzi, quite." And Celia almost fainted away with pleasure when, turning to the third doll, Laura said, "Princess Celia, how was your last visit to Paris?" For the rest of the afternoon the children were just transported, bursting with ecstasy—and they could hardly wait to tell Mam and Dadda. "Oh, slow down, lovey," Mam said to Celia. "Do slow down!" And that put the seal on the entire afternoon, for it was exactly the sort of comment that the children were constantly passing about Laura herself.

2.

One day, the children came running back from an afternoon watching *The Big House* with the news "Oh, Mam! Dadda! There's going to be a garden party! At *The Big House*! We heard Mrs. Sheridan reminding Cook! Next Saturday! Oh, can we go for the whole day? With our notebooks? In the morning? So many people have been invited! Please, Mam! Please, Dadda!" As it happened, Em had hoped the girls would mind the babes while she visited her parents but, "Let the little ones go,"

Dadda said, adding with a wink, "and I shall try to come home early in the afternoon, eh, Em love?" Trying not to blush, Em said, "All right, children, you may go," and the children clapped their hands together with glee. Then a thoughtful, twinkling look came into Mam's eyes and she suddenly left the kitchen to rummage in the glory box in the bedroom. When she came back she had some velvet and other material in her arms. "Come here, Celia lovey," Em said. "My, you've grown—" and her eyes sparkled with sadness, mingled with pride, at the thought of her eldest daughter growing into womanhood. "What are you doing, Mam?" Celia asked. "Why, measuring you, your sister and brother, of course," Mam said. "You can't go to a garden party in your everyday clothes." And Margaret said, "But Mam, we're not invited?" To which Em said, "Hush, child. We can dream, can't we?" And Jack came to hold Em close and kiss her. "That we can, Em love," he said, "that we can."

The children could hardly contain themselves. All that week they conjectured about the garden party—who would come, what food would be served, what Laura would wear, would there be a band, how many waiters—and they were so fidgety that Mam had to say, "Do keep still, Margaret, or else your dress will not be ready in time!" Then Margaret would stay very still indeed, hardly drawing breath, because green velvet was her favourite colour and she wanted to look her very best—and Mam even made a green bow for her hair! Thomas, reluctant at first, also got into the swing of things. He knew that he was going to look a proper guy—and how was he going to get up to *The Big House* and back without the other swarming children seeing him—but, oh, there was such a delicious silky feeling to the new shirt! As for Celia, she had determined, "Mam, I can make my own dress and hat." So while Mam stitched costumes for Margaret and Thomas, Celia worked on a cloth that had once been a curtain. When Celia completed her dress Mam trimmed it with a lace ribbon she had been saving for herself.

Then, when all the stitching and sewing was completed, didn't the children look just lovely, parading in front of Dadda and Mam that Friday night before the garden party? Hardly a wink was slept, so that when Dadda came to wake them, why, the children were already dressed and waiting! And wasn't Dadda the most perfect man? He had transformed the cart into a carriage and placed cushions on the seats. Then, bowing, he handed the children up, saying, "Lady Margaret, if you would be so kind—Princess Celia, charmed—Sir Thomas, delighted—" And Mam, trying not to laugh too much, came from the doorway with a hamper of cordial, sandwiches and a dear wee cake. "Oh, Mam. Oh, Dadda," was all that Celia could say because the words got caught in her throat. "Have a lovely time, children," Mam said. "And Thomas, don't worry—your Dadda will pick you all up before dark from the gateway of *The Big House*. Byeeee—" And she blew a kiss as they left.

And after all the weather was ideal. When the dawn came creeping across the sky, the children knew it was going to be a perfect day for the Sheridans' garden party. From their position under the trees they saw the garden party from beginning to end. They saw the Maori gardener already at work mowing the lawns and sweeping them. "Oh, he's missed a piece!" Margaret wailed but, joy, he returned to sweep the swathe so that the lawn looked all combed the same way—not a lick out of place. "Nothing must go wrong," Celia nodded. Then the children saw movement in *The Big House* and knew that Mr. and Mrs. Sheridan, Meg, Jose, Laura and Laurie were at breakfast. Mr. Sheridan came out the front door with a BANG to go through the gateway. At the same time the men came to put up the marquee. And who else but Laura, the little princess herself, should appear to give the men their instructions! "Oh, she's so pretty!" Thomas said, "and look, she's eating bread and butter— just like we do." The next few moments, though, were anxious ones for the children because at one point, Laura pointed to the tennis court. Yes, it was certainly the most appropriate place for the marquee but, "It will spoil our view," Celia whispered. And, why, Laura must have heard, because the workmen set the marquee near the karaka trees instead!

"Message, Laura!" a voice cried from the house, and away the little princess skimmed. But what was happening at the back door? Why, the florist had arrived and just look at the pots and pots of canna lilies—so radiant and frighteningly alive on their bright crimson stems! And then, from the drawing room, was that Meg on the piano? Pom! Ta-ta-ta Tee-ta! Oh dear, was Jose really going to embarrass herself by singing at the garden party? There she was, warming up—"This Life is Wee-ary, A Tear—a Sigh"—Oh dear, dear, dear. But now look! Someone else had arrived at the back door. Surely it was the Godber van, clattering into the yard, bringing lovely cream puffs! And there was the man from Godbers talking to Cook, and—

Suddenly the sky was filled with a soft radiance and it was almost like—like a shooting star, in the daytime though, going UP into the sky—and Celia felt such sweet pain that she wanted to weep. Her heart was so full, so overflowing, so brimming over, and in that same instant she thought of her Dadda.

Strange really, but for a while after that the house fell into silence. Laura's voice could be heard piping and alarmed. "What is happening now?" Margaret asked. "I'm not sure," Celia said. "Perhaps it is lunchtime already." Indeed it was—hadn't time passed quickly? So Margaret opened the hamper, Celia laid the food out, and Thomas said, "Lady Margaret, would you care for some wine?" Margaret clapped her hands together and, "Thank you, Sir Thomas," she said as Thomas poured some cordial into her glass. "And you, Princess Celia?" Celia inclined her head. And oh, it was so much fun to be sitting there sipping wine on the perfect day.

Lunch in *The Big House* was over by half past one. The green-coated bandsmen arrived and established themselves right next to the children near the tennis court. The man on the tuba saw them and gave a cheery wave. Would he tell? No—he was too jolly to do that. Soon after, the guests began coming in streams—one carriage after the other—the women so lovely, oh so lovely. The band struck up. The hired waiters ran from the house to the marquee. Wherever the children looked there were couples strolling, bending to the flowers, greeting, and gliding across the lawn. The children were enchanted, transported, transformed—in Heaven—by it all. There in the shadows they imitated the movements of the guests, and sometimes when the band played, Sir Thomas first asked Lady Margaret and then Princess Celia to dance with him, on and on and on. The man on the tuba smiled when he saw them dancing and, oh goodness, when the waiters came to offer the band refreshments he must have pointed out the children! Over came one of the waiters with a tray of delicious cakes and cream puffs, and he bowed gravely, saying, "Mesdames? Monsieur?" And always, far away in the sunlight was dear, darling Laura. Something was bothering her, but she was so gracious, wasn't she? "Oh, I must sketch her," Celia cried. And the perfect afternoon slowly ripened, slowly faded, slowly its petals closed. And soon it was all over.

The children were in ever such an excited state as they waited for their Dadda to pick them up. They had stayed beneath the trees until the very end when the last bandsman had packed his instrument and left. The man with the tuba had given a very cheery wave. By the time the children reached the gateway it was almost dark. "Wasn't it wonderful when—" the children would reminisce to one another. They wanted to savour every minute of the garden party and, "Oh, write that one down, Celia," Margaret would cry. "We forgot about that moment." So for a while they sat scribbling away in the gathering darkness. "Weren't the guests all so lovely?" Margaret whispered. On and on the children chattered.

The darkness deepened. The children couldn't wait for Dadda to arrive so that they could get home quickly and tell him and Mam about the garden party. When the night fell like a cloak, Celia said, "Dadda must be delayed. Come along, let's go on home. Like as not we'll meet him coming up the hill." Thomas was so happy that he didn't even think to be embarrassed should they meet any swarming children. Down, down, down into the sordid lanes the children descended. The lights were on in some of the houses. People were like silent wraiths slipping into and out of the light. All of a sudden someone came running from behind the children, passing them and turning the corner. When the children rounded the corner themselves, they saw a young man with a girl. The girl was pressed against him and she looked as if she was crying. Celia overheard the young man say, "Was it awful?" The girl shook her head—and there was something terribly familiar in the motion—but it was so dark, so dark.

Then the children were in sight of their own house and they started to run towards it. But what was this? Lamps were shining in the front parlour. A dark knot of people stood outside. Women in shawls and men in tweed caps were gathered there. Without knowing why, Celia felt an awful feeling inside her heart. She saw Gran, Mam's mother, sitting in a chair beside the gate. As the children approached, Gran gave a cry. The knot loosened and voices came out of the darkness at the children, "Oh, the poor wee children." Gran kissed the children and held them tight. "What's wrong, Gran?" Celia asked. "There's been an accident, Celia dear," Gran answered. "Your father—" Celia pulled Margaret and Thomas quickly through the crowd and into the house. Auntie May was there in the passageway, but Celia didn't want her.

"Mam? Dadda?" Celia called. "Mam?" Then another woman was there. Her face was all puffed up and red, with swollen eyes and swollen lips. "Mam?" Celia whispered, because it was indeed her mother. But she looked so — so *awful.*

"Your Dadda's gone," Mam said. "He's gone."

Margaret started to wail and Thomas bit his lip and screwed up his eyes. The two children ran to the comfort of their mother's arms. But Celia just stood there. *Oh, Dadda, was that you, that soft radiance? Was that your soul coming to say goodbye before going to Heaven?* Then, in the corner, Celia noticed a basket of fruit — the fruit looked so lovely, oh so very lovely — and she remembered the garden party. "I must tell Dadda," Celia thought. Her heart was breaking into a thousand pieces. "Where's Dadda?" she asked. Mam motioned toward the bedroom.

For a moment Celia was too frightened to go in. She didn't want to know. She didn't want to see. All of a sudden, she felt a fleeting sense of unfairness that *The Big House,* with its gilded life, should be so impervious to all the ills of the world. But no, she shouldn't think like that. Dadda wouldn't want her to think like that, would he? "Dadda?" she called from the door way. "Dadda?" She took a step and, why, there he was in his bed, and she had caught him asleep! There he was, glowing in the light of the smoky lamp, her handsome laughing Dadda. And fast asleep he was, sleeping so soundly that he didn't even stir when she knelt beside him. Curly headed Dadda, deeply, peacefully sleeping.

"Oh Dadda," Celia whispered. She put her head against his, and the first glowing tear dropped down her cheek like a golden sun. "It was a lovely garden party, Dadda, just *lovely,*" she said.

1985

Sally Ito

Sally Ito (b. 1964) was born in Alberta, Canada, of Japanese ancestry ("my mother having come from Japan and my father being a third-generation Japanese Canadian"). She studied in Japan and at the University of British Columbia. Her publications include *Frogs in the Rain Barrel* (poems, 1995), *Floating Shore* (stories, 1998), and *A Season of Mercy* (poems, 1999).

In Ito's "Of the Wave" (originally entitled in the first edition "Sisters of the Modern Mind"), the narrator is oblivious—with no sense of irony—to racial differences. She acknowledges the different paths chosen by herself and her friend but sees them as sharing a common sense of aging and a common "modern" mind. Compare this poem with Marilyn Chin's "Elegy for Chloe Nguyen (1955-1988)" and Mervyn Morris's "To an Expatriate Friend."

Of the Wave

Do you remember
when in my muddled baby English,
I called you,
"Pretty blonde fair eyes princess"
and you smiled, toothless,
without an inkling of a frown
on your five year old face?

We had laughed
high pitched peals,
in our simple nakedness once
when we were six.
Do you remember my touching you there,
when we'd thrown feather pillows
at one another, fast and furious;
hurling, hitting
as if in a blind rage,
until the white down settled onto our skin
where it lay like snow petals
on our childish cracks and curves?

We had splashed
in the bathtub once
when we were seven.
It was after our talk
about the Whelan boys across the street.

We sat prim in the tub
(for mother had put buns in our hair)
until we began to play.
Do you remember the frenzy
of white froth and bubbles
we created, crouching
like spawning pond frogs?

We grew up
congregated by telephone.
our lipstick a new weapon
heralding the moon
and her cycles of creation. And yet,
ours was a bold red scrape on white tile and mirror;
graffiti about small socialism in bathrooms
once preserved for "*Jane is a slut*" tiles.

Then, we sought after knowledge,
you and I.
Our painted nails carved deep crescents
into musty bindings.
Our hands jingled with bracelets and rings
as crinkled pages were turned, over and over,
by wettened fingertip.
Discourse passed through our reddened lips
in enthused soprano voices. Cheeks flushed
to each temperament of thought.
The knowledge became
as those pages of our skin
that we sought to caress with our own hands   too often
We could not,
though our ideas
urged us on, like heavy, masculine whispers
hot upon our lobes.

Our precious knowledge did not move
the precious opinion of the others.
Then, you were sad because Descartes was wrong
and I was happy because faith was free.
You left me then, to find perfect answers.
I waited for you. I stopped wondering.
And when you returned, you were older.
And I was with child.

You wondered at the skin of my belly,
bloated and large,
a woman's disfigured testament of love,
a prophecy generations old.
And I marvelled at the sharpness of your mind
filled with the birthing of knowledge
from the belly of experience — the new womb
in successful trial.

We have worshipped different gods,
you and I. Yet,
time and anatomy still wear
at our bones like the tide upon the sand
that tosses the jewelled shells,
you and I, sisters,
of the wave.

1986

Arnold Itwaru

Arnold Itwaru (b. 1942), poet and artist, was born in Guyana and immigrated to Canada in 1969. He has written several collections of poetry, including *Entombed Survivals* (1987) and *Body Rites: Beyond the Darkening* (1991); his fiction includes *Shanti* (novel, 1988), *Home and Back* (novel, 2001), and *Morning of Yesterday* (stories, 1999). He has several critical texts, including *The Invention of Canada: Literary Texts and The Immigrant Imagination* (1990).

Itwaru's poems "arrival" and "roomer" are short but evocative of the immigrant experience. Like Neil Bissoondath in "Man as Plaything, Life as Mockery," Itwaru provides no cultural or ethnic specifics in the poems. Does this omission work better in poetry than in fiction, where contextual details are expected? His love poem "separate ways" is similarly without identifiable ethnic details. These poems are exceptions in Itwaru's oeuvre; in his fiction and essays, Itwaru provides substantial historical and cultural specifics and explicitly censures imperial exploitation—as in his novel *Shanti*.

arrival

this is the place
mark its name
the streets you must learn to remember

there are special songs here
they do not sing of you
in them you do not exist
but to exist you must learn to love them
you must believe them when they say
there are no sacrificial lambs here

the houses are warm
there's bread there's wine

bless yourself
you have arrived

       listen
keys   rattle
locks   click
doors   slam
     silence

1987

roomer

here i cower
from the day's
drain and glare
a shadow
a wrinkled skin
cover me gently
night's linen
prepare me
prepare me

1987

separate ways

stranger in the sunset
i long to know you
to touch the poem of your presence
to dispel this loneliness
but the sun darkens
and we go our separate ways

1987

Eva Johnson

Eva Johnson (b. 1946) was born in Daly River, in Australia's Northern Territory, to the Malak Malak people. Author of several plays, she has won awards for her outstanding contribution to Aboriginal culture. A poet before she became a playwright, she has published poems in such anthologies as *Inside Black Australia* (1989). *Voices*, her third play, was performed at the Hiroshima Arts Festival in Japan in 1990.

Johnson's *Murras* (*Hands*) is about three generations of Aboriginal women and the injustices they suffer as minorities. Their closely-knit family life enables them to pick up the pieces and survive while keeping their Aboriginal spirit alive. Some critics believe that the short play has too many incidents and addresses too many issues to be dramatically effective (including the secret sterilization of women, the taking of babies from their mothers, and the denial of Australian citizenship to Aborigines until 1967). Do you agree with this evaluation? Compare this play with Archie Weller's bleak story "Pension Day." *Murras* opened at the Fringe Festival Centre during the Adelaide Festival in March 1988; it was directed by Johnson herself.

Murras[1]

CHARACTERS
>MIMI SPIRIT, a dancer
>GRANNY, an elderly woman
>RUBY, the mother, in her twenties
>WILBA, her thirteen-year-old son
>JAYDA, her sixteen-year-old daughter
>MR. RUSSEL, Department of Aboriginal Affairs worker, in his late twenties

SETTING
>This play focuses on one family and their struggle to come to grips with white Australia as they move from fringe dwelling to life in the city. The action takes place between the late sixties and mid-seventies, a time which saw the beginning of changes to laws relating to Aborigines, including the abolition of the Aborigines Protection Board.

NOTE
>Mimi is a mythical being that inhabits certain parts of the country. It can be the spirit of a dead ancestor, sometimes friendly, sometimes hostile, and the Mimi dance is very much a part of the traditional dances performed today. Mimi is a very powerful spirit who can generate magic to bring about sickness and death. It is the caretaker of the dead spirit.

---

[1] *Murras* See author's glossary (p. 215).

GLOSSARY

The Aboriginal words used in *Murras* are from the Ngarrenjeri and Pitjantjatjara languages:

MURRAS: hands
BOOGADIES: shoes
GUNDIES: underwear
NUNGARS: aboriginal people
GADJERI: aboriginal woman (friend)
WUDJELLAS: white people (non-aboriginal)
DOOLUM: head lice
INMA: special ceremony, dance
DIDJERIDU: musical instrument (traditional)
CURLEW: bird (when heard, the call of this bird means death)

ACT ONE
SCENE ONE

The MIMI SPIRIT sits in a coiled position before the Great Rainbow Serpent motif. The didjeridu[1] begins to play and the MIMI SPIRIT wakes and slides across the stage, awakening in the earth spirits. This is the birth dance of the Aboriginal Dreaming.[2] The dance ends in darkness. Blackout while props are brought on: a door, a window, an old car seat. A transistor on the window sill plays the song "I Don't Want to Play House." Fade up. Enter RUBY, carrying a bath tub. She places it on top of a kero tin[3] and begins to wash clothes. When the song ends the ABC[4] News is introduced.

ANNOUNCER: [*voice over*] This is the ABC News read by Charles Drury. There has been evidence in recent years of increasing consciousness of the rights of the Aboriginal Australian. Commonwealth and state ministers stated that: "The policy of assimilation seeks that persons of Aboriginal descent will choose to attain a similar manner and standard of living to that of other Australians and live as members of a single Australian community, and we believe that if Aboriginal Australians can be helped and encouraged to help themselves, then they will be readily attracted to and welcomed to the assimilation we aim for. Therefore, new housing will be allocated for them in different towns and cities." The Minister further commented that the move to the cities will— [*Ruby angrily switches the transistor off.*]

---

[1] *didjeridu* See author's glossary.

[2] *Dreaming* Aboriginal people accept "Dreaming" as the closest English word for the mystical insights gained in dreams into all that is known and understood in human existence.

[3] *kero tin* Kerosene tin.

[4] *ABC* Australian Broadcasting Corporation.

RUBY: [*to the radio*] Don't talk like that. We don't wanna go, what for? No good, I tell you.

[*She returns to her washing.*]

Better live here outside. We got no doors to lock out family. Look, look my murras.

[*She raises her hands out of the water.*]

All time work hard, dig for yams, make fire, make basket, dilly bag, pandana mat[1] … and carving.

[*She looks at Charlie's totem, centre stage.*]

Charlie, you were the best carver. Your murras were strong, you was the best. What I'm gonna do, Charlie? I can't leave my country. What I'm gonna do …

[*She is interrupted by her son, WILBA, who enters and goes to the door, carrying a pile of wood and a bucket of water.*]

WILBA: Mum, Mum, open the door; this bucket real heavy. Got some more wood, too, and good feed of yabbies.[2]

RUBY: [*letting him in*] Well, put that bucket down there, but get them yabbies out; we gotta drink that water. Anyway, what you doin' home from school? You gotta go to that school, Wilba, else them Government fellas come check up on us.

WILBA: I hate that school, Mum, true as God. I hate that school. Always gettin' into trouble for nothing. *wudjellas*[3] make me real mad: I all time flog them. Call me "Abo," "boong," "nigger," and all time dirty names. I'm not goin' back, Mum, true as God, I hate that school.

RUBY: Well, it probably don't matter now: we leavin' this place, anyway.

WILBA: What you saying? Mum, where? What place? Who told you?

RUBY: I heard, just now. On the wireless. Government fellas talking about new houses for Aborigines in the city.

WILBA: No way, not me. I'm not going nowhere, I ain't; just stay here and be good stockman like my father and do carving and go hunting with Jumbo.

RUBY: We gotta do what they tell us, you know that. Jumbo was good friend of your father, Wilba.

WILBA: [*looking at the sculpture*] Yeah, he use to watch my father carve; he showed

---

[1] *pandana mat* A mat made from leaves of the pandana (pandan) tree, which grows in tropical areas of Asia, Australia, and the Pacific Islands. The leaves are used for handicraft and for enhancing savoury dishes.

[2] *yabbies* Australian freshwater crayfish.

[3] *wudjellas* See author's glossary.

Jumbo how to ride, track, hunt and dance… What he have to die for, Mum? What did my father have to die, what he drink that *wudjellas* drink for, make him sick, make him die?

RUBY: Your father died because he lost his land, everything. But he never forgot how to carve, hunt and dance. But plenty more dyin', Wilba, plenty more. Dyin' here inside, for their land. When you got nothing, all you want to do is die.

WILBA: [*sadly, picking up the totem*] He taught me to dance the moon dance. Taught me to carve emu eggs. Mum, he was too good to die; he didn't hurt no-one.

RUBY: You keep his dance, his spirit, Wilba. You are the shadow of your father. He always say you be like him. Oh, my God, I almost forget: Sister coming today. She probably want check you over too. Come on now, take this—water still hot. Go give yourself good clean up.

WILBA: What Sister want to check me for? She think I got germs, all time put that purple paint on me. I got no ring worm, *doolum*.[1] No nothing.

[*RUBY hands WILBA the tub and pushes him out the door. He sticks his head in the window and yells out.*]

Mum, look here: Granny and Jayda coming.

[*He exits. GRANNY and JAYDA enter. GRANNY has a walking stick.*]

RUBY: Where you two been? Sister coming, gotta clean up. Here, Jayda, hang these clothes up.

[*GRANNY sits on the car seat. RUBY sits by the fire to make her a cup of tea in the billy.[2] JAYDA starts hanging out the clothes on a piece of string tied from the door to the window.*]

JAYDA: Mum, I thought I saw Wilba with bath tub. Don't tell me he's gonna clean up. Probably tip that water out, just wet his hair, put powder on him, just gammon have wash, aye?

RUBY: Jayda, you gotta clean up too. Sister always see you. Granny, you real quiet. You alright?

GRANNY: No, I'm not alright. Everybody leavin' this place. Jessie, Tom, they gone now, gone to city. Left yesterday. That fulla from Government reckons we all be leaving, but they just wanna try move me, I'll?

RUBY: [*interrupting*] You mean that Mr. Morton from Welfare? Granny, he right, you know. I heard them on the wireless talkin', just *wudjellas* telling us what's good for us.

GRANNY: He was tellin' all of them mob at the Kimberly reserve. Jumbo took me up to see Jessie, dropped us off just now. But he gone further up; he not goin' city, me neither. I born here, I die here, this my born place. They don't wanna try move me, I'll give it to 'em, true as God.

---

[1] *doolum* See author's glossary.

[2] *billy* Billies are used (over the campfire) for cooking or boiling water to make tea.

RUBY: Granny, we all stay together. We take care of you. Anyway, you not gonna die, you tough like old buffalo.

JAYDA: Here, Granny, have cuppa tea.

[*She sits by GRANNY's feet.*]

You want your pipe? Give me your string bag, I'll fix it. Granny, you gotta teach me more dance; anyway, you been here the longest, they can't move you. You belong this country.

GRANNY: I seen too many things changing. Too many people dyin' from wrong ways. Moving about too much, disturbin' the land. My Charlie, they move him from his land, to station, to creek bed. He finish there, in creek bed. No good, I tell you. No, something happening our people. Soon we all gone. Something happening, I tell you, no good.

RUBY: Nothing gonna happen; they know what's good for us. You'll be alright, Granny, as long as we take plendy pandana, talc stone and emu eggs. And you can still teach Jayda to dance.

JAYDA: It's gonna be different, Mum, I know. I work for that *wudjella* woman in town and I know. Sometimes she follows me around while I clean up. And she just sit and stares at me, make me eat my lunch outside. She belts her children if they talk to me. I'm not gonna work for no *wudjellas* in city, that's for sure.

GRANNY: *Wudjella* woman got different way to *gadjeri*[1] woman. They don't have woman's dreaming, special dance, *Inma*.[2] Jayda, you not forget your stories now. You keep them sacred, for your children, not *wudjellas*.

JAYDA: Mum, what was that fulla sayin' on the wireless?

RUBY: Well, that fulla reading the news just said something about Aborigines being Australians. Minister from Government saying that we should all move to the city so we can be same as white fellas. And I remember that Mr. Morton calling us "fringe dwellers" or something. People who live between the city and their own land, I think. Our land been taken over by that cattle station, so they have to find houses for us. I don't want to go, but too many dying. Maybe it's better for us.

GRANNY: You can't leave Charlie. You know that. Ruby.

[*GRANNY stands and moves forward.*]

[*Softly*]
You know who we are;
Yeah, you, Ruby, you are dugong,[3]

---

[1] *gadjeri* See author's glossary.

[2] *Inma* See author's glossary.

[3] *dugong* A species of marine mammal (sea cows).

Charlie, he moon,
Wilba, he parrotfish,
Jayda, she seagrass,
Me, I'm from water.
Dreaming say, dugong was bitten by leech.
Moon watch her.
Dugong leave her land and go into sea.
Moon follow, but he can't get wet,
So he call parrotfish, make him son.
Parrotfish look after dugong.
Both live from seagrass from bottom of the sea.
Moon always there, watch all time.
And he here, still he look for you, dugong.
Water, dugong, parrotfish, seagrass,
All same spirit, so we gotta stay together, right here.

RUBY: Charlie gone back to his Dreaming. He alright.

JAYDA: That our Dreaming. We will all return to the sea, except my father, he is moon. I'll see if I can see the moon, sometimes I talk to....

RUBY: Sit down! Sit down, Jayda. I know it's not the same now, everything is changing. All different. But we will come back here one day, just like Charlie. We will come back in our own time. Back to our Dreaming.

GRANNY: Ruby, Jayda learn a new dance; you want to see her? Come on, Jayda, do little dance for your mother.

JAYDA: You want me to, Mum?

RUBY: Yes, my baby, do a little dance for me.

[*JAYDA dances for a short while. WILBA peeps through the window and watches. There is a knock. JAYDA stops dancing and sits by GRANNY. Enter WILBA.*]

WILBA: Mum, someone here to see us.

RUBY: Well, let him in.

[*Enter RUSSEL MITCHELL, an Aboriginal liaison officer.*]

RUSSEL: Hello, my name is Russel Mitchell, and you must be Mrs. Francis.

RUBY: Yes, and this is my mother Elsie, my son Wilba and my daughter Jayda.

WILBA: You hear about Mum's new house? We heard about it, everybody movin' to the city.

RUSSEL: Yes. My God, look at this place. I mean, how long have you been living like this? I mean here?

RUBY: We've been here a few years now. We lived on a station till Charlie lost his job. Then Mr. Morton got us this place after Charlie died.

RUSSEL: Charlie. That's your husband?

RUBY: Yes, he died from too much —

WILBA: [*interrupting*] Mum! You don't have to tell him all that.

RUSSEL: Oh, it's alright, I understand. We are all the same.

JAYDA: Mum, you don't really have to, you know. Charlie's gone now. You don't have to talk about him.

RUBY: He died from too much grog. Well, that's what they said. They used to come in cars and sell it to us, flagons of grog. They made lot of money, too. That wasn't what really killed him.

GRANNY: He was the best carver: look there. He never forgot who he was; not my Charlie. He was hungry for the land. They stole it from him. He was best carver, only wanted to live blackfella way.

WILBA: He carved totem poles, for ceremony, tall ones, and strong. His *murras* were strong, had to be to carve totems.

GRANNY: No, we not the same. You ever lived in the creek bed, Mr. Russ? You sleep in sand with the sky for your blanket? Hear what the wind say to you in your sleep and what the birds' call mean at night?

RUSSEL: No, well I don't really know. But I'm sorry for your husband, Mrs. Francis. I'm sorry, it's not my business.

RUBY: Where you come from, Mr. Russel? You look like you....

RUSSEL: [*interrupting*] What I'd like to talk to you about is your new home. It's very modern, you'll notice the difference. It has electricity. Yes, you can't see it, but it's there. It's like magic; it provides power for lights, heaters, washing machines, refrigerators, almost anything. You won't hardly have to use your hands.

WILBA: "*Murras.*"

RUBY: We call them "*murras.*"

RUSSEL: What? Electricity?

JAYDA: No, these hands, our "*murras.*"

RUSSEL: "*Murras.*" Yes, well as I was saying, everything will be at your fingertips.

WILBA: As long as I can still go hunting, paint and make spears.

JAYDA: And weave baskets and mats and—

RUSSEL: [*interrupting*] You can join classes, yes, there are classes for everything these days. Look, I did: now I do my own banking, book-keeping and I can chair meetings and run seminars.

RUBY: Why does the Government want to give us a house in city?

RUSSEL: To improve your housing conditions. To enable you to live a normal life. To better yourselves.

GRANNY: But we like it just the way it is out here, how it always is.

RUSSEL: There are lots of Aborigines moving to the cities.

RUBY: Where did you say your country was?

RUSSEL: Wilba, can I see some of your carvings, please?

[*WILBA takes an emu egg to RUSSEL.*]

WILBA: This an emu egg. See, the trees, the kangaroo. Still got a lot to do yet.

RUBY: [*to RUSSEL*] Who your mother? Who your father? Where did you say you from?

RUSSEL: [*examining the egg*] There's been a lot of work put into this. The design is so intricate. You are very clever, Wilba. I could never do anything like this.

WILBA: You could if we teach you, aye, Mum?

RUSSEL: No, this is something you grow up with. It's been passed down from generation to generation. I should be able to but.... Mrs. Francis, you keep asking me where my country is. I don't know. I had an Aboriginal mother, but I was taken away. I was adopted to a white family when I was two.

RUBY: I could see you was a little *nungar*.[1]

RUSSEL: There was that policy that took all half children from their tribal mothers. I was on a mission, but I don't remember, I was too young.

GRANNY: They still doin' that now, mothers hidin' their babies. Covering them up with ash to make them look full-blood.

RUSSEL: They are kind to me — my adopted parents, they give me almost everything I want. I've had a good Christian education, a good home and a job. I haven't really missed out on much in life.

RUBY: But you are nothing if you don't know where you come from.

RUSSEL: I wanted to find out once, but now I'm married and have a family of my own. I'm happy with my life, and this job enables me to help other Aborigines that haven't had what I have.

GRANNY: That's why you got this job? You never know, you might be our relation, aye?

RUSSEL: Yes. Well you see, the Department thought that it would be easier for you people to talk to an Aborigine rather than a European. They call it self-determination. We are helping our own people, and seen as positive role models for you.

JAYDA: Will the Department give me a job?

RUSSEL: Maybe, in a hospital or working for a family.

JAYDA: See, I told you mum, working for *wudjellas* again.

WILBA: You ever been hunting? Come on then, take off them clothes and put real proper clothes on and I'll take you out now to find emu eggs, what you reckon?

RUSSEL: I really haven't got time now, as I have other calls to make.

RUBY: What's gonna happen to this land? It still belongs to our people?

RUSSEL: No, there's to be a new highway put in here and a swimming pool close by for the townspeople.

GRANNY: They just move us around like cattle. Why don't you tell them we want stay here, we not....

RUSSEL: I have to make my report and I'll tell them for you, but I'm sure that when you see your new home you will probably change your mind.

RUBY: We don't understand about this report business, but we do what they tell us. You want cuppa tea, Mr. Rus?

RUSSEL: Russel, just Russel. Yes, please.

---

[1] *nungar* See author's glossary.

[*JAYDA pours tea for all.*]

Jesus, just look at this place. How can you live here? No running water, ceiling must leak in the wet, and probably bloody cold in winter. Just look at this dirt floor, it's a breeding ground for rats and diseases; a real health hazard.

WILBA: We get water in bucket from pipeline half mile down the track, that's if they don't turn it off first. But when we have good rain, plenty water in creek, and yabbies too, aye.

GRANNY: Long time, before pipeline, river all time had water. Then cattle come, big dam come, dry 'em up all creek, water hole. Mess 'em up country real proper way.

JAYDA: [*to RUSSEL*] Your cup of tea; Mum likes it real strong; add some powdered milk if you want.

RUSSEL: Thank you. Well, I hope the referendum improves things for you. Just think, it's nineteen sixty-seven now, and in twenty years' time these places will no longer exist. They will have been abolished and we can look back on this very day. That's what the referendum means: self-determination for Aboriginal people, and a better way of life.

RUBY: Russel, you gotta find your people, you know that? They probably look for you all this time.

RUSSEL: [*standing*] Yes, well, that's something I have to think about. I'm glad to have met you, Mrs. Francis, and I will do my best to make your transition to the city easy for you. I really must go now, other calls to make. Goodbye, everyone. And thank you for the cup of tea.

[*He exits. GRANNY angrily hits her stick on the ground.*]

GRANNY: I'm not leavin, I tell you. I born here, I die here. No one gonna move me from this place, true as God, no one.

WILBA: I'm stayin' with you, Granny.

RUBY: It'll be different, we'll be real flash, aye?

WILBA: Mum, that fella, Russel, he reckon he got everything, aye, but I feel sorry for that fella. He never been in the bush. Funny for a *nungar* to get scared of the bush, aye?

RUBY: He find his mother, one day, he know he gotta. Plenty get taken from their people, but find them later on. Well, I better get ready for Sister now. Come on, help tidy up. I'll go wash up.

[*RUBY moves to the door.*]

GRANNY: Hang on, Ruby. I better come too.

RUBY: No, Granny; Sister don't want to see you.

GRANNY: I don't wanna see Sister, I wanna go Goonawalli. Else I'm in biggest trouble.

[*GRANNY and RUBY exit.*]

WILBA: [*sitting by fire carving*] Hey Jayda, what was that dance you was doin' when I come in?

JAYDA: Wilba, you not allowed to look at that dance, you cheeky, lookin' at me. Mum flog you if she finds out.

WILBA: No, she won't. I can dance too, you know.

JAYDA: Come on, show me then. You can't dance, aye?

[*WILBA gets up.*]

WILBA: This dance my father taught me. There he is: moon man, standing by sea looking for dugong. See her and he do this dance for her.

[*WILBA dances for two or three minutes, circling JAYDA. She rises slowly and joins in until the two are dancing. They dance towards the totem where the dance ends with a blackout.*]

ACT TWO
SCENE ONE

RUBY packs clothes, plates, incidentals into an old tea-chest. GRANNY smokes her pipe while weaving a mat.

RUBY: Where that Wilba? I don't like him going out with them mustering mob. Them fullas no good; all time hungry for woman. Fill 'em up with grog. Mr. Morton told them to stay away from this place.

GRANNY: School no good for Wilba. He better stockman, bushman. He gone looking for ride, to help out.

RUBY: What you gonna take to city, Mum? You want me to pack for you?

GRANNY: Never mine me, Ruby, I be alright. Ain't got much, anyway. Dillybag,[1] pipe, tobacco. What that Sister say to you yesterday, Ruby?

RUBY: Nothing, she say I'm alright. Just gave me a bit of sugar, tea, and more kero. Couldn't find that Wilba. He took off from her. She went and seen Jayda at that *wudjella*'s place.

GRANNY: I don't blame him. Wilba — takin' off from her. He hates that paint; reckon he can't get it off for days. Make him look like blue-tongue lizard. Poor fulla.

RUBY: Sister don't say much anyway, just write in her book all the time. She sticky beak, ask questions about Jayda. Don't tell her nothing, but.

---

[1] *Dillybag* (dilly bag) Traditional Australian Aboriginal mesh bag used for various food preparations and transportation.

GRANNY: Well when you go to city, you still have welfare come check up on you, you know. No good, I tell you.

[*As RUBY talks, the sound of horses galloping can be heard, first faintly, gradually becoming louder.*]

RUBY: Charlie went to the city once, I remember... what's that? Some important fulla got one of his totems for... what's that, horses?... for museum... horses and screaming. Watch out, that might be Jayda.

[*RUBY runs to the door, opens it, and JAYDA falls into her arms. She is shaken, hysterical trying to talk and panting.*]

RUBY: Jayda, what happened? Who, what they done....

[*JAYDA collapses into GRANNY's lap.*]

JAYDA: Mum, it's alright. They didn't catch us.

[*RUBY runs from door to window, looks out and shouts.*]

RUBY: You bastards, you keep away from here, you filthy hungry dogs. You hear, you *wudjella* bastards? I'll get you for this.
JAYDA: They chased Jessie and me. We was walking home from doing ironing. They was coming from the hotel way. We heard them whistle and we took off.
RUBY: What about Jessie? She alright?
JAYDA: I don't know, she went one way, I took off this way. They caught up with us, on their horses. I got a stone and hit one bloke in the eye. He got real mad and ripped my dress. Said he was gonna....
GRANNY: Shhh! Don't you talk too much my baby. You alright, just lie down and forget about it.
RUBY: [*picking up a stick and walking towards the door*] I'm gonna go find those dogs, I'll flog them, no one gonna touch my children. I better find Wilba too.
GRANNY: No, Ruby, here you stay with Jayda, I'll find Wilba and Jessie. And those fullas don't want to muck around with me, they'll be sorry, true as God, plenty sorry I'll give it to 'em.

[*GRANNY exits. RUBY comforts JAYDA. She wipes JAYDA's face with a damp rag.*]

JAYDA: Mum, I'm sorry.
RUBY: Not your fault! Now you listen, Jayda; this is not your fault. Don't you take shame for those filthy *wudjellas*. Everything alright, you rest, my baby.

[*RUBY moves away from JAYDA; crouches by the fire and looks at the totem as if talking to Charlie once again.*]

Charlie, they mess'n' up our country, puttin' shame on our children. They got no law, no shame. They no good. I'm goin', I'm goin', take Jayda away from here. They killin' our dreaming places, no good...

[*WILBA enters, followed by GRANNY.*]

WILBA: Mum, I heard screaming, and horses galloping. I was with Jumbo down by the creek, when Jessie come up running, crying, screaming. Jumbo took off after them fullas, he got them mum, gave them biggest floggin'! He gone now, taking Jessie back home. What about Jayda? She alright? Jayda?
RUBY: She alright. Granny you stay here with her. I'll go find Mr. Morton; he can take us to police station. Wilba, you come with me.
WILBA: Don't go police, mum. They won't do anything, just throw Jumbo in jail, that's all.
RUBY: We be back soon Granny.

[*RUBY and WILBA exit.*]

GRANNY: [*softly*] Jayda, your mother, she wild like wounded buffalo, but she fix up everything. *Wudjella* don't know our lore, they got no spirit. They don't have one time, like us, don't have dreaming. They nothing people, Jayda, nothing people. Jayda, listen now, I teach you one more time. Soon my time coming.
JAYDA: Granny, don't say that.
GRANNY: Shhh! Soon my time coming; no more for me to do. I seen lot a things happening, some good, but mostly bad. You know they tried to take Charlie away from me. One *wudjella* man wanted me, for himself. I told him I gave him away to 'nother woman. But I hid him, hid him in my sugar bag. I was nearly sittin' on top of him while I was lyin' to that *wudjella*. He was a good boy, kept real quiet. I kept hidin' him, until he met your mother. Hm, well, soon I'll find his spirit again. And Jayda... Jayda... you sleep? My little sea-grass, my little sea-grass. You listen for me, I sing to you, you listen now...

[*The lights fade softly to black. GRANNY hums to JAYDA.*]

SCENE TWO

GRANNY's dying scene. This scene symbolizes her return to the earth and the traditional preparation of her body to return to the spiritual world of her dreaming, returning to her ancestors. The mimi spirit is there to return her safely by dancing around her,

*calling her back into her world, her time. GRANNY sits in the centre of the motif sway-
ing, rocking to and fro, wailing as she gathers handfuls of sand and gently pours them
over herself. After the dance of the spirit is completed, he encapsulates her by stretching
over her, engulfing her. This is done to the music of the didjeridu and clapping sticks. At
the end of the dance, the lights slowly fade until the stage is totally black.*

SCENE THREE

*Slow fade up. The sounds of the bush can be heard. RUBY, WILBA, and JAYDA enter
and slowly gather all their belongings. Then they hear a bulldozer, off. The family exits.*

JAYDA runs back on.
JAYDA: [*calling*] Granny! Granny!

[*She realizes that GRANNY has gone. Blackout.*]

ACT THREE
SCENE ONE

*The year is 1970. The family have moved to the city. JAYDA is a domestic in a hospital
and WILBA is finishing school. JAYDA vacuums the living room floor. WILBA enters
with a Coke in his hand and a school bag. He flings the bag across the floor in anger,
then sits on the sofa with his head down.*

JAYDA: [*switching off Hoover*] What's up?
WILBA: Nothing, I'm alright.
JAYDA: No you not, come on, Wilba. You look real mad. Look at you. Alright, if you
    won't tell me.

[*She switches the Hoover on.*]

WILBA: Alright, alright, I'll tell you.

[*JAYDA switches the Hoover off again.*]

JAYDA: I know something's up.
WILBA: I got into trouble with headmaster. Got the cane.
JAYDA: What for this time. Fightin' again?
WILBA: I don't care, next time I'll flatten him real proper way. This fulla called me a filthy
    nigger, abo bastard. Aldo told him to shut up, but he got his face punched in.
JAYDA: Aldo always stick up for you.
WILBA: Yeah, that's why I joined in. I wasn't gonna let him get into trouble over me,
    so I dropped that fulla.

JAYDA: What did you do to him?

WILBA: Only gave him a black eye, blood nose. Should have laid him out, true as God, should have.

JAYDA: Well the three of you deserve that cane, fighting like that.

[*JAYDA unplugs the Hoover and rolls the cord up.*]

WILBA: What you talking about, Jayda? I was the only one got the cane. That *wudjella* headmaster make me real mad. He goes… "You have to learn to behave. We can't have you acting like a nomad down here."

JAYDA: Now listen Wilba, it's not that different for me, either. I work in the kitchen with Russians, Italians, Greeks, you name it, but I'm the only Aboriginal, and boy do I get it. All the dirty jobs, bossed around, and I got to stop myself from getting mad. I don't want to lose my job so I just walk away.

WILBA: Not me, I'm gonna fight.

JAYDA: It's because we different, they don't understand us. They never seen black-fullas before, probably scared of us. They'd die if they had to live in the bush like us. Come on Wilba, don't let them kill us.

WILBA: I'm not going tomorrow, I'll make out I'm sick or something.

JAYDA: Don't do that, that won't help. You just gotta be best at the things you can do. You the best runner, footballer, drawer, aren't you? Well just … shhh! That must be Mum.

[*RUBY enters carrying a bag of clothes. She flops on to the sofa.*]

RUBY: Hullo, I'm buggered, phew. These *boogadies*[1] hurt my feet.

JAYDA: Mum, you been spendin' up real good, looks like.

RUBY: Just been to the mission. Jessie and me been driving around dropping off clothes to other *nungar* families. Got few for you two. Look in there now.

[*WILBA opens the bag and spreads the clothes out on the floor.*]

WILBA: Wow, look here, jumper, jeans, socks, and look here, *gundies*,[2] real neat, aye?

JAYDA: That jumper looks good on you, Wilba, and look here, this dress real pretty, but too small for you, aye Mum?

RUBY: [*standing and picking up the dress*] No, Jayda, this dress I got specially for you, to wear to Jessie and Tom's tomorrow when?

JAYDA: [*angry and loud*] Mum, I told you before. I'm working now and I can buy my own clothes. I can't wear anything like this. Shame job.

---

[1] *boogadies* See author's glossary.

[2] *gundies* See author's glossary.

RUBY: What, you too good now? I always got clothes from there before. You didn't say anything then.

JAYDA: It's not that. I have to dress the same as....

WILBA: Mum, I think I'll go watch TV at Aldo's. See youse later.

[*Exit WILBA.*]

JAYDA: It's not that, Mum. I have to dress the same as my friends. I've got to be the same, Mum, or they'll laugh at me.

RUBY: Laugh, aye? You should be the one laughing, Jayda. You listen here, I'm not too shame. Let them think we different. I'll take them for everything they gotta offer. Jayda, it's *them* they *want* to treat us like this. I'll take them for every hand-out, ration, free pass, for every penny. As long as they *don't* think we like them, we sittin' pretty.

JAYDA: But you deserve brand-new clothes, not hand-me-downs. You will always be nobody if you let them treat you like that. Don't you see, Mum?

RUBY: When you got no money for brand-new clothes, you have to feel proud in any clothes. I'm not too shame, Jessie not too shame, I know lot of *nungars* not too shame.

JAYDA: They don't like it if you act like blackfulla, either. Sometimes I gotta be better, dress better, everything better than them. I can't be different, Mum.

RUBY: I'm same person in old dress like I am in brand-new dress. I don't change. But you, Jayda, you changin', gettin' new ways. You didn't want to come city, remember? You want to go back now, Jayda? They all gone, Jayda, our people all gone.

JAYDA: I have changed, Mum, I'm older, I'm different now.

RUBY: You don't make baskets no more.

JAYDA: [*grabbing the basket hanging on the wall*] There's no place for baskets here. It doesn't mean anything to them....

RUBY: It doesn't have to! [*She grabs the basket from JAYDA.*] This belongs to you! *This* you gotta teach your children one day.

RUBY: When you get married you will, and that's whe—

JAYDA: I can't have children, Mum.

RUBY: What? What you saying, Jayda? Who told you that?

JAYDA: Doctor at the hospital, I had a medical, a test, he told me.

RUBY: Medical? Test? What for?

JAYDA: It was a routine check-up. The doctor called me in one day. He had some special papers there, he said they were from the government, said that I was part of a programme or something, long time ago. Had to do with those injections that Sister use to give me and Jessie.

RUBY: Injections? You didn't tell me about any injections.

JAYDA: Mum, she said it was alright. I thought you knew; she said she explained it to you. She told me it was to stop diseases.

RUBY: She lied. Injections to stop disease, injections to stop babies. They lied to us; who they think they are? Boss over you, boss over me—your mother?

JAYDA: Mum, it was an experiment. We can't do anything about it now. Mum, I'm alright, it's alright.

RUBY: No, it's not alright! Jayda, you was only fourteen years old, still my baby. What kind of law they got? They mess around with our women's business; they bring death to our land, shame to our children....

JAYDA: I saw a woman from Welfare; she said there's nothing I can do. But I thought of being a nurse, Mum, and going back to make sure they still not doing this.

RUBY: Those filthy *wudjella* dogs; they knew who had those injections. That's why they chased you and Jessie.

JAYDA: How would they know, Mum? We never spoke to them.

RUBY: I remember, I remember that Sister coming around mustering time. She use to drink with them in the pub; that's how they knew.

JAYDA: Mum, come here. Remember when Granny said *wudjella* woman got different way to *gadjeri* woman? They don't have woman's dreaming, special dance, *Inma*. Then she said, "Jayda, you not forget your stories now, you keep them sacred for your children, not *wudjella*?" Granny call them nothing people, got no spirit.

RUBY: They all nothing people. Granny and I teach you your own women's business. And that Sister, she take everything away from us.

JAYDA: No, Mum, no one take you from me, or Granny. Mum, sit down, I get you a cup of tea, Mum. I'll be a good nurse, you wait and see. You be real proud of me. I gotta go back to work. You be alright?

[*She gathers her bag for work and sits beside her mother.*]

Don't worry about me.... I'll be alright. I love you, Mum, I love you.

ACT FOUR

It is some years later. WILBA is now a black activist for the Aboriginal land rights struggle which has swept the nation. There have been marches in all capital cities, and a rally which resulted in the Aboriginal Tent Embassy being set up on the lawns of Parliament House in Canberra. WILBA is often arrested in these protests.

RUBY sits on the sofa watching TV. WILBA enters, and quietly sneaks up behind his mother, startling her.

RUBY: Wilba, Wilba, what you doing home? I've been watching you on TV. You alright? Want something to eat?

WILBA: Thank you, Mum, but I'm not staying. Just getting few clothes, blankets, on my way through.

RUBY: Through to where? Where you going?

WILBA: Mum, car outside. I'm in a hurry.

RUBY: I haven't seen you for a long time. Stay and have talk, come on, Wilba.

WILBA: Mum, I don't have time, I tell you, gotta go.

[*WILBA fills clothes into a land rights bag as he talks to his mother.*]

RUBY: Wilba, you alright? Something wrong?

WILBA: I've had a gutful of this place. They got bulldozers going up, bloody bulldozers, Mum, on our land. No way no fuckin' mining company's gonna dig up my father's bones, our burial grounds.

RUBY: They can't do that, that's sacred place. They can't do that. Charlie, and Granny they....

WILBA: You better believe it, they are.

RUBY: What you gonna do? What can you do, Wilba? Don't go gettin' yourself into trouble, now.

WILBA: We gonna march, Mum. Hundreds of us, not just me. We all going up there to sit on that land when the trucks and bulldozers come in. Those politicians, mob of ignorant *wudjellas*. I'm sick to the gut of their false promises of self-determination. Sick of their shit lies, their corrupt laws, their diseases, their gaols...yeah, their chains, their chains. They handcuffed me, my *murras*, to a *wudjella* cop. The bastards...a *wudjella* pig.

RUBY: I never hear you talk like this, with so much anger. You grow like man now. Your father be real proud if he see you now. But you don't use your *murras* for the things you were taught. You do carving still, Wilba? Make boomerang, spear, emu eggs? What your father think of that if—?

WILBA: [*interrrupting*] He's dead! Mum, you not listening to me. They are going to dig up his bones to build a mining town. That's what this is all about. I can't do those things here, not in the city. We have to fight so that our traditional people can still do these things and keep their land.

RUBY: Alright, but just look after yourself. Don't worry about me, I'll be alright.

WILBA: Mum, I'll be okay, there's big mob of us.

[*A car horn sounds, off.*]

That's my lift. Mum, I gotta do this—for you, for Dad, for me. We've always been told what to do, where to live, where to go. Manipulated like cattle, just like Granny said, but you know them *wudjellas* from government, they decide what we want, what we need, where the money should be spent, but our people are still dying.

RUBY: You know what you talking about. I don't understand. I'll be here when you get back.

[*The car horn sounds again, off.*]

WILBA: That's it. Sorry, Mum, I don't want to sound too heavy, but this is what's happening. There's a lot of angry blacks out there, and I'm one of them. We are all victims of this system, but we are going to do something about it. Mum, I gotta go, and if you see Jayda, say hello for me, aye?

[*WILBA lifts RUBY to her feet and puts his arms around her.*]

I'll drop you a line, and don't worry. Come here, I love you. I'll think of you, okay? See ya, see ya ...

[*WILBA kisses RUBY and exits. RUBY looks at the door as he closes it, then slowly walks back to the sofa. She gazes around the room fixing her eyes on the artifacts that her family has made. She reminisces about her life as she gathers each piece and places it beside Charlie's totem. She stares fixedly at the totem for a long time.*]

RUBY: Charlie, I seen too many changes. Moon, water, seagrass, dugong, parrotfish ... all scattered. Granny gone. Wilba's *murras* are scarred by the *wudjella's* chains. His *murras* are clenched fists now. Jayda don't make baskets no more. She bleeds from her womb the seeds of death. She carries the scars from the *wudjella's* medicine. There's no place for baskets here, she says. And my *murras* are too weak. They no longer carve. They are empty now. Moon, water, seagrass, dugong, parrotfish ... gone. All gone.

[*The song "Visions" plays while the cast slowly move the props offstage. The MIMI SPIRIT dances around the stage until he completes a full circle.*]

THE END

1988

E. Pauline Johnson

E. Pauline Johnson, or Tekahionwake (1861-1913), born in Ontario, Canada, was the daughter of a Mohawk chief and his English wife. Caught initially between two worlds, she eventually wanted to be known by her Mohawk name, seeing herself as the "saga singer of her people" and "the sad historian of her own heroic race." Like many colonial poets, she tried to combine the traditions of English poetry and autochthonous cultural values.

In "The Cattle Thief" (1900), Johnson allies herself with the natives and censures the imperial forces that have robbed her people of land, culture, and religion. The poem employs the traditional ballad form, alternating tetrameters and trimeters, but with traditional line breaks indicated by caesuras. Does this ballad meter help to point up the defiance of the natives as embodied in the response of the cattle thief's wife? Other than "tepees," does the poem employ any Native diction or imagery? Would this make a difference on the impact of the poem?

The Cattle Thief

They were coming across the prairie, they were galloping hard and fast;
For the eyes of those desperate riders had sighted their man at last—
Sighted him off to Eastward, where the Cree[1] encampment lay,
Where the cotton woods fringed the river, miles and miles away.
Mistake him? Never! Mistake him? The famous Eagle Chief!
That terror to all the settlers, that desperate Cattle Thief—
That monstrous, fearless Indian, who lorded it over the plain,
Who thieved and raided, and scouted, who rode like a hurricane!
But they've tracked him across the prairie; they've followed him hard and fast;
For those desperate English settlers have sighted their man at last.

Up they wheeled to the tepees, all their British blood aflame,
Bent on bullets and bloodshed, bent on bringing down their game;
But they searched in vain for the Cattle Thief; that lion had left his lair,
And they cursed like a troop of demons—for the women alone were there
"The sneaking Indian coward," they hissed; "he hides while yet he can;
He'll come in the night for cattle, but he's scared to face a *man*."
"Never!" and up from the cotton woods rang the voice of Eagle Chief;
And right out into the open stepped, unarmed, the Cattle Thief.
Was that the game they had coveted? Scarce fifty years had rolled

---

[1] *Cree* The Cree are an indigenous people of North America and the largest group of First Nations people in Canada.

Over that fleshless, hungry frame, starved to the bone and old;
Over that wrinkled, tawny skin, unfed by the warmth of blood.
Over those hungry, hollow eyes that glared for the sight of food.

He turned, like a hunted lion: "I know not fear," said he;
And the words outleapt from his shrunken lips in the language of the Cree.
"I'll fight you, white-skins, one by one, till I kill you *all*," he said;
But the threat was scarcely uttered, ere a dozen balls of lead
Whizzed through the air about him like a shower of metal rain,
And the gaunt old Indian Cattle Thief dropped dead on the open plain.
And that band of cursing settlers gave one triumphant yell,
And rushed like a pack of demons on the body that writhed and fell.
"Cut the fiend up into inches, throw his carcass on the plain;
Let the wolves eat the cursed Indian, he'd have treated us the same."
A dozen hands responded, a dozen knives gleamed high,
But the first stroke was arrested by a woman's strange, wild cry.
And out into the open, with a courage past belief,
She dashed, and spread her blanket o'er the corpse of the Cattle Thief;
And the words outleapt from her shrunken lips in the language of the Cree,
"If you mean to touch that body you must cut your way through me."
And that band of cursing settlers dropped backward one by one,
For they knew that an Indian woman roused, was a woman to let alone.
And then she raved in a frenzy that they scarcely understood,
Raved of the wrongs she had suffered since her earliest babyhood:
"Stand back, stand back, you white-skins, touch that dead man to your shame;
You have stolen my father's spirit, but his body I only claim.
You have killed him, but you shall not dare to touch him now he's dead.
You have cursed, and called him a Cattle Thief, though you robbed him first of bread—
Robbed him and robbed my people—look there, at that shrunken face,
Starved with a hollow hunger, we owe to you and your race.
What have you left to us of land, what have you left of game,
What have you brought but evil, and curses since you came?
How have you paid us for our game? how paid us for our land?
By a *book*, to save our souls from the sins *you* brought in your other hand.
Go back with your new religion, we never have understood
Your robbing an Indian's *body*, and mocking his *soul* with food.
Go back with your new religion, and find—if find you can—
The *honest* man you have ever made from out a *starving* man.
You say your cattle are not ours, your meat is not our meat;
When *you* pay for the land you live in, *we'll* pay for the meat we eat.
Give back our land and our country, give back our herds of game;
Give back the furs and the forests that were ours before you came;

Give back the peace and the plenty. Then come with your new belief
And blame, if you dare, the hunger that *drove* him to be a thief."

1900

Jamaica Kincaid

Jamaica Kincaid (Elaine Potter Richardson, b. 1949) was born in St. John's, Antigua; she now lives and writes in the United States. She worked for *The New Yorker* as a staff writer until 1996. Her fiction includes *At the Bottom of the River* (short stories, 1984), *Annie John* (novel, 1985), and *The Autobiography of My Mother* (1996). She has published numerous critical and travel pieces including *A Small Place* (1988) and *Among Flowers: A Walk in the Himalayas* (2005).

Kincaid's "On Seeing England for the First Time" recalls the omnipresence of Britain in the lives of children growing up in the British Empire. On her first visit to Britain, she is able to exorcize the hold Britain had on her imagination. At least this is what she says. Do you think there is an ambivalence to her response at the end of the essay? Compare this essay with V.S. Naipaul's "Jasmine" and Fred D'Aguiar's poem "Home."

On Seeing England for the First Time

When I saw England for the first time, I was a child in school sitting at a desk. The England I was looking at was laid out on a map gently, beautifully, delicately, a very special jewel; it lay on a bed of sky blue — the background of the map — its yellow form mysterious, because though it looked like a leg of mutton, it could not really look like anything so familiar as a leg of mutton because it was England — with shadings of pink and green, unlike any shadings of pink and green I had seen before, squiggly veins of red running in every direction. England was a special jewel all right, and only special people got to wear it. The people who got to wear England were English people. They wore it well and they wore it everywhere: in jungles, in deserts, on plains, on top of the highest mountains, on all the oceans, on all the seas. When my teacher had pinned this map up on the blackboard, she said, "This is England" — and she said it with authority, seriousness, and adoration, and we all sat up. It was as if she had said, "This is Jerusalem, the place you will go to when you die but only if you have been good." We understood then — we were meant to understand then — that England was to be our source of myth and the source from which we got our sense of reality, our sense of what was meaningful, our sense of what was meaningless — and much about our own lives and much about the very idea of us headed that last list.

At the time I was a child sitting at my desk seeing England for the first time, I was already very familiar with the greatness of it. Each morning before I left for school, I ate a breakfast of half a grapefruit, an egg, bread and butter and a slice of cheese, and a cup of cocoa; or half a grapefruit, a bowl of oat porridge, bread and butter and a slice of cheese, and a cup of cocoa. The can of cocoa was often left on the table in front of me. It had written on it the name of the company, the year the company was established, and the words "Made in England." Those words, "Made in England," were written on the box the oats came in too. They would also have been written on the box the shoes I was wearing came in; the bolt of gray linen cloth lying on the shelf of a store from which my mother had bought three yards to make the uniform that I was wearing had written along its edge those three words. The shoes I wore were made in England; so were my socks and cotton undergarments and the satin ribbons I wore tied at the end of two plaits of my hair. My father, who might have sat next to me at breakfast, was a carpenter and cabinetmaker. The shoes he wore to work would have been made in England, as were his khaki shirt and trousers, his underpants and undershirt, his socks and brown felt hat. Felt was not the proper material from which a hat that was expected to provide shade from the hot sun should have been made, but my father must have seen and admired a picture of an Englishman wearing such a hat in England, and this picture that he saw must have been so compelling that it caused him to wear the wrong hat for a hot climate most of his long life. And this hat — a brown felt hat — became so central to his character that it was the first thing he put on in the morning as he stepped out of bed and the last thing he took off before he stepped back into bed at night. As we sat at breakfast, a car might go by. The car, a Hillman or a Zephyr, was made in England. The very idea of the meal itself, breakfast, and its substantial quality and quantity, was an idea from England; we somehow knew that in England they began the day with this meal called breakfast, and a proper breakfast was a big breakfast. No one I knew liked eating so much food so early in the day; it made us feel sleepy, tired. But this breakfast business was "Made in England" like almost everything else that surrounded us, the exceptions being the sea, the sky, and the air we breathed.

At the time I saw this map — seeing England for the first time — I did not say to myself, "Ah, so that's what it looks like," because there was no longing in me to put a shape to those three words that ran through every part of my life no matter how small; for me to have had such a longing would have meant that I lived in a certain atmosphere, an atmosphere in which those three words were felt as a burden. But I did not live in such an atmosphere. When my teacher showed us the map, she asked us to study it carefully, because no test we would ever take would be complete without this statement: "Draw a map of England." I did not know then that the statement "Draw a map of England" was something far worse than a declaration of war, for a flat-out declaration of war would have put me on alert. In fact, there was no need for war — I had long ago been conquered. I did not know then that this statement was part of a process that would result in my erasure — not my physical erasure, but my erasure all the same. I did not know then that this statement was meant to make me feel awe and small whenever I heard the word "England": awe at the power of its existence, small because I was not from it.

After that there were many times of seeing England for the first time. I saw England in history. I knew the names of all the kings of England. I knew the names of their children, their wives, their disappointments, their triumphs, the names of people who betrayed them. I knew the dates on which they were born and the dates they died. I knew their conquests and was made to feel good if I figured in them; I knew their defeats.

This view—the naming of the kings, their deeds, their disappointments—was the vivid view, the forceful view. There were other views, subtler ones, softer, almost not there—but these softer views were the ones that made the most lasting impression on me, the ones that made me really feel like nothing. "When morning touched the sky" was one phrase, for no morning touched the sky where I lived. The morning where I lived came on abruptly, with a shock of heat and loud noises. "Evening approaches" was another. But the evenings where I lived did not approach; in fact, I had no evening—I had night and I had day, and they came and went in a mechanical way: on, off, on, off. And then there were gentle mountains and low blue skies and moors over which people took walks for nothing but pleasure, when where I lived a walk was an act of labor, a burden, something only death or the automobile could relieve. And the weather there was so remarkable because the rain fell gently always, and the wind blew in gusts that were sometimes deep, and the air was various shades of gray, each an appealing shade for a dress to be worn when a portrait was being painted; and when it rained at twilight, wonderful things happened: People bumped into each other unexpectedly and that would lead to all sorts of turns of events—a plot, the mere weather caused plots.

The reality of my life, the life I led at the time I was being shown these views of England for the first time, for the second time, for the one hundred millionth time, was this: The sun shone with what sometimes seemed to be a deliberate cruelty; we must have done something to deserve that. My dresses did not rustle in the evening air as I strolled to the theater (I had no evening, I had no theater; my dresses were made of a cheap cotton, the weave of which would give way after not too many washings). I got up in the morning, I did my chores (fetched water from the public pipe for my mother, swept the yard), I washed myself, I went to a woman to have my hair combed freshly every day (because before we were allowed into our classroom our teachers would inspect us, and children who had not bathed that day, or had dirt under their fingernails, or whose hair had not been combed anew that day might not be allowed to attend class). I ate that breakfast. I walked to school. At school we gathered in an auditorium and sang a hymn, "All Things Bright and Beautiful," and looking down on us as we sang were portraits of the queen of England and her husband; they wore jewels and medals and they smiled. I was a Brownie. At each meeting we would form a little group around a flagpole, and after raising the Union Jack, we would say, "I promise to do my best, to do my duty to God and the queen, to help other people every day and obey the scouts' law."

But who were these people and why had I never seen them? I mean, really seen them, in the place where they lived? I had never been to England. England! I had seen England's representatives. I had seen the governor-general at the public grounds at a ceremony celebrating the queen's birthday. I had seen an old princess and I had seen a young princess. They had both been extremely not beautiful, but who among us would have told them that? I had never seen England, really seen it. I had only met a representative, seen a picture, read books, memorized its history. I had never set foot, my own foot, in it.

The space between the idea of something and its reality is always wide and deep and dark. The longer they are kept apart — idea of thing, reality of thing — the wider the width, the deeper the depth, the thicker and darker the darkness. This space starts out empty, there is nothing in it, but it rapidly becomes filled up with obsession or desire or hatred or love — sometimes all of these things, sometimes some of these things. That the idea of something and its reality are often two completely different things is something no one ever remembers; and so when they meet and find that they are not compatible, the weaker of the two, idea or reality, dies.

And so finally, when I was a grown-up woman, the mother of two children, the wife of someone, a person who resides in a powerful country that takes up more than its fair share of a continent, the owner of a house with many rooms in it and of two automobiles, with the desire and will (which I very much act upon) to take from the world more than I give back to it, more than I deserve, more than I need, finally then, I saw England, the real England, not a picture, not a painting, not through a story in a book, but England, for the first time. In me, the space between the idea of it and its reality had become filled with hatred, and so when at last I saw it I wanted to take it into my hands and tear it into little pieces and then crumble it up as if it were clay, child's clay. That was impossible, and so I could only indulge in not-favorable opinions.

If I had told an English person what I thought, that I find England ugly, that I hate England; the weather is like a jail sentence; the English are a very ugly people; the food in England is like a jail sentence; the hair of English people is so straight, so dead-looking; the English have an unbearable smell so different from the smell of people I know, real people, of course, I would have been told that I was a person full of prejudice. Apart from the fact that it is I — that is, the people who look like me — who would make that English person aware of the unpleasantness of such a thing, the idea of such a thing, prejudice, that person would have been only partly right, sort of right: I may be capable of prejudice, but my prejudices have no weight to them, my prejudices have no force behind them, my prejudices remain opinions, my prejudices remain my personal opinion. And a great feeling of rage and disappointment came over me as I looked at England, my head full of personal opinions that could not have public, my public, approval. The people I come from are powerless to do evil on a grand scale.

The moment I wished every sentence, everything I knew, that began with England would end with "and then it all died, we don't know how, it just all died" was when I saw the white cliffs of Dover. I had sung hymns and recited poems that were about a longing to see the white cliffs of Dover again. At the time I sang the hymns and recited the poems, I could really long to see them again because I had never seen them at all, nor had anyone around me at the time. But there we were, groups of people longing for something we had never seen. And so there they were, the white cliffs, but they were not that pearly, majestic thing I used to sing about, that thing that created such a feeling in these people that when they died in the place where I lived they had themselves buried facing a direction that would allow them to see the white cliffs of Dover when they were resurrected, as surely they would be. The white cliffs of Dover, when finally I saw them, were cliffs, but they were not white; you could only call them that if the word "white" meant something special to you; they were steep; they were so steep, the correct height from which all my views of England, starting with the map before me in my classroom and ending with the trip I had just taken, should jump and die and disappear forever.

1991

Thomas King

Thomas King (b. 1943) was born in Sacramento, California, USA of a Cherokee father and a Greek-German mother. He was chair of Native American studies at the University of Minnesota and now teaches at the University of Guelph, Canada. His publications include *Green Grass, Running Water* (novel, 1993), a number of short stories, poems, a children's book, and *A Short History of Indians in Canada* (2005). King gave the 2003 Massey Lectures, entitled *The Truth About Stories: A Native Narrative*.

In "A Coyote Columbus Story," King tries to evoke the Native oral tradition as far as the printed form allows him to do so. Modern historians have corrected the assumption that Columbus discovered the new world; they point out that he discovered the new world *for Europe*—that it was always there. The narrator persuades Coyote, the traditional trickster figure of Native mythology, to recognize this fact. Why does King have the narrator instruct Coyote rather than someone else? King employs humour in the telling of this story. Is the humour comic (that is, warm and accommodating), satirical (mocking), or farcical (lacking serious purpose)?

A Coyote Columbus Story

You know, Coyote[1] came by my place the other day. She was going to a party. She had her party hat and she had her party whistle and she had her party rattle.

I'm going to a party, she says.

Yes, I says, I can see that.

It is a party for Christopher Columbus, says Coyote. That is the one who found America. That is the one who found Indians.

Boy, that Coyote is one silly Coyote. You got to watch out for her. Some of Coyote's stories have got Coyote tails and some of Coyote's stories are covered with scraggy Coyote fur but all of Coyote's stories are bent.

Christopher Columbus didn't find America, I says. Christopher Columbus didn't find Indians, either. You got a tail on that story.

Oh no, says Coyote. I read it in a book.

Must have been a Coyote book, I says.

No, no, no, no, says Coyote. It was a history book. Big red one. All about how Christopher Columbus sailed the ocean blue looking for America and the Indians.

Sit down, I says. Have some tea. We're going to have to do this story right. We're going to have to do this story now.

---

[1] *Coyote* In North American Native myths, Coyote is a trickster figure and culture hero (like Anancy— see Louise Bennett's "Anancy an Ticks"). In some creation myths, she/he is the Creator.

It was all Old Coyote's fault, I tell Coyote, and here is how the story goes. Here is what really happened.

So.

Old Coyote loved to play ball, you know. She played ball all day and all night. She would throw the ball and she would hit the ball and she would run and catch the ball. But playing ball by herself was boring, so she sang a song and she danced a dance and she thought about playing ball and pretty soon along came some Indians. Old Coyote and the Indians became very good friends. You are sure a good friend, says those Indians. Yes, that's true, says Old Coyote.

But, you know, whenever Old Coyote and the Indians played ball, Old Coyote always won. She always won because she made up the rules. That sneaky one made up the rules and she always won because she could do that.

That's not fair, says the Indians. Friends don't do that.

That's the rules, says Old Coyote. Let's play some more. Maybe you will win the next time. But they don't.

You keep changing the rules, says those Indians.

No, no, no, no, says Old Coyote. You are mistaken. And then she changes the rules again.

So, after a while, those Indians find better things to do.

Some of them go fishing.

Some of them go shopping.

Some of them go to a movie.

Some of them go on a vacation.

Those Indians got better things to do than play ball with Old Coyote and those changing rules.

So, Old Coyote doesn't have anyone to play with.

So, she has to play by herself.

So, she gets bored.

When Old Coyote gets bored, anything can happen. Stick around. Big trouble is coming, I can tell you that.

Well. That silly one sings a song and she dances a dance and she thinks about playing ball. But she's thinking about changing those rules, too, and she doesn't watch what she is making up out of her head. So pretty soon, she makes three ships.

Hmmmm, says Old Coyote, where did those ships come from?

And pretty soon, she makes some people on those ships.

Hmmmm, says Old Coyote, where did those people come from?

And pretty soon, she makes some people on the beach with flags and funny-looking clothes and stuff.

Hooray, says Old Coyote. You are just in time for the ball game.

Hello, says one of the men in silly clothes and red hair all over his head. I am Christopher Columbus. I am sailing the ocean blue looking for China. Have you seen it?

Forget China, says Old Coyote. Let's play ball.

It must be around here somewhere, says Christopher Columbus. I have a map.

Forget the map, says Old Coyote. I'll bat first and I'll tell you the rules as we go along.

But that Christopher Columbus and his friends don't want to play ball. We got work to do, he says. We got to find China. We got to find things we can sell.

Yes, says those Columbus people, where is the gold?

Yes, they says, where is that silk cloth?

Yes, they says, where are those portable color televisions?

Yes, they says, where are those home computers?

Boy, says Old Coyote, and that one scratches her head. I must have sung that song wrong. Maybe I didn't do the right dance. Maybe I thought too hard. These people I made have no manners. They act as if they have no relations.

And she is right. Christopher Columbus and his friends start jumping up and down in their funny clothes and they shout so loud that Coyote's ears almost fall off.

Boy, what a bunch of noise, says Coyote. What bad manners. You guys got to stop jumping and shouting or my ears will fall off.

We got to find China, says Christopher Columbus. We got to become rich. We got to become famous. Do you think you can help us?

But all Old Coyote can think about is playing ball.

I'll let you bat first, says Old Coyote.

No time for games, says Christopher Columbus.

I'll let you make the rules, cries Old Coyote.

But those Columbus people don't listen. They are too busy running around, peeking under rocks, looking in caves, sailing all over the place. Looking for China. Looking for stuff they can sell.

I got a monkey, says one.

I got a parrot, says another.

I got a fish, says a third.

I got a coconut, says a fourth,

That stuff isn't worth poop, says Christopher Columbus. We can't sell those things in Spain. Look harder.

But all they find are monkeys and parrots and fish and coconuts. And when they tell Christopher Columbus, that one he squeezes his ears and he chews his nose and grinds his teeth. He grinds his teeth so hard, he gets a headache, and, then, he gets cranky.

And then he gets an idea.

Say, says Christopher Columbus. Maybe we could sell Indians.

Yes, says his friends, that's a good idea. We could sell Indians, and they throw away their monkeys and parrots and fish and coconuts.

Wait a minute, says the Indians, that is not a good idea. That is a bad idea. That is a bad idea full of bad manners.

When Old Coyote hears this bad idea, she starts to laugh. Who would buy Indians, she says, and she laughs some more. She laughs so hard, she has to hold her nose on her face with both her hands.

But while that Old Coyote is laughing, Christopher Columbus grabs a big bunch of Indian men and Indian women and Indian children and locks them up in his ships.

When Old Coyote stops laughing and looks around, she sees that some of the Indians are missing. Hey, she says, where are those Indians? Where are my friends?

I'm going to sell them in Spain, says Christopher Columbus. Somebody has to pay for this trip. Sailing over the ocean blue isn't cheap, you know.

But Old Coyote still thinks that Christopher Columbus is playing a trick. She thinks it is a joke. That is a good joke, she says, trying to make me think that you are going to sell my friends. And she starts to laugh again.

Grab some more Indians, says Christopher Columbus.

When Old Coyote sees Christopher Columbus grab some more Indians, she laughs even harder. What a good joke, she says. And she laughs some more. She does this four times and when she is done laughing, all the Indians are gone. And Christopher Columbus is gone and Christopher Columbus's friends are gone, too.

Wait a minute, says old Coyote. What happened to my friends? Where are my Indians? You got to bring them back. Who's going to play ball with me?

But Christopher Columbus didn't bring the Indians back and Old Coyote was real sorry she thought him up. She tried to take him back. But, you know, once you think things like that, you can't take them back. So you have to be careful what you think.

So. That's the end of the story.

Boy, says Coyote. That is one sad story.

Yes, I says. It's sad alright. And things don't get any better, I can tell you that.

What a very sad story, says Coyote. Poor Old Coyote didn't have anyone to play ball with. That one must have been lonely. And Coyote begins to cry.

Stop crying, I says. Old Coyote is fine. Some blue jays come along after that and they play ball with her.

Oh, good, says Coyote. But what happened to the Indians? There was nothing in that red history book about Christopher Columbus and the Indians.

Christopher Columbus sold the Indians, I says, and that one became rich and famous.

Oh, good, says Coyote. I love a happy ending. And that one blows her party whistle and that one shakes her party rattle and that one puts her party hat back on her head. I better get going, she says, I'm going to be late for the party.

Okay, I says. Just remember how that story goes. Don't go messing it up again. Have you got it straight, now?

You bet, says Coyote. But if Christopher Columbus didn't find America and he didn't find Indians, who found these things?

Those things were never lost, I says. Those things were always here. Those things are still here today.

By golly, I think you are right, says Coyote.

Don't be thinking, I says. This world has enough problems already without a bunch of Coyote thoughts with tails and scraggy fur running around bumping into each other.

Boy, that's the truth. I can tell you that.

1992

Rudyard Kipling

Rudyard Kipling (1865-1936) was born in British India but educated in England. He returned to India in 1882, where his father was director of the Lahore Museum. He published numerous stories and poems, the novel *Kim* (1901), and two *Jungle Books* about India. Familiar with Indian culture, he appeared at home in India, but many see an imperial trait in his writing that "The White Man's Burden" confirms. He won the Nobel Prize for Literature in 1907.

Kipling's "The White Man's Burden" was published in *McClure's* magazine (February 1899) as a response to the United States taking possession of the Philippines after the Spanish-American War. It is a very controversial poem; many find its cultural imperialism distasteful. Some defenders of Kipling have suggested that he is being ironical in the poem and is in fact censuring imperialism and Eurocentrism. Do you find any evidence of this? The American poet Ernest Crosby (1856-1907) published his parody—"The Real 'White Man's Burden'"—in the *New York Times* almost immediately after the publication of Kipling's poem (15 February 1899). Crosby also wrote *Captain Jinks, Hero* (1902), a novel that satirizes the career of Frederick Funston, the general who occupied the Philippines. Crosby's parody appears here after Kipling's poem.

The White Man's Burden

Take up the White Man's burden—
    Send forth the best ye breed—
Go, bind your sons to exile
    to serve your captives' need;
To wait, in heavy harness,
    On fluttered folk and wild—
Your new-caught sullen peoples,
    Half devil and half child.

Take up the White Man's burden—
    In patience to abide,
To veil the threat of terror
    And check the show of pride;
By open speech and simple,
    An hundred times made plain,
To seek another's profit
    And work another's gain.

Take up the White Man's burden—
    The savage wars of peace—
Fill full the mouth of Famine,

And bid the sickness cease;
And when your goal is nearest
   (The end for others sought)
Watch sloth and heathen folly
   Bring all your hope to nought.

Take up the White Man's burden —
   No iron rule of kings,
But toil of serf and sweeper —
   The tale of common things.
The ports ye shall not enter,
   The roads ye shall not tread,
Go, make them with your living
   And mark them with your dead.

Take up the White Man's burden,
   And reap his old reward —
The blame of those ye better
   The hate of those ye guard —
The cry of hosts ye humour
   (Ah, slowly!) toward the light:
"Why brought ye us from bondage,
   Our loved Egyptian night?"

Take up the White Man's burden —
   Ye dare not stoop to less —
Nor call too loud on Freedom
   To cloak your weariness.
By all ye will or whisper,
   By all ye leave or do,
The silent sullen peoples
   Shall weigh your God and you.

Take up the White Man's burden!
   Have done with childish days —
The lightly-proffered laurel,
   The easy ungrudged praise:
Comes now, to search your manhood
   Through all the thankless years,
Cold, edged with dear-bought wisdom,
   The judgment of your peers.

1899

EDITOR'S NOTE: THE POET ERNEST CROSBY WROTE THIS SATIRIC RESPONSE TO "THE WHITE MAN'S BURDEN." I DECIDED TO PLACE IT HERE (OUT OF ALPHABETICAL ORDER) AS A "COMPANION" PIECE TO KIPLING'S POEM.

The Real "White Man's Burden"

Take up the White Man's burden;
    Send forth your sturdy sons,
And load them down with whisky
    And Testaments and guns.
Throw in a few diseases
    To spread in tropic climes,
For there the healthy niggers
    Are quite behind the times.

And don't forget the factories.
    On those benighted shores
They have no cheerful iron-mills
    Nor eke department stores.
They never work twelve hours a day,
    And live in strange content,
Altho they never have to pay
    A single cent of rent.

Take up the White Man's burden,
    And teach the Philippines
What interest and taxes are
    And what a mortgage means.
Give them electrocution chairs,
    And prisons, too, galore,
And if they seem inclined to kick,
    Then spill their heathen gore.

They need our labor question, too,
    And politics and fraud,
We've made a pretty mess at home;
    Let's make a mess abroad.
And let us ever humbly pray
    The Lord of Hosts may deign

To stir our feeble memories,
    Lest we forget — the Maine.

Take up the White Man's burden;
    To you who thus succeed
In civilizing savage hoards
    They owe a debt, indeed;
Concessions, pensions, salaries,
    And privilege and right,
With outstretched hands you raise to bless
    Grab everything in sight.

Take up the White Man's burden,
    And if you write in verse,
Flatter your Nation's vices
    And strive to make them worse.
Then learn that if with pious words
    You ornament each phrase,
In a world of canting hypocrites
    This kind of business pays.

1899

Joy Kogawa

Joy Kogawa, (b. 1935) was born in Vancouver, Canada, of Japanese ancestry. She grew up in Saskatchewan, Alberta, and British Columbia. She and her family were interned during World War II. Her volumes of poetry include *A Choice of Dreams* (1974). She has written a novel, *Obasan* (1981), based on her experiences during the war. She published a sequel, *Itsuka* (1992), which she later rewrote as *Emily Kato* (2005).

Kogawa's two poems "What Do I Remember of the Evacuation" and "When I Was a Little Girl" both evoke the troubled childhood of Japanese children during World War II. The tone of the first poem is not bitter; there is no malice toward the Canadian government that caused Japanese-Canadians (after the bombing of Pearl Harbor on 7 December 1941) to be incarcerated in prison camps as enemies. The young girl remembers rather the kindness of white teachers and the excitement of the train trip. The protagonist of "When I Was a Little Girl" is more apprehensive and fearful of racial threats. Do you agree? What is the significance of their town being seen as a "ghost town" and the "white lilies" as bombers? Compare these poems with Toshio Mori's "Slant-Eyed Americans."

What Do I Remember of the Evacuation?

What do I remember of the evacuation?
I remember my father telling Tim and me
About the mountains and the train
And the excitement of going on a trip.
What do I remember of the evacuation?
I remember my mother wrapping
A blanket around me and my
Pretending to fall asleep so she would be happy
Though I was so excited I couldn't sleep
(I hear there were people herded
Into the Hastings Park[1] like cattle.
Families were made to move in two hours
Abandoning everything, leaving pets
And possessions at gun point.
I hear families were broken up
Men were forced to work. I heard
It whispered late at night

---

[1] *Hastings Park* The stables of Hastings Park racecourse in Vancouver were one of the holding areas for Japanese-Canadians.

That there was suffering) and
I missed my dolls.
What do I remember of the evacuation?
I remember Miss Foster and Miss Tucker
Who still live in Vancouver
And who did what they could
And loved the children and who gave me
A puzzle to play with on the train.
And I remember the mountains and I was
Six years old and I swear I saw a giant
Gulliver of Gulliver's Travels scanning the horizon
And when I told my mother she believed it too
And I remember how careful my parents were
Not to bruise us with bitterness
And I remember the puzzle of Lorraine Life
Who said "Don't insult me" when I
Proudly wrote my name in Japanese
And Tim flew the Union Jack
When the war was over but Lorraine
And her friends spat on us anyway
And I prayed to the God who loves
All the children in his sight
That I might be white.

1974

When I Was a Little Girl

When I was a little girl
We used to walk together
Tim, my brother who wore glasses,
And I, holding hands
Tightly as we crossed the bridge
And he'd murmur, "You pray now"
—being a clergyman's son—
Until the big white boys
Had kicked on past.
Later we'd climb the bluffs
Overhanging the ghost town

And pick the small white lilies
And fling them like bombers
Over Slocan.[1]

1974

---

[1] *Slocan* Slocan (an interior town in British Columbia) was one of the internment camps for Japanese-Canadians during World War II.

Alex La Guma

Alex(ander) La Guma (1925-85) was born in District Six, Cape Town, South Africa. He graduated in 1945 from the Cape Technical College. He was politically active against apartheid
throughout his life. In addition to his many short stories, he published such novels as *A Walk
in the Night* (novella, 1962), *And A Threefold Cord* (1964), *The Stone Country* (1967), *In the Fog
of the Seasons' End* (1972), and *Time of the Butcherbird* (1979). He left South Africa in 1966
and spent the rest of his life in exile. He died in Havana, Cuba.

La Guma's "A Matter of Taste" has little narrative action. Three men share a meal along a train
track in a remote area in South Africa. One is white and the other two coloured. They chat
about food and their impoverished lot. La Guma invariably portrays in his fiction the rampant
racism in apartheid South Africa, but in this story he shows the bond of poverty among these
hobo-like individuals. At the end of the story, the white character hops a freight train heading
for Cape Town, from where he hopes to migrate to the United States. The coloured characters
are aware that no such opportunity is available to them but they wish him well — or could
Chinaboy's comment at the end of the story be ironical?

A Matter of Taste

The sun hung well towards the west now so that the thin clouds above the ragged
horizon were rimmed with bright yellow like the spilt yolk of an egg. Chinaboy
stood up from having blown the fire under the round tin and said, "She ought to
boil now." The tin stood precariously balanced on two half-bricks and a smooth
stone. We had built the fire carefully in order to brew some coffee and now watched
the water in the tin with the interest of women at a child-birth.

"There she is," Chinaboy said as the surface broke into bubbles. He waited for the
water to boil up and then drew a small crushed packet from the side pocket of his shred-
ded wind-breaker, untwisted its mouth and carefully tapped raw coffee into the tin.

He was a short man with grey-flecked kinky hair, and a wide, quiet, heavy face
that had a look of patience about it, as if he had grown accustomed to doing things
slowly and carefully and correctly. But his eyes were dark oriental ovals, restless as a
pair of cockroaches.

"We'll let her draw a while," he advised. He put the packet away and produced an
old rag from another pocket, wrapped it around a hand and gingerly lifted the tin
from the fire, placing it carefully in the sand near the bricks.

We had just finished a job for the railways and were camped out a few yards
from the embankment and some distance from the ruins of a onetime siding. The
corrugated iron of the office still stood, gaping in places and covered with rust and
cobwebs. Passers had fouled the roofless interior and the platform was crumbled in
places and overgrown with weeds. The cement curbing still stood, but cracked and

covered with the disintegration like a welcome notice to a ghost town. Chinaboy got out the scoured condensed milk tins we used for cups and set them up. I sat on an old sleeper and waited for the ceremony of pouring the coffee to commence.

It didn't start right then because Chinaboy was crouching with his rag — wrapped hand poised over the can, about to pick it up, but he wasn't making a move. Just sitting like that and watching something beyond us.

The portjackson bush and wattle[1] crackled and rushed behind me and the long shadow of a man fell across the small clearing. I looked back and up. He had come out of the plantation and was thin and short and had a pale white face with a fine golden stubble. Dirt lay in dark lines in the creases around his mouth and under his eyes and in his neck, and his hair was ragged and thick and uncut, falling back to his neck and around his temples. He wore an old pair of jeans, faded and dirty and turned up at the bottoms, and a torn leather coat.

He stood on the edge of the clearing, waiting hesitantly, glancing from me to Chinaboy, and then back at me. He ran the back of a grimy hand across his mouth.

Then he said hesitantly: "I smelled the coffee. Hope you don' min'." "Well," Chinaboy said with that quiet careful smile of his. "Seeing you's here, I reckon I don' min' either." He smiled at me, "you think we can take in a table hoarder, pal?"

"Reckon we can spare some of the turkey and green peas."

Chinaboy nodded at the stranger. "Sit, pally. We were just going to have supper."

The white boy grinned a little embarrassedly and came around the sleeper and shoved a rock over with a scarred boot and straddled it. He didn't say anything, but watched as Chinaboy set out another scoured milk-tin and lift the can from the fire and pour the coffee into the cups.

"Help yourself man. Isn't exactly the mayor's garden party." The boy took his cup carefully and blew at the steam. Chinaboy sipped noisily and said, "Should've had some bake bread. Nothing like a piece of bake bread with cawfee."

"Hot dogs," the white boy said.

"Huh."

"Hot dogs. Hot dogs go with coffee."

"Ooh ja. I heard," Chinaboy grinned. Then he asked: "You going somewhere, Whitey?"

"Cape Town. Maybe get a job on a ship an' make the States."

"Lots of people want to reach the States," I said.

Whitey drank some coffee and said: "Yes, I heard there's plenty of money and plenty to eat."

"Talking about eating," Chinaboy said: "I see a picture in a book, one time. 'Merican Book. This picture was about food over there. A whole mess of fried chicken, mealies — what they call corn — with mushrooms an' gravy, chips and new green peas. All done up in colours, too."

---

[1] *portjackson (Port Jackson)* An invasive plant (acacia) introduced to South Africa from Australia (where it is known as wattles).

"Pass me the roast lamb," I said sarcastically.

"Man," Whitey said warming up to the discussion. "Just let me get to something like that and I'll eat till I burst wide open."

Chinaboy swallowed some coffee: "Worked as a waiter one time when I was a youngster. In one of that big caffies. You should've seen what all them bastards ate. Just sitting there shovelling it down. Some French stuff too, patty grass or something like that."

I said: "Remember the time we went for drunk and got ten days? We ate mealies and beans till it came out of our ears!"

Chinaboy said, whimsically: "I'd like to sit down in a smart caffy one day and eat my way right out of a load of turkey, roast potatoes, beet-salad and angel's food trifle. With port and cigars at the end."

"Hell," said Whitey, "it's all a matter of taste. Some people like chicken and other's eat sheep's heads and beans!"

"A matter of taste," Chinaboy scowled. "Bull, it's a matter of money, pal. I worked six months in that caffy and I never heard nobody order sheep's head and beans!"

"You heard of the fellow who went into one of these big caffies?" Whitey asked, whirling the last of his coffee around in the tin cup. "He sits down at a table and takes out a packet of sandwiches and puts it down. Then he calls the waiter and orders a glass of water. When the waiter brings the water, this fellow says: "Why ain't the band playing?""

We chuckled over that and Chinaboy almost choked. He coughed and spluttered a little and then said, "Another John goes into a caffy and orders sausage and mash. When the waiter bring him the stuff he take a look and say: 'My dear man, you've brought me a cracked plate.' 'Hell,' says the waiter. 'That's no crack. That's the sausage.'"

After we had laughed over that one Chinaboy looked westward at the sky. The sun was almost down and the clouds hung like bloodstained rags along the horizon. There was a breeze stirring the wattle and portjackson, and far beyond the railway line.

A dog barked with high yapping sounds.

Chinaboy said: "There's a empty goods going through here around about seven. We'll help Whitey, here, onto it, so's he can get to Cape Town. Reckon there's still time for some more pork chops and onions." He grinned at Whitey. "Soon's we've had dessert we'll walk down the line a little. There's a bend where it's the best place to jump a train. We'll show you."

He waved elaborately towards me: "Serve the duck, John!"

I poured the last of the coffee into the tin cups. The fire had died to a small heap of embers. Whitey dug in the pocket of his leather coat and found a crumpled pack of cigarettes. There were just three left and he passed them round. We each took one and Chinaboy lifted the twig from the fire and we lighted up.

"Good cigar, this," he said, examining the glowing of the cigarette.

When the coffee and cigarettes were finished, the sun had gone down altogether, and all over the land was swept with dark shadows of a purple hue. The silhouetted tops of the wattle and portjackson looked like massed dragons.

We walked along the embankment in the evening, past the ruined siding, the shell of the station-house like a huge desecrated tombstone against the sky. Far off we heard the whistle of a train.

"This is the place," Chinaboy said to Whitey. "It's a long goods and when she takes the turn the engine driver won't see you, and neither the rooker in the guard's van. You got to jump when the engine's out of sight. She'll take the hill slow likely, so you'll have a good chance. Jus' you wait till I say when. Hell, that sound like pouring a drink!" His teeth flashed in the gloom as he grinned. Then Whitey stuck out a hand and Chinaboy shook it, and then I shook it.

"Thanks for supper, boys," Whitey said.

"Come again, anytime," I said, "we'll see we have a tablecloth." We waited in the portjackson growth at the side of the embankment while the goods train wheezed and puffed up the grade, its headlamp cutting a big yellow hole in the dark. We ducked back out of sight as the locomotive went by, hissing and rumbling. The tender followed, then a couple of box-cars, then some coal-cars and a flat car, another box car. The locomotive was out of sight.

"Here it is," Chinaboy said pushing the boy ahead. We stood near the train, hearing it click clack past. "Take this coal box coming up," Chinaboy instructed. "She's low and empty. Don't miss the grip, now. She's slow. And good luck, pal!"

The coal car came up and Whitey moved out, watching the iron grip on the far end of it. Then as it drew slowly level with him, he reached out, grabbed and hung on, then got a foothold, moving away from us slowly.

We watched him hanging there reaching for the edge of the car and hauling himself up. Watching the train clicking away, we saw him straddling the edge of the truck, his hand raised in a salute. We raised our hands too.

"Why ain't the band playing? Hell!" Chinaboy said.

1967

Fiona Tinwei Lam

Fiona Tinwei Lam (b. 1964) was born in Scotland but grew up in Vancouver, British Columbia, where she practices law. She has published in various journals and anthologies. Her debut collection of poems is *Intimate Distances* (2002). She co-edited and contributed to the anthology *Double Lives: Writing and Motherhood* (2008). and her second book of poetry, *Enter the Chrysanthemum,* was published in 2009.

Lam's "The Hyphenated" is yet another poem dealing with the in-between status of individuals of postcolonial and multicultural communities. Lam adopts the metaphor of the hyphen itself that is used in describing her: Chinese-Canadian (perhaps Scottish-Chinese-Canadian). The Jewish-Canadian writer Mordecai Richler is one of those writers who perceive their cultural dualism as an advantage rather than a drawback. Is there any indication at all that the speaker in Lam's poem sees her duality positively? Compare Lam's poem with Jean Arasanayagam's "I Have No Country," Edward Kamau Brathwaite's "Red Rising," and Shirley Lim's "Passports."

The Hyphenated

The left side of the hyphen
lives on the side of town
you visit with tourists,
smells like parcels from Hong Kong
crammed with clothes you never wear,
eats rice every supper, sometimes two days old.
It gets you punched in the back
by the white boys at school,
sworn at by drivers,
asked by the neighbours
if you've eaten their cat.

The right side undoes
your top shirt buttons, buys tight jeans,
sings the anthem in French,
almost fails physics,
doesn't practice piano.
It bakes brownies and meatloaf,
and glories in potatoes.

In between them, the hyphen
fissures your gut
so that anything unlabelled
tumbles through.

It makes your face an imposter's,
the gold-toothed smile
of the Chinese grandmother
seeking help at the store
shutting off as if you've struck her,
your English words empty
as spilled teacups.

2004

Shirley Geok-lin Lim

Shirley Geok-lin Lim (b. 1943), born in Malaysia, immigrated to the United States in 1969 (initially as a Fullbright scholar). She is a poet, critic, and academic. Her poetry collections include *Crossing the Peninsula*, which won the 1980 Commonwealth Poetry Prize. She is co-editor of *The Forbidden Stitch: An Asian-American Women's Anthology* (1989) and author of *Among the White Moon Faces: An Asian-American Memoir of Homelands* (1996) and a novel, *Joss and Gold* (2001).

Lim's "To Li Poh" is very conscious of ethnic differences but also of similarities and shared humanity. The poem can be compared with F.R. Scott's "To the Poets of India" and Claire Harris's "Backstage at the Glenbow Museum, Calgary." In "Passports," the speaker returns to China, the home of her grandparents, with a "foreign" passport, and she experiences mixed feelings about Hong Kong, now part of China. Compare this poem with Jean Arasanayagam's "I Have No Country" and Edward Kamau Brathwaite's "Red Rising."

To Li Poh

I read you in a stranger's tongue,
Brother whose eyes were slanted also
But you never left to live among
Foreign devils. Seeing the rice you ate grow
In your own backyard, you stayed on narrow
Village paths. Only your mind travelled
Easily: east, north, south, and west
Compassed in observation of field
And family. All men were guests
To one who knew traditions, the best
Of race. Country man, you believed to be Chinese
No more than a condition of human history.
Yet I cannot speak your tongue with ease,
No longer from China. Your stories
Stir griefs of dispersion and find
Me in simplicity of kin.

1994

Passports

Having arrived at
the celestial kingdom, I
refuse to enter.

Even now they live on wet boards
    in Aberdeen,[1] once nameless,
unCeltic, an inlet of water
    safer than shore. Lured to land
sons and daughters forget the east wind
    and the north. Somewhere, grandfather
had passed through, looking for Nanyang.[2]
    A woman of my family waited
for the patched junk sails to fill.

I am walking backwards into China
    where everyone looks like me
and noone is astonished my passport
    declares I am foreign, only envious
at my good luck. Speechless, without
    a mind of China, I remember
grandfather's hands, grandma's tears.
    On Causeway Bay,[3] a hundred thousand
cousins walk beside me, ten hundred
    thousand brothers and sisters.

1999

---

[1] *Aberdeen* Aberdeen, Hong Kong, which began as a fishing village; it was well known for its boat-dwellers.

[2] *Nanyang* Nanyang, China, used to be a bustling commercial centre during the Ming and Qing Dynasties (1368–1911). Its rapid decline led to migration of its residents (including the speaker's ancestors).

[3] *Causeway Bay* A busy shopping area in Hong Kong.

Jayanta Mahapatra

Jayanta Mahapatra (b. 1928) was born and educated in Cuttack, southwest of Calcutta, India. He taught physics for many years at colleges in Orissa and Cuttack. He has written more than fourteen volumes of poetry, including *Svayamvara & Other Poems* (1971), *A Father's Hours* (1976), *Waiting* (1980), *Relationship* (1980), *Selected Poems* (1987), *Temple* (1989), and *Random Descent* (2005). He has won many prestigious awards for his poetry, including the Central Sahitya Akademi Award.

In Mahapatra's "The Abandoned British Cemetery at Balasore," the speaker tries to look beyond the bitter colonial-imperial conflict during British occupation of India and show sympathy for the many young British soldiers who lost their lives in India and are buried in forgotten cemeteries there. As he contemplates the young men's tombstones, the speaker asks, "Of what concern to me is a vanished Empire? / Or the conquest of my ancestors' timeless ennui?" The poem invites comparison with Derek Walcott's "Ruins of a Great House." Salman Rushdie noted in 1997, when India celebrated its fiftieth anniversary of freedom from British occupation, that that anniversary marked the end of the postcolonial phase in India, that India though it cannot shed its brutal colonial past is now responsible for its fate. In "Freedom" and "The Portrait," Mahapatra portrays the consequences of communal violence and sociopolitical upheavals in an independent India.

The Abandoned British Cemetery at Balasore[1]

This is history.
I would not disturb it: the ruins of stone and marble,
the crumbling wall of brick, the coma of alienated decay.
How exactly should the archaic dead make me behave?

A hundred and fifty years ago
I might have lived. Now nothing offends my ways.
A quietness of bramble and grass holds me to a weed.
Will it matter if I know who the victims were, who survived?

---

[1] *Balasore* Balasore (also known as Baleshwar) is a city in Orissa state, eastern India. It has been since colonial times a strategic military base and was seen as the foothold of British dominance of India. It is now a launching station for rockets.

And yet, awed by the forgotten dead,
I walk around them: thirty-nine graves, their legends
floating in a twilight of baleful littoral,
the flaking history my intrusion does not animate.

Awkward in the silence, a scrawny lizard
watches the drama with its shrewd, hooded gaze.
And a scorpion, its sting drooping,
two eerie arms spread upon the marble, over an alien name.

In the circle the epitaphs run: Florence R——, darling wife
of Captain R—— R——, aged nineteen, of cholera ...
Helen, beloved daughter of Mr. & Mrs. ——, of cholera,
aged seventeen, in the year of our Lord, eighteen hundred ...

Of what concern to me is a vanished Empire?
Or the conquest of my ancestors' timeless ennui?
It is the dying young who have the power to show
what the heart will hide, the grass shows no more.

Who watches now in the dark near the dead wall?
The tribe of grass in the cracks of my eyes?
It is the cholera still, death's sickly trickle,
that plagues the sleepy shacks beyond this hump of earth,

moving easily, swiftly, with quick power
through both past and present, the increasing young,
into the final bone, wearying all truth with ruin.
This is the iron

rusting in the vanquished country, the blood's unease,
the useless rain upon my familiar window;
the tired triumphant smile left behind by the dead
on a discarded anchor half-sunk in mud beside the graves:

out there on the earth's unwavering gravity
where it waits like a deity perhaps
for the elaborate ceremonial of a coming generation
to keep history awake, stifle the survivor's issuing cry.

1979

Freedom

At times, as I watch,
it seems as though my country's body
floats down somewhere on the river.
Left alone, I grow into
a half-disembodied bamboo,
its lower part sunk
into itself on the bank.
Here, old widows and dying men
cherish their freedom,
bowing time after time in obstinate prayers.
While children scream
with this desire for freedom
to transform the world
without even laying hands on it.
In my blindness, at times I fear
I'd wander back to either of them.
In order for me not to lose face,
it is necessary for me to be alone.
Not to meet the woman and her child
in that remote village in the hills
who never had even a little rice
for their one daily meal these fifty years.[1]
And not to see the uncaught, bloodied light
of sunsets cling to the tall white columns
of Parliament House.
In the new temple man has built nearby,
the priest is the one who knows freedom,
while God hides in the dark like an alien.
And each day I keep looking for the light
shadows find excuses to keep.
Trying to find the only freedom I know,
the freedom of the body when it's alone.
The freedom of the silent shale, the moonless coal,
the beds of streams of the sleeping god.
I keep the ashes away,
try not to wear them on my forehead.

1997

---

[1] *fifty years* Fifty years after India's independence (in 1947) from British occupation/colonization.

The Portrait

This evening, its face rigid
as though it had had a stroke.
A large owl burrows deep into its steamy air,
our souls hold the soft darkness when
each one of us becomes
an invalid turned stiffly to his bed.
We remain sitting together,
incapable of getting any farther.
Only the footfall of someone
approaching from the murdered land.
Only the infinite kingdom when
you can't stop anyone from a simple pain.
Does a raped sixteen-year-old girl
build a hymn of the world
where living is a flamboyant metaphor?
Just this evening,
blacked like the yin half of the symbol[1]
where death can go on proclaiming its vanity.
Walls of our world, where are you?
The evening takes whatever comes drifting in.
Aimless, I prowl through reports about justice.
All I have left is a face, rigid and helpless
as though it had a stroke.

1997

---

[1] *yin half of the symbol* The speaker is referring to the binary, complementary opposite concepts of *yin* (the dark element) and *yang* (the bright element) from ancient Chinese philosophy.

Katherine Mansfield

Katherine Mansfield (1888-1923) was born Kathleen Beauchamp in Wellington, New Zealand, to wealthy, upper-class parents. She studied art and music at Queen's College in London, which from 1908 she saw as her adopted home. Her published short-story collections include *In a German Pension* (1911), *The Garden Party and Other Stories* (1922), *The Doves' Nest and Other Stories* (1923), and *Something Childish and Other Stories* (1924). She also published *Poems* (1923).

The narrator of Mansfield's "The Garden Party" is a cloistered upper-class New Zealander who becomes aware of the impoverished lives of the working class. What she does with this awareness is unclear at the end of the story. Is she likely to remain aloof from their "weary" lives? This story can be compared with a rewriting of it by Witi Ihimaera, "This Life is Weary." Throughout his version of the story, Ihimaera sets up a contrast with "The Garden Party." For instance, his primary focus is on the life of the poor family that is peripheral in Mansfield's story; and at the end of his story it is ambiguous whether the counterpart of Mansfield's protagonist is going to accept passively her working-class life or fight against exploitation of her people.

The Garden Party

And after all the weather was ideal. They could not have had a more perfect day for a garden party if they had ordered it. Windless, warm, the sky without a cloud. Only the blue was veiled with a haze of light gold, as it is sometimes in early summer. The gardener had been up since dawn, mowing the lawns and sweeping them, until the grass and the dark flat rosettes where the daisy plants had been seemed to shine. As for the roses, you could not help feeling they understood that roses are the only flowers that impress people at garden-parties; the only flowers that everybody is certain of knowing. Hundreds, yes, literally hundreds, had come out in a single night; the green bushes bowed down as though they had been visited by archangels.

Breakfast was not yet over before the men came to put up the marquee.

"Where do you want the marquee put, mother?"

"My dear child, it's no use asking me. I'm determined to leave everything to you children this year. Forget I am your mother. Treat me as an honoured guest."

But Meg could not possibly go and supervise the men. She had washed her hair before breakfast, and she sat drinking her coffee in a green turban, with a dark wet curl stamped on each cheek. Jose, the butterfly, always came down in a silk petticoat and a kimono jacket.

"You'll have to go, Laura; you're the artistic one."

Away Laura flew, still holding her piece of bread-and-butter. It's so delicious to have an excuse for eating out of doors and, besides, she loved having to arrange things; she always felt she could do it so much better than anybody else.

Four men in their shirt-sleeves stood grouped together on the garden path. They carried staves covered with rolls of canvas and they had big tool-bags slung on their backs. They looked impressive. Laura wished now that she was not holding that piece of bread-and-butter, but there was nowhere to put it and she couldn't possibly throw it away. She blushed and tried to look severe and even a little bit short sighted as she came up to them.

"Good morning," she said, copying her mother's voice. But that sounded so fearfully affected that she was ashamed, and stammered like a little girl, "Oh — er — have you come — is it about the marquee?"

"That's right, miss," said the tallest of the men, a lanky, freckled fellow, and he shifted his tool-bag, knocked back his straw hat and smiled down at her. "That's about it."

His smile was so easy, so friendly, that Laura recovered. What nice eyes he had, small, but such a dark blue! And now she looked at the others, they were smiling too. "Cheer up, we won't bite," their smile seemed to say. How very nice workmen were! And what a beautiful morning! She mustn't mention the morning; she must be business-like. The marquee.

"Well, what about the lily-lawn? Would that do?"

And she pointed to the lily-lawn with the hand that didn't hold the bread-and-butter. They turned, they stared in the direction. A little fat chap thrust out his underlip and the tall fellow frowned.

"I don't fancy it," said he. "Not conspicuous enough. You see, with a thing like a marquee" — and he turned to Laura in his easy way — "you want to put it somewhere where it'll give you a bang slap in the eye, if you follow me."

Laura's upbringing made her wonder for a moment whether it was quite respectful of a workman to talk to her of bangs slap in the eye. But she did quite follow him.

"A corner of the tennis-court," she suggested. "But the band's going to be in one corner."

"H'm, going to have a band, are you?" said another of the workmen. He was pale. He had a haggard look as his dark eyes scanned the tennis-court. What was he thinking?

"Only a very small band," said Laura gently. Perhaps he wouldn't mind so much if the band was quite small. But the tall fellow interrupted.

"Look here, miss, that's the place. Against those trees. Over there. That'll do fine."

Against the karakas.[1] Then the karaka trees would be hidden. And they were so lovely, with their broad, gleaming leaves, and their clusters of yellow fruit. They were like trees you imagined growing on a desert island, proud, solitary, lifting their leaves and fruits to the sun in a kind of silent splendour. Must they be hidden by a marquee?

They must. Already the men had shouldered their staves and were making for the place. Only the tall fellow was left. He bent down, pinched a sprig of lavender, put

---

[1] *karakas* The karaka tree is endemic to New Zealand.

his thumb and forefinger to his nose and snuffed up the smell. When Laura saw that gesture she forgot all about the karakas in her wonder at him caring for things like that—caring for the smell of lavender. How many men that she knew would have done such a thing. Oh, how extraordinarily nice workmen were, she thought. Why couldn't she have workmen for friends rather than the silly boys she danced with and who came to Sunday night supper? She would get on much better with men like these.

It's all the fault, she decided, as the tall fellow drew something on the back of an envelope, something that was to be looped up or left to hang, of these absurd class distinctions. Well, for her part, she didn't feel them. Not a bit, not an atom.... And now there came the chock-chock of wooden hammers. Someone whistled, some-one sang out, "Are you right there, matey?" "Matey!" The friendliness of it, the—the— Just to prove how happy she was, just to show the tall fellow how at home she felt, and how she despised stupid conventions, Laura took a big bite of her bread-and-butter as she stared at the little drawing. She felt just like a work-girl.

"Laura, Laura, where are you? Telephone, Laura!" a voice cried from the house.

"Coming!" Away she skimmed, over the lawn, up the path, up the steps, across the veranda and into the porch. In the hall her father and Laurie were brushing their hats ready to go to the office.

"I say, Laura," said Laurie very fast, "you might just give a squiz at my coat before this afternoon. See if it wants pressing."

"I will," said she. Suddenly she couldn't stop herself. She ran at Laurie and gave him a small, quick squeeze. "Oh, I do love parties, don't you?" gasped Laura.

"Ra-ther," said Laurie's warm, boyish voice, and he squeezed his sister too and gave her a gentle push. "Dash off to the telephone, old girl."

The telephone. "Yes, yes; oh yes. Kitty? Good morning, dear. Come to lunch? Do, dear. Delighted, of course. It will only be a very scratch meal—just the sandwich crusts and broken meringue-shells and what's left over. Yes, isn't it a perfect morning? Your white? Oh, I certainly should. One moment—hold the line. Mother's calling." And Laura sat back. "What, mother? Can't hear."

Mrs. Sheridan's voice floated down the stairs. "Tell her to wear that sweet hat she had on last Sunday."

"Mother says you're to wear that sweet hat you had on last Sunday. Good. One o'clock. Bye-bye."

Laura put back the receiver, flung her arms over her head, took a deep breath, stretched and let them fall. "Huh," she sighed, and the moment after the sigh she sat up quickly. She was still, listening. All the doors in the house seemed to be open. The house was alive with soft, quick steps and running voices. The green baize door that led to the kitchen regions swung open and shut with a muffled thud. And now there came a long, chuckling absurd sound. It was the heavy piano being moved on its stiff castors. But the air! If you stopped to notice, was the air always like this? Little faint winds were playing chase in at the tops of the windows, out at the doors. And there were two tiny spots of sun, one on the inkpot, one on a silver photograph frame, playing too. Darling little spots. Especially the one on the inkpot lid. It was quite warm. A warm little silver star. She could have kissed it.

The front door bell pealed and there sounded the rustle of Sadie's print skirt on the stairs. A man's voice murmured; Sadie answered, careless, "I'm sure I don't know. Wait. I'll ask Mrs. Sheridan."

"What is it, Sadie?" Laura came into the hall.

"It's the florist, Miss Laura."

It was, indeed. There, just inside the door, stood a wide, shallow tray full of pots of pink lilies. No other kind. Nothing but lilies—canna lilies, big pink flowers, wide open, radiant, almost frighteningly alive on bright crimson stems.

"O-oh, Sadie!" said Laura, and the sound was like a little moan. She crouched down as if to warm herself at that blaze of lilies; she felt they were in her fingers, on her lips, growing in her breast.

"It's some mistake," she said faintly. "Nobody ever ordered so many. Sadie, go and find mother."

But at that moment Mrs. Sheridan joined them.

"It's quite right," she said calmly. "Yes, I ordered them. Aren't they lovely?" She pressed Laura's arm. "I was passing the shop yesterday, and I saw them in the window. And I suddenly thought for once in my life I shall have enough canna lilies. The garden party will be a good excuse."

"But I thought you said you didn't mean to interfere," said Laura. Sadie had gone. The florist's man was still outside at his van. She put her arm round her mother's neck and gently, very gently, she bit her mother's ear.

"My darling child, you wouldn't like a logical mother, would you? Don't do that. Here's the man."

He carried more lilies still, another whole tray.

"Bank them up, just inside the door, on both sides of the porch, please," said Mrs. Sheridan. "Don't you agree, Laura?"

"Oh, I do, mother."

In the drawing-room Meg, Jose and good little Hans had at last succeeded in moving the piano.

"Now, if we put this chesterfield against the wall and move everything out of the room except the chairs, don't you think?"

"Quite."

"Hans, move these tables into the smoking-room, and bring a sweeper to take these marks off the carpet and—one moment, Hans—" Jose loved giving orders to the servants and they loved obeying her. She always made them feel they were taking part in some drama. "Tell mother and Miss Laura to come here at once."

"Very good, Miss Jose."

She turned to Meg. "I want to hear what the piano sounds like, just in case I'm asked to sing this afternoon. Let's try over 'This Life is Weary.'"

Pom! Ta-ta-ta *Tee*-ta! The piano burst out so passionately that Jose's face changed.

She clasped her hands. She looked mournfully and enigmatically at her mother and Laura as they came in.

> This Life is *Wee*-ary,
> A Tear — a Sigh.
> A Love that *Chan*-ges,
>   This Life is Wee-ary,
> A Tear — a Sigh.
> A Love that *Chan*-ges,
> And then ... Good-bye!

But at the word "Good-bye," and although the piano sounded more desperate than ever, her face broke into a brilliant, dreadfully unsympathetic smile.

"Aren't I in good voice, mummy?" she beamed.

> This Life is *Wee*-ary,
> Hope comes to Die.
> A Dream-a *Wa*-kening.

But now Sadie interrupted them. "What is it, Sadie?"

"If you please, m'm, cook says have you got the flags for the sandwiches?"

"The flags for the sandwiches, Sadie?" echoed Mrs. Sheridan dreamily. And the children knew by her face that she hadn't got them. "Let me see." And she said to Sadie firmly, "Tell cook I'll let her have them in ten minutes."

Sadie went.

"Now, Laura," said her mother quickly, "come with me into the smoking-room. I've got the names somewhere on the back of an envelope. You'll have to write them out for me. Meg, go upstairs this minute and take that wet thing off your head. Jose, run and finish dressing this instant. Do you hear me, children, or shall I have to tell your father when he comes home tonight? And — and, Jose, pacify cook if you do go into the kitchen, will you? I'm terrified of her this morning."

The envelope was found at last behind the dining-room clock, though how it had got there Mrs. Sheridan could not imagine.

"One of you children must have stolen it out of my bag, because I remember vividly — cream-cheese and lemon-curd. Have you done that?"

"Yes."

"Egg and — " Mrs. Sheridan held the envelope away from her. "It looks like mice. It can't be mice, can it?"

"Olive, pet," said Laura, looking over her shoulder.

"Yes, of course, olive. What a horrible combination it sounds. Egg and olive."

They were finished at last, and Laura took them off to the kitchen. She found Jose there pacifying the cook, who did not look at all terrifying.

"I have never seen such exquisite sandwiches," said Jose's rapturous voice. "How many kinds did you say there were, cook? Fifteen?"

"Fifteen, Miss Jose."

"Well, cook, I congratulate you."

Cook swept up crusts with the long sandwich knife, and smiled broadly.

"Godber's has come," announced Sadie, issuing out of the pantry. She had seen the man pass the window.

That meant the cream puffs had come. Godber's were famous for their cream puffs. Nobody ever thought of making them at home.

"Bring them in and put them on the table, my girl," ordered cook.

Sadie brought them in and went back to the door. Of course Laura and Jose were far too grown-up to really care about such things. All the same, they couldn't help agreeing that the puffs looked very attractive. Very. Cook began arranging them, shaking off the extra icing sugar.

"Don't they carry one back to all one's parties?" said Laura.

"I suppose they do," said practical Jose, who never liked to be carried back. "They look beautifully light and feathery, I must say."

"Have one each, my dears," said cook in her comfortable voice. "Yer ma won't know."

Oh, impossible. Fancy cream puffs so soon after breakfast. The very idea made one shudder. All the same, two minutes later Jose and Laura were licking their fingers with that absorbed inward look that only comes from whipped cream.

"Let's go into the garden, out by the back way," suggested Laura. "I want to see how the men are getting on with the marquee. They're such awfully nice men."

But the back door was blocked by cook, Sadie, Godber's man and Hans.

Something had happened.

"Tuk-tuk-tuk," clucked cook like an agitated hen. Sadie had her hand clapped to her cheek as though she had toothache. Hans' face was screwed up in the effort to understand. Only Godber's man seemed to be enjoying himself; it was his story.

"What's the matter? What's happened?"

"There's been a horrible accident," said cook. "A man killed."

"A man killed! Where? How? When?"

But Godber's man wasn't going to have his story snatched from under his very nose.

"Know those little cottages just below here, miss?" Know them? Of course she knew them. "Well, there's a young chap living there, name of Scott, a carter. His horse shied at a traction-engine, corner of Hawke Street this morning, and he was thrown out on the back of his head. Killed."

"Dead!" Laura stared at Godber's man.

"Dead when they picked him up," said Godber's man with relish. "They were taking the body home as I come up here." And he said to the cook, "He's left a wife and five little ones."

"Jose, come here." Laura caught hold of her sister's sleeve and dragged her through the kitchen to the other side of the green baize door. There she paused and leaned against it. "Jose!" she said, horrified, "however are we going to stop everything?"

"Stop everything, Laura!" cried Jose in astonishment. "What do you mean?"

"Stop the garden party, of course." Why did Jose pretend?

But Jose was still more amazed. "Stop the garden party? My dear Laura, don't be so absurd. Of course we can't do anything of the kind. Nobody expects us to. Don't be so extravagant."

"But we can't possibly have a garden party with a man dead just outside the front gate."

That really was extravagant, for the little cottages were in a lane to themselves at the very bottom of a steep rise that led up to the house. A broad road ran between. True, they were far too near. They were the greatest possible eyesore and they had no right to be in that neighbourhood at all. They were little mean dwellings painted a chocolate brown. In the garden patches there was nothing but cabbage stalks, sick hens and tomato cans. The very smoke coming out of their chimneys was poverty-stricken. Little rags and shreds of smoke, so unlike the great silvery plumes that uncurled from the Sheridans' chimneys. Washerwomen lived in the lane and sweeps and a cobbler and a man whose house-front was studded all over with minute bird-cages. Children swarmed. When the Sheridans were little they were forbidden to set foot there because of the revolting language and of what they might catch. But since they were grown up Laura and Laurie on their prowls sometimes walked through. It was disgusting and sordid. They came out with a shudder. But still one must go everywhere; one must see everything. So through they went.

"And just think of what the band would sound like to that poor woman," said Laura.

"Oh, Laura!" Jose began to be seriously annoyed. "If you're going to stop a band playing every time someone has an accident, you'll lead a very strenuous life. I'm every bit as sorry about it as you. I feel just as sympathetic." Her eyes hardened. She looked at her sister just as she used to when they were little and fighting together. "You won't bring a drunken workman back to life by being sentimental," she said softly.

"Drunk! Who said he was drunk?" Laura turned furiously on Jose. She said just as they had used to say on those occasions, "I'm going straight up to tell mother."

"Do, dear," cooed Jose.

"Mother, can I come into your room?" Laura turned the big glass door-knob.

"Of course, child. Why, what's the matter? What's given you such a colour?" And Mrs. Sheridan turned round from her dressing-table. She was trying on a new hat.

"Mother, a man's been killed," began Laura.

"Not in the garden?" interrupted her mother.

"No, no!"

"Oh, what a fright you gave me!" Mrs. Sheridan sighed with relief and took off the big hat and held it on her knees.

"But listen, mother," said Laura. Breathless, half choking, she told the dreadful story. "Of course, we can't have our party, can we?" she pleaded. "The band and everybody arriving. They'd hear us, mother; they're nearly neighbours!"

To Laura's astonishment her mother behaved just like Jose; it was harder to bear because she seemed amused. She refused to take Laura seriously.

"But, my dear child, use your common sense. It's only by accident we've heard of it. If someone had died there normally — and I can't understand how they keep alive in those poky little holes — we should still be having our party, shouldn't we?"

Laura had to say "yes" to that, but she felt it was all wrong. She sat down on her mother's sofa and pinched the cushion frill.

"Mother, isn't it really terribly heartless of us?" she asked.

"Darling!" Mrs. Sheridan got up and came over to her, carrying the hat. Before Laura could stop her she had popped it on. "My child!" said her mother, "the hat is yours. It's made for you. It's much too young for me. I have never seen you look such a picture. Look at yourself!" And she held up her hand-mirror.

"But, mother," Laura began again. She couldn't look at herself; she turned aside. This time Mrs. Sheridan lost patience just as Jose had done.

"You are being very absurd, Laura," she said coldly. "People like that don't expect sacrifices from us. And it's not very sympathetic to spoil everybody's enjoyment as you're doing now."

"I don't understand," said Laura, and she walked quickly out of the room into her own bedroom. There, quite by chance, the first thing she saw was this charming girl in the mirror, in her black hat trimmed with gold daisies and a long black velvet ribbon. Never had she imagined she could look like that. Is mother right? She thought. And now she hoped her mother was right. Am I being extravagant? Perhaps it was extravagant. Just for a moment she had another glimpse of that poor woman and those little children and the body being carried into the house. But it all seemed blurred, unreal, like a picture in the newspaper. I'll remember it again after the party's over, she decided. And somehow that seemed quite the best plan....

Lunch was over by half-past one. By half-past two they were all ready for the fray. The green-coated band had arrived and was established in a corner of the tennis-court.

"My dear!" trilled Kitty Maitland, "aren't they too like frogs for words? You ought to have arranged them round the pond with the conductor in the middle on a leaf."

Laurie arrived and hailed them on his way to dress. At the sight of him Laura remembered the accident again. She wanted to tell him. If Laurie agreed with the others, then it was bound to be all right. And she followed him into the hall.

"Laurie!"

"Hallo!" He was half-way upstairs, but when he turned round and saw Laura he suddenly puffed out his cheeks and goggled his eyes at her. "My word, Laura! You do look stunning," said Laurie. "What an absolutely topping hat!"

Laura said faintly "Is it?" and smiled up at Laurie and didn't tell him after all.

Soon after that people began coming in streams. The band struck up; the hired waiters ran from the house to the marquee. Wherever you looked there were couples strolling, bending to the flowers, greeting, moving on over the lawn. They were like bright birds that had alighted in the Sheridans' garden for this one afternoon, on their way to — where? Ah, what happiness it is to be with people who all are happy, to press hands, press cheeks, smile into eyes.

"Darling Laura, how well you look!"

"What a becoming hat, child!"

"Laura, you look quite Spanish. I've never seen you look so striking."

And Laura, glowing, answered softly, "Have you had tea? Won't you have an ice? The passion-fruit ices really are rather special." She ran to her father and begged him: "Daddy darling, can't the band have something to drink?"

And the perfect afternoon slowly ripened, slowly faded, slowly its petals closed.

"Never a more delightful garden party..." "The greatest success ..." "Quite the most ..."

Laura helped her mother with the good-byes. They stood side by side in the porch till it was all over.

"All over, all over, thank heaven," said Mrs. Sheridan. "Round up the others, Laura. Let's go and have some fresh coffee. I'm exhausted. Yes, it's been very successful. But oh, these parties, these parties! Why will you children insist on giving parties!" And they all of them sat down in the deserted marquee.

"Have a sandwich, daddy dear. I wrote the flag."

"Thanks." Mr. Sheridan took a bite and the sandwich was gone. He took another. "I suppose you didn't hear of a beastly accident that happened today?" he said.

"My dear," said Mrs. Sheridan, holding up her hand, "we did. It nearly ruined the party. Laura insisted we should put it off."

"Oh, mother!" Laura didn't want to be teased about it.

"It was a horrible affair all the same," said Mr. Sheridan. "The chap was married too. Lived just below in the lane, and leaves a wife and half a dozen kiddies, so they say."

An awkward little silence fell. Mrs. Sheridan fidgeted with her cup. Really, it was very tactless of father....

Suddenly she looked up. There on the table were all those sandwiches, cakes, puffs, all uneaten, all going to be wasted. She had one of her brilliant ideas.

"I know," she said. "Let's make up a basket. Let's send that poor creature some of this perfectly good food. At any rate, it will be the greatest treat for the children. Don't you agree? And she's sure to have neighbours calling in and so on. What a point to have it all ready prepared. Laura!" She jumped up. "Get me the big basket out of the stairs cupboard."

"But, mother, do you really think it's a good idea?" said Laura.

Again, how curious, she seemed to be different from them all. To take scraps from their party. Would the poor woman really like that?

"Of course! What's the matter with you today? An hour or two ago you were insisting on us being sympathetic."

Oh well! Laura ran for the basket. It was filled, it was now heaped by her mother.

"Take it yourself, darling," said she. "Run down just as you are. No, wait, take the arum lilies too. People of that class are so impressed by arum lilies."

"The stems will ruin her lace frock," said practical Jose.

So they would. Just in time. "Only the basket, then. And, Laura!" — her mother followed her out of the marquee — "don't on any account — "

"What, mother?"

No, better not put such ideas into the child's head! "Nothing! Run along."

It was just growing dusky as Laura shut their garden gates. A big dog ran by like a shadow. The road gleamed white, and down below in the hollow the little cottages were in deep shade. How quiet it seemed after the afternoon. Here she was going down the hill to somewhere where a man lay dead, and she couldn't realize it. Why couldn't she? She stopped a minute. And it seemed to her that kisses, voices, tinkling spoons, laughter, the smell of crushed grass were somehow inside her. She had no room for anything else. How strange! She looked up at the pale sky, and all she thought was, "Yes, it was the most successful party."

Now the broad road was crossed. The lane began, smoky and dark. Women in shawls and men's tweed caps hurried by. Men hung over the palings; the children played in the doorways. A low hum came from the mean little cottages. In some of them there was a flicker of light, and a shadow, crab-like, moved across the window. Laura bent her head and hurried on. She wished now she had put on a coat. How her frock shone! And the big hat with the velvet streamer—if only it was another hat! Were the people looking at her? They must be. It was a mistake to have come; she knew all along it was a mistake. Should she go back even now?

No, too late. This was the house. It must be. A dark knot of people stood outside. Beside the gate an old, old woman with a crutch sat in a chair, watching. She had her feet on a newspaper. The voices stopped as Laura drew near. The group parted. It was as though she was expected, as though they had known she was coming here.

Laura was terribly nervous. Tossing the velvet ribbon over her shoulder, she said to a woman standing by, "Is this Mrs. Scott's house?" and the woman, smiling queerly, said, "It is, my lass."

Oh, to be away from this! She actually said, "Help me, God," as she walked up the tiny path and knocked. To be away from those staring eyes, or to be covered up in anything, one of those women's shawls even. I'll just leave the basket and go, she decided. I shan't even wait for it to be emptied.

Then the door opened. A little woman in black showed in the gloom.

Laura said, "Are you Mrs. Scott?" But to her horror the woman answered, "Walk in, please, miss," and she was shut in the passage.

"No," said Laura, "I don't want to come in. I only want to leave this basket. Mother sent—"

The little woman in the gloomy passage seemed not to have heard her. "Step this way, please, miss," she said in an oily voice, and Laura followed her.

She found herself in a wretched little low kitchen, lighted by a smoky lamp. There was a woman sitting before the fire.

"Em," said the little creature who had let her in. "Em! It's a young lady." She turned to Laura. She said meaningly, "I'm 'er sister, miss. You'll excuse 'er, won't you?"

"Oh, but of course!" said Laura. "Please, please don't disturb her. I—I only want to leave—"

But at that moment the woman at the fire turned round. Her face, puffed up, red, with swollen eyes and swollen lips, looked terrible. She seemed as though she couldn't understand why Laura was there. What did it mean? Why was this stranger standing in the kitchen with a basket? What was it all about? And the poor face puckered up again.

"All right, my dear," said the other. "I'll thenk the young lady."

And again she began, "You'll excuse her, miss, I'm sure," and her face, swollen too, tried an oily smile.

Laura only wanted to get out, to get away. She was back in the passage. The door opened. She walked straight through into the bedroom, where the dead man was lying.

"You'd like a look at 'im, wouldn't you?" said Em's sister, and she brushed past Laura over to the bed. "Don't be afraid, my lass"—and now her voice sounded fond and sly, and fondly she drew down the sheet—"'e looks a picture. There's nothing to show. Come along, my dear."

Laura came.

There lay a young man, fast asleep—sleeping so soundly, so deeply that he was far, far away from them both. Oh, so remote, so peaceful. He was dreaming. Never wake him up again. His head was sunk in the pillow, his eyes were closed; they were blind under the closed eyelids. He was given up to his dream. What did garden-parties and baskets and lace frocks matter to him? He was far from all those things. He was wonderful, beautiful. While they were laughing and while the band was playing, this marvel had come to the lane. Happy... happy.... All is well, said that sleeping face. This is just as it should be. I am content.

But all the same you had to cry, and she couldn't go out of the room without saying something to him. Laura gave a loud childish sob.

"Forgive my hat," she said.

And this time she didn't wait for Em's sister. She found her way out of the door, down the path past all those dark people. At the corner of the lane she met Laurie.

He stepped out of the shadow. "Is that you, Laura?"

"Yes."

"Mother was getting anxious. Was it all right?"

"Yes, quite. Oh, Laurie!" She took his arm, she pressed up against him.

"I say, you're not crying, are you?" asked her brother.

Laura shook her head. She was.

Laurie put his arm round her shoulder. "Don't cry," he said in his warm, loving voice. "Was it awful?"

"No," sobbed Laura. "It was simply marvelous. But, Laurie—" She stopped, she looked at her brother. "Isn't life," she stammered, "isn't life—" But what life was she couldn't explain. No matter. He quite understood.

"Isn't it, darling?" said Laurie.

1922

Lee Maracle

Lee Maracle (b. 1950) was born in Vancouver, Canada, of Salish and Cree ancestry. She is immersed in the social and cultural life of her people. She has been part-time writer-in-residence at the International School for Native People in British Columbia and writer-in-residence for the University of Toronto's Aboriginal Studies Program. She was one of the founders of the En'owkin International School of Writing in Penticton, British Columbia (1981), and is the cultural director of the Centre for Indigenous Theatre in Toronto. Among her books of fiction are *Sojourner's Truth and Other Stories* (1990), *Ravensong* (1993), and *Daughters Are Forever* (2002). She has a volume of poems entitled *Bent Box* (2000).

Maracle's "Charlie" is set in a Residential School in Canada's North. The story indicts the Canadian government's misguided efforts to assimilate the children of the Native people of Canada into the mainstream of Canadian society. Residential Schools flourished in Canada from 1904-73; the last one was closed in 1988. On 7 January 1998, the Prime Minister of Canada apologized to the Native people of Canada for the abuse they suffered in these schools. The white teachers who ran such schools often "othered" the Native children and perceived them as "heathen savages" incapable of learning. Maracle details the physical and emotional suffering of the children. A point worth considering is why Charlie's father complies with the law. The story can be compared with Albert Wendt's "Crocodile."

Charlie

Charlie was a quiet boy. This was not unusual. His silence was interpreted by the priests and catholic lay teachers as stoic reserve — a quality inherited from his pagan ancestors. It was regarded in the same way the religious viewed the children's tearless response to punishment: a quaint combination of primitive courage and lack of emotion. All the children were like this and so Charlie could not be otherwise.

Had the intuitive sense of the priesthood been sharper they might have noticed the bitter look lurking in the shadows of the children's bland faces. The priests were not deliberately insensitive. All of their schooling had taught them that even the most heathen savage was born in the image of their own sweet lord. Thus, they held to the firm conviction that the sons and daughters of the people they were convinced were God's lowliest children were eternally good. Blinded by their own teaching they could not possibly be called upon to detect ill in the warm broad faces of their little charges.

Charlie did not do much schoolwork. He daydreamed. Much standing in the corner, repeated thrashings and the like had convinced him that staring out the window at the trees beyond the schoolyard was not the way to escape the sterile monotony of school. While the window afforded him the luxury of sighting a deer or watching the machinations of a bluejay trying to win the heart of his lady-bird fair, the thrashing he knew could be counted on for committing the crime of daydreaming was not worth the reward. So, like the other children, he would stare hard at his work, the same practiced look of bewilderment used by his peers on his face, while his thoughts danced around the forest close to home — far away from the arithmetic sums he was sure had nothing to do with him.

He learned to listen for the questions put to him by the brother over the happy daydream. He was not expected to know the answer; repeating the question sufficed. Knowing the question meant that, like the others, he was slow to learn but very attentive. No punishment was meted out for thickheadedness.

"What is three multiplied by five, Charlie?" The brother's brisk, clipped English accent echoed hollowly in the silence.

Charlie's eyes fixed on the empty page. His thoughts followed the manoeuvres of a snowshoe hare scampering ahead of himself and his half-wild dog. The first snow had fallen. It was that time of year. The question reached out to him over the shrieks of joy and the excited yelping of his dog, but it did not completely pluck him from the scene of his snow-capped, wooded homeland.

"Three...times...five?" muttered Charlie, the sounds coming out as though his voice were filled with air. A tense look from the brother. A quizzically dull look on Charlie's face. All the children stared harder at their pages — blank from want of work. He was still staring at the teacher but his mind was already following the rabbit. Did the brother's shoulders heave a sigh of disappointment?

"Thomas," the boredom of the teacher's voice thinly disguised.

"Fifteen," clearly and with volume. Poor Thomas, he always listened.

The bell rang. The class dutifully waited for dismissal. The brother sighed. The sound of scholarly confidence carefully practiced by all pedagogues left his voice at each bell. Exasperation permeated his dismissal command. It was the only emotion he allowed himself to express.

As he stood by the doorway watching the bowed heads slink by, his thoughts wandered about somewhat. *Such is my lot, to teach a flock of numbskulls...Ah, had I only finished and gotten a degree. Then, I could teach in a real school with eager students.* Each day his thoughts read thus and every time he laid out plans to return to university, but he never carried them out. At home every night a waiting bottle of Seagram's drowned out his self-pity and steadied him for the morrow.

* * *

Charlie was bothered at meal times. The food was plain and monotonously familiar: beef stew on Monday, chicken stew on Tuesday — the days with their matching meal plan never varied. Unvarying menus did not bother Charlie though. Nor was it the plain taste of domestic meat as opposed to the sharp taste of wild meat that bothered him. He was bothered by something unidentifiable, tangible but invisible. He couldn't figure it out and that, too, bothered him.

From the line-up, he carried his plate to the section of the eating hall reserved for sixth grade boys. He looked up to watch the teenaged boys exchanging flirtatious glances with the young girls in a line opposite them. In the segregated classes of the school, boys and girls weren't permitted to mingle with, talk to, or touch one another. They sat in the same eating hall, but ate on separate sides. Charlie bored quickly of watching the frustrated efforts of youth struggling to reach each other through the invisible walls of rigid moral discipline erected by the priesthood.

His eyes began wandering about the eating room of his own home. The pot of stew was on the stove. It always had something warm and satisfying to the taste in it. He scarcely acknowledged its existence before he came to residential school. Now he saw it each day at meal time.

At home no one served you or stopped you from ladling out some of the pot's precious contents. Here at school, they lined you up to eat. Each boy at each age level got exactly the same portion. A second plate was out of the question. He felt ashamed to eat.

A stiff-backed white man appeared in the room and the low murmuring of voices stopped.

"EAT EVER-Y-THING ON YOUR PLATE!" he bellowed, clicking out the last *t* on the word plate. His entrance never varied. He said the same thing every day, careful to enunciate each word perfectly and loudly, in the manner he was sure best befitted the station of principal of a school. He marched up and down the aisles between tables in a precise pattern that was designed to impress on the boys that he was, indeed, the principal of the school. Finished with the last aisle, he marched stiff-legged out the door.

The boys were more than impressed. They were terrified. They likened the stiff-legged walk to the walk of an angry wolf. They had come to believe that whites were not quite human, so often did they walk in this wolf-like way. They knew the man who had just pranced about the eating hall to be the principal, not by the superiority of his intellect as compared to the other instructors, but by virtue of his having the stiffest walk and, hence, the fiercest temperament of the pack.

Night came and Charlie prepared for the best part of his incarceration. Between prayers and lights out, the children were left alone for fifteen minutes. Quickly into pyjamas and to the window.

The moon and the stars spread a thin blue light over the whitening ground below. Crystal flake after crystal flake draped the earth in a frock of glittering snow. As always, a tightness arose in his small boy-chest. He swallowed hard.

"LIGHTS OUT!"

Darkness swallowed the room and his little body leapt for the bunk with a willingness that always amazed him. He did not sleep right away.

"Hay, Chimmy, you got your clothes on?"

"Yeh."

"Ah-got the rope."

"Keh."

Runaway talk! Charlie hurriedly grabbed some clothes from the cupboard beneath the top of the night-table he shared with another boy.

"Ah'm comin' too," he hissed, struggling to snap up his jeans and shirt.

"Hurry, we're not waitin'."

He rushed breathless to the closet and grabbed a jacket. The older boys had already tied the rope to the metal latticing that closed the window. Each boy squeezed through the square created by one missing strip of metal lattice, and, hanging on to the rope, swung out from the window, then dropped to the ground below.

Safe in the bosom of the forest, after a tense but joyous run across the yard, the boys let go the cramped spirit that the priesthood so painstakingly tried to destroy in them. They whooped, they hollered, bayed at the moon and romped about chucking snow in loose, small balls at each other.

Jimmy cautioned them that that was enough. The faster they moved the greater the head start. They had to get through the forest to the railroad tracks by night cover.

The trek was uneventful. The older boys had run away before and knew exactly where they were going and how to get there. Stars and a full moon reflected against white snow provided them with enough light to pick their way along. As time wore by, the excited walk became dull plodding. They reached the tracks of the railroad sometime near daylight. All were serious now. They cast furtive glances up and down the track. The shelter of darkness was gone. Discovery became real in the bright light of day. Surely the priest had sent the police in search of them by now.

The boys trod light-footed and quickly along the trackline, fear spurring them on. A thin wisp of smoke curling upward from the creaking pines on their right brought the boys to a halt.

"It's mah uncle's house," Jimmy purred with contentment. The empty forest carries sound a long way in winter, so the boys spoke in whispers. It never occurred to the other boys to ask Jimmy what his uncle's reaction to their visit would be. They assumed it would be the same as their own folks' response.

A short trek through the woods brought them to the cabin's door. Uncle and aunt were already there to greet them. They were now used to the frequent runaway boys that always stopped for a day or two, then not knowing how to get home, trudged the nine and some miles back to school. The holiday, uncle mused to aunt, would do them no harm. Besides which, they enjoyed the company of happy children.

A good meal...a day's play...nightfall...heavenly sleep in this cabin full of the same sweet smells of his own cabin brought sentimental dreams to Charlie.

Charlie's dreams followed the familiar lines of his home. In the centre stood his mama quietly stirring the stew. Above her head, hanging from the rafters, were strips of dried meat. Hundreds of them, dangling in mute testimony to his father's skill as hunter and provider. A little ways from the stove hung mama's cooking tools. Shelving and boxes made of wood housed such food stuffs as flour, sugar, oatmeal, salt and the like. All here was hewn from the forest's bounty by Charlie's aging grandfather.

Crawling and toddling about were his younger brother and sister, unaware of Charlie's world or his dream of them. Completing the picture was his dad. He stood in the corner, one leg perched on a log stump used as a kindling split. He had a smoke in his hand.

No one but his wife knew how his thoughts ran. How he wondered with a gnawing tightness why it was he had to send his little ones, one after the other, far away to school.

Daily, he heard of young ones who had been to school and not returned. More often, he would come across the boys who recently finished school, hanging about the centre of the village, unwilling and poorly equipped to take care of themselves. Without hunting or trapping skills, the boys wasted away, living from hand-to-mouth, a burden on their aging parents. One by one they drifted away, driven by the shame of their uselessness.

It was not that they could not learn to hunt or trap. But it takes years of boyhood to grow accustomed to the ways of the forest, to overcome the lonely and neurotic fear it can sometimes create in a man. A boy who suddenly becomes a man does not want to learn what he is already supposed to know well. No man wants to admit his personal fear of his home.

The pull of years of priestly schooling towards the modern cities of a Canada that hardly touched their wilderness village grew stronger. For a while, family and city pulled with equal strength, gripping the youth in a listless state of paralysis. For some, the city won out and they drifted away. Charlie's father worried about the fate of his young ones.

His private agony was his own lack of resistance. He sent his son to school. It was the law. A law that he neither understood nor agreed to, but he sent them. His willingness to reduce his son to a useless waster stunned him. He confided none of his self-disgust to his wife. It made him surly but he said nothing.

In his dream, Charlie did not know his father's thoughts. He saw his father standing, leg-on-log, as he usually stood while he awaited breakfast, and he awoke contented.

Jimmy's uncle had given up wondering about the things that plagued Charlie's father. His children had grown up and left, never to return. He did not even know if there were grandchildren.

He lived his life without reflection now. Jimmy was the eldest son of his youngest brother. It was enough for his life's labours that this boy called him grandfather out of respect for the man's age.

"I'm going to check the short lines," he said, biting into his bannock and not looking at the boys.

"Can we help?" The older boys looked at their plates, studiously masking their anxiety.

"Sure." Staring at them carefully, he added, "but the small one must stay." The old man was unwilling to risk taking the coatless boy with him.

Charlie followed them to the edge of the woods. He knew that no amount of pleading would change the old man's mind and crying would only bring him shame. He watched them leave and determined to go home where his own grandfather would take him to check his short lines.

The old aunt tried to get him to stay. She promised him a fine time. It was a wasted effort. He wanted the comfort and dignity of his own cabin, not a fine time.

Charlie knew the way home. It had not taken him long to travel the distance from the tracks near his home to the school. He had marked the trail in the way that so many of his ancestors might have: a rocky crag here, a distorted, lone pine there. He gave no thought to the fact that the eight-hour trip had been made by rail and not on foot.

The creaking pines, straining under the heavy snowfall of the night before, brought Charlie the peace of mind that school had denied him. A snow-bird feeding through the snow curled Charlie's mouth into a delighted smile. A rabbit scampered across the tracks and disappeared into the forest. He had half a mind to chase it.

"Naw, better just go home." His voice seemed to come from deep within him, spreading itself out in a wide half-circle and meeting the broad expanse of hill and wood only to be swallowed by nature's huge majesty somewhere beyond his eyes. The thinness of his voice against the forest made him feel small.

The day wore by tediously slow. Charlie began to worry. He had not seen his first landmark.

"Am I going the right way?" What a terrible trick of fate to trek mile after mile only to arrive back at school. The terror of it made him want to cry.

Around the bend, he recognized a bare stone cliff. Assured, he ran a little. He coughed and slowed down again. He tired a little. He felt sleepy. He touched his bare hands. Numb.

"Frostbite," he whispered.

In his rush to leave the dormitory he had grabbed his fall jacket. The cold now pierced his chest. Breathing was difficult. His legs cried out for rest. Charlie fought the growing desire to sleep.

The biscuits aunt had given him were gone. Hunger beset him. He trudged on, squinting at the sprays of sunlight that cast a reddish hue on the snow-clad pines in final farewell to daylight.

Darkness folded itself over the land with a cruel swiftness. It fell upon the landscape, swallowing Charlie and the thread of track connecting civilization to nature's vastness, closing with maddening speed the last wisps of light from Charlie's eyes.

Stars, one by one, woke from their dreamy sleep and filled the heavens. Charlie stumbled. He rose reluctantly. His legs wobbled forward a few more steps, then gave in to his defeated consciousness that surrendered to the sparkling whiteness that surrounded him. He rolled over and lay face up scanning the star-lit sky.

Logic forsook him. His heart beat slower. A smile nestled on his full purple lips. He opened his eyes. His body betrayed him. He felt warm again. Smiling he welcomed the Orion queen—not a star constellation but the great Wendigo[1]—dressed in midnight blue, her dress alive with the glitter of a thousand stars. Arms outstretched, he greeted the lady that came to lift his spirit and close his eyes forever to sleep the gentle sleep of white death.

1980

---

[1] *Wendigo* In Algonquin mythology, Wendigo or Windigo is a man-eating ogre, used to scare unruly children. Occasionally, as in this story, the Wendigo is helpful and well-meaning.

Dambudzo Marechera

Dambudzo Marechera (1952-87) was born in Zimbabwe (then known as Rhodesia) and educated at the University of Zimbabwe and Oxford University, from both of which institutions he was expelled for his radicalism and lapses in his academic performance. He travelled extensively in Europe and Africa. He was a controversial but acclaimed writer whose publications include The *House of Hunger* (novel, 1978) and a posthumous collection of poetry, *Cemetery of Mind* (1992).

The title of Marechera's "Black Skin What Mask" is drawn from Frantz Fanon's *Black Skin, White Mask*" (1952), a text that underpins this story. Fanon analyses the feelings of dependency and inadequacy that colonial black people experience in a white world once they lose their native cultural originality and embrace the imperial culture. (See Wole Soyinka's interview with Henry Louis Gates Jr. in this text.) Marechera's story, which is basically a conversation between two students, is essentially an affirmation of Fanon's theory. Many of the stories in this anthology show characters who are caught between local and imperial cultures. Are there any stories that depict individuals (like the narrator-protagonist's friend here) who have totally rejected their native culture? Is the narrator-protagonist's portrayal of his friend fair?

Black Skin What Mask

My skin sticks out a mile in all the crowds around here. Every time I go out I feel it tensing up, hardening, torturing itself. It only relaxes when I am in shadow, when I am alone, when I wake up early in the morning, when I am doing mechanical actions, and, strangely enough, when I am angry. But it is coy and self-conscious when I draw in my chair and begin to write.

It is like a silent friend: moody, assertive, possessive, callous — sometimes.

I had such a friend once. He finally slashed his wrists. He is now in a lunatic asylum. I have since asked myself why he did what he did, but I still cannot come to a conclusive answer.

He was always washing himself — at least three baths every day. And he had all sorts of lotions and deodorants to appease the thing that had taken hold of him. He did not so much wash as scrub himself until he bled.

He tried to purge his tongue too, by improving his English and getting rid of any accent from the speaking of it. It was painful to listen to him, as it was painful to watch him trying to scrub the blackness out of his skin.

He did things to his hair, things which the good lord never intended any man to do to his hair.

He bought clothes, whole shops of them. If clothes make the man, then certainly he was a man. And his shoes were the kind that make even an elephant lightfooted and elegant. The animals that were murdered to make those shoes must have turned in their graves and said Yeah, man.

But still he was dissatisfied. He had to have every other African within ten miles of his person follow his example. After all, if one chimpanzee learns not only to drink tea but also to promote that tea on TV, what does it profit it if all the other god-created chimpanzees out there continue to scratch their fleas and swing around on their tails chattering about Rhodes and bananas?

However, he was nice enough to put it more obliquely to me one day. We were going to the New Year Ball in Oxford Town Hall.

"Don't you ever change those jeans?" he asked.

"They're my only pair," I said.

"What do you do with your money, man, booze?"

"Yes," I said searching through my pockets. Booze and paper and ink. The implements of my trade.

"You ought to take more care of your appearance, you know. We're not monkeys."

"I'm all right as I am."

I coughed and because he knew what that cough meant he tensed up as though for a blow.

"If you've got any money," I said firmly, "lend me a fiver."

That day he was equally firm:

"Neither a lender nor a borrower be," he quoted.

And then as an afterthought he said:

"We're the same size. Put on this other suit. You can have it if you like. And the five pounds."

That is how he put it to me. And that is how it was until he slashed his wrists.

But there was more to it than that.

Appearances alone — however expensive — are doubtful climbing-boots when one hazards the slippery slopes of social adventure. Every time he opened his mouth he made himself ridiculous. Logic — that was his magic word: but unfortunately that sort of thing quickly bored even the most thick-skinned anthropologist-in-search-of-African attitudes. I was interested in the booze first and then lastly in the company. But he — god help me — relied on politics to get on with people. But who in that company in their right mind gives a shit about Rhodesia?[1] He could never understand this.

And Christ! when it came to dancing he really made himself look a monkey. He always assumed that if a girl accepted his request for a dance it meant that she had in reality said Yes to being groped, squeezed, kissed and finally screwed off the dance floor. And the girls were quite merciless with him. The invitations would stop and all would be a chilly silence.

I did not care for the type of girl who seemed to interest him. He liked them starched, smart and demure, and with the same desperate conversation:

"What's your college?"

---

[1] *Rhodesia* The British colony of Rhodesia became Zimbabwe in 1980, when a new constitution introduced democratic elections and ended white minority rule.

"__.What's yours?"

"__."

Pause.

"What's your subject?"

"__.What's yours?"

"__."

Pause. Cough.

"I'm from Zimbabwe."

"What's that?"

"Rhodesia."

"O. I'm from London. Hey (with distinct lack of interest), Smith's a bastard, isn't he?"

And he eagerly:

"As a matter of fact, I have just addressed the Africa Society on the thesis that Ian Smith blah blah blah blah blah blah blah ..."

(Yawning) "Interesting. Very interesting."

"Smith blah blah blah blah blah blah ... (Suddenly) Would you like to dance?"

Startled:

"Well ... I ... yes, why not."

And that's how it was. Yes, that's how it was, until he slashed his wrists.

But there was more to it than that.

A black tramp accosted him one night as we walked to the University Literary Society party. It was as if he had been touched by a leper. He literally cringed away from the man, who incidentally knew me from a previous encounter when he and I had sat Christmas Eve through on a bench in Carfax drinking a bottle of whisky. He was apoplectic with revulsion and at the party could talk of nothing else:

"How can a black man in England let himself become a bum? There is much to be done. Especially in Southern Africa. What I would like to see blah blah blah ..."

"Have a drink," I suggested.

He took it the way God accepts anything from Satan.

"You drink too much, you know," he sighed.

"You drink too little for your own good," I said.

The incident of the tramp must have gnawed him more than I had thought because when we got back in college he couldn't sleep and came into my room with a bottle of claret which I was glad to drink with him until breakfast when he did stop talking about impossible black bastards; he stopped talking because he fell asleep in his chair.

And that's how it was until he slashed his wrists.

But there were other sides to the story.

For example: he did not think that one of his tutors "liked" him.

"He doesn't have to like anyone," I pointed out, "and neither do you."

But he wasn't listening. He cracked his fingers and said:

"I'll send him a Christmas and New Year card, the best money can buy."

"Why not spend the money on a Blue Nun?" I suggested.

The way he looked at me, I knew I was losing a friend.

For example: he suggested one day that if the Warden or any of the other tutors asked me if I was his friend I was to say no.

"Why?" I asked.

"You do drink too much, you know," he said looking severe, "and I'm afraid you do behave rather badly, you know. For instance, I heard about an incident in the beercellar and another in the dining room and another in Cornmarket where the police had to be called, and another on your staircase...."

I smiled.

"I'll have your suit laundered and sent up to your rooms," I said firmly, "and I did give you that five pounds back. So that's all right. Are you dining in Hall, because if you are then I will not, it'd be intolerable. Imagine it. We're the only two Africans in this college. How can we possibly avoid each other, or for that matter...."

He twisted his brow. Was it pain? He had of late begun to complain of insomnia and headaches, and the lenses of his spectacles did not seem to fit the degree of his myopia. Certainly something cracked in his eyes, smarting:

"Look, I say, what, forget what I said. I don't care what they think. It's my affair, isn't it, who I choose to be friends with?"

I looked him squarely in the eye:

"Don't let them stuff bullshit into you. Or spew it out right in their faces. But don't ever puke their gut-rot on me."

"Let's go play tennis," he said after a moment.

"I can't. I have to collect some dope from a guy the other end of town," I said.

"Dope? You take that — stuff?"

"Yes. The Lebanese variety is the best piss for me."

He really was shocked.

He turned away without another word. I stared after him, hoping he wouldn't work himself up into telling his moral tutor — who was actually the one who didn't like him. And that's how it was. That's how it was, until he slashed his wrists.

But there had to be another side to it: sex.

The black girls in Oxford — whether African, West Indian or American — despised those of us who came from Rhodesia. After all, we still haven't won our independence. After all, the papers say we are always quarrelling among ourselves. And all the other reasons which black girls choose to believe. It was all quite unflattering. We had become — indeed we are — the Jews of Africa, and nobody wanted us. It's bad enough to have white shits despising us; but it's a more maddening story when one kettle ups its nose at another kettle.... And this he had to learn.

I didn't care one way or the other. Booze was better than girls, even black girls. And dope was heaven. But he worried. And he got himself all mixed up about a West Indian girl who worked in the kitchen. Knowing him as I did, such a "come-down" was to say the least shattering.

"But we're all black," he insisted.

It was another claret being drunk until breakfast.

"You might as well say to a National Front thug that we're all human," I said.

"Maybe black men are not good enough for them," he protested. "Maybe all they do is dream all day long of being screwed nuts by white chaps. Maybe...."

"I hear you've been hanging around the kitchen every day."

He sat up.

I *was* finally losing a friend.

But he chose to sigh tragically, and for the first time—I had been waiting for this— he swore a sudden volley of earthy expletives.

"From now on, it's white girls or nothing."

"You've tried that already," I reminded him.

He gripped the arms of his chair and then let his lungs collapse slowly.

"Why don't you try men?" I asked, refilling my glass.

He stared.

And spat:

"You're full of filth, do you know that?"

"I have long suspected it," I said, losing interest.

But I threw in my last coin:

"Or simply masturbate. We all do."

Furiously, he refilled his glass.

We drank in silence for a long, contemplative hour.

"They're going to send me down," I said.

"What?"

It was good of him to actually sound surprised.

"If I refuse to go into Warneford as a voluntary patient," I added.

"What's Warneford?"

"A psychiatric care unit," I said. "I have until lunch this afternoon to decide. Between either voluntary confinement or being sent down."

I tossed him the Warden's note to that effect. He unfolded it.

He whistled.

The sound of his whistle almost made me forgive him everything, including himself. Finally he asked: "What have you decided to do?"

"Be sent down."

"But ..."

I interrupted:

"It's the one decision in my life which I know will turn out right."

"Will you stay on in England?"

"Yes."

"Why not go to Africa and join our guerrillas? You've always been rather more radical than myself and this will be a chance blah blah blah blah blah."

I yawned.

"Your glass is empty," I said. "But take a good look anyway, a good look at me and all you know about me and then tell me whether you see a dedicated guerrilla."

He looked.

I refilled his glass and opened another bottle as he scrutinised me.

He lit up; almost maliciously.

"You're a tramp," he said firmly, "You're just like that nigger-tramp who accosted me the other day when we...."

"I know," I said belching.

He stared.

"What will you do?"

"Writing."

"How will you live?"

"Tomorrow will take care of itself. I hope," I said.

And that was the last time we made speech to each other over bottles of claret throughout the small hours until clean sunlight slivered lucidly through the long open windows and I left him sleeping peacefully in his chair and hurried to my last breakfast in college.

1978

Sharon May

Sharon May (b. 1964) was born in California of mixed American and Iranian ancestry. She has lived and worked in Southeast Asia and is currently a Stegner Fellow at Stanford University. Her stories, essays, and interviews have appeared in numerous American journals. She is co-editor of *In the Shadow of Angkor: Contemporary Writing from Cambodia* (2004). "The Wizard of Khao-I-Dang" was first published in *TinHouse*, Fall 2005.

May's "The Wizard of Khao-I-Dang" is a story that looks at borders, the meeting point between peoples and individuals. It can be compared with Nadine Gordimer's "Is There Nowhere Else Where We Can Meet?" Gordimer has been accused by some critics of "cultural appropriation," of writing about a people (South African blacks) outside her ken; she has responded that she is concerned primarily with the meeting-point or intersection of peoples. Another justification could be that biographies (once biographers have done their homework) as well as autobiographies are needed to understand individuals and by extension peoples. In light of all this, comment on May's portraits of the protagonists in her story. May has said, "'The Wizard of Khao-I-Dang' was inspired by my experiences working in Cambodian refugee camps after the collapse of the Khmer Rouge regime. I wanted to explore the assumption that all refugees want to leave their homeland. I am interested in borders — of race, nationality, gender — the edges in between."

The Wizard of Khao-I-Dang

Tom treats me like a servant in the day, but he invites me to drink with the Australian Embassy staff in the evening. He's new on the Thai border and my least favorite of the immigration officers, arrogant and short-tempered. But I accept his offer because I consider this, too, part of my job, not only to work as a Cambodian interpreter but also to try to educate the staff, as I've been here longer than any of them. Besides, I know he'll buy the beer, and without the alcohol, I cannot sleep.

Tonight all three of them are there — Tom, Richard, Sandra — sitting at a table outside the Bamboo Garden, which caters mostly to foreigners, under a hand-lettered sign that says Bambu Gardin. I am the only Cambodian man — the only Cambodian here. The other two translators — Thais who speak Khmer with an accent, and who have their own families to return to in the evening — are absent. Only I have nowhere better to go.

My favorite of the three Australian officers, Sandra, looks about forty years old, pale and fleshy. She wears a red felt hat with a floppy brim, as if she must shield herself from the soft glow of the streetlights. Dark freckles dot her body, like bugs in a sack of rice, speckling her face, her neck, her arms. Of the three embassy officers, she is the kindest, and the most emotional, especially when she's drunk.

Tonight, after her fourth beer, she leans her face close to mine and says, "These poor people. How can you stand it?"

Her tears embarrass me.

I don't want pity. What I want is for them to understand. Of course, this is a foolish desire. I know what the Buddha teaches: desire is the cause of suffering. And so I have tried to eradicate desire from my heart. I have tried to weaken its pull on my mind. But still it remains. A wanting. A deep lake of yearning, wide as the Tonlé Sap,[1] which expands more than ten times its size during the monsoon, only to shrink again in the dry season.

Even after we have lost everything, we still want something. The people stuck in Khao-I-Dang camp, who have escaped from Cambodia to Thailand, want to get out to America or Australia—or any country that will accept them. They want this not for themselves, but for their children. I, who made it to Australia and then came back to the camps to help my people, want to go home to Cambodia. And the immigration officers, what do they want?

The next morning, Tom doesn't look at me or the Cambodian applicant, who has been bussed here from Khao-I-Dang for this interview, along with the other hundred refugees waiting outside the building for their turn. I suspect Tom is tired or hung over. He stares at the file lying on the table and absently twirls an orange Fanta bottle clockwise with his thumb and forefinger. Water drops cover the glass like beads of sweat, except near the lip, which he wipes with a handkerchief now before taking a sip. He drinks a dozen bottles of orange Fanta a day, because—as he confided to me when he first arrived a month ago, nervous and sweating—he is afraid of the water, afraid of the ice, and isn't taking any bloody chances. So every morning in the Aranyaprathet market I fill an ice chest to keep the bottles cold.

"When were you born?" Tom finally asks the applicant, who stares intently at the floor while I translate the question into Khmer. He wears the cheap, off-white plastic sandals distributed in the camp last week. One of the side straps has broken.

"I'm a Rat," the man answers, glancing up at me, not Tom.

Of course I don't translate this directly. The man, Seng Veasna according to the application, nervously holds his hands sandwiched between his knees. Seng Veasna means "good destiny." He looks about fifty, the father of the small family sitting in a half circle before the officer's wooden desk. I calculate quickly, counting back the previous Years of the Rat until I reach the one that best suits his age.

"Nineteen thirty-six," I say to Tom. He checks the answer against the birth date on the application, submitted by Seng Veasna's relatives in Australia. The numbers must match, as well as the names, or the officer will think the man is lying and reject the application. Each question is a problem with a single correct answer, only a family's future—not an exam grade—is at stake.

It is my job to solve these problems. To calculate. To resolve inconsistencies.

---

[1] *Tonlé Sap* A lake and river system in Cambodia that is of major importance to the country's economy and agriculture (and whose name means "great fresh water system").

I did not wish to become a translator or to perform these tricks. I had wanted to become a mathematician and had almost finished my baccalaureate when the Khmer Rouge took over in 1975. I'd planned to teach high school, but it was not my fate. Instead, I now work in this schoolhouse made of timber and tin, at the site of an abandoned refugee camp. This building alone still stands, used for immigration interviews. Inside, three tables for three teams are set in a wide triangle, far enough apart that we can see but not hear each other.

The arrangement reminds me of the triangle I have traveled from Cambodia to Thailand to Australia — and now back again, to Thailand, retracing my journey. After the fall of the Khmer Rouge in 1979, I left Cambodia, crossing the minefields to a camp like this one on the Thai border. Australia accepted me. In Melbourne, I washed dishes in a refugee hostel and took English classes. Language has always come easily to me, as have numbers. Before the war I'd studied French and some English. Like a fool I'd even kept an English dictionary with me after the Khmer Rouge evacuated us from the city. For this stupidity I almost lost my life; when a soldier discovered the book, I survived by claiming I used the pages for toilet paper — very soft, I told him, ripping out a few to demonstrate.

After the Khmer Rouge, I learned some Vietnamese from the occupying soldiers. In the refugee camp, I learned a little Thai. Still when I first arrived in Australia, English sounded like snake language, with so many S's, hissing and dangerous. But then the words began to clarify, not individually but in patterns, like the sequence of an equation. A door opened, and I no longer felt trapped. I still felt like a stranger, though, useless, alone. I had no wife, no children to keep me there. After three years, I got my Australian passport and returned to Thailand.

First I worked in a transit camp in Bangkok, where the refugees who have been accepted must pass medical tests before they can be sent abroad. The foreign aid workers didn't trust me, because I was Cambodian. And I didn't want to be in Bangkok. After six months, I heard the Australian embassy needed translators on the border. That's where I wanted to be, where I could be useful. I jumped at the chance. One step closer to Cambodia, to home.

I had to come back. I think it is my fate to work in a schoolhouse after all.

"Why did you leave Cambodia?" Tom asks the applicant now.

Of all the questions, I dread this one the most. When I translate it into Khmer, Seng Veasna laughs, lifting his hands and opening them in the air in a wide gesture of surrender. For the first time during the interview, he looks relaxed, as if all the tension has drained from his body.

"Doesn't he know what happened in our country?" he asks me. His tone is intimate, personal. For the moment, he has forgotten his fear. He seems to have forgotten even the presence of the embassy officer, although I have not.

"You must tell him," I say in Khmer. I understand the purpose of this question is to distinguish between economic and political refugees, but I also know that this man cannot answer, any more than the last applicant, who just looked at me in disbelief.

He cannot answer any more than I can. Still, I urge him, "Just tell the truth."

The man shakes his head, no. He cannot speak. He can only laugh. I want to tell him I know this is a nonsense question, a question they do not need to ask.

Why did you leave Cambodia?

I've told the embassy staff many times that if they ask this question, they can never get the right answer. I've explained to the other two officers—although not yet to this new one, Tom—that nearly two million people died. One-quarter of the people in Cambodia died in less than four years. Then the Vietnamese invaded. There was no food, no medicine, no jobs. Everyone has lost family. Myself, I lost my mother and father, two brothers, one sister, six aunts and uncles, seventeen cousins. The numbers I can say; the rest I cannot.

Even now, the fighting continues in Cambodia and on the border. Sometimes in this schoolhouse the muffled boom of heavy artillery interrupts the interviews.

"Why is he laughing?" Tom asks.

"He does not understand the question."

"Ask him again. How can he not know why he bloody left the country?"

I see Tom's bottle of Fanta is almost empty. I take another from the ice chest, pop off the cap, wipe the lip with a clean handkerchief, and set it on his desk before turning back to Seng Veasna to explain in Khmer. "I know, you don't want to remember. But you must tell him what you've gone through." When the man still does not speak, I add, "Uncle, if you don't answer, he will reject your application."

At that, Seng Veasna glances quickly at Tom then back to the floor and begins to talk, without raising his eyes. I repeat his story in English, the story I have heard so many times in infinite variations, the same story that is my own. And when Seng Veasna is finally through and the interview finished, to my relief the officer Tom stamps the application accepted. One done. Ten families still wait outside. The morning is not yet half over.

Here's what I don't say to the immigration officers: Try to imagine. The camp is like prison, nothing to do but wait and go crazy. Forget your iced bottles of Fanta and beer. Forget your salary that lets you live like a king while you make the decisions of a god.

Imagine. It is like magic. You wake up one morning and everything is gone. The people you love, your parents, your friends. Your home. Like in the film I saw twice in Australia, *The Wizard of Oz*. I watched it first with my second brother's son, who was six, who had been born on the border but raised in Melbourne and cannot even speak Khmer properly. The flying monkeys scared him so much I had to turn off the video. But those monkeys reminded me of home, of when I worked in the forest surrounding Lake Tonle Sap. They reminded me of the monkey god Hanuman and his army, who helped Rama rescue Sita. So, later, after my nephew went to sleep, I watched the rest of the movie. The next week I rented the video and watched it again alone. I didn't like the singing and dancing, so I fast-forwarded through those parts. But the girl's wanting to go home—that I understood. And I understood, too, the wizard who has no power, who cannot even help himself, although he also secretly wishes to return home.

I want to tell the immigration officers — imagine you are in that movie. Then maybe you will understand. You are the girl. Only there is no home to return to. And instead of Oz, you have woken up in a refugee camp.

Each day you have nothing to do but worry and, if you are lucky enough to have a ration card, to wait like a beggar for handouts of rice and canned, half-rancid fish. At night after the foreign aid workers leave, the soldiers who are supposed to protect you steal what few possessions you still have, and they rape your wives and your daughters. You want only to get out. To find a new home.

Every day you hope for an announcement on the loudspeaker that an embassy is conducting interviews. You hope for America but any country will do: France, England, Australia. You check the list on the wall, search for your name, squeezing your body in between the others. The people clustered around the wall have a certain rank smell, almost sweet. You wish you could wash this stink from your own body and purify yourself of this place, of this longing. On one side of you stands a husband who has waited for years, checking this same wall; on the other, a mother who's been rejected twice and so has little hope, yet still she comes to look. Behind you a father squats in the sun; he can't read, so his son checks for him while he waits. If you're lucky enough to be listed, you must be prepared to go to the interview the following day.

Imagine. The bus picks you up early in the morning, exiting the gate past the Thai guards with their machine guns, taking you out of the camp for the first time in the years since you arrived. As the bus rattles over the rutted road, your mind clenches in fear. The child in front of you presses her face to the window, enraptured. She points at the rice fields, the water buffalo, the cows, which she has never seen before because she was born in the camp. "What's that?" she asks, curious. "And that?" Her father names these things for her. You know he is thinking of the interview ahead, as you are, and how much depends on it, how her future depends on it; perhaps he is thinking, too, of how the shirt he has cleaned and pressed is already stained with sweat.

All the questions are difficult. Especially the ones that seem the simplest to the immigration officers: What is your name? Where were you born? How old are you?

Take, for example, this morning, when officer Richard asks a young man, "What is your brother's name?"

"Older brother Phal," the boy answers. He is skinny, frightened.

"What is his *full* name?" Richard, over six feet tall, has wide shoulders and a large belly like a Chinese Buddha. Although he smiles often, his height and massive torso scare the applicants, especially when he leans toward them as he does now, both elbows planted on the table, intently studying the boy. The young man stares at the floor. He looks like a real Khmer — wide cheekbones, full lips, chocolate skin. "Don't be scared," Richard says. "Take it easy. We're not going to do anything to you. Just try to answer correctly, honestly."

Still the boy hesitates. I worry Richard may take this as a sign he is lying about his relationship to the sponsor, although I've tried to explain to him that Cambodians don't call their relatives by their given names; it's not polite. You call them brother or sister, aunt or uncle, or you use nicknames, so you may not know the full given name. Then there are the names you may have used under the Khmer Rouge, to hide your background to save your family's lives, or your own. I have explained this all before, but it does no good.

In the end, Richard says, "I'm sorry," and stamps the front page rejected.

I can do nothing. Although siblings have lower priority, I believe the familial relationship is not the problem. Rather, the boy is dark-skinned and speaks no English. Richard, like the others, prefers the light-skinned Cambodians, who have more Chinese blood, softer features, who can speak at least some English. If they are young and pretty, and female, even better.

Just as important is the officer's mood, yet another variable I must consider. Tom is more likely to accept an applicant when he has been to a brothel the night before. Sandra is more likely to approve after she has received a letter from her children in Sydney, less likely if they happen to mention her ex-husband in Brisbane. Richard, usually in good spirits, is most dangerous when he has a hangover or digestive problems. Today, he seems to have neither trouble. He has not been running to the toilet or popping paracetamol pills for a headache, so I don't know why the day doesn't seem to get easier.

The next couple is neither young nor pretty. The wife's lips and teeth are stained red from chewing betel nut.

"When was your seventh son born?" Richard asks.

The husband and wife look at each other, confused.

"Was it eight or nine years ago?" the man asks his wife.

"Nine," she says. "No, eight."

"You sure? Wasn't it nine?"

"No, tell him eight." The wife gives her husband a scolding look, then smiles weakly at the officer, showing her stained teeth. By now Richard is laughing and shaking his head.

"Eight," I translate.

"Do they know his birth *date?*"

The husband looks again at his wife. "Dry season," she says. "I remember it had stopped raining already."

"Around December or January," I translate. Then I add, "It's not that they're lying. It's that these things aren't important. Birth dates are not registered until a child enters school, if then."

"How can you not know when your own child was born?" Richard asks me. His generous belly shakes as he laughs. He does not really want an answer, so I say nothing.

"What's wrong?" the wife asks me.

"Never mind." I say. "Don't worry."

I am forever in between.

To the people in the camp, I explain again and again, "Look, you must remember your full names and birth dates. In Cambodia it's not important, but in the West, it's very important. If you don't know, make them up. One person in the family must write all the answers down, and everyone must remember. You must practice."

They look at me funny at first, not quite believing me, like Richard watches me now, still chuckling. Because he is amused, I calculate he will accept the couple. I decide to say nothing and just smile back.

That night at the Bamboo Garden, Richard calls the owner to our table. "Your food is spot on, very *aroy*," Richard says, emphasizing and mispronouncing the Thai word for delicious, using the wrong tone. "But, mate, that sign is spelled wrong."

The owner, a slight man in his sixties, nods his head, "Yes. Thank you. Yes."

"I mean, you gotta fix that spelling." Richard points to the sign above him. "Darith, can you explain to him?"

Shit, I think, even here I have to translate. In polite language, I tell the owner in Thai that the big foreigner loves the food very much.

The owner smiles. Richard nods, happy to be understood. I think that's the end of it. But then Richard pulls a long strip of toilet paper—which is used in place of napkins—from the pink plastic container in the center of the table. In large block letters, using the pen he keeps in his shirt pocket, he writes: *BAMBOO GARDEN*. He underlines the double *O* and the *E*, then points again at the misspelled sign.

The owner's face darkens, without me having to explain. "Thank you. Yes, I fix," he says, as he takes the piece of toilet paper from Richard's outstretched hand.

The young woman sitting in front of the desk this morning is both pretty and light-skinned. Her hair, recently washed, is combed neatly into a shiny ponytail that falls below her narrow waist. As she passed me to take her seat, I could smell the faint sweet scent of her shampoo. She wears a carefully ironed white blouse, and a trace of pink lipstick, which she must have borrowed from a friend or relative to make herself up for this occasion. Officer Tom, to whom I have been assigned today, watches the girl with interest, charmed. Her sponsor is only a cousin, so normally she would have little chance of being accepted.

"What do you do in the camp?" he asks. "Do you work?"

The young lady speaks softly. Out of politeness, she doesn't meet his eyes. "Yes, I work, but ..." Her voice trails off and then she turns to me, blushing. "I don't want to say, it's a very low job."

"What is it?"

"I work in the CARE bakery, making bread."

Tom eyes me suspiciously. "Why are you talking to her?"

I could answer him straight, but I'm annoyed with him today. I did not sleep well last night. I am getting sick of this job, this place. For all I do, it seems I have done nothing. "She was talking to me," I snap back, "that's why I talked to her."

"What did she say?"

"She says she doesn't want to tell you, because she feels embarrassed." As if on cue, she turns her head away. Her pony tail ripples down her back.

"What exactly does she *do* in the camp?" Tom says this in an insinuating way, as if he suspects she's a prostitute. I don't like the way he looks at her. Maybe he is undressing her in his mind right now. For her part, the girl waits quietly in the chair, knees drawn together, looking at her hands lying still on her knees. Her fingernails are clean, cut short. This, too, she remembered to do for the interview.

"She has a wonderful job," I say to Tom. "You know the bread from the CARE bakery in Khao-I-Dang, the French bread you eat every morning? She is the baker."

"That's very good. Why didn't you say so in the first place?" He relaxes back in his chair and takes a drink from the Fanta bottle. I don't know how he can drink this stuff, or how I can watch him drink it all day. I submerge the thought and clear my head to concentrate on the task at hand. He continues, "Ask her what she is going to do if she gets accepted to Australia."

"What are you going to do in Australia — tell him you're going to open a bakery," I say, all in one sentence.

Raising her head to face him now, she answers in a sweet, composed voice, "I want to open a bakery shop in Australia."

I translate, "She wants to work in a bakery in Australia, and when she can save enough money, to open her own bread shop."

"Good, good," he says, and stamps the application accepted.

That night at dinner with Sandra and Richard, Tom asks me out of the blue, "Why did you come back here?"

The restaurant sign is gone, creating an empty space over our heads. In response to Tom's question, I shrug my shoulders and look away, hoping he'll get distracted, perhaps by the attractive waitress waiting to refill our glasses. I glance at her and she comes forward to pour more beer for everyone.

"You came back, didn't you?" Tom persists after the waitress has stepped back into the shadows. "Your mother's Australian, isn't she? And your father is Cambodian?"

I've heard this rumor, too, mostly from foreigners. I think it is their way of explaining why I can speak English.

"No, I am all Cambodian," I say. "But I have Australian citizenship."

"So you went through the Khmer Rouge and all that?" asks Richard.

"Yes. All that."

Sandra, who knows this, watches me. Her jaw tenses under the shadow of her hat.

"I don't get it," Tom says. "Why would you come back? Seems to me everyone else is trying to get out of here." He laughs, lifting his glass. "Myself included. Cheers, mate."

I lift my glass. "Cheers," I say. I should leave it at that.

Sandra is still watching me with concern, her eyebrows drawn together. "How about that storm this afternoon?" she asks to change the subject. "I couldn't hear a thing."

Maybe it is the beer. I don't know. I look straight at Tom. "You don't know how much the people feel," I say. He doesn't respond.

"I couldn't hear a thing," Sandra repeats, more forcefully this time. "I can't believe how loud rain is on a tin roof."

"Yeah," says Richard. "I even had to stop an interview."

"The way you treat people, you don't know anything," I say, still looking directly at Tom. He shifts in his chair and dips a spring roll into sweet red sauce. With his other hand he ticks the Formica tabletop. His eyes study the waitress. As if he hasn't even heard me. I often feel this way around the immigration officers, invisible. Sometimes they talk about the Cambodians, calling them lazy or stupid, as if I am not there, or as if they have forgotten that I too am Khmer.

"If you ask me, these people don't really want to come to your country," I continue. "If you open the gate, they will go back to Cambodia. They won't even say goodbye." I want to stop, but I can't. "And don't ask them why they leave the country. You think they want to leave their home? They laugh when you ask them that. You should know. The real situation is that they want to survive."

Sandra has stopped talking. Richard looks into his half-empty beer glass, then takes a sip. Tom loudly crunches on another spring roll. I don't know why they are the way they are. It's not that none of them cares. There is Sandra, and others like her. And they are sent from country to country, without time to learn the difference between Cambodia and Vietnam. It's not easy for them. I tell myself that they are just worn down, but the new arrivals have the same assumed superiority, the unquestioned belief that they know everything: what is wrong, what is right — that they are somehow more *human*. I signal to the waitress for another round.

The next night, instead of beer, Tom orders me a Fanta Orange soda, grinning as he slides the bottle across the table toward me. The restaurant sign is still gone.

"No, thanks," I say.

"Go ahead, mate."

"No, thank you," I say again.

"Why not?" asks Tom.

"Oh, leave him alone," says Sandra.

I stare at the orange bottle.

"It won't kill you," says Tom.

"No, not me." I try to make light of it. "I gave that stuff up a long time ago, in 1976."

Tom laughs. So does Richard in his booming voice. For all of their attention to dates from the applicants, for all their insistence that the numbers must match exactly, they ignore what those dates mean. But I am telling the truth. It was 1976, the second year under the Khmer Rouge regime. It was the rainy season, cold and miserable. I lived in a single men's labor camp on a hill in the rice fields. One night I heard the guards calling, "We got the enemy! We got the enemy!" *What enemy?* I thought. We were in the middle of nowhere. The real purpose of the guards was to keep the workers from trying to escape or steal food at night. When I opened my eyes, I couldn't see the man sleeping next to me. Clouds blocked the stars. Then I noticed the feeble flames from lit pieces of rubber tire, burned for lamplight, and got up to see what had happened.

Near the compound's kitchen, three Khmer Rouge leaders gathered around a skinny man kneeling in the mud, his elbows tied tightly behind his back. His shoulders were pulled back like a chicken's wings, tensing the tendons in his neck. He had dark skin and long hair that fell below his bound wrists. I'd heard rumors of resistance fighters, "long hairs" who lived in the forest around Lake Tonle Sap, but I had never seen one and did not believe until then that they really existed. I had thought them the product of our collective imagining, our wishing someone had the courage to fight back.

Comrade Sok kicked the man in his side, and he fell over into the mud. Sok was a big man, twice the size of the prisoner. When Sok kicked him again, the man's head hit a water buffalo yoke lying at the edge of the kitchen. One of the other leaders pulled his head up. The prisoner's eyes were closed. Comrade Sok said, "Why do you resist? Who do you struggle for?"

The man seemed only half-conscious. He opened his eyes briefly, then closed them again and spoke very clearly, slowly enunciating each word, "I struggle for all of you, brothers, not for myself."

"You struggle for me? We have already liberated the country." Sok kicked him again. "We have no need of your help."

The man said once more, "I struggle for you."

Then they threw him like a sack of rice into an oxcart. Everyone was watching. We couldn't help him. We couldn't do anything.

The next day, while I was cleaning the abscesses on my feet using water boiled with sour leaves, the oxcart returned — without the man, loaded instead with bottles of soft drinks and cigarette cartons. Comrade Sok explained this was our reward for capturing the enemy: one bottle for three people, one pack of cigarettes for ten people. The next time we captured the enemy, we would receive an even greater reward.

The cigarette packets were Fortunes, with a lion insignia. The soda bottles were Miranda Orange. I teased the two younger boys with whom I shared the soft drink, dividing the bottle into thirds, the top being the largest, the bottom the smallest. "What part do you want?" I asked. Of course they chose the top two portions. "Okay, I'll take the bottom," I said. "You don't mind if I drink my portion first..."

"No, that's not right," they protested together. I was only making fun. I poured the drink into three tin bowls we usually used to eat the rice ration, giving the boys most of it. They were excited about the soda, which they hadn't tasted in a long time, if ever. But all the while I was trying to make them laugh, I felt sad. A man was killed for this.

The drink was flat, not even enough liquid to fill my mouth.

The application lying on the table today in front of Sandra is a difficult case. This morning, when I dropped the files on each of the three officer's tables, I made sure this one came to her. The sponsor in Australia, a daughter, got citizenship by claiming a woman was her mother. Now that the daughter is in Australia, she claims the woman is not actually her mother, but rather her aunt, and that the woman sitting before us now is her real mother.

The mother hands me the letter from her daughter, which I translate. In it, the daughter explains that this woman is her real mother and confesses she lied before. She didn't know her mother was alive then. She was alone in the camp, with no one to take care of her. That's why she decided to lie.

Sandra asks me, "Do you think they are really mother and daughter?"

"Yes," I say, and hand her the letter, which she adds to the file lying open before her, with the previous and current applications and small black-and-white photos. "You can even see the daughter looks like her."

"Well, they can't do that," Sandra says. "She lied. The law is the law."

"I can tell you, this is a story many people face, not just these two. They do not intend to lie, but because of the circumstances they must do it, believe me. Think of your own daughter, if you were separated." And then I add, "Of course it's up to you, not me."

"She lied," Sandra says. "It's finished. I have to reject them."

"I can't tell them straight like that," I say. "Would you let me explain nicely to them the reason they are getting rejected?"

"All right, go ahead."

So I take a chance, a calculated risk. There is nothing to lose now. I know Sandra loves her own children, and also that she has a good heart. I say to the mother in a soft, even voice, "Look, your daughter lied to the embassy even though she knew what she was doing was wrong. A country like Australia is not like Cambodia. The law is the law. When you say someone is your mother, she's got to be your mother. Now she cannot change her story. So from now on, I don't think you will be able to meet your daughter anymore for the rest of your life."

Tears begin to well in the mother's eyes. I feel bad for what I am doing, but I know there is no other way. I keep my voice firm, steady, and continue, "So now, after all you've been through in Cambodia, after how hard you struggled to keep your family together, to survive, now you are separated forever."

The mother begins to wail, a long piercing sound that fills the entire room, so that the teams at the other two tables turn around to look at us. "Oh, my daughter, I will never see you again!" she cries. I translate what she says for Sandra. "After all we survived in the Pol Pot time—when you were starving, I risked my life to steal food for you. When you got sick, I looked after you. When you could not walk, I carried you in my arms. And now you lie. You lie and you are separated from me. I cannot see you for the rest of my life. *Ouey...*"

I translate it all, word for word. The father is crying now, too, but silently. He sits in a wooden chair, with his back straight. Their young son watches his mother's face and sobs as well, echoing her wails.

"Please, tell them to go now," Sandra says. She looks away and wipes her eyes with the back of her hand.

In Khmer, I dismiss the family, "Go, go. Don't cry anymore. Even if you die, nobody cares. You will never see your child anymore."

As the mother walks away, the applicants at the other tables watch her leave. The building is silent except for her voice. She cries all the way out of the building, gripping her husband's arm. Her son whimpers too, clinging to her legs through the sarong, almost tripping her.

I start to laugh. "Well, Sandra, that's it," I say. "Send them back to the Killing Fields. Don't worry. There are more coming."

Sandra looks at me, stunned. She opens her mouth and closes it again, without saying anything, like a fish gulping seawater. The freckled skin around her eyes is red and puffy. I can see the beating of her blood beneath the translucent skin of her left temple, a small pulsing disk, like the flutter of a bird's heart. She looks away, down to the table, and starts idly shifting through the papers. She isn't really looking at them.

"I'll get the next family," I say.

She nods, her face still turned away from me. I grab the list and go call the next family from the dozens of others waiting outside the building. Some stand in the sun. Others squat in the shade of three small coconut trees, fanning away flies.

"Keo Narith," I say. No one steps forward. The crowd looks agitated, nervous. The mother is still crying, "My daughter, I can never see you again!" A group has gathered around her, asking, "What happened? What happened?"

"Keo Narith!" I call again.

Still, no one answers. I remember the name because it rhymes with my own, and I saw the family members board the bus when they were called in the morning. They must be hiding somewhere now in the crowd or behind the coconut trees or around the corner of the building. I hear a man to the left of me say, "The embassy is not happy today. They reject easily." It's true, when too many people are rejected, the next applicants don't dare answer. They'd rather wait for months or years until they get back on the list again.

After we drive back to Aranyaprathet, the embassy staff meets again for dinner at the Bamboo Garden. The owner has fixed the sign: two small, oblong O's are now squeezed into the space that held the U, and the I has been changed to an E, but the shades of paint don't quite match. Tom and Richard are talking the usual bullshit. Richard expands on his most recent stomach problems. Tom no longer talks about leaving. He has a Thai girlfriend now, a prostitute he claims is a waitress at the bar who has never slept with a man before him. "She's been saving herself," he says.

Sandra looks at him, disgusted, and interjects, "Yeah, right. You really believe that?"

As the men continue talking, Sandra turns to me and whispers, "Darith, I changed it. I changed the file, when I got back. I'm letting them go."

I say quietly, "You made the right decision."

"I know," she says, her eyes shining, urgent. "I understand."

I think, there is more than any of us can understand. I feel something I cannot express: an opening, an exit. It is like the feeling I had when I first crossed the border after the end of the Khmer Rouge regime: gratitude, mixed with weariness and hunger. The day I arrived I could still taste the foul pond water I had drunk in darkness the night before, so thirsty, not seeing until morning the corpse of a woman lying in the pond, close to where I slept. I didn't know then what would come, how many years I would work to return to the border I had fled. I wonder, does Sandra — who I can see out of the corner of my eye is watching me as I glance down at my beer glass on the table — really understand? How many families will remain stuck in the camp if I can no longer do this job? I weigh all of this: duty, desire, two halves of an equation, as I turn the glass in my hand.

All the while in my heart I am thinking, hoping, I can quit now. I can leave this place. It is time to go home.

2005

Wong May

Wong May was born in Singapore and educated at the University of Singapore and the University of Iowa, which awarded her an MFA in 1968. She has published three volumes of poetry, including *A Bad Girl's Book of Animals* (1969) and *Superstitions* (1978).

Wong's "The Shroud" is set in Singapore, but the poem is void of cultural or historical details that identify the setting. Are there any specifically Singaporean elements in the poem? The poem can be compared in this regard with Arthur Yap's "2 Mothers in a HDB Playground," where cultural markers abound. Is the young girl's bitter-sweet experience of leaving school for the last time an exclusively Singaporean experience as portrayed here by the poet? Compare this poem also with Mervyn Morris's "Little Boy Crying" and Dionne Brand's "Amelia."

The Shroud

The little childish happiness
Is taken off, together
With the old school uniform.

Never will I be in that uniform again.
And who will remember
The little girl with her two pigtails
With her petticoats always too long
And her thousand naughty and silly ways?

The old school uniform
With the little childish delights and giggles
Is folded and locked up in the top drawer
Forever.

Shall I cry?
I am no longer a child
My eyes so dry
It's not easy to cry.

Yet I hear somebody weeping —
Crying louder and louder — howling
I feel her tears —
She is the girl locked up in the top drawer.

1978

Pauline Melville

Pauline Melville (b. 1948) was born in Guyana to English and Guyanese (Amerindian) parents. She immigrated to London, England, working there on stage and in film while writing poems and fiction. Her poems have appeared in various anthologies. She has published two collections of stories: *Shape-Shifter* (1990) and *The Migration of Ghosts* (1998). Her first novel, *The Ventriloquist's Tale* (1997), won the Whitbread First Novel Award.

Melville's "McGregor's Journey" offers a refreshing perspective for a postcolonial text. Set in London, it portrays a working-class Scottish man's response to his job as a construction worker in a multicultural London. Melville has written understandingly many stories about West Indians and other ex-colonials in London. Is this sympathetic tone evident in her portrait of McGregor? What does she hope to achieve in writing from the Scottish protagonist's point of view? Does she succeed? Consider this story in terms of Njabulo Ndebele's comment in the opening paragraphs of "Guilt and Atonement: Unmasking History for the Future" about depicting individuals outside your own group.

McGregor's Journey

"I'm jacking,"[1] said McGregor.

It was ten o'clock in the morning. The other scaffolder hadn't turned up. It had taken him half an hour to unload the freezing scaffolding tubes from the lorry,[2] the ringing clang of tube against tube increasingly setting his teeth on edge. That done, he set about emptying the lorry of piles of metal fittings so that the driver could get away. He banged on the side of the cab. The driver raised his thumb and backed the vehicle off the site. McGregor looked up at a sky laden with snow. Then he examined the palms of his hands. They were a shiny, raw pink where the frozen metal had taken off the first layer of skin. They burned him. Flexing his hands, he walked over to the foot of the unfinished, eight-storey building and began to base out the scaffold. On his own, he erected the first level, using the heavy, twenty-one foot tubes as uprights. With deft, experienced twists of the podger[3] on the metal nuts, he fastened the four foot tubes to the uprights, some slantwise and some horizontally so that they reached the wall. One by one, he heaved the wooden planks from the pile at the foot of the wall and laid them out along the structure. Then he decided to quit the job and go drinking.

---

[1] *jacking* A colloquial word for giving up suddenly (British).

[2] *lorry* A motor truck (British).

[3] *podger* Any of various tools that have long handles (British).

"I said I'm jacking," shouted McGregor to the site foreman, trying to make himself heard over the grinding roar of the cement-mixer. The foreman motioned to the hod-carrier,[1] showing him where the bricks were to go. Then he turned to McGregor with drooping shoulders:

"What's up, Jock?" Steam issued from his mouth.

"You can stick your fucking job up your fucking arse." McGregor grinned. "I'm jacking." The foreman looked pained for a minute and then shrugged:

"Go and tell them at the site office. Tell them to phone head office and send me down two more scaffolders."

McGregor went over and unhitched his jacket from where it hung on the end of a piece of scaffolding. He undid his belt with a mounting sense of freedom and took off the leather frogs which held his half-inch Whitworth spanner and the seven-sixteenth A.F. He chucked the podger and the spanners into his canvas tool-bag and walked over the icy, rutted ground to the portocabin by the gates. He began to whistle.

Inside the portocabin, the air was foggy from the calor[2] gas heater. Mr. Oates, the site manager, was on the telephone at a desk littered with papers. Pinned to a notice board near the door was a letter from a Mrs. Kathleen Doherty, written in a loopy scrawl, thanking the men for the collection after her husband's accident. McGregor read it idly as he waited. Mr. Oates put down the telephone. A cigarette with long ash burned between his fingers. White hair with nicotine yellow streaks lay stiffly on either side of his head like bird wings. He looked at McGregor enquiringly.

"I'm away," said McGregor. "Just phone the office and tell them to make up me cards and me wage packet. I'm on me way over to get them now."

"It's only ten o'clock. Can't you finish the morning?"

"No. I'm away now. Sammy says to tell you to ask for two more scaffolders." McGregor turned to leave.

"What's your name?" asked Mr. Oates, wearily.

"Jock the Jacker." McGregor gave a wry smile. "Mac. McGregor," he said as he left. He walked through the site gates. On the street, he took a deep breath and straightened his shoulders. Rows of mean, secretive, terraced houses stretched down the road in front of him. McGregor paused to inspect the contents of his pocket. Forty pence. He set off at a brisk pace to walk the two miles to the main office. Unexpectedly, the day felt full of promise.

"Mr. McGregor, is it?" The dumpy girl in a brown sweater greeted him from the cashier's desk in the construction company's main office.

"Ay. That's it."

She reached in the drawer and pulled out a buff wage packet and his cards:

"We've deducted the twenty pound sub. There's five weeks' holiday stamps on your holiday card and you can pick up the week in hand next Thursday. OK?"

---

[1] *hod-carrier* A builder's container for carrying mortar and brick (British).

[2] *calor* Liquified gas under pressure in containers (British).

The wage register was pushed across the desk and he signed it.

"Don't forget I done three hours this morning," McGregor reminded her.

"Well that won't be due until the Thursday after next. You see today's Thursday and the work up until today, that's your week in hand, gets paid next Thursday, but any work you do today doesn't get paid till the Thursday after that. OK?"

McGregor felt a tightening in the muscles of his neck.

"Thanks," he said. He took the wage packet and went.

At eleven o'clock precisely, the publican unlocked the doors of his Fulham pub and McGregor stepped over the threshold into the quiet, gloomy interior. The low moan of a hoover[1] came from somewhere over his head. Sleepily, the publican made his way behind the bar.

"Gi'us a double scotch there, please," said McGregor.

McGregor's drinking habit ran to a formula; two whiskies in quick succession while he stood at the bar and then straight out and onto the next pub. By the time he reached the fourth one it was snowing. He was somewhere in the back streets of Chelsea.[2] The whisky had begun to do its work, cutting a warm channel through the centre of his body. For the first time, he relaxed enough to take stock of his surroundings. The pub appeared to be empty. Then he caught sight of an old man seated round the corner, his figure half-eaten up by shadows:

"Can I get you something there?" he called across to the old man. The man's head moved a little:

"Half a pint, thank you." The voice was cracked and thin. McGregor ordered a scotch for himself and a beer for the man. They sat in silence for a while. The pensioner spilled his beer as he sipped it. He had eyes that watered permanently, the colour of faded bluebells:

"You a soldier?" he asked.

"I was once," replied McGregor. "I was slung out. Retention Undesirable in the Interest of Her Majesty's Services." He delivered the words with a flourish as if they were poetry. And laughed.

"I was in Spain," said the man.

"Oh yes?" McGregor seemed interested.

"I fought with the International Brigade in the Spanish Civil War."[3]

"Is that a fact?" McGregor waited. The old man leaned forward into a shaft of dull light from the window. McGregor saw motes of dust dancing down the light onto the amber liquid in the glass.

"I was with them in Madrid in 1936. I saw such things. Such terrible things." He

---

[1] *hoover* A vacuum cleaner (British).

[2] *Chelsea* A borough in West London.

[3] *International Brigade in the Spanish Civil War* The International Brigades, comprising mainly volunteers from different countries, were military units supporting the Republicans against General Franco's fascist National forces in the Spanish Civil War (1936–39).

wiped his chin with his checked scarf. "When I came back to England I had to tell everybody what I had seen. For thirty years, every Sunday, I took a soap-box in Hyde Park Corner and I told what I had seen to anybody who would listen. I never missed a Sunday for thirty years. And then I stopped." He leaned back into the shadows. McGregor finished his drink. The old man's glass was still nearly full.

"Will I get you another?" McGregor asked. But the old man had closed up in the darkness like a flower in the night. A restlessness overcame McGregor and he stood up:

"Good luck, then."

"And you, sir," came the voice from the invisible man.

Flakes of wet snow came to rest on McGregor's eyelashes as he walked with the urgency of a man not knowing where he is going.

An hour later, poised between conviviality and violence, McGregor stood in a bar crowded with lunch-time drinkers. He was locked in intense conversation with the father of a baby with no future, a pale young man with red hair. The young father's lack of optimism was depressing him:

"How old did you say the baby was?" asked McGregor. The man consulted his watch.

"Eight and a half hours old," he said dejectedly. "He'll never get a home of his own, poor little blighter. Look how many homeless there are."

McGregor became determined to raise the man's spirits. It was like pushing an enormous boulder uphill.

"And there's no jobs," said the man. "He'll never get a job. That's for sure. No chance."

McGregor tried harder.

"Och, I dunno. You've got a wee boy. Kids are clever these days. They understand computers. They go to college and all sorts of strange things."

"Only if they've got money."

McGregor's face was flushed. He tried again.

"They get grants. They can do anything."

Suspended in a corner of the bar was a television set with the sound turned down, showing images of soldiers chasing and firing on people somewhere in the Middle East. McGregor hoped the young man wouldn't see it.

"D'you reckon?" The red-haired man looked faintly hopeful. McGregor began to sweat:

"Jesus. Kids are magic these days. They speak out. They don't put up with any shit." Somewhere in the back of his brain, McGregor knew that if the man slipped back into despondency, he would be obliged to punch him off his stool.

"Maybe you're right," said the man, reluctantly.

McGregor's voice rose above the buzz of conversation around him as he made a final effort:

"Of course I'm fucking right. Kids have got everything. I wish I was nine hours old. All snuggly and comfy. I wish I was a fucking kid. And another thing. Kids love music. He'll be a musician. That's what's going to happen. He's going to be a great musician. They all play in bands. They make terrific music."

McGregor held his breath.

"Yeah. You're right, I suppose." The man managed a wan grin.

"Right y'are then," said McGregor, triumphantly.

The future of the child assured and the man saved from injury, McGregor made to leave. He drained the remains of his whisky:

"Slainte Mhath,"[1] he said in Gaelic.

The high street looked familiar but he did not recognize it. A lighted bus drew up beside him like an invitation and he stepped onto it. The upper deck of the bus was brightly lit. Stale smoke and a litter of cigarette ends on the floor gave it the bleakly cheerful air of a public bar that had unexpectedly taken to travelling through the dark afternoon. McGregor sat bolt upright in the back seat. The beginnings of a transformation were taking place. His hands gripped the rail in front of him as if he were on the Big Wheel of a funfair. One blazing green eye was wide open, staring ahead with fierce energy, the other was lazily half open like that of a waking child. Faint streaks of mud from the morning's work still decorated his face. Dried mud stiffened his jeans. Somewhere along the way, his jacket had taken off on a journey of its own. The same fine dusting of sand and cement that covered his navy-blue polo-neck sweater caused his hair to stick up in pointed, uneven spikes. Here and there in the spikes sat spangles of snow. Altogether, he looked like one of those creatures that has lain immobile in mud-flats for the duration of a drought waiting for the rains to come in order to return to life.

The wide-open eye focused with dislike on the passengers ahead of him. Suddenly, his expression changed. A look of intense delight spread over his face. His shoulders moved from side to side and he tapped his feet as he whistled the tune of "A Hundred Pipers an a' an a'."[2] He sang the words out, savouring each one, on his face an expression of menacing bliss. The passengers remained silent. No one looked at him. McGregor finished the song and looked expectantly round the bus. The look twisted into a sneer:

"You're all dead people," he shouted.

The man in front of him stared deliberately out of the window. McGregor rose to his feet and held onto the rail to steady himself:

"What would you say if I said 'Let's all get off the bus and light a big bonfire in the street'?" he enquired, enthusiastically.

---

[1] *Slainte Mhath* "Good health to you."

[2] *A Hundred Pipers an a' an a'* An old Scottish folk song.

There was no response. Two women at the front of the bus continued to talk, one of them in a voice as clear as a bell in winter.

"How about setting fire to the bus?" he suggested. "How about giving it a Viking's funeral?"

No one responded. Attracted by the only sign of life, the conversation at the other end of the bus, McGregor stepped carefully down the centre aisle like a seaman navigating the narrow passageway of a rolling ship. With a jerk, he sat down in the empty front seat next to the two women:

"Excuse me, lady." He spoke in the dangerously polite tones of the extremely drunk. The crippled woman with the shining face pulled her lame leg in towards her. The leg, much shorter than the other one, was fitted with a contraption of metal and leather, terminating in a shiny, black, surgical boot that seemed too solid to contain a foot.

"Never mind the leg, lady. Legs aren't important. What happened to your leg, anyway?"

The woman, unruffled by the question, began to give the history of her malformed foot. Her rational explanation and unwavering gaze horrified McGregor. He shut his eyes. When he opened them again, the woman had turned back to her friend and was discussing the essay she had to write on Jane Austen for her evening class.

"A man's a man for a' that," he mumbled, attempting to roll himself a cigarette from his tobacco tin as the bus swayed. He lit the cigarette and fished out the brown pay packet from his pocket. He took out the long, thin wage-slip:

"Forty-eight pounds fucking emergency TAX." He bellowed the last word. "I've been mugged by the government." He scrumpled up the paper and flung it down. Annoyed by the lack of impact, he ground the paper serpent into the ridged floor with his foot. Suddenly, his limbs turned to lead and a great weariness took hold of him:

"Mud. Cold. Shit. Wind. Steel. Rain. Tiredness. That's all I've got to look forward to for the rest of my life. The grants have been granted and I haven't got one," he proclaimed, bitterly. His eyelids drooped shut. To the concern of the two women, who were watching with polite attention, an extraordinary force of gravity seemed to pull McGregor's features earthwards. He forced his mouth open, baring his teeth in a fixed death's head grin. His fists were clenched. He remained like that for several moments in an epic struggle against invading tiredness. Then his face relaxed and his eyes shot open:

"A hundred pipers an a' an a'," he sang, enticingly, with the faintest of threats. The bus rounded a corner and the tobacco tin dropped from his knee to the floor. He regarded it with awe:

"Isn't it a wonderful thing," he said, "that the floor exists to stop things falling through the air?" He pocketed the tin and staggered to his feet. Eyes shut, he put both hands to his head. The mud in his hair gave it the texture of bark. McGregor enjoyed, for at least a minute, the knowledge that he had turned into a tree. He had the distinct sensation that his feet were putting down roots into the floor of the bus; his head sprouting branches that were about to push their way through the roof, each branch adorned with tingling, green buds. He shook his head and opened his eyes. The passengers sat dully before him. He regarded them with disdain and announced in the grand manner of an actor:

"I am leaving this travelling hearse!"

He made his way to the head of the stairs and turned once more, with a theatrical flourish, to address his reluctant audience:

"I hope your legs turn to gristle and chickens eat them!"

They heard his boots clattering, too fast, down the steps. The bus stopped. The word "WANKERS" drifted up to them. Nobody moved. The passengers remained pinned to their seats by this new definition of themselves as the bus drew away.

In the underground station, the driver of the tube train leaned from his window and glared at McGregor with such malevolence, such implacable hatred written on his swarthy features, that McGregor was brought to a halt on the empty platform. The doors shut in McGregor's face. The driver continued to stare. The train remained stationary. McGregor launched into a sweet, tuneful whistle. Without warning, the driver turned and pressed a button. The doors hissed open. Within minutes of boarding the train, McGregor slept a profound and dreamless sleep, his legs stretched out across the gap between the seats.

In this way, McGregor was borne, deep in the intestinal passages of the earth, across London. Through the black tunnels, under the river, he was carried along, first in one direction and then another. Overhead, the mammoth city, with its millions of citizens in their neon-lit offices, went about its business. And not a solitary soul was aware that far beneath the ground underfoot, McGregor was voyaging.

McGregor opened his eyes. The train had stopped. The doors stood open. He got off without knowing which station he was in. The platform was deserted. The air was warm. A numbness in his feet made him unsure that they were touching the ground and gave him the feeling of floating through the yellow-lit passages and hallways. For all he knew, he had slept for three days and three nights. Under one arch, a black dog that had strayed into the underground blocked his way, bristling and barking. McGregor stopped and whistled at it. The dog lost interest and padded away, sniffing at the grimy, cream-tiled walls.

And then a wondrous sight met McGregor's eyes.

Where the tunnel opened out onto the flat area below the escalators, a black woman, in her forties, was dancing vigorously on the concourse under the high, domed ceiling. All on her own, she boogied and partied to strains of music that filtered down from the station entrance, a beatific smile on her face. In one hand she held a can of lager, taking swigs from it as her hips swung from side to side. Some other black commuters passed by, giving her a wide berth. McGregor watched, enchanted, as if all his travels had been expressly to bring him to this one point at this particular moment. One side of her coat hung down lower than the other and she'd hitched up her skirt into her belt. She finished the lager and threw down the can. It skittered over the floor with an echoing rattle close to where a uniformed transport guard was sweeping. Then she bebopped over to a pile of carrier-bags, dumped where the curved wall reached the ground and rummaged for some more beer. The side of her shoe was split open by the big-toe joint:

"Lard," she said. "Look how me shoe is poppin' offa me foot." She opened the can, took a gulp and jived her way back to the centre of the hall. McGregor looked on appreciatively. Then she spotted him. Her eyes gleamed with pleasure:

"Come daalin'." She addressed him with carefree boldness. "Dance wid me, nuh."

McGregor approached bashfully:

"Och. I canna dance," he said.

"Everybody can dance," she insisted and continued to shimmy round the hall. Suddenly, McGregor joined her, leaping into the air and executing a wild, jerky Highland fling accompanied by a joyous, warlike scream. The woman shook with laughter.

"You're beautiful," said McGregor.

"Yuh lie," she screeched with laughter again and stopped to catch her breath. "It still snowin' up there?" she asked.

"I dunno," said McGregor.

"Lemme tell you sometin'." She beckoned him closer. "I was up there and a cold wind from Russia came an' fasten in me back. That damn wind bit me like a snake. So I come down here."

"And let me tell you something, lady," said McGregor. "You are the first person I have seen all day with a big smile on their face. And I love you for it."

They regarded each other with mutual approval.

"Yuh sweet, man. Yuh come to carry me way wid you?" she teased. "First yuh must gimme a kiss. Come nuh, man. Yuh gwaan kiss me or what?" she said boldly.

"Lady. You are the first real bit of humanity I've come across today, the first person with a wee bit of optimism and I'd love to kiss you." She was close to him. Her breath smelled sweet and sharp like olives. He glanced round. The station had filled up with black people. He felt a little unsure of himself.

"Wait a minute. Wait a minute, lady." He approached the guard who was still sweeping:

"Excuse me, sir. Excuse me — er this lady would like me to give her a kiss. Would that cause any bother at all?"

The guard stopped sweeping and surveyed the concourse. Three youths were lounging against the wall opposite. He scratched his head:

"Well, it just could do. A lot of these youts still hot-headed after the riots, you know. Them could jus' get hold of the wrong end of the stick, if you know what I mean. Them could jus' think 'Here is another white man who think he own a black woman like all through history.'" The guard touched McGregor kindly on the arm. "I tell you what I suggest. You go on ahead up the stairs and let the lady follow you. Then we don't have no trouble. You can go for a nice drink together somewhere and see how you get on?" He winked. "Lemme go tell her."

He walked over to the woman who was fumbling in her plastic bag. He spoke to her for a few moments and then came back:

"You jus' go on up de stairs like I said. Don't even look back. Let she jus pick up she bags and follow you."

McGregor hesitated but the woman was smiling and blowing kisses at him:

"Right y'are then," he said.

"Go on up. She will follow you. OK man?" The guard slapped him on the arm amicably.

McGregor did as he was asked. But he was hurt. Some poison had entered him. What the guard had said about history and white men went round in his head. He held onto the rail and the escalator carried him smoothly upwards. Half way up, he turned to check that she was following. Her eyes, blank with disappointment, were fixed on him and she was walking slowly backward away from him through the arched hallway, carrier-bags on each arm like white water-wings. He watched her disappearing as if she were being drawn back into the dark tunnel. Trying to get back down he slipped, cursed, stumbled and clung onto the rail. The escalator bore him steadily up towards the curtain of snow that hung in the station entrance. Something was happening to him that he did not recognize. A hot substance, like lava, crawled slowly down his cheeks.

Later that night, the police arrested a man in Camberwell.[1] He was smashing shop windows, one after the other with a scaffolding spanner. As the glass exploded in each one, he yelled:

"I want you to know that I never owned a fucking slave in my life. Never."

1990

---

[1] *Camberwell* A district of London, England, in the London borough of Southwark. A thriving multicultural community, its ethnic mix includes immigrants from Africa, the Caribbean, Cyprus, and the Middle East.

Sudesh Mishra

Sudesh Mishra (b. 1962) was born in Suva, Fiji. He received his doctorate from the Flinders University of South Australia. A fourth-generation Fijian of Indian origin, Sudesh Mishra now lives in Melbourne and teaches at Deakin University. He has published five volumes of poetry, including *Memoirs of a Reluctant Traveller* (1994) and *Diaspora and the Difficult Art of Dying* (2002). He is working on a novel set in Fiji.

The speaker of Mishra's "Mt. Abu: St. Xavier's Church" initially is troubled by the local rajah's neglect of an Anglican church in Mt. Abu, India. But the poem becomes much more personal when the speaker affects indifference to this negligence on recalling the Church's indifference years ago to his father's being "sold" into indentured labour overseas, "across the water" (see footnotes to the poem). "The Grand Pacific Hotel" has a speaker who still rankles at the thought of the humiliating colonized-colonizer relationship of the colonial days. Can we compare his response here ("Now it's easy") with Derek Walcott's "coal of [his] compassion" in "Ruins of a Great House"?

Mt. Abu:[1] St. Xavier's Church

There is an Anglican Church at Bazaar
With broken stained-glass windows and a belfry
That will crumble in less than two or three
Years, if the rajah or ruling salkaar
Continues to tread the path of negligence.
Should I be indifferent after the fact,
Being one with many axes to grind? What
Perverted sense, what religious romance
Gave rise to this house — while in Calcutta
They sold you, Father, across the water?[2]

1994

---

[1] *Mt. Abu* The town of Mt. Abu in Rajasthan is the home of many Jain and Hindu temples, with just a few churches.

[2] *across the water* This phrase is commonly "across the black water" — that is, leaving the Indian sub-continent, which results in various transformations, including losing one's caste.

The Grand Pacific Hotel[1]

A palatial building with broad verandahs and luxurious lounges, coffee rooms, etc.,
where cooling drinks or the refreshing cup of afternoon tea, are served in truly
oriental style by white-turbaned waiters.

Herald Handbook, 1921

Clumps of vesi trees[2] bob in bilge-water;
The offal-green drapery of the sea
Drapes the nothing of a louvred horizon.
The ocean is my sponsor. I forgive it
Everything—those years spent nursing ratoons[3]
Under sun's and planter's gong. Now it's easy.
I will answer to many sobriquets.
Coolie is the most familiar. Tonight
They play whist over their gins. And I wait.
As always I wait, devouring such nouns
As cricket and veranda. The trades blow
Through wicker chairs. I tire of the turban,
The looped cerements of my non-presence.
Some day I will name myself in their script.

2007

---

[1] *The Grand Pacific Hotel* There are many hotels on the Pacific shores with this name, but Mishra is referring to the "grand old lady" of Suva, Fiji, built in 1914.

[2] *vesi trees* Vesi trees were sacred among ancient Fijians; their seemingly indestructible quality was
equated with indomitable characteristics in humans.

[3] *ratoons* Plants—like sugar-cane, to which the poet is referring here—grown from stubble or shoots.

Rohinton Mistry

Rohinton Mistry (b. 1952) was born in Bombay, India, of a Parsi family, and came to Canada in 1975. He studied at the University of Bombay and the University of Toronto. His publications include *Tales from Firozsha Baag* (stories, 1987), *Such a Long Journey* (novel, 1991), *A Fine Balance* (novel, 1995), and *Family Matters* (novel, 2002).

Mistry's "Swimming Lessons" is a metafictional work in which the narrator comments on how and what he is writing, even explaining the imagery he uses, such as the dominant water image. Mistry has stated that he writes about individuals who transcend ethnic and national characteristics, achieving a human dimension. Do you think this is true of the protagonist of this story? How does this story compare with Neil Bissoondath's "Man as Plaything, Life as Mockery," which eschews cultural and historical particulars? Is the mother more traditional, less postmodern in her literary preferences? Note that the mother complains of "too much theory" in the father's discussion of their son's stories. And note how in the postcolonial period, communal conflicts are surfacing; the Parsi community is very much aware of the Shiv Sena (the advocates of Hindu nationalism).

Swimming Lessons

The old man's wheelchair is audible today as he creaks by in the hallway: on some days it's just a smooth whirr. Maybe the way he slumps in it, or the way his weight rests has something to do with it. Down to the lobby he goes, and sits there most of the time, talking to people on their way out or in. That's where he first spoke to me a few days ago. I was waiting for the elevator, back from Eaton's with my new pair of swimming-trunks.

"Hullo," he said. I nodded, smiled.

"Beautiful summer day we've got."

"Yes," I said, "it's lovely outside."

He shifted the wheelchair to face me squarely. "How old do you think I am?"

I looked at him blankly, and he said, "Go on, take a guess."

I understood the game; he seemed about seventy-five although the hair was still black, so I said, "Sixty-five?" He made a sound between a chuckle and a wheeze: "I'll be seventy-seven next month." Close enough.

I've heard him ask that question several times since, and everyone plays by the rules. Their faked guesses range from sixty to seventy. They pick a lower number when he's more depressed than usual. He reminds me of Grandpa as he sits on the sofa in the lobby, staring out vacantly at the parking lot. Only difference is, he sits with the stillness of stroke victims, while Grandpa's Parkinson's disease would bounce his thighs and legs and arms all over the place. When he could no longer hold the *Bombay Samachar* steady enough to read, Grandpa took to sitting on the veranda and staring emptily at the traffic passing outside Firozsha Baag.[1] Or waving to anyone who went by in the compound: Rustomji, Nariman Hansotia in his 1932 Mercedes-Benz, the fat ayah Jaakaylee with her shopping-bag; the *kuchrawalli*[2] with her basket and long bamboo broom.

The Portuguese woman across the hall has told me a little about the old man. She is the communicator for the apartment building. To gather and disseminate information, she takes the liberty of unabashedly throwing open her door when newsworthy events transpire. Not for Portuguese Woman the furtive peerings from thin cracks or spyholes. She reminds me of a character in a movie, *Barefoot In The Park* I think it was, who left empty beer cans by the landing for anyone passing to stumble and give her the signal. But PW does not need beer cans. The gutang-khutang of the elevator opening and closing is enough.

The old man's daughter looks after him. He was living alone till his stroke, which coincided with his youngest daughter's divorce in Vancouver. She returned to him and they moved into this low-rise in Don Mills.[3] PW says the daughter talks to no one in the building but takes good care of her father.

Mummy used to take good care of Grandpa, too, till things became complicated and he was moved to the Parsi General Hospital. Parkinsonism and osteoporosis laid him low. The doctor explained that Grandpa's hip did not break because he fell, but he fell because the hip, gradually growing brittle, snapped on that fatal day. That's what osteoporosis does, hollows out the bones and turns effect into cause. It has an unusually high incidence in the Parsi community, he said, but did not say why. Just one of those mysterious things. We are the chosen people where osteo-porosis is concerned. And divorce. The Parsi community has the highest divorce rate in India. It also claims to be the most westernized community in India. Which is the result of the other? Confusion again, of cause and effect.

The hip was put in traction. Single-handed, Mummy struggled valiantly with bedpans and dressings for bedsores which soon appeared like grim spectres on his back. *Mamaiji*, bent double with her weak back, could give no assistance. My help would be enlisted to roll him over on his side while Mummy changed the dressing. But after three months, the doctor pronounced a patch upon Grandpa's lungs, and the male ward of Parsi General swallowed him up. There was no money for a private nursing home. I went to see him once, at Mummy's insistence. She used to say that the blessings of an old person were the most valuable and potent of all, they would last my whole life long. The ward had rows and rows of beds; the din was enormous, the smells nauseating, and it was just as well that Grandpa passed most of his time in a less than conscious state.

But I should have gone to see him more often. Whenever Grandpa went out,

---

[1] *Firozsha Baag* A fictional apartment complex in Mumbai (Bombay).

[2] *kuchrawalli* A female garbage collector.

[3] *Don Mills* A neighbourhood in Toronto.

while he still could in the days before parkinsonism, he would bring back pink and white sugar-coated almonds for Percy and me. Every time I remember Grandpa, I remember that; and then I think: I should have gone to see him more often. That's what I also thought when our telephone-owning neighbour, esteemed by all for that reason, sent his son to tell us the hospital had phoned that Grandpa died an hour ago.

The postman rang the doorbell the way he always did and continuous; Mother went to open it, wanting to give him a piece of her mind but thought better of it, she did not want to risk the vengeance of postmen, it was so easy for them to destroy letters; workers nowadays thought no end of themselves, strutting around like peacocks, ever since all this Shiv Sena agitation about Maharashtra for Maharashtrians,[1] threatening strikes and Bombay bundh[2] *all the time, with no respect for the public; bus drivers and conductors were the worst, behaving as though they owned the buses and were doing favours to commuters, pulling the bell before you were in the bus, the driver purposely braking and moving with big jerks to make the standees lose their balance, the conductor so rude if you did not have the right change.*

But when she saw the airmail envelope with a Canadian stamp her face lit up, she said wait to the postman, and went in for a fifty paisa piece, a little baksheesh *for you, she told him, then shut the door and kissed the envelope, went in running, saying my son has written, my son has sent a letter, and Father looked up from the newspaper and said, don't get too excited, first read it, you know what kind of letters he writes, a few lines of empty words, I'm fine, hope you are all right, your loving son — that kind of writing I don't call letter-writing.*

Then Mother opened the envelope and took out one small page and began to read silently, and the joy brought to her face by the letter's arrival began to ebb; Father saw it happening and knew he was right, he said read aloud, let me also hear what our son is writing this time, so Mother read: My dear Mummy and Daddy, Last winter was terrible, we had record-breaking low temperatures all through February and March, and the first official day of spring was colder than the first official day of winter had been, but it's getting warmer now. Looks like it will be a nice warm summer. You asked about my new apartment. It's small, but not bad at all. This is just a quick note to let you know I'm fine, so you won't worry about me. Hope everything is okay at home.

After Mother put it back in the envelope, Father said everything about his life is locked in silence and secrecy, I still don't understand why he bothered to visit us last year if he had nothing to say; every letter of his has been a quick note so we won't worry — what does he think we worry about, his health, in that country everyone eats well whether they work or not, he should be worrying about us with all the black market and rationing, has he forgotten already how he used to go to the ration-shop and wait in line every week; and what kind of apartment description is that, not bad at all; and

---

[1] *Shiv Sena* The Shiv Sena is a right-wing militant movement that originated in Mumbai (Bombay). It favours pro-Marathi nativism (Maharastra state) and pan-India Hindu nationalism.

[2] *Bundh (bandh)* A strike by special activist groups that the community is expected to support.

if it is a Canadian weather report I need from him, I can go with Nariman Hansotia from A Block to the Cawasji Framji Memorial Library and read all about it, there they get newspapers from all over the world.

The sun is hot today. Two women are sunbathing on the stretch of patchy lawn at the periphery of the parking lot. I can see them clearly from my kitchen. They're wearing bikinis and I'd love to take a closer look. But I have no binoculars. Nor do I have a car to saunter out to and pretend to look under the hood. They're both luscious and gleaming. From time to time they smear lotion over their skin, on the bellies, on the inside of the thighs, on the shoulders. Then one of them gets the other to undo the string of her top and spread some there. She lies on her stomach with the straps undone. I wait. I pray that the heat and haze make her forget, when it's time to turn over, that the straps are undone.

But the sun is not hot enough to work this magic for me. When it's time to come in, she flips over, deftly holding up the cups, and reties the top. They arise, pick up towels, lotions and magazines, and return to the building.

This is my chance to see them closer. I race down the stairs to the lobby. The old man says hullo. "Down again?"

"My mailbox," I mumble.

"It's Saturday," he chortles. For some reason he finds it extremely funny. My eye is on the door leading in from the parking lot.

Through the glass panel I see them approaching. I hurry to the elevator and wait. In the dimly lit lobby I can see their eyes are having trouble adjusting after the bright sun. They don't seem as attractive as they did from the kitchen window. The elevator arrives and I hold it open, inviting them in with what I think is a gallant flourish. Under the fluorescent glare in the elevator I see their wrinkled skin, aging hands, sagging bottoms, varicose veins. The lustrous trick of sun and lotion and distance has ended.

I step out and they continue to the third floor. I have Monday night to look forward to, my first swimming lesson. The high school behind the apartment building is offering, among its usual assortment of macrame and ceramics and pottery classes, a class for non-swimming adults.

The woman at the registration desk is quite friendly. She even gives me the opening to satisfy the compulsion I have about explaining my non-swimming status.

"Are you from India?" she asks. I nod. "I hope you don't mind my asking, but I was curious because an Indian couple, husband and wife, also registered a few minutes ago. Is swimming not encouraged in India?"

"On the contrary," I say. "Most Indians swim like fish. I'm an exception to the rule. My house was five minutes walking distance from Chaupatty beach in Bombay. It's one of the most beautiful beaches in Bombay, or was, before the filth took over. Anyway, even though we lived so close to it, I never learned to swim. It's just one of those things."

"Well," says the woman, "that happens sometimes. Take me, for instance. I never learned to ride a bicycle. It was the mounting that used to scare me, I was afraid of falling." People have lined up behind me. "It's been very nice talking to you," she says, "hope you enjoy the course."

The art of swimming had been trapped between the devil and the deep blue sea. The devil was money, always scarce, and kept the private swimming clubs out of reach; the deep blue sea of Chaupatty beach was grey and murky with garbage, too filthy to swim in. Every so often we would muster our courage and Mummy would take me there to try and teach me. But a few minutes of paddling was all we could endure. Sooner or later something would float up against our legs or thighs or waists, depending on how deep we'd gone in, and we'd be revulsed and stride out to the sand.

Water imagery in my life is recurring. Chaupatty beach, now the high-school swimming pool. The universal symbol of life and regeneration did nothing but frustrate me. Perhaps the swimming pool will overturn that failure.

When images and symbols abound in this manner, sprawling or rolling across the page without guile or artifice, one is prone to say, how obvious, how skilless; symbols, after all, should be still and gentle as dewdrops, tiny, yet shining with a world of meaning. But what happens when, on the page of life itself, one encounters the ever-moving, all-engirdling sprawl of the filthy sea? Dewdrops and oceans both have their rightful places; Nariman Hansotia certainly knew that when he told his stories to the boys of Firozsha Baag.

The sea of Chaupatty was fated to endure the finales of life's everyday functions. It seemed that the dirtier it became, the more crowds it attracted: street urchins and beggars and beachcombers, looking through the junk that washed up. (Or was it the crowds that made it dirtier? — another instance of cause and effect blurring and evading identification.)

Too many religious festivals also used the sea as repository for their finales. Its use should have been rationed, like rice and kerosene. On Ganesh Chaturthi, clay idols of the god Ganesh, adorned with garlands and all manner of finery, were carried in processions to the accompaniment of drums and a variety of wind instruments. The music got more frenzied the closer the procession got to Chaupatty and to the moment of immersion.

Then there was Coconut Day, which was never as popular as Ganesh Chaturthi. From a bystander's viewpoint, coconuts chucked into the sea do not provide as much of a spectacle. We used the sea, too, to deposit the leftovers from Parsi religious ceremonies, things such as flowers, or the ashes of the sacred sandalwood fire, which just could not be dumped with the regular garbage but had to be entrusted to the care of Avan Yazad, the guardian of the sea. And things which were of no use but which no one had the heart to destroy were also given to Avan Yazad. Such as old photographs.

After Grandpa died, some of his things were flung out to sea. It was high tide; we always checked the newspaper when going to perform these disposals; an ebb would mean a long walk in squelchy sand before finding water. Most of the things were probably washed up on shore. But we tried to throw them as far out as possible, then waited a few minutes; if they did not float back right away we would pretend they were in the permanent safekeeping of Avan Yazad, which was a comforting thought. I can't remember everything we sent out to sea, but his brush and comb were in the parcel, his *kusti,* and some Kemadrin pills, which he used to take to keep the parkinsonism under control.

Our paddling sessions stopped for lack of enthusiasm on my part. Mummy wasn't too keen either, because of the filth. But my main concern was the little guttersnipes, like naked fish with little buoyant penises, taunting me with their skills, swimming underwater and emerging unexpectedly all around me, or pretending to masturbate— I think they were too young to achieve ejaculation. It was embarrassing. When I look back, I'm surprised that Mummy and I kept going as long as we did.

I examine the swimming-trunks I bought last week. Surf King, says the label, Made in Canada—Fabriqué Au Canada. I've been learning bits and pieces of French from bilingual labels at the supermarket too. These trunks are extremely sleek and streamlined hipsters, the distance from waistband to pouch tip the barest minimum. I wonder how everything will stay in place, not that I'm boastful about my endowments. I try them on, and feel that the tip of my member lingers perilously close to the exit. Too close, in fact, to conceal the exigencies of my swimming lesson fantasy: a gorgeous woman in the class for non-swimmers, at whose sight I will be instantly aroused, and she, spying the shape of my desire, will look me straight in the eye with her intentions; she will come home with me, to taste the pleasures of my delectable Asian brown body whose strangeness has intrigued her and unleashed uncontrollable surges of passion inside her throughout the duration of the swimming lesson.

I drop the Eaton's bag and wrapper in the garbage can. The swimming-trunks cost fifteen dollars, same as the fee for the ten weekly lessons. The garbage bag is almost full. I tie it up and take it outside. There is a medicinal smell in the hallway; the old man must have just returned to his apartment.

PW opens her door and says, "Two ladies from the third floor were lying in the sun this morning. In bikinis."

"That's nice," I say, and walk to the incinerator chute. She reminds me of Najamai in Firozsha Baag, except that Najamai employed a bit more subtlety while going about her life's chosen work.

PW withdraws and shuts her door.

Mother had to reply because Father said he did not want to write to his son till his son had something sensible to write to him, his questions had been ignored long enough, and if he wanted to keep his life a secret, fine, he would get no letters from his father.

But after Mother started the letter he went and looked over her shoulder, telling her what to ask him, because if they kept on writing the same questions, maybe he would understand how interested they were in knowing about things over there; Father said go on, ask him what his work is at the insurance company, tell him to take some courses at night school, that's how everyone moves ahead over there, tell him not to be discouraged if his job is just clerical right now, hard work will get him ahead, remind him he is a Zoroastrian:[1] manashni, gavashni, kunashni, *better write the translation also: good thoughts, good words, good deeds — he must have forgotten what it means, and tell him to say prayers and do* kusti *at least twice a day.*

Writing it all down sadly, Mother did not believe he wore his sudra *and* kusti[2] *anymore, she would be very surprised if he remembered any of the prayers; when she had asked him if he needed new* sudras *he said not to take any trouble because the Zoroastrian Society of Ontario imported them from Bombay for their members, and this sounded like a story he was making up, but she was leaving it in the hands of God, ten thousand miles away there was nothing she could do but write a letter and hope for the best.*

Then she sealed it, and Father wrote the address on it as usual because his writing was much neater than hers, handwriting was important in the address and she did not want the postman in Canada to make any mistake; she took it to the post office herself, it was impossible to trust anyone to mail it ever since the postage rates went up because people just tore off the stamps for their own use and threw away the letter, the only safe way was to hand it over the counter and make the clerk cancel the stamps before your own eyes.

Berthe, the building superintendent, is yelling at her son in the parking lot. He tinkers away with his van. This happens every fine-weathered Sunday. It must be the van that Berthe dislikes because I've seen mother and son together in other quite amicable situations.

Berthe is a big Yugoslavian with high cheekbone. Her nationality was disclosed to me by PW. Berthe speaks a very rough-hewn English, I've overheard her in the lobby scolding tenants for late rents and leaving dirty lint screens in the dryers. It's exciting to listen to her, her words fall like rocks and boulders, and one can never tell where or how the next few will drop. But her Slavic yells at her son are a different matter, the words fly swift and true, well-aimed missiles that never miss. Finally, the son slams down the hood in disgust, wipes his hands on a rag, accompanies mother Berthe inside.

Berthe's husband has a job in a factory. But he loses several days of work every month when he succumbs to the booze, a word Berthe uses often in her Slavic tirades on those days, the only one I can understand, as it clunks down heavily out of the tight-flying formation of Yugoslavian sentences. He lolls around in the lobby, submitting passively to his wife's tongue-lashings. The bags under his bloodshot eyes, his stringy moustache, stubbled chin, dirty hair are so vulnerable to the poison-laden barbs (poison works the same way in any language) emanating from deep within the powerful watermelon bosom. No one's presence can embarrass or dignify her into silence.

---

[1] *Zoroastrian* The narrator is a Parsi, and most Parsis practice Zoroastrianism.

[2] *sudra* A sacred shirt; *kusti* Both a religious rite and a sacred thread-girdle.

No one except the old man who arrives now. "Good morning," he says, and Berthe turns, stops yelling, and smiles. Her husband rises, positions the wheelchair at the favourite angle. The lobby will be peaceful as long as the old man is there.

It was hopeless. My first swimming lesson. The water terrified me. When did that happen, I wonder, I used to love splashing at Chaupatty, carried about by the waves. And this was only a swimming pool. Where did all that terror come from? I'm trying to remember.

Armed with my Surf King I enter the high school and go to the pool area. A sheet with instructions for the new class is pinned to the bulletin board. All students must shower and then assemble at eight by the shallow end. As I enter the showers three young boys, probably from a previous class, emerge. One of them holds his nose. The second begins to hum, under his breath: Paki Paki, smell like curry. The third says to the first two: pretty soon all the water's going to taste of curry. They leave.

It's a mixed class, but the gorgeous woman of my fantasy is missing. I have to settle for another, in a pink one-piece suit, with brown hair and a bit of a stomach. She must be about thirty-five. Plain-looking.

The instructor is called Ron. He gives us a pep talk, sensing some nervousness in the group. We're finally all in the water, in the shallow end. He demonstrates floating on the back, then asks for a volunteer. The pink one-piece suit wades forward. He supports her, tells her to lean back and let her head drop in the water.

She does very well. And as we all regard her floating body, I see what was not visible outside the pool: her bush, curly bits of it, straying out at the pink Spandex V. Tongues of water lapping against her delta, as if caressing it teasingly, make the brown hair come alive in a most tantalizing manner. The crests and troughs of little waves, set off by the movement of our bodies in a circle around her, dutifully irrigate her; the curls alternately wave free inside the crest, then adhere to her wet thighs, beached by the inevitable trough. I could watch this forever, and I wish the floating demonstration would never end.

Next we are shown how to grasp the rail and paddle, face down in the water. Between practising floating and paddling, the hour is almost gone. I have been trying to observe the pink one-piece suit, getting glimpses of her straying pubic hair from various angles. Finally, Ron wants a volunteer for the last demonstration, and I go forward. To my horror he leads the class to the deep end. Fifteen feet of water. It is so blue, and I can see the bottom. He picks up a metal hoop attached to a long wooden stick. He wants me to grasp the hoop, jump in the water, and paddle, while he guides me by the stick. Perfectly safe, he tells me. A demonstration of how paddling propels the body.

It's too late to back out; besides, I'm so terrified I couldn't find the words to do so even if I wanted to. Everything he says I do as if in a trance. I don't remember the moment of jumping. The next thing I know is, I'm swallowing water and floundering, hanging on to the hoop for dear life. Ron draws me to the rails and helps me out. The class applauds.

We disperse and one thought is on my mind: what if I'd lost my grip? Fifteen feet of water under me. I shudder and take deep breaths. This is it. I'm not coming next week. This instructor is an irresponsible person. Or he does not value the lives of non-white immigrants. I remember the three teenagers. Maybe the swimming pool is the hangout of some racist group, bent on eliminating all non-white swimmers, to keep their waters pure and their white sisters unogled.

The elevator takes me upstairs. Then gutang-khutang. PW opens her door as I turn the corridor of medicinal smells. "Berthe was screaming loudly at her husband tonight," she tells me.

"Good for her," I say, and she frowns indignantly at me.

The old man is in the lobby. He's wearing thick wool gloves. He wants to know how the swimming was, must have seen me leaving with my towel yesterday. Not bad, I say.

"I used to swim a lot. Very good for the circulation." He wheezes. "My feet are cold all the time. Cold as ice. Hands too."

Summer is winding down, so I say stupidly, "Yes, it's not so warm any more."

The thought of the next swimming lesson sickens me. But as I comb through the memories of that terrifying Monday, I come upon the straying curls of brown pubic hair. Inexorably drawn by them, I decide to go.

It's a mistake, of course. This time I'm scared even to venture in the shallow end. When everyone has entered the water and I'm the only one outside, I feel a little foolish and slide in.

Instructor Ron says we should start by reviewing the floating technique. I'm in no hurry. I watch the pink one-piece pull the swim-suit down around her cheeks and flip back to achieve perfect flotation. And then reap disappointment. The pink Spandex triangle is perfectly streamlined today, nothing strays, not a trace of fuzz, not one filament, not even a sign of post-depilation irritation. Like the airbrushed parts of glamour magazine models. The barrenness of her impeccably packaged apex is a betrayal. Now she is shorn like the other women in the class. Why did she have to do it?

The weight of this disappointment makes the water less manageable, more lung-penetrating. With trepidation, I float and paddle my way through the remainder of the hour, jerking my head out every two seconds and breathing deeply, to continually shore up a supply of precious, precious air without, at the same time, seeming too anxious and losing my dignity.

I don't attend the remaining classes. After I've missed three, Ron the instructor telephones. I tell him I've had the flu and am still feeling poorly, but I'll try to be there the following week.

He does not call again. My Surf King is relegated to an unused drawer. Total losses: one fantasy plus thirty dollars. And no watery rebirth. The swimming pool, like Chaupatty beach, has produced a stillbirth. But there is a difference. Water means regeneration only if it is pure and cleansing. Chaupatty was filthy, the pool was not. Failure to swim through filth must mean something other than failure of rebirth — failure of symbolic death? Does that equal success of symbolic life? death of a symbolic failure? death of a symbol? What is the equation?

The postman did not bring a letter but a parcel, he was smiling because he knew that every time something came from Canada his baksheesh was guaranteed, and this time because it was a parcel Mother gave him a whole rupee, she was quite excited, there were so many stickers on it besides the stamps, one for Small Parcel, another Printed Papers, a red sticker saying Insured; she showed it to Father, and opened it, then put both hands on her cheeks, not able to speak because the surprise and happiness was so great, tears came to her eyes and she could not stop smiling, till Father became impatient to know and finally got up and came to the table.

When he saw it he was surprised and happy too, he began to grin, then hugged Mother saying our son is a writer, and we didn't even know it, he never told us a thing; here we are thinking he is still clerking away at the insurance company, and he has written a book of stories, all these years in school and college he kept his talent hidden, making us think he was just like one of the boys in the Baag, shouting and playing the fool in the compound, and now what a surprise; then Father opened the book and began reading it, heading back to the easy chair, and Mother so excited, still holding his arm, walked with him, saying it was not fair him reading it first, she wanted to read it too, and they agreed that he would read the first story, then give it to her so she could also read it, and they would take turns in that manner.

Mother removed the staples from the padded envelope in which he had mailed the book, and threw them away, then straightened the folded edges of the envelope and put it away safely with the other envelopes and letters she had collected since he left.

The leaves are beginning to fall. The only ones I can identify are maple. The days are dwindling like the leaves. I've started a habit of taking long walks every evening. The old man is in the lobby when I leave, he waves as I go by. By the time I'm back, the lobby is usually empty.

Today I was woken up by a grating sound outside that made my flesh crawl. I went to the window and saw Berthe raking the leaves in the parking lot. Not in the expanse of patchy lawn on the periphery, but in the parking lot proper. She was raking the black tarred surface. I went back to bed and dragged a pillow over my head, not releasing it till noon.

When I return from my walk in the evening, PW, summoned by the elevator's gutang-khutang, says, "Berthe filled six big black garbage bags with leaves today."

"Six bags!" I say. "Wow!"

Since the weather turned cold, Berthe's son does not tinker with his van on Sundays under my window. I'm able to sleep late.

Around eleven, there's a commotion outside. I reach out and switch on the clock radio. It's a sunny day, the window curtains are bright. I get up, curious, and see a black Olds Ninety-Eight in the parking lot, by the entrance to the building. The old man is in his wheelchair, bundled up, with a scarf wound several times round his neck as though to immobilize it, like a surgical collar. His daughter and another man, the car-owner, are helping him from the wheelchair into the front seat, encouraging him with words like: that's it, easy does it, attaboy. From the open door of the lobby, Berthe is shouting encouragement too, but hers is confined to one word: yah, repeated at different levels of pitch and volume, with variations on vowel-length. The stranger could be the old man's son, he has the same jet black hair and piercing eyes.

Maybe the old man is not well, it's an emergency. But I quickly scrap that thought—this isn't Bombay, an ambulance would have arrived. They're probably taking him out for a ride. If he is his son, where has he been all this time, I wonder.

The old man finally settles in the front seat, the wheelchair goes in the trunk, and they're off. The one I think is the son looks up and catches me at the window before I can move away, so I wave, and he waves back.

In the afternoon I take down a load of clothes to the laundry room. Both machines have completed their cycles, the clothes inside are waiting to be transferred to dryers. Should I remove them and place them on top of a dryer, or wait? I decide to wait. After a few minutes, two women arrive, they are in bathrobes, and smoking. It takes me a while to realize that these are the two disappointments who were sunbathing in bikinis last summer.

"You didn't have to wait, you could have removed the clothes and carried on, dear," says one. She has a Scottish accent. It's one of the few I've learned to identify. Like maple leaves.

"Well," I say, "some people might not like strangers touching their clothes."

"You're not a stranger, dear," she says, "you live in this building, we've seen you before."

"Besides, your hands are clean," the other one pipes in. "You can touch my things any time you like."

Horny old cow. I wonder what they've got on under their bathrobes. Not much, I find, as they bend over to place their clothes in the dryers.

"See you soon," they say, and exit, leaving me behind in an erotic wake of smoke and perfume and deep images of cleavages. I start the washers and depart, and when I come back later, the dryers are empty.

PW tells me, "The old man's son took him out for a drive today. He has a big beautiful black car."

I see my chance, and shoot back: "Olds Ninety-Eight."

"What?"

"The car," I explain, "it's an Oldsmobile Ninety-Eight."

She does not like this at all, my giving her information. She is visibly nettled, and retreats with a sour face.

Mother and Father read the first five stories, and she was very sad after reading some of them, she said he must be so unhappy there, all his stories are about Bombay, he remembers every little thing about his childhood, he is thinking about it all the time even though he is ten thousand miles away, my poor son, I think he misses his home and us and everything he left behind, because if he likes it over there why would he not write stories about that, there must be so many new ideas that his new life could give him.

But Father did not agree with this, he said it did not mean that he was unhappy, all writers worked in the same way, they used their memories and experiences and made stories out of them, changing some things, adding some, imagining some, all writers were very good at remembering details of their lives. Mother said, how can you be sure that he is remembering because he is a writer, or whether he started to write because he is unhappy and thinks of his past, and wants to save it all by making stories of it; and father said that is not a sensible question, anyway it is now my turn to read the next story.

The first snow has fallen, and the air is crisp. It's not very deep, about two inches, just right to go for a walk in. I've been told that immigrants from hot countries always enjoy the snow the first year, maybe for a couple of years more, then inevitably the dread sets in, and the approach of winter gets them fretting and moping. On the other hand, if it hadn't been for my conversation with the woman at the swimming registration desk, they might now be saying that India is a nation of non-swimmers.

Berthe is outside, shovelling the snow off the walkway in the parking lot. She has a heavy, wide pusher which she wields expertly.

The old radiators in the apartment alarm me incessantly. They continue to broadcast a series of variations on death throes, and go from hot to cold and cold to hot at will, there's no controlling their temperature. I speak to Berthe about it in the lobby. The old man is there too, his chin seems to have sunk deeper into his chest, and his face is a yellowish grey.

"Nothing, not to worry about anything," says Berthe, dropping rough-hewn chunks of language around me. "Radiator no work, you tell me. You feel cold, you come to me, I keep you warm," and she opens her arms wide, laughing. I step back, and she advances, her breasts preceding her like the gallant prows of two ice-breakers. She looks at the old man to see if he is appreciating the act: "You no feel scared, I keep you safe and warm."

But the old man is staring outside, at the flakes of falling snow. What thoughts is he thinking as he watches them? Of childhood days, perhaps, and snowmen with hats and pipes, and snowball fights, and white Christmases, and Christmas trees? What will I think of, old in this country, when I sit and watch the snow come down? For me, it is already too late for snowmen and snowball fights, and all I will have is thoughts about childhood thoughts and dreams, built around snowscapes and winter-wonderlands on the Christmas cards so popular in Bombay; my snowmen and snowball fights and Christmas trees are in the pages of Enid Blyton's books, dispersed amidst the adventures of the Famous Five, and the Five Find-Outers, and the Secret Seven. My snowflakes are even less forgettable than the old man's, for they never melt.

It finally happened. The heat went. Not the usual intermittent coming and going, but out completely. Stone cold. The radiators are like ice. And so is everything else. There's no hot water. Naturally. It's the hot water that goes through the rads and heats them. Or is it the other way around? Is there no hot water because the rads have stopped circulating it? I don't care, I'm too cold to sort out the cause and effect relationship. Maybe there is no connection at all.

I dress quickly, put on my winter jacket, and go down to the lobby. The elevator is not working because the power is out, so I take the stairs. Several people are gathered, and Berthe has announced that she has telephoned the office, they are sending a man. I go back up the stairs. It's only one floor, the elevator is just a bad habit. Back in Firozsha Baag they were broken most of the time. The stairway enters the corridor outside the old man's apartment, and I think of his cold feet and hands. Poor man, it must be horrible for him without heat.

As I walk down the long hallway, I feel there's something different but can't pin it down. I look at the carpet, the ceiling, the wallpaper: it all seems the same. Maybe it's the freezing cold that imparts a feeling of difference.

PW opens her door: "The old man had another stroke yesterday. They took him to the hospital." The medicinal smell. That's it. It's not in the hallway any more.

In the stories that he'd read so far Father said that all the Parsi families were poor or middle-class, but that was okay: nor did he mind that the seeds for the stories were picked from the sufferings of their own lives; but there should also have been something positive about Parsis, there was so much to be proud of: the great Tatas and their contribution to the steel industry, or Sir Dinshaw Petit in the textile industry who made Bombay the Manchester of the East, or Dadabhai Nooroji in the freedom movement, where he was the first to use the word swaraj, *and the first to be elected to the British Parliament where he carried on his campaign; he should have found some way to bring some of these wonderful facts into his stories, what would people reading these stories think, those who did not know about Parsis—that the whole community was full of cranky, bigoted people; and in reality it was the richest, most advanced and philanthropic community in India, and he did not need to tell his own son that Parsis had a reputation for being generous and family-oriented. And he could have written something also about the historic background, how Parsis came to India from Persia because of Islamic persecution in the seventh century, and were the descendants of Cyrus the Great and the magnificent Persian Empire. He could have made a story of all this, couldn't he?*

Mother said what she liked best was his remembering everything so well, how beautifully he wrote about it all, even the sad things, and though he changed some of it, used his imagination, there was truth in it.

My hope is, Father said, that there will be some story based on his Canadian experience, that way we will know something about our son's life there, if not through his letters then in his stories; so far they are all about Parsis and Bombay, and the one with a little bit about Toronto, where a man perches on top of the toilet, is shameful and dis-

gusting, although it is funny at times and did make me laugh, I have to admit, but where does he get such an imagination from, what is the point of such a fantasy; and Mother said that she would also enjoy some stories about Toronto and the people there; it puzzles me, she said, why he writes nothing about it, especially since you say that writers use their own experience to make stories out of.

Then Father said this is true, but he is probably not using his Toronto experience because it is too early: what do you mean, too early, asked Mother and Father explained it takes a writer about ten years time after an experience before he is able to use it in his writing, it takes that long to be absorbed internally and understood, thought out and thought about, over and over again, he haunts it and it haunts him if it is valuable enough, till the writer is comfortable with it to be able to use it as he wants; but this is only one theory I read somewhere, it may or may not be true.

That means, said Mother, that his childhood in Bombay and our home here is the most valuable thing in his life just now, because he is able to remember it all to write about it, and you were so bitterly saying he is forgetting where he came from; and that may be true, said Father, but that is not what the theory means, according to the theory he is writing of these thing because they are far enough in the past for him to deal with objectively, he is able to achieve what critics call artistic distance, without emotions interfering; and what do you mean emotions, said Mother, you are saying he does not feel anything for his characters, how can he write so beautifully about so many sad things without any feelings in his heart?

But before father could explain more, about beauty and emotion and inspiration and imagination, Mother took the book and said it was her turn now and too much theory she did not want to listen to, it was confusing and·did not make as much sense as reading the stories, she would read them her way and father could read them his.

My books on the windowsill have been damaged. Ice has been forming on the inside ledge, which I did not notice, and melting when the sun shines in. I spread them in a corner of the living-room to dry out.

The winter drags on. Berthe wields her snow pusher as expertly as ever, but there are signs of weariness in her performance. Neither husband nor son is ever seen outside with a shovel. Or anywhere else, for that matter. It occurs to me that the son's van is missing, too.

The medicinal smell is in the hall again, I sniff happily and look forward to seeing the old man in the lobby. I go downstairs and peer into the mailbox, see the blue and magenta of an Indian aerogramme with Don Mills, Ontario, Canada in Father's flawless hand through the slot.

I pocket the letter and enter the main lobby. The old man is there, but not in his usual place. He is not looking out through the glass door. His wheelchair is facing a bare wall where the wallpaper is torn in places. As though he is not interested in the outside world any more, having finished with all that, and now it's time to see inside. What does he see inside, I wonder? I go up to him and say hullo. He says hullo without raising his sunken chin. After a few seconds his grey countenance faces me. "How old do you think I am?" His eyes are dull and glazed; he is looking even further inside than I first presumed.

"Well, let's see, you're probably close to sixty-four."

"I'll be seventy-eight next August." But he does not chuckle or wheeze. Instead, he continues softly, "I wish my feet did not feel so cold all the time. And my hands." He lets his chin fall again.

In the elevator I start opening the aerogramme, a tricky business because a crooked tear means lost words. Absorbed in this while emerging, I don't notice PW occupying the centre of the hallway, arms folded across her chest: "They had a big fight. Both of them have left."

I don't immediately understand her agitation. "What...who?"

"Berthe. Husband and son both left her. Now she is all alone."

Her tone and stance suggest that we should not be standing here talking but do something to bring Berthe's family back. "That's very sad," I say, and go in. I picture father and son in the van, driving away, driving across the snow-covered country, in the dead of winter, away from wife and mother; away to where? how far will they go? Not son's van nor father's booze can take them far enough. And the further they go, the more they'll remember, they can take it from me.

All the stories were read by Father and Mother, and they were sorry when the book was finished, they felt they had come to know their son better now, yet there was much more to know, they wished there were many more stories; and this is what they mean, said Father, when they say that the whole story can never be told, the whole truth can never be known; what do you mean, they say, asked Mother, who they, and Father said writers, poets, philosophers. I don't care what they say, said Mother, my son will write as much or as little as he wants to, and if I can read it I will be happy.

The last story they liked the best of all because it had the most in it about Canada, and now they felt they knew at least a little bit, even if it was a very little bit, about his day-to-day life in his apartment; and Father said if he continues to write about such things he will become popular because I am sure they are interested there in reading about life through the eyes of an immigrant, it provides a different viewpoint; the only danger is if he changes and becomes so much like them that he will write like one of them and lose the important difference.

The bathroom needs cleaning. I open a new can of Ajax and scour the tub. Sloshing with mug from bucket was standard bathing procedure in the bathrooms of Firozsha Baag, so my preference now is always for a shower. I've never used the tub as yet; besides, it would be too much like Chaupatty or the swimming pool, wallowing in my own dirt. Still, it must be cleaned.

When I've finished, I prepare for a shower. But the clean gleaming tub and the nearness of the vernal equinox give me the urge to do something different today. I find the drain plug in the bathroom cabinet, and run the bath.

I've spoken so often to the old man, but I don't know his name. I should have asked him the last time I saw him, when his wheelchair was facing the bare wall because he had seen all there was to see outside and it was time to see what was inside. Well, tomorrow. Or better yet, I can look it up in the directory in the lobby. Why didn't I think of that before? It will only have an initial and a last name, but then I can surprise him with: hullo Mr. Wilson, or whatever it is.

The bath is full. Water imagery is recurring in my life: Chaupatty beach, swimming pool, bathtub. I step in and immerse myself up to the neck. It feels good. The hot water loses its opacity when the chlorine, or whatever it is, has cleared. My hair is still dry. I close my eyes, hold my breath, and dunk my head. Fighting the panic, I stay under and count to thirty. I come out, clear my lungs and breathe deeply.

I do it again. This time I open my eyes under water, and stare blindly without seeing, it takes all my will to keep the lids from closing. Then I am slowly able to discern the underwater objects. The drain plug looks different, slightly distorted; there is a hair trapped between the hole and the plug, it waves and dances with the movement of the water. I come up, refresh my lungs, examine quickly the overwater world of the washroom, and go in again. I do it several times, over and over. The world outside the water I have seen a lot of, it is now time to see what is inside.

The spring session for adult non-swimmers will begin in a few days at the high school. I must not forget the registration date.

The dwindled days of winter are now all but forgotten; they have grown and attained a respectable span. I resume my evening walks, it's spring, and a vigorous thaw is on. The snowbanks are melting, the sound of water on its gushing, gurgling journey to the drains is beautiful. I plan to buy a book of trees, so I can identify more than the maple as they begin to bloom.

When I return to the building, I wipe my feet energetically on the mat because some people are entering behind me, and I want to set a good example. Then I go to the board with its little plastic letters and numbers. The old man's apartment is the one on the corner by the stairway, that makes it number 201. I run down the list, come to 201, but there are no little white plastic letters beside it. Just the empty black rectangle with holes where the letters would be squeezed in. That's strange. Well, I can introduce myself to him, then ask his name.

However, the lobby is empty. I take the elevator, exit at the second floor, wait for the gutang-khutang. It does not come: the door closes noiselessly, smoothly. Berthe has been at work, or has made sure someone else has. PW's cue has been lubricated out of existence.

But she must have the ears of a cockroach. She is waiting for me. I whistle my way down the corridor. She fixes me with an accusing look. She waits till I stop whistling, then says: "You know the old man died last night."

I cease groping for my key. She turns to go and I take a step towards her, my hand still in my trouser pocket. "Did you know his name?" I ask, but she leaves without answering.

Then Mother said, the part I like best in the last story is about Grandpa, where he wonders if Grandpa's spirit is really watching him and blessing him, because you know I really told him that, I told him helping an old suffering person who is near death is the most blessed thing to do, because that person will ever after watch over you from heaven, I told him this when he was disgusted with Grandpa's urine-bottle and would not touch it, would not hand it to him even when I was not at home.

Are you sure, said Father, that you really told him this, or you believe you told him because you like the sound of it, you said yourself the other day that he changes and adds and alters things in the stories but he writes it all so beautifully that it seems true, so how can you be sure; this sounds like another theory, said Mother, but I don't care, he says I told him and I believe now I told him, so even if I did not tell him then it does not matter now.

Don't you see, said Father, that you are confusing fiction with facts, fiction does not create facts, fiction can come from facts, it can grow out of facts by compounding, transposing, augmenting, diminishing, or altering them in any way; but you must not confuse cause and effect, you must not confuse what really happened with what the story says happened, you must not loose your grasp on reality, that way madness lies.

Then Mother stopped listening because, as she told Father so often, she was not very fond of theories, and she took out her writing pad and started a letter to her son; Father looked over her shoulder, telling her to say how proud they were of him and were waiting for his next book, he also said, leave a little space for me at the end, I want to write a few lines when I put the address on the envelope.

1987

Timothy Mo

Timothy Mo (b. 1950) was born in Hong Kong to English and Cantonese parents. He has spent much of his life in the United Kingdom. After graduating from St. John's College, Oxford, he worked as a journalist for *Boxing News* and the *New Statesman*. His works include the novels *Monkey King* (1978), *Sour Sweet* (1982), *An Insular Possession* (about the founding of Hong Kong; 1986), *Brownout on Breadfruit Boulevard* (1995), and *Renegade or Halo 2* (1999). The last two are set in the Philippines.

Mo's memoir recalls his youthful days in Hong Kong when he developed an interest in boxing under the instruction of an expatriate British instructor. Mo speaks admiringly of his instructor. Do you detect any ambivalence similar to the narrator's toward her teacher in Albert Wendt's "Crocodile"?

One of Billy's Boys: A Memoir

When I think of Hong Kong all those years ago, it's the diminutive but formidable figure of Billy Tingle which strides through my insomniac reveries, much as Blind Pew must have through those of the grown-up Jim Hawkins, while the cable drums of the upper Peak tram station (those tarry windmills of the mind) whine and Billy chases me through the dancing mists of a February evening, brandishing a cricket bat instead of a crutch or white stick, and crying not "Pieces of Eight!" but rather "Sportsman and a gentleman! Sportsman and a gentleman!"

Am I the only one who remembers Mr. Tingle? Am I the sole surviving Tingle boy in what used to be called the Crown Colony? Billy Tingle was as much a part of the expat Brit family's life here 35 years ago as taking the kids to the PG Farm and throwing streamers down from the decks of a P & O liner at the beginning of a leave.

Those were the days when you could walk under shaded granite arches the whole length of Nathan Road and Mody Road was splashed bright red with expectorated betel juice from the mouths of the Indian leather workers, and when the pug marks of confused tigers could be seen in the New Territories. The days, too, when you could still hear people speak of the waterfront as the Praya, of lunch as tiffin, and — with a strange affection — of "Camp," internment under the Japanese on Stanley peninsula.

Mr. Tingle had been flyweight champion of the Australian goldfields in the early part of the century, or it might have been the dying years of the previous one. He looked, in 1957, much like a spry, elderly, weight-trained and cross-countried version of that other Billy, Bunter. At the age of nine, when I left Mr. Tingle's academy of self-defence, I could look him straight in the eye, so I deduce he must have been about 4ft 11ins tall. Mr. Tingle was physical instructor and character builder extraordinary by appointment to the children of the expatriate gentry. He taught the Noble Art to a select few after lessons had finished at Quarry Bay School and the Peak School. On Saturday mornings droves of red and white capped boys took over the grounds of the HK Cricket Club—now concreted over as Ghater Garden—in what was known simply as Billy Tingle's.

In the summer I dreaded those Saturday mornings; tedium unmitigated from nine till twelve, interspersed with moments of fright and angst. We wore white shirts and shorts, our school summer uniforms, so the only extra item of expense was the caps—always an important consideration for the parent, as Mr. Tingle well knew. He wore one, too.

We'd troop out from the pavilion in 20-strong squads for callisthenics under the supervision of young Englishmen. There was a lot of aimless standing around. I think these off-duty schoolmasters and shipping clerks were at a loss to know what to occupy us with weekend in and weekend out. We had to call them "Sir," which was novel and unsettling, as the teachers at my coed primary school were female and to be addressed as "Mrs. Penman" (shrewd New Zealander) or "Miss Archer" (strapping English girl).

I had Mr. Partridge at Billy Tingle's, he of the handlebar moustache. For some reason we genuinely had trouble with his name, few of us being familiar with English gamebirds but all devotees of *Blackhawk* and *Superman* comics, the *77th Bengal Lancers* and *The Naked City* on black and white television (we even tried to speak with American accents, as I don't doubt they still do at KGV), so he became Mr. Cartridge to his mild irritation. "My name's Partridge, not Cartridge. Cartridge is what you fire from a gun, OK?" And he pulled out a brassy .303 case confiscated from an Andrew Jackson, who'd obtained the trophy from the firing range below Lugard Road. "Yes, Mr. Cartridge." "Right-o. You're all going to call me sir from now on."

Over to the long jump pit, a dog-defiled minefield of broken sand clods opposite what is now the front door of the Furama-Kempinski.[1] Break, eagerly looked forward to, probably by Mr. Cartridge as well, was in the Pavilion and consisted of Kit Kats, for which we had brought our 20 cents. No dried beef, no *chan pei mui* (preserved plum with orange and licorice essence). And, of course, there wasn't a Chinese boy in sight, not even a rich one, like Donald Hardoon or Raymond Woo, the only Chinese boys in class 5. Or a girl for that matter (those creatures seen outside school hours at the Ladies Recreation Club—another bastion of half-witted Anglo would-be exclusiveness—where a mob of boys and girls by lofty, high-minded, but deeply misconceived adult decree had to change for the swimming-pool in the same tiny shack. Denunciation to turn the blood cold before one's guardians. "We saw Timmy looking at Kerrie's wee-wee.").

Nor were American boys to be seen at Billy Tingle's either. They, lucky chaps—like Jimmy McDonough whose father had the most glamorous job in the world short of being a filmstar (a Pan Am pilot)—were roaming Repulse Bay or Bowen

---

[1] *Furama-Kempinski* A prominent Hong Kong hotel, known for its revolving restaurant.

Path in their jeans and basketball boots, while we were buckling musty cricket pads round our bare legs.

Cricket, unlike the callisthenics, was no lack-lustre activity. Mr. Tingle himself umpired on a no-concessions 22-yard pitch. The intensity of the attention bestowed upon you by the fielders to the sides, the wicket-keeper to the rear, the bowler charging towards you, and not least by Mr. Tingle himself, glaring behind his spectacles down a bee-line from the other wicket, would have been sufficient to shrink my own balls, had they already descended. I never lasted longer than an over and was terrified of being hit by the little red grenade of spite. Rounders with Mrs. Penman was more my line, or even the baseball games the American boys ran, with the catchers mitts to take the sting from a catch. If it was a really dire weekend, there was a Tingle official ramble, commencing at the KCR station by the Star Ferry, over the then virgin hills of the New Territories.[1]

But for all the high-minded pep talks about keeping a straight bat in life (sincere on Mr. Tingle's part), the institution was basically a ploy for getting the kids out of your hair on Saturday mornings. As an Italian once remarked to me: "It's not that the English hate children, it's just that they love animals."

Boxing, in the winter terms, was another matter. I loved that. From the start, flurries of fists held no terrors for me. It does have to be said that Mr. Tingle's method of teaching boxing, even in 1956, was already hopelessly outmoded. He coached by numbers: "Ready now. One: Left lead to the head. Two: left lead to the body. Three: knock-knock, double left lead to the head. Four: Straight right to the head. Five: straight right to the body. Six: right uppercut." That was the Tingle offence in all its rectilinear classicism. Defence was: "One: block with the right. Two: parry with the right. Three: duck."

Mr. Tingle's left lead involved shooting out the glove while taking a stormtrooper's goosestep forward, digging the heel into the ground, chin well up with shoulders thrown back like a guardsman. In its way it was the boxing equivalent of a cavalry charge into machine-gun fire.

Some 20 years previously, Joe Louis had perfected the jab, sliding pantherishly forward on the ball of his left foot, the right rear foot dragged as if it had been placed in a bucket, the chin tucked down into the hunched left shoulder, and knees well flexed. The left hook, combination punching—Mr. Tingle had the same attitude to these as admirals of the battleship era had for the aircraft carrier.

Before engaging in sparring, we would touch gloves. Mr. Tingle explained this as meaning: "I will conduct myself at all times like a sportsman and gentleman," his exact words, still echoing in my mind after nearly 40 years. Naturally, the most heinous offence in the Tingle canon was to punch one's opponent while he offered to shake hands.

Mr. Tingle wasn't a humbug. He practised what he preached. Kids penetrate

---

[1] *New Territories* A major sub-division of colonial Hong Kong; it became part of the colony in 1898 through negotiation with China.

adult flannel with ease—you forget you did as you get older yourself—and it was obvious to us that he was a tough old boy but both kindly and upright.

I was the only one who knew of his goldfield days—I think my stepfather had an Australian connection—and Mr. Tingle had reacted with asperity, while still confirming this information. A grimace came over the stubbly face. With hindsight, I think it hadn't all been sportsmanship and Queensberry rules among the prospectors. I think the fights were desperate bareknuckle affairs, with big bets going down. And, of course, what makes me smile now is the reflection that the capped, short back and sides, deeply conservative cherubs receiving the Tingle sermon would in under ten years be many of them long-haired, pot-smoking, acid-dropping hippies. And probably stockbrokers ten years after that.

Funnily enough, with all its limitations in the ring, I think now that Tingle-style boxing would be a lot safer in a street-fight than modern bob and weave. What's drummed into a kick-boxer from day one is always to stand upright with your hands up; never duck, it'll only be into a knee butt. I suspect Billy Tingle of having been a very tasty customer indeed in his day.

Came the time to examine the student and I had my first ever contest over three one-minute rounds against one Anthony Maine in a raised ring pitched in the centre of the cricket ground. The red corner was for the usual Tingle boys, the blue for Chinese boys from a less educationally advantaged institution where Mr. Tingle probably coached free. I suppose they should have put me in ring centre, with the referee.

I was given a blue sash. Without exception every boxer from this corner had lost. In the interval before the third and final round, breathless on my stool, blood leaking from my nose, I asked the two garrison sergeants who had been the blue seconds throughout, "How am I doing?" A burst of urgent instructions followed— they'd been silent till then, as had I—mostly about keeping sticking out one's left (that's what British amateur corner men always say). I think they were more pleased than I was when I scraped home on points.

Whatever the travails and eccentricities of Tingle's, it was a holiday camp compared with the Convent of the Precious Blood, the Roman Catholic school I had attended a couple of years earlier and which I called Bloody Blood. I wasn't trying to be funny. This was dominated by ferocious Chinese nuns who thought RC meant Rebarbative Confucianism.

I was the dunce of the calligraphy class who managed the characters for one, two, and three but balked at four. I got put in the corner with sticking-plaster over my mouth for asking questions. I got hit in the face ten times, very, very lightly, but still ten times. (Unfortunately Billy Tingle had yet to drill me in his one, two, three defensive routine.) The nuns instructed my amahs to feed me just white rice, without soya sauce. Little did they know it was fish fingers and chips on the menu at home.

Lord, how I hated that old-style Chinese education. Taunting and ostracism were the weapons used to break young spirits, to make them obedient to parents and, in due course, rulers, frightened to be different from all the other sniggering conformists. It was the essence of small-mindedness and Tingle, with all his ingenu-ousness, was large-minded.

I bade farewell to Mr. Tingle in 1959, the last time I saw him alive. He gave me a warm handshake and prophesied I'd startle the boxing coaches in England. With my Corinthian style, I did, of course, but not in the way he meant.

1994

Toshio Mori

Toshio Mori (1910-80) was born in Oakland, California, of Japanese ancestry. He and his family were interned at Topaz Relocation Center, Utah, during World War II. He published three volumes of fiction, including *Yokohama, California* (stories, 1949), *Woman from Hiroshima* (novel, 1979), and *The Chauvinist and Other Stories* (1979).

Toshio Mori's story "Slant-Eyed Americans" portrays the rabid stereotyping Japanese Americans faced after the bombing of Pearl Harbor by the Japanese (7 December 1941). Compare this story with Kogawa's poem "What Do I Remember of the Evacuation?" Is Mori's story different in tone from Kogawa's poem? Mori's art requires that we ask questions: Why is the narrator unnamed? Is there irony in the mother's American nationalistic feelings? Is her optimism misplaced? What is the significance of the desire of the soldier Kazuo to be a cartoonist? Is there any importance to the silence that pervades the home when Kazuo returns? What does the phrase in the last line "lost in the night of darkness" foreshadow?

Slant-Eyed Americans

My mother was commenting on the fine California weather. It was Sunday noon, December 7. We were having our lunch, and I had the radio going. "Let's take the afternoon off and go to the city," I said to Mother.

"All right. We shall go," she said dreamily. "Ah, four months ago my boy left Hayward to join the army, and a fine send-off he had. Our good friends — ah, I shall never forget the day of his departure."

"We'll visit some of our friends in Oakland and then take in a movie," I said. "Care to come along, Papa?"

Father shook his head. "No, I'll stay home and take it easy."

"That's his heaven," Mother commented. "To stay home, read the papers over and over, and smoke his Bull Durham."

I laughed. Suddenly the musical program was cut off as a special announcement came over the air: At 7:25 a.m. this morning a squadron of Japanese bombing planes attacked Pearl Harbor. The battle is still in progress.

"What's this? Listen to the announcements," I cried, going to the radio.

Abruptly the announcement stopped and the musicale continued.

"What is it?" Mother asked. "What has happened?"

"The radio reports that the Japanese planes attacked Hawaii this morning," I said incredulously. "It couldn't be true."

"It must be a mistake. Couldn't it have been a part of a play?" asked Mother.

I dialled other stations. Several minutes later one of the stations confirmed the bulletin.

"It must be true," Father said quietly.

I said, "Japan has declared war on the United States and Great Britain."

The room became quiet but for the special bulletin coming in every now and then.

"It cannot be true, yet it must be so," Father said over and over.

"Can it be one of those programs scaring the people about invasion?" Mother asked me.

"No. I'm sure this is a news report," I replied.

Mother's last ray of hope paled and her eyes became dull. "Why did it have to happen? The common people in Japan don't want war, and we don't want war. Here the people are peace-loving. Why cannot the peoples of the earth live together peacefully?"

"Since Japan declared war on the United States it'll mean that you parents of American citizens have become enemy aliens," I said.

"Enemy aliens," my mother whispered.

Night came but sleep did not come. We sat up late in the night hoping against hope that some good news would come, retracting the news of vicious attack and open hostilities.

"This is very bad for the people with Japanese faces," I said.

Father slowly shook his head.

"What shall we do?" asked Mother.

"What can we do?" Father said helplessly.

At the flower market next morning the growers were present but the buyers were scarce. The place looked empty and deserted. "Our business is shot to pieces," one of the boys said.

"Who'll buy flowers now?" another called.

Don Haley, the seedsman, came over looking bewildered. "I suppose you don't need seeds now."

We shook our heads.

"It looks bad," I said. "Will it affect your business?"

"Flower seed sale will drop but the vegetable seeds will move quicker," Don said. "I think I'll have to put more time on the vegetable seeds."

Nobu Hiramatsu who had been thinking of building another greenhouse joined us. He had plans to grow more carnations and expand his business.

"What's going to happen to your plans, Nobu?" asked one of the boys.

"Nothing. I'm going to sit tight and see how things turn out," he said.

"Flowers and war don't go together," Don said. "You cannot concentrate too much on beauty when destruction is going about you."

"Sure, pretty soon we'll raise vegetables instead of flowers," Grasselli said.

A moment later the market opened and we went back to the table to sell our flowers. Several buyers came in and purchased a little. The flowers didn't move at all. Just as I was about to leave the place I met Tom Yamashita, the Nisei[1] gardener with a future.

"What are you doing here, Tom? What's the matter with your work?" I asked as I noticed his pale face.

"I was too sick with yesterday's news so I didn't work," he said. "This is the end. I am done for."

"No, you're not. Buck up, Tom," I cried. "You have a good future, don't lose hope."

"Sometimes I feel all right. You are an American, I tell myself. Devote your energy and life to the American way of life. Long before this my mind was made up to become a true American. This morning my Caucasian American friends sympathized with me. I felt good and was grateful. Our opportunity has come to express ourselves and act. We are Americans in thought and action. I felt like leaping to work. Then I got sick again because I got to thinking that Japan was the country that attacked the United States. I wanted to bury myself for shame."

I put my hand on his shoulder. "We all feel the same way, Tom. We're human so we flounder around awhile when an unexpected and big problem confronts us, but now that situation has to be passed by. We can't live in the same stage long. We have to move along, face the reality no matter what's in store for us."

Tom stood silently.

"Let's go to my house and take the afternoon off," I suggested. "We'll face a new world tomorrow morning with boldness and strength. What do you say, Tom?"

"All right," Tom agreed.

At home Mother was anxiously waiting for me. When she saw Tom with me her eyes brightened. Tom Yamashita was a favorite of my mother's.

"Look, a telegram from Kazuo!" she cried to me, holding up an envelope. "Read it and tell me what he says."

I tore it open and read. "He wants us to send $45 for train fare. He has a good chance for a furlough."

Mother fairly leaped in the air with the news. She had not seen my brother for four months. "How wonderful! This can happen only in America."

Suddenly she noticed Tom looking glum, and pushed him in the house.

"Cheer up, Tom. This is no time for young folks to despair. Roll up your sleeves and get to work. America needs you."

Tom smiled for the first time and looked at me.

"See, Tom?" I said. "She's quick to recover. Yesterday she was wilted and she's seventy-three."

"Tom, did you go to your gardens today?" she asked him.

"No."

---

[1] *Nisei* Nisei (second generation) Japanese Americans are those who reached adulthood around the beginning of World War II. Most Japanese Americans who fought in this war were Nisei. They were allowed to fight in Europe but not in the Pacific. (Interestingly, Americans of German and Italian origins were not restricted from fighting in the European theatre.)

"Why not?" she asked, and then added quickly. "You young men should work hard all the more, keeping up the normal routine of life. You ought to know, Tom, that if everybody dropped their work everything would go to seed. Who's going to take care of the gardens if you won't?"

Tom kept still.

Mother poured tea and brought the cookies. "Don't worry about your old folks. We have stayed here to belong to the American way of life. Time will tell our true purpose. We remained in America for permanence — not for temporary convenience. We common people need not fear."

"I guess you are right," Tom agreed.

"And America is right. She cannot fail. Her principles will stand the test of time and tyranny. Someday aggression will be outlawed by all nations."

Mother left the room to prepare the dinner. Tom got up and began to walk up and down the room. Several times he looked out the window and watched the wind blow over the field.

"Yes, if the gardens are ruined I'll rebuild them," he said. "I'll take charge of every garden in the city. All the gardens of America for that matter. I'll rebuild them as fast as the enemies wreck them. We'll have nature on our side and you cannot crush nature."

I smiled and nodded. "Good for you. Tomorrow we'll get up early in the morning and work, sweat, and create. Let's shake on it."

We solemnly shook hands, and by the grip of his fingers I knew he was ready to lay down his life for America and for his gardens.

"No word from him yet," Mother said worriedly. "He should have arrived yesterday. What's happened to him?"

It was eight in the evening, and we had had no word from my brother for several days.

"He's not coming home tonight. It's too late now," I said. "He should have arrived in Oakland this morning at the latest."

Our work had piled up and we had to work late into the night. There were still some pompons to bunch. Faintly the phone rang in the house.

"The phone!" cried Mother excitedly. "It's Kazuo, sure enough."

In the flurry of several minutes I answered the phone, greeted my brother, and was on my way to San Leandro to drive him home. On the way I tried to think of the many things I wanted to say. From the moment I spotted him waiting on the corner I could not say the thing I wanted to. I took his bag and he got in the car, and for some time we did not say anything. Then I asked him how the weather had been in Texas and how he had been.

"We were waiting for you since yesterday," I said. "Mother is home getting the supper ready. You haven't eaten yet, have you?"

He shook his head. "The train was late getting into Los Angeles. We were eight hours behind time and I should have reached San Francisco this morning around eight."

Reaching home it was the same way. Mother could not say anything. "We have nothing special tonight, wish we had something good."

"Anything would do, Mama," my brother said.

Father sat in the room reading the papers but his eyes were over the sheet and his hands were trembling. Mother scurried about getting his supper ready. I sat across the table from my brother, and in the silence which was action I watched the wave of emotions in the room. My brother was aware of it too. He sat there without a word, but I knew he understood. Not many years ago he was the baby of the family, having never been away from home. Now he was on his own, his quiet confidence actually making him appear larger. Keep up the fire, that was his company's motto. It was evident that he was a soldier. He had gone beyond life and death matters, where the true soldiers of war or peace must travel, and had returned.

For five short days we went about our daily task, picking and bunching the flowers for Christmas, eating heavy meals, and visiting the intimates. It was as if we were waiting for the hour of his departure, the time being so short. Every minute was crowded with privacy, friends, and nursery work. Too soon the time for his train came but the family had little to talk.

"Kazuo, don't worry about home or me," Mother said as we rode into town.

"Take care of yourself," my brother told her.

At the 16th Street Station Mother's close friend was waiting for us. She came to bid my brother good-bye. We had fifteen minutes to wait. My brother bought a copy of *The Coast* to see if his cartoons were in.

"Are you in this month's issue?" I asked.

"I haven't seen it yet," he said, leafing the pages. "Yes, I'm in. Here it is."

"Good!" I said. "Keep trying hard. Someday peace will come, and when you return laughter will reign once again."

My mother showed his cartoon to her friend. The train came in and we got up. It was a long one. We rushed to the Los Angeles-bound coach.

Mother's friend shook hands with my brother. "Give your best to America. Our people's honor depend on you Nisei soldiers."

My brother nodded and then glanced at Mother. For a moment her eyes twinkled and she nodded. He waved good-bye from the platform. Once inside the train we lost him. When the train began to move my mother cried, "Why doesn't he pull up the shades and look out? Others are doing it."

We stood and watched until the last of the train was lost in the night of darkness.

1949

Mervyn Morris

Mervyn Morris (b. 1937) was born in Jamaica and was educated there and at Oxford University on a Rhodes Scholarship. He has published several collections of poetry, including *The Pond* (1973), *Shadowboxing* (1979), and *I Been There, Sort Of: New and Selected Poems* (2006); he has edited a number of anthologies and was also a journalist and theatre critic. He is now Professor Emeritus of Creative Writing and West Indian Literature at the Mona Campus of the University of the West Indies in Jamaica.

Morris's "To an Expatriate Friend" is set in the 1960s in a post-independence environment where former colonizer and colonized, black and white are drifting apart. In colonial Jamaica, "expatriate" invariably meant white. The speaker, evidently black, laments that the political situation has driven a wedge between himself and his white friend. Contrastingly, "Little Boy Crying," a poem about a father's response to his having punished his child, has little that is overtly political. One poem examines a sociopolitical experience that requires knowledge of a particular historical situation while the other is a much more personal experience that transcends particulars of time and place. Are there any elements in "Little Boy Crying" that identify it as a specifically Jamaican poem?

To an Expatriate[1] Friend

Colour meant nothing. Anyone
who wanted help, had humour or was kind
was brother to you; categories of skin
were foreign; you were colour-blind.

And then the revolution. Black
and loud the horns of anger blew
against the long oppression; sufferers
cast off the precious values of the few.

New powers re-enslaved us all:
each person manacled in skin, in race.
You could not wear your paid-up dues;
the keen discriminators typed your face.

The future darkening, you thought it time
to say good-bye. It may be you were right.

---

[1] *Expatriate* In Jamaican idiom, an "expatriate" invariably refers to a British or European temporary resident in Jamaica.

It hurt to see you go; but, more,
it hurt to see you slowly going white.

1973

Little Boy Crying

Your mouth contorting in brief spite and hurt,
your laughter metamorphosed into howls,
your frame so recently relaxed now tight
with three-year-old frustration, your bright eyes
swimming tears, splashing your bare feet,
you stand there angling for a moment's hint
of guilt or sorrow for the quick slap struck.

The ogre towers above you, that grim giant,
empty of feeling, a colossal cruel,
soon victim of the tale's conclusion, dead
at last. You hate him, you imagine ·
chopping clean the tree he's scrambling down[1]
or plotting deeper pits to trap him in.

You cannot understand, not yet,
the hurt your easy tears can scald him with,
nor guess the wavering hidden behind that mask.
This fierce man longs to lift you, curb your sadness
with piggy-back or bull-fight, anything,
but dare not ruin the lessons you should learn.

You must not make a plaything of the rain.

1973

---

[1] *chopping clean…down* A reference to the end of the fairy tale "Jack and the Beanstalk."

Es'kia Mphahlele

Es'kia (Ezekiel) Mphahlele (1919-2008) was born in Pretoria, South Africa. He taught at universities in the United States and South Africa, where he spent the last years of his life. His publications include *The Wanderers* (novel, 1971), *Man Must Live* (stories, 1946), and *The African Image* (essays, 1962, rev. 1974). In 2001, the University of Venda for Science and Technology, South Africa, honoured him with the opening of the Es'kia Mphahlele Centre for African Studies.

Mphahlele's "The Coffee-Cart Girl" demonstrates how individuality and individual relationships are submerged beneath group thinking in societies like apartheid South Africa. The very first sentence of the story points up the herd mentality. The two protagonists try to discover each other's individuality, but the socioeconomic and political environment is not conducive to this. Compare the story on this level with Mervyn Morris's "To an Expatriate Friend."

The Coffee-Cart Girl

The crowd moved like one mighty being, and swayed and swung like the sea. In front, there was the Metropolitan Steel Windows Ltd. All eyes were fixed on it. Its workers did not hear one another: perhaps they didn't need to, each one interested as he was in what he was saying — and that with his blood. All he knew was that he was on strike: for what? If you asked him he would just spit and say: "Do you think we've come to play?"

Grimy, oily, greasy, sweating black bodies squeezed and chafed and grated. Pickets were at work; the law was brandishing batons; cars were hooting a crazy medley.

"Stand back, you monkeys!" cried a black man pinned against a pillar. "Hey, you black son of a black hen!"

The coffee-cart girl was absorbed in the very idea of the Metropolitan Steel Windows strike, just as she was in the flood of people who came to buy her coffee and pancakes: she wasn't aware of the swelling crowd and its stray atoms which were being flung out of it towards her cart until she heard an ear-splitting crash behind her. One of the row of coffee-carts had tipped over and a knot of men fallen on it. She climbed down from her cart, looking like a bird frightened out of its nest.

A woman screamed. Another crash. The man who had been pinned against the pillar had freed himself and he found himself standing beside the girl. He sensed her predicament. Almost rudely he pushed her into the street, took the cart by the stump of a shaft and wheeled it across the street, shouting generally, "Give way, you black monkeys." Just then a cart behind him went down and caved in like matchwood.

"Oh, thank you so much, mister!"

"Ought to be more careful, my sister."

"How can I thank you! Here, take coffee and a pancake."

"Thank you, my sister."

"Look, they're moving forward, maybe to break into the factory!" When next she looked back he was gone. And she hadn't even asked him his name: how unfriendly of her, she thought...

Later that winter morning the street was cleared of most people. The workers had gone away. There had been no satisfactory agreement. Strikes were unlawful for black people anyhow.

"Come back to work, or you are signed off, or go to gaol," had come the stock executive order. More than half had been signed off.

It was comparatively quiet now in this squalid West End sector of the city. Men and women continued their daily round. A dreary smoky mist lingered in suspension, or clung to the walls; black sooty chimneys shot up malignantly; there was a strong smell of bacon; the fruit and vegetable shops resumed trade with a tremulous expectancy; old men stood Buddha-like at the entrances with folded arms and a vague grimace on their faces, seeming to sneer at the world in general and their contemptible mercantile circle in particular; and the good earth is generous enough to contain all the human sputum these good suffering folk shoot out of their mouths at the slightest provocation. A car might tear down the cross-street and set up a squall and weep dry horse manure so that it circled in the air in a momentary spree, increasing the spitting gusto ...

"Hullo."

"Hullo, want coffee?"

"Yes, and two hot buns."

She hardly looked at him as she served him. For a brief spell her eyes fell on the customer. Slowly she gathered up the scattered bits of memory and unconsciously the picture was framed. She looked at him and found him scanning her.

"Oh!" She gave a gasp and her hand went to her mouth. "You're the good uncle who saved my cart!"

"Don't uncle me, please. My name is Ruben Lemeko. The boys at the factory call me China. Yours?"

"Zodwa."

His eyes travelled from her small tender fingers as she washed a few things, to her man's jersey which was a faded green and too big for her, her thin frock, and then to her peach-coloured face, not well fed, but well framed and compelling under a soiled black beret. As he ate hungrily she shot a side-glance at him occasionally. There was something sly in those soft, moist, slit eyes, but the modest stoop at the shoulders gave him a benign appearance; otherwise he would have looked twisted and rather fiendish. There was something she felt in his presence: a repelling admiration. She felt he was the kind of man who could be quite attractive so long as he remained more than a touch away from the contemplator; just like those wax figures she once saw in the chamber of horrors.

"Signed off at the Metropolitan?"

"Hm." His head drooped and she could read dejection in the oily top of his cap. "Just from the insurance fund office." She pitied him inwardly; a sort of pity she had never before experienced for a strange man.

"What to do now?"

"Like most of us," looking up straight into her eyes, "beat the road early mornings just when the boss's breakfast is settling nicely in the stomach. No work, no government papers, no papers, no work, then out of town."

"It's hard for everybody, I guess."

"Ja."

"I know. When you feel hungry and don't have money, come past here and I'll give you coffee and pancake."

"Thanks, er — let me call you Pinkie, shall I?"

"Hm," she nodded automatically.

He shook her hand. "Grow as big as an elephant for your goodness, as we say in our idiom." He shuffled off. For a long time, until he disappeared, she didn't take her eyes off the stooping figure, which she felt might set any place on fire. Strange man Pinkie thought idly as she washed up.

China often paused at Pinkie's coffee-cart. But he wouldn't let her give him coffee and pancakes for nothing.

"I'm no poorer than you," he said. "When I'm really in the drain pipes you may come to my help."

As she got used to him and the idea of a tender playfellow who is capable of scratching blood out of you, she felt heartily sorry for him; and he detected it, and resented it and felt sorry for her in turn.

"Right, Pinkie, I'll take it today."

"You'll starve to death in this cruel city."

"And then? Lots of them starve; think of this mighty city, Pinkie. What are we, you and me? If we starved and got sick and died, who'd miss you and me?"

Days when China didn't come, she missed him. And then she was afraid of something; something mysterious that crawls into human relations, and before we know it it's there; and because it is frightening it does not know how to announce itself without causing panic and possibly breaking down bonds of companionship. In his presence she tried to take refuge in an artless sisterly pity for him. And although he resented it, he carried on a dumb show. Within, heaven and earth thundered and rocked, striving to meet; sunshine and rain mingled; milk and gall pretended friendship; fire and water went hand in hand; tears and laughter hugged each other in a fit of hysterics; the screeching of the hang-bird started off with the descant of a dove's cooing; devils waved torches before a chorus of angels. Pinkie and China panicked at the thought of a love affair and remained dumb.

"Pinkie, I've got a job at last!"

"I'm happy for you, China!"

"You'll get a present, first money I get. Ach, but I shouldn't have told you. I wanted to surprise you." He was genuinely sorry.

"Don't worry, China I'll just pretend I'm surprised really, you'll see." They laughed. Friday came.

"Come, Pinkie, let's go."

"Where to?"

"I'll show you." He led her to the cheapjack[1] down the street.

"Mister, I want her to choose anything she wants."

The cheapjack immediately sprang up and in voluble cataracts began to sing praises upon his articles.

"All right, mister, let me choose." Pinkie picked up one article after another, inspected it, and at last she selected a beautiful long bodkin, a brooch, and a pair of bangles. Naidoo, the cheapjack, went off into rhapsodies again on Pinkie's looks when China put the things on her himself, pinning the bodkin on her beret. He bought himself a knife, dangling from a fashionable chain. They went back to the coffee-cart.

From this day onwards, Naidoo became a frequent customer at Pinkie's coffee-cart. He often praised her cakes and coffee. Twice at lunch-time China found him relating some anecdotes which sent Pinkie off into peals of laughter.

"Where you work, my prend?" asked Naidoo one day.

He was one of the many Indians who will say "pore-pipty" for "four fifty," "pier foms" for "five forms," "werry wital" for "very vital."

"Shoe factory, Main Street."

"Good pay?"

"Where do you find such a thing in this city?"

"Quite right, my prend. Look at me: I was wanted to be a grocer, and now I'm a cheapjack."

"I'm hungry today, Pinkie," China said one day. He was clearly elated over something.

"It's so beautiful to see you happy, China, what's the news?"

"Nothing. Hasn't a man the right to be jolly sometimes?"

"Of course. Just wondered if anything special happened."

He looked at her almost transparent pink fingers as she washed the coffee things.

"Hey, you've a lovely ring on your finger, where's the mine?"

Pinkie laughed as she looked at the glass-studded ring, fingered it and wiped it. "From Naidoo."

"It's nothing, China, Naidoo didn't have any money for food, so he offered me this for three days' coffee and cakes." She spoke as if she didn't believe her own self. She sensed a gathering storm.

"You lie!"

"Honestly China, now what would I be lying for?"

---

[1] *cheapjack* A peddler or dealer of cheap goods.

So! he thought, she couldn't even lie to keep their friendship: how distant she sounded. His fury mounted.

"Yes, you lie! Now listen Pinkie, you're in love with that cheapjack. Every time I found him here he's been damn happy with you, grinning and making eyes at you. Yes, I've watched him every moment."

He approached the step leading into the cart.

"Do you see me? I've loved you since I first saw you, the day of the strike." He was going to say more, but something rose inside him and choked him. He couldn't utter a word more. He walked slowly; a knife drawn out, with a menacing blade, pointed towards her throat. Pinkie retreated deeper into her cart, too frightened to plead her case.

At that very moment she realised fully the ghastliness of a man's jealousy, which gleamed and glanced on the blade and seemed to have raised a film which steadied the slit eyes. Against the back wall she managed to speak.

"All right, China, maybe you've done this many times before. Go ahead and kill me; I won't cry for help, do what you like with me."

She panted like a timid little mouse cornered by a cat. He couldn't finish the job he had set out to do. Why? He had sent two men packing with a knife before. They had tried to fight, but this creature wasn't resisting at all. Why, why, why? He felt the heat pounding in his temples; the knife dropped, and he sank on to a stool and rested his head on the wall, his hands trembling.

After a moment he stood up, looking away from Pinkie. "I'm sorry, Pinkie, I pray you never in your life to think about this day."

She looked at him, mystified.

"Say you forgive me." She nodded twice.

Then she packed up for the day, much earlier than usual.

The following day China did not visit Pinkie; nor the next. He could not decide to go there. Things were all in a barbed wire tangle in his mind. But see her he must, he thought. He would just go and hug her; say nothing but just press her to himself because he felt too mean even to tell her not to be afraid of him any more.

The third day the law came. It stepped up the street in goose-march fashion. The steel on its heels clanged on the pavement with an ominous echo. It gave commands and everything came to an end at once. Black man's coffee-cart was not to operate any more in the city. "… Makes the city look ugly," the city fathers said.

For several days China, unaware of what had happened, called on Pinkie, but always found the coffee-carts empty and deserted. At last he learned everything from Naidoo, the cheapjack.

He stepped into her coffee-cart and sat on the stool.

He looked into the cheerless pall of smoke. Outside life went on as if there had never been a Pinkie who sold coffee and pancakes.

Dare he hope that she would come back, just to meet him? Or was it going to turn out to have been a dream? He wondered.

We'll meet in town, some day, China thought. I'll tell her all about myself, all about my wicked past; she'll get used to me, not be afraid of me any more ...

And still he sat in the coffee-cart which was once Pinkie's all through the lunch-hour ...

1967

Bharati Mukherjee

Bharati Mukherjee (b. 1940) was born and educated in Calcutta, India, and attended universities in India and the United States. She spent some years in Canada (teaching at McGill University) before returning to the United States in 1981. Her publications include *Wife* (novel, 1975), *Darkness* (stories, 1985), *The Sorrow and the Terror: The Haunting Legacy of the Air India Tragedy* (with Clark Blaise, 1987), *The Holder of the World* (novel, 1993), *Leave It to Me* (novel, 1997), and *The Tree Bride* (novel, 2004).

Mukherjee's "Hindus" has two well-off immigrants from India who have brought their social rivalries to the New World. Set in New York, the story underscores the multiethnic nature of the city, but ironically the Indian narrator-protagonist, Leela, identifies the secondary characters not as individuals but as ethnics: the West Indian, the Lebanese, and the Gujarati. What is Leela's tone toward her fellow immigrants? Do class differences play a role here? Does Leela recognize at the end that she is a kindred spirit of the maharajah and probably of all the other immigrants who have come to "the New World too late?"

Hindus

I ran into Pat at Sotheby's on a Friday morning two years ago. Derek and I had gone to view the Fraser Collection of Islamic miniatures at the York Avenue galleries. It bothered Derek that I knew so little about my heritage. Islam is nothing more than a marauder's faith to me, but the Mogul emperors stayed a long time in the green delta of the Ganges, flattening and reflattening a fort in the village where I was born, and forcing my priestly ancestors to prove themselves brave. Evidence on that score is still inconclusive. That village is now in Bangladesh.

Derek was a filmmaker, lightly employed at that time. We had been married three hundred and thirty-one days.

"So," Pat said, in his flashy, plummy, drawn-out intonation, "you finally made it to the States!"

It was one of those early November mornings when the woodsy smell of overheated bodies in cloth coats clogged the public stairwells. Everywhere around me I detected the plaintive signs of over-preparedness.

"Whatever are you doing here?" He engulfed me in a swirl of Liberty scarf and cashmere lapels.

"Trying to get the woman there to sell me the right catalog," I said.

The woman, a very young thing with slippery skin, ate a lusty Granny Smith apple and ignored the dark, hesitant miniature-lovers hanging about like bats in the daytime.

"They have more class in London," Pat said.

"I wouldn't know. I haven't been back since that unfortunate year at Roedean."

"It was always New York you wanted," Pat laughed. "Don't say I didn't warn you. The world is full of empty promises."

I didn't remember his having warned me about life and the inevitability of grief. It was entirely possible that he had — he had always been given to clowning pronouncements — but I had not seen him in nine years and in Calcutta he had never really broken through the fortifications of my shyness.

"Come have a drink with me," Pat said.

It was my turn to laugh. "You must meet Derek," I said.

Derek had learned a great deal about India. He could reel off statistics of Panchayati Raj and the electrification of villages and the introduction of mass media, though he reserved his love for birds migrating through the wintry deserts of Jaisalmer. Knowledge of India made Derek more sympathetic than bitter, a common trait of decent outsiders. He was charmed by Pat's heedless, old-world insularity.

"Is this the lucky man?" he said to Derek. He did not hold out his hand. He waved us outside; a taxi magically appeared. "Come have a drink with me tomorrow. At my place."

He gave Derek his card. It was big and would not fit into a wallet made to hold Visa and American Express. Derek read it with his usual curiosity.

H.R.H. Maharajah Patwant Singh
OF
Gotlah
Purveyor and Exporter

He tucked the card in the pocket of his raincoat. "I'll be shooting in Toronto tomorrow," he said, "but I'm sure Leela would like to keep it."

There was, in the retention of those final "h's" — even Indian maps and newspapers now referred to Gotla and to maharajas, and I had dropped the old "Leelah" in my first month in America — something of the reclusive mountebank. "I'm going to the Patels for dinner tomorrow," I said, afraid that Pat would misread the signs of healthy unpossessiveness in our marriage.

"Come for a drink before. What's the matter, Leela? Turning a prude in your old age?" To Derek he explained, "I used to rock her on my knee when she was four. She was gorgeous then, but I am no lecher."

It is true that I was very pretty at four and that Pat spent a lot of time in our house fondling us children. He brought us imported chocolates in beautiful tins and made a show of giving me the biggest. In my family, in every generation, one infant seems destined to be the repository of the family's comeliness. In my generation, I inherited the looks, like an heirloom, to keep in good condition and pass on to the next. Beauty teaches humility and responsibility in the culture I come from. By marrying well, I could have seen to the education of my poorer cousins.

Pat was in a third floor sublet in Gramercy Park South. A West Indian doorman with pendulous cheeks and unbuttoned jacket let me into the building. He didn't give me a chance to say where I was going as I moved toward the elevator.

"The maharaja is third floor, to the right. All the way down."

I had misunderstood the invitation. It was not to be an hour of wit and nostalgia among exotic knick-knacks squirreled into New York from the Gotla Palace. I counted thirty guests in the first quarter hour of my short stay. Plump young men in tight-fitting suits scuttled from living room to kitchen, balancing overfull glasses of gin and tonic. The women were mostly blondes, with luridly mascaraed, brooding eyes, blonde the way South Americans are blonde, with deep residual shading. I tried to edge into a group of three women. One of them said, "I thought India was spellbinding. Naresh's partner managed to get us into the Lake Palace Hotel."

"I don't think I could take the poverty," said her friend, as I retreated.

The living room walls were hung with prints of British East India Company officials at work and play, the vestibule with mirror-images of Hindu gods and goddesses.

"Take my advice," a Gujarati man said to Pat in the dim and plantless kitchen. "Get out of diamonds—emeralds *won't* bottom out. These days it *has* to be rubies and emeralds."

In my six years in Manhattan I had not entered a kitchen without plants. There was not even a straggly avocado pushing its nervous way out of a shrivelling seed.

I moved back into the living room where the smell of stale turmeric hung like yellow fog from the ceiling. A man rose from the brocade-covered cushions of a banquette near me and plumped them, smiling, to make room for me.

"You're Pat's niece, no?" The man was francophone, a Lebanese. "Pat has such pretty nieces. You have just come from Bombay? I love Bombay. Personally, Bombay to me is just like a jewel. Like Paris, like Beirut before, now like Bombay. You agree?"

I disclaimed all kinship to H.R.H. I was a Bengali Brahmin; maharajas—not to put too sharp a point on it—were frankly beneath me, by at least one caste, though some of them, like Pat, would dispute it. Before my marriage to Derek no one in my family since our initial eruption from Vishnu's knee had broken caste etiquette. I disclaimed any recent connection with India. "I haven't been home in ages," I told the Lebanese. "I am an American citizen."

"I too am. I am American," he practically squealed. He rinsed his glass with a bit of gin still left in the bottom, as though he were trying to dislodge lemon pulp stuck and drying on its sides. "You want to have dinner with me tonight, yes? I know Lebanese places, secret and intimate. Food and ambiance very romantic."

"She's going to the Patels." It was Pat. The Gujarati with advice on emeralds was still lodged in the kitchen, huddling with a stocky blonde in a fuchsia silk sari.

"Oh, the Patels," said the Lebanese. "You did not say. Super guy, no? He's doing all right for himself. Not as well as me, of course. I own ten stores and he only has four."

Why, I often ask myself, was Derek never around to share these intimacies? Derek would have drawn out the suave, French-speaking, soulful side of this Seventh Avenue *shmattiste*.

It shouldn't have surprised me that the Lebanese man in the ruffled shirt should have known Mohan and Motibehn Patel. For immigrants in similar trades, Manhattan is still a village. Mohan had been in the States for eighteen years and last year had become a citizen. They'd been fortunate in having only sons, now at Cal Tech and Cornell; with daughters there would have been pressure on them to return to India for a proper, arranged marriage.

"Is he still in Queens?"

"No," I told him. "They've moved to a biggish old place on Central Park West."

"Very foolish move," said the Lebanese. "They will only spend their money now." He seemed genuinely appalled.

Pat looked at me surprised. "I can't believe it," he exclaimed. "Leela Lahiri actually going crosstown at night by herself. I remember when your Daddy wouldn't let you walk the two blocks from school to the house without that armed Nepali, what was his name, dogging your steps."

"Gulseng," I said. "He was run over by a lorry three years ago. I think his name was really something-or-other-Rana, but he never corrected us."

"Short, nasty and brutal," said Pat. "They don't come that polite and loyal these days. Just as likely to slit your throat as anyone else, these days."

The Lebanese, sensing the end of the brave New World overtures, the gathering of the darknesses we shared, drifted away.

"The country's changed totally, you know," Pat continued. "Crude rustic types have taken over. The *dhoti-wallahs*,[1] you know what I mean, they would wrap themselves in loincloths if it got them more votes. No integrity, no finesse. The country's gone to the dogs, I tell you."

"That whole life's outmoded, Pat. Obsolete. All over the world."

"They tried to put me in jail," he said. His face was small with bitterness and alarm. "They didn't like my politics, I tell you. Those Communists back home arrested me and threw me in jail. Me. Like a common criminal."

"On what charges?"

"Smuggling. For selling family heirlooms to Americans who understand them. No one at home understands their value. Here, I can sell off a little Pahari painting for ten thousand dollars. Americans understand our things better than we do ourselves. India wants me to starve in my overgrown palace."

"Did you really spend a night in jail?" I couldn't believe that modernization had finally come to India and that even there, no one was immune from consequences.

"Three nights!" he fumed. "Like a common *dacoit*.[2] The country has no respect anymore. The country has nothing. It has driven us abroad with whatever assets we could salvage."

---

[1] *dhoti-wallahs* A derogatory term, here applied to politicians who would stoop to anything to win votes, including wearing unfashionable traditional clothing (like the *dhoti*, a loose fitting Indian loin-cloth); *wallahs* is the term for individuals associated with a particular work or service.

[2] *dacoit* A member of a robber gang in India.

"You did well, I take it." I did not share his perspective; I did not feel my country owed me anything. Comfort, perhaps, when I was there; a different comfort when I left it. India teaches her children: you have seen the worst. Now go out and don't be afraid.

"I have nothing," he spat. "They've stripped me of everything. At night I hear the jackals singing in the courtyard of my palace."

But he had recovered by the time I left for the crosstown cab ride to the Patels. I saw him sitting on the banquette where not too long before the Lebanese had invited me to share an evening of unwholesomeness. On his knee he balanced a tall, silver-haired woman who looked like Candice Bergen. She wore a pink cashmere sweater which she must have put through the washing machine. Creases, like worms, curled around her sweatered bosom.

I didn't see Pat for another two years. In those two years I did see a man who claimed to have bounced the real Candice Bergen on his knee. He had been a juggler at one time, had worked with Edgar Bergen on some vaudeville act and could still pull off card tricks and walk on his hands up and down my dining table. I kept the dining table when Derek and I split last May. He went back to Canada which we both realized too late he should never have left and the table was too massive to move out of our West 11th Street place and into his downtown Toronto, chic renovated apartment. The ex-juggler is my boss at a publishing house. My job is menial but I have a soothing title. I am called an Administrative Assistant.

In the two years I have tried to treat the city not as an island of dark immigrants but as a vast sea in which new Americans like myself could disappear and resurface at will. I did not avoid Indians, but without Derek's urging for me to be proud of my heritage, I did not seek them out. The Patels did invite me to large dinners where all the guests seemed to know with the first flick of their eyes in my direction that I had married a white man and was now separated, and there our friendships hit rock. I was a curiosity, a novel and daring element in the community; everyone knew my name. After a while I began to say I was busy to Motibehn Patel.

Pat came to the office with my boss, Bill Haines, the other day. "I wanted you to meet one of our new authors, Leela," Bill said.

"Leela, *dar-ling*!" Pat cried. His voice was shrill with enthusiasm, and he pressed me histrionically against his Burberry raincoat. I could feel a button tap my collarbone. "It's been years! Where have you been hiding your gorgeous self?"

"I didn't realize you two knew each other," Bill said.

All Indians in America, I could have told him, constitute a village.

"Her father bailed me out when the Indian government sought to persecute me," he said with a pout. "If it hadn't been for courageous friends like her daddy, I and my poor subjects might just as well have kicked the bucket."

"She's told me nothing about India," said Bill Haines. "No accent, Western clothes—"

"Yes, a shame, that. By the way, Leela, I just found a picture of Lahiri-*sahab* on an elephant when I was going through my official papers for Bill. If you come over for drinks—after getting out of those ridiculous clothes, I must insist—I can give it to you. Lahiri-*sahab* looks like Ernest Hemingway in that photo. You tell him I said he looks like Hemingway."

"Daddy's in Ranikhet this month," I said. "He's been bedridden for a while. Arthritis. He's just beginning to move around a bit again."

"I have hundred of good anecdotes, Bill, about her daddy and me doing *shikar* in the Sundarban forest. Absolutely *huge* Bengal tigers. I want to balance the politics—which as you rightly say are central—with some stirring bits about what it was like in the good old days."

"What are you writing?" I asked.

"I thought you'd never ask, my dear. My memoirs. At night I leave a Sony by my bed. Night is the best time for remembering. I hear the old sounds and voices. You remember, Leela, how the palace ballroom used to hum with dancing feet on my birthdays?"

"*Memoirs of a Modern Maharajah*," Bill Haines said.

"I seem to remember the singing of jackals," I said, not unkindly, though he chose to ignore it.

"Writing is what keeps me from going through death's gate. There are nights …" He didn't finish. His posture had stiffened with self-regard; he communicated great oceans of anguish. He'd probably do well. It was what people wanted to hear.

"The indignities," he said suddenly. "The atrocities." He stared straight ahead, at a watercooler. "The nights in jail, the hyenas sniffing outside your barred window. I will never forget their smell, never! It is the smell of death, Leela. The new powers-that-be are peasants. Peasants! They cannot know, they cannot suspect how they have made me suffer. The country is in the hands of tyrannical peasants!"

"Look, Pat," Bill Haines said, leading the writer toward his office, "I have to see Bob Savage, the sub-rights man one floor down. Make yourself at home. Just pull down any book you want to read. I'll be back in a minute."

"Don't worry about me. I shall be all right, Bill. I have my Sony in my pocket. I shall just sit in a corner beside the daughter of my oldest friend, this child I used to bounce on my knee, and I shall let my mind skip into the nooks and crannies of Gotlah Palace. Did I tell you, when I was a young lad my mother kept pet crocs? Big, huge gents and ladies with ugly jaws full of nasty teeth. They were her pets. She gave them names and fed them chickens every day. Come to me, Padma. Come to me, Prem."

"It'll be dynamite," Bill Haines said. "The whole project's dynamite." He pressed my hand as he eased his stubby, muscular body past the stack of dossiers on my desk. "And *you'll* be a godsend in developing this project."

"And what's with you?" Pat asked me. I could tell he already knew the essentials.

"Nothing much." But he wasn't listening anyway.

"You remember the thief my security men caught in the early days of your father's setting up a factory in my hills? You remember how the mob got excited and poured acid on his face?"

I remembered. Was the Sony recording it? Was the memory an illustration of swift and righteous justice in a collapsed Himalayan princely state, or was it the savage and disproportionate fury of a people resisting change?

"Yes, certainly I do. Can I get you a cup of coffee? Or tea?" That, of course, was an important part of my job.

"No thanks," he said with a flutter of his wrinkled hands. "I have given up all stimulants. I've even given up bed-tea. It interferes with my writing. Writing is everything to me nowadays. It has been my nirvana."

"The book sounds dynamite," I assured him. An Indian woman is brought up to please. No matter how passionately we link bodies with our new countries, we never escape the early days.

Pat dropped his voice, and stooping conspiratorially, said to me in Hindi, "There's one big favor you can do for me, though. Bill has spoken of a chap I should be knowing. Who is this Edgar Bergen?"

"I think he was the father of a movie actress," I said. I too, had gone through the same contortion of recognition with Bill Haines. Fortunately, like most Americans, he could not conceive of a world in which Edgar Bergen had no currency. Again in Hindi, Pat asked me for directions to the facilities, and this time I could give a full response. He left his rolled-slim umbrella propped against my desk and walked toward the fountain.

"Is he really a maharaja?" Lisa leaned over from her desk to ask me. She is from Rhode Island. Brown hasn't cured her of responding too enthusiastically to each call or visit from a literary personage. "He's terrific. So suave and distinguished! Have you known him from way back when?"

"Yes," I said, all the way from when.

"I had no idea you spoke Hindu. It's eerie to think you can speak such a hard language. I'm having trouble enough with French. I keep forgetting that you haven't lived here always."

I keep forgetting it too. I was about to correct her silly mistake — I'd learned from Derek to be easily incensed over ignorant confusions — between Hindi and Hindu — but then I thought, why bother? Maybe she's right. That slight undetectable error, call it an accent, isn't part of language at all. I speak Hindu. No matter what language I speak it will come out slightly foreign, no matter how perfectly I mouth it. There's a whole world of us now, speaking Hindu.

The manuscript of *Memoirs* was not dynamite, but I stayed up all night to finish it. In spite of the arch locutions and the aggrieved posture that Pat had stubbornly clung to, I knew I was reading about myself, blind and groping conquistador who had come to the New World too late.

1985

Gerald Murnane

Gerald Murnane (b. 1939) was born in Coburg, Melbourne, Australia. He trained briefly for the priesthood in the Roman Catholic Church but decided to pursue a career in education. He has taught creative writing at various Australian universities. His novels include *Tamarisk Row* (1974), *The Plains* (1982), *Inland* (1988), and *Emerald Blue* (1995). He has also published a book of essays, *Invisible Yet Enduring Lilacs* (2005).

Murnane's "Land Deal" is considered a short story, but in what ways does it frustrate our expectations of the short story? The story deals with Aboriginal land-rights in Australia, but it goes beyond that to suggest, using metafiction and fantasy, that it is not just land that has been taken away from the Aborigines, but their spirit and mind as well. The epigraph to the story is an extract from an actual document. Compare this story with Eva Johnson's play "Murras," in which three generations of women fight against losing their Aboriginal culture and tradition.

Land Deal

After a full explanation of what my object was, I purchased two large tracts of land from them—about 600,000 acres, more or less—and delivered over to them blankets, knives, looking-glasses, tomahawks, beads, scissors, flour, etc., as payment for the land, and also agreed to give them a tribute, or rent, yearly.

John Batman, 1835

We certainly had no cause for complaint at the time. The men from overseas politely explained all the details of the contract before we signed it. Of course here there were minor matters that we should have queried. But even our most experienced negotiators were distracted by the sight of the payment offered to us.

The strangers no doubt supposed that their goods were quite unfamiliar to us. They watched tolerantly while we dipped our hands into the bags of flour, draped ourselves in blankets, and tested the blades of knives against the nearest branches. And when they left we were still toying with our new possessions. But what we marvelled at most was worth their novelty. We had recognized an almost miraculous correspondence between the strangers' steel and glass and wool and flour and those metals and mirrors and cloths and foodstuffs that we so often postulated, speculated about, or dreamed of.

Is it surprising that a people who could use against stubborn wood and pliant grass and bloody flesh nothing more serviceable than stone? Is it surprising that such a people have become so familiar with the idea of metal? Each one of us, in his dreams, had felled tall trees with blades that lodged deep in the pale pulp beneath the bark. Any of us could have enacted the sweeping of honed metal through a stand of seeded grass or described the precise parting of fat or muscle beneath a tapered knife. We knew the strength and sheen of steel and the trueness of its edge from having so often called it into possible existence.

It was the same with glass and wool and flour. How could we not have inferred the perfection of mirrors — we who peered so often into rippled puddles after a wavering image of ourselves? There was no quality of wool that we had not conjectured as we huddled under stiff pelts of possum on rainy winter evenings. And every day the laborious pounding of the women at their dusty mills recalled for us the richness of the wheaten flour that we had never tasted.

But we had always clearly distinguished between the possible and the actual. Almost anything was possible. Any god might reside behind the thundercloud or the waterfall, any faery race inhabit the land below the ocean's edge; any new day might bring us such a miracle as an axe of steel or a blanket of wool. The almost boundless scope of the possible was limited only by the occurrence of the actual. And it went without saying that what existed in the one sense could never exist in the other. Almost anything was possible except, of course, the actual.

It might be asked whether our individual or collective histories furnished any example of a possibility become actual. Had no man ever dreamed of possessing a certain capon or woman and, a day or a year later, laid hold of his desire? This can be simply answered by the assurance that no one among us was ever heard to claim that anything in his possession resembled, even remotely, some possible thing he had once hoped to possess.

That same evening, with the blankets warm against our backs and the blades still gleaming beside us, we were forced to confront an unpalatable proposition. The goods that had appeared among us so suddenly belonged only in a possible world. We were therefore dreaming. The dream may have been the most vivid and enduring that any of us had known. But however long it lasted it was still a dream.

We admired the subtlety of the dream. The dreamer (or dreamers — we had already admitted the likelihood of our collective responsibility) had invented a race of men among whom possible objects passed as actual. And these men had been moved to offer us the ownership of their prizes in return for something that was itself not real.

We found further evidence to support this account of things. The pallor of the men we had met that day, the lack of purpose in much of their behaviour, the vagueness of their explanations — these may well have been the flaws of men dreamed of in haste. And, perhaps paradoxically, the nearly perfect properties of the stuffs offered to us seemed the work of a dreamer, someone who lavished on the central items of his dream all those desirable qualities that are never found in actual objects.

It was this point that led us to alter part of our explanation for the events of that day. We were still agreed that what had happened was part of some dream. And yet it was characteristic of most dreams that the substance of them seemed, at the time, actual to the dreamer. How, if we were dreaming of the strangers and their goods, were we able to argue against our taking them for actual men and objects?

We decided that none of us was the dreamer. Who, then, was? One of our gods, perhaps? But no god could have had such an acquaintance with the actual that he succeeded in creating an illusion of it that had almost deceived us.

There was only one reasonable explanation. The pale strangers, the men we had first seen that day, were dreaming of us and our confusion. Or, rather, the true strangers were dreaming of a meeting between ourselves and their dreamed-of-selves.

At once, several puzzles seemed resolved. The strangers had not observed us as men observe one another. There were moments when they might have been looking through our hazy outlines towards sights they recognized more easily. They spoke to us with oddly raised voices and claimed our attention with exaggerated gestures as though we were separated from them by a considerable distance, or as though they feared we might fade altogether from their sight before we had served the purpose for which they had allowed us into their dream.

When had this dream begun? Only, we hoped, on that same day when we first met the strangers. But we could not deny that our entire lives and the sum of our history might have been dreamed by these people of whom we knew almost nothing. This did not dismay us utterly. As characters in a dream, we might have been much less at liberty than we had always supposed. But the authors of the dream encompassing us had apparently granted us at least the freedom to recognize, after all these years, the simple truth behind what we had taken for a complex world.

Why had things happened thus? We could only assume that these other men dreamed for the same purpose that we (dreamers within a dream) often gave ourselves up to dreaming. They wanted for a time to mistake the possible for the actual. At that moment, as we deliberated under familiar stars (already subtly different now that we knew their true origin), the dreaming men were in an actual land far away, arranging our very deliberations so that their dreamed-of-selves could enjoy for a little while the illusion that they had acquired something actual.

And what was this unreal object of their dreams? The document we had signed explained everything. If we had not been distracted by their glass and steel that afternoon we would have recognized even then the absurdity of the day's events. The strangers wanted to possess the land.

Of course it was the wildest folly to suppose that the land, which was by definition indivisible, could be measured or parcelled out by a mere agreement among men. In any case, we had been fairly sure that the foreigners failed to see our land. From their awkwardness and unease as they stood on the soil, we judged that they did not recognize the support it provided or the respect it demanded. When they moved even a short distance across it, stepping aside from places that invited passage and treading on places that were plainly not to be intruded on, we knew that they would lose themselves before they found the real land.

Still, they had seen a land of some sort. That land was, in their own words, a place for farms and even, perhaps, a village. It would have been more in keeping with the scope of the dream surrounding them had they talked of founding an unheard-of city where they stood. But all their schemes were alike from our point of view. Villages or cities were all in the realm of possibility and could never have a real existence. The land would remain the land, designed for us yet, at the same time, providing the scenery for the dreams of a people who would never see either our land or any land they dreamed of.

What could we do, knowing what we then knew? We seemed as helpless as those characters we remembered from private dreams who tried to run with legs strangely nerveless. Yet if we had no choice but to complete the events of the dream, we could still admire the marvellous inventiveness of it. And we could wonder endlessly what sort of people they were in their far country, dreaming of a possible land they could never inhabit, dreaming further of a people such as ourselves with our one weakness, and then dreaming of acquiring from us the land which could never exist.

We decided, of course, to abide by the transaction that had been so neatly contrived. And although we knew we could never truly awake from a dream that did not belong to us, still we trusted that one day we might seem, to ourselves at least, to awake.

Some of us, remembering how after dreams of loss they had awakened with real tears in their eyes, hoped that we would somehow wake to be convinced of the genuineness of the steel in our hands and the wool round our shoulders. Others insisted that for as long as we handled such things we could be no more than characters in the vast dream that had settled over us — the dream that would never end until a race of men in a land unknown to us learned how much of their history was a dream that must one day end.[1]

1980

---

[1] *dream that... end* In this story "dream" or "dreaming" can be taken in the usual sense or in the Aboriginal sense. Aboriginals accept "dreaming" as the closest English word for the mystical insights gained in dreams into all that is known and understood in human existence.

V.S. Naipaul

Vidia(dhar) S. Naipaul (b. 1932) was born and educated in Trinidad (at Queen's Royal College). He left for Oxford University in 1950, and has lived in England since then. His novels include *The Mystic Masseur* (1957), *A House for Mr. Biswas* (1961), *The Enigma of Arrival* (1987), *A Way in the World* (1994), and *Magic Seeds* (2004). He has published several travel books and collections, including *Among the Believers* (1981), *India: A Million Mutinies Now* (1990), and a collection of letters between himself and his father, *Letters between Father and Son* (2000). He won the 2001 Nobel Prize in Literature.

The setting of Naipaul's "B. Wordsworth" is a street in a suburban section of Port of Spain, the capital of Trinidad, in the 1940s. Naipaul's narrative art raises a number of questions: Why does the story invoke William Wordsworth's name? The boy's mother is suspicious of the poet. Is this justified? Is the relationship between the poet and the boy innocent in the sense that there is no pedophilia? Does the fact that the story is given from the boy's point of view help in answering this question? Why does the poet confess that the story he told him is not true? Is it really not true? What saves the story from being sentimental—the humour and/or the innocent boy's point of view? In his later fiction, Naipaul develops a dark vision of life and is sharply critical of society. Do you see any hints of this in his story? "Jasmine" is an attempt to theorize and explore the nature of language, the nature of words, and the relationship of literature to life. What distinction is Naipaul making when he says that the "English language was mine; the tradition was not?" Compare this essay with Derek Walcott's comment on the English language in "Midsummer: LII" and Salman Rushdie's in "'Commonwealth Literature' Does Not Exist."

B. Wordsworth[1]

Three beggars called punctually every day at the hospitable houses in Miguel Street. At about ten an Indian came in his dhoti and white jacket, and we poured a tin of rice into the sack he carried on his back. At twelve an old woman smoking a clay pipe came and she got a cent. At two a blind man led by a boy called for his penny.

Sometimes we had a rogue. One day a man called and said he was hungry. We gave him a meal. He asked for a cigarette and wouldn't go until we had lit it for him. That man never came again.

The strangest caller came one afternoon at about four o'clock. I had come back from school and was in my home-clothes. The man said to me, "Sonny, may I come inside your yard?"

He was a small man and he was tidily dressed. He wore a hat, a white shirt and black trousers.

---

[1] *B. Wordsworth* William Wordsworth (1770–1850) was a British Romantic poet with whom most students in the British Empire would have been familiar.

I asked, "What you want?"

He said, "I want to watch your bees."

We had four small gru-gru palm trees and they were full of uninvited bees.

I ran up the steps and shouted, "Ma, it have a man outside here. He say he want to watch the bees."

My mother came out, looked at the man and asked in an unfriendly way, "What you want?"

The man said, "I want to watch your bees."

His English was so good, it didn't sound natural, and I could see my mother was worried.

She said to me, "Stay here and watch him while he watch the bees."

The man said, "Thank you, madam. You have done a good deed today."

He spoke very slowly and very correctly as though every word was costing him money.

We watched the bees, this man and I, for about an hour, squatting near the palm trees.

The man said, "I like watching bees. Sonny, do you like watching bees?"

I said, "I ain't have the time."

He shook his head sadly. He said, "That's what I do, I just watch. I can watch ants for days. Have you ever watched ants? And scorpions, and centipedes, and *con-gorees*[1] — have you watched those?"

I shook my head.

I said, "What you does do, mister?"

He got up and said, "I am a poet."

I said, "A good poet?"

He said, "The greatest in the world."

"What your name, mister?"

"B. Wordsworth."

"B for Bill?"

"Black. Black Wordsworth. White Wordsworth was my brother. We share one heart. I can watch a small flower like the morning glory and cry."

I said, "Why you does cry?"

"Why, boy? Why? You will know when you grow up. You're a poet, too, you know. And when you're a poet you can cry for everything."

I couldn't laugh.

He said, "You like your mother?"

"When she not beating me."

He pulled out a printed sheet from his hip-pocket and said, "On this paper is the greatest poem about mothers and I'm going to sell it to you at a bargain price. For four cents."

I went inside and I said, "Ma, you want to buy a poetry for four cents?"

---

[1] *congorees* A type of small centipede.

My mother said, "Tell that blasted man to haul his tail away from my yard, you hear."

I said to B. Wordsworth, "My mother say she ain't have four cents."

B. Wordsworth said, "It is the poet's tragedy."

And he put the paper back in his pocket. He didn't seem to mind.

I said, "Is a funny way to go round selling poetry like that. Only calypsonians do that sort of thing. A lot of people does buy?"

He said, "No one has yet bought a single copy."

"But why you does keep on going round, then?"

He said, "In this way I watch many things, and I always hope to meet poets."

I said, "You really think I is a poet?"

"You're as good as me," he said.

And when B. Wordsworth left, I prayed I would see him again.

About a week later, coming back from school one afternoon, I met him at the corner of Miguel Street.

He said, "I have been waiting for you for a long time."

I said, "You sell any poetry yet?"

He shook his head.

He said, "In my yard I have the best mango tree in Port of Spain. And now the mangoes are ripe and red and very sweet and juicy. I have waited here for you to tell you this and to invite you to come and eat some of my mangoes."

He lived in Alberto Street in a one-roomed hut placed right in the centre of the lot. The yard seemed all green. There was the big mango tree. There was a coconut tree and there was a plum tree. The place looked wild, as though it wasn't in the city at all. You couldn't see all the big concrete houses in the street.

He was right. The mangoes were sweet and juicy. I ate about six, and the yellow mango juice ran down my arms to my elbows and down my mouth to my chin and my shirt was stained.

My mother said when I got home, "Where was you? You think you is a man now and could go all over the place? Go cut a whip for me."

She beat me rather badly, and I ran out of the house swearing that I would never come back. I went to B. Wordsworth's house. I was so angry, my nose was bleeding.

B. Wordsworth said, "Stop crying, and we will go for a walk."

I stopped crying, but I was breathing short. We went for a walk. We walked down St. Clair Avenue to the Savannah and we walked to the race-course.

B. Wordsworth said, "Now, let us lie on the grass and look up at the sky, and I want you to think how far those stars are from us."

I did as he told me, and I saw what he meant. I felt like nothing, and at the same time I had never felt so big and great in all my life. I forgot all my anger and all my tears and all the blows.

When I said I was better, he began telling me the names of the stars, and I particularly remembered the constellation of Orion the Hunter, though I don't really know why. I can spot Orion even today, but I have forgotten the rest.

Then a light was flashed into our faces, and we saw a policeman. We got up from the grass.

The policeman said, "What you doing here?"

B. Wordsworth said, "I have been asking myself the same question for forty years."

We became friends, B. Wordsworth and I. He told me, "You must never tell anybody about me and about the mango tree and the coconut tree and the plum tree. You must keep that a secret. If you tell anybody, I will know, because I am a poet."

I gave him my word and I kept it.

I liked his little room. It had no more furniture than George's front room, but it looked cleaner and healthier. But it also looked lonely.

One day I asked him, "Mister Wordsworth, why you does keep all this bush in your yard? Ain't it does make the place damp?"

He said, "Listen, and I will tell you a story. Once upon a time a boy and girl met each other and they fell in love. They loved each other so much they got married. They were both poets. He loved words. She loved grass and flowers and trees. They lived happily in a single room, and then one day, the girl poet said to the boy poet, 'We are going to have another poet in the family.' But this poet was never born, because the girl died, and the young poet died with her, inside her. And the girl's husband was very sad, and he said he would never touch a thing in the girl's garden. And so the garden remained, and grew high and wild."

I looked at B. Wordsworth, and as he told me this lovely story, he seemed to grow older. I understood his story.

We went for long walks together. We went to the Botanical Gardens and the Rock Gardens. We climbed Chancellor Hill in the late afternoon and watched the darkness fall on Port of Spain, and watched the lights go on in the city and on the ships in the harbour.

He did everything as though he were doing it for the first time in his life. He did everything as though he were doing some church rite.

He would say to me, "Now, how about having some ice-cream?"

And when I said yes, he would grow very serious and say, "Now, which cafe shall we patronize?" As though it were a very important thing. He would think for some time about it, and finally say, "I think I will go and negotiate the purchase with that shop."

The world became a most exciting place.

One day, when I was in his yard, he said to me, "I have a great secret which I am now going to tell you."

I said, "It really secret?"

"At the moment, yes."

I looked at him, and he looked at me. He said, "This is just between you and me, remember. I am writing a poem."

"Oh." I was disappointed.

He said, "But this is a different sort of poem. This is the greatest poem in the world."

I whistled.

He said, "I have been working on it for more than five years now. I will finish it in about twenty-two years from now, that is, if I keep on writing at the present rate."

"You does write a lot, then?"

He said, "Not any more. I just write one line a month. But I make sure it is a good line."

I asked, "What was last month's good line?"

He looked up at the sky, and said, "*The past is deep.*"

I said, "It is a beautiful line."

B. Wordsworth said, "I hope to distil the experiences of a whole month into that single line of poetry. So, in twenty-two years, I shall have written a poem that will sing to all humanity."

I was filled with wonder.

Our walks continued. We walked along the sea-wall at Docksite one day, and I said, "Mr. Wordsworth, if I drop this pin in the water, you think it will float?"

He said, "This is a strange world. Drop your pin, and let us see what will happen."

The pin sank.

I said, "How is the poem this month?"

But he never told me any other line. He merely said, "Oh, it comes, you know. It comes."

Or we would sit on the sea-wall and watch the liners come into the harbour.

But of the greatest poem in the world I heard no more.

I felt he was growing older.

"How you does live, Mr. Wordsworth?" I asked him one day.

He said, "You mean how I get money?"

When I nodded, he laughed in a crooked way.

He said, "I sing calypsoes in the calypso season."

"And that last you the rest of the year?"

"It is enough."

"But you will be the richest man in the world when you write the greatest poem?"

He didn't reply.

One day when I went to see him in his little house, I found him lying on his little bed. He looked so old and so weak, that I found myself wanting to cry.

He said, "The poem is not going well."

He wasn't looking at me. He was looking through the window at the coconut tree, and he was speaking as though I wasn't there. He said, "When I was twenty I felt the power within myself." Then, almost in front of my eyes, I could see his face growing older and more tired. He said, "But that—that was a long time ago."

And then—I felt it so keenly, it was as though I had been slapped by my mother. I could see it clearly on his face. It was there for everyone to see. Death on the shrinking face.

He looked at me, and saw my tears and sat up.

He said, "Come." I went and sat on his knees.

He looked into my eyes, and he said, "Oh, you can see it, too. I always knew you had the poet's eye."

He didn't even look sad, and that made me burst out crying loudly.

He pulled me to his thin chest, and said, "Do you want me to tell you a funny story?" and he smiled encouragingly at me.

But I couldn't reply.

He said, "When I have finished this story, I want you to promise that you will go away and never come back to see me. Do you promise?"

I nodded.

He said, "Good. Well, listen. That story I told you about the boy poet and the girl poet, do you remember that? That wasn't true. It was something I just made up. All this talk about poetry and the greatest poem in the world, that wasn't true, either. Isn't that the funniest thing you have heard?"

But his voice broke.

I left the house, and ran home crying, like a poet, for everything I saw.

I walked along Alberto Street a year later, but I could find no sign of the poet's house. It hadn't vanished, just like that. It had been pulled down, and a big, two-storeyed building had taken its place. The mango tree and the plum tree and the coconut tree had all been cut down, and there was brick and concrete everywhere.

It was just as though B. Wordsworth had never existed.

1959

Jasmine

One day about ten years ago, when I was editing a weekly literary programme for the BBC's Caribbean Service, a man from Trinidad came to see me in one of the freelancers' rooms in the old Langham Hotel. He sat on the edge of the table, slapped down some sheets of typescript and said, "My name is Smith. I write about sex. I am also a nationalist." The sex was tepid, Maugham and coconut-water; but the nationalism was aggressive. Women swayed like coconut trees; their skins were the colour of the sapodilla, the inside of their mouths the colour of a cut star-apple; their teeth were as white as coconut kernels; and when they made love they groaned like bamboos in high wind.

The writer was protesting against what the English language had imposed on us. The language was ours, to use as we pleased. The literature that came with it was therefore of peculiar authority; but this literature was like an alien mythology. There was, for instance, Wordsworth's notorious poem about the daffodil.[1] A pretty little flower, no doubt; but we had never seen it. Could the poem have any meaning for us? The superficial prompting of this argument, which would have confined all literatures to the countries of their origin, was political; but it was really an expression of dissatisfaction at the emptiness of our own formless, unmade society. To us, without a mythology, all literatures were foreign. Trinidad was small, remote and unimportant, and we knew we could not hope to read in books of the life we saw about us. Books came from afar; they could offer only fantasy.

To open a book was to make an instant adjustment. Like the medieval sculptor of the North interpreting the Old Testament stories in terms of the life he knew, I needed to be able to adapt. All Dickens's descriptions of London I rejected; and though I might retain Mr. Micawber[2] and the others in the clothes the illustrator gave them, I gave them the faces and voices of people I knew and set them in buildings and streets I knew. The process of adaptation was automatic and continuous. Dickens's rain and drizzle I turned into tropical downpours; the snow and fog I accepted as conventions of books. Anything — like an illustration — which embarrassed me by proving how weird my own recreation was, anything which sought to remove the characters from the make-up world in which I set them, I rejected.

I went to books for fantasy; at the same time I required reality. The gypsies of *The Mill on the Floss* were a fabrication and a disappointment, discrediting so much that was real: to me gypsies were mythical creatures who belonged to the pure fantasy of Hans Christian Andersen and *The Heroes*. Disappointing, too, was the episode of the old soldier's sword, because I thought that swords belonged to ancient times; and the Tom Tulliver I had created walked down the street where I lived. The early parts of *The Mill on the Floss*, then; chapters of *Oliver Twist, Nicholas Nickleby, David Copperfield*; some of the novels of H.G. Wells; a short story by Conrad called "The Lagoon": all these which in the beginning I read or had read to me I set in Trinidad, accepting, rejecting, adapting, and peopling in my own way. I never read to find out about foreign countries. Everything in books was foreign; everything had to be subjected to adaptation; and everything in, say, an English

---

[1] *Wordsworth's...daffodil* "I Wandered lonely As a Cloud" (1804). Here are some lines from it: "When all at once I saw a crowd / a host of golden daffodils... / Ten thousand saw I at a glance, / Tossing their heads in sprightly dance."

[2] *Mr. Micawber* A character in Charles Dickens's *David Copperfield*.

novel which worked and was of value to me at once ceased to be specifically English. Mr. Murdstone worked; Mr. Pickwick and his club didn't. *Jane Eyre* and *Wuthering Heights* worked; *Pride and Prejudice* didn't.[1] Maupassant worked; Balzac didn't.

I went to books for a special sort of participation. The only social division I accepted was that between rich and poor, and any society more elaborately ordered seemed insubstantial and alien. In literature such a society was more than alien; it was excluding, it made nonsense of my fantasies and more and more, as I grew older and thought of writing myself, it made me despairingly conscious of the poverty and haphazardness of my own society. I might adapt Dickens to Trinidad; but it seemed impossible that the life I knew in Trinidad could ever be turned into a book. If landscapes do not start to be real until they have been interpreted by an artist, so, until they have been written about, societies appear to be without shape and *embarrassing*. It was embarrassing to be reminded by a Dickens illustration of the absurdity of my adaptations; it was equally embarrassing to attempt to write of what I saw. Very little of what I read was of help. It would have been possible to assume the sensibility of a particular writer. But no writer, however individual his vision, could be separated from his society. The vision was alien; it diminished my own and did not give me the courage to do a simple thing like mentioning the name of a Port of Spain[2] street.

Fiction or any work of the imagination, whatever its quality, hallows its subject. To attempt, with a full consciousness of established authoritative mythologies, to give a quality of myth to what was agreed to be petty and ridiculous — Frederick Street in Port of Spain, Marine Square, the districts of Laventille and Barataria — to attempt to use these names required courage. It was, in a way, the rejection of the familiar, meaningless word — the rejection of the unknown daffodil to put it no higher — and was as self-conscious as the attempt to have sapodilla-skinned women groaning like bamboos in high wind.

With all English literature accessible, then, my position was like that of the maharaja in *Hindoo Holiday*,[3] who, when told by the Christian lady that God was here, there and everywhere, replied, "But what use is that to *me*?" Something of more pertinent virtue was needed, and this was provided by some local short stories. These stories, perhaps a dozen in all, never published outside Trinidad, converted what I saw into "writing." It was through them that I began to appreciate the

---

[1] *The Mill on the Floss... Pride and Prejudice didn't* Supplementary information on other texts mentioned by Naipaul: George Eliot's *The Mill on the Floss* (1860); Charles Kingsley's *The Heroes* (1856); Tom Tulliver is a character in *Mill on the Floss*; Dickens's *Oliver Twist* (1838) and *Nicholas Nickleby* (1839); Mr. Pickwick is in Dickens's *Pickwick Papers* (1837); Charlotte Brontë's *Jane Eyre* (1847); Emily Brontë's *Wuthering Heights* (1847); Jane Austen's *Pride and Prejudice* (1813).

[2] *Port of Spain* Port of Spain is the capital of Trinidad and was Naipaul's home before he left for Oxford University in 1950.

[3] *Hindoo Holiday Hindoo Holiday: An Indian Journal* (1932) by J.R. Ackerly.

distorting, distilling power of the writer's art. Where I had seen a drab haphazardness they found order; where I would have attempted to romanticize, to render my subject equal with what I had read, they accepted. They provided a starting-point for further observation; they did not trigger off fantasy. Every writer is, in the long run, on his own; but it helps, in the most practical way, to have a tradition. The English language was mine; the tradition was not.

Literature, then, was mainly fantasy. Perhaps it was for this reason that, although I had at an early age decided to be a writer and at the age of eighteen had left Trinidad with that ambition, I did not start writing seriously until I was nearly twenty-three. My material had not been sufficiently hallowed by a tradition; I was not fully convinced of its importance; and some embarrassment remained. My taste for literature had developed into a love of language, the word in isolation. At school my subjects were French and Spanish; and the pleasures of the language were at least as great as those of the literature. Maupassant and Moliere were rich; but it was more agreeable to spend an hour with the big Harrap French-English dictionary, learning more of the language through examples, than with Corneille or Racine. And it was because I thought I had had enough of these languages (both now grown rusty) that when I came to England to go to university I decided to read English.

This was a mistake. The English course had little to do with literature. It was a "discipline" seemingly aimed at juvenile antiquarians. It by-passed the novel and the prose "asides" in which so much of the richness of the literature lay. By a common and curious consent it concentrated on poetry; and since it stopped at the eighteenth century it degenerated, after an intensive study of Shakespeare, into a lightning survey of minor and often severely local talents. I had looked forward to wandering among large tracts of writing; I was presented with "texts." The metaphysicals were a perfect subject for study, a perfect part of a discipline; but, really, they had no value for me. Dryden, for all the sweet facility of his prose, was shallow and dishonest; did his "criticism" deserve such reverential attention? *Gulliver's Travels* was excellent; but could *The Tale of a Tub* and *The Battle of the Books* be endured?

The fact was, I had no taste for scholarship, for tracing the growth of schools and trends. I sought continuously to relate literature to life. My training at school didn't help. We had few libraries, few histories of literature to turn to; and when we wrote essays on *Tartuffe* we wrote out of a direct response to the play. Now I discovered that the study of literature had been made scientific, that each writer had to be approached through the booby-traps of scholarship. There were the bound volumes of the Publications of the Modern Language Association of America, affectionately referred to by old and knowing young as PMLA. The pages that told of Chaucer's knowledge of astronomy or astrology (the question came up every year) were black and bloated and furred with handling, and even some of the pencilled annotations *(No, Norah!)* had grown faint. I developed a physical distaste for these bound volumes and the libraries that housed them.

Delight cannot be taught and measured; scholarship can; and my reaction was irrational. But it seemed to me scholarship of such a potted order. A literature was not being explored; it had been codified and reduced to a few pages of "text," some volumes of "background" and more of "criticism"; and to this mixture a mathematical intelligence might have been applied. There were discoveries, of course: Shakespeare, Marlowe, Restoration comedy. But my distaste for the study of literature led to a sense of being more removed than ever from the literature itself.

The language remained mine, and it was to the study of its development that I turned with pleasure. Here was enough to satisfy my love of language; here was unexpected adventure. It might not have been easy to see Chaucer as a great imaginative writer or to find in the *Prologue* more than a limited piece of observation which had been exceeded a thousand times; but Chaucer as a handler of a new, developing language was exciting. And my pleasure in Shakespeare was doubled. In Trinidad English writing had been for me a starting-point for fantasy. Now, after some time in England, it was possible to isolate the word, to separate the literature from the language.

Language can be so deceptive. It has taken me much time to realize how bad I am at interpreting the conventions and modes of English speech. This speech has never been better dissected than in the early stories of Angus Wilson. This is the judgment of today; my first responses to these stories were as blundering and imperfect as the responses of Professor Pforzheim to the stern courtesies of his English colleagues — in *Anglo-Saxon Attitudes*. But while knowledge of England has made English writing more truly accessible, it has made participation more difficult; it has made impossible the exercise of fantasy, the reader's complementary response. I am inspecting an alien society, which I yet know, and I am looking for particular social comment. And to re-read now the books which lent themselves to fantastic interpretation in Trinidad is to see, almost with dismay, how English they are. The illustrations to Dickens cannot now be dismissed. And so, with knowledge, the books have ceased to be mine.

It is the English literary vice, this looking for social comment; and it is difficult to resist. The preoccupation of the novelists reflects a society ruled by convention and manners in the fullest sense, an ordered society of the self-aware who read not so much for adventure as to compare, to find what they know or think they know. A writer is to be judged by what he reports on; the working-class writer is a working-class writer and no more. So writing develops into the private language of a particular society. There are new reports, new discoveries: they are rapidly absorbed. And with each discovery the society's image of itself becomes more fixed and the society looks further inward. It has too many points of reference; it has been written about too often; it has read too much. Angus Wilson's characters, for instance, are great readers; they are steeped in Dickens and Jane Austen. Soon there will be characters steeped in Angus Wilson; the process is endless. Sensibility will overlay sensibility: the grossness of experience will be refined away by self-awareness. Writing will become Arthur Miller's definition of a newspaper: a nation talking to itself. And even those who have the key will be able only to witness, not to participate.

All literatures are regional; perhaps it is only the placelessness of a Shakespeare or the blunt communication of "gross" experience as in Dickens that makes them appear less so. Or perhaps it is a lack of knowledge in the reader. Even in this period of "internationalism" in letters we have seen literatures turning more and more inward, developing languages that are more and more private. Perhaps in the end literature will write itself out, and all its pleasures will be those of the word.

A little over three years ago I was in British Guiana. I was taken late one afternoon to meet an elderly lady of a distinguished Christian Indian family. Our political attitudes were too opposed to make any discussion of the current crisis profitable. We talked of the objects in her veranda and of the old days. Suddenly the tropical daylight was gone, and from the garden came the scent of a flower. I knew the flower from my childhood; yet I had never found out its name. I asked now.

"We call it jasmine."

Jasmine! So I had known it all those years! To me it had been a word in a book, a word to play with, something removed from the dull vegetation I knew.

The old lady cut a sprig for me. I stuck it in the top buttonhole of my open shirt. I smelled it as I walked back to the hotel. Jasmine, jasmine. But the word and the flower had been separate in my mind for too long. They did not come together.

1972

R.K. Narayan

Rasipuram K. Narayan (1906-2001) was born in Madras, India. He spent most of his life in Mysore. He published fourteen novels, including *Swami and Friends* (1935) and *The World of Nagaraj* (1990), and numerous collections of stories, essays, and memoirs. He travelled and lectured in the United States and received India's highest literary prize, the Padma Bhushan Award.

Narayan's "Mother and Son" is a simple story that provides us with glimpses of 1960s' village life in India while relating the conflict between an Indian mother and son about whom the son should marry. Narayan examines the social and cultural changes taking place, particularly the younger generation's challenging arranged marriages. This story is void of overt postcolonial issues and could be compared in this regard with Saros Cowasjee's "His Father's Medals" and Mulk Raj Anand's "Duty."

Mother and Son

Ramu's mother waited till he was halfway through dinner and then introduced the subject of marriage. Ramu merely replied, "So you are at it again!" He appeared more amused than angry, and so she brought out her favourite points one by one: her brother's daughter was getting on to fourteen, the girl was good-looking and her brother was prepared to give a handsome dowry; she (Ramu's mother) was getting old and wanted a holiday from housekeeping: she might die any moment and then who would cook Ramu's food and look after him? And the most indisputable argument: a man's luck changed with marriage. "The harvest depends not on the hand that holds the plough but on the hand which holds the pot." Earlier in the evening Ramu's mother had decided that if he refused again or exhibited the usual sullenness at the mention of marriage, she would leave him to his fate; she would leave him absolutely alone even if she saw him falling down before a coming train. She would never more interfere in his affairs. She realized what a resolute mind she possessed, and felt proud of the fact. That was the kind of person one ought to be. It was all very well having a mother's heart and so on, but even a mother could have a limit to her feelings. If Ramu thought he could do what he pleased just because she was only a mother, she would show him he was mistaken. If he was going to slight her judgement and feelings, she was going to show how indifferent she herself could be....

With so much preparation she broached the subject of marriage and presented a formidable array of reasons. But Ramu just brushed them aside and spoke slightingly of the appearance of her brother's daughter. And then she announced, "This is the last time I am speaking about this. Hereafter I will leave you alone. Even if I see you drowning I will never ask why you are drowning. Do you understand?"

"Yes." Ramu brooded. He could not get through his Intermediate even at the fourth attempt; he could not get a job, even at twenty rupees a month. And here was Mother worrying him to marry. Of all girls, his uncle's! That protruding tooth alone would put off any man. It was incredible that he should be expected to marry that girl. He had always felt that when he married he would marry a girl like Rezia, whom he had seen in two or three Hindi films. Life was rusty and sterile, and Ramu lived in a stage of perpetual melancholia and depression; he loafed away his time, or slept, or read old newspapers in a free reading room....

He now sat before his dining leaf and brooded. His mother watched him for a moment and said, "I hate your face. I hate anyone who sits before his leaf with that face. A woman only ten days old in widowhood would put on a more cheerful look."

"You are saying all sorts of things because I refuse to marry your brother's daughter," he replied.

"What do I care? She is a fortunate girl and will get a really decent husband." Ramu's mother hated him for his sullenness. It was this gloomy look that she hated in people. It was unbearable. She spoke for a few minutes, and he asked, "When are you going to shut up?"

"My life is nearly over," said the mother. "You will see me shutting up once and for all very soon. Don't be impatient. You ask me to shut up! Has it come to this?"

"Well, I only asked you to give me some time to eat."

"Oh, yes. You will have it soon, my boy. When I am gone you will have plenty of time, my boy."

Ramu did not reply. He ate his food in silence. "I only want you to look a little more human when you eat," she said.

"How is it possible with this food?" asked Ramu.

"What do you say?" screamed the mother. "If you are so fastidious, work and earn like all men. Throw down the money and demand what you want. Don't command when you are a pauper."

When the meal was over, Ramu was seen putting on his sandals. "Where are you going?" asked the mother.

"Going out," he curtly replied, and walked out, leaving the street door ajar.

Her duties for the day were over. She had scrubbed the floor of the kitchen, washed the vessels and put them in a shining row on the wooden shelf, returned the short scrubbing broom to its corner and closed the kitchen window.

Taking the lantern and closing the kitchen door, she came to the front room. The street door stood ajar. She became indignant at her son's carelessness. The boy was indifferent and irresponsible and didn't feel bound even to shut the street door. Here she was wearing out her palm scrubbing the floor night after night. Why should she slave if he was indifferent? He was old enough to realize his responsibilities in life.

She took out her small wooden box and put into her mouth a clove, a cardamom and a piece of areca nut. Chewing these, she felt more at peace with life. She shut the door without bolting it and lay down to sleep.

Where could Ramu have gone? She began to feel uneasy. She rolled her mat, went out, spread it on the *pyol*[1] and lay down. She muttered to herself the holy name of Sri Rama in order to keep out disturbing thoughts. She went on whispering, "Sita Rama Rama ..." But she ceased unconsciously. Her thoughts returned to Ramu. What did he say before going out? "I am just going out for a stroll, Mother. Don't worry. I shall be back soon." No, it was not that. Not he. Why was the boy so secretive about his movements? That was impudent and exasperating. But, she told herself, she deserved no better treatment with that terrible temper and cutting tongue of hers. There was no doubt that she had conducted herself abominably during the meal. All her life this had been her worst failing: this tendency, while in a temper, to talk without restraint. She even felt that her husband would have lived for a few more years if she had spoken to him less ... Ramu had said something about the food. She would include more vegetables and cook better from tomorrow. Poor boy...

She fell asleep. Somewhere a gong sounded one, and she woke up. One o'clock? She called, "Ramu, Ramu."

She did not dare to contemplate what he might have done with himself. Gradually she came to believe that her words during the meal had driven him to suicide. She sat up and wept. She was working herself up to a hysterical pitch. When she closed her eyes to press out the gathering tears, the vision of her son's body floating in Kukanahalli Tank came before her. His striped shirt and mill dhoti were sodden and clung close to his body. His sandals were left on one of the tank steps. His face was bloated beyond all recognition.

She screamed aloud and jumped down from the *pyol*. She ran along the whole length of Old Agrahar Street. It was deserted. Electric lights twinkled here and there. Far away a *tonga*[2] was rattling on, the *tonga*-driver's song faintly disturbing the silence; the blast of a night constable's whistle came to her ears, and she stopped running. She realized that after all it might be only her imagination. He might have gone away to the drama, which didn't usually close before three in the morning. She rapidly uttered the holy name of Sri Rama in order to prevent the picture of Kukanahalli Tank coming before her mind.

She had a restless night. Unknown to herself, she slept in snatches and woke up with a start every time the gong boomed. The gong struck six through the chill morning.

Tears streaming down her face, she started for Kukanahalli Tank. Mysore was just waking to fresh life. Milkmen with slow cows passed along. Municipal sweepers were busy with their long brooms. One or two cycles passed her.

She reached the tank, not daring even once to look at the water. She found him sleeping on one of the benches that lined the bund. For just a second she wondered if it might be his corpse. She shook him vigorously, crying "Ramu!" She heaved a tremendous sigh of relief when he stirred.

---

[1] *pyol* A porch, balcony, verandah, or gallery (Hindi).

[2] *tonga* A horse-drawn carriage (Hindi).

He sat up, rubbing his eyes. "Why are you here, Mother?"

"What a place to sleep in!"

"Oh, I just fell asleep," he said.

"Come home," she said. She walked on and he followed her. She saw him going down the tank steps. "Where are you going?"

"Just for a wash," Ramu explained.

She clung to his arm and said vehemently, "No, don't go near the water."

He obeyed her, though he was slightly baffled by her vehemence.

1972

Mudrooroo Narogin

Mudrooroo Narogin (Colin Johnson, b. 1938) was born in Narogin, Western Australia. He changed his name to reaffirm his tribal identity. He writes poetry, fiction, and literary criticism. His publications include the novels *Wild Cat Falling* (1965), *Long Live Sandawara* (1979), and *Wildcat Screaming* (1992), and the poetry collection *The Song Circle of Jacky and Selected Poems* (1986). He has taught Aboriginal literature at Murdoch University and at the University of Queensland.

Narogin's "They Give Jacky Rights" is a lament for the lot of his people, the Aboriginals of Australia, who, deprived of opportunities for economic and social well-being, must turn to traditional spiritualism, to "dreaming," for survival. Does the ironical tone make this a stronger indictment of the powers-that-be? Compare the tone/attitude of this poem with that of Jack Davis's story "Pay Back," Eva Johnson's play "Murras," and E. Pauline Johnson's poem "The Cattle Thief."

They Give Jacky¹ Rights

They give Jacky rights,
Like the tiger snake gives rights to its prey:
They give Jacky rights,
Like the rifle sights on its victim.
They give Jacky rights,
Like they give rights to the unborn baby,
Ripped from the womb by its uncaring mother.

They give Jacky the right to die,
The right to consent to mining on his land.
They give Jacky the right to watch
His sacred dreaming place become a hole—
His soul dies, his ancestors cry:
They give Jacky his rights—
A hole in the ground!

Justice for all, Jacky kneels and prays;
Justice for all, they dig holes in his earth;
Justice for all, they give him his rights—
A flagon of cheap wine to dull his pain,
And his woman has to sell herself for that.

---

¹ *Jacky* Australian slang for an Aboriginal native; sometimes used pejoratively.

Justice for all, they give him his rights—
A hole in the ground to hide his mistrust and
What can Jacky do, but struggle on and on:
The spirits of his Dreaming[1] keep him strong!

1986

---

[1] *Dreaming* Aboriginal people accept "dreaming" as the closest English word for the mystical insights
gained in dreams into all that is known and understood in human existence.

Njabulo S. Ndebele

Njabulo S. Ndebele (b. 1948) was born in Johannesburg, South Africa. He was educated there, at Cambridge University, and at the University of Denver. He was Vice-Chancellor and Principal of the University of Cape Town. His publications include *Fools and Other Stories* (1983), *The Cry of Winnie Mandela* (novel, 2000), *South African Literature and Culture: Rediscovery of the Ordinary* (essays, 1994), and *Fine Lines from the Box: Further Thoughts About Our Country* (2007). His poetry has appeared in many anthologies. He contributes commentary regularly on issues facing South Africa in its ongoing transition to a non-apartheid nation.

Ndebele's 1994 essay "Guilt and Atonement: Unmasking History for the Future" raises a significant question about multiracial or multicultural societies: can a member of one group know the others well enough to write about them authentically? V.S. Pritchett thinks few writers can write outside their own nations or classes, pointing out that Charles Dickens caricatured the French and D.H. Lawrence the aristocracy. In post-apartheid South African society, Ndebele, drawing on his own experience, believes that it is still difficult to write across ethnic and racial lines. He proceeds to take to task the slow transition that was taking place in 1993–94. To put what he is saying in context: in 1948, white South African voters elected a government dedicated to apartheid. It became increasingly controversial, leading to international sanctions and to widespread oppression and unrest within South Africa. In 1990, the white National Party government took the initial step toward abandoning apartheid, and the first multi-racial elections were held in 1994. The predominantly black ANC (African National Congress) won by an overwhelming majority and has governed ever since. It formed The Truth and Reconciliation Commission in 1995. Ndebele believes that the Commission contributes to keeping the country together, but wonders about the long-term consequences.

Guilt and Atonement: Unmasking History for the Future

A few years ago I began to write a novel which I called "The Mask of the Fatherland." It was meant to be about a young Afrikaner[1] boy in the South African Defence Force who during the war in Angola discovers the many masks that he and his tribe have had to wear over the centuries as they tried to justify their mission on earth. After much planning and research, I found I could not write the novel. At the root of the problem was that I simply did not know my main character. I did not know the simplest things about him. What was his mother fond of saying to him? Did he dream of his childhood sweetheart? Did he have problems revealing his feelings? Who were his neighbourhood friends, and what kind of mischief as boys did they get into? Does he have any strong thoughts about TV, about the Space Shuttle? What kind of

---

[1] *Afrikaner* A South African of Dutch (or related) extraction.

home conditions his thinking? All I had was a treasure house of stereotypes for which I had no use.

I look at the times in which we live right now and I ask the question: am I in a position to write this novel? I know that I still cannot write it. At bottom is the fact that I do not know the people that my hero belongs to as a real, living community. At this time when Berlin walls of various kinds are falling, I am aware of a wall that is as formidable as ever. It is the wall of ignorance. At this time when the spirit of reconciliation is supposed to bring South Africans together, South Africans don't know one another as a people. Can we as a nation write the novel of the future under these conditions? If so, what are the preconditions for such novels to be written? What does it take for us to know one another? What *will* it take?

The African struggle for liberation was coming along. Somewhere it appeared to flounder and then it stopped to take another form. What characterises the nature of the transformation is that those who opened the prison doors were not victorious crowds pursuing a defeated enemy in flight. They were opened by an enemy who had declared that he was now a friend. To date, he still holds the keys. When it suits him, he haggles over conditions, trying to prescribe the manner in which the new friendship is to be carried out, prompting the following questions. Are those who did not forcibly bring down the doors victorious? Have those who still hold the keys been defeated? There is a stand-off that offers no certitude. We are aware of those who are driven by hope, the supposed victors, and those who are driven by fear, the supposed losers. The danger is that a situation such as this can breed the most debilitating ambiguity in which we oscillate between hope and despair with a frequency that induces undefined bitterness and cynicism.

This situation of ambiguity may very well suggest that what we see is a chaotic play of masks: the masks of conciliation or reconciliation whose colourfulness may suggest a fragile essence, the absence of an underlying form. One such mask is the expression "the new South Africa." It is a sonorous expression fraught with much meaning and meaninglessness all at once. It spawns various masks that suggest many possible forms that this "new South Africa" may take. Who, anyway, invented the phrase? Was it the anxious "defeated" or the hopeful "victors"? Whatever the case might be, at the end of the day we still ask: what exactly is behind each mask? What is the reality so steadfastly hidden by the rhetoric of hope and anxiety?

It is part of the writer's task to strive to unmask. We are confronted by so many surfaces in our day-to-day lives. So many masks. Writing enables us to crack the surface and break through to the often deliberately hidden essence. What we find may either bring joy or sadness, hope or despair, but almost always yields insight. It is this masking and unmasking that often constitutes the terrain of conflict between the writer and official culture. Writers strive to remove the blanket which officialdom insists on spreading and laying over things. When officialdom is under attack and lacks confidence, it is the new one that constructs masks.

Let us step back and reconstruct the situation briefly. It is interesting to note that we have just come from a situation in which the South African government *(this very present government*) did not even attempt to mask anything. On the contrary, it seems to have even enjoyed what most of us saw as obscene exhibitionism. It was characterised by brazen acts of public cruelty and terrible laws. It was a public dance of indecency choreographed from parliament. Some masking, of course, took place at the level of ideology. Attempts were made to justify the manifest and most observable horror through the propounding of apartheid philosophy.

Of course the oppressed had no option but to live with and to subsist in the terrible reality created. From that perspective, denied a say in matters pertaining to their health, housing, education, employment, recreation, they focused their attention on the justificatory arguments, since we cannot but respond to speech. They grappled with the logic of apartheid.

February 2, 1990 represented the strategic withdrawal of the argument. "Strategic" because, indeed, it was known all along that the argument was a lie, that it had been constructed for a purpose: to systematically entrench white power through a range of instruments of domination. Now all is in place, the red herring can be done away with and it will all seem like defeat. In fact, this is victory at the very moment that defeat is being proclaimed.

Of course, it will take generations in a normal time sequence for blacks to produce enough academics, engineers, industrialists, doctors, corporate managers, archivists, pilots, etc. to make a real competitive difference in the actual play of power in the governance of the country. Their land of milk and honey, according to the current flow of events, still seems a remote possibility.

In fact, just as they had no option but to accept the conditions of life imposed on them, if they want to experience some semblance of freedom, in the short term, they may have no option but to fit into the available business and civil service culture and rise through the ranks. Suddenly, where the various structures of such a culture represented exclusion and repulsive, exploitative white power, now they may represent opportunity. The glitter of apartheid: buildings, banks, etc., previously an index of the oppressed's powerlessness, now represent, disturbingly, the possibility of fulfilment.

But such fulfilment comes at a price. Everything has been thought out for us: our inventive capacity is harnessed according to the demands of a structured business and industrial culture. The brazen oppression of the past can now become the seductive oppression of having to build and consolidate and enjoy what was achieved at our expense. There will be the attractive tendency to accept all this as the spoils of struggle. But who are likely to take advantage of this situation?

This situation is likely to split the black community into those who, worn out by the struggle, seek immediate relief, and those who, seeing the dangers of a short-term accommodation, wish to press ahead. Indeed, the ambiguities and contradictions of the times throw up painful choices to grapple with intellectually.

Terrible choices! We can choose between absorption and accommodation on the one hand, and, on the other hand, the quest for a self-created reality. The former promises short-term relief for the few who can make it, and discontent for the vast masses who see no relief in sight. The latter choice may even prompt the question: was the armed struggle perhaps abandoned too soon? Could a year or two not have driven home more dramatically to the whites of our country the real nature of the demand of the oppressed for liberation? Did all the painful struggles of the past terminate so abruptly so that an all-white cricket team can go to India triumphantly without the baggage of guilt? Who did it represent? Certainly not me. Do people who still ask for old national emblems really know what is going on? Where is the future we have wanted to build with our hands and our imaginations from the ashes of the past?

Terrible choices! We can choose between freedom through the agony of destructive strife and struggle, on the one hand, and on the other, the anxiety born of the need for security, the choice to hang on to a known reality, no matter how problematic (after all there can be legitimate burn-out after long years of struggle and hope for deliverance); between reconstruction and accommodative consolidation; between war and negotiation.

One of the prices we can pay for choosing the illusion of freedom is to forget about the past and enjoy the present as much as we can. After all, apartheid laws are gone, what do we want now?

In fact, there is a concerted attempt by those responsible for apartheid to forget about the past and to convince everyone else to do so. Not too long ago, Roelof ("Pik") Botha, addressing the Australian press club, declared that he has also fought against apartheid. So the ANC, PAC and other liberation groups really have no special claim to the attention of the world. Of course, Pik Botha has his heroic, invisible scars to show for it: he has been banned, tortured, detained without trial, forced into exile, maimed in SADF raids in Lesotho and Botswana and then recalled to be rewarded with a cabinet post by the government of his nightmares. This tactic represents not only a brazen distortion of historical fact, but can also be regarded as an obscene attempt to appropriate the struggles of those who have been victims of his government in order to belittle the significance of the liberation struggle. What gives him the right to do this? I registered in myself the flickers of rage as I listened to our Minister of Foreign Affairs perform.

Certainly it now seems to me that the negotiation atmosphere has created a false moral equation between the Nationalist Party (the authors of our horror novel) and its government on the one hand, and the liberation movement on the other. It is an equation that has given our white compatriots a right they previously and still do not have: the right to judge our struggle. It is an equation in which the liberation movement perhaps saw the possibility of some strategic gains for the struggle. But clearly, the government saw the possibility of consolidating white power without the baggage of the past. In effect, there is no equation but conflicting interests in a balance in which one thing that is certain is the uncertainty of the future.

One should not be seen to be harping on the evils of the past. But we have to cry out when the past is being deliberately forgotten in order to ensure that what was gained by it can now be enjoyed without compunction. It is crucial at this point that the past be seen as a legitimate point of departure for talking about the challenges of the present and the future. The past, no matter how horrible it has been, can redeem us. It can be the moral foundation on which to build the pillars of the future. If so, what are the implications of keeping the past alive?

Should the oppressor now feel guilty about it? Guilt, in this situation, may be healthy. It may represent a healthy recognition of the moral flaws of the past and the extent of one's responsibility for them.

But guilt is like pain: not many of us would like or wish to inflict it on others. We cannot call forth the guilt of others. Guilty people are not pleasant people to live with. They are tense, unpredictable, and unhappy. Guilt on a massive social scale is not healthy.

And the oppressed? Should they feel shame? Yes, to the extent that they should recognise their humiliation and vow never to go through it again. Beyond that, a prolonged feeling of shame on a massive social scale may perpetuate inferiority.

Yes. It is at this point that we move away from shame and guilt to call for the atonement of justice. It is justice we must demand, not guilt. We must demand justice.

But the balance of forces at this juncture is such that we may not even be able to get justice. Is justice possible in a situation in which the following questions are still being asked? Given the current balance of forces and the need for democracy and equality in the short term:

How do we dispossess those who took the land by unfair means?
How do we remove from power those who won it by conquest?
How do we take away privileges and resources from those who
   accumulated them by unfair means?

Because of the balance of forces, I am unable to answer these questions. This inability I find debilitating. It spawns frustration and may even lead to something I have steadfastly fought in the past: bitterness. For indeed, to borrow from Jay Reddy's quotation in her address, "the end of apartheid seems to represent for the white minority a defeat in which they have lost nothing." It leads me to the uncomfortable perception that at a time when justice has to prevail (because the advent of freedom represents historical redress), there seems no objective basis on which to promote it. There is no manifest objective base to support the moral law. Entrenched privilege, entrenched and pervasive institutional and social power, entrenched poverty, ill health, joblessness, lack of opportunity, lack of housing: all these persist *with a vengeance*! All these still constitute the universal reality of our times.

Guilt? it is not something we need to spend too much time on. Guilt is irrelevant. But why is it likely to crop up in discussions of the need for redress? Essentially because the struggle is unresolved. Its end has not been decisive. Paradoxically, it may benefit the whites to keep us demanding their guilt. For guilt is a red herring that gives us the illusion that in dealing with it we are engaged in combat. It enables us to deal with the illusion while leaving the reality intact. It may even represent the reinvention of protest. The demand for justice, on the other hand, is more immediately and concretely threatening: *it keeps our attention firmly on the search for the actual process of redress.*

Those who have lost should properly experience loss, not guilt. Those who feel guilty may feel this way precisely because they have not lost, and yet see the legitimacy of the demands on them, and the possibility and even the need to lose something. The bold and the arrogant among them may even say: why should I feel guilty anyway? I deserve everything I have. Of course, yes. They deserve every bit of it, because at the individual level, people may very well have worked hard for what they possess. Of course, no. The entire social context in which those personal struggles took place was seriously flawed. Ultimately, individuals who have benefited from that flawed environment cannot deny responsibility. To deny responsibility is to affirm indirectly the perception that there has indeed been no change.

There is one area of negotiation that produces many heated words: Affirmative Action. It is designed not to make people lose jobs, but to ensure that those who have been left out previously through parliamentary injustice can find jobs. And there lie the problems.

Whenever I hear this expression, affirmative action, I boil inside. Affirmative action represents concessions that the powerful make for the oppressed. In the land of its origins, the United States of America, affirmative action is a strategy to manage the demand for redress for those who can never hope ever to seize the instruments of government as a group. The context of their struggle has been civil rights, not national liberation. In South Africa, to adopt this strategy is to distort our perceptions of the objective goal; it enables us to assume the mentality of being a dominated minority, rather than experience ourselves as a struggling, free majority, free even to make mistakes. Free, to quote Babel, to write our bad novels.

Affirmative action is a programme for the oppressed. Free people talk about the need for education and skills in a reconstructive national environment. Free people appreciate the need to learn from experience. They are not chained to keeping going something they had no part in establishing; they are not chained to the need to maintain efficiency that does not contain the content of their lives. They learn through the sweat and frustrations of reconstruction. They know that the future will not be easy; that there are new things to be learned; that during the struggle they accumulated so much experience that as a result there is so much that they are good at, and that it is that experience that must form the new society.

The maintenance of corporate efficiency will not be sufficient justification to keep people oppressed, to deny people freedom. Reference is always being made to the "chaos" in the north. One will not deny many of the allegations. But in reality, the "chaos" up north is the chaos of historically free people making their own and understandable mistakes, which they learn from. It is a much better lesson for it calls for the kind of creative involvement in the search for solutions which makes people experience themselves as true participants in history.

Paulo Freire has said that only the oppressed can free both themselves and their oppressors from the shackles of the past. But for the oppressed to feel that the moral high ground belongs to them, they have to experience themselves as having the power to be magnanimous, generous, and forgiving. Do the oppressed feel that power in our country at this point in our history?

No. I cannot and can never demand other people's guilt; but I do want justice. I cannot ask people to confess their sins, or to indulge in any kind of self-flagellation (unless they do so voluntarily—even though I would never enjoy the sight of them doing so). Guilt is too personal a feeling. To demand it of someone is to invade a personal domain that can result in humiliation. It results in no solace for both sides. Justice, on the other hand, yields not humiliation but knowledge and responsibility.

And the search for justice is the path by which the struggle for redress is dramatised, and the means by which the struggle between fairness and unfairness is made visible through a legitimate institutional instrument. It leads to decisive corrective action.

The past is knocking constantly on the doors of our perceptions, refusing to be forgotten, because it is deeply embedded in the present. To neglect it at this most crucial of moments in our history is to postpone the future.

1994

Ngitji Ngitji

Ngitji Ngitji (Mona Tur-Kennedy, b. 1936) was born in Antagaringa country in South Australia to an Aboriginal mother and an Irish father. An Antagaringa elder, she writes poetry and prose and is a teacher and translator of Aboriginal languages. She has written several critical articles on Aboriginal literature in the journal *Identity*.

Ngitji's "The Possum Woman," which clearly belongs to the oral tradition, shows that the Australian Aboriginal society operates on its own set of beliefs and myths. It can be compared with Philip Sherlock's West Indian-Amerindian creation myth "The Warau People Discover the Earth" and Buhkwujjenene's Canadian folk tale "Nanaboozhoo Creates the World."

The Possum Woman

This legend is dedicated to my late beloved mother, who passed away 9 December 1978. For many years, Mother told my sister and I this legend. Our mother was an Antagaringa Elder. — N.N.

Long ago in the Dream[1] Time, a man and his wife lived in a far-away country. These two would sleep by day. Each night, the woman would go hunting possums. She would take up her killing stick. Her husband would hear her singing in the distance: "I'm going to kill the possums by pulling them out of the hollow of the trees."

The possum woman was very tall with beautiful long hair which hung to the ground. When she caught the possums she would tie them up on top of her head with her hair and a string made of animal hair. When she returned home in the morning she would undo her hair. All of the possums fell out. Her husband then cleaned the possums, cooked meat and later on, when ready, put the meat in a bark shelter to eat.

One night the husband felt uneasy when his wife was ready to go hunting. His nose made a cracking noise, which means bad luck. Even today Aboriginals believe this. He told her to take care. That night she set off singing until she was near the hills.

Suddenly her husband heard an echo of her song, then silence. He waited all night for her return. At daybreak he followed her footprints to the rocks near a hill. There were drops of blood but no strange footprints.

He climbed the rocks. As he looked over the rocks, to his amazement he saw a great giant asleep near the fire. The bones of his wife lay nearby, pieces of her beautiful hair everywhere, her blood spilled on the ground.

The angry husband speared the giant through the heart. He was a very clever man. He said, "I'll bring her back to life."

---

[1] *Dream* For the Australian Aboriginal, "dream" is the closest English word for the mystical insights gained in dreams into all that is known and understood in human existence.

So he gathered up all the scattered bones, hair, blood, then brought her back to life as she was before. He told her, "I told you long ago not to sing while hunting. A devil or something worse can hurt you."

Later they went to live in another place. The possum woman never sang again as she hunted.

1990

Ngugi wa Thiong'o

Ngugi wa Thiong'o (James Ngugi; b. 1938) was born in Kenya and educated at Makerere University, Uganda, and Leeds University, England. A teacher, novelist, essayist, and play-wright, in the 1980s Ngugi temporarily abandoned using English as the primary language of his work in favour of Gikuyu, his native tongue. His works include *The Black Hermit* (play, 1963), *Weep Not, Child* (novel, 1964), *A Grain of Wheat* (novel, 1967), *Secret Lives, and Other Stories* (1976), *Petals of Blood* (novel, 1977), *Decolonising the Mind: The Politics of Language in African Literature* (1986), and *Wizard of the Crow: A Novel* (2006).

Ngugi's "Goodbye Africa" is written from the point of view of a British protagonist in Kenya toward the end of the colonial period. It is, on one level, an interracial love triangle. On an allegorical level, it portrays the exploitation of Africa by Europe. Consider this in light of Caryl Phillips's essay on Chinua Achebe's reading of Joseph Conrad's *Heart of Darkness*, "Out of Africa: The Case Against Conrad." Ngugi's story deliberately parallels the treatment of Africans by Europeans with the Duke's domination of his wife in Robert Browning's "His Last Duchess." Four paragraphs from the end of the story, the protagonist mentions "his thousand-year-old name"; compare this with Browning's "nine-hundred-year-old name." Note also the parallel phrasing toward the end of the official's second entry in his book in Ngugi's story (p. 387) and toward the end of Browning's poem (line 12 from the end of the poem): "I gave command/s."

Goodbye Africa

She was in the kitchen making coffee. She loved making coffee even in the daytime when the servants were around. The smell of real coffee soothed her. Besides, the kitchen was a world to her. Her husband never went in there.

He was now in the sitting room, and to him the noise from the disturbed crockery seemed to issue from another land. He picked a book from the glass-fronted shelf. He sat down on the sofa, opened the book at random, but did not read it. He just let it drop beside him.

She came in, holding a wooden tray with both hands. She enjoyed the feel of things made from wood. She put the tray on a table at the corner of the room. Then she arranged side tables, one for him and the other for herself. She sat down to her coffee, facing him. She saw his look was fixed past her. He did not seem to have noticed his cup of coffee. She stood up as if to go to him. But instead she picked up a tiny piece of paper on the floor and sat down again. She liked her house to be specklessly clean.

"The thought of leaving didn't bother me until tonight," she said, and knew it was not true. She felt the triteness of her comment and kept quiet.

He avoided her look and now played with the cup. He thought about everything and nothing. Suddenly, he felt bitter: why did she judge him all the time? Why couldn't she at least speak out her silent accusations?

And she thought he must also be sad at leaving. Fifteen years is not a small period of one's life and God, I don't make it easy for him. She was filled with sudden compassion. She made sweet, pious resolutions. I'll try to understand him. For a start, I'll open my heart to him, tonight. Now she walked up to his side, placed her left hand on his shoulder: "Come to bed, you must be tired, all that noise at the party."

He put down his cup and patted the hand on his shoulder, before removing it gently. "Go. I'll soon join you." She felt a suggestion of impatience in his voice. And he was angry because his hand was not steady.

My hands are losing their firmness, he was thinking. Or did I drink too much? No, my hand suddenly became weak, so weak. She was laughing at me. Was it my fault, what, what fault? I didn't mean to do it. I couldn't have meant it, he insisted harder now addressing himself to his absent wife. He drove me into it, he whispered uncertainly, going to the low cupboard by the wall, and taking out the only remaining bottle of whisky. Scotch, Johnny Walker born 1840 and still walking strong. He laughed a little. He poured himself a glass, and gulped it down, poured another, drank and then went back to the seat keeping the bottle beside him. Why then should a thing that never happened — well — perhaps it did happen, but he never meant it — how could it come to trouble him?

He had forgotten about the incident until these, his last months in Africa. Then he had started re-enacting the scene in his dreams, the vision becoming more and more vivid as days and months whistled by. At first the face had only appeared to him by night. His bed held terror for him. Then suddenly, these last few days, the face started appearing before him in broad daylight. Why didn't he get visitations from all the other Mau Mau[1] terrorists he had tortured and killed? Except the man, that!

Yet he knew the man was not like the others. This man had worked for him as a shamba boy.[2] A nice, God-fearing, submissive boy. A model of his type. He loved the boy and often gave him presents. Old shoes, old clothes. Things like that. He remembered the gratitude in the boy's face and his gestures of appreciation, a little comic perhaps, and it had made giving them worthwhile. It was this feeling of doing something for the people here that made the things you had to put up with bearable. Here in Africa you felt you were doing something tangible, something that was immediately appreciated. Not like in Europe where nobody seemed to care what you did, where even the poor in the East of London refused to seize opportunities offered them. The Welfare State. G-r-r-r! Such thoughts had made him feel that the boy was more than a servant. He felt somehow fatherly towards him ... responsible, and the boy was his. Then one Christmas, the boy suddenly threw back at him the gift of a long coat and ten shillings. The boy had laughed and walked out of his service. For a long time, he could never forget the laughter. This he could have

[1] *Mau Mau* The Mau Mau, led by Jomo Kenyatta, fought the British for Kenya's independence during the 1950s.
[2] *shamba boy* Shamba boys were colonial house or yard boys who hung around their white masters, imitating their behaviour.

forgiven. But the grief and the misery in his wife's face at the news of the boy's disappearance was something else. For this he could never forgive the boy. Later when the Mau Mau War broke out, he, as a screening officer, was to meet the boy.

He drank steadily as if in vengeance for years of abstinence and outward respectability. The ceiling, the floor, the chairs swam in the air. I'll be all right if I go for a drive, for a small drive, he suggested to himself, and staggered out daring the man to appear before him with that sneering laughter.

He got into the car. The headlights swept away the darkness. He did not know where he was going, he just abandoned himself to the road. Sometimes he would recognize a familiar tree or a signpost then he would go into a blackout and drive blindly. In this way, dozing, waking, telling himself to hold on to the steering wheel, he swerved round sharp corners and bends, down the valley, avoiding, miraculously, one or two vehicles from the opposite direction. What am I doing? I am mad, he muttered and unexpectedly swerved to the right, leaving the road, and just managing to avoid crashing into a passing train at the crossing. He drove through the grass into the forest; he hit into bumps, brushed against tree stumps, again miraculously avoided hitting the tree trunks. I must stop this, he thought, and to prove that he had not yet lost his head, he braked the car to a sudden standstill.

He had heard of rituals in the dark. He had even read somewhere that some of the early European settlers used to go to African sorcerers, to have curses lifted. He had considered these things opposed to reason: but what had happened to him, the visions, surely worked against the normal laws of reason. No, he would exorcise the hallucinations from his system, here, in the dark. The idea was attractive and, in his condition, irresistible. Africa does this to you, he thought as he stripped himself naked. He now staggered out of the car and walked a little distance into the forest. Darkness and the forest buzzing crept around him. He was afraid, but he stood his ground. What next? He did not know anything about African magic. At home he had heard vague things like faerie folk, rowan trees, stolen babies and kelpies. He had heard, or read, that you could make waxen images of somebody you wanted to harm and at the dead of the night stick pins into the eyes. Maybe he ought to do this; he would make an image of that man, his former shamba boy, and prick his eyes. Then he remembered that he had not brought any wax and danced with fury, alone in the forest.

No, that'll never do, he thought, now ashamed of things of the dark. I want to know what went wrong that even my wife laughs at me. He went back to the car, hoping to find out why things in Kenya, everywhere, were falling, falling apart. He had never thought a day would come when a government would retire him and replace him with a black. The shame of it. And his wife looking at him with those eyes. Another idea more irresistible than the first now possessed him. I'll write to her. I'll write to the world. He fished out a notebook and started writing furiously. Inspiration already made him feel light and buoyant within. The light in the car dimly lit the pages, but he did not mind, because words, ideas, were all in his head, he butchered his life and tried to examine it, at the same time defending himself before her, before the world.

... I know you have seen me shake before that face. You have refused to comment, perhaps not to hurt me. But you laughed at me all the time, didn't you? Don't deny it. I've seen it in your eyes and looks. I know you think me a failure. I never rose beyond the rank of Senior D.O. Africa has ruined me, but I never got a chance, really. Oh, don't look at me with those blue eyes as if you thought I lied. Maybe you are saying there's a tide in the affairs of men. O.K. I neglected it. We neglected it. But what tide? Oh, I am tired.

He stopped and read over what he had written. He turned over another page. Inspiration came in waves. His hand was too slow for what begged to come out.

... What went wrong, I keep on asking myself? Was it wrong for us, with our capital, with our knowledge, with our years of Christian civilization to open and lift a dark country onto the stage of history? I played my part. Does it matter if promotion was slow? Does it matter if there were ups and downs? And there were many moments of despair. I remember the huts we burnt. Even then I did ask myself: had I fallen so low? My life reduced to burning down huts and yet more huts? Had my life come to a cul-de-sac? And yet we could not let atavistic violence destroy all that had taken so many years and so many lives to build. When I had reached the nadir of my despair, I met that man — our shamba boy. Do you remember him? The one who spurned my gift and disappeared, maybe to the forest? He stood in the office with that sneer in his face — like — like the devil. The servile submissive face when he worked for you had gone. He had that strange effect on me — when I remembered the grief he caused you — well — made me boil inside — I felt a violent rage within such as I had never felt before — I could not bear that grin. I stood and spat into his face. And that arrogant stare never left his face even as he cleared off the spit with the back of his left hand. Isn't it strange that I forget his name now, that I never really knew his name? Did you? I only remember that he was tall and there in the office I saw the violence in his eyes. I was afraid of him. Can you believe it? I, afraid of a black man? Afraid of my former shamba boy? What happened later, I cannot remember, I cannot explain, I was not myself, I only saw the face of the man. At night, in the morning, I saw the grin, the sneer, the arrogant indifference. And he would not confess to anything. I gave command. He was taken to the forest. I never saw him again ...

He wrote in fury; images flowed, merged, clashed: it was as if he had a few days to live and he wanted to purge his soul of something. A confession to a priest before the gallows fell. He was now shivering. But he was still possessed ... I'm writing this to you, I am alone in the forest, and in the world. I want to begin a new life with you in England, after saying goodbye to Africa.... And now he discovered he had no clothes and that he was shivering. He felt ashamed of his nakedness and quickly put on his clothes. But he could not continue with his confession and he feared to read it over in case he changed his mind. He was now almost sober, but very excited at the prospect of giving his life to her, tonight.

She was not yet asleep. She too was determined to wait for him to come back so that they could share their last night in Africa. In bed, she allowed her mind to glance backwards over her life, over her relationship with him. At first, in their early days in Kenya, she had tried to be enthusiastic about his civilizing zeal and his ambitions. She too was determined to play her part, to give life a purpose. She attended a few meetings of African women in the ridges and even learnt a smattering of Swahili. Then she wanted to understand Africa, to touch the centre, and feel the huge continent throb on her fingers. In those days she and he were close, their hearts seemed to beat together. But with the passage of years, he had gone farther and farther away. She lost her original enthusiasm: the ideas that had earlier appeared so bright faded and became rusty in her eyes. Who were they to civilize anyone? What was civilization anyway? And why did he fret because he could not climb up the ladder as quickly as he wanted? She became slightly impatient with this rusty thing that took him away from her, but she would not disturb him, ruin his career. So she went to the parties, did her share of small talk, and wanted to cry. Ought she to have spoken, then, she wondered now, wriggling in bed, puzzled by his late night drive. She gave up meetings in the villages. She wanted to be alone. She did not want to understand Africa. Why should she? She had not tried to understand Europe, or Australia where she was born. No. You could never hope to embrace the meaning of a continent in your small palms, you could only love. She wanted to live her own life, and not as a prop to another's climb to a top that promised no fuller life.

So she went for walks alone in the countryside: she saw children playing and wondered what it would feel like to have a child. When would her first arrive in this strange world? She was awed by the thick crowds of banana plants, the thick bush and forests. That was just before the Emergency when you could walk down alone anywhere without fear.

It was during one of her walks that the boy had first made love to her among the banana plantations. Freedom. And afterward their fevered love-making had finally severed her from the world of her husband and other District Officers.

Arriving home, he found she was not yet asleep. He went towards her, riding on low exciting waves. He did not put on the light but sat on the bed without speaking.

"Where have you been?"

"I went for a drive — seeing the old place for the last time."

"Come into bed then, God, how cold you are! And here I was waiting for you to give me warmth."

"You know it's always chilly at night."

"Come on then."

She felt she had to tell him now in the dark, about her lover. She did not want to look into his face in case she changed her mind. She put out her hand and stroked his head, feeling for a way to start. Now. Her heart was beating. Was she scared?

"I want to tell you something," she removed her hand from his head, and paused, the next words refusing to come out. "Will you forgive me?"

"Of course I will, everything." He was impatient. What could she tell him greater than what he had written, red-hot, filling the notebook. He wanted to tell her how he had exorcised the ghost of the shamba boy from his life. He waited hoping she would finish quickly. He meant to give her the notebook and withdraw to the bathroom to give her time to see his bare soul.

"Of course I can forgive you anything," he said by way of encouragement. "Go on," he whispered gently into the dark room.

She told him about the shamba boy — her lover.

He listened and felt energy and blood leave his body.

Would he forgive her? She only wanted them to start a new life. She finished, her voice fading into dark silence. She listened to her heart-beat waiting for him to speak.

But he did not speak. A kind of dullness had crept into his limbs, into his mouth, into the heart. The man. His shamba boy. For an answer he stood up and started toward the door.

"Darling, please!" She called out, for the first time feeling dark terror at his lack of words. "Don't go. It was long way back, before the Emergency."

But he continued walking, out through the door, into the sitting room. He sat on the sofa exactly where he had earlier. Automatically, he started fingering the unfinished cup of coffee.

For all his visions of moral ideals in the service of British capitalism, he was a vain man: he never really saw himself in any light but that of an adequate husband. He had no cause, within himself, to doubt her fidelity to him as a man, or a husband. How then could this woman, his wife, bring herself to sleep with that man, that creature? How make herself so cheap, drag his thousand-year-old name to mud, and such mud?

He had followed a dream for too long. He would not let the dream go despite the reality around him. In his colonizing mission and his zeal to reach the top he had neglected his house and another had occupied it. In this, perhaps, he was not alone. But how could he know this as he sat in the middle of the room, the bare walls staring at him? The cup fell out of his hands and broke into pieces. He stood up and walked around the room, slowly, looking at nothing, seeing neither yesterday nor tomorrow. Then he took out his notebook and opened it at random:

The white man in Africa must accept a more stringent moral code in the family and in the society at large. For we must set the ideals to which our African subjects must aspire.

He closed the notebook and walked into the kitchen where he never went before. He took a match, struck it, and watched the notebook burn. He watched the flame, saw his flesh burn, but he felt no pain, nothing. The man's ghost would forever pursue him. Africa.

1975

Oodgeroo Noonuccal

Oodgeroo Noonuccal (Kath Walker, 1920–93) was born in Australia. She was a member of the Noonuccal tribe and was an activist for her people. She published several poetry volumes, including *We Are Going* (1964), children's stories, and such traditional tales as *Siradbroke Dreamtime* (1972).

Noonuccal's "Gooboora, the Silent Pool" and "The Past" are both poems about the fading Aboriginal culture and tradition in Australia. The first is a lamentation for the past, the second is a belief—perhaps a rationalization—that the past is not dead; it remains a vital part of the present. Compare this poem with Mary TallMountain's "There Is No Word for Goodbye."

Gooboora, the Silent Pool

for Grannie Sunflower, last of the Noonuccals

Gooboora, Gooboora, the Water of Fear
That awed the Noonuccals once numerous here,
The Bunyip[1] is gone from your bone-strewn bed,
And the clans departed to drift with the dead.

Once in the far time before the whites came
How light were their hearts in the dance and the game!
Gooboora, Gooboora, to think that today
A whole happy tribe are all vanished away!

What mystery lurks by the Water of Fear,
And what is the secret still lingering here?
For birds hasten by as in days of old,
No wild thing will drink of your waters cold.

Gooboora, Gooboora, still here you remain,
But where are my people I look for in vain?
They are gone from the hill, they are gone from the shore,
And the place of the Silent Pool knows them no more.

But I think they still gather when daylight is done
And stand round the pool at the setting of sun,

---

[1] *Bunyip* A mythical creature in Aboriginal mythology. There are various descriptions of it, including its possessing a snake-like tail, tusks, and flippers. Early settlers to Australia believed it to be real.

A shadowy band that is now without care,
Fearing no longer the Thing in its lair.

Old Death has passed by you but took the dark throng;
Now lost is the Noonuccal language and song.
Gooboora, Gooboora, it makes the heart sore
That you should be here but my people no more!

1970

The Past

Let no one say the past is dead.
The past is all about us and within.
Haunted by tribal memories, I know
This little now, this accidental present
Is not the all of me, whose long making
Is so much of the past.

Tonight here in suburbia as I sit
In easy chair before electric heater,
Warmed by the red glow, I fall into dream:
I am away
at the camp fire in the bush, among
My own people, sitting on the ground,
No walls about me,
The stars over me,
The tall surrounding trees that stir in the wind
Making their own music,
Soft cries of the night coming to us, there
Where we are one with all old Nature's lives
Known and unknown,
In scenes where we belong but have now forsaken.
Deep chair and electric radiator
Are but since yesterday,
But a thousand thousand camp fires in the forest
Are in my blood.
Let none tell me the past is wholly gone.
Now is so small a part of time, so small a part
Of all the race years that have moulded me.

1970

Gabriel Okara

Gabriel Okara (Imomotimi Gbaingbain, b. 1921) was born and educated in Nigeria. He worked as a schoolteacher, bookbinder, and businessman until 1953, when his poem "Call of the River Nun" won a poetry award. His publications include *The Fisherman's Invocation* (poetry, 1978), *The Voice* (novel, 1964), and two books for children, *Little Snake and Little Frog* (1981) and *An Adventure to Juju Island* (1981).

Okara's "The Snowflakes Sail Gently Down" was written when Okara was completing a degree in comparative journalism at Northwestern University in Evanston, Illinois, where he saw snow for the first time. He compares the winter-weary world with his own vibrant tropical world, which he hopes will eventually be free of the "uprooters" (imperialists?). Consider the significance of the title and of the deliberate contrasting of the image of mourners in the first stanza with that of salaaming Muslims in the last stanza. (Northern Nigeria has a large Muslim population.) Compare this poem with Dennis Brutus's "By the Waters of Babylon" and Sasenarine Persaud's "Gifting the Light of the Soul."

The Snowflakes Sail Gently Down

The snowflakes sail gently
down from the misty eye of the sky
and fall lightly on the
winter-weary elms. And the branches
winter-stripped and nude, slowly
with the weight of the weightless snow
bow like grief-stricken mourners
as white funeral cloth is slowly
unrolled over deathless earth.
And dead sleep stealthily from the
heater rose and closed my eyes with
the touch of silk cotton on water falling.

Then I dreamed a dream
in my dead sleep. But I dreamed
not of earth dying and elms a vigil
keeping. I dreamed of birds, black
birds flying in my inside, nesting
and hatching on oil palms bearing suns
for fruits and with roots denting the
uprooters' spades. And I dreamed the
uprooters tired and limp, leaning on my roots —

their abandoned roots
and the oil palms gave them each a sun.

But on their palms
they balanced the blinding orbs
and frowned with schisms on their
brows — for the suns reached not
the brightness of gold!
Then I awoke. I awoke
to the silently falling snow
and bent-backed elms bowing and
swaying to the winter wind like
white-robed Moslems salaaming at evening
prayer, and the earth lying inscrutable
like the face of a god in a shrine.

1970

Michael Ondaatje

Michael Ondaatje (b. 1943) was born in Sri Lanka (Ceylon) of mixed Tamil, Sinhalese, and Dutch parents. He immigrated to Canada by way of the United Kingdom in 1962. His many volumes of poetry and prose include *Coming Through Slaughter* (1976), *There's a Trick with a Knife I'm Learning to Do* (1979), *Running in the Family* (1982), *The English Patient* (1992), *Anil's Ghost* (2000), and *Divisadero* (2007). He is also a filmmaker and has written a critical study, *Leonard Cohen* (1970).

Ondaatje's "Light" illuminates what Oodgeroo Noonuccal says about the perennial presence of the past in her poem "The Past." Ondaatje's speaker is particularly aware of how much his extended ancestral family is a part of him. Ondaatje's thumbnail sketches of them here could be compared with fuller portraits in his 1982 memoir, *Running in the Family*. Consider the ambiguity of the title "Light" and the significance of setting the speaker's present time sequence during a stormy night punctuated by lightning.

Light

for Doris Gratiaen

Midnight storm. Trees walking off across the fields in fury
naked in the spark of lightning.
I sit on the white porch on the brown hanging cane chair
coffee in my hand midnight storm midsummer night.
The past, friends and family, drift into the rain shower.
Those relatives in my favourite slides
re-shot from old minute photographs so they now stand
complex ambiguous grainy on my wall.

This is my Uncle who turned up to his marriage
on an elephant. He was a chaplain.
This shy looking man in the light jacket and tie was infamous,
when he went drinking he took the long blonde beautiful hair
of his wife and put one end in the cupboard and locked it
leaving her tethered in an armchair.
He was terrified of her possible adultery
and this way died peaceful happy to the end.
My Grandmother, who went to a dance in a muslin dress
with fireflies captured and embedded in the cloth, shining
and witty. This calm beautiful face

organised wild acts in the tropics.
She hid the mailman in her house
after he had committed murder and at the trial
was thrown out of the court for making jokes at the judge.
Her son became a Q.C.
This is my brother at 6. With his cousin and his sister
and Pam de Voss who fell on a pen-knife and lost her eye.
My Aunt Christie. She knew Harold Macmillan[1] was a spy
communicating with her through pictures in the newspapers.
Every picture she believed asked her to forgive him,
his hound eyes pleading.
Her husband Uncle Fitzroy a doctor in Ceylon had a memory
sharp as scalpels into his 80's
though I never bothered to ask him about anything
—interested then more in the latest recordings of Bobby Darin.[2]

And this is my Mother with her brother Noel in fancy dress.
They are 7 and 8 years old, a hand-coloured photograph,
it is the earliest picture I have. The one I love most.
A picture of my kids at Halloween
has the same contact and laughter.
My Uncle dying at 68, and my Mother a year later dying at 68.
She told me about his death and the day he died
his eyes clearing out of illness as if seeing
right through the room the hospital and she said
he saw something so clear and good his whole body
for a moment became youthful and she remembered
when she sewed badges on his trackshirts.
Her voice joyous in telling me this, her face light and clear.
(My firefly Grandmother also dying at 68.)

These are the fragments I have of them, tonight
in this storm, the dogs restless on the porch.
They were all laughing, crazy, and vivid in their prime.
At a party my drunk Father
tried to explain a complex operation on chickens
and managed to kill them all in the process, the guests
having dinner an hour later while my Father slept
and the kids watched the servants clean up the litter
of beaks and feathers on the lawn.

---

[1] *Harold Macmillan* (Maurice) Harold Macmillan (1894-1986) was Prime Minister of England, 1957-63.

[2] *Bobby Darin* Bobby Darin (1936-73) was a pop music star in the 1950s and 1960s.

These are their fragments, all I remember,
wanting more knowledge of them. In the mirror and in my kids
I see them in my flesh. Wherever we are
they parade in my brain and the expanding stories
connect to the grey grainy pictures on the wall,
as they hold their drinks or 20 years later
hold grandchildren, pose with favourite dogs,
coming through the light, the electricity, which the storm
destroyed an hour ago, a tree going down by the highway
so that now inside the kids play dominoes by candlelight
and out here the thick rain static the spark of my match
                                        to a cigarette
and the trees across the fields leaving me, distinct
lonely in their own knife scars and cow-chewed bark
frozen in the jagged light as if snapped in their run
the branch arms waving to what was a second ago the dark sky
when in truth like me they haven't moved.
Haven't moved an inch from me.

1979

Sasenarine Persaud

Sasenarine Persaud (b. 1958) was born in Guyana. He lived in Toronto before relocating to Miami, Florida. He is a poet, novelist, and critic, whose publications include *The Ghost of Bellow's Man* (novel, 1992), *Demerara Telepathy* (poems, 1988), *Canada Geese and Apple Chatney* (stories, 1998), and *A Writer Like You* (poems, 2002).

Persaud's "Gifting the Light of the Soul" offers insights into an immigrant speaker's ambivalence as he longs for home as much as those left at home long for his return; yet they understand his wanting to remain to make something of himself in his adopted world. As this poem demonstrates, Persaud draws heavily on his Hindu culture while writing in the Anglo-American tradition. Do you think the poet is setting up a contrast between the "light of the world" (in the epigraph from Derek Walcott) and "the light of the soul"? Compare this poem with David Dabydeen's "Catching Crabs," Dennis Brutus's "By the Waters of Babylon," Shirley Geok-lin Lim's "To Li Poh," and Nourbese Philip's "Sprung Rhythm."

Gifting the Light of the Soul

And I had abandoned them, I knew that there
sitting in the transport, in the sea-quiet dusk…
There was nothing they wanted, nothing I could give them
but this thing I have called "The Light of the World"
        DEREK WALCOTT, "The Light of the World"

They sent me little packages of pepper and thyme,
the condiments of India in tight-lipped bottles
of mustard oil chatney pickle and brine, and once
even a coconut branch broom—but no word no note
which spoke of the land and no letter which would
uncover the hurt. I did not return, I did not return
to the picture in the August grass. K. kneeling
and aiming a toy gun at the photographer, somebody
placing a cricketer's cap on my head, another
thumbing sunlight at the camera lens; ma's smile
in the little girl's eyes near the bank of pepper
and thyme. We were once together after ma died
and they walled her in—mamoo[1] coming too late
from the bush on his face. He too returned

---

[1] *mamoo* Maternal uncle.

to the dredges and the forest like Rama in banwaas,[1]
returned to the diving on the riverbeds for
diamonds and gold: little fragments of self
remaindered in the east; the plane stuck in the
muck of a mountain airstrip, and when finally
the rain lifted and he flew to the coast again
it was too late — pa already fleshless and the pyre
down to ashes. Mamoo finally wrapped the dhoti[2]
and made offerings to the fire, puja[3] to the manes
and puja to the world.

It was too late.
I had set out for my soul with memories
of wild birds pecking from the palms
of pa standing in the wind — if the new house had
nothing it must have a verandah touching
the purple starapples closing on the grey
goldenapple branches, freckled with lemon butterflies
and fan-necked lizards wary of the slyeyed sleepy cats.

They stood aside
and let me scatter those ashes of the girdle we
had come from, unburnt pieces of pelvic bones
commingling with red hibiscus, milk-and-purple
madar,[4] mauve jasmine and pink oleander. They
set me out alone on the bow of the boat

in the ocean, let me out alone with the blessing
and the darshan:[5] I the Sanskritist uttering
the ancient prayer to the drumming waves on
wooden guardrail, salt spray on greenheart planks
on cotton on eyes on hands relinquishing the petals
and the ashed bones.

I could not return
and they wept for me. To go and be great and
come back empty hearted. Unreturning progress

---

[1] *banwaas* Forest or exile.

[2] *dhoti* Unstitched cloth wrapped about the waist and the legs, and knotted at the waist.

[3] *puja* Worship or prayer ceremony.

[4] *madar* A plant whose flowers are used in Hindu prayer ceremonies.

[5] *darshan* Vision of (and blessing from) the divine.

reports and their pride in the writing.
All the love, ah the love — but when
the returning — unuttered and unwritten.

                        They send me little
packages, parcels of pepper and thyme — and the
condiments of India in bottled pickle and brine.
But I could not return and could send them nothing
save the songs of a wandering brahmin
and the fastidious yogi silence.

1995

M. NourbeSe Philip

M. NourbeSe Philip (b. 1947) was born in Trinidad (Tobago). She moved to Canada in 1968. A lawyer and activist against racism, she has several collections of essays, including *A Genealogy of Resistance and Other Essays* (1997). Her other publications include *She Tries Her Tongue: Her Silence Softly Breaks* (poems, 1989), *Harriet's Daughter* (young adult novel, 1988), and *Looking for Livingstone: An Odyssey of Silence* (a narrative in prose and verse, 1991).

Philip's "Sprung Rhythm" is another exile or immigrant poem in which the speaker recalls nostalgically the land of her childhood and youth (which here is Tobago, if we accept that the speaker's experience derives from the poet's). The question at the end of the poem shows how conflicted the speaker is in relating to her original and her adopted homes. Compare this poem with Dennis Brutus's "By the Waters of Babylon," Gabriel Okara's "The Snowflakes Sail Gently Down," and Sasenarine Persaud's "Gifting the Light of the Soul." Do you think that Philip is drawing attention to Gerard Manley Hopkins's "sprung rhythm"—a poetic rhythm intended to imitate the rhythm of speech (with accented syllables that "spring" out) rather than regular metrical patterns?

Sprung Rhythm

It was there I learnt to walk
in sprung rhythm,
talk in syncopated bursts of music,
moulding, kneading, distorting, enhancing
a foreign language.
There, family was the whole village, if not island,
and came in all shades of black;
there, I first heard the soporific roar
of the ocean, before I grew ears to hear.
Where fear was wind and wind was fear,
and terror had branches that moved,
swayed, cracked, moaned, hissed ... bent low with the trees
There, the swollen heavy bellied sky pressed
hard against a small hand clutching
a mother's skirt, before the rains came;
and the sun was always certain,
as we were of it.
Where every yellow March, the poui mocked
Sir Walter Raleigh's gesture to his queen,

and spread its coat of sunshine for me,[1]
and the graceful ole time bougainvillea
stroked and brushed heads of boys and girls.
Colour like life was put on
thick with an artist's knife — not brush.
Red was hibiscus, cock's combs and pomeracs,[2]
and Jacob's coat was a hedge of croton.
There, where neat days patiently dovetailed
each other, glued with rituals of purgings,
school, washing and braiding of hair,
Sunday mass and blackpudding[3] breakfasts.
Was it there that I found the place
to know from,
to laugh and be from, to return and weep from?
Was it there, or was it here?

1983

---

[1] *The poui… for me* The poui tree is a large flowering tree. Its abundance of falling flowers creates a carpet that reminds the speaker of Sir Walter Raleigh gallantly spreading his coat over a puddle for Queen
Elizabeth I to step over safely.

[2] *pomeracs* Red pear-shaped tropical fruit.

[3] *blackpudding* A sausage-like food prepared usually by stuffing rice, blood, and spicy ingredients in pigs'
cleaned intestines; similar to haggis.

Caryl Phillips

Caryl Phillips (b. 1958) was born in St. Kitts, Eastern Caribbean. He left with his parents for the United Kingdom, settling in Leeds. A novelist, essayist, and playwright, he currently lives in the United States. He has published several novels, including *The Final Passage* (1985), *A State of Independence* (1986), *The Nature of Blood* (1997), *A Distant Shore* (2003), and *Dancing in the Dark* (2005). His collections of essays include *The European Tribe* (1987), *The Atlantic Sound* (2000), and *A New World Order: Selected Essays* (2001).

Phillips's "Out of Africa: The Case Against Conrad" is an engaging discussion of the perennial issue of whether Joseph Conrad's *Heart of Darkness* is racist. A prominent advocate of the affirmative is Chinua Achebe, whom Phillips interviews on this matter while offering his own views. As we read this essay, we should keep in mind that though Conrad censures colonial exploitation of Africa, he tolerates it because of the "idea" that along with the exploitation comes "civilization." Conrad's novella could be compared with E.M. Forster's *A Passage to India*, a work that demonstrates Forster's liberal criticism of British treatment of Indians but does not challenge the God-given right of Britons to be in India as proselytizers of "civilization" (advocated by many, including Lord Curzon, Viceroy of India between 1898 and 1905, and Rudyard Kipling in his piece in this anthology).

Out of Africa: The Case Against Conrad

Chinua Achebe[1] leans forward to make his point. He raises a gentle finger in the manner of a benevolent schoolmaster. "But you have to understand. Art is more than just good sentences; this is what makes this situation tragic. The man is a capable artist and as such I expect better from him. I mean, what is his point in that book? Art is not intended to put people down. If so, then art would ultimately discredit itself."

Achebe does not take his eyes from me, and I stare back at him. The face is familiar and marked with the heavy lines of ageing that one would expect to find on a 72-year-old man's face. But Achebe's lines are graceful whorls which suggest wisdom. He leans back now and looks beyond me and through the window at the snowy landscape.

We are sitting in his one-storey house in upstate New York, deep in the wooded campus of Bard College. For the past 13 years, Achebe has been a professor at this well-known liberal arts college, which has had writers such as Mary McCarthy and

---

[1] *Chinua Achebe* Achebe (see his story "Girls at War" in this anthology) gave a lecture (Chancellor's Lecture, University of Massachusetts, 18 February 1975) censuring Joseph Conrad's depiction of Africans in his novella *Heart of Darkness* (1902). It is published in Michael Harper and Robert Stepto's *Chants of Saints* (Urbana: U of Illinois P, 1979): 313-25. Given the interview format employed by Phillips in "Out of Africa: The Case Against Conrad," this essay is perhaps as much Achebe's as his.

Norman Mailer on the faculty. His house is decorated with African art and artifacts, but the landscape and the climate could not be further removed from Nigeria and the world of Achebe's fiction and non-fiction. As though tiring of the wintry landscape, Achebe turns and returns to our conversation.

"The man would appear to be obsessed with 'that' word."

"Nigger?"

Achebe nods.

"He has an admiration of the white skin. It is the whiteness that he likes, and he is obsessed with the physicality of the negro."

Again Achebe falls silent, but this time he lowers his eyes as though suddenly overcome with fatigue. I continue to look at him, the father of African literature in the English language and undoubtedly one of the most important writers of the second half of the 20th century. What I find difficult to fathom is just why Conrad's short novel, *Heart of Darkness*, should exercise such a hold on him. Achebe has taught term-long university courses dedicated to this one slim volume first published in 1902. As long ago as February 1975, while a visiting professor at the University of Massachusetts in Amherst, Achebe delivered a public lecture entitled "An Image of Africa: Racism in Conrad's *Heart of Darkness*." The lecture has since come to be recognized as one of the most important and influential treatises in post-colonial literary discourse. However, the problem is I disagree with Achebe's response to the novel, and have never viewed Conrad — as Achebe states in his lecture — as simply "a thoroughgoing racist." Yet, at the same time, I hold Achebe in the highest possible esteem, and therefore, a two-hour drive up the Hudson River Valley into deepest upstate New York would seem a small price to pay to resolve this conundrum.

Africa is presented to the reader as "the antithesis of Europe and therefore of civilization, a place where man's vaunted intelligence and refinement are finally mocked by triumphant bestiality." Achebe sees Conrad mocking both the African landscape and the African people. The story begins on the "good" River Thames which, in the past, "has been one of the dark places of the earth." The story soon takes us to the "bad" River Congo, presently one of those "dark places." It is a body of water upon which the steamer toils "along slowly on the edge of a black and incomprehensible frenzy." According to Achebe, Conrad's long and famously hypnotic sentences are mere "trickery," designed to induce a hypnotic stupor in the reader. Achebe drafts in the support of "the eagle-eyed English critic F.R. Leavis," who many years ago noted Conrad's "adjectival insistence upon inexpressible and incomprehensible mystery," whose cumulative effect is to suggest that poor Africa is inexplicable.

But it is when Achebe turns to Conrad's treatment of African humanity that he is most disparaging of Conrad's vision. He quotes from the moment in the novel when the Europeans on the steamer encounter real live Africans in the flesh:

We are accustomed to look upon the shackled form of a conquered monster, but there — there you could look at a thing monstrous and free. It was unearthly, and the men were — No, they were not inhuman. Well, you know, that was the worst of it — this suspicion of their not being inhuman. It would come slowly to one. They howled and leaped, and spun, and made horrid faces; but what thrilled you was just the thought of their humanity—like yours—the thought of your remote kinship with this wild and passionate uproar. Ugly. Yes, it was ugly enough; but if you were man enough you would admit to yourself that there was in you just the faintest trace of a response to the terrible frankness of that noise, a dim suspicion of there being a meaning in it which you—and you so remote from the night of first ages—could comprehend.

These people are "ugly," but what is even more disturbing is that they are in some way also human. A half-page later, Conrad focuses on one particular African who, according to Achebe, is rare, for he is not presented as "just limbs or rolling eyes." The problem is that the African man is, most disturbingly, not "in his place."

And between whiles I had to look after the savage who was a fireman. He was an improved specimen; he could fire up a vertical boiler. He was there below me, and upon my word, to look at him was as edifying as seeing a dog in a parody of breeches and a feather hat, walking on his hind legs.

Those critics who have defended *Heart of Darkness* against charges of racism have often pointed to both the methodology of narration and Conrad's anti-colonial purpose. The narrator of the novel is Marlow, who is simply retelling a story that was told to him by a shadowy second figure. However, in his lecture Achebe makes it clear he is not fooled by this narrative gamesmanship, or the claims of those who would argue that the complex polyphony of the storytelling is Conrad's way of trying to deliberately distance himself from the views of his characters.

"… If Conrad's intention is to draw a *cordon sanitaire* between himself and the moral and psychological malaise of his narrator, his care seems to me to be totally wasted because he neglects to hint, clearly and adequately, at an alternative frame of reference by which we may judge the actions and opinions of his characters. It would not have been beyond Conrad's power to make that provision if he had thought it necessary. Conrad seems to me to approve of Marlow…."

Achebe is, however, aware of Conrad's ambivalence towards the colonizing mission, and he concedes that the novel is, in part, an attempt to examine what happens when Europeans come into contact with this particular form of economic and social exploitation. In the lecture he remembers that a student in Scotland once informed him that Africa is "merely a setting for the disintegration of the mind of Mr. Kurtz," which is an argument that many teachers and critics, let alone students, have utilized to defend the novel. But to read the book in this way is to further stir Achebe's outrage.

"Africa as setting and backdrop, which eliminates the African as human factor. Africa as a metaphysical battlefield devoid of all recognizable humanity; into which the wandering European enters at his peril. Can nobody see the preposterous and perverse arrogance in thus reducing Africa to the role of props for the break-up of one petty European mind?"

Achebe has no problem with a novel that seeks to question both European ambivalence towards the colonizing mission and her own "system" of civilization. What he has a huge problem with is a novelist — in fact, an artist — who attempts to resolve these important questions by denying Africa and Africans their full and complex humanity.

During the two-hour drive up the Hudson River Valley through a snow-bound and icy landscape, I thought again of my own response to the novel. There are three remarkable journeys in *Heart of Darkness*. First, Marlow's actual journey up-river to Kurtz's inner station. Second, the larger journey that Marlow takes us on from civilized Europe, back to the beginning of creation when nature reigned, and then back to civilized Europe. And finally, the journey that Kurtz undergoes as he sinks down through the many levels of the self to a place where he discovers unlawful and repressed ambiguities of civilization. In all three journeys, Conrad's restless narrative circles back on itself as though trapped in the complexity of the situation. The overarching question is, what happens when one group of people, supposedly more humane and civilized than another group, attempts to impose themselves upon their "inferiors"? In such circumstances will there always be an individual who, removed from the shackles of "civilized" behaviour, feels compelled to push at the margins of conventional "morality"? What happens to this one individual who imagines himself to be released from the moral order of society and therefore free to behave as "savagely" or as "decently" as he deems fit? How does this man respond to chaos?

Conrad uses colonization, and the trading intercourse that flourished in its wake, to explore these universal questions about man's capacity for evil. The end of European colonization has not rendered *Heart of Darkness* any less relevant, for Conrad was interested in the making of a modern world in which colonization was simply one facet. The uprootedness of people, and their often disquieting encounter with the "other," is a constant theme in his work, and particularly so in this novel. Conrad's writing prepares us for a new world in which modern man has had to endure the psychic and physical pain of displacement, and all the concomitant confusion of watching imagined concrete standards become mutable. Modern descriptions of 20th-century famines, war and genocide all seem to be eerily prefigured by Conrad, and *Heart of Darkness* abounds with passages that seem terrifyingly contemporary in their descriptive accuracy.

Near the same tree two more bundles of acute angles sat with their legs drawn up. One, with his chin propped on his knees, stared at nothing, in an intolerable and appalling manner: his brother phantom rested its forehead, as if overcome with a great weariness; and all about others were scattered in every pose of contorted collapse, as in some picture of a massacre or a pestilence.

As my car moved ever closer to Bard College, I constantly asked myself, was Conrad really a racist? If so, how did I miss this? Written in the wake of the 1884 Berlin Conference, which saw the continent of Africa carved into a "magnificent cake" and divided among European nations, *Heart of Darkness* offers its readers an insight into the "dark" world of Africa. The European world produced the narrator, produced Marlow, and certainly produced the half-French, half-English Kurtz ("All Europe contributed to the making of Kurtz"), but set against the glittering "humanity" of Europe, Conrad presents us with a late-19th-century view of a primitive African world that has produced very little, and is clearly doomed to irredeemable savagery. This world picture would have troubled few of Conrad's original readers, for Conrad was merely providing them with the descriptive "evidence" of the bestial people and the fetid world that they "knew" lay beyond Europe. However, by the end of the 20th, and beginning of the 21st century, Conrad's readers are living in a decolonized—indeed postcolonial—world, and Conrad's brutal depiction of African humanity, so that he might provide a "savage" mirror into which the European might gaze and measure his own tenuous grip on civilization, is now regarded by some, including Achebe, as deeply problematic.

But is it not ridiculous to demand of Conrad that he imagine an African human-ity that is totally out of line with both the times in which he was living and the larger purpose of his novel? In his lecture, even Achebe wistfully concedes that the novel reflects "the dominant image of Africa in the western imagination." And the novel does assert European infamy, for there are countless examples throughout the text that point to Conrad's recognition of the illegitimacy of this trading mission and the brutalizing effect it is having on the Africans. However, the main focus of the novel is the Europeans, and the effect upon them of their encountering another, less "civilized," world. The novel proposes no programme for dismantling European racism or imperialistic exploitation, and as a reader I have never had any desire to confuse it with an equal opportunity pamphlet. I have always believed that Conrad's only programme is doubt; in this case, doubt about the supremacy of European humanity, and the ability of this supposed humanity to maintain its imagined status beyond the high streets of Europe. However, as I pull my car up outside Achebe's house, I already sense I had better shore up my argument with something more resilient than this.

For a moment Achebe has me fooled. He looks as though he has nodded off, but he has just been thinking. This mild-mannered man looks up now and smiles. He returns to the subject we were talking about as though he has merely paused to draw breath.

"Conrad didn't like black people. Great artists manage to be bigger than their times. In the case of Conrad you can actually show that there were people at the same time as him, and before him, who were not racists with regard to Africa."

"Who?" I ask. Achebe says nothing for a moment, and so I continue. "I find it difficult to think of any European writers who have had a benevolent view of Africa. Surely they've all used Africa as a foil."

"Well, Livingstone," suggests Achebe. "He is not a writer, but he is an explorer and Conrad admired explorers. When asked what he thought of Africans, Livingstone replied that he found them 'infuriating.' In other words, they were just like everybody else."

We both fall silent and I think back to Achebe's lecture. That Conrad had some "issues" with black people is beyond doubt. Achebe quotes Conrad who, when recalling his first encounter with a black person, remembers it thus:

A certain enormous buck nigger encountered in Haiti fixed my conception of blind, furious, unreasoning rage, as manifested in the human animal to the end of my days. Of the nigger I used to dream for years afterwards.

Conversely, when the 16-year-old Conrad encounters his first Englishman in Europe, he calls him "my unforgettable Englishman" and described him in the following manner:

[His] calves exposed to the public gaze... dazzled the beholder by the splendour of their marble-like condition and their rich tone of young ivory... The light of a headlong, exalted satisfaction with the world of men... illumined his face... and triumphant eyes. In passing he cast a glance of kindly curiosity and a friendly gleam of big, sound, shiny teeth... his white calves twinkled sturdily.

However, despite Achebe's compelling "evidence" I am still finding it difficult to dismiss this man and his short novel. Are we to throw all racists out of the canon? Are we, as Achebe suggests, to ignore the period in which novels are written and demand that the artist rise above the prejudices of his times? As much as I respect the man sitting before me, something does not ring true. We both agree that Conrad was not the originator of this disturbing image of Africa and Africans. And we both appear to agree that Conrad had the perception to see that this encounter with Africa exposed the fissures and instabilities in so-called European civilization. Further, we both agree that in order to expose European fragility, Conrad pandered to a certain stereotype of African barbarity that, at the time, was accepted as the norm. Finally, we both agree that this stereotype is still with us today. Achebe speaks quickly, as though a thought has suddenly struck him.

"You see, those who say that Conrad is on my side because he is against colonial rule do not understand that I know who is on my side. And where is the proof that he is on my side? A few statements about it not being a very nice thing to exploit people who have flat noses? This is his defence against imperial control? If so it is not enough. It is simply not enough. If you are going to be on my side what is required is a better argument. Ultimately you have to admit that Africans are people. You cannot diminish a people's humanity and defend them."

I feel as though I am walking around an impregnable fortress. However, I am losing interest in the problem of breaching the ramparts and becoming more concerned with the aesthetics of its construction.

"Which European or American writers do you feel have best represented the continent of Africa and African people?"

Achebe looks at me for a long while and then slowly begins to shake his head.

"This is difficult. Not many."

I suggest Graham Greene.

"Yes, perhaps. Graham Greene would be one because he knew his limitations. He didn't want to explain Africans to the world. He made limited claims and wasn't attempting to be too profound. After all, we can't be too profound about somebody whose history and language and culture is beyond our own."

"But you're not suggesting that outsiders should not write about other cultures?"

"No, no. This identification with the other is what a great writer brings to the art of story-making. We should welcome the rendering of our stories by others, because a visitor can sometimes see what the owner of the house has ignored. But they must visit with respect and not be concerned with the colour of skin, or the shape of nose, or the condition of the technology in the house."

It is now my turn to stare out of the window at the six-foot snow drifts and the bare, rickety arms of the trees. The light is beginning to fade and soon I will have to leave. I avert my eyes and turn to face my host.

"Chinua, I think Conrad offends you because he was a disrespectful visitor."

"I am an African. What interests me is what I learn in Conrad about myself. To use me as a symbol may be bright or clever, but if it reduces my humanity by the smallest fraction I don't like it."

"Conrad does present Africans as having 'rudimentary' souls."

Achebe draws himself upright.

"Yes, you will notice that the European traders have 'tainted' souls, Marlow has a 'pure' soul, but I am to accept that mine is 'rudimentary'?" He shakes his head. "Towards the end of the 19th century, there was a very short-lived period of ambivalence about the certainty of this colonizing mission, and *Heart of Darkness* falls into this period. But you cannot compromise my humanity in order that you explore your own ambiguity. I cannot accept that. My humanity is not to be debated, nor is it to be used simply to illustrate European problems."

The realization hits me with force. I am not an African. Were I an African I suspect I would feel the same way as my host. But I was raised in Europe, and although I have learned to reject the stereotypically reductive images of Africa and Africans, I am undeniably interested in the break-up of a European mind and the health of European civilization. I feel momentarily ashamed that I might have become caught up with this theme and subsequently overlooked how offensive this novel might be to a man such as Chinua Achebe and to millions of other Africans. Achebe is right; to the African reader the price of Conrad's eloquent denunciation of colonization is the recycling of racist notions of the "dark" continent and her people. Those of us who are not from Africa may be prepared to pay this price, but this price is far too high for Achebe. However lofty Conrad's mission, he has, in keeping with times past and present, compromised African humanity in order to examine the European psyche. Achebe's response is understandably personal.

"Conrad's presentation of me is my problem and I have a responsibility to deal with it, you understand?" I nod. "I don't come from a 'half-made' society as your 'friend' [V.S.] Naipaul would say. We're not 'half-made' people, we're a very old people. We've seen lots of problems in the past. We've dealt with these problems in Africa, and we're older than the problems. Drought, famine, disease, this is not the first time that we're dealing with these things in Africa?"

He takes a deep breath. Beyond him, and through the window, the blanket of night begins to descend over the woods.

"You know," he continues, "I think that to some extent it is how you must feel about your 'friend.' You take it to heart because a man with such talent should not behave in this way. My people, we say one palm-nut does not get lost in the fire, for you must know where it is. But if you have 20 you may lose sight of some and they will get burned, but you have others. Well, as you know, we have very few who have the talent and who are in the right place, and to lose even one is a tragedy. We cannot afford to lose such artists. It is sheer cussedness to wilfully turn and walk away from the truth, and for what? Really, for what? I expect a great artist, a man who has explored, a man who is interested in Africa, not to make life more difficult for us. Why do this? Why make our lives more difficult? In this sense Conrad is a disappointment."

2003

Sharon Pollock

Sharon Pollock (b. 1936) was born in Fredericton, New Brunswick, Canada. She lived there until she moved to Calgary in 1966. Her first play, *A Compulsory Option*, was written and performed in Calgary in 1971. She went on to write (and perform in) many other plays including *My Name is Lisbeth* (1976), *Fair Liberty's Call* (1993), and *Angel's Trumpet* (2001). She won two Governor General's Awards, for *Blood Relations* (1980) and *Doc* (1984).

Pollock's play *The Komagata Maru Incident* was first performed in the Vancouver Playhouse in 1976. Set in 1914 in a brothel near the Vancouver harbour, the play examines the nature of the immigration policy of the Dominion of Canada. Was it ethical to exclude the would-be immigrants on board the *Komagata Maru*, who were all British subjects? Of the 340 Sikhs, 24 Muslims, and 12 Hindus, why were only 20 allowed entry? After two months of negotiations, the others were forced to return to India without supplies of food or water. Some questions to consider: What is the effect of the voice of the Woman? Why does Evy identify with some of the immigrants? Should Hopkinson, the immigration officer, have been more understanding of the plight of the immigrants, considering what we find out about his ancestry in the end? Is his death justifiable? Does Pollock offer a balanced portrayal of the incident? Does she have any tangible axes to grind? Does this play transcend the time and place of the incident, acquiring a human commonality?

The Komagata Maru Incident

PLAYWRIGHT'S INTRODUCTION

The Komagata Maru Incident is a theatrical impression of an historical event seen through the optique of the stage and the mind of the playwright. It is not a documentary account, although much of it is documented. To encompass these facts, time and place are often compressed, and certain dramatic license is employed.

By the early 1900s, the Canadian government believed it had devised an airtight method to virtually exclude immigration from Asia. In 1914, the Komagata Maru, a Japanese steamer, entered Vancouver Harbour carrying 376 potential immigrants of East Indian origin. The majority were veterans of the British Army, and all were British subjects. As such, they had right of entry to Canada guaranteed by their membership in the British Empire, but they were forbidden entry by Canadian immigration officials. For the following two months, the Komagata Maru lay at anchor in Burrard Inlet, with those aboard suffering much deprivation, while political, legal, and racial skirmishes ensued. Inspector William Hopkinson of the Department of Immigration was instrumental in negotiations with those aboard and was involved in the formation of a ring of informers within the Sikh community.

The Komagata Maru returned to India in the fall of 1914, leaving behind only twenty passengers who could prove former residence in Canada. The repercussions of the government's actions — the Budge Budge riot, the radicalization of those aboard, the vigilante action against informers, the death of Hopkinson, the execution of Mewa Singh — were overshadowed by the outbreak of World War One.

As a Canadian, I feel that much of our history has been misrepresented and even hidden from us. Until we recognize our past, we cannot change our future.

CHARACTERS

T.S., The Master of Ceremonies, who plays many roles.
WILLIAM HOPKINSON, Department of Immigration Inspector.
EVY, A prostitute involved with Hopkinson.
SOPHIE, A prostitute involved with Georg.
GEORG, A German national.
A WOMAN, A Sikh immigrant, British subject.

SCENE

A brothel, Vancouver, 1914.

PRODUCTION NOTE

It is important that the scenes flow together without blackouts and without regard to time and setting. The brothel is the major playing area. Surrounding it is an arc or runway used by T.S. and HOPKINSON for most of their scenes. Although T.S. cannot intrude upon the WOMAN's space, he is free to move anywhere else on the set to observe or speak. As the play progresses, T.S.'s scenes move from the arc into the brothel area.

The characters never leave the stage. When not involved in the action, they sit on benches placed on the extreme Stage Right and Stage Left ends of the arc. The WOMAN is on a level above and behind the area used by the other characters. An open grill-like frame in front of her gives both the impression of a cage and of the superstructure of a ship. T.S. observes the audience entering. The other characters are frozen on stage; the grill-like frame, with the WOMAN behind it, is concealed by a sheet.

(*The Komagata Maru Incident* was first produced at the Vancouver Playhouse in January, 1976, and by Citadel Theatre Edmonton, in January, 1977.)

THE *KOMAGATA MARU* INCIDENT

The houselights fade out and a faint light comes up on T.S., who moves to a stool set in the centre of the arc. On this stool are his gloves, hat, and cane. He carefully puts on the gloves while surveying the audience.

T.S. Good... gooood. (*pausing for a moment*) Do you like the suit?

T.S. puts on his top hat, gives it a tap with the cane, looks toward the lighting booth, and snaps his fingers. A spot comes up on him.

Hurry! Hurry! Hurry! Right this way, ladies and gentlemen! First chance to view the *Komagata Maru*! At this very moment steaming towards picturesque Vancouver Harbour. Yes sireee! The *Komagata Maru*! A first-class—let the buyer beware—Japanese steamer, 329.2 feet in length, 2,926 gross tonnage! Captained by one Yomamoto, remember that name. And Japanese crew, carrying a cargo of coal! And 376 Sikhs, count 'em! Plus 30 East Indians, religious affiliation unknown! Add 'em all together and what do you get? That is correct, sir! Give the man a cigar! Three hundred and seventy-six is the answer! Three hundred and seventy-six Asians, to be precise, and all of them bound for Oh Canada, We stand on guard for thee!

> *T.S. salutes, holds it for a moment, then lets it drop as he moves into the brothel area.*

This is Vancouver, ladies and gentlemen, the 21st day of May, nineteen hundred and fourteen.... And may I direct your attention to my hat... I place the hat on the table... I pass my hands over the hat... and what do we have inside the hat? A pair of gloves! I give you Inspector William Hopkinson, Head of Intelligence, Department of Immigration!

> *T.S. slaps the gloves into HOPKINSON's hand, looks at him for a second, then continues.*

Ladies and gentlemen, the hand is truly faster than the eye... you see this box... and now you don't... and here it is again (*passing it behind his back*) I open it, it's empty, I close the box. (looking at EVY then placing it in her hands) May I present (*stepping back*) Miss Evy: Entrepreneur!

> *T.S. bangs his cane, spot out. EVY and HOPKINSON are lit and animated.*

EVY What is it?
HOPKINSON It's a present.
EVY Don't tell me, silly.
HOPKINSON You asked.
EVY But I don't want you to tell me.

> *HOPKINSON removes his hand from her eyes.*

Oh, Bill (*opening the box which contains a brooch*) It's beautiful. Here, pin it on me.

> *HOPKINSON bends over her to do so. T.S. bangs his cane, they freeze, spot on T.S.*

T.S. Ladies and gentlemen! Your attention, please! Now the pocket's empty. Not so now. (*taking out billfold and visa*) I have here one billfold and one German visa for one Georg Braun! (*throwing it on the floor near GEORG*) And here! Behind an ear, a chocolate! (*placing it in SOPHIE's hand*) Allow me to introduce, one Georg Braun and Sophie!

> *T.S. bangs his cane, spot out. SOPHIE goes to eat the chocolate, GEORG attempts to embrace her, and she pushes him off.*

SOPHIE Not so fast.
GEORG Eh?
SOPHIE No tickee, no washee.
GEORG I…?
SOPHIE (*putting her hand out*) Mon-ey.
GEORG Oh. (*feeling for his billfold and finding it on the floor as T.S. knocks*)
SOPHIE Somebody get the door! (*plucking billfold from GEORG's hand*) Thank you.

> *GEORG amorously tries to embrace SOPHIE again as she counts the money. T.S. knocks. SOPHIE pushes GEORG away.*

Wait a minute! Are you deaf? There's someone at the door.

> *SOPHIE moves off SR with the billfold. After a moment of indecision, his billfold gone, GEORG moves after her.*

GEORG Ah—Sophie?
T.S. (*laughing, spot on him*) Ladies and gentlemen. Lest we forget. The *Komagata Maru*. A Japanese steamer chock-full of brown-skin Hindus headed for a predominantly pale Vancouver, and entry into whitish Canada. The *Komagata Maru* in blue Canadian waters!

> *T.S. pulls cover to reveal WOMAN who bends over a child on deck. T.S. bows. Spot is out.*

WOMAN Go to sleep. Go to sleep. Shut your eyes, go to sleep.

> *It's very hot and WOMAN turns from the child, wipes her forehead and looks out with a sigh, then turns back to the child.*

Still not asleep?
HOPKINSON (*pinning brooch on*) There. Everything's forgotten. Alright?
EVY Alright.
HOPKINSON But you have to thank me for the brooch.

EVY Thank you, Billy.

HOPKINSON Don't tease. You know I don't like Billy.

EVY Thank you, Bill.

HOPKINSON That's better.

EVY Now you sit down, and I'll get you a drink.

>   *HOPKINSON checks his watch.*

>   Oh — not the time again? You just got here.

HOPKINSON Can't be helped. I'm sorry.

EVY You always have to go.

HOPKINSON Don't be mad. I won't be long, it's just an appointment.

EVY Bill?

>   *Still holding the billfold, SOPHIE crosses round to SL with GEORG following.*

SOPHIE You may as well get used to it. That's what it's like around here. Half the time I'm running messages for him.

GEORG For who?

SOPHIE Mr. Hopkinson. Evy's friend with Immigration.

GEORG Immigration?

SOPHIE I'm sick of answering that damn door for him.

GEORG Sophie, do you think — ?

SOPHIE (*at "door" SL*) There's a man out back for Mr. Hopkinson.

HOPKINSON (*from inside "room"*) Who is it?

SOPHIE He says tell Mr. Hopkinson that Bella Singh is here.

EVY Your rat again.

HOPKINSON (*preparing to leave*) Don't call him that.

EVY I don't like rats coming round.

HOPKINSON Let's not start this again.

EVY He's always coming round and when he does, off you go, poof!

HOPKINSON It'll only take a minute.

EVY My mother always said, don't snitch, and don't play with snitchers. Didn't your mother ever tell you that?

HOPKINSON Evy, we've settled all this.

SOPHIE Mr. Hopkinson! Did you hear me!

HOPKINSON Now don't pout, you'll get wrinkles.

EVY Oh, get out.

HOPKINSON I'm going. (*going to "door"*)

SOPHIE Come on, Georg.

GEORG Mr. Hopkinson?

HOPKINSON Who's this, Sophie?

GEORG Georg Braun, sir, if I could—

WOMAN See the birds? Land must be near…Mountains, trees, then the island, through the pass. Your uncle will meet us…Look! Soon we will enter the harbour. See where your uncle lives? That is where we'll live.

GEORG Thank you, sir.

SOPHIE Georg!

>GEORG *goes to the bench.* HOPKINSON *turns back into the room.*

HOPKINSON Evy? That fellow with Sophie.

EVY Georg Braun?

HOPKINSON I've, ah, asked him in for a drink when I get back.

EVY Oh?

HOPKINSON I want to meet him.

EVY You've already met him.

HOPKINSON Talk to him, then.

EVY I thought brown rats were your specialty.

HOPKINSON Bella Singh's a loyal British subject.

EVY Well, Georg Braun's no British subject! You're setting up no rats in my house!

HOPKINSON I'll do just as I please in your house! It's me that keeps you open, and don't you forget it! A nod from me, and you'd be buried under warrants. Oh Evy, Evy, Evy… what's good for me is good for you, eh?… Eh Evy? All I want to do is meet him, get to know him better…

> EVY *makes a murmur of protest.*

I get ahead, Evy, do you know how I do that? I look ahead, I'm always thinking. Now, you read the papers, you stop and think…. With Kaiser Wilhelm and all, something in here tells me a German can do me some good. Eh? Perhaps not today or tomorrow, maybe next year, who knows. Now you can understand that, can't you?

EVY I just don't like—

SOPHIE Bella Singh's at the end of the yard! He wants to see you!

HOPKINSON The German's coming in for a drink, Evy. *(exiting)*

EVY If—if you say so.

T.S. Hopkinson!

> HOPKINSON *joins* T.S., *DSR arc.*

HOPKINSON Yes, sir.

T.S. The *Komagata Maru*'s in port with three hundred and seventy-six potential immigrants.

HOPKINSON Yes sir.

T.S. So? What do you know about them?

HOPKINSON I've spoken to my man, Bella Singh, sir. He tells me they're Sikhs from India, British subjects, and as such they do have right of entry to Canada, sir.

T.S. The word is no entry.

HOPKINSON I realize that, but we may have a problem.

T.S. A what?

HOPKINSON Many are veterans of the British Army, sir; they're sure to plead consideration for military service.

T.S. You can put it this way — we don't mind them dying for us, we just don't want them living with us. (*laughing*) Get the point?

HOPKINSON (*laughing*) Yes sir … but if they should go to the courts —

T.S. They won't go to the courts. He hasn't done his homework. Have you forgotten our two orders-in-council? If an immigrant wishes to enter the country through a western port, he must make a continuous voyage from his own country to here. Have they done so?

HOPKINSON No sir, they haven't.

T.S. And that's no surprise. There's not a steamship line in existence with a direct India-to-China route and for our second ace-in-the-hole — a tax, two hundred dollars per head, to be paid before entry. Do they have it?

HOPKINSON Bella Singh says they do not, however —

T.S. Again, not surprising. In the land of his birth, the average Indian's wage is nine dollars per year. There — you see how we operate, Hopkinson? Never a mention of race, colour, or creed — and yet, we allow British subjects; yet we don't allow them to enter.

HOPKINSON Thank you, sir. However, I must inform you that Hermann Singh says —

T.S. Sh, sh.

HOPKINSON (*lowering his voice*) Hermann Singh says that the local Sikhs have raised the money for the head tax.

T.S. That's not so good.

HOPKINSON It's possible that a launch —

T.S. It is possible? Do you pay for information like that?

HOPKINSON Bella Singh says a launch will deliver the head tax to those on the ship late tonight.

T.S. The word is no entry, Hopkinson.

HOPKINSON Yes sir.

SOPHIE rushes into the room followed by GEORG.

SOPHIE Listen everybody! Here it is! (*reading from paper*) "Immigration Officials Intercept Head Tax in Vancouver Harbour."

EVY enters SR. HOPKINSON enters from arc.

WOMAN Look! A launch is coming! Maybe it's your uncle.

SOPHIE There's your name right there! Inspector William Hopkinson.

WOMAN Be careful! You'll fall!

SOPHIE Look, Georg! Look, Evy!

WOMAN The Immigration boat is stopping the launch.

SOPHIE There it is again, "Hopkinson declares—"

WOMAN Shhhhhh. Don't be afraid.

SOPHIE You read it, Evy, what's it say?

HOPKINSON I can tell you what it means. British Columbia wants no Calcutta coolies. We've Chinamen and Japs running our shops, Greeks running our hotels, Jews running our second-hand stores, and we don't want Hindus running our mills.

EVY For God's sake, Bill, have a drink.

T.S. Have a drink.

HOPKINSON (*offering bottle*) Georg?

GEORG Please. The Sikhs on the ship would pay the head tax with the money from the launch, eh? And that is legal? Can you intercept it like that?

HOPKINSON Well, we did. Another bottle, Evy. The Calcutta coolie, Georg, belongs in India.

GEORG Do you know India, sir?

HOPKINSON Do I know India? He wants to know if I know India, Evy.

EVY Does he know India!

EVY gives him a bottle, sits at the table and begins to play cards.

HOPKINSON I know India, and I know its people. When I was a child, my father was stationed in the Punjab—He had only to shout "*Quai Hai*" to summon a slave—a servant—no, goddamn it, a slave, to summon a slave, to scrawl his initials on a chit, and there was a felt carpet from Kashmir, brass ornaments from Moradabad, silver for pocket money, cigars, a horse, a dog, anything he wanted. Show him your brooch, Evy. It belonged to my father. Wonderful craftsmen, the Natives.

GEORG It's lovely.

HOPKINSON Did you know "loot" was an Indian word?

GEORG Is it?

SOPHIE (*examining the brooch*) Really beautiful.

HOPKINSON My father was a big man, blond curly hair, wonderful moustache he had, looked like a prince in his uniform. A prince—surrounded by little beige people. (*laughing*)

SOPHIE What about your mother?

HOPKINSON "*Quai Hai!*" That's all, and they'd scuttle like bugs.

SOPHIE Did your mother like it there?

HOPKINSON She never said. You've no idea, Georg, of the size, the immensity, and the millions (*smiling*). When I was a boy I used to like to read at night, alone, in a room that had dimensions.

GEORG Sophie tells me you yourself served in the Punjab.

HOPKINSON Oh, yes. Lahore Police Force. Six years' service.

GEORG And how do you end up in Canada, sir?

HOPKINSON Promotion was blocked in Lahore.

GEORG That's hard to believe for a man like... yourself.

HOPKINSON Quite simple, Georg. Cliques. And I learnt something from that. So. I answered an ad and here I am.

GEORG Your life has been very exciting—

SOPHIE Sophie can make your life exciting too, yes, she can. Let Sophie sit on Georg.

SOPHIE lifts her skirts and plunks herself on him. They both fall over on the floor as T.S. bangs his cane. They freeze.

T.S. Ladies and gentlemen! The turbaned tide is flowing! May 23rd, 1914. The first wave of an Asian Invasion sits at anchor in Vancouver Harbour!

WOMAN They won't let us land! I've told you. We've asked a judge to rule on the orders-in-council. Now go... Our food and our water are rationed. How long must we wait?

T.S. Today's lesson is taken from the Department of Immigration's handbook, Regulation 23, Paragraph 4. I am talking about Checks and Balances of Power. Now, I am the Department of Immigration, I have the power to hold proceedings, make decisions, give orders. I can detain and deport any person or potential immigrant on any grounds whatsoever, unless that person is a Canadian citizen. You are the courts. You have the power to review, reverse, and restrain, quash, and otherwise interfere with my power to hold, to make, and to give, to detain and deport. And you do. Fairly often. It's annoying. So what do I do? Quite simple. I pass Catch 22, Regulation 23, Paragraph 4, which states: "No judge and no court and no officer thereof shall have any jurisdiction to review, reverse, and restrain, quash or otherwise interfere with my holding and making and giving, detaining, deporting."

We are gathered here in the sight of God, and in the spirit of the British Empire to rule on the *Komagata Maru*'s contention that Catch 22, Regulation 23, Paragraph 4 is invalid. They maintain that the Department of Immigration has not the authority to deny immigrants access to the courts. If we give them access, then a judge or a court or an officer thereof could overthrow our orders-in-council of which we have two denying them entry—And that, my good friends, would open the floodgates!

T.S. bangs his cane. GEORG picks himself up in embarrassment, pushing SOPHIE aside.

GEORG My... my feelings are this, sir. If you examine the world and its history, you will see that the laws of evolution that have shaped the energy, enterprise, and efficiency of the race northwards have left less richly endowed the peoples inhabiting the southern regions.

HOPKINSON Go on.

GEORG Yes. This…, this process is no passing accident, but part of the cosmic order of things which we have no power to alter. The European races must administrate; all that's needed to assure their success is a clearly defined conception of moral necessity. Do you agree, sir?

HOPKINSON Agreed. It's a pleasure to talk to you, Georg. I feel as if you're a friend, a good friend.

GEORG I'm honoured.

HOPKINSON I have very few friends. A man in my position, Head of Intelligence, has very few friends.

GEORG Please consider me one of them.

HOPKINSON I'm thought of most often as a dose of salts; not palatable, but essential for the health of the body. I accept this.

GEORG You are—

HOPKINSON But! If I may make a small observation? It's truly amazing the number of people who use laxatives regularly, and lie about it. Eh? (*laughing*) You follow me, eh?

HOPKINSON laughs and GEORG joins in.

Yes, I have my job, and I do it. And damn well, if I say so myself.

GEORG You've a good network of men.

HOPKINSON Uh uh, more than that. It's a sense of responsibility, that's what it is. I take the risks, and I find my reward in the fulfillment of my task. Now there's your difference between white and coloured—the Gift of Responsibility.

EVY (*looking up from her cards*) What's the difference?

HOPKINSON You see that's why we're sitting in here, and the *Komagata Maru*'s out there scratching at the door.

EVY Why?

HOPKINSON For Christ's sake, Evy, if it weren't for the British, they couldn't construct a canoe, much less charter a steamer.

EVY (*back to her cards*) You should know, I suppose. You lived with them.

HOPKINSON I did not live with them!

EVY Well, you were there, God knows I've heard it often enough. It's hard to keep straight where you were when, and with who.

HOPKINSON I was brought up in India! I know them, if that's what you mean. Keep your mouth shut when we're talking! (*picking up bottle and starting off*). Come on, Georg, I've a chess set, hand-carved from ivory (*moving off with GEORG following*). Marvellous chess player, my father.

WOMAN I saw what you did! Do you think because I have no man you can steal food from my child? If you steal again, I will come when you sleep and I'll kill you!

T.S. (DSR, arc) Ah, Hopkinson.

HOPKINSON I have observed suffering and deprivation on the *Komagata Maru*.

WOMAN The child cries! He is thirsty!

T.S. What else?

HOPKINSON Our policy of disallowing the supplying of the ship is sound. It weakens their morale. It's only a matter of time till they question their leadership...

T.S. Continue.

HOPKINSON As... conditions deteriorate, we could, at some future date, offer supplies as an incentive to leave.

T.S. Very good. Very good.

HOPKINSON There is... a woman and child on the ship.

T.S. Irrelevant.

WOMAN It's hard to explain to a child... Your father was a soldier, he died fighting for the king, so we come to live with your uncle. But first—we must wait....

SOPHIE My feet hurt.

EVY Mmn?

SOPHIE I don't know why. I'd have thought it'd be my back.

> *EVY looks at SOPHIE and laughs.*

What? (*laughing*) Noo. Back trouble runs in the family.

EVY Oh.

SOPHIE In the women, that is. With the men it's always having to, you know, piss when they're older.

> *EVY laughs.*

Yeah, I guess if I had my druthers, I'd rather have a bad back... In the night when the pot was full, Grampa would piss out the window.... Unless the wind blew from the east. Then he pissed out the door.

EVY Why?

SOPHIE It blew back at the window. The window faced east.

EVY Oh Sophie.

> *They both laugh.*

SOPHIE It's true... I used to lie on my back in the field and Mama would scream "Sophie, Sophie!" and I'd lie there and think, "Sophie, get out of here, better yourself!"... And Mama would scream "Sophie! I know you're hidin.'"...and I'd just lie there.... Mama always said I was lazy. Maybe I am, but you don't see me emptying piss pots. I got out of there.

EVY Don't stop here, Sophie.

SOPHIE My back's not breaking from too many kids and carrying milk cans.

> (*looking at her foot*)

EVY (*as she exits*) Find a nice man, and move on.

SOPHIE Maybe I sprained it.

WOMAN bends over, retching, dry spasms. When she finished she draws in several deep breaths. She attempts a smile for the child.

WOMAN Don't worry... smile, it's only the water. Don't worry. You are a very brave boy. Your uncle will like you. Come, we'll sit on the side where there's shade.

T.S. I don't understand.

HOPKINSON I've promised them food and water.

T.S. Really?

HOPKINSON I've given my word.

T.S. And what did you hope to gain from that?

HOPKINSON Sir—

T.S. Surely not plaudits from me.

HOPKINSON Sir, when I boarded the ship for inspection, they seized me and were ready to take off in our launch and head for shore, patrol boats or not. They were desperate. They say they'd rather be shot than die of hunger and thirst. I felt it only—humanitarian to grant one week's provision.

T.S. You've enabled them to hang on. That's what you've done!

HOPKINSON I saw the mother and child—

T.S. Now where's that incentive to leave?

HOPKINSON Their case is still pending.

T.S. Never initiate action when you haven't the guts to carry it through. It's a sign of weakness, Hopkinson.

HOPKINSON Yes sir.

T.S. You disappoint us.

HOPKINSON Yes sir.

T.S. We brought you up. We can put you down.

HOPKINSON Yes sir.

T.S. We trust that our meaning's sufficiently clear?

HOPKINSON Yes sir.

EVY enters the room SL.

EVY Bill!

SOPHIE Evy!

EVY Bill!

SOPHIE Mr. Hopkinson!

　　　　HOPKINSON enters SR.

HOPKINSON What's the matter?

EVY Oh, Bill.

SOPHIE I thought you went shopping.

EVY I just—sat on the tram. A round trip. I never got off it.

HOPKINSON Come on, Evy.

SOPHIE Are you sick?

EVY I....was on the tram. I had a seat by the window. When we...

HOPKINSON Come on now.

EVY When we came round by the creek there was a queue for employment, a long line of men looking for work. They were standing in line, we'd stopped for a fare, and then... the line... all of a sudden it... there was a man in a turban at the end of the line, his eye had caught my eye as I looked out the window — he looked so — solid — and I smiled... and he smiled... and as he smiled a man stepped in front of him, and he was back at the end.... Then, I don't know, it happened so quickly, he touched the man on the shoulder, the man turned... and the long line of men, it seemed to turn. The man in the turban started to speak, he got out a few words, I didn't sense anger — and then it exploded. They knocked him down, the man in the turban they were kicking, and then pushing and shoving to get in a blow — and the tram pulled away... it was gone. As if I'd imagined it. It had never been.

HOPKINSON You were frightened, that's all.

EVY I should have done something.

HOPKINSON You should have come home and you did. Come on now, you saw a fight. You've seen fights before.

EVY No, it wasn't a fight! And I just sat on the goddamn tram and came home.

HOPKINSON (*to SOPHIE*) Get her a drink.

> *EVY goes to look out the window, at the audience, where the* Komagata Maru *sits.*

EVY There are... people at the end of Burrard, staring out at that ship... They look like the men in that line.

HOPKINSON That's why we're sending the *Komagata Maru* back, so things like your fight won't happen. We don't want them here.

> *SOPHIE exits after giving him the drink.*

EVY But why does it happen?

HOPKINSON All I know, Evy, is my father didn't die in the service for the world to be overrun by a second-rate people.

EVY You don't make sense. Who's second-rate when you run out of brown people?

HOPKINSON Drink your drink.

EVY I don't want a drink! (*speaking while exiting SR*) You belong on Burrard.

> *HOPKINSON follows her.*

HOPKINSON Evy!

T.S. Mr. Speaker; Prime Minister; Honourable Members. Today I am opening my heart to you. I am telling you my fears — fears that affect each and every Canadian today... I fear for my country, and I fear for my people... I am not ashamed, nor should you be, to state that this is white man's country! And I can tell you that our British legacy, our traditions, those things that we hold dear, that we have fought and died for, is placed in jeopardy today by a massive influx of coloured foreigners! The class of East Indian that has invaded British Columbia is commonly known as Sikh — having been accustomed to the conditions of a tropical clime, he is totally unsuited to this country. He is criminally inclined, unsanitary by habit, and roguish by instinct. The less we speak of his religion, the better. Suffice it to say that unless his ridiculous forms of worship are relinquished, he is an affront to a Christian community. His intelligence is roughly that of our Aborigines. He indeed belongs to a heathen and debased class. Honourable Members, stand up and be counted! Admit the honest fears of your constituents! Will the Sikh work for cheaper wages, and thus take away their jobs? Will he bring out his women, children, relatives and friends? Will Canadians step on a tram next week to ride from home to work and never hear a word of English spoken? And once at work, if they still have a job, who will they eat their lunch with? Men, honest and true like ourselves, whose fathers made this country what it is today — or will they be surrounded by coloured men with foreign food? Canadians have rights! Our fathers died for them! Let any man who is not willing to do the same step down! I've told you here today what's in my heart. For God's sake, show me what's in yours!

    HOPKINSON enters SL.

HOPKINSON Evy!

    EVY enters SR.

EVY I'm here.

HOPKINSON Was Bella Singh around?

EVY Don't ask me.

HOPKINSON Where's Sophie? Sophie!

    SOPHIE enters SR.

SOPHIE What?

HOPKINSON Was Bella Singh around?

SOPHIE When?

HOPKINSON Day before yesterday, goddamn it, was he here?

SOPHIE Maybe. I don't remember.

HOPKINSON What the hell do you mean, you don't remember?

EVY Look, Bill, my girls don't keep track of your rats.

HOPKINSON If they don't, they better start. Customs picked up three men at the border today. Sikhs smuggling guns for the *Komagata Maru*. And my head's on the block! That's the kind of information I'm paid to deliver! And I knew nothing. Do you hear that? Sweet bugger all! Was Bella Singh around or not?

EVY You can leave now, Sophie.

HOPKINSON She'll leave when I tell her. Did you forget a message, Sophie?

EVY You run your business, I'll run mine; Sophie, get out!

HOPKINSON (*grabbing SOPHIE*) By Jesus, I want an answer!

EVY Me! It was me! Bella Singh came round, he left a note, I threw it out!

    HOPKINSON releases SOPHIE. She leaves.

HOPKINSON Why did you do that?

EVY I don't pass notes.

HOPKINSON It's me they come down on. Don't you realize that? If I don't deliver, I'm the one that pays — not Bella Singh. Why did you do it?

EVY I'm sorry.

HOPKINSON No you're not.

EVY No, I'm not.

HOPKINSON You wanted to make me look bad, is that it?

EVY No.

HOPKINSON I look bad enough then they'll dump me. Is that what you want?

EVY No.

HOPKINSON And off we go! Something else, somewhere else, eh?

EVY What's wrong with that? People do it!

HOPKINSON Not me.

EVY Don't you like honest work?

HOPKINSON That's a funny remark from a whore!

EVY You want to know why I threw out your note? I'll tell you why! I'm a whore and what you do is offensive to me! What you do would gag me! I'm a whore and when I look at your job, I could vomit!

> *HOPKINSON slaps her.*

WOMAN Don't look at the crowd on the shore! ... don't listen, pretend they aren't there ... the sky is a blue, a beautiful blue ... look at it! Don't look at them on the shore, they are ugly!

> *WOMAN turns her back and begins to sing to the child.*

HOPKINSON I never think of the woman and child they never enter my mind.... Mewa Singh is a mill worker and priest caught crossing the border with guns. Mewa Singh is a trusted man in the Sikh community. Mewa Singh is a man I could use ... I speak to him in his jail cell. I begin with loyalty, move on to money, end up with threats. Mewa Singh says nothing. He looks me straight in the eye. I don't always like that, with some it's an act of defiance.... In Mewa Singh's eyes there is an infinite sadness, and surrounding him is a pool of silence, and as I speak and the words fall on my ears as if from a distance ... I think of an incident when I was a child ... there was trouble at the bazaar ... the soldiers had to come in on their horses ... and the next day I walked through ... I saw blood, like clots of dark jelly still on the streets ... but no people ... an empty bazaar. Do you have any conception of how strange that is? I remember standing very still, scrawny and pasty, very still, afraid to move ... in the middle of silence, listening, like a mouse on a pan, listening, for the beat of the wings of the owl ... very still. And then as I stood there, I saw a figure approaching from one of the streets. Some Native person. He stopped in the shadow of the huts ... he extended his arms towards me ... and I ... turned around ... and ran home. I was frightened ... Mewa Singh ... when I finish my mixed bag of offers Mewa Singh turns his head towards the window. It's narrow and barred. He has dismissed me. His answer is no. Goddamn it! I need a man who they trust! I'm the one who has something to lose!

T.S.   Relax! Don't worry! Congratulations are in order. The courts have come through! Catch 22, Regulation 23, Paragraph 4 still stands!

Carnival music, the air of a party. SOPHIE, GEORG, and EVY join HOPKINSON on stage.

Hurry! Hurry! Hurry! Final Immigration ruling on the *Komagata Maru*! Right this way, folks! Right this way! July 16, 1914! Last and final chance to view the *Komagata Maru*! Anchored in picturesque Vancouver Harbour these last six weeks and two days! Yes sireeee! A decision is made! Of three hundred and seventy-six Asians, twenty individuals have proven to Immigration Officials the legality of their Canadian domicile; ninety suffering from disease are ordered deported and the rest can just shove off! The Immigration Department reigns supreme! To hell with the judges, the courts and the officers thereof! Last chance to view! The *Komagata Maru*! Take it away, Bill!

Everyone's been drinking and it shows.

HOPKINSON   Fare thee well, *Komagata Maru*! Have a pleasant journey!
GEORG   Fare thee well!
HOPKINSON   *Bon voyage*! You had your day in court—
SOPHIE   Goodbye you Hindus!
HOPKINSON   Now you and yours can eat crow from here to Calcutta! Crow with seagull, crow with seaweed, or crow with seawater!
SOPHIE   (*laughing*) Crow!
HOPKINSON   Fare thee well! Fare thee well!

They're all roaring with laughter, except EVY.

HOPKINSON   Fare thee well *Komagata Maru*!
EVY   Is it moving yet?
HOPKINSON   Not yet, but any minute.
SOPHIE   That's funny.
HOPKINSON   Have a drink, Evy.
SOPHIE   That's very funny. Why would they want to eat crow with seawater?
GEORG   Who knows what Hindus eat?
          GEORG and SOPHIE are laughing still.
SOPHIE   Still, crow and seawater? It would make you sick. It would make me sick.
GEORG   You aren't a Hindu.
SOPHIE   It'd make anybody sick!
GEORG   Silly, silly, Sophie.
HOPKINSON   See, Evy? It's all over.

SOPHIE You wouldn't eat that unless you had nothing else to eat, that's for sure.
GEORG Silly, silly.
SOPHIE Hey, crow and seawater sounds awful too.
HOPKINSON Forget it, Sophie.
SOPHIE Eh?
HOPKINSON It's just an expression.
SOPHIE So what's it mean?
HOPKINSON Come on, Evy.
SOPHIE (*louder*) Eh?
HOPKINSON To submit humbly!
EVY Surely that rings a bell, I mean, it does for me.
SOPHIE What?
HOPKINSON Don't be like that. Say you're sorry. I'm sorry.
SOPHIE Come on, Georg.

GEORG embraces SOPHIE.

Where's the music — you gotta have music for a party!

HOPKINSON Sophie's right.
GEORG What we'll have is a polka!
GEORG and SOPHIE wind up the gramophone.
HOPKINSON It's a party! Come on, Evy, let's dance.
SOPHIE I love to polka! It's hard on the feet, but I love it!

They dance to the music.

T.S. Hopkinson!

HOPKINSON stops dancing.

There's someone at the end of the yard. Bella Singh's at the end of the yard!

HOPKINSON exits. EVY follows him for a step or two, then stops.
SOPHIE and GEORG dance, carry the bottle and laugh.

WOMAN We hear them rejoice on the shore. They say we are beasts; physical death
is no evil for us, it may be a blessing, else why pestilence and famine? They
say we are the enemies of Christ, the Prince of Peace; they will hate us with a
perfect hatred; the will blast us with grape shot and rockets; they will beat us
as small as dust before the wind!

The music stops. SOPHIE and GEORG collapse.

They say our appeal to the courts is dismissed. They say tonight the *Komagata Maru* will sail for India.

T.S. (*winking*) Guess again!

HOPKINSON The bastards!

WOMAN On the ship a meeting is held. I vote in the place of my son who is five. It is right that we're here!

HOPKINSON (*gazing out at the ship*) Sit tight in the harbour, will they?

EVY Drink up, everyone.

HOPKINSON The foolish bastards. They must think it's a cricket game with the officers. Fair play. Your wicket. Pass the crumpets.

GEORG So what can they do?

HOPKINSON Bugger all. A move can't be made nor a word whispered, on the street, in the temple, on the waterfront, without my knowing it.

EVY He has his men! His men produce! Eh, Bill?

HOPKINSON If they don't, they'll find themselves in steerage on the next ship out!

EVY (*drunk*) You know something?.

HOPKINSON I'll seal the *Komagata Maru* off tighter than paint on a wall.

EVY You sound worried.

HOPKINSON I'll see it wrapped round with rot and rust and manned by skeletons before one bastard disembarks!

EVY Come on, everyone! It's a party!

HOPKINSON That's right! Glasses up, glasses up! Here's to the *Komagata Maru*— stuck in picturesque Vancouver Harbour! It gives me great pleasure to extend to you the hospitality of the Canadian people! Enjoy your anchorage! Sip our rain and eat our air! And when you've had your fill—India lies westward!

T.S. Ladies and gentlemen! It walks! It talks! It reproduces! It provides cheap labour for your factories, and a market for your goods! All this, plus a handy scapegoat! Who's responsible for unemployment? The coloured immigrant! Who brings about a drop in take-home pay? The coloured immigrant! Who is it creates slum housing, racial tension, high interest rates, and violence in our streets? The coloured immigrant! Can we afford to be without it? I say "No!" It makes good sense to keep a few around—when the dogs begin to bay, throw them a coloured immigrant! It may sound simple, but it works. Remember though—the operative word's "a few"—For reference, see the Red, the White, the Blue and Green Paper on Immigration, whatever year you fancy!

EVY (*still drinking*) This place is a pigsty.

SOPHIE That's old news, Evy.

EVY This place is a pigsty.

SOPHIE At least it's a profitable pigsty—isn't it?

EVY Money isn't everything (*laughing as no one else reacts*) ... eh?

SOPHIE Don't be silly.

EVY Did you know that if a pig falls in a trough, the other pigs would eat him. (*playing cards*) Gobble, gobble gobble ... I think pigs are alright ... I've known some not bad pigs ... it's the goddamn pigstys that turn them nasty ...

GEORG (*sitting reading a German paper*) I would not want to be Kaiser Wilhelm today ...

EVY Why? Isn't he feeling well. (*laughing as no one else reacts*) Oh well ... that's too bad ... maybe tomorrow? ...

SOPHIE It's so hot. At home you always get a breeze off the water.

EVY In Manitoba you don't.

GEORG (*turning page*) If war should break out ... well ...

EVY (*brightly*) People will die, eh?

> *EVY looks at HOPKINSON who stands staring out at the ship.*

Bill? ... Bill, a watched pot never boils.

T.S. (*speaking very quietly, his stance mirroring HOPKINSON's*) What we need is a reason to board her. To mount a police action, preliminary, whatever. To arrest those aboard.

EVY Leave the window alone, Bill.

T.S. We could board them, arrest them, escort them to the open sea, and once there, release them, pointed towards India.

EVY Come talk to me.

T.S. Now if the captain and crew charged the Sikhs with mutiny, we'd be away, eh?

EVY Bill?

T.S. The captain refuses to press charges? Really? You know, I can't help but feel you don't give full vent to your powers of persuasion. One begins to wonder whose side you're on, someone should check out your file. A good man would find a reason to board her.

HOPKINSON Yes.

SOPHIE It's the heat. It's so hot.

> *SOPHIE gets up and exits.*

HOPKINSON It's July. ... It's supposed to be hot ...

> *T.S. howls in a boy scout position, on his haunches, two fingers of each hand at his temples.*

T.S. Akela says "Be Prepared." (*howling*) Akela says "Do your Duty for God and the King, and Obey the Law of the Pack." (*howling, then stopping abruptly and rising*) Akela says I have three merit badges for the boy who comes up with a first-rate reason to board the *Komagata Maru*!

EVY What're you writing?

HOPKINSON Nothing.

EVY Are you writing in German, what is it?

HOPKINSON It's nothing … now … clear off, I'm busy.

   EVY wanders off SL.

WOMAN This is not where we live … we shall not see your uncle … but we can't cross an ocean without water or food.… You must not be afraid, for hundreds of years the Khyber Pass has run with our blood, we're not afraid to spill more of it here! Do you hear me ashore! We have suffered, but we have endured! We are tempered like steel! We are ready!

HOPKINSON Georg?

GEORG Mnn? (*from behind his paper*)

HOPKINSON I was wondering.

GEORG Yes?

HOPKINSON I have a small problem … perhaps you could advise me …

GEORG Certainly. What is your problem?

HOPKINSON It's the *Komagata Maru*.

GEORG (*laughing*) You call this a small problem?

HOPKINSON (*doesn't like the laugh*) Compared to, say, Kaiser Wilhelm, of course. Compared to that of an enemy alien in this country if war should break out, yes, I think a small problem, don't you?

   GEORG gets the point.

T.S. It's not what you call subtle, but it works.

HOPKINSON I wish to make the *Komagata Maru* an offer — to give them supplies, to make some vague promise of promises, to recompense them for their cargo of coal, to entice them to sail. I wish the whole transaction kept quiet.

GEORG And what is your problem?

HOPKINSON If my offer got out, it might look like some kind of acknowledgement of their rights, and in this affair, they have none.

   GEORG goes to speak.

As for Bella Singh and the rest, well, to be blunt, I don't trust them — trustworthy as they are, have been in the past, will be in the future, I do not totally trust them in this endeavour. A very slight qualm of mistrust.

GEORG I see.

HOPKINSON What do you advise, my good friend, Georg?

   EVY enters unobserved. She's come in for a bottle but stops to listen.

GEORG You're looking for someone to carry your offer out to the ship?

HOPKINSON That's correct. (*drawing out envelope*) This particular offer — a man I can trust — a man for whom I possibly could do a small favour sometime in the future in return for this favour.

GEORG And with some small financial reward, I suppose?

HOPKINSON Correct. I will provide a boat, and one of our patrols will study the night sky as you slip through the—oh—excuse the use of the pronoun.

GEORG Quite alright. Quite—alright—in fact, is there any reason why I myself, Georg, cannot act on your behalf in this matter?

HOPKINSON Ah.

GEORG Shall we drink to it? (*moving to do so*)

HOPKINSON First the details—

> *They catch sight of EVY*

EVY Hello.

GEORG Hello, Evy.

> *HOPKINSON lowers his voice slightly as EVY hovers in background.*

HOPKINSON First the details, then the drink—Note, the envelope is sealed, and must remain so.

> *As he passes the envelope to GEORG, EVY takes it.*

EVY What's this?

GEORG (*looking to HOPKINSON*) Ah?

EVY A letter home?

GEORG Yes. May I have it?

EVY A letter to Germany—but it has no address.

HOPKINSON Give him his letter.

EVY A letter to Germany—what if—someone should open it. What's in it?

HOPKINSON Evy—

EVY Georg, where's your head? We're practically at war. The only thing worse than a letter to Germany is a letter from Germany. Governments are paranoid. Ask Bill.

GEORG Eh?

HOPKINSON She drinks too much.

EVY I just had an idea! What if—

HOPKINSON (*making a grab for her arm and missing*) Give it to me!

EVY I'm not finished! What if a letter containing—who knows what—was carried by a German national out to the *Komagata Maru*—

HOPKINSON Shut your mouth.

EVY —and intercepted by the Department of Immigration—what if, eh?

GEORG What if? (*shrugging*)

EVY A plot between the Germans and the Sikhs!

GEORG A plot between …?

> *GEORG laughs with a tinge of nervousness and a look to HOPKINSON.*

Give me the letter.

EVY He wants a good solid reason to board the *Komagata Maru* and by Jesus I'm looking at it!

HOPKINSON You're going to end up in a sailor's bar, Evy.

EVY I won't let you do this!

HOPKINSON Two-bits-a-crack in a dark alley.

EVY Georg—(*giving it to him*) Open it.

GEORG This is an offer to—

HOPKINSON That's enough.

EVY It's a trick. Open it!

HOPKINSON Return it, or deliver it sealed.

GEORG You don't understand—

HOPKINSON No trust, no deal.

EVY Don't you know who he works for?

GEORG Evy, he works for the government.

EVY Oh yes! … Oh yes … and I can tell you a story about governments … a bedtime story—

T.S. & EVY Once upon a time—

The characters freeze as T.S. moves among them. T.S. continues the story.

T.S. There was a little boy who came to Manitoba with his mummy and daddy and sisters and brothers and many others very much like him. Their skin was a pale ivory, their eyes a light blue, and their hair dark—without being too dark—and curly—but not too curly! They were running from persecution and injustice … and Canada said: "You wish to own farm land communally? No bother at all! You will not swear allegiance to the crown and the flag? Weeeellll what is it, after all, but headgear and a piece of cloth? You do not wish to fight wars? That too can be arranged; exceptions can be made." The daddies worked to earn money for seed and supplies, and the mummies harnessed themselves to the plough and pulled it, breaking the hard brown earth of Manitoba and the soft white flesh of their backs till the red blood ran down, and the little boy walked beside the plough picking bouquets of tiny blue flowers. By and by the mummies and daddies had homes and barns and food for the winter and seed for the spring and horses for the plough. Then others came and saw what they had. And Canada said—"Now about this allegiance! And which of you owns this particular piece of land? Be precise and sign here! And my goodness, friends, isn't all this worth killing and maiming for? What kind of people are you?" The mummies and daddies and sisters and brothers set out on a pilgrimage. They walked to Yorktown and along the tracks towards Winnipeg.

T.S. bangs his cane. The others unfreeze, and GEORG turns to HOPKIN-SON.

GEORG About this letter! (*extending it*)

EVY Listen to me! I watched them walk past—

> *T.S. bangs his cane. They freeze.*

T.S. It was snowing. They had little to eat, and then nothing to eat, for the Mounties cut off their supplies—and it snowed. People dropped by the tracks and a special train came along and returned everyone to Northern Manitoba. And those who would not sign and swear allegiance were driven from their land with only what they could carry! (*banging his cane*)

HOPKINSON (*snatching the letter*) I'll make other arrangements!

> *T.S. bangs the cane. They freeze.*

T.S. Then people whose skins were so fair as to be opalescent, whose eyes were so light they shone in the dark, whose hair sparkled like dust motes in the sun, with each strand hanging in a manner that can only be described as poker straight—these people stormed the land office for homesteads and barns and harvests still in the fields.

EVY My brother stood in line for three days, he got a section—next to my father's.

T.S. And they all lived happily ever after!... There now. Goodnight, sleep tight, don't let the bedbugs bite.... Shhhhhhhhhh! (*tiptoeing away*)

EVY It can happen to any of us.

HOPKINSON Go to bed.

EVY Look at him. He'd cut off his hand before he'd make the *Komagata Maru* an offer. (*laughing*) I got a thing about race, about colour, haven't you noticed?

HOPKINSON You're boring and stupid, Evy.

EVY Why do you suppose that is?

GEORG I—

EVY He goes to the temple.

GEORG Eh?

EVY Gets himself all dolled up, goes to the temple in disguise—he thinks he looks like a Sikh. I bet the Sikhs think he looks like an ass.

HOPKINSON Goodnight, Georg.

GEORG About—

HOPKINSON Goodnight.

> *GEORG gives a little bow and leaves.*

EVY I've been thinking. Funny thing, your background—

HOPKINSON That's enough.

EVY Birthplace, things like that, where were you born, Bill?

HOPKINSON Get the hell upstairs.

EVY Where?

HOPKINSON England.

EVY Where in England, be specific.

HOPKINSON Yorkshire!

EVY Yorkshire? Yorkshire! Now that's a new one, Yorkshire, eh?... That's not what I think.

HOPKINSON Evy!

EVY Quick, Georg (*pretending GEORG is still there*) without looking, what colour's his eyes, wanna bet? I'd say brown.

> *Sometime during this scene, HOPKINSON begins to subtly stalk her. She as subtly avoids him.*

HOPKINSON You filthy bitch!

EVY Blue, did you say? Well then I bet his mother's eyes were brown.

HOPKINSON My mother's dead.

EVY Born in Punjab, served by Yorkshire.

HOPKINSON Born in Yorkshire!

EVY So are they blue or brown?

HOPKINSON Blue!

EVY Your mother's eyes, now what were they?

HOPKINSON My mother's eyes were blue, you bitch! I'll kill you.

EVY First you'll have to catch me.

> *HOPKINSON chases her; she avoids him.*

You're stupid, Bill, you're stupid... it's not me that's stupid, it's you. Stupid, stupid, Bill! They all use you, Bill, yes, they do. You think that you use Georg, you think that you use Bella Singh, you think that you use me, but you're the one that's being used... they're using you and Billy Boy's too dumb to know and stupid dumbo Billy will keep on being used cause Billy Dumbo's stupid! Stupid dumbo Billy's stupid dumbo Billy.

> *HOPKINSON catches EVY; she speaks softly.*
And Billy's mother's brown.
> *HOPKINSON slaps EVY; she speaks louder.*
And Billy's mother's brown!
> *HOPKINSON slaps EVY; she speaks louder.*
And Billy's mother's brown.
> *HOPKINSON throws EVY down, kneels, and shakes her.*

HOPKINSON Don't say that. Don't say that! I'll kill you if you say that to me! (*slowing down his attack on her*) Evy, don't say that. Please don't say that... (*stopping*) I... I love you, Evy, don't say that to me...

> *EVY reaches out and draws his head to her.*

433

EVY Oh… oh… poor, poor, Billy.

T.S. Hopkinson!

> *HOPKINSON moves very slowly and speaks without expression. It's an effort for him to get up.*

T.S. What're you waiting for… where's your report?

HOPKINSON Sir.

T.S. You've come up with what?

HOPKINSON Sir.

T.S. A reason to board her, remember?

HOPKINSON Sir.

T.S. Kindly observe. (*clearing his throat*) Captain Yomamoto! Captain Yomamoto! Is there a Captain Yomamoto in the house? Ah, my dear Captain, there you are. If you wouldn't mind taking a seat.

> *T.S. indicates a chair for the Captain, who is exceedingly short.*

How many times have we had this conversation? How many times must we have this conversation? Yes, yes, I know what you said before: "strictly speaking" your passengers have not mutinied, hence you are reluctant to lay a charge…. Truly a commendable stance — however. Let us forget "strictly speaking" for a moment. How about trying "laxly speaking," "loosely speaking," "informally speaking" — could you find it in your heart to lay a charge "loosely speaking" against the passengers of the *Komagata Maru*? Nothing has changed, huh?… Not so quick, Captain, one more minute please…. While casually flipping through my classified copy of condensed Canadian law "What to Do in a Pinch" I found the most interesting — oh, I'm sure you'd be interested — you see it says right here, as I interpret this small item here…. Yes, right here in very small print — You can't see it? But my dear Captain, I assure you I can. It states: If given formal notice to sail, then sail you must, tout de suite — it's a bilingual law — or be subject to a fine of $500.00. That's per person aboard. "With-the-Power-Vested-in-Me-by-His-Majesty's-Government-I-Hereby-Give-You-Formal-Notice-to-Sail!" Now, let me see, 500 times 356, that's put down the zero, carry the three — what was that you just said? You wish to press charges? Mutiny, sedition, treason, and — blackmail? Be serious, my dear fellow, the first is sufficient….

Mutiny!

M — that's Militia for instilling fear,

U — Union jack which God knows we hold dear,

T — for a tugboat, one you can't sink,

I — for informant, a nice word for fink,

N — for our Navy of fine volunteers,

Y — for Yomamoto, who finally signed

Here!

Hopkinson! Here are your papers.

Now, my good man, do your duty.

GEORG helps HOPKINSON on with his jacket.

GEORG I'm sorry about the letter. I pay no attention to her. She's a stupid woman.

HOPKINSON Yomamoto has signed, pressed charges of mutiny. The militia is lining the dock, they are armed, they wait in reserve.... We will engage the *Komagata Maru* at sea!

GEORG In the harbour, you mean.

HOPKINSON In the harbour. (*addressing a crowd*) We will mount an attack from the *Sea Lion*, the largest ocean-going tug in the port! Police Chief MacLennan shall lead 120 policemen and 40 special Immigration Officers —

GEORG May I volunteer my services, sir?

HOPKINSON In a paramilitary attack on the ship.

GEORG Will I come under fire, sir?

HOPKINSON On board the *Komagata Maru* are veteran soldiers.

GEORG Are they armed?

HOPKINSON Reliable sources inform me that weapons abound on the ship. They have made clubs from floating driftwood, possibly spears from bamboo poles.

T.S. He's forgotten the cargo of coal.

HOPKINSON Force will be met with force. Rifles will be issued before we embark...

T.S. (*prompting*) I expect every...

HOPKINSON I expect every man to do his duty. No doubt we will meet with stubborn opposition, but remember, we are a formidable force!

T.S. In an orderly manner.

WOMAN They are coming.

T.S. Board the *Sea Lion*.

WOMAN (*softly*) *Jai Khalsa*...[1]

GEORG It was fair-sized for a tug, but not large enough for a company of men such as we were.

WOMAN Stand back from the rail.

GEORG Four reporters came along for the ride. "Hoppy," they cried, "How about a smile for the press!" Mr. Hopkinson smiled.

WOMAN Get below.

GEORG It looked like a very big ship and the closer we got —

WOMAN They have guns.

GEORG The more quiet we were... silence.... The *Sea Lion* rode low in the water...

---

[1] *Jai Khalsa* A Punjabi cheer or shout of encouragement for Sikhs. "Jai" literally is "praise"; "Khalsa" is literally "pure," and is associated with baptized Sikhs.

as we looked up we saw them … lining the rails were great turbaned figures. We stared up at them …, they stared down at us … then …

T.S. (*low*) Throw out the grappling hooks.

WOMAN (*screaming*) *Jai Khalsa*!!

GEORG All hell broke loose!

WOMAN *Jai Khalsa*!

GEORG From three hundred odd throats came a yell!

WOMAN *Jai Khalsa*!

GEORG Followed by bricks from the boiler settings, scrap iron and coal!

WOMAN Hide!

GEORG Mostly coal!

WOMAN Hide below!

GEORG Coal rains around us!

WOMAN *Jai Khalsa*!

GEORG Hopkinson's hit again and again!

WOMAN *Jai Khalsa*!

GEORG They can see the gold braid on his hat!

HOPKINSON I look for the woman and child.

GEORG Get down! For God's sake get down!

WOMAN *Jai Khalsa*!

HOPKINSON I stand as straight as I can.

GEORG Take off your hat and get down! (*raising his gun to fire*)

HOPKINSON There's no order to fire! Don't fire!

WOMAN throws the missile of coal which knocks HOPKINSON down.

WOMAN *Jai Khalsa*!

A pause with HOPKINSON lying on the floor. EVY enters slowly with SOPHIE. They help HOPKINSON to the sofa and press a cloth to his head.

GEORG It was a total and humiliating defeat. What else can you expect? It was ridiculous. We go out with rifles and then never use them. The whole thing was poorly conceived. However, compared to the execution of the scheme, the conception was an act of genius!

SOPHIE What do you mean?

GEORG It was a stupid thing to do.

EVY Hold the cloth to your head, Bill. It's cold. It'll help.

HOPKINSON I'm alright. I just want something to wash with.

SOPHIE (*laughing*) I don't wonder. He looks like a chimney sweep, doesn't he, Georg?

GEORG There you sit, a servant in His Majesty's government, battered and bruised by a bunch of Hindus.

HOPKINSON Get me some water!

SOPHIE If you yell you can get it yourself.

GEORG Tell me the point of carrying rifles if nobody uses them?... And there he stood with his hat. The smart thing to do was remove it. No there he stood. Every time he was hit, they all cheered. The air rang with cheers!

SOPHIE I just thought of something... (*laughing*) Mr. Hopkinson, I guess it was you that ate crow, eh?

> *SOPHIE nudges GEORG who chuckles after a slight effort to restrain himself.*

It was him that ate crow!

HOPKINSON Get out! Get out and leave me alone!

> *SOPHIE and GEORG move to exit SL.*

SOPHIE It was him that ate crow.

> *They're still chuckling.*

GEORG Sophie.

> *They exit. WOMAN is at a meeting on the ship.*

WOMAN We have gained nothing but time! We've driven them off for only a while, what now we must press for is food! I say it is better we starve on their doorstep than out on the sea!

HOPKINSON Do you remember when I gave you your brooch?

EVY Yes.

HOPKINSON Do you like it?

EVY Yes, I do.

T.S. Order! Order!

> *HOPKINSON begins to adjust his clothing.*

EVY Bill — this time don't go.

T.S. Order!

EVY Say to hell with it.

T.S. Are you assembled?

> *EVY speaks as HOPKINSON joins T.S.*

EVY Don't go, Bill.

T.S. The meeting will come to order.... Well now, that was a bit of a balls-up yesterday, wasn't it?...

HOPKINSON goes to speak.

However, we aren't here to assign guilt, we can do that later. What's the next
step, that's the question. Any suggestions, Hopkinson?

HOPKINSON shakes his head slowly.

I thought not. Well, luckily we have in our midst a man with courage and
foresight. He has had refurbished, refitted, and manned a second-class
cruiser at Esquimalt, the *Rainbow*, length 300 feet, 3,600 gross tonnage with
two six-inch guns and six four-inch guns. A small hand please for Harry
Stevens, our federal M.P.... I think we can do better than that.

HOPKINSON claps.

Ah, yes... Mr. Stevens has worked diligently since the arrival of the *Komagata
Maru* in our waters. Diligence, perseverance, and patriotism always pay off.
Let the *Rainbow* push through the Narrows; let her anchor near enough to
the *Komagata Maru* for the sun to glint on her guns. Let our next message be
—we won't necessarily fire on you—but we will fire on you if necessary!
(*turning to leave*)

HOPKINSON Sir!... My informants in the Sikh community inform me—

T.S. Informants inform you? (*laughing*) You're being redundant, my boy.

HOPKINSON My people in the Sikh community tell me that threats have been
made. Death threats.

T.S. You've stirred up a hornet's nest, haven't you? You've opened up Pandora's Box.
You've created a maelstrom.

HOPKINSON I was following orders.

T.S. Let me tell you something—there's someone at the end of the yard...

HOPKINSON Bella Singh?

T.S. Not Bella Singh.... Someone who's not Bella Singh waits at the end of the
yard...

EVY Who is it out there?

HOPKINSON One of my men, I imagine.

EVY Why don't you go out?

HOPKINSON Later, perhaps.... Let him wait.

WOMAN (*laughing*) Do you know something? My son's lips have swollen and
burst from the thirst—they are covered with grease from the engines. My legs
are like sticks—if I smelled a real meal I would vomit—and you think a few

guns will make our knees knock? (*stopping laughing*) *Sale Haramazaade!*[1]
Give us supplies and we'll leave!

HOPKINSON See the cruiser... it has guns trained on the *Komagata Maru.*

EVY Will they fire on it?

HOPKINSON That—is not my concern.

EVY Don't you feel anything for them?

HOPKINSON You wouldn't understand.

EVY Yes I would. I would try.

HOPKINSON One has to make decisions. Commitments. To one side or another.

EVY What side are you on?

HOPKINSON The winning side.

EVY Are you winning?

HOPKINSON This time the *Komagata Maru* will sail.

EVY Do you think then you'll have won?

HOPKINSON I'm... tired. Let's go to bed. (*starting off*)

EVY Not right now.

> *HOPKINSON stops, turns to look at EVY.*

HOPKINSON Lie beside me. That's all.

EVY I don't want to.

HOPKINSON I don't have to ask! I can order!

> *EVY looks at him, then picks up her cards, begins to lay them out. After a moment, HOPKINSON leaves. Carnival music plays.*

T.S. Hurry! Hurry! Hurry! Absolutely the last and final chance to view the *Komagata Maru*! Anchored in picturesque Vancouver Harbour for two, count 'em, two glorious months! Note the cruiser standing by to the right, see the sun on its guns, what a fantastic sight! Ladies and gentlemen, can you truly afford to bypass this splendid spectacle? Run, my good friends, you mustn't walk, you must run! Cotton candy, taffy apples, popcorn and balloons! All this and a possible plus, the opportunity to view your very own navy in action with no threat to you!

> *Music stops.*

SOPHIE It's all so exciting... now tell me what are all the little boats doing?

GEORG Some of them are harassing the Sikhs, some of them are supplying the ship—the government is giving them provisions.

SOPHIE And what about the cargo of coal—if there's any left.

---

[1] *Sale Haramazaade* A Punjabi expletive. "You bastard" is a loose translation.

GEORG I hear the government may recompense them. My friends tell me they have promised them everything and will give them nothing. That's called diplomacy, eh Bill?

SOPHIE Oh look, everybody! Look! There's black smoke coming out of the smokestack... look the *Rainbow*'s moving... it's moving in... what's it going to do... I bet it's going to shoot, I hope it's going to shoot, it's.... Look, Evy! Come look! It's.... It's... it's moving — The *Komagata Maru*'s moving — and the *Rainbow*'s going right alongside.... We won! We won! Didn't we, Georg? Didn't we, Mr. Hopkinson? Aren't you even going to look? It's over and we won!

A bang of the cane and they freeze.

T.S. Over?... A note, Mr. Hopkinson, from the man at the end of the yard... "When the affairs were past any other remedy, I thought it righteous to draw my sword."

HOPKINSON looks at the note.

WOMAN (*hard, not sentimental*) We go back. My husband is dead. He died in their war. His father is dead. He died when they cut back the famine relief. I am a British subject, and my people's taxes have gone to their King. I am not a possession, a thing. I am myself and I will fight for myself and my son and my people. I am strong.

GEORG The whole thing has been most educational. I should thank you. I have made many valuable friends and good contacts. I owe it to you, Bill... Can I get you a drink, Sophie, get him a drink.

HOPKINSON (*stepping out to T.S.*) I have good men in the Indian community... good men... they produce... Bella Singh, Baboo Singh, Hermann Singh, Gunga Ram —

T.S. Mewa Singh?

HOPKINSON Not — Mewa Singh.

T.S. For God's sake, get on.

HOPKINSON Their lives are in danger... the community feels that they're traitors, surely they're loyal British subjects, like myself.

T.S. Hurry up.

HOPKINSON My own life has been threatened... I ask for —

T.S. Extra! Extra! Read all about it! War Declared! Recession Recedes! Factories Hum the National Anthem! Send your sons overseas! See all of Europe at federal expense! Check your programme for casting — the enemy's the Kraut! The Sikh's on our side! Extra! Extra! Read all about it!

GEORG (*picking up paper*) This can't help but work nicely for me.

HOPKINSON What?

GEORG I say the war shall increase my use to your department.

SOPHIE Isn't he smart, Evy? Georg is going places — and so is Sophie.

EVY (*looking up from her cards*) Christ, Sophie, it's a war.

GEORG It's also a good business deal.

EVY spits on the floor.

GEORG You should teach her some manners.

SOPHIE You're jealous.

EVY Oh Sophie.

SOPHIE It's true—you're jealous of me—Georg's up and doing—he gets around
—we have a good time. Look at him—he doesn't do anything since the
Komagata Maru. And you're just as bad. This place is just like a morgue. Who
wants to live in a morgue? I'll leave if I want to—I can, you know—I'll leave
anytime I want.

HOPKINSON No you won't.

SOPHIE Yes I will. Won't I, Georg? Whenever Georg wants.

HOPKINSON Georg wants what I give him! When I say move, you bloody well
move, when I say jump, you say how high. In this stinking world there's two
kinds, there's the ruler and the ruled—and when I see the likes of you, I know
where I stand! (*beginning to weaken*) Some people talk, and some people
listen, but by God, I act, and if... it weren't for people like me... people like
you... would still be down in the slime... I have my... I have my...

T.S. Bill?

HOPKINSON I have...

T.S. Mewa Singh waits at the end of the yard.

HOPKINSON Yes.

EVY moves to him.

WOMAN We dock at Budge Budge fourteen miles from Calcutta. We are to be
herded aboard trains and returned to the Punjab although many of us have
not been there for years. We resist. Police, reinforced by soldiers, open fire.
Men who shared their rancid flour with my son are dead. (*threatening*) We
will remember them.

T.S. Order! Order! The court will come to order! Will the Inspector take the stand!
Do you swear to tell the truth, the whole truth, and nothing hut the truth, as
it befits this case, so help you God?

HOPKINSON I do.

T.S. Might I ask if you were acquainted with one Hermann Singh?

HOPKINSON I was.

T.S. What was his character?

HOPKINSON He was a quiet, unassuming man, intensely loyal to his King.

T.S. What was the nature of your relationship?

HOPKINSON He rendered assistance to the government in the *Komagata Maru*
Incident.

T.S. Five and one half weeks after the departure of the *Komagata Maru*, one Pirt Warnes was walking along a little used trail on the Kitsilano Indian Reserve. It was quite a pleasant trail... he noticed what at first glance appeared to be a bundle of rags behind a log close to the path. He examined it. It was the badly decomposed body of an East Indian. The turban was wrapped round the ankles. Beside the body lay a leather satchel, an empty brandy flask, and an open straight razor. When he touched the head it came off in his hand. It was Hermann Singh. Let me ask you, Inspector, from your intimate knowledge of the Asian mind, would you say the facts as related are consistent with... suicide?

HOPKINSON No, I would not.

T.S. Ah... and if indeed it were murder, can you suggest a possible motive?

HOPKINSON By informing, Hermann Singh had incurred the hatred of his people.

T.S. You may step down.

EVY Why don't we go away?... Why can't we?... Bill?... Bill, talk to me!... I can leave. I can leave. And I will. *(exiting off stage)*

T.S. Six weeks after the departure of the *Komagata Maru*, Arjun Singh shot through the back of the head from behind!

HOPKINSON Arjun Singh is dead.

GEORG *(on the sofa, feet up, reading the paper)* He'll have to get a new stable of fellows, eh?

SOPHIE *(playing cards)* Where would he find them, eh?

GEORG *(laughing)* Good point... where is he going to find them?

T.S. September 5th, 1914... early evening... Bella Singh goes to the temple. Inside the temple, people are singing. They're singing hymns for Arjun Singh, Hermann Singh... Bella Singh takes off his shoes... Bella Singh enters the temple... Bella Singh moves to the back... Bella Singh sits in a corner... Bella Singh takes out a gun... he fires ten shots, scores nine out of ten, seven wounded, two dead. He never speaks till arrested.

GEORG Do you know what he says, Sophie? He says that he acted in self-defence, he says Bill will verify that... will you testify, Bill?

HOPKINSON Yes.

T.S. October 21st, 1914... My God, what a day! Look at that sky... and the leaves all russet and gold... the mountains like sentinels, just a light breeze, the city set like a precious gem on the Pacific... breathe in... breathe out... breathe in... breathe out...

HOPKINSON I leave the house early. I walk to the court house. It's fall... I feel like a toy man walking through a toy town. Everything's working. My arms and my legs move so well together, there is... a mechanical precision to everything... I notice the houses seem neater than usual, a certain precision... at the same time, it's slower, things are slower, but very precise... there are no clouds in the sky, and it's blue, a deep blue... there's a slight breeze... the veins in the leaves protrude as if swollen... toy mountains frame my toy town... I'm just a bit late because of the walk. I enter the court house from Howe

Street. As I wait for the lift to take me up to the court, I place very carefully one hand on the wall, feeling the wall, and feeling my hand on the wall, in this tiny toy court… I open the door of the lift, I step inside, then I close it. I think of the peace of the coffin. I think of the safety of the cage. I open the door. I step out. I walk down the corridor. I see no one I know…

T.S. Mewa Singh waits in the witness room.

HOPKINSON I stop at the witness room.

T.S. Mewa Singh steps out of the witness room. In each hand he carries a gun.

HOPKINSON When I see him, I feel myself bursting. My toy town is destroyed in an instant. He is large, he encompasses my world, I feel myself racing towards eternity. They say I grapple with him. I do not. I open my arms, I say: Now!
Dazzles the sparkle of his sword
Who is utterly dreadful and is contained not
By the elements. And when he performeth
His death-dance, how dolefully his bells
toll and knell.
He, the four-armed one, of a lustrous hair bun,
He wieldeth the mace and the club,
And crushes the swollen head, even of death.
His auspicious tongue of blazing fire
Licketh all that is unholy.
When shrieks his horrid conch
The whole universe reverberates with its
raucous notes
How tintinnabulating are thy ankle bells,
And when thou movest, thou stampest the earth like a quake,
And thy immense gongs strike deep resonant notes.

T.S. Mewa Singh fires three times. A bullet pierces Hopkinson's heart.

> *T.S. touches HOPKINSON with the cane. HOPKINSON's head falls forward.*

WOMAN Mewa Singh will be hanged by the neck till he's dead. Mewa Singh says on the gallows: "I am a gentle person, but gentle people must act when injustice engulfs them. Let God judge my actions for he sees the right and the wrong. I offer my neck to the rope as a child opens his arms to his mother."

> *T.S. does a soft-shoe shuffle, stops, looks out, raises his arms, pauses and makes a large but simple bow. Black.*

THE END.

1976

Jean Rhys

Jean Rhys (1890–1979) was born in Dominica to a Welsh father and white Creole mother. She spent the first seventeen years of her life there and then left for Britain and Paris, where she spent the rest of her life. She wrote five novels, including *Voyage in the Dark* (1934) and *Wide Sargasso Sea* (1966), several short-story collections — including *The Left Bank and Other Stories* (1927) — and *Smile Please: An Unfinished Autobiography* (1979).

The likely setting of Rhys's "I Used to Live Here Once" is the Caribbean island of Dominica, where Rhys spent her girlhood with her parents. Her novel *Wide Sargasso Sea* also makes use of this locale. The protagonist of the story is someone returning after many years to a place that was possibly her home. But could she be a supernatural revenant as well? Can this be read as a gothic story? Is the story deliberately ambiguous? The crossing of the river (Jordan? Styx?) is one such ambiguous element. Are there others? Whether we see the story as natural or supernatural, what does the revenant learn? Can we identify the ethnicity of the narrator? Is it important/necessary to do so? Note that she speaks in standard English. Is there any significance to the use of the first person in the title?

I Used to Live Here Once

She was standing by the river looking at the stepping stones and remembering each one. There was the round unsteady stone, the pointed one, the flat one in the middle — the safe stone where you could stand and look round. The next wasn't so safe for when the river was full the water flowed over it and even when it showed dry it was slippery. But after that it was easy and soon she was standing on the other side.

The road was much wider than it used to be but the work had been done carelessly. The felled trees had not been cleared away and the bushes looked trampled. Yet it was the same road and she walked along feeling extraordinarily happy.

It was a fine day, a blue day. The only thing was that the sky had a glassy look that she didn't remember. That was the only word she could think of. Glassy. She turned the corner, saw that what had been the old pave had been taken up, and there too the road was much wider, but it had the same unfinished look.

She came to the worn stone steps that led up to the house and her heart began to beat. The screw pine was gone, so was the mock summer house called the ajoupa, but the clove tree was still there and at the top of the steps the rough lawn stretched away, just as she remembered it. She stopped and looked towards the house that had been added to and painted white. It was strange to see a car standing in front of it.

There were two children under the big mango tree, a boy and a little girl, and she waved to them and called "Hello" but they didn't answer her or turn their heads. Very fair children, as Europeans born in the West Indies so often are: as if the white blood is asserting itself against all odds.

The grass was yellow in the hot sunlight as she walked towards them. When she was quite close she called again, shyly: "Hello." Then, "I used to live here once," she said.

Still they didn't answer. When she said for the third time "Hello" she was quite near them. Her arms went out instinctively with the longing to touch them.

It was the boy who turned. His grey eyes looked straight into hers. His expression didn't change. He said: "Hasn't it gone cold all of a sudden. D'you notice? Let's go in." "Yes let's," said the girl.

Her arms fell to her sides as she watched them running across the grass to the house. That was the first time she knew.

1976

Kevin Roberts

Kevin Roberts (b. 1940) was born in Australia and immigrated to Canada in 1965, where he has taught creative writing for many years at Malaspina University College. In addition to his many books of poetry—including *Cariboo Fishing Notes* (1973), *Stonefish* (1982), *Nanoose Bay Suite* (1984), and *Writing the Tides: New and Selected Poetry* (2006)—he has published two books of short stories and a novel, *Tears in a Glass Eye* (1989). He lives on Vancouver Island.

Roberts's "Mah Fung," depicts the privations of an indentured Canadian Chinese coal-mine worker in 1873. Roberts has said, "There was no written history of the Chinese miners who lived and died in the coal mines in those times, so I invented this persona who was tragically exploited in both countries. His life was reduced by the Coal managers to a mere number because they could not pronounce his name." Compare this poem with F.R. Scott's "All the Spikes but the Last" and Eva Johnson's "Murras." Roberts's "Thai Logging Protest" portrays a Thai monk's belief in the sanctity of all living things; his spiritual motivation could be compared with the literary devotion to nature of the poet in V.S. Naipaul's "B. Wordsworth."

Mah Fung

And these also
Among the dead
Chinamen nos. 7,
23 and 11,
names unknown
May 3, 1887

And Lee Kung leaned forward
With the papers
And his gold rings flashed
And he said
Is it not better to labour
for ten years
among the barbarians
and gain respect upon one's return
than to live and die in poverty
here in Kiang-Tze
and be a bare branch
unremembered by one's sons?

and Mah Fung looked at Mai Wong's bright eyes
and made his mark upon the papers

and was seasick for five weeks
on the voyage

and felt his stomach rise again
to his mouth
the first time they dropped him
faster than a stone
in the cage down No 1 Mine
and in the darkness
he swung his pick and wound
the gutbuster into the black coal face
dreaming of the green
terraced rice fields Lee Kung
was buying for him every month
a day's walk from the village of
Kiang-Tze and Mai Wong's
bright eyes   and as well
the gold piece he bought
at the Hudson's Bay Bank
every two months and buried
in the dirt floor of his shack

and the seasons merged
with the dark of the pit face
and Lee Kung's letter
he folded and unfolded
and read till it fell
in squares and he could no longer
read of the new law
that took his bright
terraced rice fields and his money
and of the marriage of Mai Wong

and he dug up twenty-four gold pieces
polished them and bought land
from the barbarians and grew vegetables
and sold them and buried more gold
pieces in his land at night and coughed
in the pit face and buried more gold pieces
until each Spring when he planted
cabbages and potatoes his spade
turned the old gold pieces in
with the bright new ones and the seeds

and he leaned on his shovel
to cough up the black dust
and saw the dark mountains
above him tipped with snow and dark
trees all about the edge of his field

and looked down one day after rain
and saw in a big pool of still water
that his beard and hair were white

and went that day to buy
ship passage back to Kiang-Tze
May 3, 1887, his last shift
in No. 1 mine and coughed so much
he was on his knees
when the first explosion burst
the pit face and buried him
squatting like an ancient foetus
in the middle of the earth.

1980

Thai Logging Protest

A traffic hold up, tv cameras
on the side of the road near Ban Pong[1]

the old monk's glasses flash
as he folds his saffron robes
over his bare knees
crosslegged at the foot
of an old teak tree

his young followers fold
down into human lotuses
each at the base of a teak tree
petals of gold about the old monk

---

[1] *Ban Pong* A town in Thailand.

who listens patiently to
the policeman's rising voice
hands on hips, his Colt .45 juts out
his chin thrust forward

behind him a knot
of loggers in shorts
black singlets stand bemused,
their chainsaws
idle at their feet

as the policeman raises his hands
shouts   but the old monk
lifts both his hands
into a closed lotus bows his head

the policeman drops his hands
shrugs a *mai pen rai*[1]
what can you do?
retreats and later on Thai tv
a close up of the monk's
crinkled apple smile
and my friend translates the monk's quiet words

all living things, the monk says
must not die before their time.

1980

---

[1] Translation given in the next line.

Salman Rushdie

Salman Rushdie (b. 1947) was born in Bombay, India. He was educated at Rugby and Cambridge, England, graduating with a degree in history. His novels include *Grimus* (1975), *Midnight's Children* (1981), and the controversial *The Satanic Verses* (1988), which led to death threats (in the form of a *fatwa*) against him. Among his later publications are *The Moor's Last Sigh* (1995), *The Ground Beneath her Feet* (1998), *Shalimar the Clown (2005)*, and *The Enchantress of Florence* (2008). A prolific, engaging essayist, he has published also *Imaginary Homelands: Essays and Criticism* (1991) and *Step Across this Line: Collected Nonfiction 1992–2002* (2002).

Rushdie's essay "'Commonwealth Literature' Does Not Exist" is a thoughtful assessment of the inadequacy of this term as it relates to the new literatures written in English. He shows the difficulty of pigeonholing writers into an artificial body of writing, which was being ghettoized by "mainstream" English writers and scholars. Compare this essay with Naipaul's "Jasmine." Rushdie's "Outside the Whale" is a "writing back" to films, television shows, and novels on India, offering a corrective to their portrayal of India. It may be worth your while to examine these films and books in light of Rushdie's criticism. Compare this essay to other works that deliberately "write back to the Empire": Witi Ihimaera's "This Life Is Weary" and Ernest Crosby's "The Real 'White Man's Burden.'"

"Commonwealth Literature" Does Not Exist

When I was invited to speak at the 1983 English Studies Seminar in Cambridge, the lady from the British Council offered me a few words of reassurance. "It's all right," I was told, "for the purposes of our seminar, English studies are taken to include Commonwealth literature." At all other times, one was forced to conclude, these two would be kept strictly apart, like squabbling children, or sexually incompatible pandas, or, perhaps, like unstable, fissile materials whose union might cause explosions.

A few weeks later I was talking to a literature don—a specialist, I ought to say, in *English* literature—a friendly and perceptive man. "As a Commonwealth writer," he suggested, "you probably find, don't you, that there's a kind of liberty, certain advantages, in occupying, as you do, a position on the periphery?"

And then a British magazine published, in the same issue, interviews with Shiva Naipaul, Buchi Emecheta and myself. In my interview, I admitted that I had begun to find this strange term, "Commonwealth literature," unhelpful and even a little distasteful; and I was interested to read that in *their* interviews, both Shiva Naipaul and Buchi Emecheta, in their own ways, said much the same thing. The three interviews appeared, therefore, under the headline: "Commonwealth writers...but don't call them that!"

By this point, the Commonwealth was becoming unpopular with me.

Isn't this the very oddest of beasts, I thought—a school of literature whose supposed members deny vehemently that they belong to it. Worse, these denials are simply disregarded! It seems the creature has taken on a life of its own. So when I was invited to a conference about the animal in—of all places—Sweden, I thought I'd better go along to take a closer look at it.

The conference was beautifully organized, packed with erudite and sophisticated persons capable of discoursing at length about the new spirit of experiment in English-language writing in the Philippines. Also, I was able to meet writers from all over the world—or, rather, the Commonwealth. It was such a seductive environment that it almost persuaded me that the subject under discussion actually existed, and was not simply a fiction, and a fiction of a unique type, at that, in that it has been created solely by critics and academics, who have then proceeded to believe in it wholeheartedly... but the doubts did, in spite of all temptations to succumb, persist.

Many of the delegates, I found, were willing freely to admit that the term "Commonwealth literature" was a bad one. South Africa and Pakistan, for instance, are not members of the Commonwealth, but their authors apparently belong to its literature. On the other hand, England, which, as far as I'm aware, has not been expelled from the Commonwealth quite yet, has been excluded from its literary manifestation. For obvious reasons. It would never do to include English literature, the great sacred thing itself, with this bunch of upstarts, huddling together under this new and badly made umbrella.

At the Commonwealth literature conference I talked with and listened to the Australian poet Randolph Stow; the West Indian, Wilson Harris; Ngugi wa Thiong'o from Kenya; Anita Desai from India[1] and the Canadian novelist Aritha van Herk. I became quite sure that our differences were so much more significant than our similarities, that it was impossible to say what "Commonwealth literature"—the idea which had, after all, made possible our assembly—might conceivably mean. Van Herk spoke eloquently about the problem of drawing imaginative maps of the great emptinesses of Canada; Wilson Harris soared into great flights of metaphysical lyricism and high abstraction; Anita Desai spoke in whispers, her novel the novel of sensibility, and I wondered what on earth she could be held to have in common with the committed Marxist Ngugi, an overtly political writer, who expressed his rejection of the English language by reading his own work in Swahili, with a Swedish version read by his translator, leaving the rest of us completely bemused. Now obviously this great diversity would be entirely natural in a general literature conference—but this was a particular school of literature, and I was trying to work out what that school was supposed to be.

The nearest I could get to a definition sounded distinctly patronizing: "Commonwealth literature," it appears, is that body of writing created, I think, in the English language, by persons who are not themselves white Britons, or Irish, or citizens of

---

[1] Writings by some of the authors mentioned throughout Rushdie's essay are included in this anthology.

the United States of America. I don't know whether black Americans are citizens of this bizarre Commonwealth or not. Probably not. It is also uncertain whether citizens of Commonwealth countries writing in languages other than English — Hindi, for example — or who switch out of English, like Ngugi, are permitted into the club or asked to keep out.

By now "Commonwealth literature" was sounding very unlikeable indeed. Not only was it a ghetto, but it was actually an exclusive ghetto. And the effect of creating such a ghetto was, is, to change the meaning of the far broader term "English literature" — which I'd always taken to mean simply the literature of the English language — into something far narrower, something topographical, nationalistic, possibly even racially segregationist.

It occurred to me, as I surveyed this muddle, that the category is a chimera, and in very precise terms. The word has of course come to mean an unreal, monstrous creature of the imagination; but you will recall that the classical chimera was a monster of a rather special type. It had the head of a lion, the body of a goat and a serpent's tail. This is to say, it could exist only in dreams, being composed of elements which could not possibly be joined together in the real world.

The dangers of unleashing such a phantom into the groves of literature are, it seems to me, manifold. As I mentioned, there is the effect of creating a ghetto, and that, in turn, does lead to a ghetto mentality amongst some of its occupants. Also, the creation of a false category can and does lead to excessively narrow, and sometimes misleading, readings of some of the artists it is held to include; and again, the existence — or putative existence — of the beast distracts attention from what is actually worth looking at, what is actually going on. I thought it might be worth spending a few minutes reflecting further on these dangers.

I'll begin from an obvious starting place. English is by now the world language. It achieved this status partly as a result of the physical colonization of a quarter of the globe by the British, and it remains ambiguous but central to the affairs of just about all the countries to whom it was given, along with mission schools, trunk roads and the rules of cricket, as a gift of the British colonizers.

But its present-day pre-eminence is not solely — perhaps not even primarily — the result of the British legacy. It is also the effect of the primacy of the United States of America in the affairs of the world. This second impetus towards English could be termed a kind of linguistic neo-colonialism, or just plain pragmatism on the part of many of the world's governments and educationists, according to your point of view.

As for myself, I don't think it is always necessary to take up the anti-colonial — or is it post-colonial? — cudgels against English. What seems to me to be happening is that those peoples who were once colonized by the language are now rapidly remaking it, domesticating it, becoming more and more relaxed about the way they use it — assisted by the English language's enormous flexibility and size, they are carving out large territories for themselves within its frontiers.

To take the case of India, only because it's the one with which I'm most familiar.

The debate about the appropriateness of English in post-British India has been raging ever since 1947; but today, I find, it is a debate which has meaning only for the older generation. The children of independent India seem not to think of English as being irredeemably tainted by its colonial provenance. They use it as an Indian language, as one of the tools they have to hand.

(I am simplifying, of course, but the point is broadly true.)

There is also an interesting North-South divide in Indian attitudes to English. In the North, in the so-called "Hindi belt," where the capital, Delhi, is located, it is possible to think of Hindi as a future national language; but in South India, which is at present suffering from the attempts of central government to *impose* this national language on it, the resentment of Hindi is far greater than of English. After spending quite some time in South India, I've become convinced that English is an essential language in India, not only because of its technical vocabularies and the international communication which it makes possible, but also simply to permit two Indians to talk to each other in a tongue which neither party hates.

Incidentally, in West Bengal, where there is a State-led move against English, the following graffito, a sharp dig at the State's Marxist chief minister, Jyoti Basu, appeared on a wall, in English: it said, "My son won't learn English; your son won't learn English; but Jyoti Basu will send his son abroad to learn English."

One of the points I want to make is that what I've said indicates, I hope, that Indian society and Indian literature have a complex and developing relationship with the English language. This kind of post-colonial dialectic is propounded as one of the unifying factors in "Commonwealth literature"; but it clearly does not exist, or at least is far more peripheral to the problems of literatures in Canada, Australia, even South Africa. Every time you examine the general theories of "Commonwealth literature" they come apart in your hands.

English literature has its Indian branch. By this I mean the literature of the English language. This literature is also Indian literature. There is no incompatibility here. If history creates complexities, let us not try to simplify them.

So: English is an Indian literary language, and by now, thanks to writers like Tagore, Desani, Chaudhuri, Mulk Raj Anand, Raja Rao, Anita Desai and others, it has quite a pedigree. Now it is certainly true that the English-language literatures of England, Ireland and the USA are older than, for example, the Indian; so it's possible that "Commonwealth literature" is no more than an ungainly name for the world's younger English literatures. If that were true or, rather, if that were all, it would be a relatively unimportant misnomer. But it isn't all. Because the term is not used simply to describe, or even misdescribe, but also to *divide*. It permits academic institutions, publishers, critics and even readers to dump a large segment of English literature into a box and then more or less ignore it. At best, what is called "Commonwealth literature" is positioned *below* English literature "proper" — or, to come back to my friend the don, it places Eng. Lit. at the centre and the rest of the world at the periphery. How depressing that such a view should persist in the study of literature long after it has been discarded in the study of everything else English.

What is life like inside the ghetto of "Commonwealth literature?" Well, every ghetto has its own rules, and this one is no exception.

One of the rules, one of the ideas on which the edifice rests, is that literature is an expression of nationality. What Commonwealth literature finds interesting in Patrick White is his Australianness; in Doris Lessing, her Africanness; in V.S. Naipaul, his West Indianness, although I doubt that anyone would have the nerve to say so to his face. Books are almost always praised for using motifs and symbols out of the author's own national tradition, or when their form echoes some traditional form, obviously pre-English, and when the influences at work upon the writer can be seen to be wholly internal to the culture from which he "springs." Books which mix traditions, or which seek consciously to break with tradition, are often treated as highly suspect. To give one example. A few years ago the Indian poet, Arun Kolatkar, who works with equal facility in English and Marathi, wrote, in English, an award-winning series of poems called *Jejuri*, the account of his visit to a Hindu temple town. (Ironically, I should say, it won the Commonwealth Poetry Prize.) The poems are marvellous, contemporary, witty, and in spite of their subject they are the work of a non-religious man. They aroused the wrath of one of the doyens of Commonwealth literary studies in India, Professor C.D. Narasimhaiah, who, while admitting the brilliance of the poems, accused Kolatkar of making his work irrelevant by seeking to defy tradition.

What we are facing here is the bogy of Authenticity. This is something which the Indian art critic Geeta Kapur has explored in connection with modern Indian painting, but it applies equally well to literature. "Authenticity" is the respectable child of old-fashioned exoticism. It demands that sources, forms, style, language and symbol all derive from a supposedly homogeneous and unbroken tradition. Or else. What is revealing is that the term, so much in use inside the little world of "Commonwealth literature," and always as term of praise, would seem ridiculous outside this world. Imagine a novel being eulogized for being "authentically English," or "authentically German." It would seem absurd. Yet such absurdities persist in the ghetto.

In my own case, I have constantly been asked whether I am British, or Indian. The formulation "Indian-born British writer" has been invented to explain me. But, as I said last night, my new book deals with Pakistan. So what now? "British-resident Indo-Pakistani writer?" You see the folly of trying to contain writers inside passports.

One of the most absurd aspects of this quest for national authenticity is that — as far as India is concerned, anyway — it is completely fallacious to suppose that there is such a thing as a pure, unalloyed tradition from which to draw. The only people who seriously believe this are religious extremists. The rest of us understand that the very essence of Indian culture is that we possess a mixed tradition, a *mélange* of elements as disparate as ancient Mughal and contemporary Coca-Cola American. To say nothing of Muslim, Buddhist, Jain, Christian, Jewish, British, French, Portuguese, Marxist, Maoist, Trotskyist, Vietnamese, capitalist, and of course Hindu elements. Eclecticism, the ability to take from the world what seems fitting and to leave the rest, has always been a hallmark of the Indian tradition, and today it is at the centre of the best work being done both in the visual arts and in literature. Yet eclecticism is not really a nice word in the lexicon of "Commonwealth literature." So the reality of the mixed tradition is replaced by the fantasy of purity.

You will perhaps have noticed that the purpose of this literary ghetto — like that of all ghettos, perhaps — is to confine, to restrain. Its rules are basically conservative. Tradition is all; radical breaches with the past are frowned upon. No wonder so many of the writers claimed by "Commonwealth literature" deny that they have anything to do with it.

I said that the concept of "Commonwealth literature" did disservice to some writers, leading to false readings of their work; in India, I think this is true of the work of Ruth Jhabvala and, to a lesser extent, Anita Desai. You see, looked at from the point of view that literature must be nationally connected and even committed, it becomes simply impossible to understand the cast of mind and vision of a rootless intellect like Jhabvala's. In Europe, of course, there are enough instances of uprooted, wandering writers and even peoples to make Ruth Jhabvala's work readily comprehensible; but by the rules of the Commonwealth ghetto, she is beyond the pale. As a result, her reputation in India is much lower than it is in the West. Anita Desai, too, gets into trouble when she states with complete honesty that her work has no Indian models. The novel is a Western form, she says, so the influences on her are Western. Yet her delicate but tough fictions are magnificent studies of Indian life. This confuses the cohorts of the Commonwealth. But then, where "Commonwealth literature" is concerned, confusion is the norm.

I also said that the creation of this phantom category served to obscure what was really going on, and worth talking about. To expand on this, let me say that if we were to forget about "Commonwealth literature," we might see that there is a kind of commonality about much literature, in many languages, emerging from those parts of the world which one could loosely term the less powerful, or the powerless. The magical realism of the Latin Americans influences Indian language writers in India today. The rich, folk-tale quality of a novel like *Sandro of Chegem*, by the Muslim Russian Fazil Iskander, finds its parallels in the work — for instance — of the Nigerian, Amos Tutuola, or even Cervantes. It is possible, I think, to begin to theorize common factors between writers from these societies — poor countries, or deprived minorities in powerful countries — and to say that much of what is new in world literature comes from this group. This seems to me to be a "real" theory, bounded by frontiers which are neither political nor linguistic but imaginative. And it is developments of this kind which the chimera of "Commonwealth literature" obscures.

This transnational, cross-lingual process of pollination is not new. The works of Rabindranath Tagore, for example, have long been widely available in Spanish-speaking America, thanks to his close friendship with the Argentinian intellectual Victoria Ocampo. Thus an entire generation, or even two, of South American writers have read *Gitanjali, The Home and the World* and other works, and some, like Mario Vargas Llosa, say that they found them very exciting and stimulating.

If this "Third World literature" is one development obscured by the ghost of "Commonwealth literature," then "Commonwealth literature's" emphasis on writing in English distracts attention from much else that is worth our attention. I tried to show how in India the whole issue of language was a subject of deep contention. It is also worth saying that major work is being done in India in many languages other than English; yet outside India there is just about no interest in any of this work. The Indo-Anglians seize all the limelight. Very little is translated; very few of the best writers — Premchand, Anantha Moorthy — or the best novels are known, even by name.

To go on in this vein: it strikes me that, at the moment, the greatest area of friction in Indian literature has nothing to do with English literature, but with the effects of the hegemony of Hindi on the literatures of other Indian languages, particularly other North Indian languages. I recently met the distinguished Gujarati novelist, Suresh Joshi. He told me that he could write in Hindi but felt obliged to write in Gujarati because it was a language under threat. Not from English, or the West: from Hindi. In two or three generations, he said, Gujarati could easily die. And he compared it, interestingly, to the state of the Czech language under the yoke of Russian, as described by Milan Kundera.

This is clearly a matter of central importance for Indian literature. "Commonwealth literature" is not interested in such matters.

It strikes me that my title may not really be accurate. There is clearly such a thing as "Commonwealth literature," because even ghosts can be made to exist if you set up enough faculties, if you write enough books and appoint enough research students. It does not exist in the sense that writers do not write it, but that is of minor importance. So perhaps I should rephrase myself: "Commonwealth literature" should not exist. If it did not, we could appreciate writers for what they are, whether in English or not; we could discuss literature in terms of its real groupings, which may well be national, which may well be linguistic, but which may also be international, and based on imaginative affinities; and as far as Eng. Lit. itself is concerned, I think that if all English literatures could be studied together, a shape would emerge which would truly reflect the new shape of the language in the world, and we could see that Eng. Lit. has never been in better shape, because the world language now also possesses a world literature, which is proliferating in every conceivable direction.

The English language ceased to be the sole possession of the English some time ago. Perhaps "Commonwealth literature" was invented to delay the day when we rough beasts actually slouch into Bethlehem. In which case, it's time to admit that the centre cannot hold.

1983

Outside the Whale

Anyone who has switched on the television set, been to the cinema or entered a bookshop in the last few months will be aware that the British Raj, after three and a half decades in retirement, has been making a sort of comeback. After the big-budget fantasy double-bill of *Gandhi* and *Octopussy* we have had the blackface minstrel-show of *The Far Pavilions* in its TV serial incarnation, and immediately afterwards the overpraised *Jewel in the Crown*. I should also include the alleged "documentary" about Subhas Chandra Bose, Granada Television's *War of the Springing Tiger*, which, in the finest traditions of journalistic impartiality, described India's second-most-revered independence leader as a "clown." And lest we begin to console ourselves that the painful experiences are coming to an end, we are reminded that David Lean's film of *A Passage to India* is in the offing. I remember seeing an interview with Mr. Lean in *The Times*, in which he explained his reasons for wishing to make a film of Forster's novel. "I haven't seen Dickie Attenborough's *Gandhi* yet," he said, "but as far as I'm aware, nobody has yet succeeded in putting India on the screen." The Indian film industry, from Satyajit Ray to Mr. N.T. Rama Rao, will no doubt feel suitably humbled by the great man's opinion.

These are dark days. Having expressed my reservations about the Gandhi film elsewhere, I have no wish to renew my quarrel with Mahatma Dickie. As for *Octopussy*, one can only say that its portrait of modern India was as grittily and uncompromisingly realistic as its depiction of the skill, integrity and sophistication of the British secret services.

In defence of the Mahattenborough,[1] he did allow a few Indians to be played by Indians. (One is becoming grateful for the smallest of mercies.) Those responsible for transferring *The Far Pavilions* to the screen would have no truck with such tom-foolery. True, Indian actors were allowed to play the villains (Saeed Jaffrey, who has turned the Raj revival into a personal cottage industry, with parts in *Gandhi* and *Jewel in the Crown* as well, did his hissing and hand-rubbing party piece; and Sneh Gupta played the selfish princess but, unluckily for her, her entire part consisted of the interminably repeated line, "Ram Ram"). Meanwhile, the good-guy roles were firmly commandeered by Ben Cross, Christopher Lee, Omar Sharif, and, most memorably, Amy Irving as the good princess, whose make-up person obviously believed that Indian princesses dip their eyes in black ink and get sun-tans on their lips.

Now of course *The Far Pavilions* is the purest bilge. The great processing machines of TV soap-opera have taken the somewhat more fibrous garbage of the M.M. Kaye book and puréed it into easy-swallow, no-chewing-necessary drivel. Thus, the two central characters, both supposedly raised as Indians, have been lobotomized to the point of being incapable of pronouncing their own names. The man calls himself "A Shock," and the woman "An Jooly." Around and about them

---

[1] *Mahattenborough* Rushdie is playing with the names Mahatma and Attenborough.

there is branding of human flesh and snakery and widow-burning by the natives. There are Pathans who cannot speak Pushto. And, to avoid offending the Christian market, we are asked to believe that the child "A Shock," while being raised by Hindus and Muslims, somehow knew that neither "way" was for him, and instinctively, when he wished to raise his voice in prayer, "prayed to the mountains." It would be easy to conclude that such material could not possibly be taken seriously by anyone, and that it is therefore unnecessary to get worked up about it. Should we not simply rise above the twaddle, switch off our sets and not care?

I should be happier about this, the quietist option—and I shall have more to say about quietism later on—if I did not believe that it matters, it always matters, to name rubbish as rubbish; that to do otherwise is to legitimize it. I should also mind less, were it not for the fact that *The Far Pavilions*, book as well as TV serial, is only the latest in a very long line of fake portraits inflicted by the West on the East. The creation of a false Orient of cruel-lipped princes and dusky slim-hipped maidens, of ungodliness, fire and the sword, has been brilliantly described by Edward Said in his classic study *Orientalism*, in which he makes clear that the purpose of such false portraits was to provide moral, cultural and artistic justification for imperialism and for its underpinning ideology, that of the racial superiority of the Caucasian over the Asiatic. Let me add only that stereotypes are easier to shrug off if yours is not the culture being stereotyped; or, at the very least, if your culture has the power to counterpunch against the stereotype. If the TV screens of the West were regularly filled by equally hyped, big-budget productions depicting the realities of India, one could stomach the odd M.M. Kaye. When praying to the mountains is the norm, the stomach begins to heave.

Paul Scott was M.M. Kaye's agent, and it has always seemed to me a damning indictment of his literary judgement that he believed *The Far Pavilions* to be a good book. Even stranger is the fact that *The Raj Quartet* and the Kaye novel are founded on identical strategies of what, to be polite, one must call borrowing. In both cases, the central plot motifs are lifted from earlier, and much finer novels. In *The Far Pavilions* the hero Ash ("A Shock"), raised an Indian, discovered to be a sahib, and ever afterwards torn between his two selves, will be instantly recognizable as the cardboard cut-out version of Kipling's Kim. And the rape of Daphne Manners in the Bibighar Gardens derives just as plainly from Forster's *A Passage to India*. But because Kaye and Scott are vastly inferior to the writers they follow, they turn what they touch to pure lead. Where Forster's scene in the Marabar caves retains its ambiguity and mystery, Scott gives us not one rape but a gang assault, and one perpetrated what is more, by peasants. Smelly persons of the worst sort. So class as well as sex is violated; Daphne gets the works. It is useless, I'm sure, to suggest that if rape must be used as the metaphor of the Indo-British connection, then surely, in the interests of accuracy, it should be the rape of an Indian woman by one or more Englishmen of whatever class. But not even Forster dared to write about such a crime. So much more evocative to conjure up white society's fear of the darkie, of big brown cocks.

You will say I am being unfair; Scott is a writer of a different calibre to M.M. Kaye. What's more, very few of the British characters come at all well out of the Quartet — Barbie, Sarah, Daphne, none of the men. (Kaye, reviewing the TV adaptation, found it excessively rude about the British.)

In point of fact, I am not so sure that Scott is so much finer an artist. Like Kaye, he has an instinct for the cliché. Sadistic, bottom-flogging policeman Merrick turns out to be (surprise!) a closet homosexual. His grammar school origins give him (what else?) a chip on the shoulder. And all around him is a galaxy of chinless wonders, regimental *grandes dames*, lushes, empty-headed blondes, silly-asses, plucky young things, good sorts, bad eggs and Russian counts with eyepatches. The overall effect is rather like a literary version of Mulligatawny soup. It tries to taste Indian, but ends up being ultra-parochially British, only with too much pepper.

And yes, Scott is harsh in his portraits of many British characters; but I want to try and make a rather more difficult point, a point about *form*. The *Quartet*'s form tells us, in effect, that the history of the end of the Raj was largely composed of the doings of the officer class and its wife. Indians get walk ons, but remain, for the most part, bit-players in their own history. Once this form has been set, it scarcely matters that individual fictional Brits get unsympathetic treatment from their author. The form insists that *they are the ones whose stories matter*, and that is so much less than the whole truth that it must be called a falsehood. It will not do to argue that Scott was attempting to portray the British in India, and that such was the nature of imperialist society that the Indians would only have had bit-parts. It is no defence to say that a work adopts, in its structure, the very ethic which, in its content and tone, it pretends to dislike. It is, in fact, the case for the prosecution.

I cannot end this brief account of the Raj revival without returning to David Lean, a film director whose mere interviews merit reviews. I have already quoted his masterpiece in *The Times*; here now are three passages from his conversation with Derek Malcolm in the *Guardian* of 23 January 1984:

(1) Forster was a bit anti-English, anti-Raj and so on. I suppose it's a tricky thing to say, but I'm not so much. I intend to keep the balance more. I don't believe all the English were a lot of idiots. Forster rather made them so. He came down hard against them. I've cut out that bit at the trial where they try to take over the court. Richard [the producer] wanted me to leave it in. But I said no, it just wasn't right. They wouldn't have done that.

(2) As for Aziz, there's a hell of a lot of Indian in him. They're marvellous people but maddening sometimes, you know... He's a goose. But he's warm and you like him awfully. I don't mean that in a derogatory way — things just happen. He can't help it. And Miss Quested... well, she's a bit of a prig and a bore in the book, you know. I've changed her, made her more sympathetic. Forster wasn't always very good with women.

(3) One other thing. I've got rid of that "Not yet, not yet" bit. You know, when the Quit India stuff comes up, and we have the passage about driving us into the

sea? Forster experts have always said it was important, but the Fielding-Aziz friendship was not sustained by those sort of things. At least I don't think so. The book came out at the time of the trial of General Dyer and had a tremendous success in America for that reason. But I thought that bit rather tacked on. Anyway I see it as a personal not a political story.

Forster's lifelong refusal to permit his novel to be filmed begins to look rather sensible. But once a revisionist enterprise gets under way, the mere wishes of a dead novelist provide no obstacle. And there can be little doubt that in Britain today the refurbishment of the Empire's tarnished image is under way. The continuing decline, the growing poverty and the meanness of spirit of much of Thatcherite Britain encourages many Britons to turn their eyes nostalgically to the lost hour of their precedence. The recrudescence of imperialist ideology and the popularity of Raj fictions put one in mind of the phantom twitchings of an amputated limb. Britain is in danger of entering a condition of cultural psychosis, in which it begins once again to strut and to posture like a great power while, in fact, its power diminishes every year. The jewel in the crown is made, these days, of paste.

Anthony Barnett has cogently argued, in his television essay *Let's Take the "Great" Out of Britain*, that the idea of a great Britain (originally just a collective term for the countries of the British Isles, but repeatedly used to bolster the myth of national grandeur) has bedevilled the actions of all post-war governments. But it was Margaret Thatcher who, in the euphoria of the Falklands victory, most plainly nailed her colours to the old colonial mast, claiming that the success in the South Atlantic proved that the British were still the people "who had ruled a quarter of the world." Shortly afterwards she called for a return to Victorian values, thus demonstrating that she had embarked upon a heroic battle against the linear passage of Time.

I am trying to say something which is not easily heard above the clamour of praise for the present spate of British-Indian fictions: that works of art, even works of entertainment, do not come into being in a social and political vacuum; and that the way they operate in a society cannot be separated from politics, from history. For every text, a context; and the rise of Raj revisionism, exemplified by the huge success of these fictions, is the artistic counterpart of the rise of conservative ideologies in modern Britain. And no matter how innocently the writers and film-makers work, no matter how skilfully the actors act (and nobody would deny the brilliance of, for example, the performances of Susan Wooldridge as Daphne and Peggy Ashcroft as Barbie in the TV *Jewel*), they run the grave risk of helping to shore up the conservatism, by offering it the fictional glamour which its reality so grievously lacks.

The title of this essay derives, obviously, from that of an earlier piece (1940) by 1984's other literary phenomenon, Mr. Orwell. And as I'm going to dispute its assertions about the relationship between politics and literature, I must of necessity begin by offering a summary of that essay, "Inside the Whale."

It opens with a largely admiring analysis of the writing of Henry Miller:

On the face of it no material could be less promising. When *Tropic of Cancer* was published the Italians were marching into Abyssinia and Hitler's concentration camps were already bulging...It did not seem to be a moment at which a novel of outstanding value was likely to be written about American dead-beats cadging drinks in the Latin Quarter. Of course a novelist is not obliged to write directly about contemporary history, but a novelist who simply disregards the major public events of the moment is generally either a footler or a plain idiot. From a mere account of the subject matter of *Tropic of Cancer*, most people would probably assume it to be no more than a bit of naughty-naughty left over from the twenties. Actually, nearly everyone who read it saw at once that it was... a very remarkable book. How or why remarkable?

His attempt to answer that question takes Orwell down more and more tortuous roads. He ascribes to Miller the gift of opening up a new world "not by revealing what is strange, but by revealing what is familiar." He praises him for using English "as a spoken language, but spoken *without fear*, i.e., without fear of rhetoric or of the unusual or poetic word. It is a flowing, swelling prose, a prose with rhythms in it." And most crucially, he likens Miller to Whitman, "for what he is saying, after all, is 'I accept.'"

Around here things begin to get a little bizarre. Orwell quite fairly points out that to say "I accept" in life in the thirties "is to say that you accept concentration camps, rubber truncheons, Hitler, Stalin, bombs, aeroplanes, tinned food, machine-guns, putsches, purges, slogans, Bedaux belts, gas masks, submarines, spies, provocateurs, press censorship, secret prisons, aspirins, Hollywood films and political murders." (No, I don't know what a Bedaux belt is, either.) But in the very next paragraph he tells us that "precisely because, in one sense, he is passive to experience, Miller is able to get nearer to the ordinary man than is possible to more purposive writers. For the ordinary man is also passive." Characterizing the ordinary man as a victim, he then claims that only the Miller type of victim-books, "non political,... non-ethical,... non-literary,... non-contemporary," can speak with the people's voice. So to accept concentration camps and Bedaux belts turns out to be pretty worthwhile, after all.

There follows an attack on literary fashion. Orwell, a thirty-seven-year-old patriarch, tells us that "when one says that a writer is fashionable one practically always means that he is admired by people under thirty." At first he picks easy targets — A.E. Housman's "roselipt maidens" and Rupert Brooke's "Grantchester" ("a sort of accumulated vomit from a stomach stuffed with place-names"). But then the polemic is widened to include "the movement," the politically committed generation of Auden and Spender and MacNeice. "On the whole," Orwell says, "the literary history of the thirties seems to justify the opinion that a writer does well to keep out of politics." It is true he scores some points, as when he indicates the bourgeois, boarding-school origins of just about all these literary radicals, or when he connects the popularity of Communism among British intellectuals to the general middle-class disillusion with all traditional values: "Patriotism, religion, the Empire, the family, the sanctity of marriage, the Old School Tie, birth, breeding, honour, discipline — anyone of ordinary education could turn the whole lot of them inside out in three minutes." In this vacuum of ideology, he suggests, there was still "the need for something to believe in," and Stalinist Communism filled the void.

Returning to Henry Miller, Orwell takes up and extends Miller's comparison of Anaïs Nin to Jonah in the whale's belly.

> The whale's belly is simply a womb big enough for an adult... a storm that would sink all the battleships in the world would hardly reach you as an echo... Miller himself is inside the whale, ... a willing Jonah ... He feels no impulse to alter or control the process that he is undergoing. He has performed the essential Jonah act of allowing himself to be swallowed, remaining passive, *accepting*. It will be seen what this amounts to. It is a species of quietism.

And at the end of this curious essay, Orwell — who began by describing writers who ignored contemporary reality as "usually footlers or plain idiots" — embraces and espouses this quietist philosophy, this cetacean version of Pangloss's exhortation to "*cultiver notre jardin*." "Progress and reaction," Orwell concludes, "have both turned out to be swindles. Seemingly there is nothing left but quietism — robbing reality of its terrors by simply submitting to it. Get inside the whale — or rather, admit you are inside the whale (for you are, of course). Give yourself over to the world process... simply accept it, endure it, record it. That seems to be the formula that any sensitive novelist is now likely to adopt."

The sensitive novelist's reasons are to be found in the essay's last sentence, in which Orwell speaks of "the *impossibility* of any major literature until the world has shaken itself into its new shape."

And we are told that fatalism is a quality of Indian thought.

It is impossible not to include in any response to "Inside the Whale" the suggestion that Orwell's argument is much impaired by his choice, for a quietist model, of Henry Miller. In the forty-four years since the essay was first published, Miller's reputation has more or less completely evaporated, and he now looks to be very little more than the happy pornographer beneath whose scatological surface Orwell saw such improbable depths. If we, in 1984, are asked to choose between, on the one hand, the Miller of *Tropic of Cancer* and "the first hundred pages of *Black Spring*" and, on the other hand, the collected works of Auden, MacNeice and Spender, I doubt that many of us would go for old Henry. So it would appear that politically committed art can actually prove more durable than messages from the stomach of the fish.

It would also be wrong to go any further without discussing the senses in which Orwell uses the term "politics." Six years after "Inside the Whale," in the essay "Politics and the English Language" (1946), he wrote: "In our age there is no such thing as 'keeping out of politics.' All issues are political issues, and politics itself is a mass of lies, evasions, folly, hatred and schizophrenia."

For a man as truthful, direct, intelligent, passionate and sane as Orwell, "politics" had come to represent the antithesis of his own world-view. It was an underworld-become-overworld, Hell on earth. "Politics" was a portmanteau term which included everything he hated; no wonder he wanted to keep it out of literature.

I cannot resist the idea that Orwell's intellect, and finally his spirit, too, were broken by the horrors of the age in which he lived, the age of Hitler and Stalin (and, to be fair, by the ill health of his later years). Faced with the overwhelming evils of exterminations and purges and fire-bombings, and all the appalling manifestations of politics-gone-wild, he turned his talents to the business of constructing and also of justifying an escape-route. Hence his notion of the ordinary man as victim, and therefore of passivity as the literary stance closest to that of the ordinary man. He is using this type of logic as a means of building a path back to the womb, into the whale and away from the thunder of war. This looks very like the plan of a man who has given up the struggle. Even though he knows that there is no such thing as "keeping out of politics," he attempts the construction of a mechanism with just that purpose. Sit it out, he recommends; we writers will be safe inside the whale, until the storm dies down. I do not presume to blame him for adopting this position. He lived in the worst of times. But it is important to dispute his conclusions, because a philosophy built on an intellectual defeat must always be rebuilt at a later point. And undoubtedly Orwell did give way to a kind of defeatism and despair. By the time he wrote *Nineteen Eighty-Four*, sick and cloistered on Jura, he had plainly come to think that resistance was useless. Winston Smith considers himself a dead man from the moment he rebels. The secret book of the dissidents turns out to have been written by the Thought Police. All protest must end in Room 101. In an age when it often appears that we have all agreed to believe in entropy, in the proposition that things fall apart, that history is the irreversible process by which everything gradually gets worse, the unrelieved pessimism of *Nineteen Eighty-Four* goes some way towards explaining its status as a true myth of our times.

What is more (and this connects the year's parallel phenomena of Empire-revivalism and Orwellmania), the quietist option, the exhortation to submit to events, is an intrinsically conservative one. When intellectuals and artists withdraw from the fray, politicians feel safer. Once, the right and left in Britain used to argue about which of them "owned" Orwell. In those days both sides wanted him; and, as Raymond Williams has said, the tug-of-war did his memory little honour. I have no wish to reopen these old hostilities; but the truth cannot be avoided, and the truth is that passivity always serves the interests of the status quo, of the people already at the top of the heap, and the Orwell of "Inside the Whale" and *Nineteen Eighty-Four* is advocating ideas that can only be of service to our masters. If resistance is useless, those whom one might otherwise resist become omnipotent.

It is much easier to find common ground with Orwell when he comes to discuss the relationship between politics and language. The discoverer of Newspeak was aware that "when the general [political] atmosphere is bad, language must suffer." In "Politics and the English Language" he gives us a series of telling examples of the perversion of meaning for political purposes. "Statements like 'Marshal Pétain was a true patriot,' 'The Soviet Press is the freest in the world,' 'The Catholic Church is opposed to persecution' are almost always made with intent to deceive," he writes. He also provides beautiful parodies of politicians' metaphor-mixing:

"The Fascist octopus has sung its swan song, the jackboot is thrown into the melting pot." Recently, I came across a worthy descendant of these grand old howlers: *The Times*, reporting the smuggling of classified documents out of Civil Service departments, referred to the increased frequency of "leaks" from "a high-level mole."

It's odd, though, that the author of *Animal Farm*, the creator of so much of the vocabulary through which we now comprehend these distortions—doublethink, thoughtcrime, and the rest—should have been unwilling to concede that literature was best able to defend language, to do battle with the twisters, *precisely by entering the political arena*. The writers of the Group 47 in post-war Germany, Grass, Böll and the rest, with their "rubble literature" whose purpose and great achievement it was to rebuild the German language from the rubble of Nazism, are prime instances of this power. So, in quite another way, is a writer like Joseph Heller. In *Good as Gold* the character of the presidential aide Ralph provides Heller with some superb satire at the expense of Washingtonspeak. Ralph speaks in sentences that usually conclude by contradicting their beginnings: "This administration will back you all the way until it has to"; "This President doesn't want yes-men. What we want are independent men of integrity who will agree with all our decisions after we make them." Every time Ralph opens his oxymoronic mouth he reveals the limitations of Orwell's view of the interaction between literature and politics. It is a view which excludes comedy, satire, deflation; because of course the writer need not always be the servant of some beetle browed ideology. He can also be its critic, its antagonist, its scourge. From Swift to Solzhenitsyn, writers have discharged this role with honour. And remember Napoleon the Pig.

Just as it is untrue that politics ruins literature (even among "ideological" political writers, Orwell's case would founder on the great rock of Pablo Neruda), so it is by no means axiomatic that the "ordinary man," *l'homme moyen sensuel*, is politically passive. We have seen that the myth of this inert commoner was a part of Orwell's logic of retreat; but it is nevertheless worth reminding ourselves of just a few instances in which the "ordinary man"—not to mention the "ordinary woman" —has been anything but inactive. We may not approve of Khomeini's Iran, but the revolution there was a genuine mass movement. So is the revolution in Nicaragua. And so, let us not forget, was the Indian revolution. I wonder if independence would have arrived in 1947 if the masses, ignoring Congress and the Muslim League, had remained seated inside what would have had to be a very large whale indeed.

The truth is that there is no whale. We live in a world without hiding places; the missiles have made sure of that. However much we may wish to return to the womb, we cannot be unborn. So we are left with a fairly straightforward choice. Either we agree to delude ourselves, to lose ourselves in the fantasy of the great fish, for which a second metaphor is that of Pangloss's garden; or we can do what all human beings do instinctively when they realize that the womb has been lost for ever — that is, we can make the very devil of a racket. Certainly, when we cry, we cry partly for the safety we have lost; but we also cry to affirm ourselves, to say, here I am, I matter, too, you're going to have to reckon with me. So, in place of Jonah's womb, I am recommending the ancient tradition of making as big a fuss, as noisy a complaint about the world as is humanly possible. Where Orwell wished quietism, let there be rowdyism; in place of the whale, the protesting wail. If we can cease envisaging ourselves as metaphorical foetuses, and substitute the image of a new-born child, then that will be at least a small intellectual advance. In time, perhaps, we may even learn to toddle.

I must make one thing plain: I am not saying that all literature must now be of this protesting, noisy type. Perish the thought; now that we are babies fresh from the womb, we must find it possible to laugh and wonder as well as rage and weep. I have no wish to nail myself, let alone anyone else, to the tree of political literature for the rest of my writing life. Lewis Carroll and Laurence Sterne are as important to literature as Swift or Brecht. What I am saying is that politics and literature, like sport and politics, do mix, are inextricably mixed, and that that mixture has consequences.

The modern world lacks not only hiding places, but certainties. There is no consensus about reality between, for example, the nations of the North and of the South. What President Reagan says is happening in Central America differs so radically from, say, the Sandinista version, that there is almost no common ground. It becomes necessary to take sides, to say whether or not one thinks of Nicaragua as the United States's "front yard" (Vietnam, you will recall, was the "back yard"). It seems to me imperative that literature enter such arguments, because what is being disputed is nothing less than *what is the case*, what is truth and what untruth. If writers leave the business of making pictures of the world to politicians, it will be one of history's great and most abject abdications.

Outside the whale is the unceasing storm, the continual quarrel, the dialectic of history. Outside the whale there is a genuine need for political fiction, for books that draw new and better maps of reality, and make new languages with which we can understand the world. Outside the whale we see that we are all irradiated by history, we are radioactive with history and politics; we see that it can be as false to create a politics-free fictional universe as to create one in which nobody needs to work or eat or hate or love or sleep. Outside the whale it becomes necessary, and even exhilarating, to grapple with the special problems created by the incorporation of political material, because politics is by turns farce and tragedy, and sometimes (e.g., Zia's Pakistan) both at once. Outside the whale the writer is obliged to accept that he (or she) is part of the crowd, part of the ocean, part of the storm, so that objectivity becomes a great dream, like perfection, an unattainable goal for which one must struggle in spite of the impossibility of success. Outside the whale is the world of Samuel Beckett's famous formula: *I can't go on, I'll go on.*

This is why (to end where I began) it really is necessary to make a fuss about Raj fiction and the zombie-like revival of the defunct Empire. The various films and TV shows and books I discussed earlier propagate a number of notions about history which must be quarrelled with, as loudly and as embarrassingly as possible.

These include: The idea that non-violence makes successful revolutions; the peculiar notion that Kasturba Gandhi could have confided the secrets of her sex-life to Margaret Bourke-White; the bizarre implication that any Indians could look like or speak like Amy Irving or Christopher Lee; the view (which underlies many of these works) that the British and Indians actually understood each other jolly well, and that the end of the Empire was a sort of gentleman's agreement between old pals at the club; the revisionist theory—see David Lean's interviews—that *we, the British, weren't as bad as people make out*; the calumny, to which the use of rape-plots lends credence, that frail English roses were in constant sexual danger from lust-crazed wogs (just such a fear lay behind General Dyer's Amritsar massacre); and, above all, the fantasy that the British Empire represented something "noble" or "great" about Britain; that it was, in spite of all its flaws and meannesses and bigotries, fundamentally glamorous.

If books and films could be made and consumed in the belly of the whale, it might be possible to consider them merely as entertainment, or even, on occasion, as art. But in our whaleless world, in this world without quiet corners, there can be no easy escapes from history, from hullabaloo, from terrible, unquiet fuss.

1984

F.R. Scott

Frank R. Scott (1899–1985) was born in Quebec City, Canada. He was a Rhodes scholar at Oxford University. He studied law at McGill University and was Dean of Law there. Active in Canadian law, literature, and politics, he has published such texts as *The Eye of the Needle: Satire, Sorties, Sundries* (1957), *Essays on the Constitution: Aspects of Canadian Law and Politics* (1977), and *The Collected Poems of F.R. Scott* (1981).

Scott's "To the Poets of India" is a poetic recognition of human commonality no matter the differences in language, history, customs, flora, and fauna. "All the Spikes but the Last" was written as a response to Edward Pratt ("Ned" of the poem), whose epic poem on the building of the transcontinental railway across Canada, "Towards the Last Spike," ignores the contribution of the Chinese labourers. The builders (Canadian Pacific Railway) received millions of acres from the government of Canada on completion of this monumental achievement (see footnotes to the poem). Scott, a socialist and humanitarian, prods his friend Pratt about this "oversight" in his poem. Compare this poem with Kevin Roberts's "Mah Fung."

To the Poets of India

I read poems taken from old Indian tongues —
Bengali, Hindi, Telugu, Urdu, Kannada —
"Engraved with lines of agony"
Or with the "irrepressible desire to utter Omkar,"
The name of God,
And it seemed of me they were speaking.
When their tears fell, they poured out my anguish,
Far glories were mine on the Punjabi hills,
In the eyes of their women I saw the passion too.

Strange images were used. I do not know
"The thin branches of siris, amlaki, hocul and neem,"[1]
Nor how "A baby vulture cries out in a banyan,"

But the image of the image is the same.
Where I sit now, against this Canadian sky,
Branches of maple and of elm are thin,
A cry goes up in the night,

---

[1] *siris … neem* Various trees in India.

And over in Caughnawaga[1]
The band of Iroquois broods on what is lost
As Mohammed Iqbal mused in Sicily[2]
And wept Granada's lovely rise, and fall.

1960

All the Spikes but the Last

Where are the coolies in your poem, Ned?[3]
Where are the thousands from China who swung their picks with
    bare hands at forty below?
Between the first and the million other spikes they drove, and the
    dressed-up act of Donald Smith,[4] who has sung their story?
Did they fare so well in the land they helped to unite? Did they
    get one of the 25,000,000 CPR acres?[5]
Is all Canada has to say to them written in the Chinese
    Immigration Act?[6]

1959

---

[1] *Caughnawaga* A village in Quebec, Canada, founded in 1667 as a refuge for the Iroquois converts to the Christian faith. In the past, the Caughnawaga Indians have played significant roles in national and international conflicts. They fought in the Seven Years' War, helped to suppress the rebellion of 1837-38 in Lower Canada; and went on the Egyptian expedition to relieve Khartoum in 1884.

[2] *Mohammed Iqbal... Sicily* Iqbal (1877-1938), poet, philosopher, and politician, was an Indian Muslim, who wept when he saw Sicily, the setting of one of Islam's greatest triumphs in Europe (along with Granada).

[3] *Ned* The Canadian poet Edward J. Pratt, who wrote an epic poem "Towards the Last Spike" (1952) about the building of the CPR (Canadian Pacific Railway) transcontinental railway across Canada. Scott notes that Pratt does not mention the Chinese labourers in the poem.

[4] *Donald Smith* Smith (1820-1914) was a leading figure in the creation of the Canadian Pacific Railway (CPR).

[5] *CPR* Canadian Pacific Railway received from the government of Canada millions of acres on both sides of the track on completion of the transcontinental railway.

[6] *Chinese Immigration Act* An Act that restricted and regulated Chinese immigration into Canada. Given Royal Assent on 20 July 1855.

Samuel Selvon

Samuel Selvon (1923–94) was born in San Fernando, Trinidad. The son of an East Indian father and half-Scottish mother, he immigrated to England in 1954. He later moved to Calgary, Canada in 1978. He wrote ten novels, including *An Island is a World* (1955), *The Lonely Londoners* (1956), and *Moses Migrating* (1983), numerous short stories—including those in *Ways of Sunlight* (1957)—and screenplays and plays for radio and television, most collected in *Eldorado West One* (1988) and *Highway in the Sun* (1991).

Selvon's "Turning Christian" is set in Trinidad of the early twentieth century. It is important to know that after slavery was abolished in British colonies with the British Emancipation Act of 1834, indentured labourers were brought in—from Portugal and China, and later in large numbers from India—to relieve the labour shortage. The Afro-Trinidadians (descendants of slaves) saw the Indians as interlopers. What is the text saying about the relationship of these fellow subalterns? What does it say about the nature of religious conversion? Is it truly spiritual or pragmatic and expedient? How different is the tone of "Brackley and the Bed" from that of "Turning Christian?" How does Selvon treat the immigrant experience in London of the 1950s in "Brackley and the Bed"? Is the story comedy (kind humour), satire (mocking humour), or farce (purposeless humour)? Compare its tone with Willi Chen's "Assam's Iron Chest."

Turning Christian

Foreday morning, in the hint of pearly light preceding dawn, Changoo opened his eyes but did not stir from the floor in the corner of the barrack room he lived in with Kayshee and their son Raman. He could feel the warmth of her knee against his side. The boy was near the doorway, where he usually slept.

Changoo always woke easily, as if sleep was part of an active function except that the mind rested and the body was horizontal. It was because of what he had to do today that he lay for a minute, thinking, before he sat up and pulled on a pair of ragged khaki trousers stained with mud and the labour of the canefields, holding them up with a frayed piece of thin rope as a belt. Standing, he moved quietly to the doorway and stepped over the sleeping boy. Tomorrow morning he ain't going to be here, he thought. Kayshee got to get up earlier to catch water by the standpipe, and tie-out the goat, and do all them things what the boy had to do. But most of all she got to stop grieving for him when he gone.

Outside, Changoo walked a few steps to the road—a wide gravelly track, really, with two worn parallel grooves from the traffic of mule and buffalo-drawn carts plying from the canefields to the sugarmills. He urinated into a clump of hibiscus, splattering loudly on the leaves before directing his stream to the ground. He was convinced his urine helped to thrive the growth and keep him supplied with toothbrushes. He took one now, breaking off a twig and stripping off the bark, chewing one end to a frazzle, with which he began to scrub his mouth as he stepped onto the trail.

This was the time of day he possessed — the stillness, the pale pearly light of fore-day morning where everything loomed as imaginary shapes before the rising sun brought it all into focus. Then it would be waking sugarcane workers and their families, the clatter of buckets at the standpipe, the stir of movement and activity that was there even if he didn't see it all, because he preferred to witness the quick blur of bluejeans or listen to the raucous keskidees as they darted about the estate of Cross Crossing.

Changoo's feet were tough and did not feel the pebbly stones as he walked towards the canefields end of the barracks where his friend Gopaul lived. He was also an early riser, and had asked Changoo to do him a favour when he took Raman to San Fernando.[1] When Changoo remonstrated that he had never been to town and would not know his way about, Gopaul said it was only something he wanted from the drugstore for his cough, everybody would know where the drugstore was, and he would give him the money. That was three mornings ago, and Gopaul knew that today was the day, and that this morning was his last chance to bring the money.

Changoo would not have bothered about it except that Gopaul was his best friend and knew all his business, how he and Kayshee came to Trinidad from Calcutta because of his younger brother Jaggernauth who had himself come some years before and had settled in the town as a jeweler with a small shop. Jaggernauth's encouragement had resulted in him and Kayshee landing up in the sugar estate in Cross Crossing, along with all the other indentured labourers taking the place of the black slaves in the canefields ... and everytime he visited them, it was the same story, to join-up with the white Canadian missionary religion, as that was the only way they could get out of Cross Crossing, and come and live in town.

"You got to turn Christian," Jaggernauth said, "only those Indians who turn Christian making any headway. Is not enough to talk the language ..."

Unable to make any headway with Changoo and Kayshee, Jaggernauth had turned his attention to the boy. Raman helped his parents, like all the children in the settlement, in the fields, but he had been spending all his spare time attending the classes that a Canadian missionary from San Fernando held in a small wooden house near the main road. He even ran away sometimes to go to the school. And he was eager to show off his English and what he was learning to his uncle.

"Jesus Christ is our Saviour."

"Good, good," Jaggernauth encouraged. "What again? What about the Lord Prayer, you know the Lord Prayer?"

"Our father which art in heaven, hollow be thine name ..."

"Look at that!" Jaggernauth turned to Changoo as if he was the father showing off his son's accomplishments.

"I know hymns too," Raman said, "Onwards Christian Soldiers ..."

"Let him come and live with me in town," Jaggernauth urged. "The Canadian missionaries build a new school there, and all the smart Indians sending their children to learn and turn Christian. Give the boy a chance, Changoo."

---

[1] *San Fernando* The second-largest town in Trinidad. It is in the southern part of the island, as is Cross Crossing.

"You will keep him and support him?" Changoo asked.

"Yes. I will give him clothes and shoes to wear, and send him to school and church. Bring him to town next week." Jaggernauth wanted a feather in his cap, though he did not know what it meant; it must be something good, for the Canadian minister in the church told the congregation it would be a feather in their cap if they could persuade any heathens to be converted to the Lord and Saviour Jesus Christ.

Changoo had discussed the matter with Gopaul, who was a strict Hindu and warned the Indians that in the years to come they would regret giving up their religion and beliefs. He kept a firm hold on his own family, but there were many who were lured by the promise of an easier life and the hope of wearing shoes, and it was true that those who turn Christian seemed to prosper and do better for themselves. Changoo and Kayshee had made up their minds to let Raman go. The decision threatened, then weakened, his friendship with Gopaul.

Now, as he saw Gopaul slowly approaching — also brushing his teeth — he had a feeling that if his friend didn't need the medicine for his cough he would not have turned up.

"So." Gopaul did not waste any time in preliminary talk. "Today is the day you taking your son to town to give him away to the white people religion?" He spat a bit of hibiscus as if to emphasise his words, and spat again some phlegm which had risen in this chest.

"I just going to give him a chance," Changoo said, compromising the doubts he still held. He really wanted to ask Gopaul what it was like in town, but his friend emanated all the coldness that had come between them. Indeed, Gopaul reinforced that thought now by shoving the money at him, and saying, "Look, the money for the medicine," and Changoo put it in his pocket, and then, as Gopaul turned to go back, Gopaul said, "You sure you doing the right thing?"

And Changoo said, "Yes," though he wasn't sure, and Gopaul left him standing there ...

The police uniform doubled Norbert's concepts about himself: he felt like a giant. He did not walk, but swagger — look at me, I is the LAW, and every man-jack and his brother better get out the way, or else I lock them up and throw away the key!

Norbert grew from boyhood to manhood as a slave. When emancipation came, like many of his black countrymen, he celebrated in the intoxication of freedom by deserting the canefields for a carefree, idle life in the town of San Fernando, where they loafed about or turned their hands and wits to other means of survival. As the indentured labourers from India came in to replace the slaves, the blacks were as happy as the estate proprietors to have them. Let the coolies sweat with hoe and cutlass in the hot-sun for Massa, we done with that.

When Norbert joined the police force one of the laws he had to help enforce was to keep the Indians away from the town, unless they had a written pass from the foreman or overseer. Some of them couldn't stand the grind and absconded; others drifted away and ventured into town, or looked for another estate where conditions were not so hard. The sugar owners were concerned about this loss of labour and asked the police to watch out for them.

Norbert didn't need to be told. He was zealous in his duty; the locals cried "Call Norbert!" if they spotted an Indian looking out-of-place, or if they had an altercation with any of the few who lived legitimately in the town. Scarred with the atrocities and cruelties of slavery, Norbert had a dread that if the new labourers became rebellious, he and his friends might be called upon to return to the fields. He had nightmares about that when he couldn't sleep because the scars from the driver's whip still itched sometimes. What if the Indians gave trouble, and the white bosses and them squashed this "emancipation" business and ensnared the scattered slaves for the yoke again?

This morning, as he patrolled the one road out of the town to the nearest estate of Cross Crossing, he was looking forward to one of Tanty Matilda's sweetbreads. He could see her sitting by the wayside among a small group of women who were hawking sweetmeats and fruit and vegetables. Tanty was waving a rag over her tray of cakes to keep away the flies. In the doorway of a small shop nearby, a gang of men were gambling in a circle with a soiled pack of cards. Norbert knew the game — he played regularly before he became a policeman. The dealer turned up two cards, and after bets were placed turned up the rest of the pack until one showed up to match one of the original two. It was called *wapee*, and was illegal, but Norbert knew most of the players and turned a blind eye: one or two of the players even looked up as they saw him coming and waved out to him.

"I have your sweetbread here for you, Norb," Tanty said. She always kept a nice one for him: sweeten up the police and they go be sweet to you. Besides, she had slaved alongside Norbert's father, who had literally bled to death from a flogging a week before the emancipation thing came into force. "How things going, Tanty?" Norbert took a big bite, and winked at one of the younger women close by. She put her hand to her mouth to stifle a titter: Norbert thought he would remember her when he was off-duty.

"No thiefs and vagabonds about for you to catch, but I think I see a coolie man down the road coming? My eyesight bad in the hot sun."

"Eh-heh?" Norbert put his hand to his forehead to shade the sunlight, and looked. Like it was a coolie for true, and like he have a child with him. "You right, Tanty! On the other side of the road!"

Norbert liked public participation when he was called upon to do his duty; he pretended to be swayed by the public's reaction or opinion. So he raised his voice and shouted as Changoo and Raman drew near, "Aye, you, coolie man! Come over here!"

By the time the Indian and his son crossed the road, the gambling stopped, and the women vendors gathered around with the gamblers and idlers. There was drama in the air. They liked to watch Norbert in action, and he liked to perform for them. Furthermore, they considered themselves more as participators than spectators in what was to unfold.

"What you doing in town, coolie? You run away from the estate?"

Changoo was disconcerted by the crowd, and the black man in the police uniform. Though he had his pass safely knotted in his *dhoti*, it was the first time he had ever seen so many black people together.

"No, no," he said quickly.

"Where you from?"

"Cross Crossing."

"Where your free paper? You got a free paper?"

"Yes, yes." Changoo fumbled to undo the knot in his *dhoti* as the crowd laughed and jeered.

"He got it tie-up in he trousers!"

"You call that trousers? It look more like a sheet he got tie round he waist!" Those in the background pressed forward to see what was happening.

Norbert took the pass Changoo handed him and held it at arm's length, drawing it closer and closer to his eyes. The crowd jostled and elbowed, eager for blood.

"Take him down, Norb, take him down!"

"Lock him up and throw away the key!"

"H'mm," Norbert said, and "h'mm," and he frowned and rubbed his chin. "Cross Crossing, eh?"

Changoo was scared. The boy was gripping his arm tightly. He knew Raman was frightened, and that if he showed his own fear the boy's fright would turn to terror. Nothing was wrong with his pass, but this policeman was acting as if he had run away.

Norbert now, slowly, took a notebook out of the breast pocket of his tunic. The crowd acted silence when the notebook appeared. "I have to make a note of this." He licked the tip of the pencil. "What your name is, Ram or Singh?"

"No. Changoo."

"H'mm, that's a new one, how you spell it?"

Raman said, "C-h-a-n-g-o-o."

Norbert looked at the boy as if seeing him for the first time. "Oh, and what you call, boy?"

"I call Raman. R-a-m-a-n."

"Oho! Well, Mr. Raman, this pass is only for Mr. C-h-a-n-g-o-o. What you have to say about d-a-t?"

The witticism drew the laughter Norbert expected from his extras, and the inevitable comments:

"Is a spelling competition, Norb!"

"Ask him to spell policeman!"

"No, ask him to spell bound-coolie!"

It seemed to Changoo that the mood was changing from antagonism to derision, and suddenly his mood changed too, and he was angry.

"This boy is my son. I taking him to live by his uncle Jaggernauth who have a jewellery shop here in town."

"Aha!" Norbert cried, "this uncle sheltering runaways from the estates, eh!" For the first time, he began to write rapidly in the notebook.

"No no. He is a Christian, and the boy turning Christian too!" In a flash, Changoo thought that mention of this Christian business would end the interrogation, because Jaggernauth had told him so many times that it would take care of all his troubles.

And lo, there was a voice above the murmuring crowd. Tanty Matilda cried loudly, "Let him go, Norb, don't interfere with religious business, them coolies have their own *bassa-bassa* what work for them!"

Norbert's extras began to argue among themselves at this turn. He had never arrested a coolie who offered religion as an excuse, and was himself thinking that he would have to tote this man and boy all the way back up the road in the hot sun, to the police station. And too besides, nothing was wrong with the pass from the estate supervisor, though it ought to of had the name of the boy, too. The high-brown girl he had winked at was in front of the crowd, watching him to see what he would do. Somehow, he felt that if he let the coolie man go this time, she might favour him for future possibilities... but he felt he had to say something to save face. "Is all well and good for you to say so, Tanty, but is my job to investigate these things. If these coolies keep running away from the estates, all of we would be back to slavery!"

The word emoted a frenzied response from the crowd, shouts of: "Kill him!" and "Don't let the coolie go!"

The ultimate decision had always been to jail the coolies, and this yes-today, yes-tomorrow attitude on Norbert's part wasn't in keeping with his previous arrests. The crowd was still out for blood in spite of his unusual hesitation. The high-brown girl winked at Norbert, and shouted, "Let we see who is man today! Mr. Norbert the policeman, or the coolie from the sugar estate!"

"Don't let that woman provoke you, Norb," Tanty Matilda cried. "Let him go!"

What the girl wanted, Norbert suspected, was to see if he was man enough to challenge the mood of the crowd and not allow himself to be swayed by their emotions. I would show she who is man, he thought, and then she could show me who is woman...

"All right, all right!" He raised his arms. "Keep quiet, the whole set of you!" He waited for the hubbub to die down. "Who all-you think all-you is, eh? Who is the police here, me or you? The jail big enough to hold all of you for disturbing the peace!" He paused. The high-brown girl was watching him with wide eyes, the top of her tongue moving slowly over her slightly-parted lips. "I letting this man go about his business, and that decide the case." He turned to Changoo. "You hear what I say and you still here?" Changoo crossed the road quickly with Raman. He did not look back as he tugged the boy along, fleeing from the scene.

As the crowd slowly dispersed, arguing and discussing the incident, Norbert looked for the girl. He saw her running up the road after the man and boy...

1989

Brackley and the Bed

One evening Brackley was cruising round by the Embankment looking for a soft bench to rest his weary bones, and to cogitate on the ways of life. The reason for that, and the reason why the boys begin to call him Rockabye, you will find out as the ballad goes on.

Brackley hail from Tobago, which part they have it to say Robinson Crusoe used to hang out with Man Friday. Things was brown in that island and he make for England and manage to get a work and was just settling down when bam! he get a letter from his aunt saying that Teena want to come England too.

Teena was Brackley distant cousin and they was good friends in Tobago. In fact, the other reason why Brackley hustle from the island is because it did look like he and Teena was heading for a little married thing, and Brackley run.

Well, right away he write aunty and say no, no, because he have a feeling this girl would make botheration if she come England. The aunt write back to say she didn't mean to say that Teena want to come England, but that Teena left Tobago for England already.

Brackley hold his head and bawl. And the evening the boat train come in at Waterloo, he went there and start 'busing she right away not waiting to ask how the folks at home was or anything.

"What you doing in London?" Brackley ask as soon as Teena step off the train. "What you come here for, eh? Even though I write home to say things real hard?"

"What happen, you buy the country already?" Teena sheself giving tit for tat right away. "You ruling England now? The Queen abdicate?"

"You know where you going?" Brackley say. "You know where you is? You know what you going to do?"

"I am going straight to the Colonial Office," Teena say.

"What you think the Colonial Office is, eh? You think they will do anything for you? You have a god-father working there?"

Well, they argue until in the end Brackley find himself holding on to Teena suit-case and they on the way to the little batchy he have in Golders Green at the time.

When they get there Teena take one look at the room and sniff. "But look at the state you have this room in! You ain't ashamed of yourself?"

"Listen," Brackley say, "you better don't let me and you have contention. I know this would of happen when you come."

Teena start squaring up the room brisk-brisk.

"It making cold," she say, putting chair this way and table that way and turning everything upside down for poor Brackley. "How you does keep warm? Where the gas fire I hear so much about?"

Brackley grudgingly put a shilling in the meter and light the gas.

"What you have to eat?" But even as she asking she gone in the cupboard and begin pulling out rations that Brackley had stow away to see him through the winter.

Brackley as if he mesmerize, stand up there watching her as she start up a peas and rice on the gas ring.

"You better go easy with them rations," he say. "I not working now and money don't grow on tree here as in Tobago."

When they was eating Teena say: "Well, you have to get a job right away. You was always a lazy fellar."

"Keep quiet," Brackley say, enjoying the meal that Teena cook in real West Indian fashion—the first good meal he ever had in London. "You don't know nothing."

"First thing tomorrow morning," Teena say. "What time you get up?"

"About nine – ten," Brackley say vaguely.

"Well is six o'clock tomorrow morning, bright and early as the cock crow."

"You don't hear cock crowing in London," Brackley say. Then he drop the spoon he was eating with. "Six o'clock! You must be mad! Six o'clock like midnight in the winter, and people still sound asleep."

"Six o'clock," Teena say.

Brackley finish eating and begin to smoke, whistling a calypso softly, as if he in another world and not aware of Teena at all.

"Ah well," he say, stretching by the fire, "that wasn't a bad meal. Look, I will give you some old blankets and you could wrap up that coat and use as a pillow—you could sleep on the ground in that corner…"

"*Me*? On the floor? You not ashamed?"

"Well, is only one bed here as you see …"

"I using the bed."

"Girl, is winter, and if you think I going to sleep in the corner with two old blanket and wake up stiff…"

But, in the end, was Brackley who crouch up in the corner, and Teena sound asleep in the bed.

It look to Brackley like he hardly shut his eyes before Teena was shaking him.

"Get up," Teena say, "six o'clock."

Brackley start to curse.

"None of that," Teena say. "No bad language when I around."

Teena move around fast and give Brackley breakfast and make him dress and get out on the cold streets mumbling, "Get a job, get a job," before he knew what was happening.

It was only about ten o'clock, when he was washing dishes in a cafe where he get a work, that Brackley realize what was happening to him.

When he get home in the evening, Teena have screen put up around the bed and everything spick and span, and Brackley don't know where to look even for chair to sit down.

"I see you make yourself at home," he say maliciously.

"And what you think?" Teena flares.

"The boys come here sometimes for a little rummy."

"None of that now."

"And sometimes a girl-friend visit me."

"None of that now."

"So you taking over completely."

"Aunty say to look after you."

"Why the hell you come England, eh?"

Well, a pattern begin to form as the weeks go by, but the main thing that have Brackley worried is the bed. Every night he curl up in the corner shivering, and by the time he doze off: "Six o'clock, get up, you have to go to work."

Brackley ain't sleep on bed for weeks. The thing like an obsession with him. He window-shopping on the way home and looking at them bed and soft mattress on show and closing his eyes and sighing. Single divan, double divan, put-you-up, put-you-down—all makes and sizes he looking at.

One night when frost was forming on the window pane Brackley wake up and find he couldn't move.

"Teena."

"What?"

"You sleeping?"

"Yes."

"Teena, you want to get married?"

"Married? To who?"

"To me."

"What for?"

"So-I-could-sleep-in-the-bed—I mean, well, we uses to know one another good in Tobago, and now that you are here in London, what do you think?"

"Well, all right, but you have to change your ways."

"Yes, Teena."

"And no foolishness when we married. You come home straight from work. And I don't want you looking at no white girls."

"Yes, Teena."

No sooner said than done. Brackley hustle Teena off to the registry office as soon as things was fixed, thinking only how nice the bed would be after the hard floor and the cold, with Teena to help keep him warm.

"What about honeymoon?" Teena say after the ceremony.

"In the summer," Brackley say. "Let we go home. I am tired and I feel I could sleep for weeks."

"Bracks," Teena say as they was coming away. "I have a nice surprise for you. Guess who coming to London this evening?"

"Father Christmas," Brackley says yawning.

"No. Aunty. I write telling her to come up, as the room not so small and we could manage until we get another place. And then she and me could get a work too, and that will help."

"You putting hell 'pon jackass back," Brackley moan. But it was only when they reach home that a great fear come to Brackley. He had was to sit down in a chair before he could talk.

"But Teena," he say quietly, "we ain't have no place for Aunty to sleep?"

"Don't worry," Teena say. "She can sleep with me until we find another place."

1957

Olive Senior

Olive Senior (b. 1941) was born in Trelawny, Jamaica. She was educated there, in Canada, and in Britain. She now lives in Canada. An editor and journalist, her publications include *Talking of Trees* (poems, 1985), *Summer Lightning* (stories, 1986), *The Arrival of the Snake Woman* (stories, 1989), *Gardening in the Tropics* (poems, 1994), and *Discerner of Hearts and Other Stories* (1995).

Senior's "The Boy Who Loved Ice Cream" is a poignant story about the confusing world of a young Jamaican boy, Benjy. The narrative focuses on Benjy's relationship with his father. It is set in a remote area of the Jamaican countryside, which Senior evokes with detail after detail. Are there elements in the story that make us think the father suspects Benjy is not his child? Is the ice cream symbolic of the young boy's desires and dreams, one of which is to experience (taste) the love of his father? Does the very long unpunctuated run-on sentence (stream of consciousness?) at the end of the text effectively dramatize and evoke the boy's confusion? Do you think that Senior had James Joyce's "Araby" in mind when she wrote this story?

The Boy Who Loved Ice Cream

They walked down the path in single file, first the father carrying the baby Beatrice on his shoulder, then the mother, then Elsa. He brought up the rear. Wearing unaccustomed sandals, Benjy found it hard to keep his footing on the slippery path. Once or twice he almost fell and throwing out his hands to break his fall, had touched the ground. Unconsciously he wiped his hands on his seat, so that his new Sunday-go-to-church pants that his mother had made from cutting down one of his father's old jackets was already dirty with bits of mud and green bush clinging to him. But there was nobody behind him to see.

They were already late for the Harvest Festival[1] Sale, or so his father claimed. Papa also said that it was his fault. But then his father blamed him for a lot of things, even when he was not to be blamed. The boy wasn't sure why his father was sometimes so irritable towards him, and lived in a constant state of suspense over what his father's response to him was likely to be. Now, he had been the first ready. First his sister had taken him around to the side of the house for his bath. She held him and firmly scrubbed him down with a "strainer" covered in soap. Then she had stuck the long-handled dipper into the drum of rain water and poured it over him from head to foot. He made noises as the cold water hit him and would have run, but Elsa always had a firm grip on one of his limbs.

"Stan still yu jumbo-head bwoy or a konk yu till yu fenny," she hissed at him. Although he knew that her threats were infrequently accompanied by action

---

[1] *Harvest Festival* Harvest Festival in Jamaica is akin to North American Thanksgiving.

beyond a slap or two, still he tried to get away from her grip for he hated this weekly ritual of bathing. But Elsa by now had learned to control him and she carried the bath through without mishap for she had whispered, "Awright. Doan have yu bath and see what happen. See if yu get no ice cream."

Ice Cream! The very words conveyed to him the sound of everything in his life that he had always wanted, always longed for, but could not give a name to. He had never tasted ice cream.

It was Elsa who had told him about it. Two years ago at the Harvest Festival Sale, Mr. Doran had brought an ice cream bucket and had spent the evening the most popular man at the sale, his very customers fighting to get an opportunity to turn the bucket. According to Elsa's description, this marvellous bucket somehow produced something that, she said, was not a drink and was not food. It was hot and it was cold. Both at the same time. You didn't chew it, but if you held it on your tongue long enough it vanished, leaving an after-trace that lingered and lingered like a beautiful dream. Elsa the excitable, the imaginative, the self-assured, told him, think of your best dream, when he didn't understand. Think of it in colours, she said, pink and mauve and green. And imagine it with edges. Then imagine licking it slowly round and round the edges. That's how ice cream was.

But this description only bewildered him more. He sighed, and tried hard to imagine it. But he couldn't because he didn't have a best dream or even a good dream, only nightmares, and his mother would hold him and his father would say, "what is wrong with this pickney eh? a mampala man[1] yu a raise." Then the baby had come and he didn't have his mother's lap any more. Now imagining ice cream, he thought of sitting cuddled in his mother's arms again and saw this mysterious new creation as something as warm and beautiful. From Elsa's description, ice cream was the most marvellous thing he had ever heard of. And the strangest. For apart from anything else, he didn't know what ice was. His thoughts kept returning to the notion of ice cream throughout the year, and soon it became the one bright constant in a world full of changeable adults.

Then last year when he would have discovered for himself exactly what this ice cream was like, he had come down with measles. Elsa of course went to the sale for she had already had it, but he had to stay feverish and miserable with only toothless old Tata Maud to keep him company. And Elsa had come back and given him a description of ice cream that was even more marvellous than the first. This time Mr. Doran had brought two buckets, and she alone had had two cones. Not even the drops, the wangla,[2] and the slice of light cake they brought him could compensate for missing the ice cream.

This year he was well and nothing would keep him away.

Now with the thought of ice cream the cold water his sister kept splashing on him felt refreshing and he and she turned the bath into a game, both shrieking so

---

[1] *mampala man* An effeminate or impotent male.

[2] *wangla* Sweets made of sesame seeds.

loudly that their mother had to put her head out the window and promise to switch them both if they didn't stop.

His mother rubbed him down with an old cloth and put on his new clothes of which he was extremely proud, not noticing that the black serge was stitched very badly with white thread which was all his mother had, and the three buttons she sewed down the front were all of different sizes and colours. His shirt too, with the body of one colour, the sleeves of a print which was once part of mama's dress and the collar of yet another print, was just, Mama said, like Joseph's coat of many colours.

Then Mama had dressed the baby and she herself had got ready. By this time Papa had come up from the spring where he had had his bath and put on his Sunday suit and hat. Benjy, dressed and bored, had wandered off down to the cotton tree root to have another look at the marvellous colours and shapes of the junjo[1] which had sprung up after the rains just a few days ago. He was so busy that it took him a long time to hear them calling. They were standing all ready to go to the Harvest Festival Sale and Papa was cross for he said that Benjy was making them late.

Papa dressed in his Sunday suit and hat was a sight to see, for he only dressed up for special occasions — funerals, weddings and the Harvest Festival Sale. Papa never went to church though Mama did every Sunday. Papa complained every Sunday that there was no hot food and dinner was always late for Mama never got back from church till late afternoon. Plus Papa never liked Mama to be away from him for any length of time.

Foolishness, foolishness, Papa said of the church going.

Mama didn't say anything but she prayed for Papa every Sunday. She wasn't that religious, but she loved every opportunity to go out. She loved to dress up and she loved to talk to people and hear all the news that was happening out there in the wide world, though she didn't believe half of it. Although Mama hadn't even been to Kingston[2] in her life, if someone came along and said, "Let us go to the moon," quick as anything Mama would pick herself up and go. Or if Papa said to her "Let us give up all this hard life and move to town where we will have electric light and water out of a pipe and food out of a tin," Mama would not hesitate. Papa of course would never dream of saying anything of the sort. He was firmly wedded to the soil. She was always for Progress, though, as she sadly complained to the children, none of that ever came their way.

Now the Harvest Festival Sale was virtually the only time that Papa went into Springville these days. He hated to go into Springville even though it was where he was born for increasingly over the last four or five years, he had developed the feeling that Springville people knew something he didn't know but should, and they were laughing at him behind his back. It was something to do with his woman. It was one of those entirely intuitive feelings that suddenly occurred full-blown, then

---

[1] *junjo (jonjo)* A moss or edible fungus that grows on wood or on the ground.

[2] *Kingston* The capital of Jamaica.

immediately took firm root in the mind. Even before the child was born he had had the instinctive feeling that it was not his. Then as the boy had grown, he had searched his face, his features, to discern himself there, and had failed utterly to find anything conclusive. He could never be sure. The old women used to say you could tell paternity sure thing by comparing the child's foot with that of the supposed father: "if the foot not the spitting image of the man then is jacket." He had spent countless surreptitious hours studying the turn of his son's foot but had come away with nothing. For one thing, the child was so thin and rickety that his limbs bore no resemblance to the man's heavily muscled body.

Now he had never known of the woman being unfaithful to him. But the minute she had come back from spending three weeks in Springville that time her mother was dying, from then on he had had the feeling that something had happened. Maybe it was only because she seemed to him so beautiful, so womanly that he had the first twinges of jealousy. Now every Sunday as she dressed in her neat white dress and shoes and the chaste hat which to him sat so provocatively on her head, his heart quickened as he saw her anew, not as the young girl he had taken from her mother's house so many years before, not as the gentle and good-natured mother of his children, but as a woman whom he suddenly perceived as a being attractive to other men.

But now everyone was in a good mood again as they set off down the road to the Harvest Festival Sale. First they walked a mile and a half down their mountain path where they saw no one, until they met up with the main path to the village. Always in the distance ahead of them now they could see people similarly dressed going to the sale. Others would call out to them from their houses as they passed by:

"Howdy Mis Dinah," said Papa.

"Mis Dinah," Mama said.

"Mis Dinah," the children murmured.

"Howdy Mister Seeter. Miss Mae. Children. Yu gone on early."

"Ai. Yu coming?"

"No mus'. Jus a wait for Icy finish iron mi frock Miss Mae. A ketch yu up soon."

"Awright Mis D."

Then they would walk another quarter mile or so till they got to another house perched on the hillside.

"Owdy Mister Seeter. Miss Mae. Little ones. A coming right behin."

And another family group would come out of the house and join them. Soon, a long line of people was walking in single file down the path. The family groups got mixed. The adults would walk behind other adults so that they could talk. The children bringing up the rear instinctively ranked themselves, putting the smallest ones in front. Occasionally one of the adults would look back and frown because the tail of the line had fallen too far behind.

"Stop! Jacky! Ceddie! Mavis! Merteen! What yu all doing back there a lagga lagga so? Jus' hurry up ya pickney."

Then all the offspring chastised, the adults would soon become lost in a discussion of the tough-headedness of children.

The children paid hardly any attention and even forgot to fight or get into any mischief, for they were far too excited about the coming afternoon.

Soon, the path broadened out and joined the lane which led to the Commons where the sale was being held. Benjy loved to come out from the cool and shadows of the path, through an archway of wild brazilwood with branches that drooped so much the adults had to lift them up in order to get through. From the semi-darkness they came suddenly into the broad lane covered in marl and dazzling white which to him was the broadest street in the whole world. Today the lane was full of people as far as the eye could see, all the men in their dark suits and hats and the women, abandoning their chaste Sunday white, wearing their brightest dresses. Now a new set of greetings had to take place between the mountain people who came from a place called One Eye and were regarded as "dark" and mysterious by the people who lived in the one-time prosperous market town of Springville. Springville itself wasn't much — a crossroads with a few wooden "upstairs" houses with fretwork balconies, built at the turn of the century with quick money made in Panama or Cuba. Now even though these houses were so old they leaned in the wind together, and had never seen a coat of paint, to the mountain people they looked as huge and magical as anything they hoped to see. Two of these upstairs houses had shops and bars beneath, with their proud owners residing above, and on one corner there was a large one-storey concrete building with huge wooden shutters which housed the Chinese grocery and the Chinese. A tiny painted house served as the post office and the equally tiny house beside it housed Brother Brammie the tailor. The most imposing buildings in the village were the school and the Anglican Church which were both on the main lane. The Baptists and the Seventh Day Adventists had their churches on the side road.

At Harvest Festival time, all the people in the village forgot their differences and came together to support each other's Harvest Festival Sales. But none could compare in magnificence to the Anglicans'. The sale took place on the Monday after the Harvest Service in the church. On Monday morning at dawn, the church members travelled from far with the bamboo poles and coconut boughs to erect on the Commons the booths for the sale. Because the sale was a secular event and liable to attract all kinds of sinners, it was not held in the church yard but on the Commons which belonged to the church but was separated by a barbed wire fence. Since the most prosperous people in the area were Anglicans, this was the largest and most popular of the sales. After a while it became less of a traditional Harvest Festival Sale and more of a regular fair, for people began to come from the city with goods to sell, and took over a little corner of the Commons for themselves. The church people frowned on this at first, then gave up on keeping these people out even when they began to bring games such as "Crown and Anchor," for they helped to attract larger and larger crowds which also spent money in the church members' booths. The church members also enjoyed themselves buying the wares of the town vendors, parson drawing the line only at the sale and consumption of liquor on the premises. A few zealots of the village strongly objected to this sale, forbidding their daughters to go to this den of wickedness and vice, but nobody paid these people the slightest attention. The Mothers Union ladies who had decorated the church for the Harvest Service the day before now tied up sprays of bougainvillea and asparagus fern over the entrance into each booth and radiated good cheer to everyone in their self-appointed role as hostesses.

The sale actually started at noon, but the only people who got there early were those who were involved in the arrangements. Most people turned up only after the men had put in at least a half-day in the fields and then gone home to bathe and dress and eat. They would stay at the sale until night had fallen, using bottle torches to light their way home.

When they got to the Commons, Benjy was the only person who was worried, for he wasn't sure that they wouldn't get there too late for the ice cream. Maybe Mr. Doran would make the ice cream as soon as the sale started and then it would all be finished by the time they got there. Then another thought came: suppose this year Mr. Doran was sick, or simply couldn't be bothered with ice cream any more. He would have to wait a whole year again to taste it. Perhaps never.

"Suppose, jus' suppose," he had said to his sister many times during the past week, "suppose him doan mek enough."

"Cho! As soon as him finish wan bucket him mek anadda. Ice cream nevva done," Elsa told him impatiently, wishing that she had never brought up the subject.

But this did not console him. Suppose his father refused to buy him ice cream? It was unthinkable! And yet his father's behaviour towards him was irrational: Benjy never knew just what to expect.

As soon as they turned into the Commons they could hear the sound of Mass Vass' accordion rising shrilly above the noise of the crowd, as much a part of the Harvest Festival Sale as was Brother Shearer's fife and drum band that played at all fairs, weddings and other notable events for miles around.

There were so many people already in the Commons that Benjy was afraid to enter: the crowd was a living, moving thing that would swallow him up as soon as he crossed through the gate. And yet he was excited too, and his excitement won out over his fear so that he boldly stepped up to the gate where the ticket taker waited and Papa paid the entrance fee for them all.

"Now you children dont bother get lost," Mama warned them but not too sternly, knowing that sooner or later they would all become separated in this joyous crowd.

Benjy was in an agony just to see the ice cream. But Elsa would have none of it.

"Wait nuh," she said, grabbing his hand and steering him firmly in the direction of the fancy goods stall where Mama had headed. There were cake stalls and pickles and preserves stalls, fancy goods stalls, glass cases full of baked goods and all the finest in fruits, vegetables, yams and all the other products of the soil that the people had brought to the church as their offerings to the Harvest Service. Off to one side was a small wooden merry-go-round and all over the field were children playing and shrieking.

"Elsa, ice cream," Benjy kept saying, and finally to reduce this annoyance Elsa took him over to a corner of the field where a crowd had gathered. There, she said. But the crowd was so thick that he could see nothing, and he felt a pain in his heart that so many other, bigger people also wanted ice cream. How ever would he get any?

"Nuh mine, Benjy," Elsa consoled him. "Papa wi gi wi ice cream. When de time come."

"Suppose him forget, Elsa."

"Not gwine forget."

"Yu remin' him."

"Yes."

"Promise?"

"But wa do yu ee bwoy," Elsa cried. She angrily flung his hand away and took off into the crowd.

He did not mind being alone, for this rich crowd so flowed that sooner or later the same people passed each other.

Benjy wished he had some money. Then he would go and wiggle his way into the very centre of the crowd that surrounded the ice cream bucket. And he would be standing there just as Mr. Doran took out the ice cream. But he didn't know anything about money and had no idea what something as wonderful as ice cream would cost.

So he flowed with the crowd, stopping here and there but not really looking at anything and soon he came across his mother with Beatrice. Mama firmly took hold of his hand.

"Come. Sister Nelson bring a piece of pone fe yu."

She took him to Sister Nelson who gave him the pone which he stuffed into his mouth.

"Say tank yu chile. Yu doan have manners?" his mother asked.

He murmured thank you through the pone. Sister Nelson smiled at him. "Growing a good boy," she said and patted his head.

"But baad!" Mama said, laughing.

Mama was always saying that and it frightened him a little, for he never knew for sure just how he was "baad."

"Mama," he said, "Ice cream."

"Chile! Yu mout full an yu talking bout ice cream aready!"

Tears started to trickle down his cheeks.

"Now see here. A bawl yu wan' bawl? Doan mek a give yu something fe bawl bout, yu hear bwoy. Hm. Anyway a doan know if there is money for foolishness like cream. Have to see yu father about dat."

His heart sank, for the day before he had heard his father complain that there was not enough money to buy all the things they needed at the Harvest Festival Sale and did she think money grew on trees. But everyone knew that Papa saved all year for that day, for the town vendors came and spread out their wares under the big cotton tree — cloth, pots and pans, fancy lamps, wicks and shades, readymade clothes, shoes, shoelaces, matches, knives, cheap perfume, plastic oilcloths for the table, glasses with birds and flowers, water jugs, needles, enamelware, and plaster wall hangings with robins and favourite bible texts. Even Miss Sybil who had the dry goods store would turn up and buy from them, and months later the goods would turn up in her dark and dusty shop at twice the price as the vendors'.

Mama had announced months in advance that she wanted an oilskin cloth, a new lampshade and shoes for the children. She hadn't mentioned anything for herself, but on these occasions Mama usually came home with a pair of new shoes, or a scarf, or a hat — anything that would put her in touch with what seemed another, glamorous life.

Papa, like his son, was distracted, torn between two desires. One was to enjoy the sale and to see if he could pick up anything for the farm or just talk to the farmers whom nowadays he never saw at any other time. Then the Extension Officer was there and he wanted to catch him to ask about some new thing he had heard that the government was lending money to plant crops though he didn't believe a word of it. Then he wanted to go and buy a good white shirt from the town vendors. Mama had insisted that he should. And he wanted to see the new games they had brought. In many ways one part of his mind was like a child's, for he wanted to see and do everything. But another part of his mind was spoiling the day for him: he didn't want to let Mama out of his sight. More and more the conviction had been growing on him that if there had been another man in her life, it wasn't anyone from around here. So it had to be a townman. And where else did one get the opportunity to meet strangers but at the sale. Walking down the mountain path he had started out enjoying the feeling of going on an outing, the only one he permitted himself for the year. But as they got nearer and nearer to Springville and were joined by other people, he became more and more uneasy. The way his woman easily greeted and chatted with people at first used to fill him with pride and admiration that she could so naturally be at ease where he was dull and awkward and clumsy. But by the time they entered the lane this pride had turned to irritation, for now he had begun to exaggerate in his mind precisely those qualities for which he had previously praised her: now she laughed too loudly, chattered too much, she was not modest enough, she attracted attention to herself — and to him, for having a woman so common and so visible. By the time they got to the Commons it was clear to her that he was in one of his "moods" though she did not know why and she hoped that the crowd would bring back his good humour again, for she was accustomed to his ups and downs. But she didn't dwell on the man's moods, for nothing would make her not enjoy herself at the sale.

Now the man surreptitiously tried to keep her under his eye but it was virtually impossible because of the crowd. He saw her sometimes only as a flash in the distance and he strained to see what she was up to, but he caught her only in the most innocent of poses — with church sisters and married couples and little children. She eagerly tried on hats and shoes. She looked at pictures. She examined tablecloths. She ate grater cake and snowballs. Looking at her from afar, her gestures seemed to him so pure, so innocent that he told himself that he was surely mad to think badly of her. Then he looked at the town folk gathered around the games, hawking yards of cloth, and stockings and ties and cheap jewellery. He looked at them and their slim hard bodies and their stylish clothes and their arrogant manners and their tough faces which hid a knowledge of the world he could never have. And he felt anxious and angry again. Now he turned all his attention to these townmen to see if he could single out one of them: the one. So engaged did he become on this lonely and futile pursuit that he hardly heard at all what anybody said to him. Even the children begging for ice cream he roughly brushed aside. He was immediately full of remorse, for he had planned to treat them to ice cream, but by the time he came to his senses and called after them, they had disappeared into the crowd. He vowed that once he met up with them again he would make up for his gruffness. He would treat them not only to ice cream but to sliced cake, to soft drinks, to paradise plums and jujubs. But the moment of softness, of sentiment, quickly passed for his attention became focussed on one man in black pants and a purple shirt and wearing a grey felt hat. The man was tall, brown-skinned and good looking with dark, curly hair. He couldn't tell why this man caught his attention except that he was by far the best looking of the townmen, seemed in fact a cut above them, even though like some of the others his arms were covered from wrist to elbow in lengths of cheap chains, and his fingers in the tacky rings that he was selling. He watched the man steadily while he flirted and chatted with the girls and finally faded out of sight — but not in the direction his woman was last seen.

Now Benjy was crying and even Elsa felt let down. Papa had refused to buy them ice cream! Although she cajoled and threatened, she couldn't get Benjy to stop crying. He was crying as much for the ice cream as for being lost from even his mother so happy and animated among all the people she knew, amid crowds and noise and confusion. Now she had little time for them and impatiently waved them on to "enjoy themselves." Elsa did just that for she found everything entertaining and school friends to chatter with. But not Benjy. She could not understand how a little boy could be so lacking in joy for such long periods of time, and how his mind could become focussed on just one thing. If Benjy could not have ice cream, he wanted nothing.

Night was coming on and they were lighting the lamps. They hung up the storm lantern at the gate but all the coconut booths were lit with kitchen bitches. Only the cake stall run by Parson's wife and the most prosperous ladies of the church had a tilly lamp, though there wasn't much cake left to sell.

Benjy still stumbled along blindly, dragged by Elsa who was determined to get a last fill of everything. Benjy was no longer crying but his eyes were swollen and he was tired and his feet were dragging. He knew that soon they would have to go home. The lighting of the lamps was the signal for gathering up families together, and though they might linger for a while after that talking, making last minute purchases and plans, children were at this point not allowed to wander or stray from the group for the word of adults had once again become law, and when all the adults decided to move, woe onto the child who could not be found.

So everyone was rounding up everyone else, and in this confusion, Benjy started to howl again for he and Elsa were passing by Mr. Doran and his bucket, only the crowd was so thick around it you couldn't see anything.

But just then they ran into Papa again and, miraculously, he was the one that suggested ice cream. Although Benjy's spirits immediately lifted, he still felt anxious that Papa would never be able to get through that crowd in time. Papa left him and Elsa on the fringes, and he impatiently watched as Papa, a big man, bore his way through. What is taking Papa so long? I bet Mr. Doran has come to the end of the bucket. There is no more ice cream. Here comes Mr. Manuel and Mars Edgy asking if they aren't ready. And indeed, everyone from the mountain was more or less assembled and they and Papa now seemed the only people missing from the group. They told Mars Edgy that Papa had gone to get them ice cream, and Mars Edgy was vexed because, he said, Papa should have done that long before. Now Mars Edgy made his way through the crowd around the ice cream vendor and Benjy's hopes fell again. He felt sure that Mars Edgy would pull Papa away before he got the ice cream. Torn between hope and despair, Benjy looked up at the sky which was pink and mauve from the setting sun. Just like ice cream! But here comes Papa and Mars Edgy now and Papa is carrying in his hands three cones and Papa is coming and Benjy is so excited that he starts to run towards him and he stumbles and falls and Elsa is laughing as she picks him up and he is laughing and Mars Edgy is moving off quickly to where the mountain people are standing and Papa bends down and hands him a cone and Papa has a cone and Elsa has a cone and Benjy has a cone and the three of them stand there as if frozen in time and he is totally joyous for he is about to have his first taste of ice cream but even though this is so long-awaited so precious he first has to hold the cone at arm's length to examine it and witness the ice cream perched just so on top and he is afraid to put it into his mouth for Elsa said it was colder than spring water early in the morning and suppose just suppose it burns his tongue suppose he doesn't like it and Elsa who is well into eating hers and Papa who is eating his are laughing at him ... then he doesn't know what is happening for suddenly Papa sees something his face quickly changes and he flings away his cone and makes a grab for Benjy and starts walking almost running in the direction where Mama is standing she is apart from all the people talking to a strange man in a purple shirt and Papa is moving so fast Benjy's feet are almost off the ground and Benjy is crying Papa Papa and everything is happening so quickly he doesn't know the point at which he loses the ice cream and half the cone and all that is left in his hand is the little tip of the cone which he clutches tightly and he cannot understand why Papa has let go of his hand and is shouting and why Mama isn't laughing with the man anymore and why everyone is rushing about and why he has only this little tip of cone in his hand and there is no ice cream and he cannot understand why the sky which a minute ago was pink and mauve just like the ice cream is now swimming in his vision like one swollen blanket of rain.

1986

Vikram Seth

Vikram Seth (b. 1952) was born in Calcutta. He left India at the age of eleven to study in England. A graduate of Oxford and Stanford, he has published such texts as *Mappings* (poetry, 1982), *From Heaven Lake: Travels Through Sinkiang and Tibet* (1983), *The Golden Gate* (a novel in verse, 1986), *A Suitable Boy* (novel, 1993), and *Two Lives* (biography, 2005).

Seth's "Research in Jiangsu Province" originated in his doctoral research for Stanford University on the demography of China, elements of which are found in this poem. The narrator is collecting statistics about and from the people of Jiangsu Province, but he is mindful that statistics may be "imperfect knowledge" and may offer only "half" truths; they cannot capture the actuality of the lives of these individuals, which includes memories of the harsh brutality of the Japanese War. Compare this poem with Gerald Murnane's "Land Deal" and Rudy Wiebe's "Where Is the Voice Coming From?"

Research in Jiangsu Province[1]

From off this plastic strip the noise
Of buzzing stops. A human voice
Asks its set questions, pauses, then
Waits for responses to begin.

The questions bore in. How much is
The cost and area of this house?
I see you have two sons. Would you
Prefer to have had a daughter too?

And do your private plots provide
Substantial income on the side?
Do you rear silkworms? goslings? pigs?
How much per year is spent on eggs?

How much on oil and soya sauce
And salt and vinegar? asks the voice.
The answering phantom states a figure,
Then reconsiders, makes it bigger.

Children and contraceptives, soap
And schooling rise like dreams of hope

---

[1] *Jiangsu* A province of China, located along the east coast of the country. Jiangning (formerly Jiankang) is located west of present-day Nanjing.

To whirl with radios and bikes
Round pensions, tea and alarm clocks.

"Forty square meters. Sixteen cents.
To save us from the elements.
Miscarriage. Pickle with rice-gruel
Three times a week. Rice-straw for fuel.

Chickens and fruit-trees." In Jiangning
Green spurts the psychedelic Spring
And blossoming plum confounds the smell
Of pig-shit plastered on the soil.

Life and production, drought and flood
Merge with the fertile river mud
And maids come forth sprig-muslin drest
And mandarin ducks return to nest.

The Yangtse flows on like brown tape.
The research forms take final shape,
Each figure like a laden boat
With white or madder sails afloat.

Float on, float on, O facts and facts,
Distilled compendia of past acts,
Reveal the Grand Design to me,
Flotilla of my PhD.[1]

On the obnoxious dreary pillage
Of privacy, imperfect knowledge
Will sprout like lodged rice, rank with grain,
In whose submerging ears obtain

Statistics where none grew before
And housing estimates galore,
Diet and wealth and income data,
Age structures and a price inflator.

---

[1] *PhD* The speaker's academic experience is drawn from the poet's. In 1980-82 Seth did extensive field
work in China collecting data for his doctoral dissertation at Stanford on Chinese population planning. He was attached to Nanjing University at the time.

Birth and fertility projections,
Plans based on need and predilections.
O needful numbers, and half true,
Without you what would nations do?

I switch the tape off. This to me
Encapsulates reality,
Although the beckoning plum-trees splayed
Against the sky, the fragrant shade,

Have something tellable, it seems,
Of evanescence, light and dreams,
And the cloud-busy, far-blue air
Forms a continuous questionnaire

And Mrs. Gao herself whose voice
Is captive on my tape may choose
Some time when tapes and forms are far
To talk about the Japanese War,[1]

May mention how her family fled,
And starved, and bartered her for bread,
And stroke her grandson's head and say
Such things could not occur today.

1985

---

[1] *Japanese War* The Sino-Japanese War (before and during World War II — 1937-45) was fought between China and Japan.

Philip Sherlock

Philip Sherlock (1902–2000) was born in Jamaica. He was Vice-Chancellor of the University of the West Indies from 1963 to 1969. He is the author and editor of more than fifteen volumes of poetry, history, and folk tales, including *Anansi the Spider Man* (1954), *West Indian Folk-Tales* (1966), and *The Land and People of the West Indies* (1967).

Sherlock's "The Warau People Discover the Earth" is one of the many creation myths of the American and Caribbean Natives. This story can be compared with Ngitji Ngitji's Australian legend "The Possum Woman" and Buhkwujjenene's Canadian folk tale "Nanaboozhoo Creates the World." Sherlock's rendition is much more polished than Ngitji's and Buhkwuj-jenene's. Which style do you think is more appropriate to the folk tale? Sherlock's story is much more accessible to the non-native reader than Louise Bennett's "Anancy an Ticks," but does this accessibility work against authenticity? Would it be better to have a "literary ver-nacular"—such as Mark Twain's in *Huckleberry Finn*, in which spelling and syntax are fairly standardized but the feel and flow of the vernacular is retained? (See also Nalo Hopkinson's "A Habit of Waste.")

The Warau People Discover the Earth

The Caribs were the first people on earth. After them came the Warau from a land beyond the sky, rich in birds of rare beauty but without animals of any kind. No deer grazed on its grassy plains, no jaguar roamed through its scattered woods, no fish swam in its clear, shallow streams. Instead there were large flocks of birds of rare beauty. Some of these the Warau killed for food; and each man made for himself from the feathers of the birds a richly coloured headdress for wearing at great festivals.

One day while a young Warau hunter, Okonorote, was wandering through the fields he saw a bird more beautiful than any he had ever seen. In flight it was an exquisite jewel, the scarlet of its feathers more brilliant than those of the scarlet ibis, its green more vivid than the emerald feathers of the humming-bird. Enchanted by its rainbow loveliness, Okonorote swore not to return home until he had taken the bird. "How splendid a head-dress these feathers will make," he said to himself; "lovelier than any fashioned in ancient times. These feathers will give joy to many. I must have them."

For five days Okonorote followed the bird, using all his skill to come within bowshot while it settled to a meal of berries on some lofty branch. He crept towards the bird through the long grass, keeping out of sight, crawling, inching his way for-ward, holding his breath lest even that faint sound of breathing should startle it. Almost within range, he lifted the bow, put the arrow in place, then moved forward so gently that neither stirring of grass nor rustle of leaves told of his presence. Suddenly, even while he was pointing the arrow, the bird flew away and the pursuit began anew.

On the afternoon of the fifth day the bird settled on the low branch of a tree. Okonorote moved forward very slowly, making no sound. He kept his eyes fixed on the bird. His heart beat fast, for now he was nearer to it than he had ever been. He marvelled at the proud curve of the neck, the splendid crest of red and blue feathers, the rich hues of the rainbow plumage. He loosed his arrow. At that moment the bird flew up into the air. But it was too late. The arrow pierced the body. The bird fell back lifeless into the high grass.

Okonorote raced towards the place where the bird had fallen, shouting for joy. For five days he had watched, moving with care, making no sound, thinking only of the bird. Now he could throw caution to the winds. He raced at full speed towards the bird he had sought for so long. But it was not there. He thrust aside the daggerpoints of the thorn-bush, the keen blades of the sword-grass and tore away the thick undergrowth covering the black swollen roots of the trees, but he could not find the bird. He had seen the arrow pierce its splendid body. He had seen it fall headlong into the thorn-bushes; but it was not there. Widening his circle of search, Okonorote came not to a gleaming bird but to a deep hole. Throwing himself face downward he looked over the edge of the hole, hoping to see the bird's body. To his astonishment he saw far below him a world of sunlit savannahs, green forests, and of animals grazing quietly — cattle, the fat, slow-moving tapir, and the swift deer.

With the skill of a hunter, Okonorote noted that the hole lay at the feet of a gentle hill, under the shelter of two cedar-trees that joined hands above it. Then he hurried back to tell of what he had seen, leaving signs to show the way: an arrow scratched on the bark of a mora-tree, a little heap of stones, a broken branch.

Many of the Warau people laughed at Okonorote's tale. Some said that he had fallen asleep and mistaken a dream for reality. The elders pointed out that for many years they had wandered far and wide through their land, and had never found this deep hole. Also, surely their fathers before them would have found it. After all, Okonorote was but a young man! Perhaps he had fallen into a hole hidden in the long grass and this had so shaken him that he was confused. Besides, no bird such as he described had been seen in their land. And even if Okonorote had seen such a bird, and he had put an arrow through it, how could it have vanished, leaving neither bones nor feathers?

A few of the young men, Okonorote's friends, believed him. They set off to find the hole, threw themselves face downwards beside it, and exclaimed in wonder at the beauty of the world below them, its sparkling streams, its forests, and, most wonderful of all, at the animals grazing on the savannahs.

"But how shall we get to that world?" asked the young men.

The wise men of the Waraus came together and talked, until at last one thought of a plan.

"Let us," he said, "make a long rope-ladder down which we can climb to this other world."

"That will take many months," said one.

"And who will be the first to climb down?" asked another.

"I will climb first," replied Okonorote; "for it may be that my bird lies on those savannahs that we can see. If I fail to return, only one man is lost. If I come back you will know that the way is safe."

For many weeks the Warau girls and women picked cotton in the forest and wove it into a rope-ladder of great strength. This the men lowered through the deep hole, trying out the length of the rope. At the first trial it was too short. The women picked more cotton and lengthened the rope-ladder, but still it was too short. At the third trial it touched the trees in the forest far below.

As soon as the ladder had been made fast, Okonorote climbed down, descending first through the dark hole whose sides were smooth and damp, and then beyond towards the savannahs, the ladder swaying but holding fast; so, after half a day, he came to the trees, and finally, to the floor of the forest. Having tied the end of the rope-ladder firmly to a tree, he moved out on to the savannahs where the animals were grazing. He shot a young deer, kindled a fire, roasted the flesh and found it good. Packing up the rest of the meat, he climbed with it to his own land.

When the Waraus tasted the flesh of the deer they longed for more. When Okonorote told them of the savannahs, forests, gleaming rivers, and high mountains, and above all of the deer and cattle, the tapir and the armadillo, they cried out, "Let us go to this world below and see its wonders."

So it came about that all the Warau people descended to the earth, climbing down the rope-ladder, passing first through the deep hole and coming at last to the forest. With Okonorote they searched for the bird, but there was no trace of it. Instead, they found guavas, pineapples, sapodillas, and bananas; and animals of many kinds.

Among the Warau people there was one only, a woman named Rainstorm, who did not like the earth. In the land above the sky she had been sad and lonely, keeping to herself, often full of tears. Because she often wept, her friends called her Rainstorm. On earth the forests and the savannahs gave her no pleasure, and the animals terrified her. After some months she decided to make her way back to the land above. But Rainstorm had grown fat on earth, and while she was climbing through the hole she stuck fast. Wedged tight, she could not move. There she remains to this day, wedged tightly in the hole, so that those who live on earth cannot see through the sky. And when clouds cover the sky and the rains begin to fall, the Warau people say, "Rainstorm is weeping today."

1966

Janice Shinebourne

Janice Shinebourne (née Lowe, b. 1947) was born and educated in Guyana, relocating to London, England, in 1970. She became a university lecturer and a political and cultural activist. Her publications include two novels: *Timepiece* (1986), for which she won the Guyana Prize for Best First Novel, and *The Last English Plantation* (1988). *The Godmother and Other Stories* was published in 2004.

Shinebourne's "Red Bean Cakes: New York and London" reflects her characteristic pared, economical style and her preoccupation with memories of Guyana (or, as the narrator says, "Old British Guiana"). The memoir celebrates the multiculturalism the narrator experiences in Guyana, London, and New York, allowing her to find herself at home in most cosmopolitan communities. Compare Shinebourne's response to such communities with Bharati Mukherjee's in "Hindus" and Cyril Dabydeen's in "My Mother."

Red Bean Cakes: New York and London[1]

Soho, London

Instead of listening to my order, the waiters at The Canton in London's Soho listened to my accent and strained to place it. I used to have to repeat the order twice, even thrice. I used to catch them looking at me with intense curiosity. However, in ten years they have not asked if I am from China, Hong Kong, Malaysia, Singapore, or the Philippines. Now they accept I am a woman who likes to come here to eat. Now, the headwaiter greets me like an old friend, serves me himself and gives me his warmest smile.

I go to Soho, too, to meet different friends, to catch up on our different interests. We meet at Cranks Restaurant in Great Newport Street because there is no limit on the time they let us spend there, nor do they monitor how much we spend drinking just tea and coffee.

The Canton reminds me of my grandmother's cooking in old British Guiana. She was Chinese. Her first husband was a man from Kashmir who died young; then a man from Delhi became her devoted husband. He spoke Hindi, so did she. So did we. She wore saris he bought her as tokens of his love. Once a week, they went to the cinema to watch romantic Indian films and learn the latest love songs by Latamangeshkar.[2] He taught her to cook Indian dishes — where to buy the spices and how and when to use them — to grow all the vegetables herself, to raise her own

---

[1] This memoir/story was first published as "1957, Red Bean Cakes, Soho, London," in *Moving Worlds*, Caribbean Issue, 3.1 (2003): 119-23. It was later collected under the title given here in the author's *The Godmother and Other Stories* (Leeds: Peepal Tree, 2004) 119-21.

[2] *Latamangeshkar (Lata Mangeshkar)* Indian singer best known as a playback singer in Bollywood movies.

ducks and chickens. She made delicious duck curry. I used to chase the ducks around the garden and catch them so she could thank Allah and bless the duck while she slit its throat, drained the blood, and placed it in a tub of scalding water for the children to strip the feathers.

So while I sit at my table at The Canton, I am a secure child again in British Guiana. I am with my brothers and sister. We are chasing ducks around our backyard. I hear my grandmother trying to sing like Latamangeshkar in a Guyanese accent. I am enjoying the memory of my Delhi-born step-grandfather, who was an affectionate man who, when he visited, always remembered to bring a present for each of his stepchildren and step-grandchildren. When I eat roast duck and Chinese greens at The Canton in London, I taste East Indian duck in their Chinese duck, I taste Guyanese calaloo[1] in Chinese greens. In my memory, I am in a Guyanese garden.

Southall, London

I have a long journey to The Canton so I don't go as often as I would like. It takes thirty to forty-five minutes on London's Piccadilly Line. However, Omi's restaurant is local. It takes me ten minutes from my home in West London to drive there. I have eaten there for as long as I have at The Canton. There is no better Punjabi food in Southall, especially the curried fish, pilau rice and bhindi.[2] Guyanese curries were part of the Creole diet I grew up with — though they bear little resemblance to Punjabi cooking.

Kuldip first took me there in the early eighties. He introduced me to the owners — several brothers and their father whose BMWs were always parked in the forecourt.

When Kuldip wanted to treat comrades or journalists from the BBC or the national newspapers, he took them to Omi's. It took a couple of months for the penny to drop — they used to smile at me because they thought I was his girlfriend. When I began to turn up alone, at first I got the same curious, overprotective looks the waiters at The Canton used to give me.

At teatime, the students from the tertiary college and secondary schools fill the restaurant. They do all the things they can't do at home or in the streets where their elders can see them. They chat up boyfriends and girlfriends. They smoke, they drink beer. They listen to hip-hop, gangster rap, rag and jungle on their ghetto blasters. They live in Southall and environs — Punjabis mainly, but also Muslims, Somalis, English, Irish, African, Caribbean, Vietnamese, Chinese. In those days, I used to teach at the tertiary college. At lunchtime, it used to be all English — packed with teachers and local government staff. Those were the days of Ken Livingstone's Greater London Council when Southall attracted the white Left. It also used to attract the Black and Asian Left because it was once a front line town like Brixton, when it fought racists off its streets. On weekdays as well as on weekends, large

---

[1] *calaloo* Both a spinach-like leaf and a thick soup made from the leaves; here Shinebourne is referring to the former.

[2] *bhindi* Ochroes (Hindi).

extended Punjabi families come for early dinner. Between lunch and dinner, it is quieter. I take my friends then, and we take as long as we like, drinking cups of masala tea and mopping the gravy and chutney on our plates with the last piece of chapati or tandoori naan.[1]

In old British Guiana, my father used to travel a long way to town for Chinese cooking—although he ran his own eating-place. It was divided in two, the cake shop on the left and grocery on the right. On market days the women monopolized the cake shop when they came to cool their thirst on their way home. Then, the men had to use the grocery. On Saturday mornings, the women came to the grocery— then, the men had to use the cake shop. In the canecutting season, the whole place was a refuge for canecutters. In the mornings, it was full of workmen wanting cigarettes and loaves of bread and cheese to take to the factory and fields. In father's place, it was the times when the barriers came down that he liked, the times you would find men and women, children and adults, not in an exclusive space, but talking to each other.

Brixton, London

Mother's menu included fufu, metagee, peas and rice, plantains, yams, cassavas, eddoes, tanya, breadfruit, pepperpot made with fermented casareep, salt fish, salt beef, konki.[2] Her menu weaned me off breast milk. She also used it to teach me to cook for myself. Friends come to my table expecting Chinese. I have to explain that I prefer to eat Chinese at The Canton and Indian at Omi's because cooking them does not come to me as naturally as African Guyanese cooking.

I lived in London for over twenty-five years before I found a restaurant with a menu as evocative of my mother's tastes and lifestyle as The Canton's was of my grandmother and Omi's of my father. It took so long because I never looked for one. London was famous for its Indian and Chinese restaurants, not Caribbean ones. So I always cooked my mother's favourite dishes at home, for my family, friends and myself. Shopping for the ingredients was as integral to their power to evoke the memory of my mother as was cooking them—although she grew everything in her garden. Her gardening involved an intricate communal system: seeds, roots, shoots and their harvest, all exchanged between neighbours. When I travel to Finsbury Park, Shepherd's Bush, or Brixton[3] to find the ingredients for my mother's menu, I relive the journeys she and her friends would make *down the road* in search of a better crop of cassava or tanya root to bring back to their gardens, replant and harvest for their cooking.

---

[1] *chapati or tandoori naan* Various versions of Indian unleavened bread.

[2] *fufu ... konki* Foods endemic to the Caribbean: *fufu* (mashed plantain); *metagee* (a thick soup made of many of the items listed here); *yams, tanya, eddoes,* and *cassava* (all edible tubers); *pepperpot* (a stew made from *casareep,* which is fermented cassava juice or milk); *konki* or *conkie* (a dessert made of cornmeal).

[3] *Finsbury Park, Shepherd's Bush, or Brixton* Districts of London with large West Indian immigrant and second-generation population.

The first time I went to Cafe Jam in Brixton, the friend who took me there had no idea the chef and the menu were Guyanese. We were hungry and it was the nearest restaurant so we dropped in and made a snap decision to have lunch there. The waitress told us if we were willing to wait, she had to go *down the road* to Brixton market to bring in some of the ingredients. When our meal arrived, it was cooked in the Guyanese style, down to the black cake dessert. Now I eat at Cafe Jam regularly and I am really happy when I have to wait a long time for the ingredients to be brought in from *down the road*.

Chinatown, New York

I was trying to find my way to Chinatown in New York, which I was visiting for the first time. I had a need to find the red bean cakes my mother made. I asked a young woman the way and heard the unmistakable accent of someone from the Dominican Republic. As soon as she had given me directions, she said, "You have an English and a Caribbean accent." She wished me a good day and went on her way, waving to me as she disappeared into the crowd. It reminded me how Caribbean people have developed the skills of cultural translation. We tune our ears to accents, learning to recognize and use them to map our everyday transactions. Without that skill and other ones, we would have no maps to negotiate with. So, on my way to find my mother's red bean cake, I was reminded by a woman from the Caribbean that I was from the Caribbean, though I was looking for the home that my mother's red bean cake symbolized in Chinatown, New York.

But how different New York's Chinatown is from London's. My overriding impression was the aggressive competition for space, the number of cars and trucks, and people. People are dwarfed like ants by tall buildings and wide roads. I missed London's narrow streets, which seem to be more people-friendly. Here I saw people running for their lives as they crossed the road, with drivers oblivious to their safety. It made me think of Wild West movies, of wagons and horses stampeding through towns while people tried to get out of the way. In the communication style of some of the people of Chinatown I saw the inflections of the Wild West too — the macho John Wayne swagger in the way the owners of the jewellery shops guarded their trays of gold in open view of the pavement, daring anyone to a high noon shootout. I saw the Marlon Brando curl of the lips when they speak. I felt lost, far away from home in this version of Chinatown.

But I did not give up on my mother's red bean cake. I ventured to ask for them in a cake shop. I was shown red bean cakes I had never seen before, and the proprietor and I ended up having a conversation about the differences between the cakes I buy in London's Soho and the cakes on display in his shop. I explained to him that in London I always got my mother's red bean cakes from a shop in Soho. We were translating to each other the specificities of our different locations by talking about Chinese cakes. Cakes had become a metaphor of home to both of us. It gave me the confidence to explore a bit more, to get beyond the John Wayne and Marlon Brando macho barrier guarding the border to New York. And I came home with a bag of food much better for my diet than red bean cakes: a bag full of beautifully fresh pak choi, string beans, and spring onions, amazed at how much cheaper they are here and how much you get for a dollar. I paid three dollars for a bag of vegetables that would have set me back about eight pounds in London, that is, eleven dollars. New York wasn't so bad after all.

Later that night, I found red bean cakes, exactly like my mother's, in a Guyanese restaurant in Brooklyn. In London I get red bean cakes in Chinatown. In New York I do not find them in Chinatown but in a Guyanese restaurant in Brooklyn. I was home again.

2003, 2004

Leslie Marmon Silko

Leslie Marmon Silko (b. 1948) was born in New Mexico. She is of mixed ancestry, part Laguna, part Mexican, and part white. She is a professor of English at the University of Arizona, Tucson. Her publications include *Laguna Woman* (stories, 1974), *Ceremony* (novel, 1977), *Storyteller* (stories, 1981), *Love Poem and Slim Man Canyon* (1996), and *Garden in the Dunes* (novel, 1999).

Silko's "Yellow Woman" is another story that focuses on liminality, that is, a state of being between two cultures or two existences. Throughout the story there are hints of cultural "in-betweenness." But there are many other "third spaces" between other pairs of antitheses, including the unworldly and sensory, white and Native, sacred and secular, allegorical and literal. The setting, significantly, is close to the borderland between Texas and Mexico. Compare this poem with Claire Harris's "Backstage at the Glenbow Museum, Calgary" and Sharon May's "The Wizard of Khao-I-Dang."

Yellow Woman

I

My thigh clung to his with dampness, and I watched the sun rising up through the tamaracks and willows. The small brown water birds came to the river and hopped across the mud, leaving brown scratches in the alkali-white crust. They bathed in the river silently. I could hear the water, almost at our feet where the narrow fast channel bubbled and washed green ragged moss and fern leaves. I looked at him beside me, rolled in the red blanket on the white river sand. I cleaned the sand out of the cracks between my toes, squinting because the sun was above the willow trees. I looked at him for the last time, sleeping on the white river sand.

I felt hungry and followed the river south the way we had come the afternoon before, following our footprints that were already blurred by lizard tracks and bug trails. The horses were still lying down, and the black one whinnied when he saw me but he did not get up — maybe it was because the corral was made out of thick cedar branches and the horses had not yet felt the sun like I had. I tried to look beyond the pale red mesas to the pueblo. I knew it was there, even if I could not see it, on the sandrock hill above the river, the same river that moved past me now and had reflected the moon last night.

The horse felt warm underneath me. He shook his head and pawed the sand. The bay whinnied and leaned against the gate trying to follow, and I remembered him asleep in the red blanket beside the river. I slid off the horse and tied him close to the other horse. I walked north with the river again, and the white sand broke loose in footprints over footprints.

"Wake up."

He moved in the blanket and turned his face to me with his eyes still closed. I knelt down to touch him.

"I'm leaving."

He smiled now, eyes still closed. "You are coming with me, remember?" He sat up now with his bare dark chest and belly in the sun.

"Where?"

"To my place."

"And will I come back?"

He pulled his pants on. I walked away from him, feeling him behind me and smelling the willows.

"Yellow Woman," he said.

I turned to face him. "Who are you?" I asked.

He laughed and knelt on the low, sandy bank, washing his face in the river. "Last night you guessed my name, and you knew why I had come."

I stared past him at the shallow moving water and tried to remember the night, but I could only see the moon in the water and remember his warmth around me.

"But I only said that you were him and that I was Yellow Woman—I'm not really her—I have my own name and I come from the pueblo on the other side of the mesa. Your name is Silva and you are a stranger I met by the river yesterday afternoon."

He laughed softly. "What happened yesterday has nothing to do with what you will do today, Yellow Woman."

"I know—that's what I'm saying—the old stories about the ka'tsina spirit and Yellow Woman can't mean us."

My old grandpa liked to tell those stories best. There is one about Badger and Coyote who went hunting and were gone all day, and when the sun was going down they found a house. There was a girl living there alone, and she had light hair and eyes and she told them that they could sleep with her. Coyote wanted to be with her all night so he sent Badger into a prairie-dog hole, telling him he thought he saw something in it. As soon as Badger crawled in, Coyote blocked up the entrance with rocks and hurried back to Yellow Woman.

"Come here," he said gently.

He touched my neck and I moved close to him to feel his breathing and to hear his heart. I was wondering if Yellow Woman had known who she was—if she knew that she would become part of the stories. Maybe she'd had another name that her husband and relatives called her so that only the ka'tsina from the north and the storytellers would know her as Yellow Woman. But I didn't go on; I felt him all around me, pushing me down into the white river sand.

Yellow Woman went away with the spirit from the north and lived with him and his relatives. She was gone for a long time, but then one day she came back and she brought twin boys.

"Do you know the story?"

"What story?" He smiled and pulled me close to him as he said this. I was afraid lying there on the red blanket. All I could know was the way he felt, warm, damp, his body beside me. This is the way it happens in the stories. I was thinking, with no thought beyond the moment she meets the ka'tsina spirit and they go.

"I don't have to go. What they tell in stories was real only then, back in time immemorial, like they say."

He stood up and pointed at my clothes tangled in the blanket. "Let's go," he said.

I walked beside him, breathing hard because he walked fast, his hand around my wrist. I had stopped trying to pull away from him, because his hand felt cool and the sun was high, drying the river bed into alkali. I will see someone, eventually I will see someone, and then I will be certain that he is only a man—some man from nearby—and I will be sure that I am not Yellow Woman. Because she is from out of time past and I live now and I've been to school and there are highways and pickup trucks that Yellow Woman never saw.

It was an easy ride north on horseback. I watched the change from the cotton-wood trees along the river to the junipers that brushed past us in the foothills, and finally there were only piñons, and when I looked up at the rim of the mountain plateau I could see pine trees growing on the edge. Once I stopped to look down, but the pale sandstone had disappeared and the river was gone and the dark lava hills were all around. He touched my hand, not speaking, but always singing softly a mountain song and looking into my eyes.

I felt hungry and wondered what they were doing at home now—my mother, my grandmother, my husband, and the baby. Cooking breakfast, saying, "Where did she go?—maybe kidnapped," and Al going to the tribal police with the details: "She went walking along the river."

The house was made with black lava rock and red mud. It was high above the spreading miles of arroyos and long mesas. I smelled a mountain smell of pitch and buck brush. I stood there beside the black horse, looking down on the small, dim country we had passed, and I shivered.

"Yellow Woman, come inside where it's warm."

II

He lit a fire in the stove. It was an old stove with a round belly and an enamel cof-feepot on top. There was only the stove, some faded Navajo blankets, and a bedroll and cardboard box. The floor was made of smooth adobe plaster, and there was one small window, facing east. He pointed at the box.

"There's some potatoes and the frying pan." He sat on the floor with his arms around his knees pulling them close to his chest and he watched me fry the pota-toes. I didn't mind him watching me because he was always watching me—he had been watching me since I came upon him sitting on the river bank trimming leaves from a willow twig with his knife. We ate from the pan and he wiped the grease from his fingers on his Levis.

"Have you brought women here before?" He smiled and kept chewing, so I said, "Do you always use the same tricks?"

"What tricks?" He looked at me like he didn't understand.

"The story about being a ka'tsina from the mountains. The story about Yellow Woman."

Silva was silent, his face was calm.

"I don't believe it. Those stories couldn't happen now," I said.

He shook his head and said softly, "But someday they will talk about us, and they will say, 'Those two lived long ago when things like that happened.'"

He stood up and went out. I ate the rest of the potatoes and thought about things — about the noise the stove was making and the sound of the mountain wind outside. I remembered yesterday and the day before, and then I went outside.

I walked past the corral to the edge where the narrow trail cut through the black rim rock. I was standing in the sky with nothing around me but the wind that came down from the mountain peak behind me. I could see faint mountain images in the distance miles across the vast spread of mesa and valleys and plains. I wondered who was over there to feel the mountain wind on those sheer blue edges — who walks on the pine needles in those blue mountains.

"Can you see the pueblo?" Silva was standing behind me.

I shook my head, "We're too far away."

"From here I can see the world." He stepped out on the edge. "The Navajo reservation begins over there." He pointed to the east. "The Pueblo boundaries are over here." He looked below us to the south, where the narrow trail seemed to come from. "The Texans have their ranches over there, starting with that valley, the Concho Valley. The Mexicans run some cattle over there too."

"Do you ever work for them?"

"I steal from them," Silva answered. The sun was dropping behind us and shadows were filling the land below. I turned away from the edge that dropped forever into the valleys below.

"I'm cold," I said; "I'm going inside." I started wondering about this man who could speak the Pueblo language so well but who lived on a mountain and rustled cattle. I decided that this man Silva must be Navajo, because Pueblo men didn't do things like that.

"You must be a Navajo."

Silva shook his head gently. "Little Yellow Woman," he said, "you never give up, do you? I have told you who I am. The Navajo people know me, too." He knelt down and unrolled the bedroll and spread the extra blankets out on a piece of canvas. The sun was down, and the only light in the house came from outside — the dim orange light from sundown.

I stood there and waited for him to crawl under the blankets.

"What are you waiting for?" he said, and I lay down beside him. He undressed me slowly like the night before beside the river — kissing my face gently and running his hands up and down my belly and legs. He took off my pants and then he laughed.

"Why are you laughing?"

"You are breathing so hard."

I pulled away from him and turned my back to him.

He pulled me around and pinned me down with his arms and chest. "You don't understand, do you, little Yellow Woman? You will do what I want."

And again he was all around me with his skin slippery against mine, and I was afraid because I understood that his strength could hurt me. I lay beneath him and I knew that he could destroy me. But later, while he slept beside me, I touched his face and I had a feeling—the kind of feeling for him that overcame me that morning along the river. I kissed him on the forehead and he reached out for me.

When I woke up in the morning he was gone. It gave me a strange feeling because for a long time I sat there on the blankets and looked around the little house for some object of his—some proof that he had been there or maybe that he was coming back. Only the blanket and the cardboard box remained. The .30-30 that had been leaning in the corner was gone, and so was the knife I had used the night before. He was gone, and I had my chance to go now. But first I had to eat, because I knew it would be a long walk home.

I found some dried apricots in the cardboard box, and I sat down on a rock at the edge of the plateau rim. There was no wind and the sun warmed me. I was surrounded by silence. I drowsed with apricots in my mouth, and I didn't believe that there were highways or railroads or cattle to steal.

When I woke up, I stared down at my feet in the black mountain dirt. Little black ants were swarming over the pine needles around my foot. They must have smelled the apricots. I thought about my family far below me. They would be wondering about me, because this had never happened to me before. The tribal police would file a report. But if old Grandpa weren't dead he would tell them what happened— he would laugh and say, "Stolen by a ka'tsina, a mountain spirit. She'll come home— they usually do." There are enough of them to handle things. My mother and grandmother will raise the baby like they raised me. Al will find someone else, and they will go on like before, except that there will be a story about the day I disappeared while I was walking along the river. Silva had come for me; he said he had. I did not decide to go. I just went. Moonflowers blossom in the sand hills before dawn just as I followed him. That's what I was thinking as I wandered along the trail through the pine trees.

It was noon when I got back. When I saw the stone house I remembered that I had meant to go home. But that didn't seem important any more, maybe because there were little blue flowers growing in the meadow behind the stone house and the gray squirrels were playing in the pines next to the house. The horses were standing in the corral, and there was a beef carcass hanging on the shady side of a big pine in front of the house. Flies buzzed around the clotted blood that hung from the carcass. Silva was washing his hands in a bucket full of water. He must have heard me coming because he spoke to me without turning to face me.

"I've been waiting for you."

"I went walking in the big pine trees."

I looked into the bucket full of bloody water with brown-and-white animal hairs floating in it. Silva stood there letting his hand drip, examining me intently.

"Are you coming with me?"

"Where?" I asked him.

"To sell the meat in Marquez."

"If you're sure it's O.K."

"I wouldn't ask you if it wasn't," he answered.

He sloshed the water around in the bucket before he dumped it out and set the bucket upside down near the door. I followed him to the corral and watched him saddle the horses. Even beside the horses he looked tall, and I asked him again if he wasn't Navajo. He didn't say anything; he just shook his head and kept cinching up the saddle.

"But Navajos are tall."

"Get on the horse," he said, "and let's go."

The last thing he did before we started down the steep trail was to grab the .30-30 from the corner. He slid the rifle into the scabbard that hung from his saddle.

"Do they ever try to catch you?" I asked.

"They don't know who I am."

"Then why did you bring the rifle?"

"Because we are going to Marquez where the Mexicans live."

III

The trail leveled out on a narrow ridge that was steep on both sides like an animal spine. On one side I could see where the trail went around the rocky gray hills and disappeared into the southeast where the pale sandrock mesas stood in the distance near my home. On the other side was a trail that went west, and as I looked far into the distance I thought I saw the little town. But Silva said no, that I was looking in the wrong place, that I just thought I saw houses. After that I quit looking off into the distance; it was hot and the wildflowers were closing up their deep-yellow petals. Only the waxy cactus flowers bloomed in the bright sun, and I saw every colour that a cactus blossom can be: the white ones and the red ones were still buds, but the purple and the yellow were blossoms, open full and the most beautiful of all.

Silva saw him before I did. The white man was riding a big gray horse, coming up the trail toward us. He was traveling fast and the gray horse's feet sent rocks rolling off the trail into the dry tumbleweeds. Silva motioned for me to stop and we watched the white man. He didn't see us right away, but finally his horse whinnied at our horses and he stopped. He looked at us briefly before he loped the gray horse across the three hundred yards that separated us. He stopped his horse in front of Silva, and his young fat face was shadowed by the brim of his hat. He didn't look mad, but his small, pale eyes moved from the blood-soaked gunny sacks hanging from my saddle to Silva's face and then back to my face.

"Where did you get the fresh meat?" the white man asked.

"I've been hunting," Silva said, and when he shifted his weight in the saddle the leather creaked.

"The hell you have, Indian. You've been rustling cattle. We've been looking for the thief for a long time."

The rancher was fat, and sweat began to soak through his white cowboy shirt and the wet cloth stuck to the thick rolls of belly fat. He almost seemed to be panting from the exertion of talking, and he smelled rancid, maybe because Silva scared him.

Silva turned to me and smiled. "Go back up the mountain, Yellow Woman."

The white man got angry when he heard Silva speak in a language he couldn't understand. "Don't try anything, Indian. Just keep riding to Marquez. We'll call the state police from there."

The rancher must have been unarmed because he was very frightened and if he had a gun he would have pulled it out then. I turned my horse around and the rancher yelled, "Stop!" I looked at Silva for an instant and there was something ancient and dark—something I could feel in my stomach—in his eyes, and when I glanced at his hand I saw his finger on the trigger of the .30-30 that was still in the saddle scabbard. I slapped my horse across the flank and the sacks of raw meat swung against my knees as the horse leaped up the trail. It was hard to keep my balance, and once I thought I felt the saddle slipping backward; it was because of this that I could not look back.

I didn't stop until I reached the ridge where the trail forked. The horse was breathing deep gasps and there was a dark film of sweat on its neck. I looked down into the direction I had come from, but I couldn't see the place. I waited. The wind came up and pushed warm air past me. I looked up at the sky, pale blue and full of thin clouds and fading vapor trails left by jets.

I think four shots were fired—I remember hearing four hollow explosions that reminded me of deer hunting. There could have been more shots after that, but I couldn't have heard them because my horse was running again and the loose rocks were making too much noise as they scattered around his feet.

Horses have a hard time running downhill, but I went that way instead of uphill to the mountain because I thought it was safer. I felt better with the horse running southeast past the round gray hills that were covered with cedar trees and black lava rock. When I got to the plain in the distance I could see the dark green patches of tamaracks that grew along the river; and beyond the river I could see the beginning of the pale sandrock mesas. I stopped the horse and looked back to see if anyone was coming; then I got off the horse and turned the horse around, wondering if it would go back to its corral under the pines on the mountain. It looked back at me for a moment and then plucked a mouthful of green tumbleweeds before it trotted back up the trail with its ears pointed forward, carrying its head daintily to one side to avoid stepping on the dragging reins. When the horse disappeared over the last hill, the gunny sacks full of meat were still swinging and bouncing.

IV

I walked toward the river on a wood-hauler's road that I knew would eventually lead to the paved road. I was thinking about waiting beside the road for someone to drive by, but by the time I got to the pavement I had decided it wasn't very far to walk if I followed the river back the way Silva and I had come.

The river water tasted good, and I sat in the shade under a cluster of silvery willows. I thought about Silva, and I felt sad at leaving him; still, there was something strange about him, and I tried to figure it out all the way back home.

I came back to the place on the river bank where he had been sitting the first time I saw him. The green willow leaves that he had trimmed from the branch were still lying there, wilted in the sand. I saw the leaves and I wanted to go back to him—to kiss him and to touch him—but the mountains were too far away now. And I told myself, because I believe it, he will come back sometime and be waiting again by the river.

*   *   *

I followed the path up from the river into the village. The sun was getting low, and I could smell supper cooking when I got to the screen door of my house. I could hear their voices inside—my mother was telling my grandmother how to fix the Jell-o and my husband, Al, was playing with the baby. I decided to tell them that some Navajo had kidnapped me, but I was sorry that old Grandpa wasn't alive to hear my story because it was the Yellow Woman stories he liked to tell best.

1974

Wole Soyinka

Wole Soyinka (b. 1934) was born in Nigeria and educated at universities in Ibadan and Leeds. He has published several novels and volumes of essays, plays, and poetry, including *A Dance of the Forest* (play, 1963), *The Interpreters* (novel, 1965), *Poems from Prison* (1969), *The Man Died: Prison Notes of Wole Soyinka* (1972), *Mandela Earth and Other Poems* (1988), and *The Open Sore of a Continent: A Personal Narrative of the Nigerian Crisis* (1996). He was awarded the Nobel Prize for Literature in 1986.

Soyinka's "Chimes of Silence" was written when he was imprisoned by the Nigerian government, which misconstrued as traitorous his unsuccessful negotiations with the secessionist Igbos to avert civil war (known as the Biafran War, 1967–70). In spite of being deprived of reading and writing material in prison, Soyinka managed to write this and a number of other poems (published in a 1972 volume, *A Shuttle in the Crypt*). Soyinka considers the "Chimes of Silence" section of the book to be central to his experience in jail, particularly the loss of human contact that he found more "corrosive" than "purely physical loss," as he notes in the Preface to the volume. In his 1975 interview with Henry Louis Gates, Jr., Soyinka mentions many of the issues that continue to concern African (and postcolonial) writers today. Soyinka comments on Africa's relationship with Europe in such contentious areas as education, language, religion, racism, Marxism, Freudianism, pan-Africanism, and African diaspora. Consider this interview in relation to Salman Rushdie's essay on "'Commonwealth Literature' Does Not Exist," Njabulo Ndebele's on "Guilt and Atonement: Unmasking History for the Future," and V.S. Naipaul's on "Jasmine." The Nigerian Civil War that Soyinka mentions is the setting of Chinua Achebe's "Girls at War." The interviewer, Henry Louis Gates, Jr., is a distinguished United States scholar of African diaspora and African-American studies. His books (authored and edited) include *The Signifying Monkey* (1988), *Thirteen Ways of Looking at a Black Man* (1997), *Africana: The Encyclopedia of the African and African American Experience* (1999), and *Lincoln on Race and Slavery* (2009).

Chimes of Silence

At first there is a peep-hole on the living.[1]

It sneaks into the yard of lunatics, lifers, violent and violated nerves, cripples, tuberculars, victims of power sadism safely hidden from questions. A little square hole cut in the door, enough for a gaoler's fist to pass through and manipulate the bolt from either side. Enough also for me to — casually, oh so casually — steal a quick look at the rare flash of a hand, a face, a gesture; more often a blur of khaki, the square planted rear of the guard on the other side.

---

[1] *At first ... living* Soyinka wrote this prose poem when he was in solitary confinement in a Nigerian jail during the Biafran War (1967-70).

Until one day, a noise of hammering. All morning an assault of blows multiplied and magnified by the unique echoing powers of my crypt. (When it thunders, my skull is the anvil of gods.) By noon that breach is sealed. Only the sky is now open, a sky the size of a napkin trapped by tall spikes and broken bottles, but a sky. Vultures perch on a roof just visible from another yard. And crows. Egrets overfly my crypt and bats swarm at sunset. Albino bats, sickly pale, emitting radio pips to prowl the echo chamber. But the world is dead, suddenly. For an eternity after ceasing the hammers sustain their vehemence. Even the sky retracts, dead.

Buried alive? No. Only something men read of. Buoys and landmarks vanish. Slowly, remorselessly, reality dissolves and certitude betrays the mind.

Days weeks months, then as suddenly as that first death, a new sound, a procession. Feet approach, dragging to the clank of chains. And now another breach that has long remained indifferent, blank, a floodhole cut in the base of the wall, this emptiness slowly, gracelessly, begins to frame manacled feet. Nothing has ever passed so close, so ponderously across the floodhole of the Wailing Wall. (I named it that, because it overlooks the yard where a voice cried out in agony all of one night and died at dawn, unattended. It is the yard from which hymns and prayers rise with a constancy matched only by the vigil of crows and vultures.) And now, feet. Bare except for two pairs of boots which consciously walk deadweight to match the pace of manacles on the others. Towards noon the same procession passes the other way. Some days later the procession again goes by and I count. Eleven. The third day of this procession wakes into the longest dawn that ever was born and died of silence, a silence replete and awesome. My counting stops brusquely at six. No more. In that instant the ritual is laid bare, the silence, the furtive conspiracy of dawn, the muffled secrets hammer louder than manacles in my head, all all is bared in one paralysing understanding. Five men are walking the other way, five men walking even more slowly, wearily, with the weight of the world on each foot, on each step towards eternity. I hear them pause at every scrap of life, at every beat of the silence, at every mote in the sun, those five for whom the world is about to die.

Sounds. Sounds acquire a fourth dimension in a living crypt. A definition which, as in the case of thunder becomes physically unbearable. In the case of the awaited but unheard, physically punishing. Pips from albino bats pock the babble of evensong — moslem and christian, pagan and unclassifiable. My crypt they turn into a cauldron, an inverted bell of faiths whose sonorities are gathered, stirred, skimmed, sieved in the warp and weft of sooty mildew on walls, of green velvet fungus woven by the rain's cunning fingers. From beyond the Wall of Mists the perverse piety of women, that inhuman patience to which they are born drifts across to lash the anguish from the Wall of Purgatory. A clap of wings — a white-and-ochre bolt, a wood-pigeon diving and crossing, a restless shuttle threading sun-patches through this darkest of looms. Beyond and above the outside wall, a rustle of leaves — a boy's face! A guileless hunter unmasks, in innocence—an evil labyrinth. I shall know his voice when children's songs invade the cauldron of sounds at twilight, this pulse intrusion in the home of death.

The sun is rising behind him. His head dissolves in the pool, a shuttle sinking in a fiery loom.

1972

An Interview with Wole Soyinka

(with Henry Louis Gates, Jr.)

Truly a Renaissance man, Wole Soyinka is poet, playwright, novelist, critic, actor, teacher, editor, philosopher. Born in 1934 in West Nigeria, the "Yoruba Pantheon" attended Government College in Ibadan (then the University of Ibadan) and received an honors degree in English from Leeds University, England, in 1957. Beginning in 1958, he spent 18 months as a Play Reader at the Royal Court Theatre in London, where he produced *The Invention*, one of his earliest satirical pieces. In 1960, he returned home to Africa to produce, with The 1960 Masks, his drama troupe, his play A *Dance of the Forests*, which won the competition to commemorate Nigeria's Independence in October of that year.

Four years later, Soyinka formed a new group, Orisun Theatre, which became a vehicle for the more serious political satire, teaming up with the older group for major productions. In 1965, his play, *The Road*, won first prize for published drama at the first Festival of the Negro Arts at Dakar, Senegal. That same year, he was awarded, together with Tom Stoppard, the John Whiting Award for Drama. Shortly after his return from the Commonwealth Arts Festival in Britain at which *The Road* was performed, he was arrested and imprisoned.

Soyinka's first term in prison seems almost humorous. In the Western Region Assembly in 1965, the corrupt ruling party, led by one Chief Akintola, was being challenged for the first time by the opposition Action Group. By "blatant and unrestrained thuggery and ingenious treachery," wrote Ruth First in her *The Barrel of a Gun*, Akintola and his boys snatched away electoral officers before opposition candidates could lodge their nominations. Ballot boxes were stuffed, ditches dug around polling stations so that people couldn't vote.

Just as the local radio station prepared to broadcast the good Chief's prerecorded victory speech, a pirate tape interrupted and announced, "This is the voice of Free Nigeria!" and proceeded to advise, in no uncertain terms, Chief Akintola to leave the country after his startling upset at the polls! On the evidence of a producer,

Soyinka was arrested and charged. His first trial was a farce. At the end, he was acquitted, but not before he had gone on a hunger strike in prison to protest the delay in bringing his case to court.

Undaunted, the following year Soyinka took his play *Kongi's Harvest* to the Festival in Dakar. In August 1967, just after his first volume of poems, *Idanre*, was published, again he was arrested. This time, though, there was no humor.

Three weeks into the Nigerian Civil War, Soyinka issued a poignant appeal for a cease-fire. Gen. Odumegwu Ojukwu (leader of the Biafran secessionists), he argued, had at best made a miscalculation; the Federal Government, for its part, was obligated to re-examine its acts of war, since it must accept a sense of responsibility for the massacre in the North of the Ibo people and for the future of the people of Nigeria. The Federal Government, he continued, was faced with a no-win situation: either it had to destroy completely the Ibo people, or it would be faced with the unappealing prospects of attempting to "govern" an implacably embittered people. All this at the moment when it had appeared that "the new generation was about to march together." There had emerged, he wrote in the *Nigerian Daily Sketch*, in August 1967, "the by now familiar brigade of professional congratulators, opportunists, patriots, and other sordid racketeers, the cheer-leaders of a national disaster whose aim was to exploit Ojukwu's blunders to camouflage their own game of power and positions."

In August, returning from a visit to Ojukwu in Biafra, Soyinka was arrested for "spying" for the secessionists. The authorities said he had confessed to helping to buy arms "for the overthrow of the Federal Government." No trial. Two years in solitary confinement, where only the briefest fore-knowledge foiled at least one attempt on his life.

Released in 1969, he assumed a position at the University of Ibadan as Head of the Department of Theatre Arts. He resigned his position and published *The Man Died*, the brilliant and powerful account of his incarceration. Advised that it was unwise to return to Nigeria, he spent a year as a Fellow at Churchill College, Cambridge, England. Recently, he returned to his home in Africa—this time to Accra, where he assumed editorship of the controversial African journal, *Transition*.

He hopes to return to the Chair of Dramatic Literature at the University of Ife in Nigeria sometime in the next two years. He has helped produce one film, *Kongi's Harvest*, which he has vigorously denounced. He has written over a dozen plays, collected by Oxford Press. And his *The Fourth Stage*, an essay on the African tragic arts, is destined to mold the definitive theory of African poetics for the next generation.

Gates: You spent three years in prison for allegedly conspiring with the Ibo during the Nigerian Civil War. After two years of freedom, just before the publication of your description of your prison experience, called *The Man Died,* you left Nigeria, some say rather abruptly. Why?

Soyinka: My decision to leave Nigeria still carries with it some kind of *considered* action. I left Nigeria about two years ago to catch up with some work of mine, to be away by myself, considering a number of things. It just happens that a number of problems have developed from some writings of mine, that have made it necessary to stay out longer than I planned. I don't consider myself as having *left* Nigeria.

Gates: Why exactly were you incarcerated during the War?

Soyinka: Let me say this: there is a lot of confusion over this visit of mine to the secessionist region during the war. In fact, there is a lot of confusion over my role in the war. There have been some categorical statements which have astonished me. I am always rather amused at the certainty with which certain allegations are made. But then, as I think the American press have more recently discovered, I think journalists tend to go more by the statements made by regimes than by individuals or by minorities, or minority opinions within society. I think the expression "clandestine," as my visit to the secessionist region was widely labeled, really belongs to the propaganda machinery of the Federal Nigerian Government, during the war. It's a very false expression, however; I did not make a clandestine visit to the Eastern region. It was a deliberate visit. I consulted a number of people, even those actually connected with the regime. The risk was mine and the decision was mine, and that of a group of people with whom I was actively involved. And again, it has been suggested that I went on a "peace" mission. So far as one of the purposes of my visit was to put an end to the war which had only just begun, you could, I suppose, call it a peace visit. But—and this I suppose was what really bothered the Federal military regime—the real motivation of the visit was to present viable and very concrete alternative solutions to the solution by war. It was a political visit in that sense; I didn't go to the East just to ask the Biafrans to lay down their arms; that would be daft. In any case, that's an impractical idea once guns start firing. No, I went there to present a definite political alternative which had been worked out by quite a number of influential people, including my own contributions. It could very well have been another individual entirely who paid the visit. But, for particular reasons, I was in a position to present these alternatives to the secessionist regime. And I went.

Gates: What were the root causes of the Nigerian Civil War?

Soyinka: Let me say what the root causes were *not*. The root cause of the Civil War certainly was not secession. Secession was merely a sort of critical event in their long line of national betrayal, desecration of values in the community, an inequitable society, clannishness, petty chauvinism, personal ambition—but, most important of all, the emasculation, the negation, of certain restraining and balancing institutions within the society, by cliques and caucuses within the community. All of which were definitely inimical to the aspirations of the masses of people.

If you want me to be even more elaborate, I would suggest—and I think this is quite tenable—that the root causes of the War can be found in the very lack of egalitarianism within the community. In other words, very deep seated dissatisfactions within the community which were of such a nature that they *could* be manipulated or diverted *into* what I call the "scapegoat syndrome." In other words, if you have succeeded in robbing society blind you can persuade the robbed and the dissatisfied sections of society that the real causes of their dissatisfaction can be traced to a particular sector of the community. And this was what, this was the policy which was very actively pursued by one or the other of the various power-holding sectors of the community. It was not merely tribal—when I talk about this segmentation, it was not merely tribal segmentation; it was, if you like, *class* segmentation. There is nothing *new* about it. The whole history of societies all over the world has always demonstrated this capacity of a very small minority—an elite, or a momentarily privileged and power-holding group within society to manipulate the masses of people into a belief that injustices which really are due, which have been created by them, have in fact been created by completely innocent groups within society. So the Civil War, the act of secession by the Biafrans, was really a kind of culminating result of very many factors within society. And it really is very distressing to find the very simplistic attitudes taken by so-called intelligentsia within Nigerian society and, of course, outside commentators, almost as if a group of people got up suddenly and decided: "Okay, we want to be part no longer of the Nigerian polity." Of course this is absolute nonsense. In fact, my association and active collaboration with this group, which in certain circles has been dubbed the "Third Force" of the Civil War, was dictated by a conviction that the roots of the Civil War were not to be found in the act of secession of the Ibos or even in the hideous massacre of the Ibo people; but that they reached far deep down into the very fundamental disjunction within the total society.

Gates: Given your incarceration and the unpopularity in official circles of *The Man Died*, did you intend originally to live in Europe when you left Nigeria?

Soyinka: No. I did not come to Europe to live. Since my absence from Nigeria, if you add up the amount of time I've spent in Europe, I think you'll find—with the exception of the year I spent on a fellowship and some teaching at Churchill College, Cambridge—I think you'll find that I spent less time in Europe than in Africa.

Gates: But having lived here at least for the last year, and, one assumes, having associated yourself with some of the more original minds in Europe, how would you evaluate the intellectual climate in Europe?

Soyinka: I think I had better first emphasize that I do not consider Cambridge, or even England for that matter, a place to apply the intellectual barometer for Europe. But I take it your question is really meant in far more general terms. I will say quite candidly that I have always considered the whole of European intellection, I suppose naturally, Euro-centered: because of this, it is a very inaccurate and therefore a very untruthful system of analysis and conceptualization—in fact, of human beginnings and development, thought and ideas. I don't think this is a wholly personal prejudice. You will find there have been quite a number of formidable scholars—Cheikh Anta Diop is a name that comes easily to mind, and also Chancellor Williams—have questioned and backed by research the assumptions regarded as the foundation of "human" civilization, what constitutes "human" development. They have re-evaluated, in fact, the whole theory of social origins which have been postulated by European thinkers and scholars.

I find myself very much preoccupied—if you like, naturally prejudiced—in favor of a wholesale re-examination, re-evaluation of European ideas. In fact, I question very much the intellectual value of a number of the preoccupations of European scholars. And taking as the foundation of my thinking the ideas, the world-view, the philosophical concepts of my society, I find that Europe has for too long browbeaten the rest of the world, and especially the African world, into an acceptance of the very fundamental system [of evaluation] which is, I suppose, natural to Europe. It is time the paths which have been blazed by a number of very serious African scholars should be followed up very rigorously. And the damage which has already been done—the waste of toil which has been indulged in by universities—seems very ridiculous. Tiny, really minuscule, academic studies, with no relevance at all, to a true understanding of man's situation within the universe—which I think is at the root the most fundamental aspect of all intellectual inquiry. I believe that one of the primary duties of African intellectual institutions is really not merely to question the system of thought of Europe, but to question the *value* of these systems, the *value* of these particular patterns of thought in European thinking.

Now one ready example, of course, is the old question of social development—the idea, the Darwinian idea of human evolution, for instance, which has been applied in a very racist and negative way to a comparative study of societies in the world, always of course to the detriment and the belittlement of Black societies: The deliberate suppression of facts, of historical facts, which are dug up by anthropologists; the biased, the very dishonest selectiveness of material, which then becomes the basis of supposedly rigid structuralism in analyzing social systems; the habit of ignoring or merely treating as curious the systems, the metaphysical systems, the philosophical ideas of African society. In other words, these are made sort of adjuncts to the European artificial systems. I think all of these would make me feel far too prejudiced, really, to make any comment on the European intellectual climate. I find myself completely outside of it. I find a lot of European intellectual structures really of irrelevance to myself as a member of my own society. In fact, the only justification for being preoccupied with these systems seems to me to be a need to recognize what they are, in order to protect ourselves; in order to undo, as far as we can, the immense damage which has been done to our society, and also to retrieve our centers of learning—our schools even, and our universities—from the wrong emphasis, from the time-wasting irrelevancies which have been given a very special badge of erudition, intellectualism and so on. All these things which really have distorted not just the abstract thinking of African scholars, but the *application* of such thinking to social and intellectual development in an African society.

Gates: The motif of self-sacrifice is a common one in your works. Although you apparently reject membership in the European intellectual community, do you think that, perhaps, this motif is a result of the undue influence of a Judeo-Christian tradition?

Soyinka: This, again, I believe is part of the pattern of acceptance of European thought and ideas—this idea of attributing the concept of self-sacrifice to the Christian, to the Euro-Christian or Judeo-Christian world, simply because a single figure emerged from that particular culture to espouse, in very beautiful mythological terms, the cause of the self-sacrificing individual as a kind of, as the surrogate for world suffering, social unhappiness, and general human unhappiness. It is often forgotten that the idea of individual sacrifice—the principle of the surrogate individual—is, in fact, a "pagan" one. Those who attribute this concept to Europe forget that Christianity itself is not a European religion. And that Christ, the central figure of Christianity, is really a glamorization of very "paganistic" ideas: the idea of personalizing the dying old year, the dying season; to insure the sprouting, the fertility, the idea of the emergence, in fact the very resurrection, of Nature. All this is "pagan"—"pagan" as an expression used by the Christian world to describe the fundamentally natural, Nature religions. I see Christianity merely as another expression of nature religion. I cannot accept, I do not regard the principle of sacrifice as belonging to the European world. I completely reject the idea that the notion of the scapegoat is a Christian idea. This scapegoat idea is very much rooted in African religion.

If I may just leave religion aside for a moment. I would like to comment on the peculiar isolation of creativity—the peculiar isolation of the artist as an expression of certain principles, including the principle of individual self-sacrifice. The isolation, if you will, of the artist from the rest of society. If we look at this politically, I think we will find the greatest social manipulators have been individuals who have not scrupled to sacrifice themselves on behalf of the rest of the community. They have also been tremendous organizers. But it is when they failed that the concept of sacrifice begins. To take a modem example: if Fidel Castro had failed in his war of revolutionary struggle in Cuba, he would have been regarded literally as another romantic artist who, in spite of being a member of the *bourgeoisie,* saw himself as Christ did, as a savior of the people, the masses of the people. This transposition always takes place, and the *key* to the particular nature of this transposition—to the concepts and the terminology used—depends very much on whether the practical, organizing aspect (whether in a military sense, or the political sense, or even the propagandizing sense)—whether the sheer political technology of the struggle becomes a successful thing. But if the leader, the visionary—and this really is what is common to all these figures of sacrifice, the visionary—if he fails, then of course he becomes another Christ figure. The moment he seems to struggle—all revolutionary struggles, do not forget, commence by the action of visionaries against supposedly impossible odds. But of course if it succeeds, then you have the transposition of terminologies, which takes place *immediately.* And you now have a revolutionary figure, you now have a man of the masses. So I'm not at all impressed by this distinction.

The writer has—I won't even call it a duty; I would say the field, the scope of the writer involves a true recording of this element, of this *blurred* transition between, if you like, the Christ-like figure of self-sacrifice and the successful revolutionary. I do not think that the writer should be limited if he writes about a particular aspect of this figure, because inherent — and this is the important thing — inherent in all struggle on behalf of society is always the element of self-sacrifice. I don't think Garcia-Lorca set out to be deliberately self-sacrificing anymore than Lenin did, for instance. It is too sharp a division for me to accept. This is a subject I have had to confront more and more. Only recently, for instance, I was giving a lecture at Sheffield University, and one of the members of the audience remarked that he noticed in my recent writing a move from what he called the artist as self-sacrificial, the notion of the artist as a revolutionary member of the community. And this, for me, was a very great simplification of the motivations and the actual futurist goals which move the artist as a member of society into action.

Gates: But many of the "Keepers of Blackness" in America insist on the subjugation of self — all, that is, except *their* self — for what they call the "collective good of the community." Do you think it is an African notion that the individual will of the artist must be subjugated to the will of the community, as is claimed by said Keepers of the said Faith?

Soyinka: You know, fascism takes all sorts of shapes and forms of expression. We have to be very, very cautious always when we are confronted by those who say a certain group of people within the community — either as individuals or as species of some strange animal — should always submit themselves, bury themselves within a certain totality. There is always a germ of fascism in the mental preoccupation of individuals, of certain groups of people — their preoccupation with this. I think it is the intensity of this preoccupation which we have to watch.

Of course, the artist, whether he likes it or not, is a member of the community. His concerns, his preoccupations — even his calling, his very profession — depend very much on the security of society. I think he recognizes this. I can count, for instance, on a couple of hands, artists whom I know in African society who consider themselves *separate*, and not a part, of the totality. But while I can say I can count the *artists* on one hand, I can count on both hands and toes and a lot of borrowed digits the number of civil servants, the army hierarchy, plus what I call the colonial aristocracy of African society — in fact, I cannot enumerate them totally, there are so many who do not regard themselves at all as being part of the commonality of African society. So when I hear this concern, this unequal preoccupation with artists, I first of all ask myself what the protestors are hiding above all about *themselves*, what they are hiding about their own personal ambitions; this is very important. In our society we've had artists who've died, who've sacrificed themselves on the altar of war; we've had those, unsung, who have been tortured silently in prisons.

Finally, and this is the most important point: when you listen especially — and I am glad you quoted Black American observers — when you listen to these Black American observers, you find that very often they are those who come to Africa and immediately ally themselves with the power structure. They view the entire society through the spectacles of those who are in power. It's very amusing; but it shouldn't be amusing. It's really tragic and destructive in many ways, because they are the same people who *shout* about the totality of society. They're the ones who complain about writers and artists standing aside. And when they talk about the polity, when they talk about the entire society, they really are talking about a very small hierarchy.

I wish to suggest to you that the first exercise always is to study the background of these complainants, these great champions of the collectivity, these "more revolutionary-than-thou" members of the collectivity. You find they are usually pampered, idle members of the *bourgeoisie,* who have been toasted, wined and eliticized by the ruling powers within society. These commentators, very often who come to aid the revolution in our society, have figures—human figures—in their heads— the top, the leaders in their heads. I don't wish to be cruel, but I would suggest that most of the time these commentators are suffering from a slave mentality. They have not totally eradicated in their mind a slave mentality. They have merely substituted a Black master for the ole white massa.

Not so long ago I had an argument in Kenya over the whole question of our dear friend, General Idi Amin. Now I found out that this [American] brother was not interested in the masses of Ugandans. He was nicely, comfortably situated in Kenya, by the way, and had paid a fleeting official visit to Uganda, had in fact met the "genial" figure of General Amin. And I asked him, "Have you visited some of the refugee camps, have you visited Kisuimu," which is on the Lake [Victoria] and is one of the favorite places for escaping Ugandans.... No, he hadn't. All that concerned him was that somebody had made a statement publicly criticizing the head, the leader of Uganda. Now this is their sense of collectivity: when a writer, an artist within that society has the courage to expose certain realities, they cannot stand it, because it is a rebuke on themselves....

Now, and the question is: is the leadership of African society today the collectivity? Until those who are so passionately concerned with African collectivity, until they can apply the same rules to *all* sections of society, whether it is the military class, or the civil-service class, or the very top leadership hierarchy—until they learn to study very carefully what is the voice, what really is the aspiration of the masses, and whose articulation is closest to this, I think some people will finally be condemned by the very realities which are constantly taking place within our society.... To take the most recent and obvious example: the collective good of the Ethiopian masses, as defined and as recognized by default by the intelligentsia of Africa—this "collective good" has been the benign imperial neglect by the privileged minority.

The magazine I have just begun editing, *Transition,* carried an eyewitness report, a month before the movement against Haile Selassie, of a famine in Ethiopia. In fact, it was more than an eye-witness report. It was a document which also demanded the mobilization of intelligent opinion within Ethiopian society and in the outside world on behalf of the neglected masses against the corrupt arrogance of Haile Selassie. I would like to ask—because I don't really know—how many Black

American magazines ever thought fit to publicize and to criticize this criminal neglect of the Ethiopian masses? I want to ask how many intellectual magazines in Africa thought it necessary or saw fit to criticize the banquetry and the junketry and the thoughtless dissipation of the wealth of the Ethiopian people while hundreds of thousands of people were dying of starvation? I want to ask how many African leaders themselves thought it fit while they were wining and dining in the Ethiopian Palace during the O.A.U. conferences, while just a few miles away the people of Ethiopia were dying? How many thought it necessary even to utilize, however indirectly, journals they control to call attention to the plight of the Ethiopian masses? Very, very few.

But the moment a spokesman, a writer, insists that his commitment is to the masses of the people, he is described as a privileged minority who is exploiting a European concept of freedom of speech. I call this *a slave mentality. I* call it a refusal really to be truthfully emancipated as a human being, as a member of society. I use "emancipation" in the Fanonist sense, the revolutionary antidote to Marx's "alienated man." I cannot accept the definition of collective good as articulated by a privileged minority in society, especially when that minority is in power. And when I hear expressions like "collective good," I always want to know whose definition this is? Is collective good to be equated with the self-consolidation, the self-perpetuation of an exploiting minority, just in order to satisfy either our Black brothers from the States, or even to satisfy the constantly proliferating privileged so-called intelligentsia of our own African societies? I insist on reading "collective good" as an expression which refers to the total, to the masses of society, not as expressed, as defined by the propaganda machinery of a privileged minority....

Gates: But how could you concretize this idea of self-sacrifice in your work?

Soyinka: Two things I said regarding your questions earlier: first of all the theme of self-sacrifice, let me try and concretize it a little with examples from my work. In *The Strong Breed*, I utilize a ritual which is a very common one which takes many forms among the riverine people on the West Coast of Africa, certainly in Nigeria what we call the "river people" there. There is the idea there of the ritual. The principle of it is that a person takes on himself the entire burdens of society; very often it takes the symbolic form of a canoe-shaped object which is then taken to the river or to the sea and floated away. Other times it takes the form of a mysterious lump which is taken to the river bank or to the sea shore and buried. In certain Yoruba areas the carrier takes the object and dives into the water and disappears for quite a while; he goes down there to bury the object right in the sea bed. Again among the Yoruba people you have a festival called the Eyo festival at which certain human masquerades parade the city.

There is a particular masquerade who is called a Eyo Adimu, who is considered a very dangerous masquerade. He carries the evils of the year in his person: all the diseases, the unhappiness, the evil, all the curses which have hung around society. He takes this away, disappears into a grove or bushes somewhere and all the collective evils of society are taken in his own person and are thrown away. Now the point about all these various forms is that the individuals who carry, who serve as carriers for the rest of the community, are not expected to survive very long. The whole demand, the stress, the spiritual tension, as well as the forces of evil which they trapped into their own person are such that after a few years they either go insane, or they catch some mysterious disease, or they simply atrophy as human beings and die. Their life span is very short; they cease to be useful members of the community quite early. This is recognized, and the Eyo Adimu in particular is ex*posed* to a very lingering illness of the sort that incapacitates him completely after one or two journeys of this nature, journeys on which he saves society.

Now these individuals whom I have mentioned, they are not artists, or teachers, or any of these special classifications of society; they are just ordinary human beings like you or me. There hasn't been any concept within society that these are poor, Christian, deluded individuals. For me it is a great misconception to suggest that the principle of self-sacrifice, or the principle of individual sacrifice is something alien to African traditional societies. This is nonsense. I am not interested in whether the concept of individual sacrifice is valid or not; obviously these are things which have to be considered on their own terms, depending on the particular historic or political necessity in which an individual — whether he is a mason, an athlete, a bricklayer — finds himself within his community.

I think the obsession with individual salvation — which, if you like, is on the opposite end of the axis to self-sacrifice — is a very European thing. I am not aware that it occupied the minds of our people. I think it is a very European literary idea; in fact, the obsession itself is a very Christian principle. In our society, this kind of event, this process, is inbuilt into the very mechanism which operates the entire totality of society. The individual who acts as this carrier and who knows very well what is going to become of him is really no different, is doing nothing special, from other members of society who build society and who guarantee survival of society in their own way. I think there is one principle, one essential morality of African society which we must always bear in mind, and that is the greatest morality in what makes the entire society survive. The actual detailed mechanism of this process merely differs from group to group and from section to section, but it is the totality that is important. I think there is far too much concern about this business of the Christian ethic of individual self-sacrifice.

On the subject of collectivity, I think maybe after all I should use a very pertinent example. It sums up entirely what I consider the hypocrisy of these "more-collectivized-I's-than-thou" revolutionaries who spout these fashionable themes so readily. There is a criticism of my book, *The Man Died,* in *Black World* magazine [August 1974 "Books Noted"] which you have just shown me, and this is an illustration of what I consider to be indecisive, the insincerity of many "collective I's" propagandists we have in our midst. On one level this would-be critic [reviewer Carrie Sembene] accuses me of separating myself from the collectivity, from the social collectivity, by certain stands which I take in society and stands which I took in the book and also the very language of the book. In my book, I use an expression to describe what I considered an outrage during the suffering of hundreds of thousands of our people and the self-sacrifice which was being made by our people during the War. I referred to the very elaborate, extravagant wedding of the Nigerian leader [President Yakubu Gowon] as "grandiloquent vomit," and she objects to this. There is no recognition in her piece that that wedding event was a kind of a slap in the face for the sacrificing masses of Nigeria.... Not only that, but [Gowon] also says that the fall of a town just around the time of his wedding was literally meant to be a wedding present for him, but regretted that it did not happen on the very day of his wedding.

In what I consider a mood of moral outrage (which I know many of my countrymen shared, by the way, even the so-called intelligentsia) — if this critic had read some of the Nigerian newspapers she would have found that one or two actually had the moral courage to criticize in stronger terms this insulting waste of our revenue, especially at a time of national self-sacrifice. It was not just the artist-writer who criticized this. But what strikes me is the fact that the whole of this lady's attitude is governed entirely by the idea that one should dare criticize the first member of the Nigerian society. I don't know if she carried in her head some fantasies of becoming married to some head of state or not,[1] and resents the idea that some impertinent artist should call such an occasion "grandiloquent vomit." I don't really understand. But it is remarkable that she is applying one set of laws to the power structure, one set of laws to the artist within society. Now it is this contradiction which makes me always question these facile propagandists for so-called collectivism. They don't know what collectivism really is. To believe in a collective society, to believe in genuine communalism means you do not tolerate any act of arrogance or of exploitation from any side of the community: you do not accept the setting aside by itself of a particular class of society. And you have the courage to criticize and to articulate the voice and the protest of society in this respect. I think people should be a little more honest and regard it as their duty if they are genuine spokesmen for the masses of the people, which is what I understand when they talk about a collectivized society. If they are genuine spokesmen, then they cannot afford this revelation of slave mentality, which says it is all right for the power structure to be elitist but it is criminally elitist for the artist to criticize the elitism of the power structure.

By the way, I think I also ought to take this opportunity to correct a misconception which has been repeated in Sister [Carrie Sembene's review]: that I supported the Biafran cause. Again, this is a result of falling victim to the propaganda of the power structure which, of course, is supposed to be gospel truth. Well *I did not* support the Biafran cause, but I was also very much opposed to the Federal cause. I believe that the Federal regime was responsible for the affairs going as far as they did, for matters reaching the edge of civil war, because of the Federal Government's criminal negligence. In fact, I would prefer to call it tacit approval, by default — let me make it as generous as that — tacit approval by default of the act of genocide committed

---

[1] Ms. Sembene is married to Sengalese novelist-filmmaker Ousman Sembene. [Gates's note]

on the Ibos. But I did not support the act of secession, for the simple reason that I felt that it was not the solution; it was not the way to create a viable society. I believe very strongly that the Biafrans should stay in Nigeria and, therefore, give Nigeria an opportunity to cleanse itself thoroughly of the crime which was committed. In other words, punish those who were responsible and completely re-organize society on principles which would not perpetuate the inequities within society, and the systematic exploitation by a small group of people of the majority.

Gates: How would you appraise the value — spiritual, political or otherwise — of the diasporan Black man's proverbial return to mother Africa?

Soyinka: The move back to Africa by the Brothers from the diaspora is in itself, without any question, a valid desire. By move, of course, I do not really mean the physical move, although this can be a very fruitful and necessary experience or solution for a number of Black Americans. I am more interested in what you might call the cultural move, the spiritual move, even the intellectual move; the rediscovery of the social system, the beliefs, the philosophy of our own society, because this in itself means a long overdue rejection of European habits of thought and life-approach. It is quite true that quite a few who do come, Richard Wright for example, find that they are already far too conditioned to benefit, or even to successfully penetrate the, well, I wouldn't call them secrets — the basic tenets and values of African society. I do not find this strange. I notice that some Brothers tend to criticize others for failing to find "themselves," so to speak, in Africa; I do not consider it strange at all. Those who do, then, it means that there is a gap within — a hiatus within their soul — which needs to be filled from this. I find that to those who are already complete beings in themselves, the rediscovery of Africa would only be an additional bonus if they do rediscover it. Well, they can still survive as revolutionary members of society without actually putting on a dashiki. I am never overly concerned.

I think it's a good thing, this internal movement back to Africa. I think it is one which we in Africa should respond to very seriously. I notice its influence in the cultural product at the moment of Black America in the drama. Again, there are some misbegotten examples of the experimentation, unfortunately. It manifests itself also in the arts, in painting and sculpture; and there is a very, very sadly commercialized aspect of this return, when everything is geared to the business of artifacts and even spiritual commerce and so on. All these distortions are part of a movement of this kind. You will find that even the Roman Catholic pilgrimages to their Holy Lands always carry with them a certain commercial aspect, so let's not worry too much about the negative aspects of this return. It is unfortunate, it is very irritating, it's very often disgusting and it makes Africans — I mean the "home" brothers — very cynical about Americans in general, and I am afraid, occasionally more prejudiced about their Black brothers than about the white Americans. But all in all I think that what we are witnessing is a complete rejuvenation of long accepted cultural forms, concepts, ideas; images, artistic images, even the poetry has benefited a lot from this move.

Gates: How do we gain control of the means of dissemination of information—especially when we are evaluating European concepts?

Soyinka: Now, first of all, I think the most fundamental means is the complete reorganization of our educational system. Some national governments are already aware of this. One recent example is Ghana, whose government has already commissioned a number of educationists, teachers and writers to take time off. Literally, they have been invited to completely rewrite, recreate the textbooks which are used in schools; offer new ideas where they cannot actually get to work on them, and try and attune them to the African background, the truthful African reality, and prune away the exocentric ideas of training and mental development which are very often insidiously slipped into these texts. That is one method. And, of course, you move on from the primary level, secondary level to the university level.

When I look at our universities—this, perhaps, apart from the primary-school level—the university level is where the real fight is. I have taught in several universities in Africa, both as a member of staff and as a guest lecturer, and the closer I get, the more experience I have of African universities, the more I become convinced that perhaps nothing short of a *cultural revolution* on the lines of China would do. It's a very drastic method, but I think, not just myself, but a number of my colleagues with whom I speak have a feeling that very little can be done, internally.

Universities are very much the slaves of the system of a bureaucratization. It is impossible really to rid the university of old brigades and old, jaded ideas and Eurocentric evaluation of ideas, even of learning, of discoveries, of research: the emphasis on trivia—on scholastic-sounding trivia—the waste of time, the waste of energy, the waste of intellect on the most irrelevant and generally immaterial details of learning. Sometimes I think nothing short of a real militant movement against the universities—if necessary, the closing down of universities for a number of years while we start over from scratch; I sometimes think that nothing less than this will serve. There may be other methods, but I am afraid I have failed to think of them.

Evolution within our universities is going to take, at the pace it is going, another 1,000 years and will probably just travel the full circle and come back to the colonial system which we have inherited, not only inherited, but *enshrined*—the very pride which a lot of unproductive intelligentsia take in the principle of nonproductivity. By "nonproductivity" I refer to this business of glorification of trivia-independent, autonomous trivia. So, for the process of evaluation and the process of the dissemination of new, valid ideas for our society, I think we must literally gain control ourselves—that is, the real people, the masses of the people, the parallels of the power structure must somehow gain control of the universities.

A third method of course is again to gain control of journals of thought, of ideas, which probably gives away why I was interested in taking this job of the editorship of *Transition* in Africa.

Gates: Granted that we *can* gain control of the dissemination of ideas, what sort of re-evaluations do you deem necessary?

Soyinka: Just one rudimentary example, regarding the revaluation or re-orientation of values necessary for the African world, the African intelligentsia. You see, I do not consider it necessary to wait for the Claude Levi Strauss' of the world to undo the centuries of Eurocentric blasphemy that have placed the Black man, the so-called primitive man, under the categorization of some kind of semi-human creature possessing some sort of "prelogical mentality." It is for me not very important that a Levi-Strauss comes along and tries to undo the heresy of the Gobineaus, the Humeses—those who try to glamorize this presumed, this very conceited and racist idea about the Black man's incapacity for thought. That is a task which belongs quite naturally to the intelligentsia of the Black world itself. But again, there can be a level of exaggeration about this. It is as serious, I think, is as *erroneous* an emphasis of direction to spend time trying to disprove this fallacy as to try and glorify it as, let us say, some Negritudinists have done—to try and suggest, to try and agree with the European racist scholars that the Black man is incapable of analytical thought or ratiocination. To suggest that this is, however, as laudible a faculty—a faculty of emotion, thought, intuition, as *opposed* to rationality—to try and laud it and glorify it is to accept, first of all, the dichotomy between rationality and intuition—subjectivity and objectivity—which is postulated by European scholars.

When I talk about the true intellectual liberation of the Black man, I speak of a complete rejection, a refusal *even to begin* from the untried axioms of the white academic—you know, bored with his own society or seeking some kind of validation for his presumed superiority of his own people before he attempted to come to terms, in a very self-validating way, with African society. [My position] is to believe very implicitly that the African peoples live a very complete, rounded, self-sufficient existence, both emotionally and intellectually, and that all the postulations of the European scholar are either irrelevant, in fact have no bearing whatever—except perhaps in some peripheral cases—or contradict the reality of the African peoples. It amuses me to find African scholars considering themselves very proud to be Freudians or Jungians. It betrays a kind of basic inferiority; a lack of self-assurance, which can only be compensated by recourse to European terminologies. I mean, Freud was *a bourgeois* psychologist whose entire, whose very presumptuous analysis of the human psyche was based on a peculiar, European, *bourgeois* society. If we accept the fact that the human psyche can be understood not only from a study of individuals, but by a study of society, then we must—coming from a completely different matrix of ideas, of social relationships—must look warily at the findings of Freud.

The same thing, of course, applies to Marx. For individuals and students and scholars who are concerned with the reform of society in general, a Marxist analysis of European society is of course a very useful base for trying to plumb the various contradictions, the anomalies within our own society which have been picked up and developed as a result of our contact with European society. It is important to try and understand the various, profound, fundamental analyses of European society. But to accept all the tenets of Marx, *carte blanche,* without any intelligent adaptation for the peculiarities of our own society, is really to betray a lingering desire to be accepted on the European intellectual level. There have, of course, been various intellectuals in Black society in the Third World who have been very conscious of this: Fanon is a very obvious example, Amilcar Cabral is another and he, of course, is both a praxist as well as a theorist of African revolution. But all those who inhabit, who *infest*, our intellectual institutions in the majority prove themselves uncritical slaves of European ideas, incapable of critical application to the uniqueness of their own society. They fail to accept this fundamental fact: that theories and ideas *do not exist in vacuo,* but are based on empirical observations of society and tempered by the idealist vision of which every serious and profound thinker is capable.

Gates: What African institutions would you say facilitate the most organic reassociation between the diasporian African and his brothers on the continent?

Soyinka: On the subject of the internal return of our Afro-American Brothers to the Mother Continent, there is yet one more positive advantage which should not be ignored. For a long time, and quite rightly, fortunately the most militant and the most cleansing force for the Black American in the United States has been the force of Islam. The sense of a kind of Islamic nationalism. For us, let me say this quite frankly—for us on the Mother Continent, this has always been a kind of half-way house, a station through which the Brothers had to pass before finding their true, authentic Black soul in Africa. What I am trying to say is this: that we must not underestimate, we must always be grateful for a force which the Islamism of the Black Muslims, the redeeming role it played in recalling the Black American to himself, to a spirituality, a personality, a dignity, which could no longer be tainted or corrupted by the decadent values of American white society. But it must be understood that this is only a half-way house, and that when we in Africa encounter supposedly serious and intelligent Black Americans who have failed to move beyond this point, we get an uncomfortable feeling that there is a genuine fear in such people really to come deep down to where *home is.*

Islam is not an African religion, anymore than Christianity is. For many of us, having repudiated Christianity, we are not about to accept a religion, a way of life, an outlook on life, which is in many ways basically contradictory to the authentic African religions. When we speak of religions, we are not merely talking about an act of worship; we are talking about a whole pattern of cultural mores, a whole metaphysical outlook, a philosophic approach to the world. We are talking about a political attitude as well. There is a very sad lack of understanding, or even curiosity, in many Black Brothers in America about what is the *true* spiritual reality of Africa. And one encouraging fact about this movement back to Africa among our Brothers is that there is now today a lot more genuine commitment to finding out about the true Black African past. I am not apologetic at all about making this distinction; in fact, I think it has become crucial—very crucial—to make this distinction, to emphasize the fact that there does exist a true, an authentic African spirituality, a religiosity if you like, a Black metaphysical outlook. I use the expression "African World," the African World, in preference to others. And this is distinct from both Christianity and from Islam.

To move away slightly from the role, the present commitment of Brothers on the American Continent, to move away from their commitment to what after all was a kind of salvationist ideal for them, to go now to the political emphasis a bit: I sometimes detect to my great discomfort a fear of the true Black heritage discovery. It is something which can be paralleled to the much earlier social distortion in the minds of the slaves, which is that to be quadroon or octaroon is much better than to be *pure* Black. I think that there are still too many Brothers who are very content and who feel very secure in this half-way house. They cannot make the final plunge toward a true, a complete, full-rounded, uncompromising Black authenticity.

Gates: What did you think of the so-called symbolic value of holding the Ali [-George Foreman Heavyweight Championship] Fight in Mobutu's Zaire?

Soyinka: Muhammad Ali, by the way, is one of my favorite heroes, if I may use that expression—which is always a dangerous one. But he's one of my true heroic figures of this century. And I have no doubt in my mind that his Islamic conviction, for instance, is absolute and total. And I don't expect him *ever* to discover the African religions that are a source of his own spiritual strength, his own dignity, because I get the feeling—and this is why I admire the man—that he is grounded in his Islamic calling. But I do wish he would discover some day gods like Shango and Ogun, and find in them sources of strength and the reality of his own being. Very optimistically. I hope a character like this would find that while the Islamic religion was useful to him up to a point, it is merely a transitional, though combative, alternative to the hypocritical, exploitative and racist self-affliction of the Christian Ethic. If Ali had lost his match on African soil, it would have been because he was not viscerally tuned to the Gods who make the energies of the Black Continent. He won because his opponent was even more alienated from those demonic sources of African strength. Ali's psychology was pure African; he stuck pins in Foreman's effigy, then finished the job in the ring. So you see, either way, the African Deities won against the twin usurpers of African spirituality. And that, of course, was the only thing which kept the fight from being a total farce against Africa, against the Mother Continent.

1975

Subramani

Subramani (b. 1943) was born in Fiji. He has studied in Suva, New Zealand, and Canada. His publications include *The Fantasy Eaters* (1988), a collection of stories, and a number of critical essays. He now teaches at the University of the South Pacific in Suva. The publication of his novel, *Dauka Puran* (2001), is considered a literary event since it is the first major work to be written in the Indo-Fijian vernacular.

Subramani's "Sautu" is set in the Indian community of Fiji. The Indians were brought there as labourers ("girmits") from India by British plantation owners during the colonial period. "Sautu," a native Fijian word, is the name of the village; it means "plenty" and "peace," and is evidently ironically used in both senses. There is little that is peaceful in the lives of the protagonist and his family and friends. At the end of the story, the protagonist loses his land and is committed to a mental asylum. Subramani captures well the quotidian life of the Indo-Fijian community (and their tenuous relationship with the native Fijian community). Like many Indo-Fijian writers, Subramani is very aware of his Indian heritage in his writing, incorporating Indian language and mythology. Compare this story with Ama Ata Aidoo's "No Sweetness Here," and Sam Selvon's "Turning Christian."

Sautu[1]

That evening Dhanpat returned early from the mill barracks. Most of the night, lying on his string bed, he struggled with Kanga's remarks. He felt immensely uneasy and distressed.

His friend had brought out the tobacco and, wrapped up in their blankets, they filled their clay pipes and smoked. They talked of indenture but the period was no longer clearly defined; it seemed like a labyrinth full of shadows and memories.

Then Kanga told him a story he had read in a Hindi paper. It was about an old Hindu who was afraid of dying. Is it true, he asked Dhanpat, that a man's memory sharpens before death?

It didn't take long for Dhanpat to notice that his friend wasn't his usual self. He was less jocular and more introspective. Consequently there were long stretches of silence in their conversation when Kanga seemed tense and irascible one moment (the prattling of women and children next door seemed like an irritation which grated upon his nerves) and next moment he sank into a state of acute depression.

When Dhanpat saw him to bed, his friend held his arm and tried to talk. But Kanga's mouth merely opened and shut like that of a stranded fish.

Dhanpat couldn't sleep though he felt weary and his limbs ached. He coughed badly. After rubbing on some pain balm he slept. But not for long. Soon he was awakened by the barking of dogs and harsh whispers outside his hut. He went out with

---

[1] *Sautu* (Fijian) A quality of life characterized by much accomplishment, peace, good health, and wealth.

his lantern to see what was amiss: they were carrying Bansi's wife to the hospital.

And then he had those nightmares again: Ratni's madness, the pool of blood in dry sugar cane leaves, the frightening pursuit by apparitions on horse-back and Ratni's dismembered limbs in the *machaan*.[1]

Dhanpat got up early. The minah birds were squawking angrily again on the bare branches of the tamarind tree. It made the cattle and goats restless. He donned his *dhoti*,[2] picked his white cotton shirt, now coarsely patched and mildewed, from a nail and staggered to the window to shoo the birds away.

Dulari was up early too; she was already milking the cows. After her mother Ratni's death, Dulari looked after the animals for her father. In return, she took some milk for her baby.

A cloud had descended on Dhanpat's life after the simultaneous departure of Ratni and the children. Immediately after Ratni's death, Dulari was married. Then Dhaniram found work with a tailor and he shifted to town with his wife. And Somu disappeared from Sautu. With these exits a great deal of love was banished from Dhanpat's life.

When he had Ratni and the children, he saw the need for the body to be fine and the mind strong. Now his body was without motives or consequences. Detachment and acceptance of life came easily and quickly to him. He had read in the Gita "Desire nothing so that you'll have everything." Once this was a line he quoted in *mandali*[3] debates; now it was held with conviction.

The village was stirring again. It stirred only in mornings and evenings with departure and arrival of men from the fields and the sugar mill. The women hurried in and out of their huts minding their *orhini*,[4] while the bare-backed children squatted and rolled in the dirt-yard.

Dhanpat had observed the unchanging life of that village for nearly fifty years. Sautu wasn't an old village. After indenture a group of men and women scratched a little clearing from which the present squalid little huts sprang up.

The site was badly chosen. There were no rivers and the sea was thirty miles away. The village was hemmed in by an irregular stretch of unprosperous sugar cane fields in the south and in the north by partly barren soapstone hills bearing occasional guava bushes and stunted rain trees and reeds.

Sautu was regarded as insignificant, and it turned its back on the world beyond. More thatch and bamboo structures appeared as the families became larger. They continued to till the obstinate earth; there was nowhere else to go. Besides they were

---

[1] *machaan* Shed.

[2] *dhoti* The traditional Indian male garment consisting of a long piece of unstitched cloth wrapped about the waist and the legs, and tied at the waist.

[3] *mandali* Council.

[4] *orhini* A female veil used as a head cover as well.

no longer moved by a momentum of their own. Habit and custom held them fettered to the place. Ultimately, Sautu, like its inhabitants, became an aberration, a contortion of history, on that landscape.

Near the coast, in the west, there were several small Fijian villages. Much of the land was owned by local chiefs. When Dhanpat came with Ratni, who was in late stages of pregnancy, he looked desperately for land to build a hut. The villages counselled him to see Ratu Epeli who gave Dhanpat a plot at the edge of Sautu, and sent Tomasi to help build his hut.

Dhanpat's reverie was broken: a waft of breeze brought the damp odour of old hay and cowdung from the pen. He turned from the window and sat heavily on his string bed.

Now in disarray, his hut spoke of a past order in the faded limewash on matted bamboo walls, in the arrangement of dull, discoloured photographs, and ripped up crepe on soap-box shelves.

The reeds in the roof had thinned and the walls sagged. Cobwebs hung in shabby strands from rafters. The mud floor was uneven. Where it was damp the cowdung plaster had come off and the red earth showed.

It was always dismal and dark in the hut. The windows and doors rarely opened completely. The years had added nothing significant to his worldly possessions. A much-battered grey heavy tin suitcase under his string bed held his and Ratni's old clothes and odd cups and saucers, glass jugs, a large looking-glass and several combs and some jewellery—their wedding presents.

In a corner, where the wall and rafters were black with soot from cooking, lay copper and aluminum utensils and earthenware. His broken *dholak*,[1] brought from India, stood on an empty wooden box in another corner.

He looked reflectively at his earthly belongings: a great emptiness seemed to unfold within him.

Then he did something he hadn't done for a long time—he pulled out his suitcase and picked up the large jagged mirror, a gift from Kanga, and examined himself.

The piercing brown eyes, narrow and heavily wrinkled, an aquiline nose and the thin line of his rather well-formed lips were the only visible parts; the rest of his face and head were concealed behind grey tangled hair.

Long years in the fields had bent his constitution. His long and bony arms and legs cracked and creased like the earth outside. He was reminded of Kanga— his withered and shrunken husk—and the mask of death on his face.

He felt old, exhausted and bereft.

Ignoring the bowl of milk Dulari had left for him, he scrambled out, and went behind the hut to urinate.

Now slumped back against the wall of his hut, he watched the somnolent village minding its dull business.

---

[1] *dholak* Small drum.

He was relieved when Bhairo, the village barber, greeted him. He went inside the hut to get a mat. Bhairo pulled off his dusty canvas shoes, and squatted on the mat in the hot sun, resting his elbows on his scrawny legs.

"Acha, Dhanpat, I don't see you at *mandali* these days. Why?" he asked, fanning himself vigorously with his skull cap.

This was the correct way to begin. Bhairo knew it would lead, by way of discourse on comparative merits of illness and treatment, ancient and modern, to the scriptures. Bhairo trusted his own knowledge of Vedic literature. He often embellished his arguments, secretly elated, with learned quotations from the ancient books.

Bhairo, like most other villagers, respected Dhanpat less for his knowledge than his common sense and fairness. But he was too much of a free thinker, too much at times like the despicable *Samajis*. No wonder, thought Bhairo, he bred a renegade (according to the norms of Sautu, the highest form of delinquency) for a son.

Bhairo was disappointed when Tomasi appeared. He hurriedly opened his bundle and took out a wedding card for Dhanpat. It caught Tomasi's eyes.

"Aha, Bhairo. This modern thing catching fast. Where's the yellow rice?" asked Tomasi in broken Hindi.

Bhairo frowned. This wedding card was an odiously un-Hindu custom which he regretted but nevertheless propagated. But he understood well Tomasi's sinister fondness for asking awkward questions. He didn't answer.

Tomasi watched him and waited to be contradicted. Bhairo simply wilted under his stare, his face revealing the expression of self-denigration which unmistakably showed whenever he lost a verbal duel.

Bhairo resented the way Tomasi seemed to be appraising him. He resented most of all the way Tomasi's nostrils stared at him. Bhairo's effort to keep up an appearance of good companionship with Tomasi was inevitably resulting in suppressed hostility.

He observed this at a *Kali Puja*.[1] Bhairo was the protagonist in the rituals. He was in a trance, singing and dancing in complete abandon round and round the grotesque brass idol. When he turned a corner his eyes arrested a familiar figure in the crowd —a ponderous head with thick fuzzy hair and a dark face. And those nostrils—they stared at him. When their eyes met, Tomasi grinned. The trance was broken.

Bhairo gathered his bundle, nodded and slipped away.

Dhanpat, however, derived certain pleasure from Tomasi's friendly antagonism. Tomasi, eager to test Dhanpat's response to his newly acquired ideas (from the visiting *misnari*[2]) waited for an opportunity to begin. But today, scenting a certain dullness and abstract preoccupation in his friend, he asked instead after Somu.

Somu was planning to come back. "Only for a visit. At Christmas," Dhanpat told his friend with a nonchalance which wasn't real. He hadn't told anyone, however, that Somu wanted to take him to Canada. He waited to burst it on them when it became a recognized and established fact.

---

[1] *Kali Puja* A prayer service to the goddess Kali.

[2] *misnari* Missionary.

Tomasi didn't take this aspect of Dhanpat's conversation seriously. He couldn't conceive of Dhanpat and Somu in any other setting. He was convinced that Somu was hiding in another village.

Tomasi flapped his large hands against his sleeveless blue coat in disappointment. For a moment he gazed, with a kind of proprietorial concern, at the sagging hut and the bare garden patch. The kasava sticks he had given Dhanpat for planting still lay under the tamarind.

Dhanpat anticipated Tomasi's half-patronizing, half-admonitory glance.

Tomasi stood there without saying anything while Dhanpat's mangy dog licked the sores on Tomasi's ankles. He crossed the yard to the tamarind tree where the ground was thick with leaves and tamarind fruits in various stages of decomposition. He examined a handful of fruits, dropped a couple into his coat pocket, and left.

In the pelting heat of two o'clock sun, Dhanpat picked up his walking stick and turban and headed for the village school. With his head slightly in advance of his body, he walked like one balked with a nagging problem.

He trudged on a ribbon of well-beaten dusty soapstone path, past the straggle of huts where women went listlessly about their tasks or sat under a mango or a tamarind tree picking lice from their hair.

The huts looked desolate and the dirt-yards showed ugly cracks. There were no gardens to speak of, no decorative trees, except occasional marigold plants which bore small gawdy flowers. For the first time Dhanpat was overwhelmed by the dereliction.

He rested for a while at Rambaran's store where the latter sold groceries from the front door and very bad rum from the back. Some men were drinking *kava*[1] and smoking *bidi*[2] cigarettes on the veranda. Two or three others were snoring on empty sugar bags. Rambaran was inside, in his black shorts, chewing a match-stick with which he picked his teeth.

In a dilapidated *bure*[3] outside the shop, Rambaran's attractive daughter-in-law was in her customary hammock singing mournfully a song from *Barsaat*. Bhairo's deaf-mute son was sitting in front devouring her with his gaze. Now and then Bimla would throw a mischievous glance at him, seductively, fluttering her eyelids. In response, his toothless grin would stretch from ear to ear, revealing the spittle at the corner of his mouth.

From somewhere inside the shop Rambaran's wife whispered reproachfully "Dulahin!" And Bimla straightened her *orhini*, slowly and deliberately, over her ample bosom, studiously avoiding her mother-in-law's eyes.

Dhanpat was distressed. He climbed down the veranda and took the path towards the swamp. At the swamp, Bansi was peeling pandanus[4] leaves under a tree.

---

[1] *kava* A Fijian herbal drink with anti-depressant elements.

[2] *bidi* Self-made cigarettes.

[3] *bure* Thatched hut.

[4] *pandanus (pandan)* Leaves of the pandana tree, which grows in tropical areas of Asia, Australia, and the Pacific Islands. These leaves are used for handicraft and for enhancing savoury dishes.

The swamp had swallowed several animals and children when it was wet and soggy. Mangal's eldest son had buried himself alive here twenty years ago. Now the swamp was dry. It carried only pandanus trees. And cattle and goats searched for anything edible all day.

Dhanpat waited for Bihari on a crooked wooden bench outside the school room. Bihari was inside prowling behind rows of exceptionally silent learners hoping to catch someone talking. There was a loud clamour when the bell rang. Bihari dismissed his class and came straight to Dhanpat.

He had a letter for Dhanpat. Dhanpat limped along with Bihari across a parched playground, strewn with lunch wrappings, as the schoolmaster translated the letter, his reading punctuated by a regular asthmatic wheeze. Bihari prided himself upon his knowledge of Hindi and English and his ability to translate from both languages. He glowed in his superior knowledge as he explained every nuance, every shade of meaning in Somu's letter.

The letter was sad. It was unlike those letters Somu wrote from New Zealand. Those early letters mainly described landscapes and expressed bewilderment at the complexity of social life. They were enthusiastic letters.

Dhanpat didn't hear from Somu for a long time after he stowed away to India. However, he received reports of his levity with women and money, and the frequent bouts of depression he suffered. Rambaran once spread the story that Somu was in a mental hospital in India.

Dhanpat was alarmed; he worried about his son. Now more than ever when he heard so regularly from him. This was strange. He never had much affection for Somu. He wasn't like Dhaniram who went through all stages of life like a true Hindu. Dhanpat could trust Dhaniram. But his younger son invited only suspicion. He was far too restless, discontented and given to secret thinking.

The villagers regarded Somu as special. He didn't go to Bihari's school; instead he was taken into a mission school in town. They shook their heads in amazement and disbelief when he talked about books and ideas. This attitude changed to perplexity when he abruptly left his father. Finally, they were comforted in their initial belief that Somu was always a renegade.

Dhanpat saw quite early that Somu refused to be absorbed in the life of the village. These letters from Somu told more than he ever expected to know about his son. They were not addressed to him; it was always Somu talking to himself. At times he had wished that his son would come back. Life would change; it would become whole and fine again for both.

Somu, of course, didn't return. But in a curious way Dhanpat's life was changing. There were words in the letters which echoed, and arguments which festered, in his mind. It seemed that some unknown force had confronted him with truths he had hidden from himself.

His world was becoming rapidly disorientated. Things didn't seem to regroup again. His days oscillated between a past order and new anguish. At times he felt his life hovering at the edge of new perceptions.

There was, however, a loneliness now which was intense and complete. Was it because he feared desolation — that he wanted Somu back?

The pale amber of receding sunlight rested on the distant Makai Hills and on top of tired and empty trees. It sharpened the grim profiles of the lugubrious huts.

The village was stirring again: the men were back from the fields and the mill. Dhanpat was at his prayer house under the tamarind tree. The door was open and the mixed smell of camphor and sandalwood paste was sharp and, to Dhanpat, reassuring. But when he confronted the icons and the brass idols the momentary exhilaration, like a sudden inspiration, was followed by corresponding hopelessness. The gods looked old and ravaged.

He heard someone stir behind him. It was Bhairo.

"Aré, Aré[1] Dhanpat, you carry on. Don't worry about me," he protested, gesticulating.

Dhanpat placed the lota[2] he was carrying at the door, and turned towards Bhairo.

They sat on the ground in front of the prayer house, and talked in low whispers. When Bhairo had left, Dhanpat sat there for a long time feeling old and withered.

This drought had laid so many old people in their graves, among them some of his closest acquaintances from the indenture days. Now it was Kanga's turn. How was he, thought Dhanpat, to regard all these deaths as quirks of fate?

Dhanpat had always considered himself inviolate. That is why he moved through life with such splendid reassurance. Now sitting in front of the temple, he saw how the protective armour had gradually disintegrated. The tenuous bond that existed among disparate items of his life was breaking. More than ever he felt the pointlessness of daily rituals of toil and rest, prayer and persistence. Once they were, however, the only affirmations of his existence.

He felt oddly defeated and humiliated.

Dhanpat hurried into his hut like one excited over an unknown thing or one expecting an eruption. He fretfully closed the doors and windows and crept onto his string bed, and lay there in a delirium, his energies completely drained.

That night there was more looting and stone throwing in the neighbouring village. More sugar cane was burnt.

It was Bimla's husband who, creeping and crawling home after a rum party, noticed the fire in Dhanpat's hut. He dragged himself from hut to hut yelling for help.

The villagers came with their machetes and cane knives, and with whatever water they could spare. They broke the door with their machetes and pulled Dhanpat out of the blaze.

The dry and brittle thatch and bamboo crackled, wilted and then flared into flames. They were soon reduced to cinders. The rafters and poles also came down with an explosion, and burnt on the ground giving off a pale glow.

---

[1] Aré An exclamation usually of surprise or impatience.

[2] lota A brass goblet used in Hindu religious ceremonies.

A moment ago there was total hush. Now the village broke into a tumult and then pandemonium.

Dhanpat sat silently amidst wailing and shrieking women and children. Someone had thrown an old blanket around him. A couple of urchins crept close to him and stared, their faces revealing a mixture of fear and mute incomprehension.

Bhairo searched hard for any indication of guilt or shame on Dhanpat's face.

There was no sign of stress: he was stoic and inscrutable like the gods in the prayer house.

Dulari consoled her father in a low and husky voice, blowing her nose, and wiping her tears with the corner of her *orhini*. She helped him to his feet and directed him towards her hut.

Dhanpat felt something cold and damp on his thighs and down his legs. He examined his *dhoti*: he was wet.

In the weeks that followed, Dhanpat's insanity was argued and disputed. Then those outrageous stories began circulating. Bimla complained that she found Dhanpat peeping into her bath-shed. Henceforth the women moved in pairs or groups, and avoided him at the village well.

Bansi's son reported to his mother that the old man tried to molest him at the marshes. As a result the children refused to walk through the marshes to school. And Bimla's husband said one night when he was slouching back after a rum party he met Dhanpat, apparently sleep-walking. He was stark naked.

Other stories were equally scandalous. Finally, the village elders met at the *mandali* and proclaimed Dhanpat imbecile. They agreed he was bent on inviting the wrath of the gods on the entire village.

Dulari wept with shame. Her husband was embarrassed. One morning, instead of going to the fields, he left for town. When he came back late in the evening, he was angry and disappointed.

The following day he took a village elder with him. Weeks later a government van halted in the village amidst great shouting and clamour.

Dhanpat was taken away for observation. And the chief took possession of his land.

1988

Mary TallMountain

Mary TallMountain (Mary Randle, 1918–94) was born in Alaska. The daughter of a Koyukon-Athabascan Indian mother and Scottish-Irish father, she published several collections of poems and short stories, including *Nine Poems* (1979), *There Is No Word For Goodbye* (1981), *Light on the Tent Wall* (1990), and a posthumous collection, *Listen To the Night* (1995).

In TallMountain's "There Is No Word for Goodbye," the speaker is being instructed on a particular aspect of Athabascan culture and language. It is possible that she is someone who is familiarizing herself with her ancestry, a characteristic experience of postcolonial individuals caught between cultures. Compare this poem with Shirley Lim's "Passports" and Oodgeroo Noonuccal's "Gooboora, the Silent Pool."

There Is No Word for Goodbye

Sokoya, I said, looking through
   the net of wrinkles into
   wise black pools
   of her eyes.

What do you say in Athabaskan[1]
   when you leave each other?
   What is the word
   for goodbye?

A shade of feeling rippled
   the wind-tanned skin.
   Ah, nothing, she said,
   watching the river flash.

She looked at me close.
   We just say, Tlaa. That means,
   See you.
   We never leave each other.
   When does your mouth
   say goodbye to your heart?

---

[1] *Athabaskan* The name of a large group of closely related Native American peoples living mainly in Western North America.

She touched me light
   as a bluebell.
   You forget when you leave us,
   You're so small then.
   We don't use that word.

We always think you're coming back,
   but if you don't,
   we'll see you some place else.
   You understand.
      There is no word for goodbye.

1981

Edwin Thumboo

Edwin Thumboo (b. 1933) was born in Singapore to a Tamil father and a Chinese mother. He was professor in the Department of English Language and Literature and Dean of the Faculty of Arts and Social Sciences at the National University of Singapore. He has also been a visiting professor and fellow at universities in the United States, the United Kingdom, and Australia. He has published several volumes of poetry, including *Gods Can Die* (1977), *Ulysses by the Merlion* (1979), *The Third Map: New and Selected Poems* (1993), and *Still Travelling* (2008).

Thumboo's "Ulysses by the Merlion" is an example of a nationalistic poem of newly independent countries. Here Thumboo envisages the classical Ulysses seeing the unique Merlion (a creature that is half-lion, half-fish) as a symbol of a unique Singapore. (See the footnote to the poem.) Why does the poet give us the point of view of a Mediterranean adventurer? Is this a form of postcolonial writing back to the Empire, proclaiming the ex-colony's achievements, or does the use of Ulysses' perspective complicate this? Compare Thumboo's echo of Homer with Ngugi wa Thiong'o's of Robert Browning in "Goodbye Africa."

Ulysses by the Merlion[1]

for Maurice Baker

I have sailed many waters,
Skirted islands of fire,
Contended with Circe
Who loved the squeal of pigs;
Passed Scylla and Charybdis
To seven years with Calypso,[2]
Heaved in battle against the gods.
Beneath it all
I kept faith with Ithaca,[3] travelled,
Travelled and travelled,
Suffering much, enjoying a little;
Met strange people singing
New myths; made myths myself.

But this lion of the sea
Salt-maned, scaly, wondrous of tail,

---

[1] *Merlion* A statue with the head of a lion and the body of a fish, used by the Singapore Tourist Board as their trademark icon and adopted unofficially (and reluctantly by some) as a Singaporean symbol.

[2] *Circe, Scylla and Charybdis, and Calypso* Mythical figures encountered by Ulysses in Homer's *Odyssey*. Note that Thumboo employs the mythical Ulysses as his speaker.

[3] *Ithaca* Ulysses' home city.

Touched with power, insistent
On this brief promontory ...
    Puzzles.

Nothing, nothing in my days
Foreshadowed this
Half-beast, half-fish,
This powerful creature of land and sea.

Peoples settled here,
Brought to this island
The bounty of these seas,
Built towers topless as Ilium's.[1]
    They make, they serve,
    They buy, they sell.

Despite unequal ways,
Together they mutate,
Explore the edges of harmony,
Search for a centre;
Have changed their gods,
Kept some memory of their race
In prayer, laughter, the way
Their women dress and greet.
They hold the bright, the beautiful,
Good ancestral dreams
Within new visions,
So shining, urgent,
Full of what is now.

Perhaps having dealt in things,
Surfeited on them,
Their spirits yearn again for images,
Adding to the dragon, phoenix,
Garuda, naga, those horses of the sun,
This lion of the sea,
This image of themselves.

1979

---

[1] *Ilium* This city is also known as Troy in Homer's *Iliad*, which relates the Trojan War. When Thumboo
mentions Ilium's topless towers, he is making an inter-textual reference to Faustus's admiration for
Helen of Troy in Christopher Marlowe's *Dr Faustus* (1592).

Alafina Vuki

Alafina Vuki was born in Suva, Fiji. Vuki is a graduate of the University of the South Pacific and has taught at Dudley High School in Fiji.

Vuki's "Four-Year Wisdom" is yet another poem that transcends place and time. There are few if any cultural signifiers that mark this poem as a specifically Fijian poem. Here an older sibling must learn to cope with failure. Compare this poem with Mervyn Morris's "Little Boy Crying" and Wong May's "The Shroud."

Four-Year Wisdom

Yesterday
My kid sister
asked me
why the sun
was dying
into the sea?

Inside
I was bleeding
red
into
Pure misery.

The sun
I sobbed
has run
across the sky
not to die
but to sleep
deep
in the sea.

Lips of four-year
wisdom
ask
"Why do you cry?
If you say the
sun does not die?"

In my hand
a telegram
that ran
"ALL UNITS FAILED"
Efforts gone to sand.

Eyes of four-year
wisdom

piercing
waiting
searching
needing
an answer
While I fumbled
the paper
stuttered
stammered
could not stop
the crying
choking
"I wish I was the
sun
asleep forever in the sea."

Hand of four-year
wisdom
holding my hand
crying along with
me
as we watched the
fiery kingdom
slipping into the
sea.

1985

Fred Wah

Fred Wah (b. 1939) was born in Saskatchewan, Canada. He has written several collections of poetry, including *Selected Poems* (1980), *Breathin' My Name with a Sigh* (1981), *Waiting for Saskatchewan* (1986), which won the Governor General's Award for Poetry, *Rooftops* (1988), and *Sentenced to Light* (2008). He has taught at the University of Calgary.

Fred Wah's poem "Breathin' My Name with a Sigh" is a short poem that raises the issues of hybridity and liminality inherent in postcolonial writers. It is a moving account of a father's sadness when his cultures and mores (even types of food) disappear from the consciousness and the daily lives of his children, who struggle with dual ethnicities. Compare this poem with Fiona Tinwei Lam's "The Hyphenated" and Leslie Marmon Silko's "Yellow Woman."

Breathin' My Name with a Sigh

my father hurt-
ing at the table
sitting hurting
at suppertime
deep inside very
far down inside
because I can't stand the ginger
in the beef and greens
he cooked for us tonight
and years later tonight
that look on his face
appears now on mine
my children
my food
their food
my father
their father
me mine
the father
very far
very very far
inside

1981

Derek Walcott

Derek Walcott (b. 1930) was born in St. Lucia. He has lived there, in Trinidad, and the United States, and has taught at Boston University. His volumes of poems include *25 Poems* (1948), *In a Green Night: Poems* (1962), *Midsummer* (1984), *Omeros* (1989), and *Selected Poems* (2007). He has written several plays, including *Henri Christophe* (1950), *Dream on Monkey Mountain* (1970), *Pantomime* (1978), and *The Capeman* (lyrics, in collaboration with Paul Simon, 1997). He received the Nobel Prize for Literature in 1992.

Walcott's "Ruins of a Great House" is a poignant look at the colonial past of the Caribbean and the speaker's feeling of "rage" at the injustice done to slaves in this period: "The river flows, obliterating hurt." Does the speaker show that this is possible? Does he try to overcome his anger? Note how he moves from the historical and the political to the personal at the end of the poem as he confronts his own anger toward his brutal colonial past. In "A Letter from Brooklyn," an old woman's recollection of the speaker's deceased father moves him to tears but also rekindles his faith and strengthens him. Is this poem as political as "Ruins of a Great House?" In "Midsummer: LII," are the sentiments expressed about the English language and English literature reminiscent of Naipaul's in "Jasmine?" Is it true that, as Walcott says here, "No language is neutral?" How appropriate is the image of the oak tree for reflecting the relationship of the English language and its various versions today? Compare the oak symbol with that of the banyan tree (whose vines or branches when they touch the ground become major trunks)—an image that some think is more indicative of the individual histories and development of the different "Englishes" around the world.

Ruins of a Great House

> *though our longest sun sets at right*
> *declensions and makes but winter*
> *arches, it cannot be long before we*
> *lie down in darkness, and have our*
> *light in ashes ...*
> BROWNE: *Urn Burial*[1]

Stones only, the *disjecta membra*[2] of this Great House,
Whose moth-like girls are mixed with candledust,
Remain to file the lizard's dragonish claws;
The mouths of those gate cherubs streaked with stain.

---

[1] *Browne: Urn Burial* Sir Thomas Browne (1605-82), British writer, wrote *Hydriotaphia, Urn-Burial* (1658), a treatise on the funeral rites of ancient nations.

[2] *disjecta membra* Scattered fragments (Latin).

Axle and coachwheel silted under the muck
Of cattle droppings.

    Three crows flap for the trees,
And settle, creaking the eucalyptus boughs.
A smell of dead limes quickens in the nose
The leprosy of Empire.

      "Farewell, green fields"
      "Farewell, ye happy groves!"[1]

Marble as Greece, like Faulkner's[2] south in stone,
Deciduous beauty prospered and is gone;
But where the lawn breaks in a rash of trees
A spade below dead leaves will ring the bone
Of some dead animal or human thing
Fallen from evil days, from evil times.

It seems that the original crops were limes
Grown in the silt that clogs the river's skirt;
The imperious rakes are gone, their bright girls gone,
The river flows, obliterating hurt.
I climbed a wall with the grill ironwork
Of exiled craftsmen, protecting that great house
From guilt, perhaps, but not from the worm's rent,
Nor from the padded cavalry of the mouse.
And when a wind shook in the limes I heard
What Kipling[3] heard; the death of a great empire, the abuse
Of ignorance by Bible and by sword.

A green lawn, broken by low walls of stone
Dipped to the rivulet, and pacing, I thought next
Of men like Hawkins, Walter Raleigh, Drake,[4]
Ancestral murderers and poets, more perplexed

---

[1] *Farewell ... groves* This is an adaptation of a line from William Blake's poem "Night": "Farewell, green fields and happy groves."

[2] *Faulkner* William Faulkner, American novelist (1897-1962), set his novels in the American South; exploitation of people and land is a recurring theme in his work.

[3] *Kipling* Rudyard Kipling (1865-1936); see his poem "The White Man's Burden" in this anthology.

[4] *Hawkins ... Drake* The British explorers Sir John Hawkins (1532-95), Sir Walter Raleigh (1554-1618), and Sir Francis Drake (1545-96).

In memory now by every ulcerous crime.
The world's green age then was a rotting lime
Whose stench became the charnel galleon's text.
The rot remains with us, the men are gone.
But, as dead ash is lifted in a wind,
That fans the blackening ember of the mind,
My eyes burned from the ashen prose of Donne.[1]

Ablaze with rage, I thought
Some slave is rotting in this manorial lake,
And still the coal of my compassion fought:
That Albion[2] too, was once
A colony like ours, "Part of the continent, piece of the main"
Nook-shotten, rook o'er blown, deranged
By foaming channels, and the vain expense
Of bitter faction.

      All in compassion ends
So differently from what the heart arranged:
"as well as if a manor of thy friend's ..."

1962

A Letter from Brooklyn[3]

An old lady writes me in a spidery style,
Each character trembling, and I see a veined hand
Pellucid as paper, travelling on a skein
Of such frail thoughts its thread is often broken;
Or else the filament from which a phrase is hung

---

[1] *Donne* John Donne (1572-1631), from whose "Meditation XVII" Walcott takes the next two quotations. Donne says: "No man is an island, entire of itself; every man is a piece of the continent, a part of the main; if a clod be washed away by the sea, Europe is the less, as well as if a promontory were, as well as if a manor of thy friend's or of thine own were; any man's death diminishes me, because I am involved in mankind, and therefore never send to know for whom the bell tolls; it tolls for thee."

[2] *Albion* An ancient name for Britain.

[3] *Brooklyn* Brooklyn, New York. If the speaker's experience is drawn from the poet's, he is likely reading the letter in St. Lucia, home of the poet.

Dims to my sense, but caught, it shines like steel,
As touch a line, and the whole web will feel.
She describes my father, yet I forget her face
More easily than my father's yearly dying;
Of her I remember small, buttoned boots and the place
She kept in our wooden church on those Sundays
Whenever her strength allowed;
Grey haired, thin voiced, perpetually bowed.

"I am Mable Rawlins," she writes, "and know both your parents;"
He is dead, Miss Rawlins, but God bless your tense:
"Your father was a dutiful, honest,
Faithful and useful person."
For such plain praise what fame is recompense?
"A horn-painter, he painted delicately on horn,
He used to sit around the table and paint pictures."
The peace of God needs nothing to adorn
It, nor glory nor ambition.
"He is twenty-eight years buried," she writes, "he was called home,
And is, I am sure, doing greater work."

The strength of one frail hand in a dim room
Somewhere in Brooklyn, patient and assured,
Restores my sacred duty to the Word.
"Home, home," she can write, with such short time to live,
Alone as she spins the blessings of her years;
Not withered of beauty if she can bring such tears,
Nor withdrawn from the world that breaks its lovers so;
Heaven is to her the place where painters go,
All who bring beauty on frail shell or horn,
There was all made, thence their lux-mundi[1] drawn,
Drawn, drawn, till the thread is resilient steel,
Lost though it seems in darkening periods,
And there they return to do work that is God's.

So this old lady writes, and again I believe,
I believe it all, and for no man's death I grieve.

1962

---

[1] *lux-mundi* Latin for "light of the world." In Matthew 5:14, Jesus says to his followers, "You are the light of the world."

Midsummer: LII[1]

I heard them marching the leaf-wet roads of my head,
the sucked vowels of a syntax trampled to mud,
a division of dictions, one troop black, barefooted,
the other in redcoats bright as their sovereign's blood;
their feet scuffled like rain, the bare soles with the shod.
One fought for a queen, the other was chained in her service,
but both, in bitterness, travelled the same road.
Our occupation and the Army of Occupation
are born enemies, but what mortar can size
the broken stones of the barracks of Brimstone Hill[2]
to the gaping brick of Belfast? Have we changed sides
to the mustached sergeants and the horsy gentry
because we serve English, like a two-headed sentry
guarding its borders? No language is neutral;
the green oak of English is a murmurous cathedral
where some took umbrage, some peace, but every shade, all,
helped widen its shadow. I used to haunt the arches
of the British barracks of Vigie.[3] There were leaves there,
bright, rotting like revers or epaulettes, and the stenches
of history and piss. Leaves piled like the dropped aitches
of soldiers from rival shires, from the brimstone trenches
of Agincourt to the gas of the Somme. On Poppy Day
our schools bought red paper flowers. They were for Flanders.[4]
I saw Hotspur[5] cursing the smoke through which a popinjay
minced from the battle. Those raging commanders
from Thersites to Percy,[6] their rant is our model.
I pinned the poppy to my blazer. It bled like a vowel.

1984

---

[1] Walcott has mentioned in "A Far Cry from Africa" (1962) that he is "divided to the vein." Both his grandfathers were white, both grandmothers black. In this poem, we can see how divided he is in speaking about the influence on him of British society, culture, and language.

[2] *Brimstone Hill* Ruins of British barracks in St. Kitts, West Indies.

[3] *Vigie* A resort town in St. Lucia (West Indies), Walcott's homeland.

[4] *Agincourt, Somme, and Flanders* Places of famous/infamous battles: Agincourt (1415) is a crucial locale in Shakespeare's *Henry V* (1599); Somme and Flanders feature in World War I. Note the reference in the last line to poppies (associated with Flanders Fields).

[5] *Hotspur* Military figure in Shakespeare's *Henry IV* (1597).

[6] *Thersites to Percy* Thersites was a bow-legged, disrespectful soldier in the Trojan War; the Percys rebelled against Henry IV (1403).

Archie Weller

Archie Weller (b. 1957) was born in Perth, Western Australia. He has worked as a dishwasher, hospital orderly, broadcaster, scriptwriter, and lecturer. He spent a short time in jail, allegedly for reasons linked to his part-Aboriginal background. His publications include *Nidjera: Children Crying Softly Together: A Play Exploring the Emotions of a Modern Day Koori Family* (1990) and two novels, *The Day of the Dog* (1989) and *Land of the Golden Clouds* (1998). His volume of stories, *Going Home* (1986), is the first collection by an Aboriginal writer in Australia. He has edited *Us Fellas: An Anthology of Aboriginal Writing* (with Colleen Glass, 1987).

Weller's "Pension Day" is an uncompromising depiction of the degradation, poverty, and harshness of Australia's Aboriginal life. Using the flashback technique, Weller tells the sad story of Snowy Jackson, who dies alone, having spent his last days drinking cheap liquor. It is one of the bleakest stories in this anthology. Does Weller's narrative offer any hope that Aboriginals can avoid his protagonist's dismal fate, pick up the pieces, and survive? Does he espouse Eva Johnson's advocacy in "Murras" that Aboriginals can do so by adhering to the traditional values of family and community?

Pension Day

All day the old black man sits, away from everyone else. He wears the same old black coat every day. Once it had silver buttons and a silk collar and was worn in the best society—with speeches, silver and champagne.

Now it has no buttons and sits upon the hunched back of the leader of the red-back people. The people who hug the dark corners and scuttle hideously from rusted hiding place to rusted hiding place. Away from the pale blue eyes that are like the sun, burning everything away so all is stark and straight and true, and there are no cool secrets left.

No one wants to know any of the secrets, anyway.

He sits in the park, the old man, like one of the war cannons that guard the perimeter and stick their long green noses out threateningly at the cars that swish by, not even knowing they are there. Today's children leap and laugh over silent steel to further demolish yesterday's pride.

There is no room for yesterday's people.

He is a Wongi[1] from out near Laverton,[2] and he can hardly speak English. When he first came to Perth many years ago, he huddled in the back of the police Land

---

[1] *Wongi* The Wongi Aboriginal community of Western Australia.

[2] *Laverton* An Australian outback mining town on the western edge of the Great Victoria Desert. It was a gold-mining town until the 1950s, when it had the reputation of being a wild place. It is now the centre of a major nickel-mining operation.

Rover and moaned in terror as the ground swept away before him and trees and rocks and mountains and towns and his whole universe disappeared in a blur. Had it not been for the handcuffs around his great wrists, he would have leaped out the door and ended it all then.

The white men had torn him away from his red land's breast for a crime he could not understand.

A life for a life. That was how the law had worked since before everything. The law was the law.

Yet the Land Rover lurched out to the camp and the three policemen had sprung upon him, taking him by surprise as he sat, singing softly, by his campfire.

The dogs had barked, the children screamed, his young girl-woman, already full with a child-spirit, cried, and he had fought with all his strength.

The old men had watched with silent, all-knowing eyes as he was overpowered and two policemen held him while the sergeant clipped on the handcuffs triumphantly.

He took one last look at his night-blackened land and the black shut faces in the red firelight. Rubbed red dust over his horny feet before being pushed gently into the hard, hot Land Rover. A tear slid out of his frightened, puzzled eyes before he closed his mind and hunched into himself.

He was only about eighteen then and although he wore a pair of scuffed grubby moleskins (and an army slouch hat he kept for special occasions) he had only seen white men six times in his whole life.

So that was that.

When he came out of jail seven years later, he was still strong and proud. No one had been able to touch him in there. He had worked all day and at night he had willed himself out over the walls back to his country.

Red dust and thin mulga bushes and glittering seas of broken glass from the miners' camps. Yellow-sided holes many metres deep. Black open mouths gulping in the hot air and holding white man secrets and dreams.

Just the place to hide a body snapped in two by powerful hands.

He could never go home again. He would have been killed out at the gabbling, dusty camp, if not by the relatives of his victim, certainly by the new husband to whom the elders would long ago have given his woman.

So he had no country. He had no home. He decided to learn more about the white man's ways that had so awed him.

But what could he do? A young man with big muscles, a quick temper, not much knowledge of English—and a black skin? After a few fights in a few country towns, he settled down, working for a produce store deep down south and doing some shearing on the side.

He loved that town. His boss was a good man who protected the angry giant from the taunts that sometimes whipped through the air. It was his boss, too, who found him a good half-caste girl from the nearby mission.

They called him "Jackie Snow" and the name stuck: Snowy Jackson, the straight-shouldered, black colossus among his brown, sharper brethren. There was no love lost between the full-blood and the half-castes. They jeered at the way he worked so hard and refused to share his money around. But they were afraid of his physical and spiritual powers. For wasn't he one from the shimmering emptiness of the desert, a man who came with laws and secrets the brown staggering people had lost or only half-remembered?

He did not tell them that he had lost those, too.

At the produce store he was always cheerful and he kept out of trouble. His educated half-caste wife taught him a little more English, but he never learned how to read or write.

They got their citizenship rights and a little house, just off the track to the town's reserve. Every evening, especially in winter, his wife read the Bible and he stared into the searing heart of the fire with thoughtful, quiet eyes, and tried to remember before.

But this was his life now.

At shearing time they put him on the yard work. He loved to stride through the greasy, grey sea, shouting in his own language and clapping his huge hands so they sounded like the echoes from the thunder in the sky above. He would fling his head back and flare his nostrils like a wild black horse, and the sheep would pour into the darkened tin woolshed with a furious clicketty-clatter on the wooden grating floor. He felt like a king then, a leader of the people.

The other shearers respected Snowy Jackson for his size and strength. Who else could lift a bleating struggling sheep up above his head and still flash the huge white grin he wore (like his slouch hat for special occasions).

But he used to grow angry sometimes, and picking the stupid sheep up by their shaggy necks he would hurl them into the yard, sometimes killing them.

Then they put him on the shearing team alongside all the white men. He was at last one of them, and he took great pride in his new position. After he got over his first hesitation at the whining shears, he became quite skilled at peeling off the curly wool so it lay, wrinkled and ready, around his feet. Each bald, skinny, white sheep that he pushed down the chute was a new piece of juicy fruit for him to chew up, until his belly was full of white man respect.

Every night when he went home, he would try to explain his joyful day to his little wife, just as once, as a successful hunter, he had recounted his stories to his young woman way away up in the red, swirling Dreaming. But he could not tell the half-caste anything and, after a while, he would stop his broken, happy mumbling and stare into his fire. He would smile softly at things that had happened that day, while the stories came out of his eyes and nestled amongst the coals so he could see them again the next night.

Dreams, dreams.

One year, his young wife died giving birth to her fourth child.

All her relatives came down for the funeral. They sat around talking and remembering, and catching up on the news. Then they all got back in their old cars and trucks and left.

He just has the rain now, turning the sky grey and the world cold. He used to love the rain. He could stand for hours in the soft drizzle and let all the secrets from the heavy black clouds soak into his soul. But he hated the rain, that day, for it was there and his little quiet wife was dead.

He just has the rain — and his tears. All his secrets and the love the half-caste girl had taught him, dripping from his puzzled eyes.

When he was alone, he became roaring drunk and smashed up his house that he and the girl had been so proud of then went and started a brawl amongst the Nyoongah people.

He might have been getting older, but his huge angry fists put three of the men in hospital. He was put in jail.

The next morning the boss came and got him out. As he walked down the muddy street in the sultry sun, everyone stared at him, shocked or disgusted at the damage he had done. He followed his boss's footsteps like a huge dog.

So he lost even his pride and gave up.

He worked at the store for a few more years. Every time he thought of his woman he went out and got drunk. He lived in a little humpy in the bush, where no one could find him.

The Community Welfare took away his children one day whilst he was out hunting. All except the baby, whom Mrs. Haynes the boss's wife was looking after.

He never saw his children again.

He did not shear any more, as he was getting too old. Beer fat lay over him, like bird dung greening a famous statue.

Just as he had been shearing beside the white men and had gained a type of pride, now he could drink beside white men with another sort of pride. They were all brothers now — getting drunk together.

He left to wander.

He has memories of countless tin-and-asbestos towns with cold white people and whining brown people. He has memories of crowded hotels and fights, and falling asleep, drunk in the slimy gutter or under a tree. He tried his hand at boxing on a showground troupe. But soon he fell down, forever. His body was left to moulder where it lay, while the laughter bored into him like busy constant ants.

Boys drag lazily past, going nowhere. Cigarettes hang from their thin lips, phallus-like, to prove they are men.

The old man would like to beg for a smoke, but the wine he has drunk today thickens his tongue. All that comes out of his mouth is a thin dribble of saliva that hangs off his scraggly grey beard.

Devils dance out of the boys' black eyes. They swagger, shout and laugh loudly. The words and laughter are caught by the fingers of the Moreton Bay fig trees. Later, they will be dropped to rot away with the stinking, sticky fruit. But the boys don't know that.

Two peel away from the sly dark group and squat down beside him.

"G'day, ya silly ole black bastard. Gettin' stuck into th' gabba at this time a day? Hey, ya wanna tell us 'ow ya was the state boxer, ole man?"

"Look at the metho e's got 'ere, Jimmy."

"Unna? 'E got no sense."

"Look out, Snowman! Featherfoot comin' your way, ya ole murderer."

"Jesus, don't 'e stink, but?"

They laugh.

He smiles, uncomprehending, and nods his head. He knows they are laughing at him. Once he would have leaped to his feet and pulverised the whole group. That was a long time ago, though. He cannot remember.

They steal $20 from him with quick black fingers. They always do, every pension day. Where they had been afraid of his powers before, now they laugh and steal from him. He has no people to look after him. Only himself.

He sits under the tree, surrounded by empty wine bottles. He staggers over to the tap and bumps into two young girls, who shriek and squeal with mirth at him.

"The Snowman's drunk!" they shriek.

Once, they would have had to respect and admire him, as he told them about the ways and laws of their tribe.

Once.

Now they have no tribe, and he has no ways.

He half-fills a bottle with water and pours the last of his methylated spirits into it. He sits and drinks, lonely.

He watches as the groups gather in circles. People wander from one group to another or stagger across to the hotel, waiting on the corner. The tribe goes walkabout. They stumble over to the brick toilets, as lonely as he is. They clutch onto the tight circles and pass the drink and words around.

Drink gets hot, words get hot in the cold wind.

The boys strip off their shirts and fight out their quarrels, while the women join them or egg them on.

The people play jackpot or two-up or poker. Some grow rich, some grow poor; almost everyone grows drunk.

Everyone goes home, to wherever home is. He stays.

The sky gets darker and more oppressive. Then it rains.

First there are the whipcracks rattling across the sky, rolling and growling like puppies playing in the fleeciness of the clouds. The lightning leaps and bounces like children; here, there and gone. The rain starts off fat and slow but becomes faster and leaner.

He just sits there, finishing off his metho and wishing he had a smoke. He suddenly vomits up all his pension day money. All over his coat and face and trousers.

Time to sleep.

The old Aboriginal lies underneath his tree that cannot help him, for it, too, is old and sparse of gentle green leaf. The tree and the man get wet; neither cares, though.

So cold. That rain runs in streaks down his face and body. It washes the vomit off him, with soft hands. The pattering of the rain is interrupted only occasionally by short harsh coughs.

In the early hours of the morning, the cruising police van that, like the gardener, is searching for a few weeds to pull up by the roots and throw in the bin, finds him.

His rain has taken him away from his useless, used-up life. Perhaps back to the Dreamtime[1] he understood.

No one knew the old Wongi was dead until the next pension day.

1986

---

[1] *Dreamtime* Aboriginal people accept "dreaming" as the closest English word for the mystical insights gained in dreams into all that is known and understood in human existence.

Albert Wendt

Albert Wendt (b. 1939) was born in Western Samoa, of Samoan and German ancestry. He has taught at the University of the South Pacific in Fiji and at the University of Auckland. His novels include *Pouliuli* (1976), *Leaves of the Banyan Tree* (1979), and *Black Rainbow* (1992). He has published several collections of stories and poems, including *The Best of Albert Wendt's Short Stories* (1999), *The Book of the Black Star* (2002), and *The Songmaker's Chair* (2004).

Wendt's "Crocodile" is based on the schooling of some students from Western Samoa in boarding schools in New Zealand, where they were exposed more to Western culture than to their own Polynesian culture. Ola is one such student. Here is a story that intertwines the human and the sociopolitical. Ola appears to exhibit an ambivalence toward her teacher. Do you agree with this view? Are there hints of her ambivalence throughout the story? The author, a male, attempts to write from a female point of view. Does he succeed in authenticating this point of view? The residential schooling experience of Ola could be compared with Charlie's in Lee Maracle's "Charlie."

Crocodile

Miss Susan Sharon Willersey, known to all her students as Crocodile Willersey, was our House Mistress for the five years I was at boarding school. I recall, from reading a brief history of our school, that she had been born in 1908 in a small Waikato farming town and, at the age of ten, had enrolled at our Preparatory School, had then survived (brilliantly) our high school, had attended university and graduated MA (Honours in Latin), and had returned to our school to teach and be a dormitory mistress, and, a few years later, was put in charge of Beyle House, our House.

So when I started in 1953, Crocodile was in her fit mid-forties, already a school institution more myth than bone, more goddess than human (and she tended to behave that way!).

Certain stories, concerning the derivation of her illustrious nickname, prevailed (and were added to) during my time at school.

One story, in line with the motto of our school (which is: Perseverance is the Way to Knowledge), had it that Miss Willersey's first student called her Crocodile because she was a model of perseverance and fortitude, which they believed were the moral virtues of a crocodile.

Another story claimed that because Miss Willersey was a devout Anglican, possessing spiritual purity beyond blemish (is that correct?), an Anglican missionary, who had visited our school after spending twenty invigorating years in the Dark Continent (his description), had described Miss Willersey in our school assembly as a saint with the courage and purity and powers of the African crocodile (which was sacred to many tribes). Proof of her steadfastness and purity, so this story went, was her kind refusal to marry the widowed missionary because, as she reasoned (and he was extremely understanding), she was already married to her church, to her school and students, and to her profession.

The most unkindly story attributed her nickname to her appearance: Miss Willersey looked and behaved like a crocodile—she was long, long-teethed, long-eared, long-fingered, long-arsed, long-everythinged. Others also argued she had skin like crocodile hide, and that her behaviour was slippery, always spyful, decisively cruel and sadistic and unforgiving, like a crocodile's.

As a new third-former and a naive Samoan who had been reared to obey her elders without question, I refused to believe the unfavourable stories about Miss Willersey's nickname. Miss Willersey was always kind and helpful (though distant, as was her manner with all of us) to me in our House and during her Latin classes. (Because I was in the top third form I *had* to take Latin though I was really struggling with another foreign language, English, and New Zealand English at that!) We felt (and liked it) that she was also treating all her "Island girls" (there were six of us) in a specially protective way. "You must always be proud of your race!" she kept reminding us. (She made it a point to slow down her English when speaking to us so we could understand her.)

During her Latin classes, I didn't suffer her verbal and physical (the swift ruler) chastisements, though I was a dumb, bumbling student. Not for ten months anyway.

However, in November, during that magical third-form year, I *had* to accept the negative interpretations of Miss Willersey's nickname.

I can't remember what aspect of Latin we were revising orally in class that summer day. All I remember well were: Croc's mounting anger as student after student (even her brightest) kept making errors; my loudly beating heart as her questioning came closer and closer to me; the stale smell of cardigans and shoes; Croc's long physique stretching longer, more threateningly; and some of my classmates snivelling into their handkerchiefs as Croc lacerated them verbally for errors (sins) committed.

"Life!" she called coldly, gazing at her feet. Silence. I didn't realize she was calling me. (My name is Olamaiileoti Monroe. Everyone at school called me Ola and *translated* it as Life which became my nickname.) "Life!" she repeated, this time her blazing eyes were boring into me. (I was almost wetting my pants, and this was contrary to Miss Willersey's constant exhortation to us: ladies learn early how to control their bladders!)

I wanted desperately to say, "Yes, Miss Willersey?" but I found I couldn't, I was too scared.

"Life?" She was now advancing towards me, filling me with her frightening lengthening. "You *are* called Life, aren't you, Monroe? That *is* your nickname?"

Nodding my head, I muttered, "Yes—yes!" A squeaking. My heart was struggling like a trapped bird in my throat. "Yes, yes, Miss Willersey!"

"And your name is Life, isn't it?"

"Yes!" I was almost in tears. (Leaking everywhere I was!)

"What does Ola mean exactly?"

"Life, Miss Willersey."

"But Ola is not a noun, is it?" she asked.

Utterly confused, leaking every which way, and thoroughly shit-scared, I just shook my head furiously.

"Ola doesn't mean Life, it is a verb, it means 'to live,' 'to grow,' doesn't it?" I nodded furiously.

"Don't you know even your own language, young lady?" I bowed my head (in shame); my trembling hands were clutching the desk-top. "Speak up, young lady!"

"No, Miss Willersey!" I swallowed back my tears.

"Now, Miss Life, or, should I say, Miss To-Live, let's see if you know Latin a little better than you know your own language!" Measuredly, she marched back to the front of our class. Shit, shit, shit! I cursed myself (and my fear) silently. Her footsteps stopped. Silence. She was turning to face me. Save me, someone!

"Excuse me, Miss Willersey?" the saving voice intruded.

"Yes, what is it?"

"I think I heard someone knocking on the door, Miss Willersey." It was Gill, the ever-aware, always courageous Gill. The room sighed. Miss Willersey had lost the initiative. "Shall I go and see who it is, Miss Willersey?" Gill asked, standing up and gazing unwaveringly at Miss Willersey. We all focused our eyes on her too. A collective defiance and courage. For a faltering moment I thought she wasn't going to give in.

Then she looked away from Gill and said, "Well, all right and be quick about it!"

"You all right, Miss To-Live?" Gill asked me after class when all my friends crowded round me in the corridor.

"Yes!" I thanked her.

"Croc's a bloody bitch!" someone said.

"Yeah!" the others echoed.

So for the remainder of my third-form year and most of my fourth year I *looked* on Miss Susan Sharon Willersey as the Crocodile to be wary of, to pretend good behaviour with, to watch all the time in case she struck out at me. Not that she ever again treated me unreasonably in class despite my getting dumber and dumber in Latin (and less and less afraid of her).

In those two years, Gill topped our class in Latin, with little effort and in courageously clever defiance of Crocodile. Gill also helped me to get the magical 50% I needed to pass and stay out of Crocodile's wrath.

Winter was almost over, the days were getting warmer, our swimming pool was filled and the more adventurous (foolhardy?) used it regularly. Gill and I (and the rest of Miss Rashly's cross-country team) began to rise before light and run the four miles through the school farm. Some mornings, on our sweaty way back, we would meet a silent Crocodile in grey woollen skirt and thick sweater and boots, striding briskly through the cold.

"Morning, girls!" she would greet us.

"Morning, Miss Willersey!" we would reply.

"Exercise, regular exercise, that's the way girls!"

In our fourth-form dormitory, my bed was nearest the main door that opened out to the lounge opposite which was the front door to Crocodile's apartment, forbidden domain unless we were summoned to it to be questioned (and punished) for a misdemeanour, or invited to it for hot cocoa and biscuits (prefects were the usual invitees!). Because it *was* forbidden territory we were curious about what went on in there: how Croc lived, what she looked like without her formidably thick make-up and stern outfits, and so on. As a Samoan I wasn't familiar with how papalagi[1] (and especially Crocodile) lived out their private lives. I tried but I couldn't picture Miss Willersey in her apartment in her bed or in her bath in nothing else (not even her skin) but in her make-up, immaculately coiffured hair and severe suits. (I couldn't even imagine her using the toilet! Pardon the indiscretion which is unbecoming of one of Miss Willersey's girls!)

The self-styled realists and sophisticates among us — and they were mainly seniors who had to pretend to such status — whispered involved and terribly upsetting (exciting) tales about Crocodile's men (and lack of men), who visited (and didn't visit) her in the dead of night. We, the gullible juniors, inexperienced in the ways of men and sex, found these lurid tales erotically exciting (upsetting) but never admitted publicly we *were* excited. We all feigned disgust and disbelief. And quite frankly I couldn't imagine Miss Willersey (in her virgin skin) with a man (in his experienced skin) in her bed in the widely lustful embrace of *knowing each other* (our Methodist Bible-class teacher's description of the art of fucking!). No, I really tried, but couldn't put Crocodile into that forbidden but feverishly exciting position. At the time I *did* believe in Miss Willersey's strict moral standards concerning the relationship between the sexes. (I was a virgin, and that's what Miss Willersey and my other elders wanted me to retain and give to the man I married.)

One sophisticate, the precociously pretentious and overweight daughter of a Wellington surgeon and one of Crocodile's pet prefects, suggested that Croc's nightly visitors *weren't* men. That immediately put more disgustingly exciting possibilities into our wantonly frustrated (and virgin) imaginations.

"Who then?" an innocent junior asked.

"What then?" another junior asked.

"Impossible. Bloody filthy!" the wise Gill countered.

"It happens!" the fat sophisticate argued.

"How do you know?" someone asked.

"I just know, that's all!"

"Because your mother is a lesbian!" Gill, the honest, socked it to her. We had to break up the fight between Gill and the Wellington sophisticate.

---

[1] *papalagi* White Europeans.

"Bugger her!" Gill swore as we led her out of the locker room. "She sucks up to Miss Willersey and then says Croc's a les!"

"What's—what's a les...lesbian?" I forced myself to ask Gill at prep that evening. She looked surprised, concluded with a shrug that I didn't really know, printed something on a piece of paper and, after handing it to me, watched me read it.

A FEMALE WHO IS ATTRACTED TO OTHER FEMALES!!!

"What do you mean?" I whispered. (We weren't allowed to talk during prep.)

She wrote on the paper. "*You Islanders are supposed to know a lot more about sex than us poor pakehas.*[1] *A les is a female who does it with other females. Savvy?*"

"*Up you too!*" I wrote back. We started giggling.

"Gill, stand up!" the prefect on duty called.

"Oh, shit!" Gill whispered under her breath.

"Were you talking?"

"Life just wanted me to spell a word for her!" Gill replied.

"What word?"

"Les—," Gill started say. My heart nearly stopped. "Life wanted to know how to spell 'lesson'?" Relief.

"Well, spell it out aloud for all of us!" And Gill did so, crisply, all the time behind her back giving the prefect the up-you sign.

After this incident, I noticed myself observing the Crocodile's domain more closely for unusual sounds, voices, visitors, and, though I refused to think of the possibility of her being a lesbian, I tried to discern a pattern in her female visitors (students included), but no pattern emerged. Also, there were no unusual sounds. (Croc didn't even sing in the bath!)

Some creature, almost human, was trapped in the centre of my head, sobbing pitifully, mourning an enormous loss. It was wrapping its pain around my dreaming and I struggled to break away from its tentacles. I couldn't. I woke to find myself awake (and relieved I wasn't strangling in the weeping) in the dark of our dormitory. Everyone else was fast asleep.

Then I knew it was Miss Willersey. I knew it and tried not to panic, not to give in to the feeling I wasn't going to be able to cope. I wrapped the blankets round my head. It was none of my business! But I couldn't escape.

I found myself standing with my ear to Miss Willersey's door. Shivering. Her light was on, I could tell from the slit of light under the door. The sobbing was more audible but it sounded muffled, as if she was crying into a pillow or cushion. Uncontrolled. Emerging from the depths of a fathomless grief. Drawing me into its depths.

My hand opened the door before I could stop it. Warily I peered into the blinding light. My eyes adjusted quickly to the glare. The neat and orderly arrangement of furniture, wall pictures, ornaments, and bookcases came into focus. Miss Willersey

---

[1] *pakehas* New Zealand Europeans.

was enthroned in an armchair against the far wall, unaware of my presence, unaware of where she was and who she was, having relinquished in her grief all that was the Crocodile. She was dressed in a shabby dressing-gown, brown slippers, hair in wild disarray, tears melting away her thick make-up in streaks down her face, her long-fingered hands clasped to her mouth trying to block back the sound.

Shutting the door behind me quietly, I edged closer to her, hoping she would see me and order me out of her room and then I wouldn't have to cope with the new, fragile, vulnerable Miss Willersey. I didn't want to.

All around us (and in me) her grief was like the incessant buzzing of a swarm of bees, around and around, spiralling up out of the hollow hive of her being and weaving round and round on my head, driving me towards her and her sorrow which had gone beyond her courage to measure and bear.

And I moved into her measure and, lost for whatever else to do, wrapped my arms around her head, and immediately her arms were around me tightly and my body was the cushion for her grief.

At once she became my comfort, the mother I'd never had but had always yearned for, and I cried silently into her pain. Mother and daughter, daughter and mother. A revelation I hoped would hold true for as long as I was to know her.

Her weeping eased. Her arms relaxed around me. She turned her face away. "Please!" she murmured. I looked away. Got the box of tissues on the table and put it in her shaking hands. I looked away. Tearing out a handful of tissues, she wiped her eyes and face.

I started to leave. "It is Ola, isn't it?" she asked, face still turned away. In her voice was a gentleness I have never heard in it before.

"Yes."

"Thank you. I'm ... I'm sorry you've had to see me like this." She was ripping out more tissues.

"Is there anything else I can do?" I asked.

"No, thank you." She started straightening her dressing-gown and hair. The Crocodile was returning. I walked to the door. "Ola!" she stopped me. I didn't look back at her. "This is our secret. Please don't tell the others?"

"I won't, Miss Willersey. Good-night!"

"Good-night, Ola!"

I shut the door behind me quietly, and on *our* secret.

Next morning there was a short article in the newspaper about her mother's death in Hamilton, in an old people's home. Miss Willersey left on the bus for Hamilton that afternoon.

"The Croc's mother's crocked!" some girls joked at our table at dinner that evening.

Yes, Crocodile Willersey remained married to her school and students until she died in 1982. By becoming a school tradition and a mythical being in the memories of all her students (generations of them) she has lived on, and we will bequeath her to our children.

Miss Susan Sharon Willersey, the Crocodile, I will always think of you with genuine alofa.[1] (And forgive me — I've forgotten nearly all the Latin you taught me!) By the way, you were wrong about the meaning of Ola; it can also be a noun, Life.[2]

1986

---

[1] *alofa* Love and commitment.

[2] *can also be a noun, Life* Samoan dictionaries confirm this; *ola* is a verb meaning "to live" and it is a noun meaning "life."

Rudy Wiebe

Rudy Wiebe (b. 1934) was born in Saskatchewan, Canada. Educated in Canada and Germany, he was a professor of English at the University of Alberta. He is the author of four short story collections, three essay collections, and nine novels including *The Temptations of Big Bear* (1973). He has published (with Yvonne Johnson) *Stolen Life: The Journey of a Cree Woman* (1998) and his memoir, *Of This Earth: A Mennonite Boyhood in the Boreal Forest* (2006).

Wiebe's "Where Is the Voice Coming From?" is based on a historical incident—the killing of Almighty Voice, a Native accused of stealing a cow and evading arrest. Wiebe's construction of this incident raises many questions about the relative nature of truth in literary and historical texts. From the very beginning the narrator warns us that he is "making" the story and may have his own biases and agendas in telling it. At the end of the story, he says that he could have been "more accurate if I had a reliable interpreter who would make a reliable interpretation. For I do not, of course, understand the Cree myself." Compare this story with Gerald Murnane's "Land Deal," which raises the question of what is real and unreal in discussing Aboriginal issues.

Where Is the Voice Coming From?

The problem is to make the story.

One difficulty of this making may have been excellently stated by Teilhard de Chardin:[1] "We are continually inclined to isolate ourselves from the things and events which surround us...as though we were spectators, not elements, in what goes on." Arnold Toynbee[2] does venture, "For all that we know, Reality is the undifferentiated unity of the mystical experience," but that need not here be considered. This story ended long ago; it is one of finite acts, of orders, of elemental feelings and reactions, of obvious legal restrictions and requirements.

Presumably all the parts of the story are themselves available. A difficulty is that they are, as always, available only in bits and pieces. Though the acts themselves seem quite clear, some written reports of the acts contradict each other. As if these acts were, at one time, too well known; as if the original nodule of each particular fact had from somewhere received non-factual accretions; or even more, as if, since the basic facts were so clear perhaps there were a larger number of facts than any one reporter, or several, or even any reporter had ever attempted to record. About facts that are still simply told by this mouth to that ear, of course, even less can be expected.

---

[1] *Teilhard de Chardin* A French Jesuit priest who was a philosopher, biologist, and paleontologist (1891-1955).

[2] *Arnold Toynbee* A British historian (1889-1975).

An affair seventy-five years old should acquire some of the shiny transparency of an old man's skin. It should.

Sometimes it would seem that it would be enough—perhaps more than enough—to hear the names only. The grandfather One Arrow; the mother Spotted Calf; the father Sounding Sky; the wife (wives rather, but only one of them seems to have a name, though their fathers are Napaise, Kapahoo, Old Dust, The Rump)—the one wife named, of all things, Pale Face; the cousin Going-Up-To-Sky; the brother-in-law (again, of all things) Dublin. The names of the police sound very much alike; they all begin with Constable or Corporal or Sergeant, but here and there an Inspector, then a Superintendent and eventually all the resonance of an Assistant Commissioner echoes down. More. Herself: Victoria, by the Grace of God etc., etc., QUEEN, defender of the Faith, etc., etc.; and witness "Our Right Trusty and Right Well-beloved Cousin and Councillor the Right Honorable Sir John Campbell Hamilton-Gordon, Fan of Aberdeen; Viscount Formartine, Baron Haddo, Methlic, Tarves and Kellie, in the Peerage of Scotland; Viscount Gordon of Aberdeen, County of Aberdeen, in the Peerage of the United Kingdom; Baronet of Nova Scotia, Knight Grand Cross of Our Most Distinguished Order of Saint Michael and Saint George, etc., Governor General of Canada." And of course himself: in the award proclamation named "Jean-Baptiste" but otherwise known only as Almighty Voice.

But hearing cannot be enough; not even hearing all the thunder of A Proclamation: "Now Hear Ye that a reward of FIVE HUNDRED DOLLARS will be paid to any person or persons who will give such information as will lead... (etc., etc.) this Twentieth day of April, in the year of Our Lord one thousand eight hundred and ninety-six, and the Fifty-ninth year of Our Reign..." etc. and etc.

Such hearing cannot be enough. The first item to be seen is the piece of white bone. It is almost triangular, slightly convex—concave actually as it is positioned at this moment with its corners slightly raised—graduating from perhaps a strong eighth to a weak quarter of an inch in thickness, its scattered pore structure varying between larger and smaller on its perhaps polished, certainly shiny surface. Precision is difficult since the glass showcase is at least thirteen inches deep and therefore an eye cannot be brought as close as the minute inspection of such a small, though certainly quite adequate, sample of skull would normally require. Also, because of the position it cannot be determined whether the several hairs, well over a foot long, are still in some manner attached or not.

The seven-pounder cannon can be seen standing almost shyly between the showcase and the interior wall. Officially it is known as a gun, not a cannon, and clearly its bore is not large enough to admit a large man's fist. Even if it can be believed that this gun was used in the 1885 Rebellion[1] and that on the evening of

---

[1] *The 1885 Rebellion* Known also as The North-West Rebellion or the Saskatchewan Rebellion of 1885. This was an unsuccessful uprising by the Métis under Louis Riel against the Canadian government. The Métis (that is, people of mixed Native and European descent) believed the government was indifferent to their survival as a people.

Saturday, May 29, 1897 (while the nine-pounder, now unidentified, was in the process of arriving with the police on the special train from Regina), seven shells (all that were available in Prince Albert at that time) from it were sent shrieking into the poplar bluffs as night fell, clearly such shelling could not and would not disembowel the whole earth. Its carriage is now nicely lacquered, the perhaps oak spokes of its petite wheels (little higher than a knee) have been recently scrapped, puttied and varnished; the brilliant burnish of its brass breeching testifies with what meticulous care charmen and women have used nationally-advertised cleaners and restorers.

Though it can also be seen, even a careless glance reveals that the same concern has not been expended on the one (of two) .44 calibre 1866 model Winchesters apparently found at the last in the pit with Almighty Voice. It also is preserved in a glass case: the number 1536735 is still, though barely, distinguishable on the brass cartridge section just below the brass saddle ring. However, perhaps because the case was imperfectly sealed at one time (though sealed enough not to warrant disturbance now), or because of simple neglect, the rifle is obviously spotted here and there with blotches of rust and the brass itself reveals discolorations almost like mildew. The rifle bore, the three long strands of hair themselves, actually bristle with clots of dust. It may be that this museum cannot afford to be as concerned as the other; conversely, the disfiguration may be something inherent in the items themselves.

The small building which was the police guardroom at Duck Lake, Saskatchewan Territory, in 1895 may also be seen. It had subsequently been moved from its original place and used to house small animals, chickens perhaps, or pigs — such as a woman might be expected to have under her responsibility. It is, of course, now perfectly empty, and clean so that the public may enter with no more discomfort than a bend under the doorway and a heavy encounter with disinfectant. The door-jamb has obviously been replaced: the bar network at one window is, however, said to be original; smooth still, very smooth. The logs inside have been smeared again and again with whitewash, perhaps paint, to an insistent point of identity-defying characterlessness. Within the small rectangular box of these logs not a sound can be heard from the streets of the, probably dead, town.

Hey Injun you'll get hung for stealing that steer
Hey Injun for killing that government cow you'll get three weeks on the woodpile
Hey Injun

The place named Kinistino seems to have disappeared from the map but the Minnechinass Hills have not. Whether they have ever been on a map is doubtful but they will, of course, not disappear from the landscape as long as the grass grows and the rivers run. Contrary to general report and belief, the Canadian prairies are rarely, if ever, flat and the Minnechinass (spelled five different ways and translated sometimes as "The Outside Hill," sometimes as "Beautiful Bare Hills") are dissimilar from any other of the numberless hills that everywhere block out the prairie horizon. They are bare; poplars lie tattered along their tops, almost black against the straw-pale grass and sharp green against the grey soil of the plowing laid in half-mile rectangular blocks upon their western slopes. Poles holding various wires stick out of the fields, back down the bend of the valley; what was once a farmhouse is weathering into the cultivated earth. The poplar bluff where Almighty Voice made his stand has, of course, disappeared.

The policemen he shot and killed (not the ones he wounded, of course) are easily located. Six miles east, thirty-nine miles north in Prince Alberta, the English Cemetery. Sergeant Cohn Campbell Colebrook, North West Mounted Police Registration Number 605, lies presumably under a gravestone there. His name is seventeenth in a very long "list of non-commissioned officers and men who have died in the service since the inception of the force." The date is October 29, 1895, and the cause of death is anonymous: "Shot by escaping Indian prisoner near Prince Albert." At the foot of this grave are two others: Constable John R. Kerr, No. 3040, and Corporal C.H.S. Hockin, No. 3106. Their cause of death on May 28, 1897 is even more anonymous, but the place is relatively precise: "Shot by Indians at Min-etch-inass Hills, Prince Albert District."

The gravestone, if he has one, of the fourth man Almighty Voice killed is more difficult to locate. Mr. Ernest Grundy, post master at Duck Lake in 1897, apparently shut his window the afternoon of Friday, May 28, armed himself, rode east twenty miles, participated in the second charge into the bluff at about 6:30 p.m., and on the third sweep of that charge was shot dead at the edge of the pit. It would seem that he thereby contributed substantially not only to the Indians' bullet supply, but his clothing warmed them as well.

The burial place of Dublin and Going-Up-To-Sky is unknown, as is the grave of Almighty Voice. It is said that a Métis named Henry Smith lifted the latter's body from the pit in the bluff and gave it to Spotted Calf. The place of burial is not, of course, of ultimate significance. A gravestone is always less evidence than a triangular piece of skull, provided it is large enough.

Whatever further evidence there is to be gathered may rest on pictures. There are, presumably, almost numberless pictures of the policemen in the case, but the only one with direct bearing is one of Sergeant Colebrook who apparently insisted on advancing to complete an arrest after being warned three times that if he took another step he would be shot. The picture must have been taken before he joined the force; it reveals him a large-eared young man, hair brush-cut and ascot tie, his eyelids slightly drooping, almost hooded under thick brows. Unfortunately a picture of Constable R.C. Dickson, into whose charge Almighty Voice was apparently committed in that guardroom and who after Colebrook's death was convicted of negligence, sentenced to two months hard labour and discharged, does not seem to be available.

There are no pictures to be found of either Dublin (killed early by rifle fire) or Going-Up-To-Sky (killed in the pit), the two teen age boys who gave their ultimate fealty to Almighty Voice. There is, however, one said to be of Almighty Voice, Junior. He may have been born to Pale Face during the year, two hundred and twenty-one days that his father was a fugitive. In the picture he is kneeling before what could be a tent, he wears stripped denim overalls and displays twin babies whose sex cannot be determined from the double-laced dark bonnets they wear. In the supposed picture of Spotted Calf and Sounding Sky, Sounding Sky stands slightly before his wife; he wears a white shirt and a stripped blanket folded over his left shoulder in such a manner that the arm in which he cradles a long rifle cannot be seen. His head is thrown back; the rim of his hat appears as a black half-moon above eyes that are pressed shut in, as it were, profound concentration; above a mouth clenched thin in a downward curve. Spotted Calf wears a long dress, a sweater which could also be a man's dress coat, and a large fringed and embroidered shawl which would appear distinctly Dukhobour[1] in origin if the scroll patterns on it were more irregular. Her head is small and turned slightly towards her husband so as to reveal her right ear. There is what can only be called a quizzical expression on her crumpled face; it may be she does not understand what is happening and that she would have asked a question, perhaps of her husband, perhaps of the photographers, perhaps even of anyone, anywhere in the world if such questioning were possible for an Indian lady.

There is one final picture. That is one of Almighty Voice himself. At least it is purported to be of Almighty Voice himself. In the Royal Canadian Mounted Police Museum on the Barracks Grounds just off Dewdney Avenue in Regina, Saskatchewan, it lies in the same showcase, as a matter of fact immediately beside, that triangular piece of skull. Both are unequivocally labelled, and it must be assumed that a police force with a world-wide reputation would not label *such* evidence incorrectly. But here emerges an ultimate problem in making the story.

There are two official descriptions of Almighty Voice. The first reads: "Height about five feet, ten inches, slight build, rather good looking, a sharp hooked nose with a remarkably flat point. Has a bullet scar on the left side of his face about $1\frac{1}{2}$ inches long running from near corner of mouth towards ear. The scar cannot be noticed when his face is painted but otherwise is plain. Skin fair for an Indian." The second description is on the Award Proclamation: "About twenty-two years old, five feet ten inches in height, weight about eleven stone, slightly erect, neat small feet and hands; complexion inclined to be fair, with wavey dark hair to shoulders, large dark eyes, broad forehead, sharp features and parrot nose with flat tip, scar on left cheek running from mouth towards ear, feminine appearance."

So run the descriptions that were, presumably, to identify a well-known fugitive in so precise a manner that an informant could collect five hundred dollars — a considerable sum when a police constable earned between one and two dollars a day. The nexus of the problems appears when these supposed official descriptions are compared to the supposed official picture. The man in the picture is standing on a small rug. The fingers of his left hand touch a curved Victorian settee, behind him a photographer's backdrop of scrolled patterns merges to vaguely paradisiacal trees and perhaps a sky. The moccasins he wears make it impossible to deduce whether

---

[1] *Dukhobour* A religious group whose members choose to live communally.

his feet are "neat small." He may be five feet, ten inches tall, may weigh eleven stone, he certainly is "rather good looking" and, though it is a frontal view, it may be that the point of his long and flaring nose could be "remarkably flat." The photograph is slightly over-illuminated and so the unpainted complexion could be "inclined to be fair"; however, nothing can be seen of a scar, the hair is not wavy and shoulder-length but hangs almost to the waist in two thick straight braids worked through with beads, fur, ribbons and cords. The right hand that holds the corner of the blanket-like coat in position is large and, even in the high illumination, heavily veined. The neck is concealed under coiled beads and the forehead seems more low than "broad."

Perhaps, somehow, these picture details could be reconciled with the official description if the face as a whole were not so devastating.

On a cloth-backed sheet two feet by two and one-half feet in size, under the Great Seal of the Lion and the Unicorn, dignified by the names of the Deputy of the Minister of Justice, the Secretary of State, the Queen herself and all the heaped detail of her "Right Trusty and Right Well Beloved Cousin," this description concludes: "feminine appearance." But the pictures: any face of history, any believed face that the world acknowledges as *man*—Socrates, Jesus, Attila, Genghis Khan, Mahatma Gandhi, Joseph Stalin—no believed face is more *man* than this face. The mouth, the nose, the clenched brows, the eyes—the eyes are large, yes, and dark, but even in this watered-down reproduction of unending reproductions of that original, a steady look into those eyes cannot be endured. It is a face like an axe.

It is now evident that the de Chardin statement quoted at the beginning has relevance only as it proves itself inadequate to explain what has happened. At the same time, the inadequacy of Aristotle's much more famous statement becomes evident: "The true difference [between the historian and the poet] is that one relates what *has* happened, the other what *may* happen." These statements cannot explain the storyteller's activity since, despite the most rigid application of impersonal investigation, the elements of the story have now run me aground. If ever I could, I can no longer pretend to objective, omnipotent disinterestedness. I am no longer *spectator* of what *has* happened or what *may* happen: I am become *element* in what is happening at this very moment.

For it is, of course, I myself who cannot endure the shadows on that paper which are those eyes. It is I who stand beside this broken veranda post where two corner shingles have been torn away, where barbed wire tangles the dead weeds on the edge of this field. The bluff that sheltered Almighty Voice and his two friends has not disappeared from the slope of the Minnechinass, no more than the sound of Constable Dickson's voice in that guardhouse is silent. The sound of his speaking is there even if it has never been recorded in an official report:

hey injun you'll get
hung
for stealing that steer

hey injun for killing that government
cow you'll get three
weeks on the woodpile hey injun

The unknown contradictory words about an unprovable act that move a boy to defiance, an implacable Cree warrior long after the three-hundred-and-fifty-year war is ended, a war already lost the day the Cree watch Cartier hoist his gun ashore at Hochelaga[1] and they begin the long retreat west; these words of incomprehension, of threatened incomprehensible law are there to be heard just as the unmoving tableau of the three-day siege is there to be seen on the slopes of the Minnechinass. Sounding Sky is somewhere not there, under arrest, but Spotted Calf stands on a shoulder of the Hills a little to the left, her arms upraised to the setting sun. Her mouth is open. A horse rears, riderless, above the scrub willow at the edge of the bluff, smoke puffs, screams tangle in rifle barrage, there are wounds, somewhere. The bluff is so green this spring, it will not burn and the ragged line of seven police and two civilians is staggering through, faces twisted in rage, terror, and rifles sputter. Nothing moves. There is no sound of frogs in the night; twenty-seven policemen and five civilians stand in cordon at thirty-yard intervals and a body also lies in the shelter of a gully. Only a voice rises from the bluff:

We have fought well
You have died like braves
I have worked hard and am hungry
Give me food

but nothing moves. The bluff lies, a bright green island on the grassy slope surrounded by men hunched forward rigid over their long rifles, men clumped out of rifle-range, thirty-five men dressed as for fall hunting on a sharp spring day, a small gun positioned on a ridge above. A crow is falling out of the sky into the bluff, its feathers sprayed as by an explosion. The first gun and the second gun are in position, the beginning and end of the bristling surround of thirty-five Prince Albert Volunteers, thirteen civilians and fifty-six policemen in position relative to the bluff and relative to the unnumbered whites astride their horses, standing up in their carts, staring and pointing across the valley, in position relative to the bluff and the unnumbered Indians squatting silent along the higher ridges of the Hills, motionless mounds, faceless against the Sunday morning sunlight edging between and over them down along the tree tips, down into the shadows of the bluff. Nothing moves. Beside the second gun the red-coated officer has flung a handful of grass into the motionless air, almost to the rim of the red sun.

And there is a voice. It is an incredible voice that rises from among the young poplars ripped of their spring bark, from among the dead somewhere lying there,

---

[1] *Hochelaga* The old name for Montreal, Canada.

out of the arm-deep pit shorter than a man; a voice rises over the exploding smoke and thunder of guns that reel back in their positions, worked over, serviced by the grimed motionless men in bright coats and glinting buttons, a voice so high and clear, so unbelievably high and strong in its unending wordless cry.

The voice of "Gitchie-Manitou Wayo" — interpreted as "voice of the Great Spirit" — that is, The Almighty Voice. His death chant no less incredible in its beauty than in its incomprehensible happiness.

I say "wordless cry" because that is the way it sounds to me. I could be more accurate if I had a reliable interpreter who would make a reliable interpretation. For I do not, of course, understand the Cree myself.

1971

Arthur Yap

Arthur Yap (1943–2006) was born in Singapore and educated at the University of Singapore and the University of Leeds, England. He taught in various institutions, including the National University of Singapore. He wrote several collections of poetry, such as *Only Lines* (1971), *Commonplace* (1977), *Man Snake Apple and Other Poems* (1986), and *The Space of City Trees: Selected Poems* (2000).

Yap's "2 Mothers in a HDB Playground" identifies in its very title the setting as Singapore (HDB is the Housing and Development Board of Singapore). The form of English used ("Singlish" or Singapore English) and other cultural markers in the poem confirm this. The poem can be compared with Wong May's "The Shroud," in which cultural markers are virtually absent. Do the two mothers (one distinguished from the other in the poem by indentation of lines) exhibit particularly Singaporean traits? Or do they illustrate what in Western societies is seen as "keeping up with the Joneses?" In dramatic monologues, readers have to establish the context in which the monologues are given (Who is speaking? To whom? When?). Do you think that this poem would justify coining the term "dramatic dialogue?"

2 Mothers in a HDB Playground

ah beng is so smart,
already he can watch tv & know the whole story.
your kim cheong is also quite smart,
what boy is he in the exam?
this playground is not too bad, but i'm always
so worried, car here, car there.

    at exam time, it's worse.

because you know why?

    kim cheong eats so little.

give him some complan.[1] my ah beng was like that,
now he's different. if you give him anything
he's sure to finish it all up.

    sure, sure. cheong's father buys him
    vitamins but he keeps it inside his mouth

---

[1] *complan* A nutritional food supplement (proprietary brand name).

& later gives it to the cat.
i scold like mad but what for?
if i don't see it, how can i scold?

on saturday, tv showed a new type,
special for children. why don't you call
his father buy some? maybe they are better.

money's no problem. it's not that
we want to save. if we buy it
& he doesn't eat it, throwing money
into the jamban[1] is the same.

ah beng's father spends so much,
takes out the mosaic floor & wants
to make terazzo or what.

we also got new furniture, bought from diethelm.[2]
the sofa is so soft, i dare not sit. they all
sit like don't want to get up. so expensive.
nearly two thousand dollars, sure must be good.

that you can't say. my toa-soh[3]
bought an expensive sewing machine,
after 6 months, it is already spoilt.
she took it back but.... beng,
come here, come, don't play the fool.
your tuition teacher is coming.
wah! kim cheong, now you're quite big.

come, cheong, quick go home & bathe.
ah pah wants to take you chyahong[4] in new motorcar.

1986

---

[1] *jamban* Toilet bowl.

[2] *diethelm* Furniture store.

[3] *toa-soh* "Wife of an elder brother" (Hokkien: a Chinese dialect used in Singapore).

[4] *chyahong* Literally "to eat the wind" (a Hokkien idiom for "joy-riding").

Acknowledgements/Permissions

Chinua Achebe. "Girls at War," from *Girls at War and Other Stories*. London: Heinemann, 1972. Reprinted by permission of the author.

Ama Ata Aidoo. "No Sweetness Here," from *No Sweetness Here*. New York: The Feminist Press, 1995. Copyright © 1970 Ama Ata Aidoo. Reprinted by permission of The Feminist Press at the City University of New York, <www.feministpress.org>. All rights reserved.

Meena Alexander. "Port Sudan," from *Illiterate Heart*. Evanston, IL: Northwestern University Press, 2002. Reprinted by permission of the author.

Agha Shahid Ali. "Snowmen," from *The Half-Inch Himalayas*. Middleton, CT: Wesleyan University Press, 1987. Copyright © 1987 Agha Shahid Ali. Reprinted by permission of Wesleyan University Press.

Lillian Allen. "Rub A Dub Style Inna Regent Park," from *Women Do This Every Day*. Toronto: Women's Press, 1993. Reprinted by permission of the author.

Mulk Raj Anand. "Duty," from *The Barber's Trade Union and Other Stories*. London: Cape, 1944. Reprinted by permission of the Estate of Mulk Raj Anand.

Jean Arasanayagam. "I Have No Country," from *Reddened Water Flows Clear*. London: Forest Books, 1991. Reprinted by permission of the author.

Louise Bennett. "Anancy an Ticks," from *Anancy and Miss Lou*. Kingston: Sangster's Book Stores Ltd., 1979. Reprinted by permission of Sangster's Book Stores Ltd.

Neil Bissoondath. "Man as Plaything, Life as Mockery," from *Digging Up the Mountains*. Toronto: Macmillan, 1985. Reprinted by permission of the author.

Dionne Brand. "Return I," from *No Language is Neutral*. Toronto: McClelland & Stewart, 1998. Copyright © 1990 Dionne Brand; "Amelia," from *Chronicles of a Hostile Sun*. Stratford: Williams-Wallace, 1984. Reprinted by permission of McClelland & Stewart, Ltd.

Edward Kamau Brathwaite. "Red Rising," from *Sun Poem*. Oxford: Oxford University Press, 1982. Copyright © 1982 Edward Kamau Brathwaite. Reprinted by permission of Oxford University Press.

Dennis Brutus. "By the Waters of Babylon," from *7 South African Poets: Poems of Exile Collected and Selected by Cosmo Pieterse*. London: Heinemann Educational Books, 1971. Reprinted by permission of the author.

Buhkwujjenene. "Nanaboozhoo Creates the World," from *First People, First Voices*. Toronto: University of Toronto Press, 1983. Reprinted by permission of University of Toronto Press.

Willi Chen. "Assam's Iron Chest," from *King of the Carnival and Other Stories*. London: Hansib, 1988. Reprinted by permission of the author.

Marilyn Chin. "Elegy for Chloe Nguyen (1955–1988)," from *The Phoenix Gone, the Terrace Empty*. Minneapolis, MN: Milkweed Editions, 1994. Reprinted by permission of Milkweed Editions.

Austin Clarke. "The Man," from *When Women Rule*. Toronto: McClelland & Stewart, 1985. Reprinted by permission of the author.

Saros Cowasjee. "His Father's Medals," from *More Stories from the Raj and After*. London: Grafton Books, 1986. Reprinted by permission of the author.

Rienzi Crusz. "Roots" and "In the Idiom of the Sun," from *A Time for Loving*. Toronto: TSAR, 1986. Reprinted by permission of TSAR Publications.

Cyril Dabydeen. "My Mother," from *Stoning the Wind*. Toronto: TSAR Publications, 1994. Reprinted by permission of the author.

David Dabydeen. "Catching Crabs" and "The New Poetry," from *Coolie Odyssey*. London: Hansib, 1988. Reprinted by permission of the author.

Fred D'Aguiar. "Home." Reprinted by permission of *ARIEL* and of the author. "A Son in Shadow: Remembering, in Fragments, a Lost Parent," from *Harper's Magazine* March 1999. Copyright © 1999 by Harper's Magazine. Reproduced from the March issue with special permission. Reprinted by permission of Harper's Magazine. All rights reserved.

Kamala Das. "An Introduction," from *Summer in Calcutta*. London: Heinemann, 1965; "The Looking Glass," from *The Descendants*. London: Heinemann, 1967. Reprinted by permission of the author.

Jack Davis. "Pay Back" and "White Fantasy—Black Fact," from *Paperbark: A Collection of Black Australian Writing*. St Lucia, Qld.: University of Queensland Press, 1990. Reprinted by permission of the author.

Anita Desai. "Surface Textures," from *Games at Twilight*. London: Penguin, 1978. Copyright © 1978 Anita Desai. Reprinted by permission of the author c/o Rogers, Coleridge & White Ltd., 20 Powis Mews, London W11 1JN.

Eunice de Souza. "Catholic Mother" and "Return," from *Indian English Poetry*. Hyderabad: Longman, 1990. Reprinted by permission of the author.

Nissim Ezekiel. "In India," from *The Unfinished Man*. Calcutta: Writer's Workshop, 1960. Reprinted by permission of the author.

Lorna Goodison. "Survivor," from *Heartease*. London: New Beacon Books, 1988. Reprinted by permission of New Beacon Books Ltd.; "Lessons Learned from the Royal Primer," from *Controlling the Silver*. Chicago: University of Illinois Press, 2005. Reprinted by permission of University of Illinois Press.

Nadine Gordimer. "Is There Nowhere Else Where We Can Meet?," from *The Soft Voice of the Serpent*. London: Gollancz, 1953. Copyright © 1951 by Nadine Gordimer, renewed in 1979 by Nadine Gordimer. Reprinted by permission of Russell & Volkening as agents for the author and of AP Watt, Ltd. for the author.

Jessica Hagedorn. "The Song of Bullets," from *Danger and Beauty*. New York: Viking Penguin, 1993. Copyright © 1993 by Jessica Hagedorn. Reprinted by permission of Viking Penguin, a division of Penguin Group (USA) Inc.

Kaiser Haq. "Strange Pleasures," from *ARIEL* 29.1 (1998). Reprinted by permission of *ARIEL*.

Claire Harris. "Death in Summer," from *The Conception of Winter*. Stratford, ON: Williams-Wallace, 1989. Reprinted by permission of Goose Lane Editions; "Backstage at the Glenbow Museum, Calgary." Reprinted by permission of the author and of *ARIEL*.

Wilson Harris. "Kanaima," from *Black Orpheus Anthology*. Akoka: Mbari Ibadan, 1964. Reprinted by permission of the author.

Bessie Head. "The Collector of Treasures," from *The Collector of Treasures and Other Botswana Village Tales*. Oxford: Heinemann, 1977. Reprinted by permission of Jack Johnson Ltd. on behalf of the author.

A.D. Hope. "Man Friday," from *Collected Poems 1930-1965*. New York: Viking Penguin, 1968. Copyright © 1963, 1966 by A.D. Hope. Reprinted by permission of Viking Penguin, a division of Penguin Group (USA) Inc.

Nalo Hopkinson. "A Habit of Waste," from *Skin Folk*. New York. Warner Books, 2001. Reprinted by permission of the author.

Keri Hulme. "Hooks and Feelers," from *New Zealand Listener* (17 January 1976). Reprinted by permission of the author.

Witi Ihimaera. "This Life Is Weary," from *Dear Miss Mansfield: A Tribute to Kathleen Mansfield Beauchamp*. Auckland, NZ: Viking, 1989. Reprinted by permission of the author.

Sally Ito. "Of the Wave." Originally appeared in *Fireweed* 23 (Summer 1986). Copyright © 1986 Sally Ito. Reprinted by permission of the author.

Arnold Itwaru. "arrival," "roomer," and "separate ways," from *Entombed*. Stratford: Williams-Wallace, 1987. Reprinted by permission of the author.

Eva Johnson. "Murras," from *Plays from Black Australia*. Sydney: Currency, 1992. Copyright © 1988 Eva Johnson. Reprinted by permission of Currency Press.

Jamaica Kincaid. "On Seeing England for the First Time," from *Harper's Magazine* (August 1991). Reprinted by permission.

Thomas King. "A Coyote Columbus Story," from *One Good Story, That One*. Toronto: Harper Perennial Canada, 1993. Copyright © 1993 by Thomas King. Reprinted by permission of Westwood Creative Artists on behalf of the author.

Joy Kogawa. "What Do I Remember of the Evacuation?" and "When I Was a Little Girl," from *A Choice of Dreams*. Toronto: McClelland & Stewart, 1974. Reprinted by permission of the author.

Alex La Guma. "A Matter of Taste," from *A Walk in the Night and Other Stories*. Evanston, IL: Northwestern University Press, 1968. Reprinted by permission.

Fiona Tinwei Lam. "The Hyphenated," from *Intimate Distances*. Roberts Creek, BC: Nightwood Editions, 2002. Reprinted by permission of Nightwood Editions.

Shirley Geok-lin Lim. "Passports," from *ARIEL*; "To Li Poh," from *Bridges: Literature Across Cultures*. NY: McGraw-Hill, 1994. Reprinted by permission of the author.

Jayanta Mahapatra. "Freedom" and "The Portrait." Reprinted by permission of the author; "The Abandoned British Cemetery at Balasore," from *The False Start*. Bombay: Clearing House, 1980. First published in *Sewanee Review*. Reprinted by permission of the author.

Lee Maracle. "Charlie," from *Sojourner's Truth and Other Stories*. Vancouver: Press Gang, 1980. Reprinted by permission of the author.

Dambudzo Marechera. "Black Skin What Mask," from *The House of Hunger*. London: Heinemann, 1978. Reprinted by permission.

Sharon May. "The Wizard of Khao-I-Dang," from *Tinhouse* Issue 25 (Fall 2005). Reprinted by permission of the author.

Wong May. "The Shroud," from *Critical Engagements*. Singapore: Heinemann, 1986. Reprinted by permission.

Pauline Melville. "McGregor's Journey," from *Shape-Shifter*. London: The Women's Press, 1991. Copyright © 1991 by Pauline Melville. Reprinted by permission of The Wylie Agency, LLC.

Sudesh Mishra. "Mt. Abu: St. Xavier's Church," from *Memoirs of a Reluctant Traveller*. Adelaide: CRNLE, Flinders University, 1994; "The Grand Pacific Hotel," from *Tandava*. Melbourne: Meanjin Press, 1992. Reprinted by permission of the author.

Rohinton Mistry. "Swimming Lessons," from *Tales from Firozsha Baag*. Toronto: McClelland & Stewart, 1987. Copyright © 1987 by Rohinton Mistry. Reprinted by permission of Westwood Creative Artists on behalf of the author.

Timothy Mo. "One of Billy's Boys: A Memoir," from *Eastern Express Weekend* 5 (February 1994). Reprinted by permission of the author.

Toshio Mori. "Slant-Eyed Americans," from *Yokohama, California*. Caldwell, ID: Caxton Printers, 1949. Reprinted by permission of Caxton Press.

Mervyn Morris. "To an Expatriate Friend" and "Little Boy Crying," from *The Pond*. London: New Beacon, 1973 & 1997. Reprinted by permission of New Beacon Books Ltd.

Es'kia Mphahlele. "The Coffee-Cart Girl," from *Short Stories*. Dar es Salaam: East Africa Publishing House, 1967. Reprinted by permission of the author.

Subramani. "Sautu," from *The Fantasy Eaters*. Washington: Three Continents Press, 1988. Reprinted by permission of the author.

Mary TallMountain. "There Is No Word for Goodbye," from *There Is No Word for Goodbye*. Marvin, SD: Blue Cloud Quarterly, 1981. Reprinted by permission of the literary executor of the TallMountain estate.

Edwin Thumboo. "Ulysses by the Merlion," from *Ulysses by the Merlion*. Oxford: Heinemann, 1979. Reprinted by permission of the author.

Alafina Vuki. "Four-Year Wisdom," from *Creative Writing*, ed. Satendra Nandan. Suva: Fiji Writers' Association, 1985. Reprinted of permission of the editor.

Fred Wah. "Breathin' My Name with a Sigh," from *Breathin' My Name with a Sigh*. Vancouver: Talon Books, 1981. Reprinted by permission of the author.

Derek Walcott. "Ruins of a Great House," "A Letter from Brooklyn," and "LII," from "Midsummer," from *Collected Poems 1948-1984*. New York: Farrar, Straus & Giroux, 1987. Copyright © 1986 by Derek Walcott. Reprinted by permission of Farrar, Straus & Giroux, LLC and of Faber and Faber Ltd.

Archie Weller. "Pension Day," from *The Australian Short Story*. St Lucia, Qld.: University of Queensland Press, 1990. Reprinted by permission of Mrs. Weller c/o University of Queensland Press.

Albert Wendt. "Crocodile," from *The Birth and Death of the Miracle Man*. London: Penguin, 1986. Copyright © 1986 by Albert Wendt. Reprinted by permission of Curtis Brown Ltd., London on behalf of Albert Wendt.

Rudy Wiebe. "Where Is the Voice Coming From?," from *River of Stone*. Toronto: Knopf Canada, 1995. Copyright © 1995 Jackpine House Ltd. Reprinted by permission of Knopf Canada.

Arthur Yap. "2 Mothers in a HDB Playground," from *Critical Engagements*, ed. Kirpal Singh. Singapore: Heinemann Asia, 1986. Reprinted by permission of the author.

The publisher has made every effort to locate all copyright holders of the texts published in this anthology and would be pleased to hear from any party not duly acknowledged.

Index by Title

Index by Genre

Essays

Fiction

Poetry

Plays

Index by Region

Africa

Canada

Caribbean

The Indian Subcontinent

South-East Asia/Pacific

South Pacific

United States and United Kingdom